MANAGING EDUCATION

Managing Education
The System and the Institution

Edited by

Meredydd Hughes
Peter Ribbins
Hywel Thomas

CASSELL

Cassell Educational Ltd: Artillery House
Artillery Row
London SW1P 1RT

British Library Cataloguing in Publication Data

Managing education: the system and the institution.
1. Education—Great Britain—Management
I. Hughes, Meredydd   II. Ribbins, Peter
III. Thomas, Hywel
379.1'54'0941   LB3011

ISBN: 0 304 31448 X

Phototypeset by Macmillan India Ltd, Bangalore
Printed in Great Britain by Mackays of Chatham Ltd

Last digit is print no: 9 8 7 6 5 4 3 2

ACKNOWLEDGEMENTS

It is impossible to thank individually the many people who have made this book possible. We should, however, like to express our gratitude to our students on advanced and shorter courses of the past several years, with whom we have learned so much. We must also acknowledge our great debt to those members of the secretarial staff associated with the Department of Social and Administrative Studies in Education at the University of Birmingham—Penny Austin, Cathy Baker and Jenny Neave. They have typed and retyped the several drafts of this manuscript with patience, good humour and care. Finally, we dedicate this book to our wives, Glenys Hughes, Maureen Ribbins and Christine Thomas.

LIST OF CONTRIBUTORS

David Elliott   Having taught in a secondary school, a college of further education and a college of education, David Elliott is currently Head of the School of Curriculum Studies, Wolverhampton Polytechnic. His main research interests lie in the management of higher education, with special reference to teacher training.

Don Field   Don Field is head of a large urban comprehensive school. Having been head of department in grammar schools and senior master in a comprehensive school, he became head of a multi-racial inner-city school. His is currently researching into policy-making in the local government of education.

Meredydd Hughes   At Birmingham University Meredydd Hughes is Professor and Head of Department of Social and Administrative Studies in Education, and has recently served as Dean of the Faculty of Education. A former secondary-school head, head of mathematics and barrister-at-law, he contributed as Foundation Editor of *Educational Administration* to the early development of the British Educational Management and Administration Society, later becoming the Society's National Chairman. He is a Fellow and currently Senior Vice-President of the Commonwealth Council for Educational Administration.

Ken Lambert   Ken Lambert taught in schools for thirty years, of which twenty-three were as headmaster of schools ranging in size from 300 on the roll to 2000. In 1983–84 he was seconded to Birmingham University as tutor for the School Organisation and Management Course and from 1984 has been Management Development Co-ordinator for the Birmingham LEA.

Keith Lloyd   After teaching in the West Riding of Yorkshire, and two headships in Oxfordshire primary schools, Keith Lloyd is currently a General Adviser for Primary Education in Derbyshire. His recent professional activities have included involvement with the Open University as a contributor to 'Management and the School' and research into the role of the primary head.

Michael Matthewman Michael Matthewman is Examination Secretary and Head of Department for Religious Education at Great Barr School, Birmingham. He has taught in grammar, secondary modern and comprehensive schools and has also been head of an adult education centre.

Peter Ribbins Peter Ribbins is a lecturer in the Department of Social and Administrative Studies in Education, University of Birmingham. Previously he taught in secondary schools and an institute of higher education and was an education officer in an LEA. Since 1975 he has been researching into various aspects of secondary schooling, including a study of pastoral care and of the subject department.

Derek Slater Derek Slater has worked in both a sixth-form centre under schools' regulations and a college of further education, and he is currently a Faculty Head at Bilston Community College, a tertiary college in the West Midlands. He has tutored seminar groups on the MEd. course in educational management at the University of Birmingham.

Hywel Thomas Hywel Thomas has been a lecturer in the Department of Social and Administrative Studies in Education, University of Birmingham, since 1979. In addition to applying economics to teaching education management, he has been researching into economic aspects of upper secondary provision. He previously taught in comprehensive secondary schools.

John Thorp John Thorp is Headteacher of Glaisdale CP School in North Yorkshire. He was previously a deputy head in the Midlands. He has published work on the transfer of children to secondary school and his current interests include the theory and practice of community education.

Patricia Twyman Patricia Twyman is Assistant to the Principal (Personnel) and Head of the Community Studies Department at Bournville College of Further Education, Birmingham. She is currently researching into alternative management structures for further education colleges.

Jim Waddington Following teaching experience principally in further education and schools, together with some work in universities, Jim Waddington entered educational administration and is currently Assistant Education Officer in Bedfordshire.

CONTENTS

Introduction
    Meredydd Hughes, Peter Ribbins and Hywel Thomas   xi

PART ONE   EDUCATIONAL MANAGEMENT: AN APPLIED DISCIPLINE

1   Theory and Practice in Educational Management
    Meredydd Hughes   3

PART TWO   MANAGING THE SYSTEM

2   The Education Sub-Government: Structure and Context
    Derek Slater   43
3   Teacher Supply: Problems, Practice and Possibilities
    Hywel Thomas   68
4   The School Curriculum in Contention: Content and Control
    Jim Waddington   99
5   Provision, Process and Performance in Compulsory Education:
    An Economic Perspective on Changing Enrolment
    Hywel Thomas   125
6   Comprehensive Secondary Reorganisation: A Case of Local Authority
    Policy-making?
    Peter Ribbins   148
7   Sixteen to Nineteen: Towards a Coherent Policy?
    Derek Slater   177
8   Higher Education: Towards a Trans-Binary Policy?
    David Elliott   198

ix

PART THREE   MANAGING THE INSTITUTION

9   Organisation Theory and the Study of Educational Institutions
    Peter Ribbins   223
10 Leadership in Professionally Staffed Organisations
    Meredydd Hughes   262
11 Management and Leadership in the Primary School
    Keith Lloyd   291
12 Headship in the Secondary School
    Don Field   308
13 Management and Leadership in Further Education
    Patricia Twyman   325
14 The Role of the Middle Manager in the Secondary School
    Peter Ribbins   343

PART FOUR   THE MANAGEMENT OF EVALUATION AND CHANGE

15 Perspectives on Evaluation
    Hywel Thomas   373
16 The Practice of Evaluation
    Ken Lambert, Peter Ribbins and Hywel Thomas   394
17 Accountability versus Participation?
    John Thorp   414
18 Sustaining Vigorous Educational Institutions in a Period of Retrenchment
    Michael Matthewman   428
19 The Management of Change: The Theory and the Practice
    Derek Slater   445

CONCLUSION AND INDEXES   469

Conclusion
    Meredydd Hughes, Peter Ribbins and Hywel Thomas   471

NAME INDEX   478

SUBJECT INDEX   483

INTRODUCTION

Meredydd Hughes, Peter Ribbins and Hywel Thomas

As the twenty-first century comes ever closer, the challenges and opportunities which are emerging in the management of education in all parts of the world are of increasing complexity and diversity. Managers and administrators of education — whether their work is based in the classroom or lecture room, in the study of the headteacher or college principal, or in the local authority office or national department — all face major and generally increasing pressures. These result from a number of factors: the ever-widening horizons of education itself, the rapidly changing economic, social and political context of educational management, and the continuing significant change in social expectations concerning the education service. To all who are concerned with maintaining, developing and improving understanding in educational management, and thereby improving its practice, the challenges and opportunities are both daunting and exciting. It is to clarifying these challenges, and the opportunities they provide, that this volume is addressed.

We have referred above to both managers and administrators, and it may be helpful to begin by clarifying what we mean by the terms 'management' and 'administration'. Ron Glatter (1972) reflected a well-established tradition in this country when he claimed that 'we see no difference in practice between "administration" and "management"' (p. 5), and suggested that in much of the literature the two terms are used interchangeably. From such a viewpoint we might take them both to mean 'the process of securing decisions about what activities the organisation (or unit of an organisation) will undertake, and mobilizing the human and material resources to undertake them'.

Glatter observed, however, that two different levels of activity were involved and that such a division was well entrenched in the public consciousness, the terms 'management' and 'administration' then being used differentially: 'We have found that sometimes "management" and sometimes "administration" carries the greater implication of directing in policy-making functions, with the other word implying more *routine* work. In the private sector, though, "management" generally has the connotation of *higher level work*' (emphasis added). A source of further confusion, as Glatter also noted, has been a tendency to use 'administration' for high-level work in central and local government, while 'management' is more often applied to directing and organising educational institutions.

In a helpful paper which is critical of earlier taxonomies of administrative process, the Canadian philosopher Hodgkinson (1980) also distinguishes between two levels of activity. Administration, he claims, is a philosophy in action, which becomes activated in two ways: 'by means of *administrative* processes which are abstract, philosophical, qualitative, strategic and humanistic in essence, and by means of *managerial* processes which are concrete, practical, pragmatic, quantitative and technological in nature' (emphasis added).

These ideas are developed in the form of an *ideal type* sequence, in which administration is made up of three successive processes (*philosophy*, *planning* and *politics*); 'each of these three process phases can be subsumed under the rubric of *policy making*' (p. 9). The next three phases in the sequence involve *mobilizing*, *managing* and *monitoring*, and taken collectively they may be classified as management 'and subsumed under the rubric of policy implementation' (p. 9). What are the implications of such an analysis? Hodgkinson argues that:

> If there is truth, as opposed to merely some form of aesthetic order, in the above taxonomy then I think the major implications have to do with the preparation of administrators and the division of executive functions within the organisation . . . Not to do all the six things, not to have them done by the right people, not to be aware and self conscious of the stages, and not to articulate them is simply not to be firing on all six cylinders (pp. 16, 17).

Hodgkinson (1980) still felt it helpful to have a single generic term to cover the three phases of policy making and the three phases of policy implementation. Not surprisingly he opted to use the word 'administration' for this purpose, this being the term predominantly used in an educational context in North America. Facing the same problem, but writing in a British context, we have chosen to use 'management' as the general term applicable to both levels of activity, though the other usage will emerge in quotations from North American sources.

The general approach adopted can be simply stated. The aim is to increase understanding of the interrelated dynamic complexities of educational management. In the main the treatment is focused specifically on education at national, local and institutional levels in England and Wales, though much of it is also relevant to Scotland and Northern Ireland. The emphasis, however, is on critical analysis and on the use of conceptual tools to assist the understanding of complex issues.

The primary aim therefore is not to describe the present educational system and the way it operates; that would be a mammoth and formidable task, and a frustrating one in that some of the detail would be out of date even before publication, as tends to happen to comprehensive handbooks on any matter which is subject to rapid change. Some description will obviously be necessary, and it is hoped that description and analysis have been combined in such a way as to provide a timely perspective on some current major problems, for those who may not be entirely familiar with recent developments, as well as for readers from overseas who may welcome some informed discussion in a British context of issues of world-wide significance. Nevertheless, providing information is a secondary aim.

Neither is this a management text which aims directly to enhance managerial skills through offering simple prescriptive guides to action. We take the view that educational management can benefit substantially from management studies conducted in other contexts, as several chapters amply demonstrate, but any application of concepts or processes should be carried out cautiously and with sensitivity to the special characteristics of educational management. This is a consideration which will be found relevant on several occasions in the present volume.

In its emphasis, then, on seeking understanding through critical analysis rather than through detailed description or general prescription, there is an implicit assumption that achieving such understanding is at least a first step towards becoming a better educational manager. The claim is stated modestly, for there is no guarantee that reading this volume from cover to cover will instantly result in enhanced proficiency in educational management. On the other hand we do believe that, given the diversity of specific problems and broader issues in a constantly changing environment, an analytical approach provides a powerful and flexible conceptual tool, which will be of use over a longer period than an approach stressing description or managerial guides to action. We turn, therefore, to the social sciences to find appropriate conceptual frameworks to assist our analysis of educational systems and institutions. The various chapters draw, as appropriate, upon economics, political science and sociology to illuminate the areas which are examined.

There is thus a basic paradox in the way in which we respond to the constantly recurring and legitimate challenge to relate theory to practice. On the one hand, this is a book which is *theoretical*, in the sense that its concern is to assist readers to reflect more critically upon their own management practice and that of others, and to use concepts and theories from the social sciences when doing so. On the other hand it is also *practical* in its intention, first that such reflection should contribute to better management practice, and second that practitioner experience and viewpoints should be taken into account to a substantial extent in the text, so that the reader's critical reflection can have a broader practitioner base than it would otherwise have, and thus contribute more effectively to an appreciation of better managerial practice. With these points in mind the four parts of the volume will be briefly surveyed.

The relationship of theory to practice is appropriately the theme of the single chapter of Part 1. It begins by examining the empirically-based work of early writers in the field of management, who often drew upon their own experience as managers. It then considers, by contrast, the development of the theoretically inclined New Movement in US educational administration, and proceeds to a discussion of the rich diversity of social science perspectives now applied to this field of study (as reflected in later chapters). The final section emphasises the potential creativity of tension between theory and practice, a theme to which we return in our concluding comments at the end of the book. There we argue the need for an interactive two-way relationship to achieve both relevance and rigour in management education for the education service.

Part 2 is concerned with system management, and explores some of the major policy issues in the government of education in England and Wales, giving attention selectively to matters perceived to be of considerable significance within the system and its institutions. The first of the seven chapters (Chapter 2) identifies the main features nationally and locally, giving attention to the wider context at both levels. A framework for analysis is provided by adapting to education a structural model first used to interpret developments in housing policy, a key concept being that of a national local government system. Channels of *influence flows* are considered in relation to issues such as educational finance and accountability, and the part played by various interest and pressure groups in modifying outcomes. The model thus performs two functions: first, it enables much of the basic factual information concerning educational provision to be given systematically, albeit in compressed form, to those whose knowledge is incomplete outside their own area of experience, and to overseas readers who wish to be informed of recent educational developments in England and Wales; second, it enables changes in the pattern of influence flows to be noted, and pertinent questions asked concerning the effect on the system of changing circumstances. The following chapters explore some of these policy issues.

The crucial educational resource of teacher supply is the first issue considered (Chapter 3), and a planning model is described which identifies the main factors determining the number of teachers required and the number available. The assumptions made in the DES manpower planning model are critically examined with regard to successes and failures over the past thirty years. The influence of the DES, the LEAs and the teacher unions upon policy outcomes in the areas of subject shortage and social priority schools are then analysed, and an alternative planning model is proposed which incorporates a more market-oriented approach. Finally, the consequences (for learners) of ignoring the realities of the labour market are demonstrated.

In Chapter 4 the complex and contentious subject of the content and control of the school curriculum is examined, and major changes since the 1944 Education Act are identified. Recognising that the monolithic hierarchical model of classical management theory would be inappropriate, the author has chosen to structure his analysis in terms of a 'loose coupling' model. Loose coupling is a contemporary social science approach, briefly introduced in Chapter 1 as an example of structural relativism, and it enables the author to take full account of variations and ambiguities in the relationships of the several agents which influence the school curriculum. The issue of increased central intervention is considered, and the conclusions reached challenge much contemporary thinking on the control of curriculum.

The subject discussed in Chapter 5 is changing pupil enrolment in compulsory education, the input-process-output model of the economist being adopted as a framework for analysis. The consequences of increased enrolments from 1986 in the primary sector are considered, while enrolments at the secondary stage will still be falling for some years. In order to consider how, in a period of resource scarcity, significant variables can be altered in an attempt to achieve multiple ends (which may not be wholly compatible), attention is directed in the latter part of the chapter to the relevance to pupil needs of alternative curricula. The interesting conclusion is reached that, in meeting future patterns of paid and unpaid work, and post-school education and leisure, a more vocationally-oriented curriculum is likely to be *less* economic than a more general curriculum.

The next two chapters consider, in turn, secondary reorganisation and 16- to 19-year-old provision. Continuing discussion of the merits of an institutional break at 16, and of possible re-introduction of selection at 11, show that secondary reorganisation remains a live policy issue in the mid-1980s. In examining the considerations involved, Chapter 6 draws on a number of theories and models and notably applies a 'political systems' model to local authorities, treating them as administrative and political systems in their own right. The author's detailed review of the many case studies available demonstrates the helpfulness of analysis, as indicated by the model, in terms of the conversion of general wants into specific demands, and the subsequent reduction of those demands through the recognised processes of the system. It is shown that, in achieving such reduction, the roles of senior officers and elected representatives are usually critical. Chapter 7 is then concerned specifically with the initial post-compulsory stage, whether in the secondary school, in further education or elsewhere. The main developments since 1944 are identified in terms of three sets of key issues — institutional, governmental and curricular. The writer then reinterprets the history using an incrementalist model. The explanatory power of the model is thus tested, policy-making for 16- to 19-year-olds being revealed as a series of disjointed responses to recurring problems, including — notably — the tensions within and between the education and training sub-governments.

The final chapter in Part 2 (Chapter 8) traces the fluctuating fortunes of higher education, as policy-making for universities and comparable public sector institutions has developed since the early 1960s. The much discussed binary policy is analysed and appraised. The more recent convergent trend is then discussed in terms of a model of policy change, which sees the emergence — or the 'manufacture', as one commentator (Reynolds 1983, p. 68) prefers to call it — of a new ideology as a necessary intermediate phase between the build-up of pressure for change and the final establishment of new structures. The model enables the author to interpret current developments in terms of growing adherence to a trans-binary ideology.

It will be evident from the above that each chapter in Part 2 provides factual material to inform and guide the reader on complex policy matters in relation to system management in education. Issues of current concern relating to each of the main sectors, from compulsory schooling to higher education, have been included, but we do not claim to have covered all the major questions which could have qualified for inclusion. Considerations of space made selectivity obligatory.

It will also be evident that the underlying emphasis is on analysis, each chapter introducing, explaining and applying influential theoretical perspectives, mainly from economics and political science. The structures of the chapters vary: some begin with an account of the situation, then introduce the principal features of the analytical model, and finally apply the model to problematic aspects of the situation; others develop the descriptive material and the analytical perspectives together. The nature of the topic often suggests suitable structures, but the style of the writer is also a factor. In the interests of clarity and rigorous analysis, the individual authors were encouraged to organise their treatments largely in terms of the critical application of a single policy model, following a well-established precedent in the literature (see, for example, Howell and Brown 1983). A contributory factor in the choice of subject areas was thus our desire to illustrate appropriately a range of different models. The aim is to contribute to learning about educational management at two distinct levels: elucidating salient systemic issues in the management of education, on the one hand, while simultaneously providing an introduction, through demonstration and practical application, to some of the alternative frameworks available to analyse such problems. Such action learning can be taken a stage further by the reader, who is encouraged to strengthen personal understanding of the issues and models and to enhance analytical skills by using the knowledge gained of each model to reinterpret at least one of the factual accounts of policy issues given in other chapters. Part 3 and Part 4 may be reviewed more briefly.

Part 3, which consists of six chapters, switches attention to managing the individual educational institution. It begins with a wide-ranging chapter (Chapter 9) broadly concerned with relating contemporary organisational theory to the study of schools and colleges. Such theory, as Part One has already made evident, is far from monolithic, and the chapter identifies, describes and explains three competing paradigms from sociological theory which offer quite different perspectives on the nature of organisations. Two of these paradigms are developed at some length, to make clear their contrasting interpretations of the nature of schools and colleges and to suggest ways in which they lead to quite different implications for action by their members. The discussion is illustrated by reference to material drawn from a case study largely based on the author's own research in schools.

The following chapter (Chapter 10) also has a wide scope, investigating the implications for leadership of educational institutions (at different levels) of the fact that they are staffed by persons who, to varying degrees, claim to be professionals. An initial review of the social science literature on leadership and professionalism reveals a significant contemporary growth of external pressures on professionals, and an increased emphasis on political skill as an essential characteristic of effective leadership. A role model for the professional-as-administrator, based on the writer's personal research, is then outlined, which involves the interpenetration (rather than the complete separation) of professional and managerial aspects. Its application to practice is considered in the three broad areas of task achievement, group development and external representation, the political dimension again being emphasised.

The next three chapters make use, in different ways, of concepts and structures developed in Chapters 9 and 10. Chapter 11 explores the relationship of management and leadership in the primary school, considering in particular the issues of curriculum development, staff involvement and accountability. The chapter draws on the writer's personal experience of primary headship and on his personal research, which uses a three dimensional role model, to illuminate the head's leadership role. Chapter 12, on headship in the secondary school, is structured in terms of four categories of heads' tasks — technical (i.e. educational), conceptual, human relations and external management — which are derived from an Open University project on the selection of secondary heads (Morgan, Hall and Mackay 1983). It also draws extensively on the author's personal experience of the frustrations and challenging opportunities of contemporary headship in an urban, cosmopolitan environment. Chapter 13, which focuses on leadership and management in further education, is similarly underpinned by practitioner experience, in this case from the perspective of a further education college head of department. The turbulence, complexity and change which have been characteristic of provision over the last decade are examined, together with the extent to which they have been accompanied by attitudinal change. Implications are considered for the roles of the principal and the head of department, and finally for identifying the management training needs of further education.

The final chapter of Part 3 (Chapter 14) provides an analysis of middle management roles in educational institutions, specifically in secondary schools. The complexities of structures and systems in modern comprehensive schools are first explored, and the roles of pastoral and academic middle managers are then located and analysed. Illustrations are provided from the growing literature now available, prescriptive and behavioural accounts being clearly distinguished. In developing his theme, the writer finds it helpful to discuss in greater depth the concepts of bureaucracy and role which were briefly considered in Chapters 1 and 9. This enables him to examine critically the horizontal and vertical divisions in the contemporary secondary school and, finally, to adopt an appropriately sceptical stance in relation to the decontextualised concept of role which frequently appears in the management literature. An interactionist conception of role, based on an ethnographic research methodology, is commended.

Throughout Part 3 institutional management and leadership are thus considered in ways which seek to take full account of particular contexts, while at the same time deepening understanding of commonalities and concepts of general application. The primary, secondary and further education chapters should thus not be considered to be aimed exclusively at those whose experience is in that particular field, but should prove to be of interest and relevance to those concerned with management in other sectors. By the same token the whole section should be of interest to those whose immediate concern is with system management, whether at local or national level, just as we would consider the system-wide issues of Part 2 to be essential elements in 'the appreciative systems' (to borrow the term popularised by Sir Geoffrey Vickers (1965)) of the senior and middle managers of educational institutions. In the final part we turn to management issues relating to evaluation and change, which have important implications for both the system and the institution.

Part 4, consisting of five chapters, begins with two chapters on evaluation. The first of these (Chapter 15) firmly establishes evaluation as a continuing activity essential to the entire planning and implementation process: it is present in the initial judgement that change is either necessary or desirable; it happens in parallel with the change process as progress is monitored; and it occurs at the final stage when conclusions are drawn concerning outcomes, the whole sequence often being re-activated if outcomes are unacceptable. The author proposes a new three-dimensional model which notably clarifies the structures of relationships within educational evaluation. He is thus able to identify significant examples in common experience of each of his eight categories, his further analysis being concerned with the conduct of evaluation and its techniques. The succeeding chapter (Chapter 16) has a joint authorship, and is concerned specifically with the practice of evaluation. It applies the model introduced in the previous chapter successively to three distinct evaluative activities of current significance in education: evaluation by HMI and LEA inspectors and advisers; departmental review by senior managers in schools; and the use of LEA-inspired evaluation documents which represent an important initiative towards achieving institutional self-evaluation. In the subsequent analysis, the significant concept of professionalism, previously discussed in relation to institutional leadership in Chapter 10, reappears in a different context. The question of whose interest is primarily served by the evaluation becomes a key issue, and 'professional independence' is seen as a necessary quality of those who seek simultaneously to be agents of control and agents of change.

In the last three chapters of the book the management of change becomes increasingly the dominant theme. Chapter 17 seeks to relate the desire to improve standards, to inevitable tensions between insistent demands both for external accountability and for professional participation. Drawing on concepts introduced in earlier chapters, the writer discusses the interpenetration of the institution's internal and external domains and makes out a strong case for a considerable measure of teacher autonomy. This is followed appropriately by a chapter (Chapter 18) which considers how educational institutions can be organised for the formidable task of seeking to improve education in a period of contracting resources. The chapter discusses the meaning which can be given to the concept of a vigorous educational institution, identifies sectoral differences, and examines ways in which good management can contribute to an institution's morale and achievement.

The final chapter (Chapter 19) provides a broad survey of theory and practice in the management of change, drawing to a considerable extent on the international literature. It thus systematically brings together a number of ideas, some of which have been touched on or implied in earlier parts of the book. To facilitate his analysis, the author distinguishes in broad terms between *rational* and *political* approaches to the management of change. Three kinds of rational approach are identified: instrumental (as in the Research, Development and Diffusion model); interactive, the emphasis being on dissemination; and individual, in the sense that a problem-solving model can be applied to a 'user' of any size or complexity, such as to an institution or department deciding to adopt an organisation development strategy. Political approaches, it is suggested, take account of ways in which individuals and groups with different resources of power act in accordance with their particular perceptions of reality and conceptions of interest. Three ways are proposed in which change is then legitimated: through the authority of management, through an appeal to democracy and through reliance on professionalism. The chapter ends with a critical assessment of the rational models of change which effectively assume consensus and order, and a similarly realistic appraisal of control issues in respect of the three kinds of political approach discussed. The writer's analysis is clear and convincing, and experienced managers will no doubt appreciate the significance of his initial pregnant observation that the rational/political division is, 'for heuristic purposes', readily recognising that situations (ostensibly) entirely governed by rational processes can sometimes only be effectively handled by those with a firm grasp also of political overtones. The relevance for improving practice in the management of change is thus very evident. Other implications, relating to the issues of power and legitimation, are further discussed in our own conclusion to the volume.

Whether used informally or as part of a planned course of study, it is hoped that this book will be found useful in the study of educational management: it may serve both as an introduction to contrasting perspectives currently available to illuminate the field of study, and as an analytical account of the complex interrelationships of salient aspects of educational management, at system and institutional levels, in England and Wales today. The latter aspect should make it of use to the interested general reader, particularly school parents and governors, and also to overseas students seeking to make sense of a rapidly changing educational system to which the old stereotypes no longer apply. As a book of reference, it will provide background for BEd. and PGCE students, particularly, in relation to their educational and professional studies, and it should certainly be of relevance for one-term and shorter in-service courses on educational management and related topics. In the more detailed systematic study of educational management we envisage that the analytical approach adopted, which seeks to draw on concepts and perspectives from the social sciences, will prove to be of particular value. By providing valid means to describe and analyse issues of management practice as they emerge, such study enables action to be firmly based on a critical appreciation of relevant factors and their interrelationships. We have particularly in mind students from all parts of the education service, taking the increasing number of advanced undergraduate and specialised diploma courses, as well as the various taught master's degrees which have educational management components.

The latter point is made with some confidence, as the book is essentially the outcome of specialised and general MEd. degrees, by course work and dissertation, in educational management and administration for both home and overseas students at Birmingham University, in which all three of the editors have been closely involved for several years. Though the courses involve some lecturing in large groups, perhaps the most rewarding aspect has been the structured discussion in small seminar groups based on papers prepared and circulated in advance by each group member in turn. It was this experience which gave us the idea of a book, which would be more than a disjointed collection of readings, and a substantial part of which would consist of contributions from those who have either taught with us or been our higher degree students at Birmingham. Ken Lambert and Derek Slater have made substantial contributions to our taught MEd. course. Derek Slater and other contributors are former MEd. students, who bring a wide range of practitioner experience to their writing (as described in the separate list of contributors).

It may finally be noted that in bringing together the work of experienced practitioners, who have been involved in systematic study, with that of academics who themselves have practitioner experience in educational management, this book provides an example of the productive relationship which can and should exist between the theory and the practice of educational management.

April 1985

REFERENCES

Glatter, R. (1972) *Management Development for the Education Profession.* London: Harrap.

Hodgkinson, C. (1980) 'A New Taxonomy of Administrative Process'. Paper presented to the Canadian Association for the Study of Educational Administration, Congress of Learned Societies, Montreal, June.

Howell, D. A. and Brown, R. (1983) *Educational Policy Making: An Analysis.* London: Heinemann.

Morgan, C., Hall, V. and Mackay, H. (1983) *The Selection of Secondary School Headteachers.* Milton Keynes: Open University.

Reynolds, D. (1983) 'Review of Salter, B. and Tapper, T., *Education, Politics and the State'. Educational Management and Administration,* **11**(1), 67–8.

Vickers, Sir G. (1965) *The Art of Judgement.* London: Chapman and Hall.

PART ONE

EDUCATIONAL MANAGEMENT: AN APPLIED DISCIPLINE

1

THEORY AND PRACTICE IN EDUCATIONAL MANAGEMENT

Meredydd Hughes

INTRODUCTION

Theory and practice are uneasy, uncomfortable bedfellows, particularly when one is attempting to understand the complexities of human behaviour in organisational settings, and still more so if the purpose in seeking to achieve such insight is to influence and improve the practice.

Such issues have been faced for nearly a century in industrial management and public administration. The main traditions in these areas are considered in the first section of the chapter, ending with a brief review of their application in education.

A sustained attempt to develop an explicit theory of educational management or administration, which was initiated in the USA in the late 1950s, is then considered because of the challenging and innovative way in which it sought to tackle the relationship of theory and practice. Later development in the UK and in other parts of the world, both developed and developing, has inevitably been influenced, whether positively or negatively, by the US experience.

The third section of the chapter adopts a more catholic and flexible approach and seeks to show the kind of theorising within the social sciences on which contemporary students of educational management are able to draw. An attempt is made to examine in some depth the extent to which the ever-present challenge to lessen the gap between theory and practice has led to the development of new perspectives, which provide different kinds of insight, helpful to participants in appreciating the complexities of the diverse facets of organisational experience.

The final section briefly reviews the continuing tension between theory and practice, which is seen as an opportunity for further development rather than as a cause for despair.

THE EMPIRICAL ROOTS OF TRADITIONAL MANAGEMENT STUDIES

It has often been noted that the pioneering works on the management and functioning of organisations were written by engineers, managers and industrial consultants who were very familiar with the practical problems encountered in operating large productive organisations. There were later developments on similar lines in business management and in public administration, but it was the managers of industry who first sought to derive management principles of general application from their personal experience in factories and foundries. Some of the milestones celebrated in traditional management texts will be briefly mentioned.

The scientific management movement of Frederick Taylor

The leading figure of the scientific management movement, which was influential in the early decades of the century, was Frederick Taylor. He trained as a mechanical engineer and rose from labourer to foreman, and then to chief engineer at a US steelworks, subsequently becoming a management consultant. In his definitive work Taylor (1911) called for a systematic study of working practices to discover the most efficient means of performing every task, and a corresponding study of management to determine the most efficient means of controlling the workers. Such 'scientific' management, resulting in low labour costs and high wages, would be in the interest of both employers and workers, and would lead, it was claimed, to the general elimination of all causes of dispute between them.

Taylor favoured time and motion studies, involving systematic observation and measurement of workers, coupled with incentive payment schemes. He applied similar ideas to management also, insisting on the advantages of maximum specialisation and separation of functions. All organisational members, in his view, could be regarded as essentially rational beings who, with appropriate instructions and agreed incentives, could be expected to operate like machines to increase productivity.

The scientific management movement had many supporters, and Taylor's methods achieved wide currency on both sides of the Atlantic. They also gave rise to bitter resistance and controversy among those who regarded his analysis of human motivation as inadequate and crude, so that the pejorative overtones of the term 'scientific management' are still not entirely dispelled.

Classical management theory

A number of writers, also from a practitioner background, developed a more general analysis of organisations than is implied in scientific management. An early example was a French mining engineer, Henri Fayol, whose major work (Fayol 1916) was the outcome of thirty years' experience as an industrial managing director. He defined the fundamental elements of management as being 'to forecast and plan, to organise, to command, to co-ordinate and to control'. Pugh, Hickson and Hinings (1971, p. 65) identify him as the earliest known proponent of a theoretical analysis of management activities. He formulated what have become known as Fayol's general principles of management, which begin with an insistence on division of work and specialisation and end by proclaiming the desirability of management actively fostering the morale of employees.

Fayol's writings on management may be described as classical both for their concern with form and structure and because of their emphasis on management principles of general application. He has been praised for his clarity and criticised for his apparent rigidity and authoritarianism. Baker (1980, p. 15) perceived him as a kind of Napoleon of industrial and general organisation theory: 'immensely creative in opening up clear straight lines through hitherto not easily penetrable jungles; and hence, like Napoleon, stimulating the creativity of others'.

Among those others was Colonel Urwick in Britain, who drew substantially on Fayol's work and on his own military experience in his treatment of principles of administration (Urwick 1947). In the USA James Mooney, a General Motors vice-president, and Luther Gulick, a prominent public administrator, were among the enthusiastic advocates of general management principles. Gulick (1937), in a volume which he edited jointly with Urwick, described the work of a top executive as consisting of seven distinct tasks: planning, organising, staffing, directing, co-ordinating, reporting, and budgeting. In countless management lecture rooms these have since been recalled by means of the well known acronym, POSDCORB.

It may be noted that the readiness with which the generalisations of Fayol and other classical writers were widely and uncritically accepted owed much to their impeccable practitioner credentials. Their robust and wide-ranging commonsense pronouncements, relying more on individual personal experience than on systematic study, were usually expressed clearly and authoritatively. They gave little attention, however, to constraints and qualifications, or to the conditions which would need to be satisfied for their propositions to be of value in predicting future performance. They were pioneers whose confident generalisations provided a basis for conceptual clarification and further refinement.

Organisations as bureaucracies

The word 'bureaucracy', which may be traced back to pre-revolutionary France of the mid-eighteenth century (Albrow 1970, p. 16 ff.), belongs to a different world, the world of government departments. It referred to the rule of officials in public administration, and was discussed in such terms by a succession of writers, including John Stuart Mill. Described as 'the giant power wielded by pigmies', bureaucracy was both popularised and castigated by Balzac (1836) in his novel, *Les Employés*.

In the late nineteenth century the German sociologist and jurist, Max Weber, offered a succinct and influential statement of the essentials of a bureaucracy which had a profound influence on later writers on organisation, and was in close accord with the ideas independently promulgated by the classical management writers. As conceived by Weber (1947), a bureaucracy has the following characteristics:

(a)   a clear-cut division of labour leading to specialisation;
(b)   a hierarchical authority structure, the scope of such authority being specified;
(c)   a comprehensive system of rules and regulations to ensure uniformity and continuity in organisational decisions;

(d)   impersonal relationships among officials and between officials and clients;

(e)   employment and advancement based on objective criteria.

Underlying Weber's classic formulation is a concept of authority which is *legal* and *rational*, carefully distinguished by Weber from both *charismatic* authority, which is dependent on the personal quality of the leader, and from *traditional* authority, which is based on custom and precedent. In contrast to social groupings involving charismatic and traditional authority, a bureaucracy, according to Weber, can be relied upon to ensure rational decision-making which is neither arbitrary nor compromised by inappropriate and irrelevant considerations.

Silverman (1970, p. 74) has suggested that it was 'in an uncharacteristic moment of dogmatism' not typical of Weber's general emphasis on understanding and interpreting the subjective meaning of situations to individuals, that Weber boldly asserted that bureaucracy is the most efficient form of administrative organisation. The claim was not based on empirical research, and it has been noted by several commentators (e.g. Blau and Scott 1963, p. 34) that Weber's characterisation of bureaucracy was intended as a conceptual construct or 'ideal type' rather than as a composite description of actual organisations.

Whereas Weber was concerned to explain the contribution of formal structure to efficient organisational functioning (and may thus be regarded as adopting a 'structural–functionalist' viewpoint, as described by Ribbins in Chapter 9), subsequent research and theoretical analysis (Gouldner 1955; Merton 1957; Blau and Scott 1963) have focused attention in contrast on the *dys*functional consequences of bureaucracy, which are more apparent to the general public. Some later empirical studies, as will be noted, have questioned more basically the unitary assumptions of the ideal-type conceptualisation. These further developments, however, in no way diminish the intellectual power of Max Weber's precise and perceptive characterisation of bureaucracy rooted in the world of European officialdom, or lessen the profound and far-reaching influence it has exerted indirectly on society in general and, more specifically, on the thinking of both practising administrators and organisational theorists.

Human relations perspectives

It could be argued that the tenets of scientific management, the general principles of the classical management writers and the impersonal structures of bureaucratic theory give only cursory recognition of the fact that organisations basically consist of people with varied personalities, purposes and perceptions. The Human Relations Movement, which developed and gained recognition within industrial management in the 1920s and 1930s, was a conscious attempt to redress the balance and modify the emphasis of the earlier theorists.

The research conducted by Elton Mayo and his associates from 1927 to 1932 at the Hawthorne Plant of the Western Electrical Company in Chicago has been frequently cited and is well documented (Mayo 1933; Roethlisberger and Dickson 1939). Mayo concluded that the relationship of workers with management and each other may be more significant in affecting productivity than the streamlined procedures and incentive schemes proposed by Taylor or the rational management principles advocated by the classical theorists. The potent influence of informal groups on motivation and behaviour came to be appreciated, so that organisational goals were modified in practice through the pressure on members of their peers' expectations.

The concept of *informal* organisation, defined as 'the aggregate of the personal contacts and interactions and associated groupings of people', was introduced by Barnard (1938, p. 115) as a necessary concomitant of every *formal* organisation. In an influential text on the functions of the executive, based on his experience in commerce and government, Barnard's emphasis was on team-work and communication: 'Authority depends upon a co-operative personal attitude of individuals on the one hand; and the system of communication in the organisation on the other' (1938, p. 175). Paradoxically, he also referred to a need for managers to indoctrinate those at the lower levels with general purposes and major decisions (p. 233). In order to strengthen the influence of the formal organisation, he suggested, the informal organisation should be manipulated by management through friendship ties and deliberate leaks of information.

Not surprisingly Barnard has been criticised for the basic inconsistency in his approach (Perrow 1970; Greenfield 1975; Burrell and Morgan 1979). More broadly, his work provides an apt illustration of two general criticisms which can be made of the human relations approach: *first*, that because of a managerial bias human relations adherents tend to disregard genuine conflicts of interest between workers and their employers (Clegg and Dunkerley 1980, p. 134); and *second*, that human relations studies tend to ignore external factors such as mobility aspirations, market forces and union membership (Silverman 1970, p. 76).

On the other hand, human relations theory may be regarded in retrospect as an approach which directed attention to important personal variables in organisations, which had previously been neglected. As such the theory has been seen, particularly by practitioners, to provide a valuable corrective to views of management which rely exclusively on the abstractions of organisational charts and bureaucratic structures.

Management ideas applied to education

In a subtle and pervasive way the management ideas briefly indicated in preceding sections have become part of the intellectual currency of our time. Most people will readily appreciate what is involved in time and motion studies, lines of command and faceless bureaucracy, and a good number will be familiar with the Hawthorne effect. Those with responsibilities in educational management during the last half-century or so are likely to have had a broad familiarity with the main issues involved, though probably few of them would have studied the texts of industrial management or public administration. It is of interest to note some examples of educational management practice which may be regarded as anticipating, or more frequently echoing, the management traditions which have been described.

The level of funding of the new elementary schools in England and Wales in the latter part of the nineteenth century depended directly on the performance of pupils in oral and written examinations administered by HM Inspectors. The resulting slogan, 'payment by results', was in common usage some thirty years before Frederick Taylor's workers' incentive schemes, but was very much in the spirit of scientific management. The mounting opposition to the scheme, which finally led to its abandonment by the turn of the century, may be compared to the resistance often engendered by scientific management crudely applied in industrial concerns.

In the USA, performance-based accountability in education came a little later, as Callahan (1962) has shown in fascinating detail. It was evidently as committed advocates both of scientific management, and of the wholesale application of general principles of management to education, that the early professors of educational administration, Bobbitt, Spaulding and Cubberley, gained nationwide recognition. According to Cubberley (1916, p. 338), education had to have its corps of efficiency experts like 'every manufacturing establishment that turns out a standard product or series of products', while 'it is the business of the school to build its pupils according to the specifications laid down'.

Such ideas might nowadays be regarded as crude and simplistic. It is salutary to note, however, that some of the thinking about assessing educational outcomes — which has led to competency-based training for educational administrators in North America (Lipham 1975; Project ASK 1980) and to the progressive development of objective testing techniques in Britain on lines already well established in the USA (Becher and Maclure 1978; Holt 1981) — is essentially similar to that of the scientific management advocates of the early years of the twentieth century.

An updated version of Taylorism is also (arguably) implicit in recent detailed studies of managerial activities in industry, as Hodgkinson (1978, p. 17) suggested in commenting on Mintzberg's (1973) influential study, which involved the intensive systematic observation of five chief executives. Similar studies in education, mainly relying for their data on diary entries (Webb and Lyons 1982), on structured interviews (Jenkins 1983) and on structured observation (Martin and Willower 1981; Duignan 1980; Willis 1980; Thomas, Willis and Phillips 1981) respectively, have all drawn to some extent on Mintzberg's work. They provided support in an educational context for his conclusion that managers are not reflective planners, and that their activities 'are characterised by brevity, variety and fragmentation . . . with the trivial interspersed with the consequential' (Mintzberg 1973, p. 51). The observational studies, which followed Mintzberg in incorporating a time-study element, were among those criticised by Gronn (1982; 1984) for introducing 'Neo-Taylorism' into educational management, a charge rebutted by Willower (1983). From the lively interchange between the two writers it may at least be concluded that the ideas of Frederick Taylor are still meaningful in current controversy.

A similar conclusion may be reached concerning Max Weber's ideas about bureaucracy. Over the years, the terms bureaucracy and bureaucratic, which are almost invariably used pejoratively by frustrated participants, have been found relevant in describing the functioning of educational systems and institutions. Schools and colleges, particularly if they are large, conform to a considerable degree to Weber's specification of bureaucracy, as judged by their division of work, their hierarchical structures, their rules and regulations, their impersonal procedures and their employment practices based on technical criteria (Anderson 1968; Jones 1974).

Adopting a historical perspective, Musgrove (1971) has written of the advantages of bureaucracy in education, and has argued that the bureaucratisation of schools has given more dignity and power both to school heads and to assistant staff (p. 98). It has been shown that some aspects of bureaucracy, such as the precise definition of individual responsibilities, are not necessarily unwelcome to school staff (Hughes 1977). There is evidence that the heads of larger schools tend to be bureaucratic, in the sense that they lay greater emphasis on the application of rules and regulations to govern procedures (Cohen 1970), though the same study also indicated that they appeared no less concerned than the heads of smaller schools for the individual child, the individual teacher or the particular parental request.

Cohen's study is thus an example of both a bureaucratic and a human relations viewpoint, and the strength of the latter emphasis is further illustrated in the work of Bates (1970) and Bernbaum (1976), both of whom show heads of schools giving priority to the traditional human relations aspect of their work. There have also been many studies of staff morale and satisfaction in educational institutions — sometimes explicitly drawing on similar work in industry — which have typically explored the relationship between satisfaction and staff participation in decision-making (Chase 1952; Sharma 1955; Belasco and Alutto 1972; Nias 1980).

The influence on education of the human relations movement of the 1930s, occasionally with specific reference to the Hawthorne studies, was soon evident in books advocating democracy in educational administration (Koopman 1943; National Society for the Study of Education 1946; Hughes 1951), and was reflected in texts on school management (Yauch 1949; Griffiths 1956; Bassett, Crane and Walker 1963). A generation later, staff development and involvement and participative leadership continue to receive close attention in texts on the management of educational institutions (Newell 1978; Bush et al. 1980; John 1980; Gray 1982).

It is also of interest that a model for higher education recently proposed by Becher and Kogan (1980) distinguishes at four levels (individual, basic unit, institution and central authority) between an *operational* and a *normative* mode, concerned respectively with what people actually do and what they count as important. Their normative mode at the individual level is specified in terms of job satisfaction, personal wants and expectations and subscription to group norms (Figure 2.1, p. 19), i.e. in terms of basic concepts which today are familiar and generally accepted, but which were new and unexpected when put forward by the human relations management consultants of the Hawthorne Studies era.

The extent to which general management theory can be applied to schools has been considered on a number of occasions, e.g. by Thomason (1974), Landers and Myers (1980), Paisey (1981) and Handy (1984), to name only a few. It has been maintained by Everard (1984) and in publications of the Industrial Society for heads of schools (Warwick 1984; Trethowan 1984) that school management has much to learn from industry, a view challenged by Fielding (1984) and White (1984). Research by Jenkins (1983) has identified a number of similarities, but also some significant differences in the ways in which managers in manufacturing industry and those in schools in England and Wales actually perceive their job.

In concluding this section it may thus be claimed that the various concerns and emphases of management writers, ranging from scientific management to human relations theory, have found expression in a variety of ways in the management of education and in the related literature. To begin with, this happened in a very piecemeal and haphazard manner. Even in the USA, where courses in educational administration had been mounted since early in the century (generally staffed by former administrators drawing anecdotally on their past experience), there was, for a long time, little attempt to integrate or reconcile the various disparate approaches available, or to consider how, if at all, the management of education differed from other kinds of management. From the mid-1950s the position changed significantly with the emergence in the USA and Canada of what came to be known as the 'New Movement' in educational administration. Its influence in Britain and other Commonwealth countries was somewhat indirect and came later.

This was a period, as Culbertson (1980, p. 326) later recalled, of 'an intense romance with theory'. The New Movement sought to provide coherence in educational management by emphasising the importance of theory. Sceptical practitioners were assured, in the oft-quoted words of John Dewey (1929, p. 17), that 'theory is in the end . . . the most practical of all things'. It involved nothing less than a new paradigm and a new approach to the relationship of theory and practice in educational management. Its aspirations, achievements and limitations are considered in the next section.

THE THEORETICAL BIAS OF EDUCATIONAL MANAGEMENT'S 'NEW MOVEMENT' PARADIGM

In this section the emergence and major achievements of the New Movement in US educational administration will be described, followed by an account of some of the doubts and challenges to its basic viewpoint which later developed. But first it will be helpful to clarify the meaning of the term 'paradigm' as used in the title of this section.

Paradigm: a term of multiple meanings

The word 'paradigm' is defined in the Concise Oxford Dictionary as 'example, pattern, especially of inflexion of noun, verb, etc.', and thus has a very specific, concrete meaning as used by philologists. Nowadays the term is widely used with very different connotations, this being largely a result of the work of Thomas Kuhn, a historian and philosopher of science. As he later recalled in a volume of selected papers (Kuhn 1977, pp. XVII and 318), the concept of paradigm was first extended by him in 1959 to refer by analogy to shared examples of successful practice within a scientific community, as distinguished from agreed rules and definitions. Acquiring an arsenal of exemplars, according to Kuhn (1977, p. 307), is 'integral to the process by which a student gains access to the cognitive achievements of his disciplinary group'.

In Kuhn's influential book, *The Structure of Scientific Revolutions* (1962), the concept of paradigm is progressively broadened from its original meaning, so that one commentator (Masterman, 1970) has identified at least 21 different usages of the term. As Kuhn later admitted, paradigms took on a life of their own:

> they expanded their empire to include, first, the classic books in which these accepted examples initially appeared and, finally, the entire global set of commitments shared by members of a particular scientific community (1977, p. XIX)

The essential point which Kuhn made in his major work is that what is called normal science involves the solving of problems without questioning the assumptions, explicit or implicit, of the generally accepted frame of reference or paradigm of the scientific community. There are, however, other periods of revolutionary science in which the paradigm itself is called into question, because of deep-seated anomalies which it cannot resolve. Such transitional periods, it was suggested, lead in due course to the emergence and acceptance of a new paradigm.

The concept has been broadened even further within the social sciences with the recognition that alternative frames of reference may be available simultaneously. Thus Burrell and Morgan (1979, p. 36) argue that 'social theory can be conveniently understood in terms of the co-existence of four distinct and rival paradigms defined by very basic meta-theoretical assumptions in relation to the nature of science and society'.

The progressive extension in meaning of the term paradigm is thus itself a potent reminder of the essential inter-penetration of theory and practice. 'Paradigm' was originally introduced into scientific discourse to signify the specific examples of problems and their solutions. It is these exemplars which provide the constituents of the shared understandings embedded in alternative views of reality presented by paradigmatic theorists.

The emergence in US educational administration of a 'New Movement'

The mid-1950s may be identified as a period of intellectual ferment in relation to educational management studies in the USA, as evidenced by a number of significant publications (Coladarci and Getzels 1955; Campbell and Gregg 1957; Griffiths 1959a, 1959b). There was a significant infusion of new ideas, propogated by a new breed of able enthusiasts whose expertise in educational management was derived more from study and research in the social sciences than from long practitioner experience. Andrew Halpin, Ronald Campbell and Dan Griffiths were among those who called for a more rigorous theoretical approach in the study of educational administration.

In his contribution to the Campbell and Gregg volume, Halpin (1957 p. 197) vigorously rejected 'naked empiricism' and rebuked those scholars who spent their time on practical problems rather than doing the research on theoretical issues, which he regarded as much more important. The term 'theory' itself had to be rescued: it would not be used by Halpin 'as a euphemistic synonym for any speculation about administrator behaviour—no matter how vaguely formulated—but in the restrictive sense employed by the social scientist' (Halpin 1957, p. 156). He quoted with approval a rigorous definition of theory as 'a set of assumptions from which can be derived by purely logico-mathematical procedures a larger set of empirical laws. The theory thereby furnishes an explanation of these empirical laws . . .' (Feigl 1951, p. 182).

The ideal which Griffiths enthusiastically envisaged was the development of a general theory of human behaviour, within which the theory of administrative behaviour in education would be a sub-system. The natural sciences, and particularly physics, would provide the model, Kepler's Laws of Planetary Motion being the prototype of the yet undiscovered laws of educational administration (Griffiths 1957, p. 388). He added later that he agreed with Halpin's suggestion that Feigl's definition of theory be adopted, and observed that this 'would mean that theoretical work would be more narrowly limited than previously' (1959a, p. 28).

A necessary consequence of the new determination to rely exclusively on a natural science methodology was that, in accordance with the philosophical tenets of logical positivism which Feigl advocated, the concepts used were to be defined operationally, i.e. their meanings were to correspond, as Herbert Simon (1947, p. 37) had also insisted, 'to empirically verifiable facts or situations'. Value judgements as to the desirability of policies and behaviours were therefore to be firmly resisted in the new studies being initiated, which would concentrate on determining what *is* rather than what *ought to be* (Culbertson 1965, p. 4). Similarly, Gregg (1965, p. 46), writing approvingly of a National Society for the Study of Education Year-Book (1964) which was an outcome of the New Movement, supported its emphasis on validated operational concepts within a theoretical context:

> Such concepts help to illuminate the nature of administration. They do not prescribe rules for administrative action, but they may enable the administrator to analyse administrative problems more penetratingly and accurately, to view events in different perspectives, and to reflect in ways which would not be possible without such concepts . . . The current scientific approach to administration is directed to identifying and describing the variables of administration and their relationships, so that an administrator can have a better understanding of them and thus control them in terms of whatever goals and policies he chooses.

The new ideas gained international currency in the 1960s, the initial impetus for Commonwealth development coming largely from William Walker, who founded *The Journal of Educational Administration* in Australia in 1963, two years before the US-based *Educational Administration Quarterly* was established. The first major UK involvement was in 1966 in Canada and the USA, at the first of what have become quadrennial International Intervisitation Programmes (IIP) in educational administration (Baron, Cooper and Walker 1969).

The early writings of the leaders of the New Movement paradigm were critical and perceptive papers which provided a welcome, astringent antidote to the unsupported generalisations — often based on dated and untypical experience — that had been customary in the educational administrative literature. What was actually achieved through this new style of research is more problematic. Three major areas of development will be briefly described: a framework for conceptualising organisations as social systems, some examples of role studies, and studies of organisational climate.

The Getzels-Guba social systems model

An example from the early days of the New Movement of an abstract formulation intended to generate hypotheses as a basis for empirical study, is provided by a model of educational administration as a social process, which was developed jointly by two social psychologists, J. W. Getzels and E. G. Guba (1957). Basically the model proposed that a social system be conceived in terms of two types of phenomena, involving respectively an organisational (or nomothetic) dimension and a personal (or ideographic) dimension. Observed behaviour is then regarded as the result of the interaction of elements located on each of the two axes.

The organisational dimension permits analysis successively in terms of the *institution*, its constituent *roles*, and the specific *expectations* attached to each role. Implicit is a structural view of organisation, such as Fayol or Weber might have proposed, with a clear division of tasks among official positions or roles. It is assumed that the obligations and responsibilities which these roles involve can be specified in terms of explicit expectations, which serve as an agreed prescription for the particular role. The various roles are interdependent and complementary, and it is to their interrelationship that the term 'organisational structure' applies.

The personal dimension takes account of the human aspect which the organisational dimension ignores, and thus accords with a human relations emphasis. It focuses on the *individual* members of the system, the analysis being successively in terms of the concepts of *personality* and *need-disposition*. Need-dispositions are described as a person's 'individual tendencies to orient and act with respect to objects in certain manners and to expect certain consequences from these actions'.

Though the justification for the use of the term 'dimension' is somewhat obscure, it may be granted that the model neatly accommodates the two main strands in traditional management theory, the classical and the human relations, and suggests three levels at which interaction can be considered: institution and individual, role and personality, role expectation and need-disposition.

An extension to the model (Getzels and Thelen 1960) took account of the fact that every social system is embedded in a wider environment. This was conceptualised in terms of a further anthropological dimension, of which the constituent elements are: *culture, ethos* and *values.*

In its original two-dimensional form the model generated a number of research studies of the correlates of role–personality conflict and of conflict within the organisational and personal dimensions, some of which are described by Campbell, Corbally and Ramseyer (1966, pp. 189–216). Personal satisfaction was found to be positively related to the extent to which need-dispositions are congruent with role expectations. The extended model led to studies being undertaken of the influence of value conflicts on relationships between school administrators and their school boards. The sensitive position of the administrator was thus highlighted, first as the mediator of intra-organisation conflict, and second as the organisational representative exposed to diverse external measures.

Commenting on the model, Trow (1959, p. 124) noted that Getzels used it to illuminate empirical problems. Trow saw it as being 'likely to be useful to administrators both in their thinking and practice', and suggested that its 'simplicity and clarity' derived from 'its close connection with his (i.e. Getzels') empirical research'. More recently it has been severely criticised for *excessive* simplicity, in that 'it manages to reduce the puzzles, conflicts and pain of life in organisations to a few neatly-working regularities by applying some very special assumptions to the mysteries of existence' (Greenfield 1979/80, p. 222). Such criticism is well-founded in terms of the perspectives now available, and can justifiably be extended to the methodological limitations of the associated research. Nevertheless, the Getzels-Guba model deserves to be recognised as a conceptual framework which generated a succession of hypotheses which were subject to empirical test. Within the parameters of the New Movement paradigm it thus contributed to developing a closer relationship between theory and practice.

Role studies in educational management

Apart from role studies conducted within the Getzels-Guba framework, numerous studies of the roles of the US superintendent (responsible, for education territorially, to a school board) and of the principal (responsible, for an individual school, to the superintendent) were undertaken in the early 1960s from the standpoint of role theory, i.e. that social behaviour is to a significant extent socially determined.

The most comprehensive of the role studies were those in which Neal Gross and his associates at Harvard University were involved. These included a study of the superintendency role (Gross, Mason and McEachern 1958) which explored differences in the expectations of superintendents and their board members. It was found, as hypothesised, that in defining the division of responsibilities between the two positions, each group assigned greater responsibility to their own position (p. 141). The study also explored the incidence and resolution of role conflict.

A study by Carlson (1962) of a sample of recently appointed school superintendents introduced an overt sociological perspective into a field which had hitherto been dominated by psychologists. Carlson showed that superintendents promoted from within the system (the 'insiders') and those brought in from other systems (the 'outsiders') tended to differ in their organisational behaviour. The outsiders were more likely to introduce major innovations and to accept the possible risk of community disapproval; the insiders, wishing to stay in the community, were more cautious and adapted themselves to survive. Though Carlson concluded that 'there is no reason to expect that one type is more capable than the other type' (p. 14), the study has been recognised as having implications for achieving organisational change.

A large-scale research project may also be mentioned, which Halpin and Hayes (1977, p. 269) later singled out as 'perhaps the most monumental single study ever conducted within the field of educational administration'. Using sophisticated simulation techniques and a formidable battery of psychological tests and assessment procedures, Hemphill, Griffiths and Fredericksen (1962) studied intensively the personality characteristics of a sample of 232 elementary school principals. The final conclusions, arrived at by elaborate statistical treatment, were ambiguous and obscure. From the viewpoint of practical application the best that can be said is that the array of situational exercises developed in the research were resourcefully converted by the University Council for Educational Administration (1960) into the 'Whitman School' simulation, and used in the in-service training of thousands of US elementary school principals.

A general criticism which can be made of the educational role studies which appeared in the 1960s is that they did not take heed of misgivings already expressed concerning the basic assumptions of role theory. Levinson (1959) had vigorously challenged the 'unitary' assumption that there is necessarily a close correspondence between the expectations of 'society' for a given role and those of the role incumbents, and between such expectations and actual behaviour, these being assumptions which do not accord with empirical evidence. Likewise Gross, Mason and McEachern (1958, pp. 21–47) had clearly rejected 'the postulate of role consensus', i.e. the assumption that there is general agreement in society regarding expectations for different roles. It is paradoxical that, in their empirical studies, Gross and his colleagues seem not to have fully appreciated the potency of the explosive device, with slow-burning fuse attached, which they had unwittingly planted within the corpus of management studies (cf Chapters 9 and 13).

With the benefit of hindsight and the alternative perspectives now available, the host of meticulously undertaken role studies may be seen at best as providing static, statistical composite snapshots, which ignore many of the subtle differences which really matter, and which afford little insight into the dynamics of changing perceptions and relationships.

Organisational climate studies

The organisational climate of schools is an imprecise notion which falls well short of the rigorous conceptual standards to which Halpin and his colleagues originally aspired. It has been loosely defined as that set of internal characteristics which distinguishes one school from another, and which influences the behaviour of people in each school (Hoy and Miskel 1978, p. 137); the idea has received considerable attention from researchers in the USA and elsewhere working within the New Movement paradigm.

Foremost was Halpin and Croft's pioneering study (1963) of 71 elementary schools, which was based on a simple comparison. As Halpin later recalled (1967, p. 6), 'Croft and I began with the obvious analogy that personality is to the human individual as 'organisational climate' is to the organisation'. He added that they might just as easily have chosen the term 'organisational personality' for what they had in mind. Their approach was to develop a questionnaire to explore various aspects of teacher–teacher and teacher–principal relationships. In its final form their definitive instrument, the ubiquitous Organisational Climate Description Questionnaire (OCDQ), contained 64 items. Addressed specifically to teachers, it invited them to indicate for each item, on a four point scale from 'rarely occurs' to 'very frequently occurs', their answer to the question, 'To what extent is this true of your school?'

Using factor analytic techniques Halpin and Croft were able to arrange the OCDQ items so as to provide eight sub-tests measuring particular variables. Four of these scales related to perceptions of the principal's behaviour, namely, production emphasis, aloofness, consideration and thrust; the other four related to perceptions of staff behaviour, namely, hindrance, intimacy, disengagement and esprit. It was thus possible to provide an eight-dimensional profile of the organisational climate of each school in terms of the mean perceptions of its teaching staff. The researchers found that these profiles clustered in six groups, and consequently 'invented' (the term is that of Halpin himself, 1967, p. 6) a typology of six climates, arranged along a continuum from an 'open climate' at one end to a 'closed climate' at the other. The *open* climate is characterised by 'authenticity' on the part of both principal and staff: the principal leading by example and the staff showing commitment and working well together, so that acts of leadership emerge naturally as needed. The *closed* climate is in stark contrast: the principal provides no effective leadership and is preoccupied with formalities and trivia, while the teachers are frustrated and apathetic, responding at a minimum level.

Later research has thrown doubt on the usefulness of the four intermediate categories which were identified, but the idea of assessing educational organisations on a climate continuum from open to closed has generated substantial research activity in many parts of the world. Such research should be treated with caution, however, for the OCDQ research instrument, originally developed and tested in a small sample of US elementary schools, has sometimes been used 'with greater zeal than wisdom', as Halpin (1977, p. 7) has sadly observed; i.e. in very different institutional and cultural contexts and without adaptation or further validation.

In spite of his caveats concerning misuse, Halpin (1977, p. 270) interestingly included the OCDQ research in his selection of the five studies which, in his view, best characterise research within the New Movement in its first decade. (It may be added in parentheses that his other nominations included the Getzels-Guba study, the Carlson insider/outsider study, and the large-scale Hemphill, Griffiths and Fredericksen study of elementary school heads, each of which has been noted above. His fifth nomination was his own earlier study of leadership styles, to which reference is made in Chapter 10).

The inclusion of the OCDQ in the top five may not be surprising in view of its wide currency and obvious appeal, especially to those favourably disposed to greater staff participation. Matched against the initial claims of the New Movement, however, the theoretical basis of the study is slight, relying on the simple analogy of personality, which is presumably a reflection of the fact that Halpin's specialist field was psychology. One may speculate that if Halpin's training had been in sociology, he would have linked the climate concept firmly to the literature on 'culture', allowing for the identification and inter-relating of the equivalents of sub-cultures, rather than submerging all differences in a single holistic concept of *one* organisational climate.

The *post facto* specification of six discrete organisational climates was soon challenged on empirical grounds by Brown (1965) whose computer printout, using a sample of schools in Minnesota, identified *eight* climates. Replication by Andrews (1965), using Canadian schools, also raised fundamental questions about the concept operationally defined by the OCDQ. He observed that an instrument completed only by teachers, and concerned essentially with the interaction of teachers and principal, does not effectively recognise the contribution to the distinctive culture of the school of relationships which involve the pupils and the parents. It is of interest that a subsequent National Foundation for Educational Research (NFER) study of school climate in the UK (Finlayson, Banks and Loughrans 1971) included the perceptions of pupils as well as of teachers. This has been replicated in Australia (Deer 1980).

A further point, which relates to the shallow theoretical underpinning of organisational climate research, is that it provides no insight as to how a particular organisational climate comes into existence or how a closed climate can be made more open. As Halpin (1967, p. 11) himself frankly admitted, 'The blunt truth is that we do not yet know very much as to how to change a climate'. It is thus tantalising that, though organisational climate can be seen by practitioners as a useful rough and ready means of generalising about their organisations, it is not a concept which theorists have been able to define with any precision. Because of its lack of clarity it has failed to generate powerful hypotheses and has done little to increase understanding. It appears that it is the inadequacy of organisational climate as theory which has lessened its usefulness for practice.

A paradigm partly accepted, variously challenged

While a cursory reading of the literature might suggest that the rigorous, theoretical epistemology of the New Movement writers had quickly been accepted as the new orthodoxy of the field, a survey by Jean Hills (1965), later confirmed by a more extensive study (Campbell and Newell 1973), showed that even among US academics the commitment was less than total. Professional associations of administrators were supportive, but in somewhat general terms (American Association of School Administrators (AASA) 1963).

Substantial discrepancy between theoretical aspirations and research achievement made the original optimistic forecast, that a comprehensive general theory was about to emerge, less convincing. At the same time it could be argued that the large-scale, statistically sophisticated research projects, and the more modest doctoral dissertations which were copiously produced, shared a hidden paradigmatic assumption to which the

New Movement implicitly subscribed. This was the belief that social science research is essentially concerned with random samples (the larger the better) with mean responses and standard deviations, and with the statistical significance of differences. The varying perceptions and qualified answers of particular respondents tended to be disregarded, scientific methodology having no means readily available to handle unique individual cases.

A tendency to advocate, and to make some use of, general systems theory was perhaps the nearest that the New Movement got to the adoption of a universal conceptual framework. An extensive theoretical treatment, drawing on the work of Talcott Parsons, was provided by Hills (1968), and made evident the underlying reliance on the analogy of a living organism in the discussion of pattern maintenance, integration, goal attainment and adaptation. Practical applications of considerable sophistication were developed, notably at the University of Oregon. These involved the adaptation to educational planning of system analytic techniques such as planning, programming and budgeting systems (Piele, Eidell and Smith 1970; Eidell and Nagle 1970), but they were not always successful in enlisting wholehearted practitioner co-operation, as Wolcott's evaluative study (1977) makes clear.

The ideal of a science of educational administration, based on a single grand theory, appeared to become less compelling by the mid-1960s. Schwab (1964, p. 47) cogently argued that 'contrary to the burden of recent literature on administration, the pursuit of one sufficing theory of administration is a manifest impossibility in the foreseeable future. and *an uncritical aping of the wrong model*' (emphasis added). He further observed that 'a sophisticated and cynical grasp of about a dozen separate and distinct bodies of "theory" are indispensable to deliberately good, intelligent administration', a sentiment broadly in harmony with the viewpoint adopted in the latter part of this chapter, though the epithet 'cynical' would not necessarily be endorsed.

At the 1966 International Intervisitation Programme, Griffiths counselled that 'the search for one encompassing theory (if anyone is searching) should be aban-doned . . . We have learned that a modest approach to theory pays off' (Baron, Cooper and Walker 1969, p. 166). Similarly Erickson (1967, p. 376) reported that 'the field is very much in flux. The erstwhile search for "administrative theory", for example, seems virtually abandoned today . . .'.

Robin Farquhar (1977, p. 356), referring to 'some disarray' in administrator preparatory programmes in the mid-1970s, called for more attention to be given to 'grounded' theory, and ended his survey 'on a note of cautious optimism'. Donald Willower (1975, p. 3), who continued to be a consistent upholder of the broad principles of the New Movement paradigm when others were expressing doubts and reservations, argued that highly abstract, large-scale theory had not been an issue and that 'in spite of its use as a straw man by some writers, there has been no real effort to construct a "grand theory" of educational administration'. His own cautious defence of theory prudently excluded Feigl's rigorous definition, previously mentioned, which 'sets a standard that would exclude virtually everything done in educational administration to date' (p. 3). He commended Merton's more modest view that a large part of what is called theory 'consists of general orientations toward data, suggesting types of variables which theories must somehow take into account rather than clearly formulated, verifiable statements of relationships between specified variables' (Merton 1957, p. 52). The notion of theory as a general orientation towards data was, of course, a significant retreat from the position boldly proclaimed in the heyday of the New Movement (Griffiths 1959a), but it enabled Willower to maintain some optimism concerning future development.

In stark contrast was the bleak disillusion expressed by Halpin (1969, 1970, 1977) in papers drawing variously on the imagery of a foggy view from Olympus, a fumbled torch and a broken ikon. The papers were, regrettably, less convincing in their suggestions for the future.

More constructively Jean Hills (1980), while recognising that the field was in disarray, called for an appreciation that educational administration is an applied science which draws on many disciplines. 'Any concrete, common sense object or event', he observed, 'is of such infinite diversity that its full richness cannot be grasped in terms of any system of abstract concepts' (p. 226). He proposed arrangements to facilitate socialisation with regard to clinical values in administrator preparation, an emphasis at variance with the positivist separation of facts and values characteristic of the New Movement. Similarly Culbertson (1980), who — like Hills — was addressing the 1978 IIP in Canada, called for the development of a new 'Theory for Practice'.

In concluding this section it is appropriate to recall Kuhn's differentiation between a period of normal science, when the assumptions of the accepted paradigm of a scientific community are not questioned, and a transitional period when the paradigm itself is under attack. By the mid-1970s two US scholars, Oliver Gibson (1975; 1977) and Donald Erickson (1977), were, in fact, writing about the need for a 'paradigm shift' in educational administration. In neither case was the kind of change desired clearly indicated, while the basic assumptions of the prevailing paradigm were not fundamentally questioned.

At the 1974 IIP, held in the UK, Tom Greenfield (1975) made an assault on the accepted tenets of the New Movement in a paper which has come to be recognised by supporters and opponents as a landmark in theory development. He rejected 'the apparent assumption that organisations are not only real but also distinct from the actions, feelings and purposes of people' (p. 71), and that organisational structures are invariate while 'people occupy organisations in somewhat the same way that they inhabit houses' (p. 72). Organisations are not, he suggested, real entities with a life of their own or governed by a generally accepted set of values; they are invented social reality reflecting the values of people with access to power. The emphasis should therefore be on 'discovering how different people interpret the world in which they live' rather than on 'discovering the universal laws of society and human conduct within it' which had been the ideal of the New Movement academics (p. 77).

The underlying assumptions of the pervasive social science paradigm associated with 'structural-functionalism' and 'natural systems theory', which Greenfield was directly challenging in his repudiation of the New Movement orthodoxy, will be considered further in Chapter 9, together with the various alternative viewpoints which have been proposed, and which are still emerging.

The new perspectives debate, conducted in the USA in *Educational Administration Quarterly* and in the UK in *Educational Administration*, in the wake of Greenfield's paper, has been lively and generally constructive. The result to date, as well illustrated by Griffiths' analysis (1979) of the intellectual turmoil within educational administration, has been a sharpened appreciation of the strengths and weaknesses of competing perspectives and paradigms. For the student of educational management the current situation is as stimulating as it is demanding. As compared with the undisputed emergence and wide acceptance of a single new orthodoxy — which Kuhn appeared to envisage when a period of normal science is replaced by a transitional phase — a diverse, less predictable prospect is revealed, which may well presage a more productive, interactive and critical relationship between theory and practice.

The account, given in some detail, of the achievements and disappointments of what have been called 'the developing decades' (Cunningham, Hack and Nystrand 1977) in the study of educational management and administration, provides both an instructive case study in theory–practice relationships in an emerging field and some of the necessary background for appreciating the significance of more recent developments.

THE CONTEMPORARY APPLIED SCIENCE, FIELD OF APPLICATION, PERSPECTIVE

A variety of potentially relevant modes and areas of knowledge is today available to all who are concerned to improve educational management through better understanding of its concepts, processes and structures. In the UK a cautiously pragmatic, multidisciplinary approach has characteristically been generally adopted. It is, incidentally, also an approach which is currently more widely favoured internationally, as the monodisciplinary aspirations of the North American New Movement appear less attainable (Griffiths 1982). In this section the implications of a multidisciplinary approach will be considered, followed by an inevitably selective survey of some of the models and constructs of possible relevance for application to educational systems and institutions.

The multidisciplinary approach

An important early landmark in the development of educational management and administration as a field of study in the United Kingdom was the publication of *Educational Administration and the Social Sciences*, edited by George Baron and William Taylor (1969). The editors acknowledged 'the influence of recent American, Canadian and Australian thinking', but claimed that 'the dominant note is that of English pragmatism; this is perhaps as it should be in a book emanating from a country in which the *practice* of administration has long been held in high esteem and in which its theory is only now receiving serious attention' (p. vii).

Several chapters of the book drew substantially on the US literature, familiar names such as Halpin, Getzels and Guba and Griffiths being frequently cited. The theoretical bias of the New Movement, however, was not endorsed, Baron noting that 'to the practitioner in England . . . writing of this kind can appear highly remote from his concerns' (p. 12). Hoyle, in a chapter on organisational theory and the sociology of organisations, referred to shortcomings of the New Movement due to its 'over-ambitious approaches to theory construction' (p. 38), and was sceptical about the use of general systems theory as a source of hypotheses. He concluded that 'a more limited approach to theory construction would enable us to handle the problems arising from the unique or limited characteristics of educational administration' (p. 45).

The approach adopted in the Baron and Taylor volume was that educational management is a field of application and that its study should draw widely, but with discrimination, on the social science disciplines and on already recognised applied fields such as organisational theory. Multidisciplinary study, rather than interdisciplinary study, was the preferred descriptor, since the latter 'could suggest an approach which, in its generality, falls between the interstices of the disciplines and adds nothing solid' (Hoyle p. 47).

The multidisciplinary standpoint was further developed by Ron Glatter (1972) in a survey of approaches to management development in education, which endorsed Snyder's warning to the 1966 IIP concerning the art of 'squeezing disciplines': 'Only on the basis of rigorous specification of need and an equally rigorous grasp of how a particular discipline organises its knowledge can one establish relevance and borrow safely and productively' (Snyder 1969, p. 297).

Both the priority given to substantive practical issues and the multidisciplinary emphasis in theoretical analysis have been much in evidence in the expansion of UK provision in educational management (Hughes, Carter and Fidler 1981), in the parallel growth of the British Educational Management and Administration Society as an association bringing together the practitioners and the academics, and in the increasing availability of relevant books and journals.

A field of application

As Hills (1980, p. 225) reminded his US colleagues at IIP 1978, an applied science is required to pay close attention to the special characteristics of its field of practice, which need to be thoroughly and sympathetically understood. One cannot automatically assume, without further testing, that intellectual currency minted for other economies will be acceptable in the educational market place. Research and analysis has to be done in an educational context, which may reveal the need for substantial modification of concepts and methodologies developed elsewhere. The need for awareness and sensitivity in relation to the problems and concerns of practice as defined by practitioners makes it particularly appropriate that most of the contributors to this book regard themselves primarily as practitioners rather than as academics.

A multidisciplinary study

In the past, organisational studies in education have drawn mainly on social psychology, sociology and economics. The range of borrowings has broadened to include philosophy, political science, anthropology, a diversity of micro-social sciences, and the methods of qualitative, as well as quantitative, research. Also recognised as of interest are the many-sided contemporary studies of organisational structures and change processes, in schools of management studies which have long superseded the simplicities of the traditional management writers.

Indiscriminate borrowing, however, resulting in the accumulation of an undigested aggregation of discrete bits of incompatible theory, is likely to be unproductive in achieving understanding. In choosing an eclectic mode of proceeding, Snyder recognised that it is essential to be aware of the strengths and limitations of the concepts and methodologies of the particular discipline or sub-discipline one is using, and also of the underlying assumptions of the perspective adopted.

Given such understanding, a pragmatic approach which is prepared, circumspectly and critically, to make use of more than one perspective, is likely to provide greater insight into the complexities of an educational system than a methodology which confines attention to one kind of problem or one mode of inquiry. In similar vein Gareth Morgan (1980) has advocated 'a theoretical and methodological pluralism which allows the development of new perspectives for organisational analysis' (p. 605). He called for uncontested assumptions to be exposed to the challenge of alternative ways of seeing. A cosmopolitan outlook would enable the practitioner and the theorist to avoid being imprisoned by a single set of metaphors.

In the present volume various aspects of current interest in the management of educational systems and institutions will be described and considered using a variety of models and approaches, the models providing a framework for coherent analysis. In some cases alternative models might also be appropriate, and it would be a rewarding exercise for the reader to test out such possibilities. To give some indication of the vitality and rich diversity of the ideas available, selected areas of recent and continuing theory development, which may be of use as sources of concepts and models applicable to educational management, will now be briefly described.

A diversity of structural models

A considerable body of empirical research and theory development on organisational structure may be interpreted as a vigorous rejection by later structuralists of the classical doctrine, equally upheld by Fayol and Weber, that there is *one* right model of organisation. The universal acceptance of the ideal of a tight hierarchical structure has given way to the concept of *structural relativism*, which permits alternative, more differentiated, and more flexible structures.

Burns and Stalker (1961), on the basis of their pioneering study of innovation in Scottish electrical companies, had come to the conclusion that 'the beginning of administrative wisdom is that there is no optimum type of management system' (p. 125). They identified a pair of contrasting ideal-type management structures, a *mechanistic* form appropriate to stable conditions and an *organic* or *organismic* form to handle less predictable problems more flexibly. Litwak (1961) showed that different types of structure may be appropriate even within the same organisation, a human relations model being applicable in handling work of a non-uniform nature and a Weberian model in dealing with uniform work of a routine nature.

A comparative study by Lawrence and Lorsch (1967) of ten varied industrial organisations led to the construction of a 'contingency model', which developed further the implications of the view that structures are contingent upon the problems with which they have to deal. They identified and produced measures of distinct organisational sub-environments, matching each sub-environment to an appropriate sub-unit structure. 'Goodness of fit' became the important issue. The more turbulent and uncertain the environment, the greater the tendency for a high level of performance to be associated with high differentiation among sub-units, coupled with effective integration achieved by means of shared information, flexible procedures and open decision-making.

Another approach also challenged the unitary concept of bureaucracy by seeking to identify and measure a number of independent dimensions of organisational structure. Work by Hall (1963) in the USA was followed by an impressive array of systematic empirical studies by the Aston group in England, which have been brought together in a series of volumes (Pugh and Hickson 1976; Pugh and Hinings 1976; Pugh and Payne 1977). The dimensions identified in these studies were: specialisation of activities, standardisation of procedure, formalisation of documentation, centralisation of authority, and configuration of role structure. They also developed measures of contextual and performance variables, and explored relationships between variables, using factor analysis and correlational induction. The studies originally used heterogeneous samples of commercial and governmental organisations to develop general propositions connecting structure and context, and the group's exclusive preoccupation in such studies with variables involving objective quantifiable data at the expense of political and ideological factors has been severely criticised (Burrell and Morgan 1979; Clegg and Dunkerley 1980).

Interestingly, some later but loosely related cross-institutional studies of local authorities (Greenwood, Hinings and Ransom 1975) and of churches (Hinings 1979), using a contingency theory approach, have led to the conclusion that belief systems and ideologies, which had previously been regarded as irrelevant, deserved detailed study. A theoretical model has been proposed which includes the conceptual categories of provinces of meaning and power dependencies, as well as contextual constraints (Ransom, Hinings and Greenwood 1980). Whereas the more technical aspects of the research produced as a result of the original Aston studies may not be directly relevant to educational management, the methodological flexibility which their dimensional approach entailed is certainly of interest, as is the recent move to develop a framework to incorporate 'ostensibly disparate perspectives' with a view to 'searching for the relations between cause and meaning, between what is determinant and what voluntary in the relation of structure and action' (Ransom, Hinings and Greenwood, 1980, p. 14).

In selectively reviewing structural models, it is appropriate finally to refer to two theoretical contributions which substantially widen the meaning of the term 'structural relativism'. The metaphor of a rigid invariant structure is fundamentally challenged both by Karl Weick's (1976) perception of organisations as 'loosely coupled systems' and by the closely related 'organised anarchies' of Cohen, March and Olsen (1972), which appear to provide the ultimate antithesis to Weberian bureaucracy.

Loose coupling, a term previously used by March and Olsen (1975), is intended to signify that the parts of an organisation are in *some* relationship to each other, but that the linkage is limited, uncertain and weak, and certainly much looser than the tight hierarchical control of bureaucratic theory. Weick added that loose coupling also 'carries connotations of impermanence, dissolvability and tacitness all of which are potentially crucial properties of the "glue" that holds organisations together' (1976, p. 3). He argued specifically that educational organisations can be viewed as loosely coupled systems. In Chapter 4 of the present volume the applicability of the model is tested in relation to policy-making for the school curriculum.

Meyer and Rowan (1977), who used the concept in an empirical study of school structures, concluded that loose coupling helps to maintain the facade that formal structures are really working when they are not. In a later paper Weick (1980) accepted that loose coupling can be seen as having a stabilising function, in that the connection points of sub-systems act as shock absorbers which internalise pressures rather than transmitting them to other parts of the system. A further factor is that feedback is neutralised as a result of incomplete information being available concerning the effects of previous action. Because of such considerations Foster (1983) has argued that the flexibility claimed for loosely coupled systems is illusory, and that the concept is not essentially different from the 'exception principle' of Frederick Taylor's Scientific Management, which allows for attention to be focused on exceptions to the smooth flow of work (Foster 1983, pp. 20–21).

Writing from an educational management viewpoint, Willower (1980, p. 6) repeated the suggestion in Weick's original paper that the extent of coupling should be investigated as a dependent variable, subject to the influences of organisational and environmental factors. As Weick further observed, 'If an organisation faces a scarcity of resources its pattern of couplings should differ from when it faces an expansion of resources . . .' (1976, pp. 13–14). It may be noted that scarcity in the resources currently available to the maintained school system in the UK is likely to be one factor, among others, contributing to the tightening of curriculum control at national level which is noted by James Waddington in Chapter 4.

The term 'organised anarchy' is intended to signify structural looseness in an extreme form. It is a fair description of the 'Garbage Can Model of Organisational Choice' described by Cohen, March and Olsen (1972), and further developed by Cohen and March (1974), and by March and Olsen (1976). In such an organisation the goals are inconsistent and ill-defined, the technology for achieving them is unclear to the members, and those involved in decision-making vary unpredictably. Thus problems, solutions and decision-makers are not systematically related to each other. Problems may be created in order to provide opportunities for applying previously discovered solutions, and decision-making serves purposes other than the production of decisions. Organisational choice may be viewed as being achieved by various participants unpredictably throwing various kinds of problems and solutions into a 'garbage can'. Such an organisation, in brief, is characterised by severe ambiguity and irrationality.

The creators of the model applied it in a university context. Colin Turner (1977, p. 8) has argued that it also applies to further education colleges and polytechnics operating within turbulent, unpredictable environments. The model has attracted wide interest because of its vivid portrayal of the fact that the completely rational organisation is no more likely to exist in real life than its antithesis. Padgett (1980) operationalised the theory to show how variable ambiguity impinges on decision-making at different levels in a traditional Weberian bureaucracy, and showed that the model is potentially applicable even when the system is not highly decoupled. Lutz (1982) argued that universities are differentially coupled, 'tightly coupled in some aspects and uncoupled in others'. It is the informal system, he suggested, which can best be described as an organised anarchy. 'Academe is not so fragile', he concluded, 'that it could not survive tighter coupling' (1982, p. 668).

In this section a diversity of approaches to organisational structure have been described which may be regarded as portraying different ways of bringing the ideal rational structures of traditional management theory into closer touch with the 'brute facts' of real life. The different models can each provide significant insight in particular circumstances. Even the most sophisticated model, however, can only provide partial enlightenment. Structural approaches of themselves, as Ransom, Hinings and Greenwood (1980) came to appreciate, do not take account of the values, motivations and power relationships of organisational participants.

Policy-making models

Grant Harman (1980), in his study of the policy process in education, found it necessary to take account of twelve different models taken from political science and other disciplines. Here brief reference will be made to three different frameworks: Easton's political systems model, Simon's modified rational model, and Lindblom's incremental model.

A political systems model was proposed by David Easton (1965) as a framework for political analysis. It was developed as a means of considering the process of policy-making at national level, Easton's distinctive insight being that the political system can be conceptualised as the means for the authoritative allocation within society of valued things. The output of the system is thus the allocation of benefits and resources made through the enunciation of government policies, consequent decisions and the implementation of actions.

The system's inputs are of two kinds. First, there are the demands which finally reach the political agenda as items for political decision. A sophisticated and often protracted process is involved, by which general wants are crystallised into specific demands, which are then progressively modified, combined, and reduced in the interest of 'realism' by interest groups, political parties and officials. The second type of input consists of the general support which the political system requires in order to function effectively. This involves the concept of a political community which is supportive of the political system generally, of the regime of rules and regulations by which decisions are made, and of those in authority who make the decisions. Feedback mechanisms, providing information concerning reactions within society to allocations made or proposed, enable the system in normal circumstances to adapt and regulate its processes as necessary to cope with disturbance and potential conflict. There is thus an assumption, which is a basic feature of the systems viewpoint, that there is sufficient stability and consensual agreement on values in the society for the allocative decisions of the authorities to be generally accepted.

Though developed in a national context, the model clearly has potential for more general application, such as to policy-making in the local education service (cf Chapter 5). In this context it is of interest that Easton himself has recently referred appreciatively, in a foreword to Howell and Brown's (1983) twin studies of policy-making in education, to the conceptual novelty, daring, and genuine promise of regarding educational organisations as parapolitical systems, the scope of the term 'political' being thereby broadened.

While Easton's model thus provides an appropriate framework for appreciating the essentially political nature of policy-making, it does not provide an analysis of the different stages involved in the decision-making process. A number of approaches to the process of decision-making are possible, ranging from the comprehensively rational to the modestly incremental.

The classical or rational approach, as described by March and Simon (1958), may be regarded as the ideal if time and resources are plentiful. Three phases are involved, the first being that of problem recognition. This may be no simple matter in a complex situation, as Vickers (1967) has noted; it would require judgement based on experience and an alertness of mind. The second phase is the search for solutions, which may be a routine matter if the problem can be computer-programmed. If the problem is novel and unusual, creative solutions along completely new lines may have to be sought. The third and final phase is that of choosing a particular solution, having regard to the costs and benefits of alternative solutions. This requires not only a technical appraisal of feasibility but also a judgement of what is practical and politically expedient in the given circumstances, having regard to demands and supports.

A modification to the rational model, first proposed by Simon (1947), has been named the 'satisficing' model. This takes account of the constraints and pressures on those involved in decision-making by limiting the search for solutions to those considered most promising and ending the search as soon as a solution is found which is regarded as reasonably satisfactory in the circumstances. 'Satisficing' is the term introduced to indicate that the policy-maker accepts the first alternative regarded as satisfactory rather than continuing the search for an optimum solution. In this way Simon conceded that the splendid rationality of 'economic man' assumed in the classical theory has to give way in practice to the more modest notion of the bounded rationality of 'administrative man'.

A hard-headed appreciation of what actually happens in many real life situations is even more evident in the 'disjointed incrementalism' model of Lindblom (1959; 1979). This accepts the idea that in practice it is often only a small step, rather than a radical change, which is likely to be acceptable to the diverse groups that the policy-maker has to satisfy. The policies considered are therefore only slightly, or incrementally, different from those previously followed, but a small move in the desired direction may be possible. As external conditions permit or internal changes take place, it becomes possible to make further small advances, so that improvement is achieved not by a continuous process but by a patient strategy of 'disjointed incrementalism'. The process is also 'exploratory in that goals of policy-making continue to change as new experience with policy throws new light on what is possible or desirable' (Braybrooke and Lindblom 1963, p. 71).

Such a mode of proceeding, well known to experienced educational managers, has been dubbed 'the science of muddling through'. It involves cultivating a political awareness of what can be achieved in the short term, but without necessarily compromising commitment to long-term objectives. In this respect it differs markedly from the random separation of problems and solutions which is a characteristic of Cohen, March and Olsen's organisational anarchy.

The examples of policy-making models that have been given serve to illustrate some of the ways that theories are structured or are modified to take account of the specifics of practice. They also suggest that different approaches are not necessarily to be treated as exclusive alternatives, but may complement each other by illuminating different facets of complex reality.

Emerging perspectives in the economics of education

Though educational finances have always been a concern of educational administrators at the system level, it may be claimed that sustained academic study of economic aspects of education both in the UK and in the USA began in the late 1950s. An early UK outcome was John Vaizey's (1958) *The Costs of Education*, while in the USA 'Investment in Man' was the significant title of Theodore Shultz's presidential address to the American Economic Association in 1960. The rapid development of empirical studies which then took place in the USA, involving the analysis by computer of elaborate census returns, also inspired more modest studies in the UK (Woodhall, 1972).

That the new subject had implications for educational policy-making and educational management was soon appreciated. Mark Blaug (1983, p. 7) recently referred to the decade of the 1960s as the golden years 'when no self-respecting Minister of Education would have dreamed of making educational decisions without an economist sitting at his right hand'. By the middle of the decade Innes, Jacobson and Pellegrin (1965) were already reporting to US educational administrators the human capital and economic growth findings of Schultz, Becker, Denison and others, which were endorsed as 'highly significant research on the economic benefits accruing to the individual and to society from investment in education' (p. v). Similarly Peston (1969, p. 63), in a chapter linking economics with the administration of education in the Baron and Taylor volume, argued that the economics of education is of value to the administrator in the way it formulates problems and in its methods of research, and because of its substantive empirical contributions.

The rapid worldwide growth of the subject owed much to the interest of international agencies and of governments in both developed and developing countries in the part played by education in economic growth. Interest was particularly focused on the key concept of human capital, the invention of which, according to Blaug (1976), could be regarded as a very significant paradigm change in the Kuhnian sense. Reviewing the field, Williams (1982, p. 98) concluded that to most authors 'human capital theory is at the heart of the economics of education'.

According to human capital theory, education enhances productivity so that educational expenditure is as much a form of investment, for both the individual and the society, as capital investment in industrial installation and equipment. From this perspective the resource requirements of education and training (i.e. the capital outlay) are viewed exclusively in terms of the increased income to be derived from that outlay. The propositions underlying the theory were amenable to empirical investigation, which was undertaken on a massive scale in the United States. Some work was also done in the UK, mainly by special surveys to compare the average earnings of persons with different levels of education.

Peston (1969), while admitting that research in Britain was 'still in a most primitive condition' (p. 62), provided a summary of substantive findings as follows:

> That having allowed for all the other variables which are likely to influence the distribution of income and having attributed the remaining income difference to education, the value of education in producing income differences may be calculated as a rate of return. This return is typically in the range 6–12 per cent per annum and compares favourably with returns to investment in the public and private sectors. From the point of view of the individual this formulation is adequate. From the national standpoint an additional assumption has to be made, namely, that incomes measure productivities (more strictly, that income differences measure differences in marginal productivities). (p. 63)

Peston himself was prepared to make such an assumption, as is evident from a later passage:

> Using work of this kind it is possible to calculate what share of a country's growth is attributable to improvements in human capital as opposed simply to the quantity of labour,

physical capital and technical progress. As much as fifty per cent of growth is attributable to human capital. (p. 63)

Reviewing the situation over a decade later, Williams (1982, p. 99) was distinctly more cautious. He warned that, since relative earnings are to some extent dependent on supply and demand, which change with time, past experience was an unreliable guide to future development. He conceded, however, that 'expenditure on education has in the past been, and is seen to be, a worthwhile *private* investment' (p. 99). Whether it is also a worthwhile *social* investment was in his view a more debatable proposition.

Similar doubts have been expressed by Blaug (1983) in his exposition of what he called a second-generation economics of education, which developed the subject in new directions in the 1970s but did not 'perhaps deliver the same firm pronouncements on matters of educational policy as did the first generation' (p. 9). He singled out two new directions of particular relevance to human capital theory: first the recognition, stimulated by the neo-Marxian critique of Bowles and Gintis (1976), that schools have a significant socialising function, i.e. the transmitting of specific values and attitudes, which is overlooked by teachers and orthodox economists whose emphasis is on the imparting of cognitive knowledge; and second the challenge to human capital theory, as formulated in 1960s, which is presented by the so-called 'screening hypothesis'. Each requires some elaboration.

If the second-generation view is accepted — that socialisation, rather than the acquisition of skills and knowledge, is the primary economic function of education — there are implications to be drawn for practice which differ significantly from the standpoint traditionally expected of economists. First, it would appear that attempts, in the presumed interest of the labour market, to make secondary education more specifically vocational at the expense of general education may be misguided and irrelevant. Second, doubts are raised about the wisdom of educational planning, whether in developed or developing countries, which relies on precise forecasts of manpower requirements for different kinds of educational attainment.

The screening hypothesis adds another dimension to the conceptual framework, by proposing a further economic function for education. Education appears to assist employment agencies by separating out, at different stages, those regarded as less suitable for positions of responsibility and higher salary. A strong version of the hypothesis therefore claims that education is no more than a filtering device, conveniently regarded by all concerned as fair and appropriate, which identifies those with the attributes required in different positions but which does nothing to create or develop those attributes. Blaug concluded, after reviewing the empirical evidence, that this strong version of the hypothesis is untenable. If education were simply a screening mechanism, it would obviously be cheaper and simpler, as Blaug observed (1983, p. 15), to replace it by a battery of personality tests.

A weaker interpretation of the hypothesis, which recognises that educational qualifications (whatever their other functions and merits) are in fact used as predictors of future job performance, can hardly be disputed, as Blaug also admitted. He further suggested that, because promotions usually involve the operation of an 'internal labour market' rather than external competition, advantages at initial appointment tend to be perpetuated throughout working life.

The extent to which a modified human capital theory can accommodate the new insights of Blaug's second-generation economists of education is a matter of continuing debate, which clearly has direct relevance for government policy and for the management of education. If, as advocates of stronger versions of the screening hypothesis claim, increased educational expenditure for further and higher education simply gives salary and employment advantages to the better qualified, it is difficult to justify continued total dependence on public funding which, as Williams (1982, p. 101) notes, 'provides able individuals with additional lifetime benefits at the expense of their contemporaries'. On the other hand, if educational expenditure can be shown to be a significant factor in increasing national productivity, the case for relying in the main on public finance for the provision of further and higher education will continue to be strong.

Educational costs, resource utilisation and manpower forecasting and planning can be cited as further areas of theory development and research of relevance to both the study and the practice of educational management, the economist's constant concern being to analyse the implications and explore the consequences of alternative uses of resources. The concepts and methodologies of economics are thus likely to have a contribution to make to the professional development of educational managers. It may be instructive for the reader to consider, in view of the previous discussion, whether this would be as human capital investment or as part of a sophisticated occupational screening device.

Micropolitics and other micro-perspectives

New directions which have recently emerged in the social sciences, potentially of significance for educational management practice, have in common a concern with individual persons and their perceptions of the events in which they are involved, rather than a primary emphasis on collectivities and institutions. Such studies, which may collectively be called the micro-social sciences, vary in theoretical background, basic assumptions and areas of specific interest. Their methodologies differ to some extent, but broadly rely on ethnographic research methods, i.e. on qualitative research, including participant observation (Hammersley and Atkinson 1983).

In particular, the significance for educational management of *micropolitics* has been recognised in the UK (Pratt 1982), the term being used to embrace 'those strategies by which individuals and groups in organisational contexts seek to use their resources of power and influence to further their interests' (Hoyle 1982, p. 88). In responding to Hoyle's paper, Bailey (1982 p. 101) suggested that 'degree of legitimacy' is a useful concept in considering the propriety of political strategies, while Glatter (1982 p. 162) warned against regarding micropolitical analysis as prescriptive as well as descriptive.

The concepts of micropolitics, significantly gaining currency in a period of worldwide resource constraint, throw into relief the limitations of theories which virtually ignore the issue of power, through their reliance on rational choice and bureaucratic models of organisation (Pfeffer 1978; Bacharach and Lawler 1980; Pfeffer 1981). It was proposed that more attention should be given to the micro-events of organisational politics, defined by Pfeffer (1981, p. 7) as 'those activities taken within organisations to acquire, develop and use power and other resources to obtain one's preferred outcomes in a situation in which there is uncertainty or dissensus about choices'. A similar suggestion had been made by Zaleznik (1970), as noted by Handy (1976), and by Baldridge (1971).

The micropolitical model begins by recognising the diversity of perspectives and goals within organisations, which are pluralistic in terms of values and beliefs and are divided into various interests, sub-units and sub-cultures (Baldridge 1971, p. 25). In contrast to classical and human relations management models — which rely respectively on structural control devices and on normative influences to achieve consensus on organisational objectives and models of implementation — the political model accepts that, in practice, general agreement on goals and technology cannot be taken for granted. In this respect it is similar to the garbage can model previously discussed, but does not accept the anarchic view that decisions are the adventitious result of the interplay of opportunities, problems, persons and solutions. The randomness implied in the garbage can model, according to Pfeffer (1981, p. 30), 'is inconsistent with the observation that in organisational decision-making, some actors seem usually to get the garbage, while others manage to get the can'. At least some organisational participants, it appears, know what they want and have the power to get it.

The key themes, as identified by Bacharach and Lawler (1980), are power, coalitions and bargaining. Shifting coalitions promote the opposing interests of different organisational sub-groups. Decisions are the result of bargaining and compromise; they are unlikely to satisfy completely the preferences of any individual or sub-group, but will tend to favour the preferences of those with most power and influence. Attention has thus been given to the measurement of intra-organisational power within organisations, considered as bargaining and influence systems (Abell 1975).

Whereas power is, in part, structurally related, it is claimed that structures are themselves to some extent politically determined. 'To understand organisational design, one must examine the distribution of power and the preferences of those in the organisation's dominant coalition' (Pfeffer 1981, p. 271). Similarly Child (1984) recommends a 'political contingency approach' to organisational design. Among the political skills which are then helpful in operating within the structure are an ability to assess the issues which can be won and those which are hopeless, and an ability, taking account of changes in power distribution, to form new coalitions and structures.

Several writers (Peters 1978; Mangham 1979; Pfeffer 1981) have given attention to the crucial role of political language and symbolic action, involving ceremonies, symbols and settings. This applies both in mobilising support and quieting opposition, and, as in Mangham's action research, in encouraging, guiding and sustaining organisational change. Mangham draws on the symbolic interactionist viewpoint of Blumer (1969) to illuminate the self-reflective character of human relationships in organisations, involving interpretive interaction and tentative definitions of situations, in which non-verbal language may be as significant as what is actually said.

Blumer's *symbolic interactionism* is one of a number of micro-sociologies which may now be briefly noted. Its relevance to Mangham's work may be surmised from the following quotation:

> Symbolic interaction involves *interpretation*, or ascertaining the meaning of the actions or remarks of the other person, and *definition*, or conveying indications to another person as to how he is to act. Human association consists of a process of such interpretation and definition. Through this process the participants fit their own acts to the ongoing acts of one another and guide others in doing so. (Blumer 1966, p. 538)

In its more subjective form symbolic interactionism claims that it is through the process of interacting, and only so, that participants create for themselves a meaningful social world.

The resulting research task is to discover how participants come to agree upon certain meanings and definitions for co-ordinated action (Denzin 1970).

Ethnomethodology switches the focus of enquiry from the interactive situation to the methods by which everyday life situations are organised, perceived and understood. It has sought, 'by paying to the most commonplace activities of daily life the attention usually accorded extraordinary events . . . to learn about them as phenomena in their own right' (Garfinkel 1967, p. 1). The use of language has been studied, as has the fact that conversations convey meanings beyond what is actually said (Cicourel 1972). The way in which social contexts are negotiated has been examined, and organisational concepts such as structure and efficiency are taken as problematic, i.e. as topics to be investigated rather than terms to be taken for granted (Bittner 1965).

Other micro-social approaches of potential relevance include: *ethogenics* (Harré 1977) which analyses social episodes through the verbal accounts which people give to explain their actions; *hermeneutics* (Gadamer 1975), which seeks to understand situations by an iterative process — the hermeneutic circle — such as is used cumulatively in the interpretation of literary texts; and *critical theory*, which — as developed by Habermas (1974) — might be described as a radical version of hermeneutics. The relevance of critical theory for educational administration practice has been strongly advocated by Bates (1982) and challenged by Lane (1983).

There are thus a number of different approaches which overlap in their areas of interest, but differ in theoretical background and ideological assumptions. A common feature is that they seek to come to terms, as has happened in modern physics in the wake of Heisenberg's uncertainty principle, with the inescapable fact that the investigators themselves and their methodologies are in integral part of the situation being investigated (Hammersley and Atkinson 1983). Though the philosophical debate will long continue, it appears that the customary sharp differentiation, between the assumed objectivity of a positivism based on an outmoded view of natural science and the admitted subjectivity of the micro-social sciences (some of which have been described above), may prove to have been an over-simplification.

An early integration of micro- and macro-perspectives does not seem to be at hand, in spite of Cicourel's recent optimism and his injunction that 'we must study the way human decision-making in complex micro-settings contributes to the creation of macro-structures by routine problem solving activities necessary for the simulation or realisation of basic organisational goals' (1981, p. 67). It may be, however, that those involved in educational organisations, whether primarily as practitioners or as students, will be disposed to accept the validity of the seeming paradox enunciated in the same volume by Knorr-Cetina. She suggests that 'it is through micro-social approaches that we will learn most about the macro-order, for it is these approaches which through their unashamed empiricism afford us a glimpse of the reality about which we speak' (1981, pp. 41–2).

THEORY AND PRACTICE IN TENSION

For Thomas Kuhn (1977) the essential tension was between tradition and innovation in scientific research — the tension that leads in time to paradigm change within a scientific community. There is a sense, however, in which Kuhn's tension is subsumed within that more basic tension between theory and practice which has been the underlying theme of this chapter.

It has been customary for practitioners to state the dichotomy in robust terms: airy-fairy theory versus down-to-earth practice. Sir Edward Bridges (1956, p. 23), when he was Permanent Secretary to the Treasury, put his emphasis squarely on the value of 'working with or working under people who have far more experience, far more wisdom in handling affairs and dealing with people than I had'. Similarly it has been suggested that understanding the pupils, having commonsense, and being able to profit by experience are the only essential requirements for school headship (Thomas 1927).

Lest it be thought that such views would be exceptional today, it is salutary to note, from a Birmingham University dissertation (Turner 1981), the results of a survey of 66 recently appointed first-time secondary school heads. Placing little reliance on 'concepts, techniques, theories, perspectives', the new head teachers

> stress operational problems and their practical solution strictly in terms of the educational context. Moreover they prefer to rely upon personal qualities and wide experience rather than the findings of observation and research to inform the decision-making process. (p. 75)

Such a viewpoint would presumably not preclude learning from the experience of others, as suggested by Bridges, or from common sense, as recommended by Thomas. It thus involves an acceptance of the distilled wisdom of past experience as concentrated in the precepts of common sense. Commonsense knowledge, however, inevitably carries with it unspoken assumptions and unrecognised limitations. Theorising is taking place without it being acknowledged as such.

In contrast, the theorising about management of Taylor, Fayol, Gulick and the rest, the engineers and captains of industry who produced the pioneer management texts, was quite explicit. It was essentially a commonsense extention of their own considerable and relevant practical experience. Generalisations were then often made with unwarranted assurance, and there was little appreciation, even by proponents of scientific manage-ment, that attention needs to be given to the critical conditions which have to be satisfied for propositions found to be tenable in one context to be relevant also in an entirely different situation. This last observation is particularly applicable, as Fielding (1984) has noted, when attempts are made to apply general principles of management developed in an industrial context to other areas, such as education.

Such strictures are less applicable to the human relations tradition, which drew on a number of carefully conducted research projects. Though these may be criticised with hindsight for methodological and conceptual defects, they were successful in drawing attention to human variables inadequately recognised in traditional management theory. As applied to education, human relations ideas found a ready response, as has been noted, because of the support they provided for more participative and democratic forms of management.

For both the classical and the human relations management writers, the immediacy of the claimed connection with practice was paramount. Theory consisted essentially of generalisations from past experience and field observation, whether by scientific management efficiency experts or human relations industrial psychologists.

The New Movement in educational administration and comparable developments in other management areas, such as those which resulted in the founding of the journal,

Administrative Science Quarterly, in 1956, provided a very different kind of justification for theory and for its relationship to practice. Henceforth, as with the laws of motion of Newtonian dynamics, theory was to consist of assumed relationships between operationally defined concepts, from which empirical laws would be defined and tested. From this viewpoint it is theory which gives meaning to facts, rather than the reverse. The point was clearly made by Griffiths:

> Facts, to be of value, must bear a relationship to one another. The use of theory in the gathering of facts provides this relationship . . . But over and above the search for new facts is the concept that theory gives meaning to the facts which are uncovered. (1959a, p. 26)

It does this by providing practitioners with sets of concepts which enable them to organise the facts with which they have to deal in a systematic and orderly manner. According to Goldhammer (1963), social science concepts provide the tools 'through which the administrator finds the meaning and the significance of events which confront him' (p. 15), and hence provide the means necessary 'for the development of an independent science of educational administration' (p. 21).

Even in the early days of the New Movement, misgivings were expressed concerning the dangers of excessive abstraction. 'There are scientists, and administrators too', stated Halpin (1958), 'who consistently soar in the clouds. They forget that theory must be rooted in the actual world of experience'. He later complained (Halpin 1960) that 'the theoretical models are too rational, too tidy, too aseptic' and that the school superintendent feels that they omit 'much of the palpable stuff which quickens his pulse in his daily job'.

What the practitioners were in fact saying was that the theories they were being offered, far from providing new perspectives for ordering their experience, were ignoring aspects of that experience which they regarded as important. The rather modest success achieved within the New Movement paradigm has already been described, research findings relying more on statistical techniques than on insightful conceptualisation. As Iannaconne (1973) observed, 'We have rigorously tested a lot of poor ideas in educational administration'.

The latter part of the chapter has sought to show how the recognition of educational management as a field of application, rather than a unitary science, has enabled more productive relationships to be developed with the world of practice. This has taken place partly because of the diversity of perspectives in the social sciences and other disciplines, such as philosophy (Hodgkinson 1978), on which an applied field may nowadays draw, and partly because the theories and models currently available make it possible to come closer to the irreducible 'brute facts' of real life of which Whitehead (1926) wrote.

The trend to take closer account of the reality of practice has been demonstrated in a number of areas. Whereas the high abstraction of Weber's ideal-type conceptualisation of bureaucracy contributed immensely to clarifying the concept of organisation as a structure, the various models introduced under the heading of structural relativism, from the binary construct of Burns and Stalker to the organised anarchy of March, Cohen and Olsen, provide examples of ways in which different aspects and assumptions of the classical model can be challenged from the viewpoint of practice. Contrasting models of policy-making for different kinds of situations have been similarly described. Human capital theory in the economics of education provides an example of the modification of a powerful concept of relevance in educational policy-making to take account of perspectives and mechanisms identified by second generation economists of education.

Micropolitics has been shown to illuminate an aspect of organisational life, very familiar to practitioners, which is inadequately handled in mainstream theories mainly concerned with the rational achievement of agreed objectives. The related micro-social sciences, by careful analysis of events, language and behaviour, provide insights into how individuals perceive and create their own organisational life and contribute to that of others. The intensely human nature of organisational involvement is highlighted, its implications for understanding and for practice being matters of continuing debate. A further matter for debate is the extent to which reconciliation is possible between macro- and micro-approaches to educational management.

The tension between theory and practice in educational management and in cognate areas of applied social science shows little sign of abating. Such tension can be dissipated and wasted in uncomprehending, sterile debate, but this is not inevitable. Tension can also be dynamic and creative, leading to deeper understanding and to a consequent improvement in the practice of educational management. May it always be so.

REFERENCES

Abell, P. (ed.) (1975) *Organisations as Bargaining and Influence Systems*. London: Heinemann.

Albrow, M. (1970) *Bureaucracy*. London: Macmillan.

American Association of School Administrators (1963) *The Education of a School Superintendent*. Washington, D.C.: AASA

Anderson, J. G. (1968) *Bureaucracy in Education*. Baltimore: Johns Hopkins Press.

Andrews, J. H. M. (1965) 'What school climate conditions are desirable?' *The Council on School Administration Bulletin* (Calgary, Alberta), 4(5), 4–20.

Bacharach, S. B. and Lawler, E. J. (1980) *Power and Politics in Organisations*. San Francisco: Josey Bass.

Bailey, T. (1982) 'The question of legitimation: a response to Eric Hoyle'. *Educational Management and Administration*, 10(2) 99–105.

Baker, R. J. S. (1980) *Organisation and Management Theory*. Sheffield: Sheffield City Polytechnic.

Baldridge, J. V. (1971) *Power and Conflict in the University*. New York: Wiley.

Balzac, H. de (1836) *Les Employés*, quoted by Albrow, M. (1970) in translation by Marriage, E. (1898) *Bureaucracy*.

Barnard, C. I. (1938) *The Functions of the Executive*. Cambridge, Mass.: Harvard University Press.

Baron, G., Cooper, D. H. and Walker, W. G. (ed.) (1969) *Educational Administration: International Perspectives*. Chicago: Rand McNally.

Baron, G. and Taylor, W. (ed.) (1969) *Educational Administration and the Social Sciences*. London: Athlone.

Bassett, G. W., Crane, A. R. and Walker, W. G. (1963) *Headmasters for Better Schools*. St. Lucia: University of Queensland Press.

Bates, A. W. (1970) 'The administration of comprehensive schools'. In Monks, T. G. (ed.) *Comprehensive Education in Action*. Slough, Bucks: NFER.

Bates, R. J. (1982) 'Towards a critical practice of educational administration', *Studies in Educational Administration*, CCEA, 27, 1–15.

Becher, T. and Kogan, M. (1980) *Process and Structure in Higher Education*. London: Heinemann.

Becher, T. and Maclure, S. (ed.) (1978) *Accountability in Education*. Windsor, Berks: NFER Publishing.

Belasco, J. A. and Alutto, J. A. (1972) 'Decisional participation and teacher satisfaction'. *Educational Administration Quarterly*, 8(1) 44–58.

Bernbaum, G. (1976) 'The role of the head'. In Peters, R. S. (ed.) *The Role of the Head*. London: Routledge and Kegan Paul.

Bittner, E. (1965) 'The concept of organisation'. *Social Research*, **32**, 239–55.

Blau, P. M. and Scott, W. (1963) *Formal Organisations: a Comparative Approach*. London: Routledge and Kegan Paul.

Blaug, M. (1976) 'The empirical status of Human Capital Theory: a slightly jaundiced view'. *Journal of Economic Literature*, **14**(3) 827–55.

Blaug, M. (1983) 'Where are we now in the Economics of Education?', *Special Professional Lecture*. London: University of London Institute of Education.

Blumer, H. (1966) 'Sociological implications, of the thought of George Herbert Mead'. *American Journal of Sociology*, **71**(5) 535–48.

Blumer, H. (1969) *Symbolic Interactionism: Perspectives and Method*. Englewood Cliffs, N.J.: Prentice-Hall.

Bowles, S. and Gintis, H. (1976) *Schooling in Capitalist America*. London: Routledge and Kegan Paul.

Braybrooke, D. and Lindblom, C. E. (1963) *A Strategy of Decision*. New York: Free Press.

Bridges, E. (1956) 'Administration: what is it? and how can it be learnt?' In Dunsire, A. (ed.) *The Making of an Administrator*. Manchester: Manchester University Press.

Brown, R. J. (1965) 'Identifying and classifying organizational climates in twin cities area elementary schools'. Paper quoted in Halpin (1967).

Burns, T. and Stalker, G. M. (1961) *The Management of Innovation*. London: Tavistock.

Burrell, G. and Morgan, G. (1979) *Sociological Paradigms and Organisational Analysis*. London: Heinemann.

Bush, T., Glatter, R., Goodey, J. and Riches, C. (ed.) (1980) *Approaches to School Management*. London: Harper and Row.

Callahan, R. E. (1962) *Education and the Cult of Efficiency*. Chicago: University of Chicago Press.

Campbell, R. F., Corbally, J. E. and Ramseyer, J. A. (1966) *Introduction to Educational Administration*, 3rd edition. Boston: Allyn and Bacon.

Campbell, R. F. and Gregg, R. T. (ed.) (1957) *Administrative Behavior in Education*. New York: Harper.

Campbell, R. F. and Newell, L. J. (1973) *A Study of Professors of Educational Administration*. Columbus, Ohio: University Council for Educational Administration.

Carlson, R. O. (1962) *Executive Succession and Organisational Change*. Chicago: University of Chicago.

Chase, F. S. (1952) 'The teacher and policy making: how democratic can you get?'. *Administrator's Notebook*, **1**(1) 1–4.

Child, J. (1984) *Organisation: a guide to problems and practice*, 2nd edition. London: Harper and Row.

Cicourel, A. V. (1972) *Cognitive Sociology: Language and Meaning in Social Interaction*. Harmondsworth, Middlesex: Penguin.

Cicourel, A. V. (1981) 'Notes on the integration of micro- and macro- levels of analysis'. In Knorr-Cetina, K. and Cicourel, A. V. (ed.) *Advances in Social Theory and Methodology*. London: Routledge and Kegan Paul.

Clegg, S. and Dunkerley, D. (1980) *Organization, Class and Control*. London: Routledge and Kegan Paul.

Cohen, L. (1970) 'School size and head teachers' bureaucratic role conceptions'. *Educational Review*, **23**, 50–58.

Cohen, M., March, J. and Olsen, J. (1972) 'A garbage-can model of organisational choice'. *Administrative Science Quarterly*, **17**(1) 1–25.

Cohen, M. and March, J. (1974) *Leadership and Ambiguity: The American College President*. New York: McGraw Hill.

Coladarci, A. P. and Getzels, J. W. (ed.) (1955) *The Use of Theory in Educational Administration*. Stanford, California: Stanford University.

Cubberley, E. P. (1916) *Public School Administration*. Boston: Houghton Mifflin.

Culbertson, J. A. (1965) 'Trends and issues in the development of a science of administration'. In *Perspectives on Educational Administration and the Behavioural Sciences*. Eugene, Oregon: Centre for the Advanced Study of Educational Administration, University of Oregon.

Culbertson, J. (1980) 'Educational administration: where we are and where we are going'. In Farquhar, R. and Housego, I. E. (ed.) *Canadian and Comparative Educational Administration*. Vancouver: University of British Columbia.

Cunningham, L. L., Hack, W. G. and Nystrand, R. O. (ed.) (1977) *Educational Administration: The Developing Decades*. Berkeley: McCutchan.

Deer, C. E. (1980) 'Measuring organisational

climate in secondary schools'. *Australian Journal of Education*, **24**(1) 26–43.

Denzin, N. K. (1970) 'Symbolic interactionism and ethnomethodology'. In Douglas, J. D. (ed.) *Understanding Everyday Life*. London: Routledge and Kegan Paul.

Dewey, J. (1929) *Sources of a Science of Education*. New York: Liveright.

Duignan, P. (1980) 'Administrative behaviour of school superintendents: a descriptive study'. *Journal of Educational Administration*, **18**(1) 5–26.

Easton, D. A. (1965) *A Framework for Political Analysis*. Chicago: University of Chicago Press.

Eidell, T. L. and Nagle, J. M. (1970) *Conceptualization of PPBS and Data-Based Educational Planning*. Eugene, Oregon: Centre for the Advanced Study of Educational Administration, University of Oregon.

Erickson, D. A. (1977) 'Foreword'. *Review of Educational Research*, **37**, 4.

Everard, K. B. (1984) *Management in Comprehensive Schools — What can be learned from Industry?* 2nd edition. Centre for the Study of Comprehensive Schools. University of York.

Farquhar, R. H. (1977) 'Preparatory programmes in educational administration, 1954–1974'. In Cunningham, L. L., Hack, W. G. and Nystrand, R. O. (ed.) *Educational Administration: The Developing Decades*. Berkeley, California: McCutchen.

Farquhar, R. H. and Housego, I. E. (ed.) (1980) *Canadian and Comparative Educational Administration*. Vancouver: University of British Columbia.

Fayol, H. (1916) *Administration Industrielle et Générale*. Translated by Storrs, C. (1949) as *General and Industrial Management*. London: Pitman.

Feigl, H. (1951) 'Principles and problems of theory construction in psychology'. In *Current Trends in Psychological Theory*. Pittsburg: University of Pittsburg Press. Quoted in Griffiths, D. E. (1959a, p. 28).

Fielding, M. (1984) 'Asking different questions and pursuing different means: a critique of the new Management Training Movement'. In White, J. (ed.) *Education plc?*. Bedford Way Papers 20, London: University of London Institute of Education.

Finlayson, D. S., Banks, O. and Loughran, J. L. (1971) *Administrative Manual for Pupil Questionnaire for School Climate Index*. Slough: National Foundation for Educational Research.

Foster, W. (1983) *Loose Coupling Revisited: a critical view of Weick's contribution to educational administration*. Victoria, Australia: Deakin University.

Gadamer, H. G. (1975) *Truth and Method*. London: Sheed and Ward.

Garfinkel, H. (1967) *Studies in Ethnomethodology*. Englewood Cliffs, N.J.: Prentice-Hall.

Getzels, J. W. and Guba, E. G. (1957) 'Social behavior and the administrative process'. *School Review*, **65**, 423–41.

Getzels, J. W. and Thelen, H. A. (1960) 'The classroom group as a unique social system'. In National Society for the Study of Education, *The Dynamics of Instructional Groups*. Chicago: University of Chicago Press.

Gibson, R. O. (1975) 'Research trends in the United States'. In Hughes, M. (ed.) *Administering Education: International Challenge*. London: Athlone.

Gibson, R. O. (1977) 'An approach to paradigm shift in educational administration'. In Immegart, G. L. and Boyd, W. L. (ed.) *Problem-Finding in Educational Administration*. Lexington, Massachusetts: Heath.

Glatter, R. (1972) *Management Development for the Education Profession*. London: Harrap.

Glatter, R. (1982) 'The micropolitics of education: issues for training'. *Educational Management and Administration*, **10**(2) 160–65.

Goldhammer, K. (1963) *The Social Sciences and the Preparation of Educational Administrators*. Edmonton, Alberta: University of Alberta.

Gouldner, A. W. (1955) *Patterns of Industrial Bureaucracy*. London: Routledge and Kegan Paul.

Gray, H. L. (ed.) (1982) *The Management of Educational Institutions: Theory Research and Consultancy*. Lewes, Sussex: The Falmer Press.

Greenfield, T. B. (1975) 'Theory about organisation: a new perspective and its implications for schools'. In Hughes, M. (ed.) *Administering Education: International Challenge*. London: Athlone.

Greenfield, T. B. (1979/80) 'Research in Educational Administration in the United

States and Canada'. In Hughes, M. and Ribbins, P. (ed.) *Research in Educational Administration* in *Educational Administration*, **8**, 1.

Greenwood, R., Hinings, C. R. and Ransom, S. (1975) 'Contingency Theory and the Organisation of Local Authorities: Parts I and II'. *Public Administration*, **53**, 1–23 and 169–90.

Gregg, R. T. (1965) 'Essay Review: *Behavioral Science and Education Administration*'. *Education Administration Quarterly*, **1**(1) 42–49.

Griffiths, D. E. (1956) *Human Relations in School Administration*. New York: Appleton-Century-Crofts.

Griffiths, D. E. (1957) 'Toward a theory of administrative behavior'. In Campbell, R. F. and Gregg, R. T. (ed.) *Administrative Behavior in Education*. New York: Harper.

Griffiths, D. E. (1959a) *Administrative Theory*. New York: Appleton-Century-Crofts.

Griffiths, D. E. (1959b) *Research in Educational Administration*. New York: Columbia University.

Griffiths, D. E. (1979) 'Intellectual turmoil in educational administration'. *Educational Administration Quarterly*, **15**(3) 43–65.

Griffiths, D. E. (1982) 'Theories: Past, Present and Future'. Paper given at the 5th IIP in Nigeria (Mimeo).

Gronn, P. (1982) 'Neo-Taylorism in educational administration?'. *Educational Administration Quarterly*, **18**(4) 17–35.

Gronn, P. C. (1984) 'On studying administrators at work'. *Educational Administration Quarterly*, **20**(1) 115–29.

Gross, N., Mason, W. S. and McEachern, A. W. (1958) *Explorations in Role Analysis: Studies of the School Superintendency Role*. New York: Wiley.

Gulick, L. and Urwick, L. F. (1937) *Papers on the Science of Administration*. New York: Columbia University Press.

Habermas, J. (1974) *Theory and Practice*. London: Heinemann.

Hall, R. H. (1963) 'The concept of bureaucracy'. *American Journal of Sociology*, **69**(1) 32–40.

Halpin, A. W. (1957) 'A paradigm for research on administrative behavior'. In Campbell, R. F. and Gregg, R. T. (ed.) *Administrative Behavior in Education*. New York: Harper.

Halpin, A. W. (1958) 'The development of theory in educational administration', Chapter 1. In Halpin, A. W. (ed.) *Administrative Theory in Education*, 1–19. Chicago: University of Chicago.

Halpin, A. W. (1960) 'Ways of knowing', Chapter 1. In Campbell, R. F. and Lipham, J. M. (ed.) *Administrative Theory as a Guide to Action*. Chicago: University of Chicago.

Halpin, A. W. (1967) 'Change and organization climate'. *Journal of Educational Administration*, **5**(1) 5–25.

Halpin, A. W. and Croft, D. B. (1963) *The Organizational Climate of Schools*. Chicago: University of Chicago.

Halpin, A. W. (1969) 'A foggy view from Olympus'. *Journal of Educational Administration*, **7**(1) 3–18.

Halpin, A. W. (1970) 'Administrative theory: the fumbled torch'. In Kroll, A. M. *Issues in American Education*. New York: Oxford University Press.

Halpin, A. W. and Hayes, A. E. (1977) 'The broken ikon, or whatever happened to theory?'. In Cunningham, L. L., Hack, W. G. and Nystrand, R. O. (ed.) *Educational Administration: The Developing Decades*. Berkeley, California: McCutchan.

Hammersley, M. and Atkinson, P. (1983) *Ethnography: Principles in Practice*. London: Tavistock.

Handy, C. B. (1976) *Understanding Organisations*. Harmondsworth, Middlesex: Penguin.

Handy, C. B. (1984) *Taken for Granted? Understanding Schools as Organisations*. London: Longman.

Harman, G. (1980) 'Policy-making and the policy process in education'. In Farquhar, R. F. and Housego, I. E. (ed.) *Canadian and Comparative Educational Administration*. Vancouver: University of British Columbia.

Harré, R. (1977) 'The ethogenic approach: theory and practice'. In Berkowitz, L. (ed.) *Advances in Experimental Social Psychology*, **10**. New York: Academic Press.

Hemphill, J. K., Griffiths, D. E. and Fredericksen, N. (1962) *Administrative Performance and Personality*. New York Teachers College, Columbia University.

Hills, J. (1965) 'Educational administration: a field in transition'. *Educational Administration Quarterly*, **1**(1) 58–66.

Hills, R. J. (1968) *Towards a Science of Organisation*. Eugene, Oregon: Centre for the Advanced Study of Educational Administration, University of Oregon.

Hills, J. (1980) 'Critical issues in the preparation of educational administrators in North America'. In Farquhar, R. H. and Housego, I. E. (ed.) *Canadian and Comparative Educational Administration*. Vancouver: University of British Columbia.

Hinings, C. R. (1979) 'Continuities in the study of organisations: churches and local government'. In Lanemers, C. and Hickson, D. J. (ed.) *Organisations alike and unalike*. London: Routledge and Kegan Paul.

Hodgkinson, C. (1978) *Towards a Philosophy of Administration*. Oxford: Blackwell.

Holt, M. (1981) *Evaluating the Evaluators*. London: Hodder and Stoughton.

Howell, D. A. and Brown, R. (1983) *Educational Policy Making: An Analysis*. London: Heinemann.

Hoy, W. K. and Miskel, C. G. (1978) *Educational Administration: Theory, Research and Practice*. New York: Random House.

Hoyle, E. (1982) 'Micropolitics of educational organisations'. *Educational Management and Administration*, **10**(2) 87–98.

Hughes, A. G. (1951) *Education and the Democratic Ideal*. London: Longman.

Hughes, M. G. (ed.) (1974) *Secondary School Administration: A Management Approach*, 2nd edition. Oxford: Pergamon.

Hughes, M. G. (ed.) (1975) *Administering Education: International Challenge*. London: Athlone.

Hughes, M. G. (1977) 'Consensus and conflict about the role of the secondary head'. *British Journal of Educational Studies*, **25**, 1.

Hughes, M. G., Carter, J. and Fidler, B. (1981) *Professional Development Provision in Schools and Colleges: A DES Supported Research Project*. Birmingham: University of Birmingham. (Summarised in *Educational Management and Administration* (1982) **10**(1), 1–15).

Iannaconne, L. (1973) 'Interdisciplinary theory guided research in educational administration'. *Teachers College Record*, **75**.

Innes, J. T., Jacobson, P. B. and Pellegrin, R. J. (1965) *The Economic Returns to Education*. Eugene, Oregon: University of Oregon.

Jenkins, H. O. (1983) *Job Perceptions of Senior Managers in Schools and Manufacturing Industry*. Unpublished Ph.D. thesis, University of Birmingham.

John, D. (1980) *Leadership in Schools*. London: Heinemann.

Jones, R. (1974) 'The application of manage-

ment principles in schools. In Hughes, M. G. (ed.) *Secondary School Administration: A Management Approach*, 2nd edition. Oxford: Pergamon.

Knorr-Cetina, K. (1981) 'The micro-sociological challenge of macro-sociology: towards a reconstruction of social theory and methodology'. In Knorr-Cetina, K. and Cicourel, A. V. (ed.) *Advances in Social Theory and Methodology*. London: Routledge and Kegan Paul.

Koopman, G. R. (1943) *Democracy in School Administration*. New York: Appleton-Century-Crofts.

Kuhn, T. S. (1962) *The Structure of Scientific Revolutions*. Chicago: University of Chicago Press.

Kuhn, T. S. (1977) *The Essential Tension: Selected Studies in Scientific Tradition and Change*. Chicago: University of Chicago Press.

Landers, T. and Myers, J. (1980) 'Organisational and administrative theory'. In Bush, T. et al (ed.) *Approaches to School Management*. London: Harper and Row.

Lane, T. J. (1983) 'How critical is critical theory?'. *Studies in Educational Administration*, CCEA, **32**, 1–7.

Lawrence, P. R. and Lorsch, J. W. (1967) *Organisation and Environment*. Boston: Harvard University Press.

Levinson, D. J. (1959) 'Role, personality and social structure in the organisational setting'. *Journal of Abnormal and Social Psychology*, **58**, 170–80.

Lindblom, C. E. (1959) 'The science of "muddling through" '. *Public Administration Review*, **19**, 79–88.

Lindblom, C. E. (1979) 'Still muddling, not yet through'. *Public Administration Review*, **39**, 517–26.

Lipham, J. M. (1975) 'Competency/Performance-Based Administrator Education (C/PBAE): recent developments in the United States'. In Hughes, M. (ed.) *Administering Education: International Challenge*. London: Athlone.

Litwak, E. (1961) 'Models of bureaucracy which permit conflict'. *American Journal of Sociology*, **67**, 177–84.

Lutz, F. W. (1982) 'Tightening up loose coupling in organisations of higher education'. *Administrative Science Quarterly*, **27**(4) 653–69.

Mangham, I. (1979) *The Politics of*

Organisational Change. London: Associated Business Press.

March, J. and Olsen, J. P. (1975) 'Choice situations in loosely coupled worlds'. Unpublished paper, Stanford University.

March, J. and Olsen, J. (ed.) (1976) *Ambiguity and Choice in Organisations.* Bergen, Norway: Universitetsforlaget.

March, J. G. and Simon, H. A. (1958) *Organisations.* New York: Wiley.

Martin, W. J. and Willower, D. J. (1981) 'The managerial behaviour of high school principals'. *Educational Administration Quarterly,* **17**(1) 69–90.

Masterman, M. (1970) 'The nature of a paradigm'. In Lakatos, I. and Musgrave, A. (ed.) *Criticism and the Growth of Knowledge.* Cambridge: Cambridge University Press.

Mayo, E. (1933) *The Human Problems of an Industrial Civilization.* New York: Macmillan.

Merton, R. K. (1957) *Social Theory and Social Structure* revised edition. Glencoe, Illinois: The Free Press.

Meyer, J. W. and Rowan, B. (1977) 'Institutionalised organisations: formal structure as myth and ceremony'. *American Journal of Sociology,* **83**(2) 340–63.

Mintzberg, H. (1973) *The Nature of Managerial Work.* New York: Harper and Row.

Morgan, G. (1980) 'Paradigm, Metaphors, and Puzzle Solving in Organisation Theory'. *Administration Science Quarterly,* **25**(4) 605–22.

Musgrove, F. (1971) *Patterns of Power and Authority in English Education.* London: Methuen.

National Society for the Study of Education (1946) *Changing Conceptions in Educational Administration.* Forty-fifth Year Book, Part II. Chicago: University of Chicago Press.

Newell, C. A. (1978) *Human Behaviour in Educational Administration.* Englewood Cliffs, New Jersey: Prentice-Hall.

Nias, J. (1980) 'Leadership styles and job-satisfaction in primary schools'. In Bush, T. et al. (ed.) *Approaches to School Management.* London: Harper and Row.

Padgett, J. F. (1980) 'Managing garbage can hierarchies'. *Administrative Science Quarterly,* **25**(4) 583–602.

Paisey, A. (1981) *Organisation and Management in Schools.* London: Longman.

Perrow, C. (1970) *Complex Organisations: A Critical Essay.* Chicago: Scott, Foresman.

Peston, M. (1969) 'Economics and Administration of Education'. In Baron, G. and Taylor, W. *Educational Administration and the Social Sciences.* London: Athlone.

Peters, T. J. (1978) 'Symbols, patterns and settings: an optimistic case for getting things done'. *Organizational Dynamics,* **7**, 3–23.

Pfeffer, J. (1978) 'The micropolitics of organisations'. In Meyer, M. W. et al. (ed.) *Environments and Organisations.* San Francisco: Jossey-Bass.

Pfeffer, J. (1981) *Power in Organisations.* Marshfield, Massachusetts: Pitman.

Piele, P. K.. Eidell, T. L. and Smith, S. C. (1970) *Social and Technological Change: Implications for Education.* Eugene, Oregon: Centre for the Advanced Study of Educational Administration, University of Oregon.

Pratt, S. (ed.) (1982) 'The micropolitics of educational improvement'. *Educational Management and Administration,* **10**, 2.

Project ASK (1980) *Development of Administrative Skills and Knowledge:* Phase 1 Summary Report. Edmonton: University of Alberta.

Pugh, D. S., Hickson, D. J. and Hinings, C. R. (1971) *Writers on Organisations.* Harmondsworth, Middlesex: Penguin.

Pugh, D. S. and Hickson, D. J. (1976) *Organisational Structure in its Context: The Aston Programme I.* London: Saxon House.

Pugh, D. S. and Hinings, C. R. (1976) *Organisational Structure, Extensions and Republications: The Aston Programme II.* London: Saxon House.

Pugh, D. S. and Payne, R. L. (1977) *Organisational Behaviour in its Context: The Aston Programme III.* London: Saxon House.

Ransom, S., Hinings, C. R. and Greenwood, R. (1980) 'The structuring of organisational structures'. *Administrational Science Quarterly,* **25**(1) 1–17.

Roethlisberger, F. G. and Dickson, W. J. (1939) *Management and the Worker.* Cambridge, Mass.: Harvard University Press.

Schultz, T. W. (1961) 'Investment in Human Capital'. *American Economic Review,* **51**, 1–17.

Schwab, J. J. (1964) 'The professorship in educational administration: theory-art-practice'. In Willower, D. J. and Culbertson, J. A. (ed.) *The Professorship in Educational Administration.* Columbus,

Ohio: University Council for Educational Administration.

Sharma, C. L. (1955) 'Who should make what decision?'. *Administrator's Notebook,* **3**(8) 1–4.

Silverman, D. (1970) *The Theory of Organisations.* London: Heinemann.

Simon, H. A. (1947) *Administrative Behaviour.* New York: Macmillan.

Snyder, R. C. (1969) 'The preparation of educational administrators: some problems reconsidered in the context of the establishment of a new Graduate School of Administration.' In Baron, G., Cooper, D. H. and Walker, W. G. (ed.) *Educational Administration: International Perspective.* Chicago: Rand McNally.

Taylor, F. W. (1911) *Principles of Scientific Management.* New York: Harper.

Thomas, A. R., Willis, Q. and Phillips, D. (1981) 'Observational studies of Australian school administrators: methodological issues'. *Australian Journal of Education,* **25**.

Thomas, W. J. (1927) 'Letter' in Thomas, W. J. and Bailey, C. W., *Letters to a Young Headmaster.* London: Blackie.

Thomason, G. (1974) 'Organisation and management'. In Hughes, M. G. (ed.) *Secondary School Administration: A Management Approach.* Oxford: Pergamon.

Trethowan, D. (1984) *Target Setting and Delegation.* London: Industrial Society Booklets.

Trow, M. (1959) 'Book Review: *Administrative Theory in Education*'. Administrative Science Quarterly, **4**, 122–26.

Turner, C. (1977) 'Organising educational institutions as anarchies'. *Educational Administration,* **5**(2) 6–12.

Turner, L. T. (1981) *Preparation for Headship.* Unpublished B.Phil.(Ed.) dissertation, University of Birmingham.

University Council for Educational Administration (1960) *Simulation in Administrative Training.* Columbus, Ohio: UCEA.

Urwick, L. F. (1947) *The Elements of Administration.* London: Pitman.

Vaizey, J. E. (1958) *The Costs of Education.* London: Allen and Unwin.

Vickers, G. (1967) *Towards a Sociology of Management.* London: Chapman.

Walker, W. G. (1963) Founder Editor, *The Journal of Educational Administration.*

Warwick, D. (1984) *Effective Meetings, Staff Appraisal and Decision-Making.* London: Industrial Society Booklets.

Webb, P. C. and Lyons, G. (1982) 'The nature of managerial activities in education'. In Gray, H. L. (ed.) *The Management of Educational Institutions.* Lewes, Sussex: The Falmer Press.

Weber, M. (1947) *The Theory of Social and Economic Organisation,* translated by Henderson, A. M. and Parsons, T. Glencoe, Illinois: The Free Press.

Weick, K. (1976) 'Educational organisations as loosely-coupled systems'. *Administrative Science Quarterly,* **21**(1) 1–19.

Weick, K. E. (1980) 'Loosely coupled systems: relaxed meanings and thick interpretations'. Paper presented at the Annual Meeting of the American Educational Research Association, Boston. Quoted by Foster, W. (1983).

White, J. (1984) 'Managing heads'. In White, J. (ed.) *Education plc?.* Bedford Way Papers 20, London: University of London Institute of Education.

Whitehead, A. N. (1926) *Science and the Modern World.* London: Cambridge University Press.

Williams, G. (1982) 'The economics of education: current debates and prospects'. *British Journal of Educational Studies,* **30**(1) 97–107.

Willis, Q. (1980) 'The work activity of school principals: an observational study'. *Journal of Educational Administration,* **18**(1) 27–54.

Willower, D. J. (1975) 'Theory in educational administration', *University Council for Educational Administration Review,* **16**(5) 2–10.

Willower, D. J. (1980) 'Contemporary issues in theory in educational administration'. *Educational Administration Quarterly,* **16**(3) 1–25.

Willower, D. J. (1983) 'Analogies gone awry: replies to Hills and Gronn. *Educational Administration Quarterly,* **19**(1) 35–47.

Wolcott, H. F. (1977) *Teachers Versus Technocrats.* Eugene, Oregon: Centre for Educational Policy and Management, University of Oregon.

Woodhall, M. (1972) *Economic Aspects of Education: a review of research in Britain.* Slough: National Foundation for Educational Research.

Yauch, W. A. (1949) *Improving Human Relations in School Administration.* New York: Harper.

Zaleznik, A. (1970) 'Power and politics in organisational life'. *Harvard Business Review.*

PART TWO

MANAGING THE SYSTEM

2

THE EDUCATION SUB-GOVERNMENT: STRUCTURE AND CONTEXT

Derek Slater

THE EDUCATION SUB-GOVERNMENT: A FRAMEWORK FOR STUDY

A definition of the education sub-government

The term 'education sub-government' was coined by Manzer (1970). He used it to describe what he called a 'tripartite structure' between the DES,[1] LEAs and organised teachers (Manzer 1970, pp. 1–2). He argued that this structure was a sub-system of the UK political system and was the one in which most decisions about national educational policy were made. Manzer was studying specifically the influence of one of the three components (organised teachers) over a specific time scale (the 1950s). But the phrase has entered the vocabulary of analysis of educational policy-making as a useful shorthand.

However, the term as Manzer used it needs some refinement. It is clear that Manzer is referring to educational policy-making in England and Wales, and it is also with these that this particular chapter is concerned.[2] A separate, if related, sub-system applies each to Scotland and Northern Ireland as regards educational policy-making.

Furthermore, this chapter will be equally concerned with the other components of the educational sub-government (the DES and LEAs), and the relationships between them in the face of the changing context in which they operate.

An approach to a structural analysis of the education sub-government

There are few accounts which have attempted to discuss the relationships within the education sub-government in a theoretical framework. Accounts which do contain

43

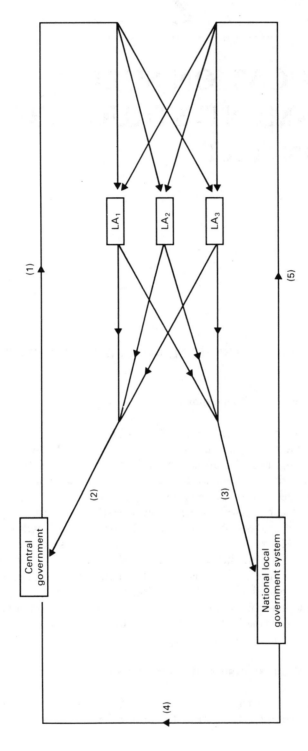

Figure 2.1 *The structure of governmental relations involved in the high-rise housing issue. Source: Dunleavy, P. J. (1981) The Politics of Mass Housing in Britain, p. 179. Oxford: Oxford University Press. (Reproduced with permission.)*

LA_1 = Local authority$_1$, etc.

theoretical approaches have usually concentrated on relationships between the DES and LEAs in the framework of central–local government relationships, and therefore do not take into account organised teachers.

A recent attempt to construct a model of general intergovernmental relationships which would take into account the relationships of the DES and LEAs, not only with each other but also with organised teachers, has been made by Dunleavy (1980 and 1981). Although this model was constructed to explain developments in housing policy (see Dunleavy 1981, p. 179; and Figure 2.1), Pattison (1980, pp. 64–66) has suggested that it can be usefully applied to policy-making as regards education. Ribbins, in Chapter 6, has further refined it[3] to apply it specifically to the issue of comprehensive re-organisation.

The novel feature of Dunleavy's model is its concept of the 'national local government system', which incorporates not only organised professionals but also other informal as well as formal agencies. This, with respect to education, will be examined in detail later.[4]

Dunleavy's model (1981 p. 179) contains five influence flows (Figure 2.1), to which Pattison (1980) has added a sixth. I, in my turn, am adding a seventh:

(1)   central government on LEAs;
(2)   LEAs on central government;
(3)   LEAs on the national local government system;
(4)   the national local government system on central government;
(5)   the national local government system on LEAs;
(6)   one LEA on another or others;
(7)   one central government agency on another or others.

Pattison (1980) has included the sixth influence flow (one LEA on another or others) and I have added the seventh (one central government agency on another or others). In addition, I have modified the terminology to emphasise the distinction, legally, between the local authority and the local education authority.[5] I shall discuss each of these influence flows in the rest of the chapter, but for convenience I shall not deal with them in the above order.

As can be seen in Figure 2.2, I have also used a simplified version of Dunleavy's model to give an overview of the structure and functions of the education system in the UK. More detailed discussion of the institutional levels will take place in Chapters 9–14.

THE INFLUENCE FLOW OF ONE CENTRAL GOVERNMENT AGENCY ON ANOTHER OR OTHERS

Although the DES is the main executive agency for education, it is the cabinet which initiates policy-making, even if it has in general shown little interest in educational questions since 1944 (see, for example, Fowler 1974, para. 4.2; Kogan 1971, pp. 104 and 162; Kogan and Bowden 1975, p. 151; Mann 1979, p. 28).

Nor does Parliament significantly fill the vacuum in this respect. Certainly it is the legitimising force: from the 1944 Education Act which laid down the main structure of the

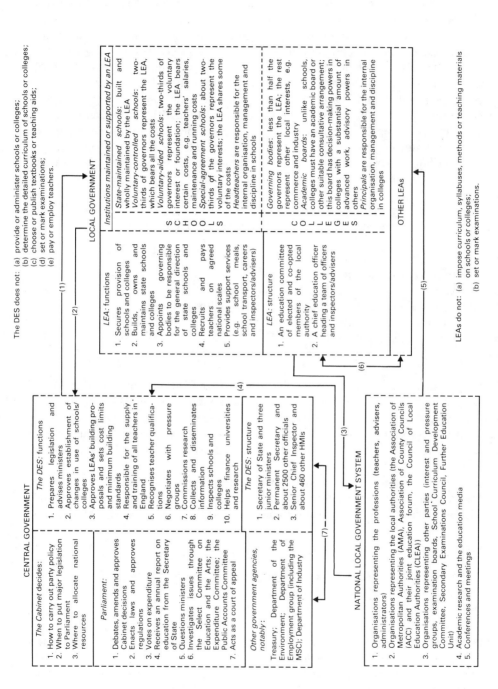

Figure 2.2 *An overview of the education system in England and Wales.*

educational system and whose architect was R.A. (later Lord) Butler, Parliament passed, up to 1976, 17 Education Acts relating to England and Wales alone (Mann 1979, p. 29). On the other hand, if Parliament legitimates policy decisions, its contribution to the actual formulation of such policy has been more debatable.

Kogan and Bowden (1975, p. 234), after studying Parliament and education, concluded by confirming the doubts that other writers have expressed ' . . . on the contribution Parliament makes to decisions or to whether it effectively reviews and criticizes the authority structure.'

Specifically, they argue earlier (p. 233) that the relationship between parliamentary activity and policy formulation is episodic rather than systematic, despite the potential for the Select Committee system. They opine that the most that can be said about parliamentary activity is in its contribution to the environment in which policy is made and the way it serves partly 'to aggregate local feelings and project them onto a national screen' (p. 182).

In 1979, the Select Committee system was revamped and strengthened. While retaining all the traditional powers of the old Select Committees, several new features were added. Notable among these new features was that there were now to be Select Committees shadowing the fourteen major departments of state. Furthermore, members were to be appointed for the whole of a Parliament, and they were given a small clerk's department and the power to appoint specialist advisers.

One such former specialist adviser to the Select Committee which shadows the DES — the Education, Science and Arts Committee — in a review of the work of that Committee, took a more sanguine view than Kogan and Bowden's judgement on the work of earlier committees. He considers that its most important achievement has been in revealing information which might otherwise have remained concealed; while, in addition, it has been effective in exploring remote corners of the system, like prison education, and has provided a new focus for pressure groups and a new forum for critical analysis of government policy. While he argues that the committee's existence seems to have changed the way the government behaves, if only indirectly, he concedes, however, that 'The achievement was less evident when it came to getting the Government to follow [the Committee's] recommendations.' (Lightfoot 1983)

Thus the influence flow between, respectively, the cabinet and the DES, and Parliament and the DES, in terms of policy-making, is perhaps more limited than may be thought to be the case. Indeed, it is not too much to say that much of the policy-making process, including its initiation, has been for a considerable amount of the time since 1945 in the hands of the education sub-government itself. Certainly that is one implication behind the statement of one Education Secretary (Shirley Williams) in 1977 when she said that there was little prospect of a major education act as there was not sufficient agreement about what such an act should say (quoted in Mann 1977, p. 29); as Mann comments: 'In education, it appears, legislation tends to follow informed opinion not to shape it.'

What is of greater magnitude is the size and number of influence flows between other government departments and the DES. And those influence flows tend to be one way, in that other government departments have greater influence on the DES rather than the other way round. The Treasury has historically been an important influence on the DES in determining each year the amount of money that will be available to education; more recently, the Department of the Environment has had a key role in changing the basis of calculating projected local government expenditure. In addition, there has been an increasing influence of the Manpower Services Commission (MSC) on the DES and the LEAs (see also Chapter 7). What is qualitatively different about this latter influence flow is not only its magnitude but its direction. Unlike the other influence flows which have operated on the other components of the educational sub-government through the DES, the MSC has dealt directly with others in the education sub-government.

THE INFLUENCE FLOWS OF CENTRAL GOVERNMENT ON LEAs AND LEAs ON CENTRAL GOVERNMENT

It is worth noting that just as at central level it is necessary to distinguish between the DES and other agencies, so at local level there is a distinction between local authorities and local education authorities: a distinction which is important in the light of the development of corporate management structures in local government in the 1970s.[6]

The 1944 Act based all LEAs on what were then counties and county boroughs, and by so doing reduced the number of LEAs in England and Wales from 315 to 147. However, although this brought education more into line, organisationally, with the administration of other local authority services, the special and distinct place of education at local level which long predated 1944[7] was retained. On the one hand, under s. 6 of the Act, the full councils of either the counties or the county boroughs became the local education authorities. On the other hand, Sch. 1(2) of the Act required these councils to appoint education committees whose composition had to be approved by the minister. These committees, according to the Act, had to 'include persons of experience in education and persons acquainted with the educational conditions prevailing in the area for which the committee acts'.

The special place of the education committee was further emphasised by the condition that councils had to consider reports from their education committees before exercising their education powers. Further, s. 88 of the Act required every LEA to appoint a 'fit person to be the chief education officer of the authority'.

Developments since 1944 in reshaping the local government structure in England and Wales have served to confirm the special place of education. In 1964, re-organisation took place in London: 20 outer London boroughs remained, or became, full LEAs, while 12 inner London boroughs were covered by one LEA — the unique Inner London Education Authority (ILEA).[8] In 1974, the rest of England and Wales underwent changes in the local government structure, based on the 1972 Local Government Act. Thus, outside London, LEAs were now based on the councils of 47 Shire Counties (a considerable number of which were based on the previous 51 English and Welsh counties) and the Metropolitan Districts (many of which were based on the previous county boroughs). The new tier of local government erected by the 1972 Act — the Metropolitan Counties — were not LEAs.[9]

Although the net result of these changes has been to reduce the number of LEAs to 104[10] at present, the special position of LEAs has been structurally confirmed, even if the changing context in which this structure has been operating has put strains on its functioning in practice.[11] Despite some opposition from other local authority interests, s. 192 of the 1972 Local Government Act confirmed s. 6 of the 1944 Act: it is still incumbent upon the relevant councils to have, and consider reports from, their education committees. Indeed Circular 8/73 from the DES went further than the 1944 Act in two respects: it made it clear that the Secretary of State would only approve the composition of committees which included at least two-thirds elected members but between one-quarter and one-third co-opted members; and it stressed that

> a local authority which is a local education authority may not arrange for the discharge of any of its functions in respect to education by any committee or sub-committee other than its education committee.

This requirement has come under increasing strain as corporate management structures have in practice often encroached on educational matters. Nevertheless, the 1972 Local Government Act also confirmed the requirement to have a chief education officer. Thus, education's special position in the local government structure was confirmed: there is no requirement for local authorities to appoint any other special committees except a Social Services and a Police Committee: and there is no requirement to appoint any other specified official except a director of social services and a financial officer. Given this, then, it is possible to examine the mutual influence flows between central government and LEAs both in the context of centre–local relations in general; and in the context of the specific structure, based on the 1944 Education Act, of education in particular.

There has been much debate on the nature of central–local relationships in England and Wales.[12] The history of centre–local relationships in their English and Welsh context has resulted, through custom and convention, in a constitutional relationship of checks and balances which is in a continual state of mutual re-adjustment; and whose equilibrium has been summed up by Hartley (1971 p. 450):

> It is possible for a local authority to escape with serious deviations from national policy by 'overdoing' an existing policy, or by not acting at all. But a policy which is active . . . can be checked in one devious way or another. Positive action can be controlled eventually, but inaction is not so easily handled by central departments. This means that an innovating active authority can often be most easily controlled. It can be eventually frustrated by central control of the detail of policies. But a deliberately inactive authority cannot be so checked.

This point is made again in the specific context of education by Pattison (1980 p. 81):

> Coercive measures are probably sufficient simply to block change . . . but in a competitive period of adversary politics they may prove too limited for a reforming central government.

The interplay between these checks and balances may be seen through the example of finance. As regards both capital and current expenditure, although the centre controls the source of finance, it cannot in the end control its specific use by local authorities. Thus, although it may reduce the options open to a local authority by withholding finance, it cannot actually order a local authority to spend money in specific ways. Even when there are cases of specific grants, it cannot force the local authority to take up that grant if it chooses to forgo it.

In terms of capital expenditure, an LEA is unable to borrow sums for capital expenditure without 'loan sanction' from the DES, in the granting of which the latter acts as the agent of the Treasury.[13] The DES can and does indicate the sort of project acceptable at any point in time,[14] and by changing the priorities, the major building programme has acted not only as a financial regulator but as a steering mechanism ensuring, as governments have come and gone, that the truly massive resources ploughed into school building have promoted their policies – political as well as educational. (Brooksbank 1980, p. 57)

Fowler (1979, p. 49) opines that, in a period of continuous expansion — such as obtained from 1945 to at least the mid-1960s — control of the school building programme was the strongest mechanism of DES control.

However, it is still open to LEAs to resist this control by inaction: the refusal to submit building plans. Even in a period of expansion when LEAs' need for such programmes was acute, the apparent control of the DES, through capital expenditure, over LEAs must need be viewed with caution, as Ribbins below in Chapter 6 demonstrates in connection with the issue of comprehensive education: those LEAs opposed to comprehensive education merely refused to submit schemes, or submitted schemes unacceptable to the DES at that time (Pattison 1980, p. 709).

A similar position can be seen in relation to current expenditure. LEAs depend for revenue on two sources: local rates, supplemented by a central government grant. The latter has changed its form considerably. Ad hoc subsidies were replaced in 1919 by a system of annual grants on a percentage basis, which remained as the principle behind the central government grant until 1958, though rationalised by s. 100 of the 1944 Act.[15] The main grant was calculated by a formula that related to the number of children and the capacity of the area covered by an LEA to pay. In 1958, there was again a change of principle: the specific education grant made to LEAs, with the exception of the grants for school meals and milk, was subsumed into a general grant towards the main services provided by local authorities. This was part of a policy designed to give LEAs a greater degree of autonomy over their services. This meant that, though the DES calculated the education component of the general grant, it was up to local authorities to decide how they spent it: it was no longer specifically earmarked for education. Though the mechanism for calculating and distributing the grant was changed in 1966 with the creation of the rate support grant (RSG), the principle underlying the general grant remained: the centre could no longer earmark particular parts of the RSG for particular services such as education.

Fowler (1979, p. 52) noted how, since the ending of the percentage grants in 1958, it was possible for local authorities to ignore central guidelines on policy priorities; and this is indeed what happened. For example, when central government put money into the RSG for the expansion of nursery education as a result of the programme outlined in the 1972 White Paper (DES 1972) and continued when a Labour government was returned to office in 1974, a number of local authorities took up the money but did not spend it on nursery education. In 1977–78, £17.8 million was put into the RSG for the In-Service Training (INSET) of teachers; but LEAs spent only £14.6 million on INSET and the rest on other priorities (Cohen 1978).[16] Indeed, LEAs are quite overt in arguing their constitutional rights to use RSG money as they see fit: the Director of Education for Clwyd in 1979 made it clear that, whatever the Secretary of State wished as regards the INSET component of the RSG, INSET would not have the same priority within LEAs that was accorded it by the DES, and other priorities, such as staffing, capitation and capital basic needs, would continue to have precedence (Davies 1979). It was this inability to ensure that any money put into the RSG for Educational Maintenance Allowances (EMAs) — for 16–19-year-olds in full-time education — was spent by LEAs for that purpose which prevented a fully-blown EMA scheme being put into operation in 1979.[17]

However, even if the central government did reduce the amount of the RSG, it was still open to local authorities to make up any shortfall from the rates. Although the level of RSG rose progressively from 54 per cent of local authority expenditure in 1967–8 to 66 per cent by 1975–6 (Pile 1979, p. 49),[18] this served to heighten the lack of central government power to ensure that the money was spent in line with its, rather than a local authority's, priorities.

But the 1980 Local Government Planning and Land Act has given the centre more leverage. It changed the basis of calculation to a unitary grant system,[19] which is in turn based on the cost of providing local services. The unit allocation on local authority services is decided by central government using various indicators of local authority need which are given weightings. In this way, the grant-related expenditure (GRE) of each service in each local authority is calculated. The intention is to redistribute money away from those authorities deemed to be 'over-spenders' by central government criteria and towards those deemed to be 'under-spenders'. More than this, central government can exert greater leverage as the level of grant — unlike before — is linked to rating decisions, to try to prevent those authorities judged to be 'over-spenders' on a particular service (and whose grant is therefore reduced) from making up the deficit from the rates. The higher an authority raises its rates, the more its grant for a service is reduced, to try to curb expenditure and produce a national standard of service.

Furthermore, in 1985 central government introduced 'rate capping', which can be used to prevent local authorities from 'over-spending' on central government criteria.[20] 'Rate-capping' will effectively remove the power to raise rates above levels determined by central government from local authorities. In the first instance, central government has taken 'selective powers' to deal with a number of local authorities which refuse to meet central government spending targets. Progressive reductions in the RSG and rate-capping, taken together, will undoubtedly reduce the scope for local authorities to use their discretion in spending.

Nevertheless, although this puts a strain on local authorities and may indeed reduce, in the end, the amount an individual authority has available to it, the conventions that Hartley has outlined as governing local–central relations still hold true: there is no attempt to impinge directly on local decisions and priorities by forcing a local authority to spend, for example, the GRE for education on that particular service. Despite the new pressure, it is still left to local authorities to decide how they spend their grant.

There are, however, certain areas of expenditure which are governed by specific grants: under s. 11 of the 1966 Local Government Act, for example, there are 75 per cent grants available to local authorities designed to meet the needs of ethnic minorities. The central government, in 1982, also discovered that it had the power — in the 1962 Act — to make specific grants for INSET for teachers. The Education (Grants) Act (1984) extended the areas covered by specific grants, at the discretion of the Secretary of State by means of education support grants (ESGs). In deference to centre-local conventions, the sums involved initially are modest: such DES direct-financing is limited to under £40 million, which will be taken out of the RSG. Also, in the further education sector, the MSC has, since the mid-1970s, been increasingly directly funding work-related courses, and it is intended that by 1986–87, MSC funding will account for 25 per cent of the total provision of work-related courses.[21] Moreover 'The resultant reduction in the need for local authority expenditure will be taken into account in settling the rate support grants;' (DE/DES 1984, para. 46).

Again, this may place pressure on the existing conventions; but it is still open to an LEA not to take up the grant on a particular area if it so wishes. Thus an LEA may choose a particular pattern of grants to deal with what it views as its priorities; another LEA may choose a completely different pattern.

The checks and balances in the general conventions governing centre-local relations are mirrored in the specificity of legislation as regards education. What is notable is the degree of ambiguity or vagueness in much of the legislation when it comes to defining relationships between the DES and LEAs, reflecting the constitutional conventions. Sloman (1980) notes the 'elegance and balance' of the 1944 Act in its detail; yet it is a detail which, it may be argued, achieves as much by omission as by inclusion. Brooksbank (1980, pp. 5 and 8) comments that at the core of the Act is the fact that 'education' is nowhere defined, except in tautologous terms; and Mann (1979, p. 193) notes that, in the arrangements for education in England there is neither any formal and public machinery to agree the aims, content, outcomes or evaluation of the curriculum, nor is there any systematic machinery for the direction and methodology of teaching. Thus he concludes that 'How the education service moves forward remains an impenetrable mystery' (p. 240).

Though this may be a debatable exaggeration, it does highlight the spaces in the legislation which have been filled by conventions and understandings which challenge systematic analysis.

In part, this stems from uncertainty as to the degree of power that the Secretary of State possesses actually to influence LEAs; and from the fact that this power is negative — reflecting the checks and balances in Hartley's analysis — rather than positive. It is useful here to note Glatter's comments on the relationships between responsibilities, powers, influences and control (Glatter 1979a, paras. 3.4 and 3.6; 1979b, paras. 2.5–2.8): an agency may be given powers to carry out its tasks or duties, but the degree of power it has is no guarantee that it is either willing to use it or skilful in its use. Its degree of influence is therefore determined by its actual use or exercise of those powers in practice.

In this connection, the degree of apparent power that the DES has to influence LEAs seems great, particularly in ss. 1, 68 and 99 of the 1944 Act. Dunleavy (1981, p. 180) notes how central government exerted a strong and direct influence on local authority decision-making through major policy-making as regards housing; and in education, too, LEAs operate in a framework of national policies such as the length of compulsory schooling, teachers' salaries, building standards etc. There is evidence that ministers, under the powers that they were given in the 1944 Act, were intended to develop a much more active role in policy-making than they have, in practice, undertaken (see, for example, Raison 1976, pp. 14 and 16; and Sloman 1980): in other words, their influence — that is, their actual use of power — has been far less than the powers that they apparently have been given.

As regards s. 1 of the Act, for example, whereas up to 1944 the President of the Board of Education merely 'supervised' the education service, the 1944 Act firmly gave the new minister the duty 'to *promote* the education of the people of England and Wales . . . ' [my emphasis]. The implication of this term was that he would take the initiative; moreover, he further had a duty 'to *secure* the effective execution by local authorities, under his control and direction, of the national policy' [my emphasis].

However, one of the reasons[22] for the discrepancy between these apparent powers and the actual influence successive ministers have had may be that, as Raison (1976, p. 14) points out, the sweeping powers implied in s. 1 are not supported in the rest of the Act.

Sections 68 and 99 are perhaps the most important 'enforcement' sections. As Sloman (1980) observes, s. 68 deals with 'sins of commission': the Minister is given the power to decide that a local authority is acting 'unreasonably', in some way that it is not covered by statute or regulation, and to intervene to give directions as he sees fit. Section 99, on the other hand, deals, in Sloman's phrase, with 'sins of omission': the Minister is given the power to proceed by mandamus in the case of default by an LEA (or managers or governors of a school[23]).

But two points may be made about these powers. On the one hand, they are negative rather than positive: they can be used to prevent rather than to initiate, and are thus in line with the conventions which have developed to regulate centre–local relationships, and which Hartley has outlined. Second, they may be more apparent than real. As Pile (1979, p. 29) points out, the existence of a power may be as important as its use, and that it is probable that records would show a number of cases where an active LEA, threatened with its use, 'chose discretion as the better part of valour'. Thus, for example, the threat of the use of s. 68 in 1952 led to Durham County LEA backing down in its attempts to enforce trade union membership on its staff. However, when one LEA — Tameside — did challenge the Secretary of State's definition of 'unreasonably', the courts took the view that the powers of the Secretary of State under s. 68 are something of a chimera: as Sloman (1980) points out, the courts in 1976 decided that s. 68 does not mean what Parliament and ministers intended it to mean in 1944. In between, however, the perception of the power implied in s. 68 undoubtedly influenced the behaviour of LEAs in deciding not to risk a challenge.

There has, as of yet, been no attempt by the Secretary of State to use his powers under s. 99 of the 1944 Act,[24] which would involve the DES in getting a High Court writ if it was judged that an LEA was in default of its duties. But this option, too, is beset by difficulties. Again, it is a negative rather than a positive power: unlike health legislation, s. 99 does not give central government the power to send in commissioners to run the service in an LEA, except — possibly — in the most extreme circumstances. Also, since the DES cannot specify the exact nature of an LEA's provision, the definition of 'default' is as fraught with difficulties as is the definition of 'unreasonably' under s. 68.

If the DES has had any success in using its essentially negative and regulatory powers, it has been rather under s. 13 of the 1944 Act. Where an LEA proposes to establish, discontinue or (since the 1968 Education Act) make a significant change in the character, or significant enlargement to the premises, of a county school, the Secretary of State has the power of veto. There are similar powers of veto over voluntary schools. Although s. 13 of the 1980 Education Act means that the Secretary of State's approval for such a change is no longer automatically required, he can still call in any proposals for his decision if he so chooses; and if there are any local objections, he once again has to give his approval before plans can go ahead. The substantial veto powers contained in s. 13 have been used to limit innovating LEAs: as Ribbins points out in Chapter 6, in the period 1970–4 the Secretary of State prevented the closure of over 300, mostly grammar, schools; and in so doing could effectively wreck an LEA's whole scheme for comprehensive re-organisation.

The checks and balances that the 1944 Act, in reflecting the general pattern of local–

centre relations imposed on the influence flow from DES to LEA, have also meant that a number of strategies have emerged which the DES uses in its dealings with LEAs. In general terms, Griffith (1966) has constructed a conceptual framework of attitudes which central government departments adopt as regards local authorities: 'laissez-faire', 'regulatory' and 'promotional'. Regan (1977) argues that the relations between DES and LEAs are an example of the third of these attitudes and is instrumental in explaining, in part, why LEAs are not merely agents of the DES. Weaver (1979, paras. 9.22 and 9.23) sees promotion as an aspect of control, arguing that the concept of control contains not just a sense of constraint but also of promotion. He suggests a typology of strategies: advocacy, guidance, encouragement, exhortation, and request.

The problem with basing strategies on a view of relationships based on a concept of promotion is that it is difficult to incorporate any strategy which takes into account the conflicts that have been outlined above: Weaver's typology virtually denies the DES any sanctions — albeit negative ones.

I am therefore going to attempt a typology of strategies which allows for notions of conflict as well as consensus in the influence flow from centre to local levels in education (Figure 2.3). While not as 'finely-tuned' as Weaver's typology towards the consensus end of the spectrum, I would argue that the strategies 'Advice — Exhortation — Encouragement' do, in fact, subsume Weaver's typology.

Coercion ◄— Prescription —— Advice —— Inducement —— Exhortation —— Encouragement —► Pleading

Figure 2.3   *A typology of strategies in the influence flow of central government on LEAs.*

The DES can coerce recalcitrant LEAs in those areas where it is accepted that the centre lays down the rules. An LEA cannot, for example, allow children in its area to leave school before the minimum school-leaving age laid down in law. But, usually, before laws are passed there has been extensive consultation through the national local government system to ensure that there will be no massive outcry if a particular measure is passed. Moreover, as has been demonstrated, the elegance of legislative language conceals some conceptual obfuscation that — as in the case of s. 68 — can only be clarified by the courts, and there is no guarantee that the DES's interpretation will be accepted. Again, as Pattison (1980, p. 81) has noted, in a competitive two-party system, ' . . . the "force of law" may not be as powerful and decisive as it sounds'. New laws can be repealed; and this is especially true if, in the national local government system, there is considerable opposition to a particular measure which opposition parties may take up. Thus, the 1976 Education Act, passed by a Labour Government and empowering the Secretary of State to require LEAs to submit detailed plans for comprehensive re-organisation, was repealed in 1979 when the Conservatives took office.

As regards prescription, the Minister can, under the 1944 Act, ss. 100 and 111, convey his policy to local and other authorities by means of statutory rules, regulations and instruments all of which specify in detail what is required in general terms of the Act, and which have the force of law. If the authority fails to comply, the Minister is able to refuse to authorise Exchequer payments towards the cost of the service concerned. Though deriving from existing Acts, regulations and instruments are in effect delayed phases of Acts themselves and take their statutory effects from the Acts. Again, the text and content of such rules are usually fully discussed, in draft form, in the national local government system before they are formally issued.

Circulars and memoranda, on the other hand, are not legally effective, and are the means by which the DES advises, exhorts, encourages — and sometimes virtually pleads — with LEAs. Here, perhaps, style and decorum are very important — not just in the degree of consultation which is carried out in the national local government system, but also in the very language of the circulars. Thus, Anthony Crosland was persuaded by officials in the DES and others in the national local government system, particularly the Association of Education Committees, to substitute the word 'request' for 'require' in Circular 10/65, in which LEAs were asked to submit schemes for comprehensive re-organisation (Kogan and Bowden 1975, p. 100; Fowler 1974, para. 7.20; Saran 1979, para. 7.5). However, since there was no statutory obligation on LEAs to comply with the request, many did not do so, despite the additional lever of Circular 10/66 which declared that no funds would be available for secondary building projects other than for comprehensive re-organisation. On the other hand, when a newly elected Conservative government abruptly withdrew Circular 10/65 and replaced it with Circular 10/70, allowing LEAs to make their own decisions on comprehensive education, this brought considerable protest from the national local government system because, as Kogan and Bowden (1975, p. 100) point out, of the then Secretary of State: ' . . . it was not what she did but the way she did it that was objectionable.'

Circulars confirm the negative role of the DES: they can be used — as in 10/70 — to try to prevent change, but they cannot compel change in the direction the DES wants. As Griffiths (1971) concludes, the process of government by circular is a statement of national policy without the means to enforce it.[25]

As regards the influence flow from LEAs to the centre, Dunleavy notes how, in connection with housing, local authorities were able to constrain central government's influence between major policy changes by ignoring non-mandatory advice (Dunleavy 1981, p. 180). In the same way, by ignoring the advice, encouragement or exhortation of circulars, LEAs are able to constrain government influence from the centre. It is possible, therefore, to construct a typology of strategies which LEAs use to influence central government (see Figure 2.4).

Innovation ◄— Collaboration —— Prevarication —— Delay —— Passive resistance —— Inaction —► Active resistance

Figure 2.4 *A typology of strategies in the influence flow of LEAs on central government.*

Innovation is the most direct way in which individual LEAs can influence the DES. Raison (1976, p. 27) comments that ' . . . the ability to experiment is one of the justifications of local freedom.' Similarly, Milroy et al (1979, p. 55) opine that one of the principal ways that LEAs influence central government is through successful pioneering activities of individual LEAs. Ribbins, in Chapter 6, shows how the trend towards comprehensive re-organisation was pioneered by a small number of LEAs in the late 1940s. Milroy et al (1979, p. 18) note how a number of LEAs brought pressure to bear on the DES to be allowed to introduce 'middle' schools spanning part of both primary and secondary sectors as defined by the 1944 Act; and this eventually led in 1964 to the amendment of the 1944 Act to make middle schools legal. A later example of such pioneering was the introduction of tertiary colleges by some LEAs in the early 1970s.[26]

On the one hand, as has been noted, the response of the centre may be to prevent, or at least delay, the development of these innovations. However, there may be a more positive response if the innovation is taken up in the national government system, so that the DES may promote and enhance local developments, bringing them eventually into the formal mainstream of national policy.

However, the strategy of collaboration may be both a strategy of co-operation or of resistance to the centre by individual LEAs. If an LEA's own thinking corresponds with the particular schemes which the centre is promoting, then the LEA is likely to collaborate with the DES.[27] On the other hand, LEAs may adopt a strategy of tactical collaboration, which may be an elaborate form of stalling: calling for further discussions; submitting, in the case of comprehensive education, incomplete schemes or schemes which they knew would be rejected,[28] and so on. In this way, tactical collaboration often shades into prevarication and delay. But there comes a point when an LEA, having used up one or all of these strategies, must move either towards a strategy of active resistance—such as challenging the DES's interpretation of the law in the courts—or to a strategy of inaction. The adoption of each or any of these strategies may well depend on the issue in question; but, as has been shown, a strategy of inaction on the part of an LEA is often an effective constraint on the influence of the DES which cannot compel an LEA, say, to spend its block grant in a certain way, or re-organise its education according to a specific DES plan.

THE INFLUENCE FLOW OF ONE LEA ON ANOTHER OR OTHERS

There are few examples of joint administrative arrangements which impinge on individual LEAs' autonomy, although Sch. 1(1) of the 1944 Act gave the Minister the power to set up a 'joint education board' for the areas of two or more counties or county boroughs judged too small or poor to carry by themselves the full burden of a comprehensive education service. There are, of course, administrative arrangements for inter-authority recoupment of fees where they are obliged to educate one another's pupils or students (see, for example, Brooksbank 1980, p. 78). But the actual influence flow of one on another seems relatively limited.

Although part of the reason for this may lie in the different complexion of the political groups controlling different LEAs, there may well be technical reasons behind this relatively muted influence flow. Becher and Maclure (1978, pp. 73–4) have suggested that, at an institutional level, there are problems of lateral communication in that there is no easy channel of communication between institutions and that the easiest way is to go through vertical channels first, such as a teachers' centre. They suggest that a possible reason for this is that the technology of education is very unstable: the effectiveness of any given approach varies from one situation to another, especially as there are no agreed means of assessment. It may well be that the same condition applies between LEAs: the different circumstances—or the belief in different circumstances—which obtain as between LEAs with their different patterns of development mean that schemes which suit the circumstances of one LEA would be unsuitable for another, even neighbouring, LEA.[29]

There are other factors which may also be posited. First, the influence flows between LEAs seem to be strongest under conditions of common resistance to an initiative from the centre. Ribbins, in Chapter 6, points out that the decision in the courts in favour of Tameside seems to have emboldened other prevaricating LEAs to challenge the Secretary of State in the courts. A second factor is that of geography: there does appear to be what Dunleavy calls a 'multiplier' effect of resistance across neighbouring authorities (Pattison 1980, pp. 73 and 80) when one 'leader' LEA made a stand. Third, size seems to be an important variable: smaller rather than larger LEAs are more willing to resist the centre's influence. However, there have been too few studies of direct lateral influence flows between LEAs to make these other than tentative conclusions.

THE NATIONAL LOCAL GOVERNMENT SYSTEM DESCRIBED

Before considering the influence flows in to, and out of, the national local government system, it is worth considering the composition of the national local government system in more detail.

Although informally constituted it has a number of formal institutions in it. It provides a forum—in different guises—where representatives of the DES, LEAs and organised teachers—the third component of Manzer's educational sub-government—meet. As Scribbins (1980, p. 648) remarks, it is one of the remarkable features of education that teachers' pay and conditions of service are determined separately.

As regards teachers' pay, the Burnham Committee was set up in 1919 to negotiate teachers' salaries nationally, and in 1945 the Burnham Committee accepted the principle of the same basic salary scale for primary and secondary teachers. Following an acrimonious dispute which concluded in the Remuneration of Teachers' Act (RTA) in 1965, the Secretary of State made an agreement with LEAs which gave them the final say on the distribution of salaries in return for the ultimate decision on the global sum to be offered each year. To the teachers, the Secretary of State conceded a binding system of arbitration in the event of a deadlock—a device which has been increasingly used in recent years. Thus, in 1981, the system was changed so that arbitration was no longer binding. Moreover, various changes and rationalisations over the years have resulted in only two Burnham Committees, one dealing with the salaries of primary and secondary teachers, and the other dealing with the salaries of teachers in further education (including adult education, and agricultural education).

Conditions of service, on the other hand, are dealt with by the Council of Local Education Authorities (CLEA). The latter was created in 1975 after the local government re-organisation of 1974.[30] Until then, the representative of the LEAs had been the influential Association of Education Committees (AEC), whose strength derived as much from the personal influence of its long-standing secretary, William Alexander, as from other factors. But after 1974, the newly-created Association of Metropolitan Authorities (AMA) and Association of County Councils (ACC) were determined to curb what they perceived as the relative independence of the education interests, and created CLEA to represent common educational interests.[31] The AEC soon declined and was disbanded in 1977.

However, the national local government system is much broader than this: as Pattison (1980, p. 65) points out, there are also representatives of the local authority advisers and officers, operating through their respective organisations—the National Association of

Inspectors and Educational Advisers (NAIEA) and the Society of Education Officers (SEO). HMIs also move in and out of the national local government system. Other organisations are also influential within the national local government system: examples include the Secondary Examinations Council, the School Curriculum Development Committee, the National Development Centre for school management training at Bristol, various examining boards and research bodies like the National Foundation for Educational Research (NFER); and the educational press, such as the *Times Educational Supplement* and *Education*. In addition, there are numerous conferences and meetings where opinion can be 'sounded out': sometimes a junior minister, HMI or senior official like the Permanent Secretary at the DES, will make a speech which hints at a possible course of action to see how it is received.

It is not surprising that this complex matrix of formal and informal relationships is volatile and dynamic over time, sucking in and legitimising new elements and transforming relationships between existing elements.

On the one hand, the case of organised teachers is an example of changing relationships. Manzer's (1970) study of organised teachers' politics in the 1950s presents a picture of a dominant organisation — the NUT — operating in a relatively stable network of conditions and even personal relationships, representing a relatively closed sub-system: William Alexander, secretary of the AEC from 1946 to 1977; Ronald Gould, general secretary of the NUT from 1947 to 1970; and the two Permanent Secretaries at the DES from 1945 to 1959 — John Maud (1945–1952) and Gilbert Flemming (1952–1959).[32] Successive ministers in these years — there were seven[33] — emerge, with the possible exception of Eccles, as relatively marginal figures in respect of policy-making. But Manzer (1970, p. 9) notes the discontent which was welling up in the ranks of the NUT in the later 1960s with the leadership. By contrast with Manzer's study, Coates' (1972) study of teacher politics in the 1960s notes how imperatives external to the educational sub-government were increasingly important: the NUT lost its previously commanding position as other, more aggressive groups, like the NAS attempted to move into the wider political system to gain access to greater political leverage, particularly on the question of pay; and the NUT then followed suit. This move, according to Coates, took the form of four strategies: a search for professional self-government; increasing militancy; an alliance with other bodies for educational advance; and an alliance with organised labour.

A different perspective is given by Tipton (1975) who links teacher unionism to social stratification; similarly, Kogan and Bowden (1975, p. 124) argue that instability has been created by teachers' greater awareness of their position as salary earners which in turn has interacted with changes in their social and economic values so that 'Teachers associations have moved from policies that are institutionally continuous to far more disjunctive and tempestuous issues of social distribution and control'.

Just as the balance within the traditional educational sub-government has been changed by teachers themselves, so also the degree of influence exercised through the national local government system by other organised professional groups, like the Society of Education Officers, gives them an increasing claim to be a part of the educational sub-government. Meanwhile, the traditional educational sub-government has been faced with other boundary problems. Again, just as at central level the MSC, among other government agencies, has since the mid-1970s had an increasing influence in education, so too at local level the MSC has been able to bypass local authorities, giving them a representative but not controlling interest on MSC area boards.[34] Then again, the hostility manifested in the national local government system through the local authority associations — the AMA and the ACC — to the special position of education in local government[35] (see, for example, Mann 1979, p. 89; Price 1980) has been reflected since the mid-1970s within local authorities. The Bains Report (1972) recommended the adoption of corporate management structures by the new local authorities after the re-organisation of local government in 1974, with the setting up of a powerful Policy and Resources Committee to oversee and control the allocation of resources and priorities across the whole range of services within each local authority. This again threatens the special position of the LEA within the local government structure (see, for example, Bayliss 1983; Browning 1976; Gretton 1974; Pritchett 1976; Salter and Tapper 1981, pp. 96–110).

Moreover, the tensions between these groups representing the providers in the national local government system have been complicated, since the 1960s, by other groups, acting as either interest or pressure groups,[36] which have emerged to represent the consumers of educational services.[37] Many of these groups represent centrifugal rather than centripetal forces in the national local government system: Kogan (1978, pp. 68–9) has argued that the aims of many of these groups have been

> . . . essentially atomistic or particular. They allowed different groups not so much to seek consensus as to represent directly their own particular viewpoint without any logical or moral requirement to state the needs of all.'

Kogan and Bowden (1975, p. 232) attempted a classification of both provider and consumer groups, and this was updated and slightly amended by Mann (1979, pp. 124–6). The classification takes the form of a matrix based on degrees of conflict, legitimacy and managerial style; and whether or not groups are government sponsored. Kogan (1979a) noted the hostility of existing, legitimised groups — usually representing providers — to the newer groups; and elsewhere, Kogan (1979b) has suggested a model of the impact of interest and pressure groups. He suggests that, chronologically, an initial model where decisions come from political inputs at the head of the system at both central and local levels was then modified by the addition of provider groups in the decision-making process, whereby professionals 'read' recipients' value preferences for them. This, Kogan suggests, is now being further modified as consumer groups become legitimised in the decision-making process, so that recipients are now transformed into clients, and power diffused to a much greater degree.

Although as a description of what may happen — or even what ought to happen — this model is of undoubted value, the evidence does not suggest that this has yet happened to any great degree. On the one hand, at the local level of decision-making, Ribbins, below in Chapter 6, confirms Saran's (1979, para. 6.27) view that even a component of the educational sub-government — organised teachers — has had, with few exceptions, little influence on policy-making as regards comprehensive re-organisation; and this was even truer of the consumer element — parents. On the other hand, even at central level, Saran (1979, para. 8.7) concludes that pressure groups seem to have had far less influence than is often attributed to them. The implication, therefore, is that even provider groups, though having representation in the decision-making process, have limited influence.

An example may be seen in the case of school governors.[38] Even before 1944, school governors had in general become moribund (for a brief but lucid account, see Baron 1979). Despite the attempts in ss. 17 and 18 of the 1944 Act to revive the status of governors by decreeing a 'constitution' in the form of instruments and articles of government[39] which had to be approved by the Minister, the effect was limited, and most governors continued to show little independence of heads (Sallis 1979). Indeed Baron and Howell's (1974) survey of school government in the 1960s found that in nearly three-quarters of the boroughs and half the counties many schools had no individual governing bodies at all: these authorities had grouped some or all of their secondary and primary schools under one governing or managing body. Where individual school governors or managers did exist, they were usually controlled by the LEA or its dominant party.

When increasing pressure from consumer groups became more vocal and strident in the early 1970s, the then government set up, in 1975, the Taylor Committee to report on the whole issue of school government. Its report (Taylor 1977), recommended strengthening school government, suggesting that a quarter of school governing bodies should be elected by parents, and another quarter should represent the staff of the school. However s. 2 of the 1980 Education Act, which took into account the Taylor recommendations, specifies only that there be two parent governors (one in voluntary-aided and special-agreement schools) and one elected teacher governor (two in schools of more than 300 pupils). The effects of increasing the numbers and responsibilities of parent governors are examined in Chapter 17, together with the proposals made in May 1984 and March 1985 for extending further the role of parents on governing bodies.

If, on the one hand, the activities of provider and consumer groups can be regulated through this process of representative government, on the other hand there is also a process of self-regulation at work. Eckstein (1960, p. 21) notes how pressure groups often come to resemble the organisations they are trying to influence. Kogan and Bowden (1975, pp. 118–19) show how the NAS[40] — until 1961 a teacher organisation on the boundary of the national local government system — failed to obtain a seat on the Burnham Committee[41] because its declared objective was to oppose established government policy on salary negotiations. But when, by tactical error on the government's side, it was admitted to Burnham in 1961,

> . . . the NAS increasingly acquired the characteristics of other interest groups . . . On some matters, indeed, the NAS became closer to the DES than had the NUT.

Thus the national local government system has become at once more complex and more heterodox. There has been the development of a number of groups, some representing providers and many representing consumers seeking, initially, entry into the national local government system by a recognition that they represent genuine interests or causes, and thence to influence decisions, in some cases to such a degree that they can be regarded as a part of the educational sub-government.

However, how great that influence is in reality is debatable. Doubt must also be cast, not only on the influence of more recent groups, but also those — like organised teachers — who have long been a part of the educational sub-government. Glatter (1977b, paras. 3.30 and 4.3) has suggested that two parallel processes are at work: on the one hand, some pressures are tending towards greater control by both DES and LEAs[42]; while, on the other hand, other pressures, notably the enlargement of the role of consumers, are tending towards wider dispersion of influence. But the logical extension of the greater dispersion of influence is that it is spread more thinly across the groups in the national local government system, unless existing power relationships are altered. Significantly Fiske (1978, p. 75), noting the growth of demands for participation, suggested that one of the new roles that chief education officers of LEAs must learn is the 'orchestration of consumer voices' — with all that is implied in that metaphor. Perhaps the illusion of a degree of influence greater than that which is in fact the case is both a necessary and sufficient condition for satisfying both provider and consumer groups in the national local government system.

INFLUENCE FLOWS INTO AND OUT OF THE NATIONAL LOCAL GOVERNMENT SYSTEM

Having considered the changing structure and context of the national local government system, it is now possible to go on to consider the mutually re-inforcing influence flows connected with it (see Figures 2.3 and 2.4).

LEAs on the national local government system

Dunleavy (1981, p. 180) argues that, as regards housing, local authority outputs into the national local government system (Figure 2.1, influence flow 2) contributed to, and in some cases even served to define, trends in that system. As has been argued,[43] innovation by a number of pioneering LEAs influences central government; but also LEAs can begin or accelerate trends, such as those towards comprehensive re-organisation, middle schools or tertiary colleges. Here, the multiplier effect through the national local government system can be important as pioneering LEAs 'link up' via the informal networks.

The national local government system on LEAs

Trends in the national local government system influence individual LEAs' decision-making (Dunleavy 1981, p. 180; Figure 2.1, influence flow 3). Thus the national local government system has a homogenising or magnifying influence on LEAs, reinforcing the experiments of innovators and persuading others to take up favourable trends, which thus take on a self-reinforcing aspect. In this connection, Huberman (1973, p. 9) suggests that, in triggering change, a 'critical mass' factor is important: pressure to change becomes critical relative to the normal operating conditions (the mass) of the system. Thus, in the national local government system, there comes a transition point when what has been singular and unusual becomes a trend. Ribbins, in Chapter 6, argues that, after the pioneering efforts of individual LEAs in the late 1940s in comprehensive re-organisation, the period 1957–67 saw comprehensive re-organisation established as the prevailing orthodoxy. Similarly, as regards middle schools, the pioneering efforts of the West Riding of Yorkshire, Hull, Bradford and Wallasey in the early 1960s, combined with the recommendations of the Plowden Committee in 1967 which favoured middle schools, meant that the years 1969–76 saw a rapid growth in the numbers of pupils at middle schools, peaking in 1976 (Milroy et al. 1979, p. 18; *Times Educational Supplement Briefing* 1981). The pioneering development of tertiary colleges in a number of LEAs in the early 1970s (e.g. Exeter, Richmond-upon-Thames, Lancashire) led to a surge in schemes being presented to the DES from 1980, especially among the metropolitan districts.[44]

In each case, there seems to be an important factor operating through the national local government system which triggers it: in the case of comprehensive re-organisation, a consensus between Labour and Conservatives nationally on the benefits of comprehensive re-organisation; the Plowden Report in favour of middle schools; falling secondary school rolls and a static post-16 staying-on rate as regards tertiary colleges.

The national local government system on central government

In his study of housing policy, Dunleavy (1981, p. 180) found that trends in the national local government system could reinforce constraints on central government, generalising the control problems facing central government and so strengthening the constraints that individual local authorities put on central government initiatives.

Pattison's (1980) study of resistance to comprehensive re-organisation by the London borough of Sutton illustrates how its multiplier effect across other boroughs was instrumental in building up a consensus of resistance in the national local government system among the 22 LEAs who by 1969 had still not presented re-organisation schemes along comprehensive lines which were acceptable to the then Labour government (p. 70); and the tide turned against comprehensive re-organisation around this time.[45] As regards middle schools, the problem of falling rolls in the secondary sector, which made many middle schools vulnerable, turned the tide against them between 1976 and 1981 when pupil numbers in middle schools remained fairly constant; but 1981 saw the first large-scale middle school closures (*Times Educational Supplement Briefing* 1981). There is already a considerable tide of resistance to tertiary colleges in the national local government system which made itself felt in 1980.[46]

That the national local government system can have a considerable constraining effect on the DES is recognised by a former Permanent Secretary at the DES, William Pile, when he noted that educational planners ' . . . could not go against the tide of educational feelings. The Department [of Education and Science] saw its planning function as identifying existing trends in evolutionary fashion' (OECD 1975, p. 49). It is the network which goes to make up the national local government system which both formulates and expresses this tide of educational feeling.

CONCLUSION: THE EDUCATION SUB-GOVERNMENT RE-DEFINED?

Fowler (1979, p. 54) suggests that, while a description of DES, LEAs and organised teachers as an 'educational sub-government' may help policy analysis in one period, it may actually hinder analysis in another if it is not suitably amended. He argued that this is especially true when there are demands from other claimants to a share in policy-making, notably parents and training interests. Glatter (1979b, para. 3.14) also suggests that there has been a profound shift in the realities of power which the concept of 'partnership' may be unable to reflect.

It is certainly true that the 'triangle of power', as Briault (1976) terms it, between DES, LEAs and organised teachers is no longer so visible as it seemed to Manzer (1970) in the 1950s and 1960s. Then, the national local government system consisted largely of these three components operating in a powerful informal and personal network, where individuals like Alexander and Gould were able to exert personal influences, as well as the influence ascribed to them by their roles in the education sub-government.

However, since at least the early 1970s[47] there has been a change in the previous conditions under which conflict had been stabilised. The machinery and framework through which conflict was institutionalised and contained for some 20 or 25 years since 1945 have been increasingly strained and fragile; the 1970s and perhaps the 1980s are seeing a struggle to find new conditions in which new forces can be accommodated, to re-invent the stability of previous decades.

For the 'education sub-government' of DES, LEAs and organised teachers no longer neatly overlies the national local government system: there are a number of sharp discontinuities as new components attempt to assert themselves. The traditional education sub-government has therefore been faced with a number of boundary problems as these newer groups or interests press claims.

But the amount of influence that these new groups exert differs sharply. On the one hand, the emergence of the MSC at the centre of what may be termed a 'training sub-government' has undoubtedly had an important effect, and resulted in a shift of power away from the DES in certain areas.[48] On the other hand, the changing conditions have probably made the influence of some interests more visible than they were before, notably the Treasury and the Department of the Environment in connection with the central financing of education. But the emergence of new, largely consumer, interests demanding a share of power does not necessarily mean that they have obtained that power. By shifting its boundaries to admit consumer interests on representative terms, the educational sub-government may still maintain a degree of hegemony under new conditions.

AFTERWORD

It seems clear from the White Paper, *Better Schools* (DES 1985), that only limited changes are intended to the legislative framework within which the education sub-government works. Indeed, parts of the document read as a forceful re-statement of the division of responsibilities defined in the 1944 Act. For example, on the curriculum:

> . . . the headteacher will be responsible for the organisation and delivery of the curriculum, including detailed syllabuses and the teaching approaches and materials employed, within the available resources and having regard to the statement of aims and objectives determined by the governing body; (p. 68)

Proposals to alter the composition of school governing bodies are detailed in Chapter 17, and Chapter 4 examines the Government's view of the division of responsibility on the curriculum. Other proposals include plans to increase central influence on in-service training, by introducing a centrally controlled specific grant to replace existing allocations within the general grant to local authorities (p. 54). The Government also hopes to introduce a scheme for a more systematic performance appraisal of teachers, and is in consultation with the local authority and teacher associations on this issue (pp. 55–56). How this and the other proposed changes will develop remains to be seen.

NOTES

(1) The Department of Education and Science (DES) succeeded the Ministry of Education in 1964. However, for convenience the term 'DES' is used in this chapter to cover the whole period since 1944.

(2)   This chapter considers England and Wales together, but two important constitutional differences between the countries should be noted. First, there is the Welsh Joint Education Committee (WJEC), a body of unique constitutional status established by Order of the Minister of Education under a provision of the 1944 Education Act. Each LEA in Wales has representation on the WJEC which has three main roles: co-ordinator and initiator on many aspects of education, a regional advisory council on education and an examining body. Second, there is the Welsh Office, which has been given progressively greater responsibility for education since the appointment, in 1964, of the first Secretary of State for Wales.

(3)   Ribbins identifies a number of features, such as 'educational opinion' as being outside the national local government system. In my analysis, after Pattison (1980), I have considered these as a part of the national local government system.

(4)   See below, pp. 57–61.

(5)   The information in Figure 2.2 is derived largely from DES (1982a and 1982b), and Burgess (1969).

(6)   See below, p. 59.

(7)   For brief surveys of the development of the place of education in local government up to the late 1970s, see, for example, Brooksbank (1980, pp. 14–18); Gray (1980b, pp. 387–8); Mann (1979, pp. 62–70).

(8)   Technically, the ILEA is a committee of the Greater London Council (GLC). However, at the time of writing, the government was proposing to abolish the ILEA and replace it with a joint board of representatives from the boroughs which presently come under the aegis of ILEA.

(9)   The metropolitan counties will be abolished in 1985, and their powers either devolved to their constituent boroughs or carried out under alternative arrangements yet to be fully worked out.

(10) 105, if the Isle of Man is included; a somewhat special case.

(11) See below, p. 59.

(12) For a survey of references and useful commentary, see Pattison (1980); and Ribbins, below, Chapter 6.

(13) For detailed analysis of the mechanisms of capital expenditure see, for example, Brooksbank (1980) pp. 54–74; Fowler (1979) p. 49; Gray (1980b) pp. 172–3; Mann (1979) pp. 107–9; Raison (1976) pp. 15 and 22–3; Salter and Tapper (1981) pp. 106–7.

(14) For a history of changing DES priorities since 1945, see in particular Brooksbank (1980) pp. 56–7; and Fowler (1979) p. 49.

(15) For a history of the central government grant system to 1980, see Mann (1979) pp. 93–107; Pile (1979) pp. 45–61; and Bennett (1983). For a specific account of the operation and calculation of the RSG down to 1980, see Weir (1977).

(16) This was before central government discovered its powers to make specific grants for INSET under the 1962 Education Act.

(17) See below, Chapter 7.

(18) In recent years, however, this percentage has been progressively reduced: in 1983–4, only 52.8 % of current local authority expenditure was met by central grant; in 1984–5, 51.9 %.

(19) For detailed but lucid explanations of the mechanism of the system since 1980, see Burgin (1982), or Venning (1980).

(20) Scotland already has rate-capping. In 1981, the Secretary of State for Scotland was empowered to reduce the central government grant when a council's budget was "excessive and unreasonable". In 1982, the additional power to order a reduction in the rate was added.

(21) See also Chapter 7.

(22) See below, pp. 54–55 for a consideration of other possible factors.

(23) Sections 17 and 18 of the 1944 Act continued the then existing distinction between "managers" of primary schools and "governors" of secondary schools. Section 1 of the 1980 Education Act abolished this distinction: all schools now have governors.

(24) On the one hand, a parent unsuccessfully tried to persuade the Secretary of State that, under Sections 68 and 99, the county of Hereford and Worcester in 1982–83 was in default of its duty in that it was not providing the number of staff sufficient to teach the curriculum in a

particular school. On the other hand, the urgent need to re-organise Liverpool's secondary provision in the light of falling rolls was made critical by political deadlock which prevented re-organisation; and the possibility of a Section 99 order was considered in 1982.

(25) See also Ribbins in Chapter 6, below.

(26) See below, Chapter 7.

(27) See below, Chapter 6; and Pattison (1980) p. 69.

(28) ibid.

(29) The influence flows between LEAs are mediated, for the most part, through the national local government system.

(30) See above, p. 48.

(31) For details of relationships between local authority organisations and education before 1975, see, for example, Kogan and Bowden (1975) pp. 88–97; and Mann (1979) pp. 87–9.

(32) There have been seven Permanent Secretaries at the DES since 1945:
John Maud (13th November 1945–30th September 1952)
Gilbert Flemming (1st October 1952–30th September 1959)
Mary Smieton (1st October 1959–21st July 1963)
Herbert Andrew (22nd July 1963–31st July 1970)
William Pile (1st August 1970–28th May 1976)
James Hamilton (29th May 1976–30th April 1983)
David Hancock (1st May 1982–   )

(33) For a list of the eighteen ministers between 1945 and 1976, see Pile (1979) p. 241.

(34) See below, Chapter 7.

(35) The AMA, representing metropolitan authorities seems more hostile than the ACC, representing the shire counties: in 1982, for example, the AMA initially decided that its policy committee, not its education committee, should represent it on the national supervisory board to oversee the Youth Training Scheme (YTS). The ACC, by contrast, nominated its education committee chairman.

(36) An interest group may be defined as one whose main concern is to defend the professional, social or economic interests of its members, and will therefore attempt to shape policy-making in its chosen direction for only a part of the time. By contrast, a pressure group may be defined as a group which is concerned less with an interest and more with a cause of some sort. Once its aim is achieved it will go out of existence, but this does not necessarily happen. (See Finer [1966] and [1968]). However, the terms 'interest group' and 'pressure group' are often used interchangeably in the literature.

(37) Examples of such groups have been the Confederation for the Advancement of State Education (CASE), the Advisory Centre for Education (ACE), and the Child Poverty Action Group (CPAG). For a discussion of the activities of such groups, see, for example: Education Digest (1980); Kogan and Bowden (1975) especially Chapter 8; Kogan (1978); Locke (1974); Mann (1979), especially Chapter 6; and Saran (1979).

(38) The term "governors" is used here to include the pre-1980 "managers" of primary schools.

(39) or instruments and articles of management in primary schools.

(40) now the National Association of Schoolmasters/Union of Women Teachers (NAS/UWT).

(41) See above, p. 57.

(42) For a detailed discussion of these pressures, see Salter and Tapper (1981).

(43) See above, pp. 55–56.

(44) See below, Chapter 7.

(45) Ribbins, below, Chapter 6, dates the change from 1967.

(46) See below, Chapter 7.

(47) Some writers see a change in atmosphere or conditions from the mid-sixties (e.g. Kogan and Bowden [1975] pp. 36–8; Saran [1979] para 7.13), while Manzer (1970) p. 26 sees a steady erosion of consensus throughout the fifties. But cf Fowler (1974) para. 10.23 and (1979) pp. 73–4, who dates the changes from the early seventies.

(48) See below, Chapter 7.

REFERENCES

Bains Report (1972) *The New Local Authorities: Management and Structure.* London: HMSO.

Baron, G. (1979) 'Governors and Managers: origins of the species'. *Education* 24th September, 264–5.

Baron, G. and Howell, D. A. (1974) *The Government and Management of Schools.* London: Athlone.

Bayliss, S. (1983) 'Corporate Management "is sapping public confidence"'. *Times Educational Supplement* 21st January.

Becher, T. and Maclure, S. (1978) *The Politics of Curriculum Change.* London: Hutchinson.

Bennett, R. J. (1983) *Central Grants to Local Governments. The Political and Economic Impact of the Rate Support Grant in England and Wales.* Cambridge: Cambridge University Press.

Briault, E. W. H. (1976) 'A distributed system of education administration: an international viewpoint'. *International Review of Education*, **22**(4) 429–39.

Brooksbank, K. (ed.) (1980) *Educational Administration.* London: Councils and Education Press.

Browning, P. (1976) 'Corporate Planning: the Myth and the Reality'. *Education Administration* **4**(2) Spring 28–34.

Burgess, T. (1969) *A Guide to English Schools.* Harmondsworth: Pelican.

Burgin, K. L. H. (1982) 'Calculating Education Spending Need, 1976–82'. *Public Money* March 49–55.

Coates, R. D. (1972) *Teachers' Unions and Interest Group Politics.* London: Cambridge University Press.

Cohen, S. (1978) 'Cash released to create 18,000 more jobs'. *Times Educational Supplement* 16th November.

(CPRS) Central Policy Review Staff (1975) *A Joint Framework for Social Policies.* London: HMSO.

Davies, J. H. (1979) 'Progress on INSET: Clwyd'. *Education* 11th May, 544–5.

(DE/DES) Department of Employment/Department of Education and Science (1984) *Training for Jobs.* Cmnd. 9135. London: HMSO.

(DES) Department of Education and Science (1972) *Education: A Framework for Expansion.* Cmnd. 5174. London: HMSO.

(DES) Department of Education and Science (1982a) *The Educational System of England and Wales.* London: DES.

(DES) Department of Education and Science (1982b) *The Department of Education and Science — a brief guide.* London: DES.

(DES) Department of Education and Science (1985) *Better Schools*, Cmnd. 9469. London: HMSO.

Dunleavy, P. J. (1980) *Urban Political Analysis: The Politics of Collective Consumption in Contemporary Britain.* London: Macmillan.

Dunleavy, P. J. (1981) *The Politics of Mass Housing in Britain 1945–1975: A Study of Corporate Power and Professional Influence in the Welfare State.* London: Oxford University Press.

Eckstein, H. (1960) *Pressure Group Politics.* London: Allen and Unwin.

Education Digest (1980) 'Consumer Movements'. *Education* 8th August.

Finer, S. E. (1966) *Anonymous Empire.* London: Pall Mall Press.

Finer, S. E. (1968) 'Great Britain'. In Macridis, R. and Ward, J. (ed) *Modern Political Systems.* New Jersey: Prentice-Hall.

Fiske, D. (1978) 'S.E.O. Presidential'. *Education* 27th January, 74–7.

Fowler, G. (1974) 'Central Government of Education 1'. Unit 2 of Course E221: *Decision-Making in British Education Systems.* Milton Keynes: The Open University Press.

Fowler, G. (1979) 'The Politics of Education'. In Bernbaum, G. (ed.) *Schooling in Decline.* London: Macmillan.

Glatter, R. (1979a) 'An Introduction to the Control of Education in Britain'. Unit 1 of Course E222: *The Control of Education in Britain.* Milton Keynes: The Open University Press.

Glatter, R. (1979b) 'Conclusion'. Unit 16 of Course E222: *The Control of Education in Britain.* Milton Keynes: The Open University Press.

Gray, L. (1980a) 'Education Finance'. In Waitt, I. (ed) *College Administration — A Handbook.* London: National Association of Teachers in Further and Higher Education.

Gray, L. (1980b) 'Local Authorities'. In Waitt, I. (ed) *College Administration — A*

Handbook. London: National Association of Teachers in Further and Higher Education.

Gretton, J. (1974) 'Corporate Management Ways'. *Times Educational Supplement* 18th October.

Griffith, J. A. G. (1966) *Central Departments and Local Authorities*. London: Allen and Unwin.

Griffiths, A. (1971) *Secondary School Reorganisation in England and Wales*. London: Routledge and Kegan Paul.

Hartley, O. A. (1971) 'The Relationship between Central and Local Authorities'. *Public Administration*, **49** Winter 439–56.

Huberman, A. M. (1973) *Understanding Change in Education: an Introduction*. Paris: UNESCO Press.

Kogan, M. (ed.) (1971) *The Politics of Education: conversations with Edward Boyle and Anthony Crosland*. Harmondsworth: Penguin.

Kogan, M. (1978) *The Politics of Educational Change*. London: Fontana.

Kogan, M. (1979a) 'Sir William's Department'. *Times Educational Supplement* 21st December.

Kogan, M. (1979b) 'Different Frameworks for Educational Policy Making and Analysis'. *Educational Analysis*, **1**(2) Winter, 5–14.

Kogan, M. and Bowden, K. (1975) *Educational Policy-Making: A Study of Interest Groups and Parliament*. London: Allen and Unwin.

Lightfoot, M. (1983) 'The new interrogators'. *Times Educational Supplement* 27th May.

Locke, M. (1974) *Power and Politics in the School System*. London: Routledge and Kegan Paul.

Mann, J. (1979) *Education*. London: Pitman.

Manzer, R. A. (1970) *Teachers and Politics: the role of the National Union of Teachers in the making of national educational policy in England and Wales since 1944*. Manchester: Manchester University Press.

Milroy, P. *et al* (1979) 'The Local Government of Education'. Unit 4 of Course E222: *The Control of Education in Britain*. Milton Keynes: The Open University Press.

(OECD) Organisation for Economic Co-operation and Development (1975) *Educational Development Strategy in England and Wales*. Paris: OECD.

Pattison, M. (1980) 'Intergovernmental Relations and the Limitations of Central Control: reconstructing the politics of Comprehensive Education'. *Oxford Review of Education*, **6**(1) 63–89.

Pile, W. (1979) *The Department of Education and Science*. London: Allen and Unwin.

Price, C. (1980) 'Everyone in the garden?'. *Times Educational Supplement* 25th April.

Pritchett, G. R. (1976) 'Municipal Malaise'. *Times Educational Supplement* 12th November.

Raison, T. (1976) *The Act and the Partnership — an essay on educational administration in England*. London: Bedford Square Press.

Regan, D. (1977) *Local Government and Education*. London: Allen and Unwin.

Sallis, J. (1979) 'The sixties and seventies: stirrings of change'. *Education* 5th October, 367–8.

Salter, B. and Tapper, T. (1981) *Education, Politics and the State. The Theory and Practice of Educational Change*. London: Grant McIntyre.

Saran, R. (1979) 'The Politics of Educational Policy-Making: Pressures on Central and Local Government'. Unit 6 of Course E222: *The Control of Education in Britain*. Milton Keynes: The Open University Press.

Scribbins, K. (1980) 'Conditions of Service: Agreements Affecting Teaching Staff'. In Waitt, I. (ed.) *College Administration — A Handbook*. London: National Association of Teachers in Further and Higher Education.

Sloman, P. (1980) 'When is unreasonableness reasonable?'. *Education* 13th June, 503.

Taylor, T. (1977) *A New Partnership for our Schools*. London: HMSO.

Times Educational Supplement Briefing (1981) 'Middle Schools decline due to haphazard development'. *Times Educational Supplement* 13th November, 9.

Tipton, B. F. A. (1975) 'The hidden side of teaching: the teachers' unions'. *London Educational Review*, **3**(2).

Venning, P. (1980) 'Block Grant: beginner's guide'. *Times Educational Supplement* 21 November.

Weaver, T. (1979) 'The Department of Education and Science: Central Control of Education?'. Unit 2 of Course E222: *The Control of Education in Britain*. Milton Keynes: The Open University Press.

3

TEACHER SUPPLY: PROBLEMS, PRACTICE AND POSSIBILITIES

Hywel Thomas

INTRODUCTION

Apart from learners, the single most important resource within schools is teachers, with analyses of school financial budgets showing teachers as the major resource, often absorbing two-thirds of all financial resources.[1] Responsibility for ensuring that there is an adequate supply of suitably-trained teachers lies with the Secretary of State (DES 1977) who is given substantial powers to discharge these obligations. These powers arise from the 1944 Education Act and subsequent regulations, which give the Secretary of State authority to control the numbers of students on initial training courses as well as making available places for in-service training courses.

Ministers and senior officials recognise the importance of this role. A former Permanent Secretary has written that ' . . . for most of the decades following the 1944 Act the securing of an adequate supply of teachers to meet the needs of a growing school population was one of the Department's major preoccupations' (Pile 1979). Anthony Crosland, a former Secretary of State, explaining his decision to abolish the National Advisory Council on the Training and Supply of Teachers (NACTST) argued:

> I did not reappoint the NAC after its *Eleventh Report*, despite continuing protests, and I would never have done so. It was concerned with the future supply and demand for teachers. I thought that was a job that should be done inside the Department and not by an amorphous outside body. If the Department couldn't do that job, which was central to all its activities, it ought to pack up. (Kogan 1971)

Thus any investigation of the successes and failures of teacher supply policy is, simultaneously, an examination of the supply of a crucial educational resource and an appraisal of policy-making and planning within the DES. That post-war teacher supply policy has had its successes and its failures becomes evident when we begin to examine the record.

Possibly the first items which should be regarded as indicators of successful policy are the improvement in the pupil–teacher ratios and the reductions achieved in class size. By January 1983 the combined pupil–teacher ratio for maintained primary and secondary schools stood at 18:1 and was the lowest level ever achieved. Moreover, despite the pressures to cut public expenditure, the government's plans show an intention of improving this ratio into the mid-1980s (HM Treasury 1984). This does not alleviate anxieties about redundancies because with the declining school age population biting into school rolls, fewer teachers are needed even to support improvements to the ratio. Almost twenty years earlier, in 1962, a one-year hiatus in the output of teachers from the training colleges was a sign of another policy goal achieved. The interruption in supply was a consequence of the lengthening of training from two to three years for those who entered the colleges in 1960, and was seen by the teacher associations as an opportunity for strengthening and improving the professional preparation of the non-graduate part of the teacher force (Crispin 1979). This was followed later in the 1960s by the introduction of the BEd. degree which in the 1970s, in its three- and four-year variants, gradually replaced the non-graduate certificates and diplomas. This up-grading of the professional qualification was matched in the later 1970s by the up-grading of entry qualifications, a task made easier by the reduction in the number of training places available.

An important part of the explanation for the achievement of most of these policy goals lies with the performance of the UK economy. The slow but steady economic growth in the 25 years up to 1970 was sufficient to allow more resources to be made available for education, thereby financing longer training and the larger teaching force needed to improve pupil–teacher ratios and reduce class sizes. There was also much optimism in the capacity of education to generate an improved economic performance, and the 1960s produced substantial studies like those of Denison (1967) which seemed to support this belief. In such a context it is possible to understand why the education sub-government was so successful in attracting more resources and why teacher associations such as the NUT were able to gain support for their initial objective of longer professional training and a subsequent objective of an all-graduate profession. The poorer performance of the economy after 1970, allied to falling rolls, can also explain the more recent improvement in the qualifications of entrants to training courses. Both act to make fewer places available and allow the training institutions, all other things being equal, to be more selective.

While the successes of post-war supply policy can be readily understood, the failures and partial successes of the past, as well as the uncertainties of future supply policies, are more complex. They are best introduced in two parts which distinguish the macro-level tasks of controlling the total stock of teachers from the micro-level tasks concerned with the composition and distribution of the teaching stock.

The concern of those responsible for the macro-level task of controlling the total stock of teachers is to ensure that a sufficient number of suitably qualified teachers are available to meet the requirements of schools. Anyone tempted by the notion that this does not seem to be too difficult a task would be advised to think again. Matching the numbers of teachers supplied to numbers required entails making predictions about the behaviour of some hard-to-predict variables, such as future births or the number of teachers who will choose to leave the profession. From these predictions forecasts can then be made of the future school-age population and the number of teachers likely to be in post. These forecasts offer guidance for decisions about the number of places needed in the training institutions and it is these decisions which were productive of some prominent failures in policy-making and planning. An example of this planning failure can be seen in the consequences of the decision, made in 1957, to extend the training period to three years for students first entering colleges in 1960. Ahamad (1970) notes the effect of errors in the 1956 forecast of demand and supply of teachers:

> In retrospect, this turned out to be a very bad time for introducing the change. The lengthening of the training period caused a reduction in the supply of teachers from 1962 and hence at exactly the time that the underestimation errors in the demand projections became substantial. The council's recommendation therefore served to increase the shortage of teachers and caused a worsening of staffing standards.

The principal factors underlying these forecast errors was an underestimate, both of future births and of the rate at which teachers left the profession, variables which were to cause further difficulties for the planners. The eighth and ninth Reports of the NACTST, published in 1962 and 1965 respectively, warned of the need for rapid expansion of training places to produce more teachers, not only to meet the needs of a growing school population, but also to meet anticipated future growth (Hencke 1978). A rapid expansion of training places began in the early 1960s in order to overcome the shortage of teachers, and continued until 1972 when forecasts of future growth somewhat abruptly changed to forecasts of a declining school population. The expansion of training places was thrown into sharp reverse and college closures were announced. This sudden and unexpected change from expansion to contraction is vividly illustrated by the case of Hereford College of Education, where the last buildings were completed in 1975, only four years before the scheduled closure of the college in 1979 (Hencke 1975). The 1970s almost certainly mark the nadir of failures in the macro-level management of teacher supply and, as Crispin (1979) appropriately writes, ' . . . a situation where an apparent shortage of teachers in the early 1970s, with part-time schooling in some urban areas, was quickly followed by teacher unemployment from the mid-1970s, is hardly likely to inspire public confidence in planning.'

Failures to achieve policy objectives also occurred in the management of the composition and distribution of the teaching stock, summarised above as micro-level issues. The longest running failure, and perhaps the most important, concerns the supply of shortage subjects. In the case of maths and science teachers, the chronic shortage which continued through the post-war years persists in the 1980s despite teacher 'surplus' and unemployment. The consequences of this failure are by no means negligible with its immediate effect on the learning opportunities of children and its subsequent implications for career choice and skills at work. An apparently more successful micro-level policy was the quota scheme introduced in the late 1950s and continued through the next decade during a time of general teacher shortage. This was a voluntary rationing scheme with the aim of enabling each local education authority to obtain a fair share of the total number of teachers available (DES 1968). It was a scheme widely regarded as successful but, as will be discussed later, it may be that its consequence was a net loss of teachers from an already inadequate stock. This general shortage affected some parts of the education system much more seriously than others, particularly schools with a high proportion of disadvantaged and underprivileged children, and also schools in the London area. Special measures were introduced to meet these particular difficulties, beginning with the Schools of Exceptional Difficulty (SED) allowance in November 1968 and followed in 1971 by the first London allowance. The initial impact and later changes to these allowances will be examined more fully later in the chapter but it is important to note here that their immediate effect was to produce outcomes *opposite* to those intended by the policy-makers, creating rather than solving problems for the schools.

As indicated earlier, these policy failures require more complex explanations than the policy successes and will occupy much of the remaining chapter, which is divided into three further parts. The first of these, dealing with the macro-level task of controlling the teaching stock, is divided into six sections, the first of which describes the many variables affecting the demand for and supply of teachers. The second section examines three perspectives from which DES planning has been criticised and is followed by a section analysing the assumptions underlying the DES' planning methodology; an alternative to this methodology is described in the fourth section. The last two sections deal first with DES planning for teacher supply into and beyond the 1980s, and second with procedures which could be adopted to improve existing practice. This is followed by a discussion of the micro-level issues of managing the composition and distribution of supply. This is divided into four sections, beginning with an account of the different agencies involved in these issues. Later sections are case studies describing and analysing the many initiatives aimed at resolving the above-mentioned micro-level problems. The chapter ends with a brief concluding discussion.

CONTROLLING THE TEACHING STOCK

The planning model

The need to plan

The need to plan teacher supply in the UK arises because government (central and local) operates an administered market in which it has the responsibility of maintaining and staffing the schools (demand), ensuring an appropriate number of training places exist (supply) and fixing the salary scales for teachers (price). The DES has the final responsibility for determining the future numbers of teachers required and from this it calculates the necessary numbers of teacher training places which must be provided. The length of the training cycle allied to the need, in some circumstances, to provide new buildings for an increased number of training places means that forecasts of the numbers of teachers required have to be made some years ahead of the time when the teachers will actually be needed in the schools.

While the decisions based on the forecasts are made by the Secretary of State, the Department has often drawn upon advice from advisory committees with membership representing a wide range of education interests. Between 1949 and its abolition by Anthony Crosland in 1965, NACTST produced nine reports on teacher demand and supply. After an interval of eight years the Advisory Committee on the Supply and Training of Teachers (ACSTT) was established. This continued until 1978, to be followed in September 1980 by the Advisory Committee on the Supply and Education of Teachers (ACSET), which was disbanded in April 1985.

The planning problem

The statistical information required by these advisory committees was, and is, supplied by the Department and Figure 3.1 attempts to represent diagrammatically the main variables which must be estimated when tackling the critical planning problem of equalising the stock of teachers in employment to the number of teachers required. It is appropriate to acknowledge that some parts of this diagram are inspired by the earlier work of Crispin (1979). Discussion of these variables will be illustrated by examples drawing principally upon the history of teacher supply in the 1970s. The diagram will be examined in two parts, first the top part showing the factors determining the numbers required (demand), and then the bottom part showing the factors affecting the stock of teachers (supply).

The teachers required

The number of pupils.   Figure 3.1 shows that all the variables affecting the number of teachers required are affected by government policy, though the level of effect varies considerably, with many of the variables more affected by non-governmental decisions. The most significant variable is birth rate and it is fluctuations in this difficult-to-predict factor which has caused so much trouble for DES planners. It is the Office of Population and Census Surveys (OPCS) which produces information for the DES on actual births and expected trends. For many years, the consistently optimistic assessments of the OPCS suggested that the fall in birth rate which began in 1964 was temporary and would soon reverse itself. Not until 1972 did concern grow that the fall would continue. The scale of the decline in births was substantial, from 876 000 in 1964 to 568 000 in 1977 and it is this fall which underlies the declining school population of the 1980s.[2] While there is a close relationship between births and the size of the compulsory school-age population, other factors, such as expected patterns of migration, must be incorporated into calculations. Changes in government policy can also have a substantial impact on the compulsory school-age population, as with the raising of the compulsory leaving age in 1972–3.

Pupils over 16 in full-time education normally have a choice of institution in which to continue their studies. This adds to the uncertainty in calculating what is called the age participation rate (APR) for schools (the proportion of the age cohort choosing to continue their studies in the schools sector). The APR can also be influenced by government policy. For example, the prevailing economic circumstances and the likelihood of employment can affect the decisions of fifth-formers to leave school or continue; government decisions on entitlement to social security payments can also affect decisions to continue at school or leave and follow part-time courses in colleges of further education. These decisions by 16-year-olds have a greater impact on the number of teachers required than changes in younger age cohorts because of the increased weighting of the sixth-former in calculations of pupil–teacher ratios.

A further factor which must be included when calculating the numbers of pupils within the maintained systems is the number of under-fives. While their total numbers depend upon birth rate the scale of provision lies within an area of LEA policy discretion. The number of under-fives within the schooling system depends partly upon the expressed preferences of parents but also on the willingness of local authorities to make provision. As junior

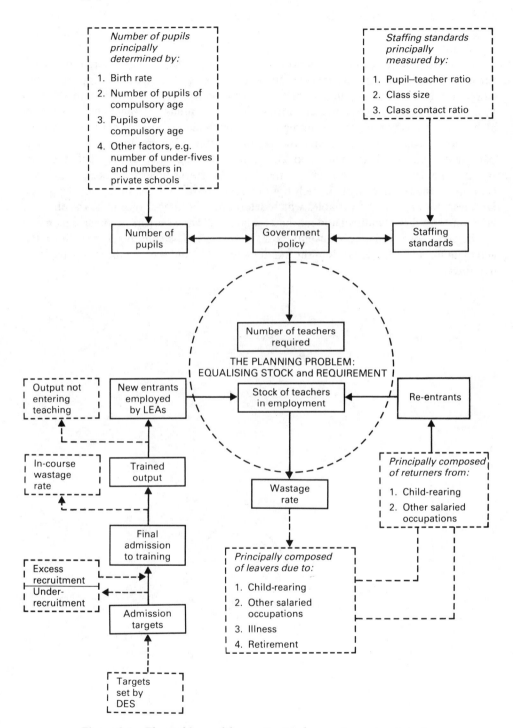

Figure 3.1 *The problems of forecasting teacher requirement and stock.*

school heads compensate for falling rolls by enrolling a greater proportion of this age group, the effect of the rising-fives on teacher requirement has probably become more significant.

This account of the factors which principally determine the number of pupils has made some reference to instances where government policy is significant, but it is appropriate to emphasise the wide-ranging impact of government policy. Thus, legislation on abortion law, the availability of free contraception and changes in family allowance entitlements will all have some effect on birth rate; immigration policy will have an impact on the numbers of pupils of compulsory age, and the possible effect of unemployment on the age participation rate has been mentioned. Decisions on the eligibility for tax relief of fees for private schools, as well as decisions on the charitable status of such schools, will have a bearing on the relative costs of such options for parents and, in turn, their decisions. However, for *most* of the variables which determine the number of pupils, the effect of government policy is indirect and marginal. Figure 3.2 shows errors in forecasting made by the OPCS over a period of twenty years from 1955. The solid black line shows the actual figures of 5–14 year olds in the maintained sector and they can be compared with five forecasts.

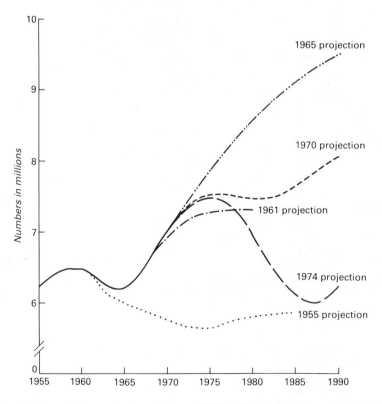

Figure 3.2 *Pupil population projections. Source: CPRS (1977) Population and the Social Services. London: HMSO. (Reproduced with permission.)*

Staffing standards. Unlike many of the factors which determine the numbers of pupils, government policy directly determines staffing standards. For many years the principal measures used for determining staffing standards were the pupil–teacher ratio (PTR) and class size. PTR measures the number of pupils per teacher and is widely accepted in education as one yardstick for assessing change, with improvements in the ratio interpreted as indicating improvements in the standards of educational provision. Class size is another favoured indicator of standards of provision and governments, as well as teacher unions, have adopted policy targets for reducing class sizes. The relationship between these two measures is by no means straightforward and improvements in PTR need not, necessarily, either eliminate oversize classes or even reduce average class size. This, perhaps surprising, outcome can be explained. Improvements in PTR can be utilised by schools in two principal ways. One option is to use the extra teachers to increase provision for particular children. For example, the provision of small teaching groups for the least able (e.g. extra remedial reading) and the most able (e.g. an extra modern language), or providing a wider range of options for the 14 + age group. These decisions will reduce the *average* size of classes but do not necessarily reduce *maximum* class size. The second option is to deploy teachers into extra administrative tasks. Thus, extra pastoral responsibilities and more liaison with out-of-school agencies may be resourced by reducing the classroom time required by teachers. These changes in the proportion of teaching time (contact ratio) could be such that an improvement in PTR might reduce neither average class size nor the number of oversize classes. School-based discretion over the allocation of staff time was not recognised as a significant variable by the NACTST when, in its ninth report in 1965, it suggested suitable PTR targets for effecting reductions in the number of classes of more than 30 pupils. Later reports by the DES (1975) indicates a more cautious view on the relationship between PTR and class size: '. . . there is no exact relationship between pupil–teacher ratio and class size.' Recognising the effect of teacher contact ratio on policies aimed at reducing average class size and the elimination of over-size classes, the DES has incorporated measures of contact ratios when attempting to calculate the number of teachers required. Longman (1977), a statistician with the DES, offers a useful discussion of the use of this measure, along with other school-based measures. In the paper he comments on the non-availability of much of the necessary data and mentions plans for a proposed survey of secondary schools, in order to '. . . provide a much more complete picture than at present exists of the existing stock of teachers and how they are deployed. . . .' (Longman 1977). This took place in the autumn of 1977 and basic data from the survey was published in *Statistical Bulletin 6/80* (DES 1980).

Projection of pupil and teacher numbers. The Department, or its Advisory Committees, is able to make projections of the number of teachers required by combining forecasts of pupil numbers with the policy-determined judgement about desirable staffing standards. For example, with a given number of pupils, to achieve an overall PTR of 1 : 20 will need fewer teachers than would be needed to meet a PTR target of 1 : 19. The difficulty of attempting these forecasts of teacher numbers required is emphasised by the figures shown in Table 3.1.

In each of the years shown in the first column of the table the DES published forecasts of the expected schools population in 1981 (second column), together with forecasts of the number of teachers required in 1981 (third column). In the thirteen years (1965–1978)

Table 3.1   *Projections of pupil and teacher numbers in England and Wales, 1955–1978.*

Projection made in:	Projected number of pupils in 1981 (000s)	Teacher target in 1981 (000s)
1965	9898	590
1971	9562	540
1972	9447	510
1973	9107	510
1974	8670	510
1975	8584	480–490
1976	8522	449
1977	8500	450–460
1978	8497	456

Source: Crispin A., (1979) *Providing the Teachers*, Unit 8 of E222 'The Control of Education', Milton Keynes: Open University (reproduced with permission).

during which forecasts for 1981 were made the expected number of pupils projected was revised downwards by 14 per cent and the required number of teachers forecast was revised downwards by over 22 per cent. Change in birth rate is the principal explanation for revision of projected pupil numbers. The downward revision of teachers required, however, is only partly explained by the fall in pupil numbers; the larger drop in teacher target numbers is caused by changes in government policy on staffing standards. From 1965 to 1972 there was only a 4.6 per cent fall in expected pupil numbers for 1981 but a 13.6 per cent fall in the teacher target for 1981. The figures produced in 1972 show a major shift in government policy from the targets set for staffing standards by the NACTST's ninth report.[3] A further retreat from the ninth report's projected staffing standards occurred in 1976 as a result of the Labour Government's expenditure cuts of that year: between 1975 and 1976 the projected number of pupils was revised downwards by only 0.7 per cent but the forecast number of teachers was revised downwards by 7.4 per cent. These departures from the 1965 targets for staffing standards may offer an explanation of Crosland's decision (see above) to scrap the NACTST, since a body with its status, responsibility and voice would have been a continuous and uncomfortable reminder to the Department of the targets it had set for improving staffing standards.

Deciding upon the numbers of teachers required for any target year is only the first stage of planning teacher numbers. The second stage is concerned with ensuring that the required number of teachers are available and the next section examines the supply side of the planning process.

Producing the teachers

How the DES determines the target for the number of teachers required was described above, but achieving this target requires judgement and decisions concerning the variables shown in the bottom part of Figure 3.1. The total stock of teachers in employment is affected by the flows into and out from the stock, as in the diagram. Some of these flows are more open to DES control or influence than others.

Control of training. It is on flows from initial training that the DES is able to exercise the greatest control. Calculating the level of trained output is the area of greatest certainty because the Department determines admission targets, and levels of in-course wastages (drop-outs and failures) are small and predictable. Uncertainty increases beyond this level for three reasons, each of which have their origin in developments in the past ten years. First, the re-organisation of public-sector teacher education in the 1970s transferred teacher training from monotechnic, vocationally oriented colleges of education into multipurpose institutions where, as Crispin (1979) argues, students may become less committed to their proposed profession so that they emerge as trained output but do not wish to enter employment as teachers. He adds that the economic circumstances of the 1970s may counterbalance this tendency as students, in the context of historically high levels of unemployment, may be more eager to find employment in the area for which their training has prepared them. However, whether local education authorities will have the resources to employ all the trained output seeking employment seemed doubtful to Crispin, writing before 1979. This last reservation has been borne out in the wake of public expenditure cuts of the late 1970s and early 1980s. The problem of predicting the recruitment levels of local authorities has been worsened by changes in methods of controlling public expenditure announced in 1981 (HM Treasury 1981) where, in future, *cash* will be the primary constraint on public spending and not *volume*.

The change of emphasis to cash has significant implications for teacher supply policy, since projections of numbers required will only be possible after making estimates for changes in teacher salaries.

Wastage and re-entrant rates. The total stock of teachers is also affected by flows leaving the profession (wastage rate) and those returning to the service after an interval elsewhere (re-entrants). The fact that wastage rates are an area of great uncertainty is reflected in various DES commentaries on teacher supply as with: 'Wastage is and will remain an element of major uncertainty' (DES 1973). A later report (DES 1975) describes the basis for estimating wastage rates:

> Wastage rates differ between teachers of different ages and qualifications and between men and women. The individual wastage rates for most ages and most categories of teachers have, in general, been declining since about 1969. Were this decline to continue right through to 1985, the overall rate could fall to as low as 5.3 per cent from its 1972 level of 9.5 per cent. If the individual wastage rates were to remain constant at about the 1972 levels, there would still be a fall . . . because of the shifting composition by age, sex and category of teacher . . . to about 8.0 per cent in 1985. Projections of the potential supply of teachers have been calculated on the two alternative hypotheses of constant or of declining wastage rates.

The same DES report explains the basis for calculating re-entrants:

> Separate projections have been made for married women returning to service after a break of at least a year and for other re-entrants. The calculations have assumed that:
>
> i   the number of married women returning to teaching (after a break in service of at least a year) will rise from the present figure of 3500 to some 5000 in the early 1980s;
> ii other re-entrants to teaching will be equivalent to some 30 per cent of the leavers of the previous year (the historical figure).

Managing the flows. Given the circumstances where the DES controls initial training but feels it cannot ever reliably predict wastage and re-entrant rates, it is not surprising that, in seeking to manage flows of entry and exit to attain targets for the teaching force, the DES has laid emphasis on the numbers in initial training. This emphasis partly explains the very rapid increase in initial training numbers in the 1960s, to be followed by almost equally rapid contraction in the 1970s. Table 3.2 shows levels of annual intake and the total numbers in initial training for selected years between 1964 and 1982. It shows an 82 per cent growth of total numbers from 1964 to 1972, followed by a contraction of 70 per cent from 1972 to 1980, a contraction which is not yet complete. The near doubling in size in eight years, of a whole sector of the UK education system, followed in terms of numbers by a more dramatic contraction is clear evidence of the use, by the DES, of initial training as the principal variable for controlling the size of the teaching stock. Less clear is first, whether the expansion and contraction of the training system was a consequence of bad planning or a regrettable byproduct illustrative of the difficulties of planning and second, whether managing initial training is the most appropriate way of controlling the size of the teaching stock. These issues will be considered in the following three sections.

Table 3.2   *Initial teacher training in England and Wales, 1964–1982.*

	1964	1966	1968	1970	1972	1974	1976	1978	1980	1982[a]
Annual intake	30.4	39.5	46.6	46.5	50.6	43.3	30.9	21.7	18.9	17.0
Total numbers enrolled	65.9	88.8	109.6	115.6	119.6	111.2	89.0	49.6	35.8	30.4

[a] 1982 figures show England only.
Sources: DES (1976b; 1979b; 1981b; 1982b; 1984a).

The causes of planning failures

There appear to be three alternative explanations of DES planning failures. One perspective is very critical of the planners, suggesting that it is their competence which is most in doubt. Consider David Hencke's (1978) comments on the extension of training to three years,

> Unfortunately such a decision could not have been made at a worse time. From 1957 the birth rate began climbing rapidly again and it continued remorselessly until 1964. At the same time the children born immediately after the war were reaching university age. It was quite clear that there would not be enough places for this new generation in universities and colleges. Thus a growing teacher shortage in the schools was combined with an obvious shortage of places in higher education.

This quotation suggests that the planners apparently failed to recognise rather obvious demographic trends. Later, in his account of the training cutbacks of the 1970s, Hencke suggests that the Department had information about the decline in the birth rate and recognised its implications but chose to suppress the figures. The long-term aim of this tactic was to enable the DES to link the reorganisation of teacher training with public sector higher education,

> At this stage there can be no doubt that the reorganization of teacher education had been replaced with a plan to reorganize higher education into a firm binary system. The 'problem' of the colleges was to be solved by almost abolishing them as a significant separate sector. At this point the Department can take great credit for introducing a major change unnoticed,

without publishing the full background and ensuring that no machinery existed outside the Department for monitoring its implementation.

This perspective is not shared by Crispin (1979)[4] who, in fact, challenges Hencke's criticisms. For example, he admits that the government could have delayed the extension of training but asks,

> It was the government's determination to press ahead with what, after all, many believed to be a much needed reform that is surely the debatable point: was it sheer expediency, rigidity of policy or concern for standards of educational provision?.

As for the suppressed figures, Crispin advances the argument that a sudden check to the falling birth rate in mid-1971 is a more convincing explanation for delaying the cutbacks than 'the mysterious figures of June 1971 mentioned by Hencke', the existence of which he obviously has some doubts about. Crispin's view of the quality of DES planning seems to be in three parts. First, the failures must be seen against the difficulty of planning which, in this area, includes so many uncertain, unreliable, but critical variables. Second, critics must recognise the limits which exist on the powers of the DES to manage the training system and that blame for failures must be shared with the institutions who were slow to introduce a Dip.HE. Finally, planners can produce projections and memoranda but ministers are crucial to the *policy* decisions which emerge and, 'In giving their advice, DES officials may have difficulty in convincing the minister of the reality and probability of what might happen. It should not be forgotten that the minister may act without adhering to the submissions of officials and without consulting the advisory committee.' Set against these observations it is worthwhile noting that Pile (1979) is so reluctant to address the issues of the training cutbacks that he mentions them in only two short paragraphs, a strangely muted response to events described by John Mann (1979) as a 'debacle'.

It may be, however, that a convincing explanation lies neither in the charge of ineptitude or the difficulties of planning, but in the limitations of the *manpower planning methodology* used by the DES and their reluctance, probably abetted by other partners in the education service, to use other planning instruments. Criticism of the assumptions and methodology of manpower planning is well established (see Blaug 1967; 1970) and it has been related to the management of teacher supply by Ahamad (1970; 1973) and Woodhall (1977). The assumptions which manpower planners make about the world suggest that they assume certain rigidities about the way the world works, and what is being suggested is that if planners accept and use a methodology which has a fairly rigid world view then the policies and projections which emerge also tend to be rigid. These assumptions are examined further in the next section before turning to the more flexible approach to planning advocated by these critics.

The assumptions of manpower planning

Introduction

Detailed manpower planning entails making precise forecasts of the future number of teachers needed, sub-classified by sector and subject, and ensuring the right number and type of training places are available to meet the requirements of the schools. By the *future* is meant a period of at least ten years, and perhaps as many as 15 and 20 years from the date of the plan (Parnes 1962). It has a strong appeal for policy-makers because it *appears* to offer certainty, an attractive quality for those with the responsibility of making resource allocation decisions to their alternative uses. In the UK it has long existed as a planning technique for teachers,[5] underlying the advice of the NACTST and its successors. Its continued use is reflected by the reductions announced in teacher training for the mid-1980s. The critics argue that the promise of certainty is bogus and is but one reflection of a 'view of the world' which is unrealistically rigid. These rigidities are examined in the following analyses, concentrating on the three assumptions of manpower planning of greatest significance for the case of teacher supply.

The significance of time

An important assumption is that it is possible to make reliable predictions 15 years into the future. Now consider the task of the planners at the DES who begin with a five-year warning period of first-year enrolment into primary schooling. This means that while they can make a very reliable projection of the total school population five years into the future, the reliability of the projections decline as we go beyond that time. Thus, a 16-year projection, as with the ninth report (DES 1965) and the interim report on training needs into the 1990s (DES 1981a), includes few children actually born at the time of the projection, only those who will stay on beyond 16. Now the question which needs to be considered is whether a 16-year projection is actually needed. The flow through training takes only one year for the postgraduate certificate and three to four years for the BEd. Certainly, in a time of expansion new buildings must be provided, but even this brings the planning horizon to within ten years and close to the eight years which one reviewer of manpower forecasts (Ahamad 1973) says may be important, since the evidence suggests that up to an eight-year period forecasts were better than no forecasts, but beyond that they were no use at all. For planning purposes it would seem appropriate to adapt the training system to the planning horizon, placing greater emphasis on the one-year postgraduate certificate and pressing more strongly for the failed innovation of the James Report for the two-year professional preparation programme following a diploma of higher education, as both qualifications have a shorter production cycle than the BEd.

However, such considerations are scarcely important if you *believe* it is possible to make reliable estimates up to 16 years ahead. Indicative of the belief that it was possible to make such reliable projections, recommendations for policy were made on the basis of single-value forecasts, rather than presenting a range of projections which would have, simultaneously, recognised the uncertainty involved in predicting the future and, appropriately, would have reduced the impression of high statistical reliability provided by the single-value forecast (Ahamad 1973). A further illustration of the excessive reliability placed on these forecasts is the failure to subject data to sensitivity analysis which entails examining how sensitive the forecasts are to slight changes in the assumptions:

> For example, a small change in the average pupil—teacher ratio in 1960—from 27.0 to 26.5—would have increased the demand for teachers by 3000. Allowance of a margin of error of ±5 per cent in the forecasts for 1968 would have implied a shortage of up to 30 000 instead of the predicted balance between demand and supply. (Woodhall 1977)

Recognition of the uncertainties involved in these forecasts may not only have led to an earlier change to the policy of emphasising the one-year training schemes for graduates but may have occasioned an earlier appraisal of the disadvantages of the structural rigidities of monotechnic training institutions.

The importance of relative wages

While manpower forecasters recognise that prices do have an effect upon the demand for and the supply of a commodity (and wage and salary levels are, in this respect, the price levels for particular occupational categories) they choose to ignore their significance for planning purposes. Estimating future manpower requirements is identified as a technological concept rather than an economic one and the idea is to work out the required occupational composition of employment necessary to achieve targets. For teacher supply this entails deriving the number and subject composition of teacher-training places from the projections of pupil numbers at primary and secondary levels and from the forecast teacher numbers required to meet the policy-determined staffing levels. Theoretically, the outcomes should equal the target number of teachers in the schools with the appropriate qualifications for the subjects being taught. It does not work. And one of the reasons why it does not work is that it is not possible to achieve these policy targets by ignoring the impact of relative wages upon the decisions of teachers and prospective teachers. Relative wages have an impact on teacher supply in a number of ways, affecting the wastage rate, the staffing levels of shortage subjects, the regional distribution of teachers and the distribution of teachers amongst schools of different types. The significance of relative wages on the wastage rate will be examined fully in this section, in order to demonstrate that its effects cannot be ignored by those responsible for managing teacher supply.

Earlier in this chapter the uncertainty prevalent in DES calculations of wastage rates was described, with a commentary concerned with the substantial impact which changes in these rates can have on the total size of flows into and out of the teaching force. The Department's view (DES 1973) was that this 'is and will remain an element of major uncertainty.' By contrast, one part of a recent study of the economics of teacher supply set out to test the hypothesis that 'relative earnings and unemployment rates have a predictable influence on leaving rates' (Zabalza et al 1979). It would certainly be of some significance if it could be shown that a predictable influence exists, because it may then be possible to improve the reliability of forecast wastage rates by incorporating some economic analysis into the process of planning teacher supply. Before describing the results of the study of leaving rates some preliminary observations on the underlying economic theory may be appropriate.

Human capital theory provides the framework for the theoretical analysis. This suggests that certain elements of human behaviour can be predicted on the assumption that people in education are investing in themselves and seek the best possible return available from that investment: 'people spend on themselves in diverse ways, not for the sake of present enjoyments, but for the sake of future pecuniary and nonpecuniary returns' (Blaug 1976). In terms of analysing (and predicting) behaviour in an occupation such as teaching it assumes (and makes predictions on that basis) that teachers make choices in terms of the comparative net advantages of alternative occupations. That is, if an individual in a particular post recognises that, by moving to an alternative post which is open, he or she will make some pecuniary and/or nonpecuniary gain, then he or she will make the change.

In practice, economic analysis of occupational decisions tends to rely upon relative wage levels as the main explanatory variable in occupational choice. When economists make this assumption they are not suggesting that you can only explain decisions on occupational choice in terms of relative wage levels. On the contrary, they recognise that other considerations are significant, such as the appeal of continuing to live in one particular area which restricts the choice of some individuals, while a desire to live close to family may be another explanation of occupational choice. Alternatively, the attraction of a job may be for its interest or for its inherent status. When economists set these factors aside they do not imagine that they do not exist, but they are saying that the effect of other factors is marginal and that the influence of relative wages is so great that it can be relied upon, almost exclusively, as a variable for predicting the behaviour of defined occupational groups and sub-groups. In the study by Zabalza et al, unemployment levels in alternative occupations are added to relative wages to provide two explanatory variables for occupational choice. The study covers a period of 'teacher shortage' (1963–1972) but this does not invalidate some of the lessons to be drawn from a study of this type because if teachers are shown to respond to changes in salaries in predictable ways, then this has implications for the management of teacher supply even during a period of 'teacher surplus'.

How do changes in relative wage levels and employment prospects in alternative occupations affect the leaving rates from teaching? Understanding the behaviour of leavers requires a recognition that they be classified into a number of sub-groups. There are those who leave because of retirement, while a second group of leavers transfer to other branches of grant-aided education, leaving a third group who left employment in the primary and secondary sector and did not transfer to other branches of grant-aided education. These last two sub-groups of leavers must be further classified, first by sex and then by qualifications and levels of training. The sub-classification by sex is necessary because the survey results showed that men and women respond in different ways to changes in wage and levels of employment. With regard to the leaving decision women teachers, unlike men teachers, appear to be quite strongly influenced by unemployment elsewhere, with the rate of leaving falling as employment prospects deteriorate. The sub-classification by levels of training distinguishes three categories, non-graduates, trained graduates and untrained graduates.[6] This classification is necessary because these groups can be expected to respond differently:

> In terms of human capital theory, teachers with specific training will have a considerably higher productivity inside teaching than outside, and the wages they will be able to obtain in the profession will be larger than those offered by alternative employments. For teachers with more general training, on the other hand, earnings opportunities inside and outside teaching will be similar. . . . Non-graduate teachers are probably those with the highest component of specific training, followed by trained graduates, and finally by untrained graduates. If this argument is correct we should expect to find the lowest rates of leavers for non-graduates, and the highest for untrained graduates. (Zabalza et al 1979)

This is borne out by the results of the survey, with the leaving rates of untrained graduates always being significantly higher than rates for trained graduates which is, in turn, always higher than the leaving rates for non-graduate teachers. However, *changes* in salary levels and alternative employment prospects produce rather different results: trained graduates are more responsive to changes in salary levels than non-graduates, but both these groups are more responsive than untrained graduates who, it would appear, enter teaching while 'job-shopping' and then move on to other employment.[7] The response of male teachers to changes in relative salary levels is so sensitive that the two-year intervals between salary settlements which was then the norm produces a wave-like oscillation with a fall in the leaver rate after a salary settlement followed by a rate of leaving which progressively increases during the settlement period as the relative value of the salary progressively deteriorates against other salaries. As indicated earlier women teachers are more responsive to changes in employment opportunities than to changes in salary levels, but they also show a systematic and predictable response to this economic indicator.

These findings are significant in a number of respects. First, they demonstrate that the practice of ignoring economic factors when making forecasts of teacher supply adds to the unreliability of the forecasts because economic factors do affect the entry and leaving decisions of prospective and experienced teachers. Second, with regard to wastage rates, the results demonstrate that the rate at which teachers leave the profession, in response to changes in salary levels and employment prospects, is more systematic and predictable than has hitherto been recognised by the DES. This means that, by integrating techniques from economic analysis with demographic data and information about the internal labour market for teachers, the estimation of wastage rates could have been improved upon, replacing the DES practice described earlier, which made two alternative assumptions about wastage which were either that it would remain constant, or that it would continue to decline because of known changes in the characteristics of the teaching force. Third, since this study shows that teachers entering and leaving the profession are influenced by alternative employment opportunities and changes in the level and structure of salaries, it becomes appropriate to consider in what ways salary policy can be used as a means of *deliberately* influencing other aspects of teacher supply policy. The emphasis is important because, since salaries *do* affect the decisions and behaviour of teachers, policy-makers must now recognise that they have the option of using salaries as one device, among others, for trying to achieve their objectives. Alternatively, they can continue to allow salary decisions to be determined by other criteria, the consequences of which may conflict with important objectives of supply policy. Clearly, it is possible to ignore salaries when formulating policies for teacher supply but that does not mean that salaries will have no effect upon the supply policies. How salary policy has sometimes aggravated problems for which policy-makers have sought and are seeking answers is explored later in this chapter, but it is appropriate to end this section with a warning from the study by Zabalza et al that even in a period of teacher 'surplus', planners 'will make just as many mistakes as they did in the earlier situation if they ignore the effects of economic incentives on overall teacher supply and its distribution', an issue developed further in Chapter 5.

The relationship between inputs and outputs

A further reason for the crises of teacher shortages and surpluses may well lie with the consequences of the widespread and strong belief in the idea that the way to improve standards in education is to improve the pupil–teacher ratio. In other words, it is unnecessary to go to all the trouble of measuring outputs because an *input* measure (PTR) offers such a reliable guide to the state of educational standards. This widespread belief explains the importance attached to policies designed to increase the number of teachers and reduce class sizes in primary and secondary schools. It also explains the desperate rush to expand training facilities in the time of teacher shortage in the 1960s; its influence persists during the retrenchment of the later 1970s and 1980s when building maintenance programmes and budgets for educational books, materials and equipment suffer more, in relative terms, than the budget for teachers. These circumstances are advantageous for the teaching profession because during times of economic expansion they can always make a case for expanding their numbers and, in times of contraction, a case for being protected or, at least to be cut last and least. This unwillingness to accept that factor substitution is possible leads to an inflexibility in planning, which must then be able to anticipate changes in pupil numbers so as to produce the necessary number of teachers. But is it not possible to maintain and improve educational outputs by substituting sub-professional assistants who can assist in the classroom and clerical assistants outside the classroom who can relieve teachers of mundane tasks and allow them to concentrate on their professional tasks? Are televisions or self-instructional materials never learning substitutes for the conventional classroom teaching situation? To the extent that such substitution *is* possible so it becomes practical to have a more flexible policy of resourcing in education.

It would seem to this writer that this emphasis on improving pupil–teacher ratios is to be explained by a combination of self-interest and conventional wisdom within the teaching profession which has been accepted by educational planners and policy-makers. To the extent that educational planners work within a manpower planning methodology it is not surprising that they accept this emphasis on the link between 'standards' and the pupil–teacher ratio, in that it reflects the rigidity identified earlier.

The purpose of this analysis of three principal assumptions of manpower planning is to demonstrate that it is the characteristics of the planning methodology used by the DES which offers the most convincing explanation of its planning failures. If this is the case then DES planning failures can only be legitimately criticised if there exists an alternative and superior approach to planning. The next section examines just such an alternative.

An alternative planning model?

While the existence of an administered teacher market means that there is a need to plan teacher supply, *how* to plan is a problem over which choice may be exercised. This choice can be made from a continuum ranging from, at one extreme, a detailed manpower planning policy and, *towards* the other extreme, a market-orientated policy. We have seen that detailed manpower planning entails making precise forecasts of the number of teachers needed, sub-classified by sector and subject and ensuring that the right number and type of training places are available to meet the requirements of schools. In contrast, a more market-orientated approach to planning recognises the uncertainty of the future and the impossibility of making precise forecasts. Naturally, this perspective encourages adaptability and substitution in the use of teachers and other resources and aims to develop flexibility in the training system. It is also prepared to use the price mechanism as a means of eliminating shortages of particular skills. Even within the administered UK teacher market there is scope for introducing some market-orientated policy instruments and also managing supply in a way which recognises the difficulties inherent in planning under conditions of uncertainty.

In order to understand the reasons for the different policy advice which comes from these two approaches to planning, it is necessary to clarify their contrasting assumptions about how the labour market works. Essentially, the difference is that, unlike manpower planners, the advocates of a stronger market-orientation emphasise, first, the responsiveness of labour to the price signals of the market and, second, the scope and level of labour and factor substitution. What these can mean for the problems of managing the teacher labour market is considered below.

The earlier discussion on the importance of relative wages began with the assumption of manpower planners that it is possible to ignore the effect of wage and salary changes when forecasting future teacher numbers. We then saw that making this assumption is unsound because teachers do respond to changes in their wages relative to that in other occupations. Moreover, this response is systematic and predictable, affecting entry and leaving decisions. Consequently, planning processes which ignore economic factors are likely to produce unreliable forecasts. Thus, there is a need for integrating techniques from economic analysis into planning practice so that more reliable estimates of wastage rates can be produced. The evidence that teachers do respond to changes in salary levels also provides grounds for a much closer integration of salary policy and teacher supply policy. A consequence of such integration for the management of macro-level supply is that salary structures can be devised which optimise total expenditure on salaries, an application which will be explored in the section on 'Areas of potential improvement'. Integration may also have led to policies which could have averted the probable consequences of the Houghton Report's (1974) increases in relative salaries, of which Zabalza et al comment,

> ... the implications of this increase were a further reduction in demand, due to additional labour costs, and an overall increase in supply due to the more favourable pay conditions. Given these circumstances it is not surprising that by the mid-1970s, for the first time since the war, the supply of teachers was larger than actual demand. What would have occurred a few years later was brought forward by the public expenditure cuts. There is an important difference between the two situations; whereas the eventual outcome would have implied a fulfilment of the desired staffing standards in terms of educational criteria, the actual outcome stopped short of that target.

Changes in relative wages also have implications for the composition and distribution of the teaching force, as we shall see in the third part of this chapter.

Proponents of a market-orientated influence on teacher supply also have a strong belief in the scope for factor substitution. This means recognising the possibilities of using teaching and non-teaching ancillaries as *substitutes* for some parts of a teacher's job, thereby releasing the teacher to concentrate on those parts of the job which require their professional skills. This flexibility can be particularly valuable during times of teacher shortage, but it also has a wider relevance. It highlights the idea that there are various ways of combining resources for learning and that reducing PTR is not the only way of increasing educational outputs, a notion that runs counter to the assumptions of manpower planners.

The twin effects of responsiveness to wage change and the possibilities of factor substitution means that a market-orientated approach need be *less* concerned with forecasting the future than the manpower planning approach. Added to this is their greater sense of realism about predicting the future, which leads to their support of a more flexible training system, able to adapt relatively quickly to changing circumstances. In this respect we can discern considerable change in the approach of the DES to planning for the 1980s and 1990s. However, and as the next two sections will argue, while the DES has increased the flexibility of its plans, there remains scope for further change and improvement.

Planning for the 1980s and 1990s

It is scarcely surprising that the teacher training 'debacle' of the 1970s led to some re-appraisal by the Department of its plans and planning processes. Changes were introduced in the presentation of data and, simultaneously, the case for a more flexible training system was advanced. Projections for the numbers of teachers needed in the 1980s (DES 1975) included forecasts for pupils and teachers based upon a basic projection, with high and low variants. The Report also emphasised the difficulties entailed in planning when so much uncertainty surrounded crucial variables. In turn, this led to support for a more flexible training system. A later document (DES 1976a) notes the uncertainty of pupil projections which include only a small proportion of children yet born and even, for

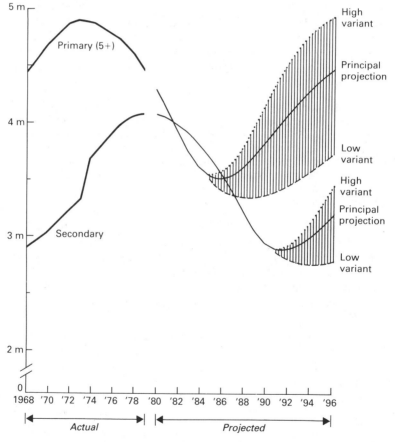

Figure 3.3 *Primary and secondary pupil numbers. Source: DES (1979) Trends in School Population, Report on Education No. 96. London: HMSO. (Reproduced with the permission of HMSO.)*

the later part of the projection, figures which include no children yet born. This same publication suggested a need for greater flexibility on the part of schools, which should be prepared to accept year-by-year variations in the pupil–teacher ratios. The use of alternative assumptions for post-compulsory APR (DES 1976a; 1978) is a further recognition of the uncertainties involved in the planning process. Figure 3.3 is included to show this emphasis on uncertainty in data presentation.

Structural changes to the training system were introduced and the proportion of places provided for the one-year graduate training programme was increased at the expense of the BEd. The size of the change in the proportion of places on the one-year training courses is given in Table 3.3. The benefit of this structure can be seen in the Secretary of State's decision to reduce the 1982 intake to PGCE courses by 20 per cent (*Education* 1981a). The advantage of cuts in PGCE numbers, as opposed to BEd. numbers, is that these have a quicker impact on output, a valuable quality when the context of central and local government decision-making is so dominated by short-term expenditure plans. In the event, the actual reduction of enrolments to all initial training courses was not as great as expected, the principal explanation being the increased numbers entering BEd. courses which, in 1982, were closer to filling their quota of places. This reduction in PGCE numbers followed advice in an interim report published by ACSET (DES 1981a), a document which merits some examination for the insights it gives us into the DES's approach to planning teacher supply for the 1980s and beyond[8].

Table 3.3 *One-year courses as a percentage of intake to initial teacher training, 1968–1982.*

	1968	1970	1972	1974	1976	1978	1980	1982[a]
(1) Total annual intake	46 648	46 519	50 632	43 257	30 851	21 672	18 894	17 028
(2) PGCE and other one-year courses	8 363	10 017	13 251	12 069	12 326	11 785	11 955	8 977
(3) (2) as a percentage of (1)	17.9	21.5	26.2	27.9	40.0	54.4	63.27	52.7

[a] 1982 figures show England only.
Sources: DES (1981b; 1982b; 1984a)

Emphasis on the uncertainty of assumptions concerning crucial variables and forecasts based upon them is pervasive. Arising from this, the Committee 'felt it appropriate to consider a number of possible projections' and much of the Report discusses the effect of various assumptions about: the state of the economy and government expenditure policy; levels of wastage rates; levels of recruitment of 'returners' to the teaching force. The Committee's advice for action is restricted to the short term, that PGCE recruitment in 1982 be cut 25 per cent below 1981 targets (see the Secretary of State's decision). Such a decision allows ACSET to think further about its long-term advice, an option made possible only because of the greater flexibility of the training structure. The Committee does *suggest* that, in the long term, it will be necessary to reduce training output by 10 per cent but offers no immediate advice for action.

While this ACSET advice reflects valuable improvements in the planning process it is also possible to detect areas where little real change has occurred. These will be discussed in the next section.

Areas of potential improvement

Zabalza et al (1979) conclude their study of teacher supply with these comments and advice

> Decisions about teacher supply ought to be based on an appreciation of the fact that although it is a public sector activity with administered salary scales, there is a labour market for teachers. The system is a complex one and warrants careful monitoring. We believe that a *teacher supply research unit* should be established to keep under permanent review the relationships between teachers' salary policies, economic factors affecting the demand for teachers and teacher training and supply policies. At present these appear to be treated as separate issues and surprise is expressed when, for example, a shortage of teachers apparently suddenly becomes a surplus. Such a body could provide data to both sides of the Burnham salary negotiating Committee and the Advisory Council on the Training and Supply of Teachers, it could monitor policy initiatives to investigate their effectiveness in achieving desired staffing objectives, and it might undertake applied research into the operation of the labour market along the lines suggested in the present study.

The absence of advice based upon such an approach is all too evident in the continuing manpower planning practices of the DES. For example, the range of wastage rates included in the 1981 ACSET advice takes no account of possible changes in the wages of teachers relative to those in comparable occupations. There is, instead, an assumption that an improved economic performance will lead to an increase in wastage, an outcome which need not follow if teachers' relative salary levels were to improve. Restricting estimates of wastage to assumptions about the *general* economic climate overlooks the specific effects of *relative* changes. Assumptions and judgements about *returners* also overlook the importance of relative wages in these decisions. The decisions of returners are also seen as ones on which policy-makers can have no effect, thereby discounting the potential use of salary policy on increments as a means of encouraging or discouraging returners.

A 'Teachers Supply Research Unit' could advise on levels of wastage and returners, but it could also do more. Since we now know that teachers do respond to changes in salary and market conditions, it becomes possible to consider using salary policy as a means of influencing the size and pattern of the supply of teachers. This is not to suggest something entirely new. For example, before the Houghton settlement, the NAS used to campaign for a salary structure which appealed to experienced 'career' teachers; moreover, various salary settlements have had this rather ill-defined group in mind. However, all such salary settlements have only been able to *intuit* the appropriate structure because there has been no empirical evidence to calculate an optimal salary. This is no longer the case. The work of Zabalza et al shows that it is possible to construct optimal profiles which would appeal to teachers with particular characteristics. There is no space here to give an extended example of how it is possible to construct the 'best' salary profile, but it does instance yet another case where teacher supply policy could be improved by incorporating more expertise drawn from economic analysis. Such an approach would be appropriate for the restructuring talks taking place in 1984 but there is no evidence of its use in providing information for the Burnham salary-structure working party. Instead, the working party has more sophisticated information on staffing in schools which enables officials to calculate quickly the cost consequences of alternative proposals (*Education* 1984). The limitations of this approach are considered in Chapter 5, which examines the quality consequences of change in the composition of the teaching force in the coming decade.

Integrating economic analysis with the current manpower planning process would require a closer relationship between the bodies responsible, on the one side, for the macro-level management of supply and those bodies which, on the other, are influential in determining policies for the micro-level issues of the composition and distribution of the teaching force. It is appropriate to consider some of these micro-level issues and, through their study, learn more of the attitudes of the local authorities and the teachers to integrating economic analysis into planning for teacher supply.

THE COMPOSITION AND DISTRIBUTION OF SUPPLY

The partnership

Controlling the stock of teachers so that there are sufficient to meet the requirements of the school population is only one part of the teacher supply problem. Other aspects of a successful policy include the micro-level issues of ensuring that teachers with suitable subject qualifications are available for employment and, also, that they are reasonably fairly distributed among the schools. These micro-level problems, because they refer to *patterns* of employment, brings our attention to the other 'partners' in the education service, the employers (the LEAs) and the teacher unions. Decisions on ways and means of resolving problems of distribution often requires the co-operation of the LEAs and also, if it includes the Burnham salary negotiating process, the teacher unions. In this part of the chapter attention will be given to the major micro-level issues of teacher supply, beginning with the management of subject shortage. This will be followed by a case study of the effect of special allowances in schools with a large proportion of disadvantaged children, and the last section will include some brief comments about the teacher quota and the London allowance.

Subject shortage and salary policy

Ensuring that the subject composition of the profession is suitable for staffing the curriculum preferences of the school is an area of supply policy notable for its long-running failure, with reports on the shortage of maths and science teachers stretching back thirty years and continuing into the 1980s. A major survey of secondary schools carried out by HMI (DES 1979a) noted that 22 per cent of maths teaching was being done by those lacking a main or subsidiary qualification in the subject. Headteachers' estimates of the maths teacher shortage produced figures ranging from 2500 to 4500. The shortage of secondary science teachers was less dramatic and, of all the sciences, the most poorly staffed was physics, where 5 per cent of those whose main teaching subject was physics had no qualification in science or mathematics. Another problem was that in 'at least 10 per cent of the schools one or more of the science teachers did not know the subject sufficiently well and false information was taught.'

One way of increasing the number of graduate science teachers and qualified mathematics teachers would be to pay teachers with these qualifications higher salaries. If market conditions were allowed to determine the salaries of teachers with qualifications in shortage subjects, the existing conditions of excess demand relative to supply would cause salaries to rise. This would bring forth an increase in supply attracting into teaching scientists and mathematicians who, at present, seek employment elsewhere. Salaries would continue to rise until there was a sufficient flow of suitably qualified teachers to meet the demand for them in schools. At that point, salaries would stabilise at an equilibrium level at which the number of qualified teachers entering teaching would meet the demand for that particular type of teacher. In practice, market conditions do not determine the salaries of these teachers and the explanation for this lies, in part, with the rigidities of an administered salary system. However, and as we shall see, it is also necessary to recognise the hostility within the education service to using salary differentials as a means of overcoming subject shortages.

Despite the inflexibility of the salary structure there is some evidence that teachers of shortage subjects receive higher earnings. The pre-1971 salary structure provided very little flexibility but, despite this, mathematics and chemistry graduates received superior earnings to other graduates suggesting that heads offered these teachers quicker and higher promotions as a means of attracting them. (Zabalza et al 1979) The post-1971 salary structure deliberately allows more flexibility and the DES has suggested that teachers of shortage subjects do obtain accelerated promotion and are sometimes recruited above scale one. (Saran 1981) The change introduced in 1971 is one of a number of initiatives designed to pay more to teachers in shortage subjects. While opposition to these initiatives from within the education service should not be underestimated there is some evidence of important changes, in the years between 1955 and 1980, in the views of management and teacher representatives. In 1955 the Burnham Committee considered the shortage of graduate maths and science teachers after receiving a letter from the Minister of Education, referring to a report by the NACTST, which suggested that relatively poor financial prospects were a major factor explaining this shortage. The management side stated their reluctance to make distinctions between teachers on the basis of their subjects and this was later supported by NUT leaders who said there was no support in the profession for subject differentials. An attempt at resolving the problem was the introduction of allowances for teachers doing a proportion of advanced work but which made no subject distinction. Of this, the Chairman of Burnham, in a rare intervention, commented that it was a response which was not likely to carry much conviction with the Minister.

By 1971 the management side were showing some willingness to use salary differentials to help with this chronic problem but the leaders of the teachers in negotiations remained opposed. Indeed, the change in the salary structure introduced in 1971 was opposed by Edward Britton on the NUT, partly because of the fear that shortage subject teachers would be put on higher scales. In evidence to the arbitration body he cited remarks by the Secretary of State (Margaret Thatcher) 'that one of the objects of the Management Panel's new scales is to enable LEAs to pay higher salaries to teachers of maths and science.' The basis for his opposition to this was its violation of the McNair principle which Britton interpreted to mean that two teachers doing the same sort of job should be paid the same, a comment which ignored the graduate, honours and class of degree differentials. His suspicions concerning the management's objectives in 1971 are borne out by the views of some participants on the management side and there is also evidence that, at the official level, the DES was not only very keen on restructuring but also in using the market mechanism to attract maths and science teachers. Others on the management side, such as Lord Alexander, consistently opposed the use of the market mechanism believing that the answer to shortages lies on the training side.

The next important initiative came in 1979/80 when the problem of teachers' pay was referred to the Standing Committee on Pay Comparability. In its Report, the Committee recommended that extra scale posts in schools, and level 2 posts in further education, be made available to assist with shortage subjects. This has been accepted by the Burnham Committee and local authorities now have the discretion to allocate additional points to schools to recruit and retain shortage subject teachers. The actions of Fred Jarvis, successor to Britton as general secretary of the NUT, shows a greater pragmatism and a willingness to accept a differential if it entails more scale posts for schools than would otherwise exist. He insists, though, that it is a proposal which is not welcomed by most teachers or, for that matter, the local authorities and that the principal advocate of differentials is the DES, a view endorsed by these three cases. The normal hostility of the unions to shortage differentials is exemplified again in Fred Jarvis' hostility (*Education* 1982) to the proposals of the Cockcroft Committee (DES 1982a) to give extra increments for maths teachers with two or more years in post: for Jarvis such ideas were 'diversionary and divisive'. The common feature of these initiatives is that they have yet to resolve the problem of shortage. The 1955 and the 1971 proposals are piecemeal alternatives to dealing with the problem in a more overt way and while the 1980 'Clegg' initiative is better and more openly directed at the problem, it may have too little money to be effective. Moreover, the salary restructuring proposals of 1984 seem designed to move away from such differentiation (see Chapter 5). The failure to solve this problem over almost 30 years suggests more concern by the salary negotiators for equality of treatment for teachers than allowing pupils greater access to suitably qualified teachers. If this is the case, it not only ignores the divisive reality of graduate differentials but, and more important, results in some pupils, on the evidence of HMI, receiving poor and inadequate teaching. We can, in turn, assume an immediate effect upon their learning and a subsequent effect on their levels of skills upon entering employment.

An intriguing contrast exists between the failure *to* act on subject shortage and the failures *of* action on social priority allowances. The next case study, which draws on the work of Zabalza et al (1979), demonstrates the need for salary initiatives to be guided by a suitable analysis of their market implications.

The social priority allowance

An important consequence of the Plowden Report (DES 1967) was the introduction of special payments designed to attract and keep well-qualified and experienced teachers in schools containing a significant proportion of underprivileged and under-achieving children. It was one part of a package of measures designed to discriminate in favour of these children. The recommendation of Plowden was that there should be a £120 salary allowance for all teachers serving within areas designated as EPAs (Educational Priority Areas) but, in practice, the allowance was lower and distributed rather less widely. The final designation 'Schools of Exceptional Difficulty' was made by November 196 , included 1.8 per cent of the total pupil population (compared with the 2 per cent advocated by Plowden), and the allowance for teachers was fixed at £75. It could not be anticipated as having any significant effect on schools until the 1969/70 academic year. Only a small number of *eligible* schools received the allowance because the budget was limited and it was left to the DES to select the chosen few. The original allowance was raised to £83 in

April 1971, £105 in April 1972 and £114 in April 1974. (Zabalza et al 1979)

There have been few attempts at evaluating the effects of these allowances, or the later modifications, which gave LEAs more discretion over school unit totals (1973) and introduced the two-step 'Social Priority' allowance (1974). An earlier inquiry into EPAs (Halsey et al 1972) reported the results of an investigation of the response of teachers in the ILEA to the £75 supplement. It reported that the initial decline in resignation rates for designated schools was followed by a subsequent increase in resignations to a rate higher than comparable schools which effectively cancelled the favourable initial response.

Modifications to the scheme, mentioned above, have increased its flexibility and moved away from the original flat-rate addition to salary but such changes were introduced without any study appraising the relative effectiveness of one scheme as against another. Similarly, no study appears to have been undertaken in relation to proposals to abandon the Social Priority Allowance (*Education* 1981b). Evaluating the effects of these changes would be a difficult task, not least because of the way changes have been superimposed on each other, and the Zabalza study has attempted an evaluation only of the teacher response to the first innovation, from 1969 to 1972, when the SED allowance paid to staff in the 572 designated schools was unaffected by other changes. The evaluation concentrated only upon the primary schools receiving the allowance (which accounted for almost 90 per cent of all the *teachers* receiving the allowance) and made comparisons with a sample of non-SED primary schools. Three areas were examined, covering the three years before the introduction of the allowance and the four years following: first, the characteristics of the teaching force in SED and non-SED schools were compared; second, comparisons of the earnings of teachers in the two groups of schools were made; finally, changes in the composition of the flow of teachers into and out from the two groups of schools were examined.

This analysis can be followed in detail in Chapter 8 of the Zabalza study. Its principal conclusions are that there was an increase in numbers of teachers under 30, while there was a decrease in relative numbers in the 30–49 age group, thereby worsening the already unbalanced age distribution of the SED schools. There was also an increase in the proportion having less than five years' teaching experience. Evidence on relative earnings and promotion performance of male teachers suggests a deterioration over time in the perceived quality of men teachers in SED schools which was not halted by the introduction of the allowance. A comparative analysis of the flow of teachers in and out of SED schools, with the non-SED schools, allows us to examine not only the rate of staff turnover, but its composition. The rate of turnover was reduced only for 1969/70, confirming the temporary effect of the allowance identified in the earlier study in the ILEA (Halsey 1972). However, there was an increase in the proportion of graduates, mainly women recruited from other schools and from those re-entering the profession.

It was suggested in the earlier discussions on the importance of relative wages that the act of occupational choice can be understood in terms of the comparative net advantage of alternative occupations. This analysis was extended to include the choice of one post over another, suggesting that individuals would move to alternative posts if they would make some pecuniary and/or non-pecuniary gain by the change. From this theoretical analysis some of the outcomes of the flat-rate allowance were predictable. A flat-rate allowance has a proportionately greater effect on the salary of a young teacher low on the incremental scale than on an experienced teacher well advanced on the incremental scale. Thus, the effect of the allowance on the balance of pecuniary and non-pecuniary advantage of the

SED schools is greater for younger and more inexperienced teachers. And, as seen above, these formed a greater proportion of the teaching force of SED schools following the introduction of the allowance, exactly the opposite outcome to that intended by the advocates of the policy. Predicting the outcome on teacher turnover of the flat-rate allowance is more problematic. The direction of the effect could be predicted and some of its distribution, but the time effect of its impact could not have been adequately predicted purely at the theoretical level. It could be anticipated that the effect of the allowance would have been a decline in the rate of turnover, but how long this lasted could not have been predicted without information on the responsiveness of the teaching force to changes in relative wages. It could also be predicted that the allowance would affect the rate of turnover of some groups of teachers more than others (for instance, younger rather than older and more experienced teachers would be more responsive, for the reasons of proportionate salary effect explained above) but how this would have affected total turnover could not have been reliably predicted without more information on the composition of the teaching force in the SED schools. However, even this limited theoretical analysis would have led to the suggestion that a percentage allowance would be more likely to keep teachers at the school than a flat-rate allowance.

The foregoing paragraph illustrates the advantages to policy-makers with responsibility for the different aspects of teacher supply of drawing upon advice from a wider range of policy-relevant methodologies than is the case. Even at the level of theoretical analysis labour market economists would have advised against a flat-rate SED allowance and in favour of a percentage allowance, thus avoiding the adoption of a salary innovation which ran counter to the objectives of policy. But such a theoretical analysis of the problem is not the limit of the contribution which labour market economists could have made. Theory may offer some insights to guide policy-making in areas of uncertainty but more insight can be obtained, and better advice given, if it is based upon greater knowledge of the characteristics of the particular labour market being studied. By analysing the particular characteristics of the teaching staff of SED schools it becomes evident that one of the major problems of these schools was that they had a large proportion of relatively poorly-qualified staff who, in any school, have a high rate of turnover. As one aim of the SED policy was to improve the average level of experience of the teachers in such schools, a policy instrument was needed to attract the type of teachers to the school who, if new teachers, had the characteristics of stayers or, and more immediately effective, already had experience. The means of attracting the latter would have been to give SED schools more graded posts which would have improved the relative position of the SED schools in the market for experienced teachers. Another feature of the SED teaching force highlighted by empirical analysis is the uninterrupted decline in 'quality' of men teachers between 1966 and 1971, the full period of the study. The introduction of the allowance seemed to have no effect on this decline and this suggests the need for alternative policies. The most appropriate policy would be to use any extra money selectively, improving the availability of graded posts. This option offers flexibility with its opportunity of paying extra only to those staff which the schools wishes to keep or attract. The case for maximising rather than minimising the flexibility of salary instruments at the level of the school is considerable since the head is the best-placed person for making qualitative judgements concerning members of staff.

The 1973 Burnham agreement introduced more generous staffing allowances, giving LEAs the discretion to increase the unit totals which determine the number of above Scale

1 posts. The discretion applied to all schools meeting the criteria agreed for the SED allowance but it was already four-and-a-half years after the counterproductive SED allowance. A year later, the modification of the SED allowance to the two-stage social priority allowance seemed an improvement on the pre-existing arrangement but the condition that the higher rate should be payable only after three years' service was counter to the need of the schools, in the first place, to attract experienced teachers.

Reviewing the years between the introduction of the first educational priority allowance and its likely demise as a special allowance (leaving the more selective LEA discretion on unit totals), a notable omission is any systematic attempt by the DES or the LEAs to analyse the labour market implications of alternative salary strategies in this area, while another is any evaluation of the effectiveness of the salary strategies adopted. The consequences of this intuitive approach to policy-making is that for five-and-a-half years scarce resources were allocated in such a way that outcomes achieved were the opposite to those intended. This reliance on intuition can also be seen with the initiatives designed to affect the regional distribution of teachers.

The regional distribution of teachers

Two main policy initiatives have been adopted in order to ensure some reasonable equality in the regional distribution of teachers, the teacher quota and the London allowance. The teacher quota was a voluntary rationing scheme, adopted by LEAs and administered by the DES, at the time of teacher shortage in the 1950s and 1960s. By setting an upper limit on the number of new entrants which an LEA could employ, it was the aim of the quota to direct any newly-qualified teachers away from the most popular LEAs, which rapidly recruited their quota, and towards the less popular authorities. The implication of the quota, Zabalza et al argue, is that teachers will search for jobs in areas outside their chosen location. If some do not, then the effect of the quota is a net loss of supply. The equalising of PTR between LEAs at the time of the quota suggests that teachers did move, but there was no study to ascertain the level if any, of any net loss of supply. The quota was not the only way of redistributing supply — an alternative would have been to allow a regional wage differential to equalise the distribution of teachers. The absence of any study of the required size of such a differential prevents the drawing of any final conclusions on the merits and de-merits of these policy alternatives. Nevertheless, two relevant observations can be made. The first is from Zabalza et al,

> The quota system could only be justified in a situation where the policy-maker regards the redistribution of supply . . . as of sufficient priority to outweigh the disadvantages of reduced overall supply, but not of sufficient priority to overcome objections to the existence of salary differentials.

The second comment is that here again we see the scope for adopting other perspectives for managing teacher supply.

The effects of the London allowance were evaluated by Zabalza et al, although space prevents more than a summary of their findings. The first flat-rate allowance brought about effects similar to the SED allowance discussed earlier, reducing the average age and experience of teachers, outcomes the opposite to those intended. Even subsequent variants of the allowance apparently failed to close, ' . . . a residual "quality" gap between teachers in schools receiving allowances and others.' The most appropriate policy for London would seem to be a mixture of special allowances to meet the higher cost of living and much larger promotion premiums, paid to keep and attract better quality staff.

The study of micro-level supply indicates again the value of an economic perspective on policy-making. However, it has also shown the hostility of the teachers and, to some extent, the LEAs towards a greater market orientation, an issue to be discussed with others in the conclusion.

CONCLUSION

This chapter has described some of the principal successes and failures of post-war teacher supply policy. It suggested that the policy successes can be explained by the performance of the UK economy in that period and, also, the success of the education sub-government in attracting a substantial share of the economy's resources. It then argued that the failures of policy with regard to controlling the total stock of teachers lies with the planning methodology adopted by the DES, and its refusal to integrate prespectives drawing on economic analysis to improve its planning processes. In order to understand the failures of policies for micro-level supply, it is necessary to recognise the role of the 'partnership', with the LEAs and the teacher unions more reluctant than the DES to adopt suitable market-orientated initiatives for the resolution of supply problems. When any market-orientated policy was adopted, the scheme reflected the *intuition* of decision-makers as to the appropriate nature of the initiative and was not the result of systematic inquiry into its labour market implications.

It is necessary to conclude this account of the past and present of teacher supply policy by noting that many of the factors crucial to past failures are still deeply embedded in the current practice of policy-making and planning for teacher supply. The failure to take account of, and adapt to, the realities of the labour market for teachers in no way diminishes the effect of the workings of that market. Hostility to market-orientated policies on the basis that they are diversionary, and divisive for the teaching profession, ignores their effect on learners. Under existing salary and supply policies some learners are not only diverted from effective learning by inadequately-qualified teachers (e.g. maths) but obtain unequal (divisive) access to educational opportunities. And it is learners who are the *most* important resource in schools.

NOTES

1. A major study of secondary school costs by Hough (1981) showed teachers' salaries without 'on-costs' ranging from 48 per cent to 66 per cent of recurrent expenditure.
2. The difficulty of making reliable forecasts of births is illustrated by the figures for the years after 1977. Increases in the number of births in 1978 (596 000), 1979 (638 000) and 1980 (656 000) was followed by declines in 1981 (635 000) and 1982 (626 000). 1983 showed a slight rise (628 000), although the fertility rate continued to show a decline (OPCS 1984).

3. Thus, the 10 per cent improvement in staffing standards proposed for 1981 in the White Paper, *A Framework for Expansion*, (DES 1972) was based on the staffing standards of 1971. As these figures were a cut on the Ninth Report targets, the White Paper could be viewed as a 'Framework for Contraction'. For a full discussion of this and the inappropriateness of abandoning class size as a guide on staffing standards see Ryba and Drake (1974).

4. See also Blackstone and Crispin (1982) for an analysis of the complexities of the management of teacher supply and the challenges and problems of the 1980s. The proposals canvassed are rooted largely in a *manpower planning* methodology.

5. It has also been used as a technique for forecasting future requirements of doctors and dentists and has underpinned the claims of several reports (Jones 1967; Dainton 1968; Swann 1968; Finniston 1980) that deficiencies of skilled manpower (particularly scientists and engineers) is an important cause of the UK's economic decline. A review of these reports as a reflection of the work of a science lobby can be obtained from Gannicott and Blaug (1969) and Mace (1980).

6. It will be noted that the study covers the period before the growth of the BEd. and when the entry of the untrained graduate into the teaching force was much more common than in the present.

7. This group of untrained graduates is gradually dwindling following the change in regulation, with regard to training, in 1969.

8. The committee was able to draw upon the Department's 'Teacher Manpower Model' and received advice on the judgements underlying the Department's own projections. In some instances, as with the numbers of expected re-entrants, the Committee's judgement differed from the Department's. The significance of judgements on the level of government spending for the future numbers of teachers is again made clear in a more recent DES (1984b) document on teacher deployment in the longer term. Its Table 2 (p. 19) shows the sensitivity of modestly differing policy assumptions about expenditure levels on teacher numbers: one assumption would mean 362 000 teachers in schools in England by 1991 and another 387 000 teachers.

REFERENCES

Ahamad, B. (1970) 'A post mortem on teacher supply forecasts'. *Higher Education Review*, **2**(3), Summer.

Ahamad, B. (1973) 'Teachers in England and Wales'. In Ahamad, B. and Blaug, M. (ed) *The Practice of Manpower Forecasting*. Amsterdam: Elsevier.

Blackstone, T. and Crispin, A. (1982) *How Many Teachers? Issues of Policy, Planning and Demography*. Bedford Way Papers No. 10: University of London Institute of Education.

Blaug, M. (1967) 'Approaches to Educational Planning'. *Economic Journal*, **77** June.

Blaug, M. (1970) *An Introduction to the Economics of Education*. London: Penguin.

Blaug, M. (1976) 'The Empirical Status of Human Capital Theory: A Slightly Jaundiced View. *Journal of Economic Literature*, **14**, September.

CPRS (1977) *Population and the Social Services*. Report, London: HMSO.

Crispin, A. (1979) *Providing the Teachers*. Unit 8 of E222: The Control of Education in Britain. Milton Keynes: The Open University.

Dainton Report, The (1968) *Enquiry into the Flow of Candidates in Science and Technology into Higher Education*. Cmnd. 3541. London: HMSO.

Denison, E. F. (1967) *Why Growth Rates Differ. Postwar Experience in Nine Western Countries*. Washington DC: Brookings Institution.

DES (1965) NACTST 9th Report. *The Demand and Supply of Teachers, 1963–1986*. London: HMSO.

DES (1967) Central Advisory Council for Education (England). *Children and their Primary Schools: a report* (The Plowden Report). London: HMSO.

DES (1968) 'The Distribution of Teachers'. *DES Reports on Education No. 42*. January.

DES (1972) *Education: A Framework for*

Expansion. Cmnd. 5174. London: HMSO.

DES (1973) 'The Supply of Teachers'. *DES Reports on Education No. 78.* July.

DES (1975) 'Teachers for the 1980s: Statistical Projections and Calculations.' *DES Reports on Education No. 82.* March.

DES (1976a) 'The Future School Population.' *DES Reports on Education No. 85.* June.

DES (1976b) 'Teachers'. *Statistics of Education, 1974, 4.* London: HMSO.

DES (1977) *Education in Schools: a Consultative Document.* Cmnd. 6869. London: HMSO.

DES (1978) 'School Population in the 1980's'. *DES Reports on Education No. 92.* June.

DES (1979a) *Aspects of Secondary Education in England: a Survey by HM Inspectors of Schools.* London: HMSO.

DES (1979b) 'Teachers'. *Statistics of Education, 1977, 4,* London: HMSO.

DES (1979c) 'Trends in School Population'. *DES Reports on Education No. 96.* November.

DES (1980) 'The Secondary School Staffing Survey.' *Statistical Bulletin 6/80.* July.

DES (1981a) ACSET *The Future of the Teacher Training System.* ACSET 81/24. August.

DES (1981b) 'Teachers'. *Statistics of Education, 1979, 4,* London: HMSO.

DES (1982a) *Mathematics Counts; Report of the Committee of Inquiry into the Teaching of Mathematics in Schools* (The Cockcroft Committee). London: HMSO.

DES (1982b) *Statistics of Education, Further Education November 1980, England and Wales.* London: DES.

DES (1984a) *Statistics of Education, Further Education November 1982, England.* London: DES.

DES (1984b) *School Teacher Numbers and Deployment in the Longer Term, A Discussion Paper.* London: DES, September.

Education (1981a) **158**(19) 6 November, 348.

Education (1981b) **158**(20) 13 November, 362.

Education (1982) **159**(5) 29 January, 78.

Education (1984) **163**(19) 11 May, 378.

Finniston Report, The (1980) *Committee of Enquiry into the Engineering Profession: Engineering Our Future.* Cmnd. 7794. London: HMSO.

Gannicott, K. and Blaug, M. (1969) 'Manpower Forecasting Since Robbins: A Science Lobby in Action'. *Higher Education Review,* **2**(1).

Halsey, A. H. (ed) (1972) *Educational Priority, Vol 1: EPA Problems and Practice.* London: HMSO.

Hencke, D. (1975) 'Teacher Supply: a case of manpower planning'. *Higher Education Review,* **8**(1).

Hencke, D. (1978) *Colleges in Crisis.* London: Penguin.

HM Treasury (1981) *The Government's Expenditure Plans, 1981–82 to 1983–84.* London: HMSO.

HM Treasury (1984) *The Government's Expenditure Plans, 1984–85 to 1986–87.* Cmnd. 9143-II. London: HMSO.

Hough, J. R. (1981) *A Study of School Costs.* Windsor: NFER–Nelson.

Houghton, Lord (1974) *Report of the Committee of Inquiry into the Pay of Non-University Teachers.* London: HMSO.

Jones Report, The (1967) *The Brain Drain. Report of the Working Group on Migration.* Cmnd. 3417. London: HMSO.

Kogan, M. (1971) *The Politics of Education.* London: Penguin.

Longman, B. (1977) 'Secondary School Teachers — a new survey and mathematical model for assessing demand'. In *Statistical News,* 88, August.

Mace, J. (1980) 'The Finniston Report: An Economist's View'. *Education Policy Bulletin,* **8**(1), Spring.

Mann, J. (1979) *Education.* London: Pitman.

OPCS (1984) *OPCS Monitor.* Ref FM1, 84/1, 21 February.

Parnes, H. S. (1962) 'Planning Education for Economic and Social Development'. In Baxter, C., O'Leary, P. J. and Westoby, A. (ed) (1977) *Economics and Education Policy: a reader.* London: Longman and The Open University.

Pile, Sir William (1979) *The Department of Education and Science.* London: George Allen and Unwin.

Ryba, R. and Drake, K. (1974) 'Teacher Training: to cut or not to cut?'. In *Higher Education Review,* **6**(2) Spring.

Saran, R. (1981) For information on the salary-related initiatives between 1955 and 1980, and of the views expressed by some of those involved, I am indebted to Dr. R. Saran, who kindly made available unpublished information arising from her studies of the "Burnham Committees since 1945".

Swann Report, The (1968) *The Flow into Employment of Scientists, Engineers and Technologists. Report of the Working Group on Manpower for Scientific Growth*, Cmnd. 3760. London: HMSO.

Woodhall, M. (1977) 'Manpower Planning and the Demand for Qualified Manpower'. In *The Planning of Higher Education, The*

Social Demand, Block II of ED. 322, Economics and Education Policy.

Zabalza, A., Turnbull, P. and Williams, G. (1979) *The Economics of Teacher Supply*. Cambridge: University Press.

ACKNOWLEDGEMENT

I am very grateful to Dr Rene Saran of the City of London Polytechnic for providing me so readily with unpublished information relating to salary initiatives on the problem of shortage subjects. Responsibility for the use made of this information, and for any interpretations made, is my own.

4

THE SCHOOL CURRICULUM IN CONTENTION: CONTENT AND CONTROL

Jim Waddington

INTRODUCTION

Between 1944 and the early 1970s it would have been somewhat unusual to think in terms of a system of control for the school curriculum. Outside purely professional circles, content of the school curriculum was essentially non-controversial. The Ruskin College Speech of the then Prime Minister, James Callaghan, in October 1976 radically transformed this perspective, leading to claims that the government was moving in the direction of a centralised curriculum for pupils of compulsory school age, strengthening the hand of the DES (Becher and Maclure 1978; Lawton 1980 and 1984) at the expense of professional autonomy.

It is the purpose of this chapter to assess the shifts in the balance of power related to control of the school curriculum, and also to examine attitudes towards its content held by actors in the political arena. Yet delineating the changing politics of the school curriculum is no easy task: rather, using Weick's (1976) imagery, it may be likened to observing an unconventional football match in which the boundaries of the field of play are diffuse, and goalmouths scattered haphazardly around the pitch. Players may enter or leave at will, negotiating rules with a multiplicity of referees and yet interacting in a manner which is assumed by participants and observers alike to be intelligible.

The analysis given below comprises three strands. In the first an attempt will be made to outline some key issues of content and control post-1944. The need for an appropriate theoretical model will then be established, with the underpinning assumption being that preoccupation with a tidy 'rational' perspective of curriculum policy-making is of limited value. Finally, selected features of the chosen model will be applied to the topography of the curriculum landscape, with particular reference to the years since 1970.

It would be prudent to commence, however, with a cautionary note concerning the manner in which 'curriculum' and 'policy-making' are to be operationally deployed. When discussing 'curriculum', two definitions come readily to mind. The first is that it represents an agglomeration of subjects (see, for example, DES 1979b): echoing the *Oxford English Dictionary*'s explanation of curriculum being synonymous with 'course'. A second, broader perspective would follow that contained in *A View of the Curriculum*, ie:

> . . . the curriculum in its full sense comprises all the opportunities for learning provided by a school. It includes the formal programme of lessons . . . 'extracurricular' activities deliberately promoted or supported by the school; and the climate of relationships, attitudes, styles of behaviour and the general quality of life established in the school community as a whole. (DES 1980b)

Each of these definitions has limited analytical value; the idea of curriculum being simply a kind of syllabus is clearly too narrow, while 'all the opportunities for learning' makes curriculum virtually interchangeable with education (Becher and Maclure 1978). In this paper it is held that the curriculum is best portrayed as a conceptual matrix whose form and boundaries vary according to the stance of the observer.

In policy terms it represents a medium through which social values are prioritised and authoritatively allocated, and in post-war Britain it is inextricably linked with wider politico-educational issues, including the central–local relationship, mechanisms of selection for both further/higher education and employment, the allocation of (scarce) financial resources, rapidly expanding and contracting school populations, and demands for professional autonomy.

Space precludes more than tangential reference to 'policy-making': for present purposes the interim definition offered by Heclo (1972) will be utilised:

> . . . policy does not seem to be a self-defining phenomenon . . . There is no unambiguous datum constituting policy and waiting to be discovered in the world. A policy may usefully be considered as a course of action or inaction rather than specific decisions or actions, and such a course has to be perceived and identified by the analyst in question. Policy exists by interrogating rather than intuiting political phenomena.

THE SCHOOL CURRICULUM SINCE 1944: SOME SALIENT ISSUES

The agents of change and control

At least twelve groupings exercising to a greater or lesser extent influence over the school curriculum may be identified. Of peripheral significance has been the Prime Minister and the Cabinet, for as Boyd-Barrett (1982) has argued: ' . . . educational issues tend[ed] to appear on their agendas relatively infrequently, curricular issues least of all'.

Most commentators (Becher and Maclure 1978; Kogan 1971; Lawton 1980; et al) have agreed that governments prior to 1976 adopted a laissez-faire approach. This is not to say that Prime Ministers did not enter into dialogue with other authorities on the subject of curriculum control — especially broad philosophies. Speaking to the Society of Education Officers Conference in 1973, Edward Heath argued:

We try as a society to indicate to the professionals the human values, the social attitudes, the cultural traditions, the range of skills we wish them to foster . . . Thereafter we leave it to their professional responsibility and expertise to decide how to translate our wishes into courses and syllabuses.

However, during the 1940s and 1950s Ministers of Education followed the dictum of knowing 'nowt about curriculum', and carefully avoided pronouncements on either content or control. This is perhaps less surprising when it is remembered that few Ministers/Secretaries of State for Education held their posts for any significant period between 1945 and 1970 — Eccles being a notable exception (Pile 1979). Some incumbents have been only too aware of this constraint. Crosland admitted (Kogan 1971):

I reckon it takes you six months to get your head properly above water, a year to get the general drift of most of the field, and two years really to master the whole of a Department.

Prior to Sir Keith Joseph's North of England Education Conference Address (*Education* 1984a) and Callaghan's dramatic intervention at Ruskin in 1976, the initiation of David Eccles' controversial Curriculum Study Group (1962) represents the best-documented instance of Ministers exercising initiative within the field of curriculum control (Lawton 1980).

Parliament's role can easily be underestimated. While legislation such as the 1980 Education Act, which resulted in LEAs having to make public a greater array of information about its schools (Boyd-Barrett 1982), generates predictable debate and questions to Ministers, Parliament has sustained a more detailed interest via Select Committees. In February 1982 the Select Committee for Education, Science and the Arts produced a wide-ranging report on the secondary curriculum, dealing particularly with the 14–16 age group, and making some 65 recommendations, including amending the 1944 Act to give the Secretary of State powers to intervene when 'nationally agreed' levels of provision appeared endangered. Elements of these recommendations were subsequently reflected in DES Circular 8/83 (sec. 5). An earlier Select Committee expressly recommended a much greater degree of involvement on the part of the DES with 'substantive educational issues', including curriculum (see Tenth Report of Expenditure Committee 1976).

For much of the post-1944 period the Ministry of Education and its successor, the DES, can be said to have exercised distant and infrequent involvement in curricular matters. The 1944 Act conferred powers to establish Central Advisory Councils, standing advisory councils, and 'ad hoc' departmental committees of inquiry. The duties of the two Central Advisory Councils (ie, for England and Wales) were to:

. . . advise the Minister upon such matters connected with educational theory and practice as they think fit, and upon any questions referred to them by him. (1944 Education Act sec. 4 (i))

These Councils were at their most active between 1959 and 1967, when they reported on 15–18 provision (Crowther), education 13–16 (Newsom), and lastly 'primary education in all its aspects' (Plowden). However, from the early 1960s the DES turned more towards specialised advisory bodies: for example, the Schools Council and other standing committees dealing with handicapped children and educational technology, to 'ensure a measure of consensus amongst all concerned with the implementation of policies' (Pile 1979 pp. 37–38).

The 1970s saw a spate of publications emanating from 'ad hoc' bodies dealing with language/communication in the school curriculum (Bullock Report), school government (Taylor Report), and special education (Warnock Report). According to Mann (1979) the function of these bodies was not just to create a consensus, but to allow the identification of problems in public, and enable central government to test ideas in a wider educational arena.

Another arm of DES influence has been Her Majesty's Inspectorate. Until the late 1960s, however, HMI's role as a central 'authority' in curricular matters at the policy-making level was circumscribed. Rather, the Inspectorate acted as a disseminator of good practice, as reflected in the 'Handbook of Suggestions' (1959) which gave advice to those engaged in primary school teaching. This role expanded significantly after 1968, when full-scale formal inspections of schools appeared effectively to have ended, and a House of Commons Select Committee commented critically on the role of HMI, including its function vis-à-vis the school curriculum (see Her Majesty's Inspectorate (England and Wales) Report, Part I 1968). These events triggered the publication of a series of subject-focused documents, which began to plot curriculum trends, and which had been presaged in 1967 by the paper *Towards World History* (see, for example, Booth and Porter, 1971/2, reprinted in Hopkinson (ed.), 1978). By 1977 nearly a quarter of the Inspectorate were engaged on national surveys and studies, such as *Aspects of Secondary Education in England*, published in 1979, which attempted an account of 'how well schools provide and their pupils respond in the fourth and fifth years of secondary education'.

At the local level it could be argued that for most of the period 1944–1974, LEAs abdicated any direct curricular responsibilities, despite the fact that the 1944 Act stated that both curriculum content and organisation came within their remit. As recently as 1979 it was possible for the Secretary of State, addressing the Annual Conference of the Secondary Headteachers Association, to suggest that some authorities were insufficiently briefed about the curricula of schools, and that they were thereby failing in their statutory responsibilities. The impact of falling school rolls, as well as exhortations from central government — for example Circular 6/81 — served to sensitise an increasing number of LEAs to investigate, if not necessarily rationalise, curricular provision within both primary and secondary sectors. For example, Cheshire established a Curriculum Reappraisal Group, which subsequently recommended an explicit curriculum-led staffing model (see various SEO papers (EMIE) for other examples). The proposals contained in the Hargreaves Report (ILEA 1984) on the curriculum and organisation of Secondary Schools in the ILEA represents another important example of local authority initiatives in the area.

For practical purposes, supervision of curriculum policy has been delegated to two subordinate agencies, namely, Advisory Services and Governing Bodies. There has been little research on the former (Bolam et al 1978), and the depth of involvement of local inspectors and advisors in curriculum policy-making would appear to depend on the nature of the structural relationship between themselves and other professional officers of the individual authority concerned.(See also Chapter 16.)

Both the Taylor Report (DES 1977d) and a subsequent ACE survey conducted by Sallis (1977) concluded that the contribution of governors to the form and substance of school curricula was minimal. A number of LEAs took advantage of the 1944 Act to introduce 'consortia' governing bodies, while others operated sub-committees of the education committee as governing bodies for all the county schools in the area. Brooksbank and Revell (1981) suggest that:

... in the struggle to provide and maintain an efficient education service in the face of enormous difficulties, it is small wonder that little priority should have been accorded to the attainment of an effective system of school governing bodies.

Although firm evidence is scarce, there are indications that in the consultations forming the basis of LEAs' response to 'The School Curriculum' (1981a), governing bodies simply ratified the drafts prepared by LEA officers, rather than initiating their own proposals. The 1980 Education Act committed LEAs to move away from consortia arrangements, and to broaden representation on governing bodies with the election of parent and teacher governors. However, it remains to be seen whether the effectiveness of governing bodies in determining curriculum issues will have been enhanced by this legislation.

Operating within and between central and local levels of curriculum policy making have been the professional agencies. Boyd-Barrett (1982) has argued that:

'. . . to a significant degree the machinery of curriculum control in the United Kingdom is under the influence of the professionals themselves, the teachers'.

On occasion the power of this group has been both considerable and overt. The attempt by Eccles between 1961 and 1964 to establish a greater ministerial involvement in the curriculum, ie, the Curriculum Development Group, was thwarted by teacher interests: in particular, Sir Ronald Gould, the then General Secretary of the NUT. The replacement of the Secondary Schools Examinations Council, which had been directed by the Ministry, with the Schools Council meant that teachers in general and the NUT in particular were to have a major voice in national discussions on curriculum matters in the 1960s. This influence was consolidated by constitutional changes in voting arrangements introduced in 1968 (Becher and Maclure 1978; see also comment contained in the Trenaman Report, DES 1981d).

During the 1970s this teacher-led body was responsible for a number of initiatives, most notably the moves towards a common system of examining at 16+, appraising the need for new courses and examinations for sixth-formers not likely to proceed to higher education, and revision of the 'A' level examination system. The 1977 Green Paper, 'Education in Schools: a consultative document', heralded a check on unfettered teacher power, however (DES 1977b). In the following year a convocation was established along with a seemingly innocuous Finance and Priorities Committee. Between 1978 and the demise of the Schools Council in 1983, teacher interests were effectively subordinated to those of the DES and local authority representatives (Trenaman Report, DES 1981d; Mann 1982).

A more consistent and pervading professional influence has been via the examination system. Although GCE boards have been controlled by the universities, the role of school teachers has been significant in acting as examiners and moderators, and participating, to a greater degree than university interests, at the level of subject committees. The advent of CSE examinations in 1965 acted as a catalyst for Mode II and Mode III examination syllabuses in which the power of the classroom teacher was extant (Boyd-Barrett 1982). However, it should be remembered that in legal/constitutional terms the DES never relinquished its control over the examination structure (Lawton 1980). It was to the respective Secretaries of State that various Schools Council proposals for examinations reform at 16+, 17+ and 18+ were submitted in the 1970s, paralleling the power of the Ministry in the 1950s to plot the future of a single-subject system of examining in GCE.

At the institutional level the ability of teachers, particularly head teachers, to influence curriculum change, has been paramount, and it could be argued that the freedom to act both as a force for innovation and a barrier to change has remained largely unaltered by national developments. In 1975 a Schools Council Working Party Report stated:

> British schools have for long been jealous of their independence in curricular matters. However much they may turn to outside bodies for resources, information and advice, they insist that the curriculum must be of their own making. (Schools Council, 1975a)

This may, as Becher and Maclure (1978) suggest, have been a largely historical perspective even by 1975. The definition of what counts as curriculum knowledge and the status of approved knowledge and its presentation were beginning to be questioned as early as 1969 (Hopkins 1978). Nevertheless, using Eggleston's typology of curriculum decision areas, it could still be maintained that the selection and organisation of knowledge, the use of specialist disciplines, and more particularly the structuring of knowledge, how much should be taught, in what order and relationship, were still matters for the classroom practitioner, and even the student (Eggleston 1973).

The focuses of curriculum control

For the purposes of this chapter, these focuses may be taken to include the development of the curriculum and its content, as well as examination structures and the evaluation of standards.

The dynamics of curriculum development between the mid-1950s and early 1970s are complex, and were shaped by ideological, methodological and practical considerations. During much of this period consensus reigned among agencies involved in the curriculum that there was a direct relationship between the social and economic health of the nation and the financial resources allocated to education (Bernbaum (ed.) 1979). Exponential growth in space technology between the superpowers also encouraged educationalists in the UK as well as the USA to believe that shortcomings in scientific/technological achievement could be traced to defects in the school curriculum (Becher and Maclure 1978). The Labour governments of the 1960s thus promoted science teaching in schools via a variety of Nuffield projects, and during the 1970s funding from the Department of Industry and other government agencies enabled primary and secondary schools to invest in computers and other microprocessor hardware.

The strategies for achieving curriculum change were generally subject-based rather than system-based, reflecting the roles of specific interest groups such as the Association for Science Education, and also the relatively narrow remit of the Schools Council, which did not include an in-service training brief for school staff. However, despite the fact that this resulted in a continuing dichotomy between traditional and heuristic forms of curriculum development, there were significant changes within subject areas. Projects such as the Schools Council 13–16 History project, introduced into schools in the early 1970s, propounded a skills-based problem-solving documentary approach to learning, where content was of illustrative rather than structural significance. This represented a comparatively radical departure from a fact-oriented textbook-based curriculum that had hitherto prevailed in many secondary schools.

Another salient force in shaping both primary and secondary schools curricula was belief in the 'efficacy of educational investment as a force for social equalisation' (Fowler, in Bernbaum (ed.) 1979). Contrary to much received opinion (Kogan 1975; Boyd-Barrett 1982), ideological pessimism in relation to educational investment did not suddenly wane with the arrival of the General Election of June 1970, and the subsequent Barber Axe of December 1973. Belief in the social value of educational development was reflected in both the major parties' election manifestos of 1970. 'A Better Tomorrow' (*TES* 1970b) identified primary education as essential to social welfare: ' . . . where an inadequate start could so easily destroy the chances that every child must have to develop its talent to the full . . . ' while in the Labour alternative, Short promised that ' . . . in the next five years we shall put more resources . . . into primary schools and expand nursery schools inside and outside educational priority areas'. (*TES*, 1970a)

The challenge to education as 'an undisputed good' came both prior to 1970 and after. Cash-limiting for the education service was introduced during the financial stringencies of 1968, and with the freezing of the RSG to local authorities during 1968–9. The re-allocation of resources favouring the secondary sector at the expense of both primary and higher education predated the 1973 oil crisis, and was not consequent upon it (see HC Select Committee, Public Expenditure to 1979–80 1976). Much of Margaret Thatcher's 'new' strategy was a logical follow-on from the reprioritising of values contained in Labour's 1969 Green Paper, *The Task Ahead* (see Fowler et al 1973). Ideological shifts away from unquestioning faith in the utility of education owed as much to the widely publicised work of Jencks et al (1974) as to the £200 million budget cuts instituted by Anthony Barber in December 1973. In *Equality: A reassessment of the effect of family and schooling in America*, the authors concluded:

> . . . the claims of students and teachers on the public purse are no more legitimate than the claims of highway users who want to get home a few minutes faster . . . or medical researchers who hope to extend to man's life expectancy another year or two.

By February 1974 the link between education and resources allocated to it had been weakened. Heath's statement in commenting on the Conservative Party's manifesto that:

> Above all we are concerned to provide not merely more education but better education. Better education is not *only* a matter of resources. (my emphasis) (*TES* 1974)

was not refuted by politicians from other parties.

One of the consequences of such ideological shifts was an increasing questioning of a single-subject curriculum approach as opposed to a system-based perspective. According to some commentators, (eg, Boyd-Barrett 1982; Becher and Maclure 1978) the period 1976–1981 was distinguished by an awareness at both central and local levels of curriculum development, which recognised the needs of *all* schools as well as the total curriculum of any *one* school. Arguing for greater professional and lay consideration of a 'common core' of subjects in schools, Callaghan suggested:

> . . . the basic purposes of education require the same essential tools. These are basic literacy, basic numeracy, the understanding of how to live and work together . . . this means acquiring certain basic knowledge and skills and reasoning ability. (Ruskin Speech, quoted in *Education*, 22.10.1976)

His sentiments were subsequently echoed in follow-ups by HMI and the DES. *Aspects of Secondary Education*, published in 1979, was critical of over-elaborate option systems for pupils in their fourth and fifth years of secondary schooling; while the *Red Book — Curriculum 11–16*, (DES 1977c) highlighted experiments within five LEAs where 'core focused' curricula were being developed. By 1983 the final HMI Report on Curriculum 11–16 concluded that a common curriculum was not only desirable but feasible (DES 1983b). One reviewer commented acidly that the 'entitlement curriculum': . . . cuts across the tribal loyalties of the education service: subject territories, examination syllabuses, teaching methods, and local government autonomy. (*Education* 1983)

The issues of 'standards' and the relationship of the examination system to the curriculum represented dormant concerns for curriculum policy-making for much of the post-war period to 1970. The tripartite system set up by the 1944 Act did not effectively restrict access by pupils to the external examination system, even prior to the introduction of CSE, because of local variations in the allocation of grammar school places and the freedom allowed by LEAs for secondary modern schools to enter pupils for GCE. The status of public examinations was not seriously questioned in the broader public arena — success in GCE was equated with upward social mobility by many parents and teachers. The setting-up of the Schools Council similarly satisfied professional interests. Largely teacher-dominated, the Council's joint responsibility for examinations and continuous assessment encouraged by the CSE — which was also teacher-controlled — meant that examination techniques kept pace with curriculum innovation.

But from the early 1970s a number of factors were coalescing to make both standards and examinations an increasingly emotional subject for debate. Several, essentially non-curricular, developments may be cited related to the examination system. The extension and consolidation of comprehensive education made the dual system of examining increasingly anomalous. Parents and employers alike were confused by the respective status of GCE and CSE, especially comparability of grades. The raising of the school-leaving age to 16 in 1973 meant that there was a much broader spectrum of ability in the 15–16-year age band than the external examination system had been designed for, despite the continued evolution of Mode III assessment procedures. The governmental response to reform of the examination system is discussed later.

The emergence of 'standards' as an articulated, if initially undirected, political demand, can be traced to 1969–1970 and the publication of the first three 'Black Papers'. Initially the writings of Amis et al (see Hopkins 1978) were relatively indiscriminate, denouncing student activism in higher education, and presenting selective justification for 'traditional' style university education. In *Fight for Education* (1969) Cox and Dyson quoted approvingly an article by a prospective Conservative parliamentary candidate, Timothy Raison, who had suggested that a potential catalyst for student unrest had been the introduction of 'informal learning environments' in primary schools during the 1960s. Subsequently the press seized on suggestions that 'progressive' ideas had produced student illiteracy and other shortcomings — a claim to which the then Secretary of State could not resist a riposte at the NUT's Easter 1970 Conference. This guaranteed continuing publicity for the Black Paperites who possessed the added media attraction that Amis, Murdoch and other contributors were already acknowledged literary celebrities.

Confidence in primary schooling was further sapped — in the eyes of the general public, if not the teaching profession — by the 'scandal' of William Tyndale School in London. This had resulted in ILEA Inspectors assuming the roles of classroom teachers, and the dismissal of the head teacher. The Auld Inquiry (1976) which followed was extensively reported, as were the politics of four teachers subsequently dismissed from Tyndale. Hopkins (1978) argued that: ' . . . it is quite clear that they were committed to teaching methods aimed at transforming, rather than endorsing, the structure of society'.

Superimposed on the aspect of 'standards' outlined above, was professional and lay interest in the *trend* of 'standards' in the basic tool subjects of mathematics and English, particularly in the context of comprehensive education (see Ross 1972; DES 1977a). Although HMI were to conclude in their preparatory paper for the great debate that was to follow Callaghan's Ruskin speech: ' . . . there appears to be very little to choose between the attainments of those who have followed traditional and modern cour- ses . . . ' 'standards' were now at the centre of political debate, and hence in a position to influence subsequent curriculum policy-making. Outlining his causes for concern at Ruskin, Callaghan argued: ' . . . there is concern about the standards of numeracy of school leavers. Is there not a case for a professional review of the mathematics needed by industry at different levels?'

The debate over standards post-1976 was not internalised, but continued to be influenced by two other concerns: namely, 'value for money' and lack of participation. Each of these strands had been emphasised and linked to the question of educational standards in the Ruskin speech. Callaghan had stressed that expenditure on education had increased both in absolute terms and as a proportion of the gross national product in the thirty years after 1944, and concluded: 'There is a challenge to us all in these days, and a challenge in education is to examine its priorities and to secure as high efficiency as possible'.

In practical terms the response of government was to strengthen for a time the role of the newly-established Assessment of Performance Unit in analysing skill attainment and implementing some of the recommendations of the Taylor Report (DES 1977d). Thus the 1980 Education Act helped to legitimise the concept that the community at large should exercise a guiding role vis-à-vis the curriculum, and that schools should be 'accountable' to such a community. Reviewing the decade 1970–1980, Boyd-Barrett (1982) argued:

> . . . the desirability of a much more explicit definition and assessment of stan- dards . . . developed . . . from a narrow concern about *measurement* towards a more fundamental concern about *defining* what standards should be, and for *community evaluation* of the continuing maintenance and relevance of existing standards.

THE NEED FOR A MODEL: A LOOSE-COUPLED APPROACH

Recent analysts of policy-making and the school curriculum in England (Lawton 1980; Kogan 1966; Becher and Maclure 1978) are generally agreed that control over curricular matters is decentralised compared to Western Europe and even other parts of the United Kingdom. It may thus be fruitful to look for theoretical approaches which acknowledge an untidy reality (Howell 1981), ie, that elements within the policy process — for example, the DES, LEAs, teachers, etc — as well as the process itself, function as attached but separate agencies in a 'loose-coupled' relationship.

As a concept, 'loose-coupling' is a relative newcomer, delineated first by Glassman (1973) and more recently March and Olsen (1975). To date the model has received only cautious acceptance, and application to educational systems at both macro and micro levels has been scarce (Weick 1976). Reviewing Weick's contribution, Daft and Becker

(1978) suggest that loose-coupling:

> . . . evokes many rich images but . . . is not yet well enough elaborated to escape the 'either-this-or-that' nature of the propositions – richness in description is achieved at the cost of precision in prediction.

Yet the explanatory potential of Weick's approach is considerable, not least because it is more ready to accept the intrinsic complexity of organisations than 'traditional' Eastonian systems approaches. The weaknesses of such perspectives relate to premises made concerning participants in the policy-making process. For example, the 'authorities' within the 'political community' are seen to be tightly linked and operating within one all-embracing political system. The policy process itself is presented as an essentially linear phenomenon where adequately supported 'demands' are converted into policy 'outputs' by the political system, and processed 'outcomes' are fed to the 'environment'. A fuller account of Easton's (1957) process of demand reduction is given by Peter Ribbins in Chapter 6.

Weick et al accept the possibility of disconnection of data and process at the outset, but what are the main components of a loose-coupled perspective? Building on the work of Meyer (1975), Weick argued that to a greater or lesser extent policy-making systems and organisations exhibit the following characteristics:

(a)   slack times — times when there is an excessive amount of resources relative to demands;

(b)   occasions when any one of several means will produce the same end;

(c)   richly connected networks in which influence is slow to spread and/or is weak while spreading;

(d)   a relative lack of co-ordination, slow co-ordination, or co-ordination that is dampened as it moves through a system;

(e)   a relative absence of regulations;

(f)   planned unresponsiveness;

(g)   actual causal independence;

(h)   poor observational capabilities on the part of a viewer;

(i)   infrequent inspection of activities within the system;

(j)   decentralisation;

(k)   delegation of discretion;

(l)   the absence of linkages that should be present based on some theory — for example, in educational organisations the anticipated feedback linkage from outcome back to inputs is often non-existent;

(m)   the observation that an organisation's structure is not coterminus with its activity;

(n)   those occasions when no matter what strategy is adopted, the outcome is always the same: for example, when, despite changes in the structure and delivery of an element of the school curriculum, the outcomes in an educational situation remain the same;

(o)   curricula or courses in educational organisations for which there are few prerequisites: the longer the list of prerequisites, the tighter the coupling.

The attractiveness of loose-coupling stems from the focus it places upon the 'glue' which holds together the sub-systems of educational government. According to proponents of the theory, loose-coupling carries with it connotations of impermanence, dissolvability and tacitness, as well as the concept that organisations consist of building blocks which can either be grafted on or severed with relatively little disturbance to either the blocks or the organisation.

To take an example, it may be that in curriculum policy-making at the level of the Local Education Authority the education committee is loose-coupled with the governing body of a school or college. The image is that the committee and governing body are attached, i.e., there is a constitutional relationship consisting of devolved responsibilities on the monitoring of subject development, as well as a political relationship, i.e., councillors who act both as governors and committee members. Nevertheless each retains some individual identity and separateness. Thus despite the existence of committee pronouncements that schools' curricular practices be regularly reviewed and agreed by governing bodies, this may not occur. It may well be that the initiative as to which aspects of curriculum subject, content, method, performance development are discussed, and the frequency with which they are debated or simply 'received' via the head teacher's report, remains with the individual governing body. As a consequence there may well be a wide gap between the intention of the committee and the practice of governors, ie, in reality the attachment of these two agencies may be . . . 'circumscribed, infrequent, weak in [their] mutual effects, unimportant and slow to respond'. (Weick, 1976).

It is now necessary to apply the key features of the model to selected issues of curriculum content and control, and thus to test the viability of loose-coupling as an explanatory tool.

THE APPLICATION OF 'LOOSE-COUPLING' TO ISSUES OF CURRICULUM CONTENT AND CONTROL

A relative absence of regulations

Weick's analysis (1976) stresses 'authority of office' as a key coupling element: ' . . . the elements include positions, offices, responsibilities, opportunities, awards and sanctions'. For March and Olsen (1975), regulatory control represents an important part of the 'glue' which holds organisations together. How far can it be argued that there had been an identifiable framework for curriculum control since 1944, and to what extent was this framework being consolidated or weakened?

The backcloth to any analysis of policy-making regarding the school curriculum is undoubtedly the 1944 Education Act. Despite the fact that this statute never uses the term 'curriculum', it overtly and covertly established much of the present legal framework of control, and successive legislation (see Education Acts 1980 and 1981, for example) can be seen as adjustments to Butler's Act rather than radical innovations.

Specifically, the Act made sustained reference to only one area of the curriculum, i.e., 'religious education' or 'religious instruction', which as Gordon and Lawton (1978) have suggested, are used interchangeably. Thus s. 25 (i) states: 'Subject to the provisions of this section, the school day . . . shall begin with collective worship on the part of all pupils in attendance at the school . . . ' There were also vague references in s. 53 of the Act to 'adequate facilities for recreation and social and physical training'.

In broad terms the 1944 Act outlined the participants in curriculum policy-making, albeit sketchily. Section 23 determined that in institutions other than aided secondary schools, secular instruction: ' . . . shall . . . be under the control of the Local Education Authority', and the powers of LEAs were amplified in ss. 7 and 8 with the responsibility to:

> . . . contribute towards the spiritual, moral, mental and physical development of the Community by securing that efficient education at all stages should be made available to meet the needs of their areas,

and there should be sufficient schools:

> . . . to afford for all pupils opportunities for education offering such variety of instruction and training as may be desirable in view of their differing ages, abilities and aptitudes . . . including practical instruction and training appropriate to their respective needs.

Governing and managing bodies were also ascribed a role, which was stated with further precision in the ensuing administrative memorandum (Ministry of Education 1945): 'Subject thereto the governors shall have the general direction of the conduct and curriculum of the school'. Any reports that the head made regarding curricular matters also had to be presented to the governing body.

Three further participants were identified by the Act. The parental role was fairly circumscribed, relating mainly to attendance (see s. 36, 1944 Education Act). Duties and powers were placed upon the Minister, particularly in his dealing with LEAs (see s. 1, 1944 Act). He could issue regulations subject to Parliamentary approval, and some of these impinged directly, if narrowly, on the curriculum of the school (Ministry of Education 1959; DES 1972). These powers were refined but not tightened by the reorganisation of local government in 1974. The Minister/Secretary of State also had powers of mediation and adjudication in disputes between LEAs and its governors or managers (ss. 67 and 68, 1944 Act). Finally, two other sections should not be overlooked. Section 77 emphasises that the Minister should cause inspection to be made of every educational establishment at such intervals as appeared to him to be appropriate, thus involving the Inspectorate, and under s. 93 he had the ability to direct local inquiries into any matter connected with the Act. In curriculum terms, however, the latter has remained a dead letter.

Until the mid-1970s it could not really be argued that the foregoing strategy framework was either comprehensive or tightly linked. The ambiguity inherent in the 1944 Act was noted by the House of Commons Select Committee on Expenditure in 1976, where one contributor stated succinctly: ' . . . the location of responsibility for curriculum . . . is obscure and governed less by law than by custom and myth.'

Between 1976 and 1981 it seemed likely that controls would be tightened (DES 1977d; DES 1979a; DES 1980a; Education Act, DES 1980d), supporting Lawton's thesis (1980) that there was growing centralised control of the curriculum in the aftermath of the 'Great Debate'.

But Circular 6/81 and subsequently Circular 8/83 appeared to be moving away from prescriptive legislation and a tightening of regulatory instruments. Following-up s. 8 of the 1980 Act and the DES consultative document (DES 1981a), Circular 6/81 asked each LEA, somewhat blandly:

> . . . to review its policy for the school curriculum . . . its arrangements for making that

policy known to all concerned; [and] to review the extent to which current provision in its maintained . . . schools was consistent with that policy.

While Circular 6/81 had implied that further legislation was probable, Circular 8/83 stated: ' . . . recognis[ing] that reappraisal . . . inevitably takes time . . . [and] . . . a good deal of planning and consultation . . . ' and asserted that the Secretary of State now regarded 'the process of implementing 6/81 as a continuing one'. The DES would thus act as a recipient of detailed information for future unspecified action other than simply further dissemination and dialogue (DES 1983a, s. 8). The later statement on the 'Organisation and Content of the 5–16 Curriculum' (DES, 1984) offers further support for this view. Whilst the early part of the document appears prescriptive the annex, which contains five examples of existing 11–16 curricular patterns, supports diversity and school discretion: ' . . . each of the five examples contain some uneasy arrangements that limit the time and status given to some subjects in comparison with others and reflects a series of decisions taken by particular schools, in particular parts of the country . . . each of these schools succeeds in providing a generally broad and balanced curriculum for all its pupils . . . ' (DES 1984, Annex, p. 1). Such diversity is regarded as satisfactory by the DES; it provides some support for Boyd-Barrett's view (1982): 'If there was a system of curriculum control . . . it was a system that largely went unacknowledged . . . or was at best seen as a malfunctioning system . . . '.

The more recent White Paper, *Better Schools* (DES 1985), may be interpreted as further evidence of the weakness of the system of central control of the curriculum. While claiming an entitlement for the Government ' . . . to be more precise about, for example, the balance between curricular elements . . . ', it also insists that ' . . . the detailed organization and content of the programme for any particular school should be a matter for the headteacher and his staff.' Moreover, 'The Government does not propose to introduce legislation affecting the powers of the Secretaries of State in relation to the curriculum.' Thus, while the White Paper can be interpreted as moving towards increasing central prescription, it can also be understood as leaving schools with great flexibility as to how these prescriptions are to be translated into particular curriculum practice. It becomes a matter of fine judgement which is the more significant form of control.

Occasions when any one of several means will achieve the same end

According to Weick (1976):

> An interesting set of elements that lends itself to the loose-coupling imagery is means and ends. Frequently, several different means lead to the same outcome. When this happens, it can be argued that any one means is loosely coupled to the end in the sense that there are alternative pathways to achieve that same end.

A number of examples of this process in the field of curriculum development and control may be identified. For much of the postwar period, agencies concerned with reforming the curriculum have pursued three developmental models, each overlapping in chronological terms. During the late 1950s and early 1960s there was some professional enthusiasm for the research, development and diffusion model, which in Schon's terms was essentially a centre-periphery construct (Schon 1971). The Nuffield 'O' level Physics course reflected this approach in the sector of secondary education. Dissatisfaction with the ability to create 'teacher-proof' learning materials (Havelock 1970; 1971), amongst other, theoretically-based shortcomings, meant that the RD and D model lost ground to the social interaction model. This periphery–periphery approach stressed the significance of the teacher rather than the pupil, and secured support at the primary level with the establishment of Nuffield Junior science and mathematics teams. Even in the late 1970s, however, instances of RD and D curriculum innovations could be found: for example, the 'Children's Awareness of the Past' project aimed at pupils aged 7–11 (West 1980; 1981). By the mid-1970s the resource implications of the social interaction model, which required the maintenance of local networks of teachers often based on LEA-supported teachers' centres, was being increasingly questioned at a time of economic stringency. Continued diffusion of ideas once central planning teams were disbanded was also a weakness (Becher and Maclure 1978). A third strategy of curriculum development which burgeoned under the auspices of the Schools Council was the 'problem-solving' approach. Project teams at both national and local levels experimented with information 'item banks': for example, the Schools Council 'Sixth Form General Studies Project' (1974) and 'Local History and Radio Project' (1976). Subsequent experience indicated that considerable fragmentation and lack of coherent objectives could result from this approach. Thus schemes moved towards more comprehensive, centrally-produced materials organised on a modular thematic basis.

It could be argued, however, that the proliferation of 'means' vis-à-vis 'ends' typified by Weick's model is less tenable for the period post-1976, when some characteristics of a system-based approach to curriculum development began to emerge. The Ruskin Speech publicised a change of direction which had begun in April 1975 with the establishing of a Curriculum Publications Group (CPG) by HMI. A significant element in this group's thinking was the concept of measuring curricular provision against 'areas' of experience, i.e., a core curriculum (DES 1978a). This was articulated later in 'Aspects of Secondary Education':

> We see that common curriculum as a body of skills, concepts, attitudes and knowledge, to be pursued . . . by all pupils in the compulsory years of secondary education for a substantial part of their time . . . (DES 1979b)

More significant, the 'Red Book' (DES 1977c) triggered a major experiment in curriculum reappraisal involving 41 secondary schools in five LEAs (DES 1981b). While the feedback served to broaden the inquiry into areas of resources, staff training, etc, it would be true to state that the 'linking of elements' (Weick 1976), i.e., between the agencies of HMI and LEAs, was being tightened rather than loosened.

Paradoxically, 1976–1983 witnessed a multiplying of 'means' to achieve 'ends' in terms of curriculum control. Several strands in this process may be identified. One of the keynotes of Callaghan's speech at Ruskin had been the assertion that it was the duty of schools to boost the nation's economic fortunes by fostering favourable attitudes to industry. The inauguration of the Manpower Services Commission two years earlier did not, in the short term, have implications for the schools sector. But by 1977 rapidly escalating youth unemployment — there were 120 000 young persons under 18 out of work in January of this year, compared to 27 000 in July 1973 — generated demands for an appropriately swift political response (*Education* 1977). For central government the lessons of channelling £168 million per annum via the MSC, catering for approximately

230 000 young persons aged 16–17, was clear. Specific grants which the DES could not, for constitutional reasons, give, offered a seemingly 'instant' return in training terms, with associated political benefits for the government. By 1982 there were 630 000 16–17-year-olds taking advantage of the special measures included in the Youth Opportunities Programme (YOP). Although the education/training element within YOP took second place to work experience, and dealt exclusively with the 16 + school leaver, it was within the temporary expedient of the YOP that MSC established a claim to act as a formative influence on the school curriculum. In December 1981, one of the three national objectives contained in the government's Training White Paper (DE 1981), was: ' . . . better preparation in schools and colleges for working life and better arrangements for the transition from full-time education to work'. This was given substance in 1983, when 14 LEAs received funding to the sum of £70 million to formulate experimental technically oriented courses for the 14–18 age group in full-time education at either school or college, under the auspices of the Technical and Vocational Education Initiative, which aimed to ' . . . open to young people within education, across the whole range of ability, a technical and vocational route to recognised national qualifications'. (DE/DES 1984)

Claims to have a formative influence in the securing of a relevant vocational curriculum for the secondary sector were also made between 1976 and 1981, with funding of education/industry liaison officers via the industry/education unit of the Department of Trade and Industry. The DTI was also ascribed a role within TVEI in both staff and curriculum development terms by the 1984 White Paper, *Training for Jobs*. The DES counter to such trends was to announce a certificate of pre-vocational education for the 16–17-year-old in full-time education, with pilot schemes commencing in 1984 (see DES 1982, for initial moves towards this).

A relative lack of co-ordination

A premise of loose-coupling is that coupled events are responsive, but that each event also preserves its own identity and some evidence of its physical or logical separateness. It is tempting to view the period of the 'great debate' as a closely-linked chain of events leading to a greater public and professional understanding of curricular issues requiring resolution. Two case studies, however — outlined below — would serve to temper such a perspective.

The publications of HMI and those of the DES between 1976 and 1981 suggest a marked lack of integration, and the sequence of appearance of a number of documents owed more to chance than planning. The DES Green Paper, 'Education in Schools' (DES 1977b), appeared several months before the issuing of 'Curriculum 11–16' (DES 1977c) — the so-called 'Red Book' — logically the reverse of what might have been expected. The latter introduced three topics as a 'contribution to the current debate', i.e., common curriculum, the relationship of school to society, and vocational preparation undertaken by schools. Significantly, however, the Red Book disclaimed any notion that its contents reflected either the views of HMI as a whole or the DES (Boyd-Barrett 1982). Similarly, 'Curriculum 11–16: A review of Progress' (DES 1981b) was published nearly two months *after* the DES policy document, Circular 6/81, 'The School Curriculum' (DES 1981a). The foreword to 'Review of Progress' stated that the timing was 'fortuitous' but that the emergence of 'The School Curriculum' belonged to 'another chain of events'. Finally, although the DES policy document, 'A Framework for the School Curriculum' (DES 1980b) shared a common conception of the curriculum for the 14–16 age range, it was obvious that yet again policy had not developed out of the initial work undertaken by HMI. Only in relation to 'Aspects of Secondary Education' (DES 1979b) could the anticipated causal chain be established in relation to 'A Framework for the School Curriculum'. 'Separateness' rather than 'integration' was also displayed in the relationship between the DES and the Schools Council in the period 1975–1983. Although the Schools Council could legitimately argue that it was the precursor of 'whole curriculum thinking' (Schools Council 1975a), the DES was sharply critical of the report of that Schools Council working party (see DES 1977a) to the extent that Callaghan at Ruskin had felt obliged to distance himself from a potentially damaging division of opinion (*Education* 22.10.1976). The DES preferred the advice of the Waddell Committee (DES 1978b) to that of the Schools Council (1975b) on the reform of 16 + examinations (see DES 1980c).

There were marked differences of both tone and content between 'The School Curriculum' and the Schools Council-sponsored 'The Practical Curriculum', published in 1981. The DES effectively delayed the launch of 'The Practical Curriculum' (Schools Council 1981) in order that it would not coincide with its own publication. To some extent these differences have been reduced by two subsequent statements, i.e., '17 +: A new qualification' (DES 1982), and more recently the Schools Council Pamphlet 21, 'Planning One-year Courses' (1983), which was a follow-up to 'The Practical Curriculum'. In giving their respective prescriptions for a vocationally biased programme of general education, both documents drew heavily on FEU research, especially 'A Basis for Choice' (FEU, 1979).

Decentralisation/delegation of discretion

In their analysis of the English examination system, Becher and Maclure (1978) argue, somewhat ambivalently, for increased intervention and control by the DES/Secretary of State, particularly after 1976. Yet for much of the postwar period this view is not really tenable, i.e., central government retained a residual authority, and effectively delegated discretion to intermediate agencies.

Between 1944 and 1963 this authority devolved on the Secondary Schools Examination Council, whose ancestry could be traced to the setting up of the School Certificate Examination of 1917. Although the Ministry envisaged that the SSEC would act to implement its own policies on examinations, this did not occur: rather, the SSEC became more independent once the GCE system replaced School Certificate during the 1950s. The reconstituted Council now approved all syllabuses at both 'O' and 'A' level, and there was little interplay either between the SSEC and the Ministry, or, more surprisingly, between the Council and the eight GCE Boards (Bruce 1969).

There was further fragmentation of control following the Beloe Report (Secondary School Examinations Council 1960), which recommended the introduction of a new secondary school examination for the 15 + age range, encompassing the next 40 per cent below GCE 'O' level. Despite the fact that the report, which was legitimised by Circular 9/63, endeavoured to stem the trend towards a proliferation of examining bodies providing for the secondary leaver, the outcome did not reflect this aim. The new CSE introduced greater teacher involvement in both course content and assessment, and 14 additional regionally based examination boards were inaugurated.

'Delegation of discretion' was sustained with the setting up of the Schools Council in 1964 — an independent body undertaking curriculum development work and advising the Department of Education and Science on examination policy. However, the rhetoric of the Lockwood Report (1964) aimed to forestall concern within the teaching profession that the new Council, whose remit absorbed that of the SSEC, was a restructured Curriculum Study Group, with aims of centralised control of the examination system:

> No-one is consciously seeking to erode the schools' responsibilities. Indeed, great strides have been made since the turn of the century in freeing schools from detailed supervision . . . by local and central government . . . (Lockwood, DES 1964; also Lawton 1980)

Funded jointly by the DES and LEAs, the Schools Council initiated over 160 curriculum development projects between 1964 and 1980, and did succeed in integrating some examination syllabuses with such development work. But supervision of the examination system was now notional. As Becher and Maclure suggest, it was impossible to monitor the 'cafeteria' type offerings of the CSE Boards — in particular, Mode II and Mode III schemes, whose diversity was such that comparability was difficult to assess. During the period after the publication of the first Black Paper in 1969 (Hopkins 1978) the issue of how well the comprehensive system was faring (Pedley 1969; Ross 1972; Baldwin 1975) stimulated the debate over 'standards' and accentuated interest in comparability not simply within the CSE sector but also between subjects and boards at GCE. Although research (Forrest 1971; Nuttall 1982) did not provide incontrovertible statistical evidence for the 'pessimists' (see JMB 1978), it did suggest that some subjects, e.g., art and geography, were comparably 'easier' to do well in than, say, physics or chemistry.

The impact of the dialogue on standards vis-à-vis the examination system was to place evaluation of examining at 16+ firmly on the political agenda. Thus at Ruskin, Callaghan argued: 'Another problem is the examination — a contentious issue' but, equally important, he continued:

> The Schools Council have reached conclusions about its future after a great deal of thought, but it would not be right to introduce such an important change until there has been further public discussion.

From 1976 a number of instances of increasing centralisation regarding control of the examination system may be cited. As Secretary of State for Education, 1976–1979, Shirley Williams adopted an interventionist stance, by setting up a steering group to look at the issue of examinations at 16+ rather than relying on the machinery of the Schools Council (Becher and Maclure 1978). During this period the DES, and in particular HMI, resurrected the issue of national criteria for external school examinations. Discussing the possibility of a common 16+ examination, Sheila Browne, Senior Chief Inspector, stated:

> . . . the exercise to establish criteria for the common examination system at 16+ offers yet another chance — perhaps the last this century — to embody in the examination system aims long aspired to. (quoted in Nuttall 1982)

By the end of 1983 it was clear that the DES was moving in the direction of criterion-referencing rather than norm-referencing for examinations at 16+. This was legitimised in the much-publicised North of England Conference speech given by Sir Keith Joseph at Sheffield in January 1984, indicating that measurement of absolute rather than relative performance would be introduced nationally by 1989.

> We need reasonable assurance that pupils obtaining a particular grade will know certain things, possess certain skills or have achieved a certain competence . . . we need to move towards a system of grade-related criteria.

These views were manifested in the announcement by Sir Keith, in June 1984, of the decision to replace the existing 'O' level, CSE and joint 16+ examinations in England and Wales with a General Certificate of Secondary Education (GCSE), with its first examination in Summer 1988 (*Education* 1984b). The new grades, A to G, will *eventually* all be criterion-referenced and based upon national criteria, to be approved by the Secretaries of State, for syllabuses, procedures of assessment and grading. Since these national criteria will need to discriminate effectively by ability it is also proposed to allow for this, ' . . . by requiring either differentiated papers or differentiation within papers in examinations for all subjects' (*Education* 1984b). The significance of these changes in terms of the debate over centralised control will be examined in the conclusion.

Similarly, the 1983 Education (Awards and Grants) Bill, subsequently the Education Act 1984, created the opportunity for the Secretary of State to introduce a pilot scheme to develop a national model system of recording achievement based on a profile approach in order to: ' . . . confer on records of achievement a measure of national uniformity in all parts of the country'. (DES 1983c).

Such profiles would encompass information on personal achievements and characteristics, graded results in public examinations, and other evidence of academic attainment. There is thus some foundation for the belief that the principle that each school should have:

> . . . the fullest possible measure of responsibility for its own work with its own curriculum and teaching methods based on the needs of its own pupils and evolved by its own staff, (Skilbeck 1983)

was being eroded.

The period 1978–1984 did not represent a uniform trend towards greater centralisation regarding the examination system, however. Although the DES had pressed for, and secured, a reduction in the number of groupings of CSE/GCE examination boards to four for England by 1981, the feasibility studies for the new national criteria at 16+ were to be undertaken by the examination boards themselves and not by a more direct DES instrument, such as the APU. Similarly the demise of the Schools Council in 1982 did not necessarily herald greater DES control. The new structure which comprised two agencies, one for examinations at 16+ and 18+, and the other for curriculum, effectively divided the responsibilities that had previously come within the ambit of the Schools Council which had been increasingly dominated by the DES after 1978. Representation on both the Secondary Examinations Council and Schools Curriculum Development Committee was to be within the remit of the Secretary of State. Although teacher representation was not to comprise a majority on either the SEC or SCDC, it was clear that the power to appoint had resulted in a wider 'public' representation rather than an enhanced role for the DES. Many of the 39 organisations approached to submit nominees for ten appointed places on the SEC included those who had never had a place on the original Schools Council, for example, the Standing Conference of Regional Advisory Councils for

Further Education, and CGLI (City & Guilds of the London Institute). The extent to which these bodies will be allowed to act independently of the Secretary of State remains to be seen, but even prior to the creation of the SEC/SCDC the government had made it clear that the Central Advisory Councils were not to be revived. In a written answer, Sir Keith Joseph stated that it was the government's intention:

> . . . to repeal at the first opportunity which presents itself that section of the 1944 Act which provides for the establishment of central advisory councils. (9 November 1982)

Infrequent inspection of activities within the system

For Weick, a related feature of decentralised organisations such as those concerned with educational policy-making is that the monitoring of activities within the system is comparatively weak.

With few exceptions the period post-1944 substantiates such an argument. It is true that the two central advisory councils for England and Wales, which in theory were free to advise the Minister 'upon any matters connected with educational theory and practice, as they thought fit', were much underused between 1945 and 1971 (Pile 1979). The Plowden Report (1967) was the product of the only occasion when primary education was examined during this period, and comparatively few of its 197 recommendations were taken up. Sir William Pile, who served as Permanent Under Secretary of State at the DES, 1970–76, testified to the 'ad hoc' practice of CACs (Pile 1979). Crosland commented, somewhat complacently, that:

> . . . we've got to the point now where this general theme of education and social background . . . has been taken in, and it doesn't need more enquiries to drive it home. We've got a large body now of active educationalists who can carry this discussion on themselves. (Kogan 1971)

By 1971 the Central Advisory machinery was effectively moribund.

Although formal school inspections by the Inspectorate were effectively abolished after 1968, this represented a shift in the focus of monitoring rather than a termination of interest. As Boyd-Barrett (1982) has argued, there was during the 1970s an intensification of survey work which: ' . . . functioned to improve the quantity and quality of publicly available information on how curriculum decisions were actually implemented across the country'. Thus the Primary and Secondary Surveys made available a more defined picture of the structure and diversity of curriculum practice in these sectors than had been available at any time since 1944.

From the early 1970s the DES began to assert hitherto comparatively latent rights to monitor pupil performance. The Bullock Committee (DES 1975) assumed a wide-ranging brief related to reading standards, utilising in part data collected by the Start and Wells reading survey of 1970–1971 (Start and Wells 1972). Despite the fact that the statistical base of both this and the Committee's report was challenged (Hopkins 1978), the conclusion of 'A Language for Life' was clear: 'We are in no doubt of the importance of monitoring standards of achievement in literacy, and of doing so to as sophisticated an extent as possible'.

Second, in August 1974 it was announced that the DES was to establish an Assessment of Performance Unit (APU). It would be too simplistic to link the gestation of the unit directly with the later debate over 'standards' in schools. The setting up of the unit was in response to a report on education by the House of Commons Select Committee on race relations and immigration, and as the 1974 White Paper made clear, it was to operate in liaison with the Educational Disadvantage Unit. As Dennison (1978) has suggested, however, ' . . . the creation of the unit resulted from a complex mixture of internal and external pressures, developments in evaluative techniques and considerations of potential benefits'.

Between August 1974 and July 1975 when the APU started work, 'internal pressures' moved the unit into a broader arena. Brian Kay, who served as Chairman of the APU co-ordinating group between 1975 and 1977, was instrumental in shifting the emphasis from 'discerning and seeking' a remedy for 'under achievement among ethnic minorities', to assessing the performance of pupils of all levels of ability across a wide spectrum of the curriculum (Simon 1979). In an ostensibly casual contribution to *Trends in Education* in June 1975, Kay suggested some lines of development:

> Initially one might identify . . . six such areas of pupil performance — though this is not to suggest either that there are no more than six, and . . . their sum will form a wholly satisfactory description of the curriculum.

The main objective of the APU, post-1975, was to develop machinery for assessment of national standards of educational performance at age levels 11–15. By 1982 subjects tested included maths, language, science and foreign language (Gipps and Wood 1982), though controversial plans to test the attainment of West Indian school children were hastily abandoned by the DES in May 1981.

The impact of the Department's foray into educational attainment between 1975 and 1983 should not, however, be over-emphasised. In operational terms the APU ran into a number of difficulties. The original plan for a cross-curricular model was narrowed for financial reasons, and the light sampling practices and supporting techniques came in for considerable criticism (Boyd-Barrett 1982). By the summer of 1981 the DES was emitting signals that it would be scaling down the scope of future APU activity. Reporting in *Primary Education Review*, Gipps and Wood (1982) were able to state confidently that LEAs now had less grounds for fearing that an 'accountability through testing' movement was being inspired by central government.

Actual causal independence

When considering the issue of curriculum control and the examination structure in the context of the 'Great Debate', commentators have been swift to connect events in England with those north of the border. Becher and Maclure (1978) state that: 'It was noticeable that the search for new conventions generated occasional sidelong glances at Scotland' while Boyd-Barrett (1982) postulated that:

> In Scotland there had been a much longer history, and a greater degree of curriculum control from the 'centre' than in the case of control exercised by the DES.

To what extent, therefore, can change in the central–local policy-making relationship in Scotland be viewed as providing a blueprint for a more interventionist DES in England?

The establishment of a Consultative Committee on the Curriculum (CCC) had given the Scottish Education Department direct influence over both primary and secondary school curricula as early as 1965, reinforced by its dominant representation on the Scottish Certificate of Education Examinations Board (Wilson 1978). The SED also stimulated discussion of the 'great debate' and ensuing regional conferences. This was illustrated by the Ruthven Report (SED 1967), which initiated a dialogue on both the structure and balance of the total curriculum at the secondary level, and ten years later produced the Munn and Dunning Reports (SED 1977a; b). These were comparatively sophisticated, the former:

> . . . identified curriculum aims, criteria for determining the scope of curriculum, the modes of activity . . . that were appropriate to the aims, and the balance between compulsory and optional elements. It even specified minimum time allocations . . . (Boyd-Barrett 1982)

But however tempting the analogy between such trends of 'relevant' curricula and 'credible' monitoring of school-leavers in Scotland with, for example, the content of Callaghan's Ruskin speech, there are a number of theoretical and practical weaknesses. First, there was no evidence in statements emanating from the DES, Secretaries of State, or other government Ministers, to suggest that changes in the direction of Scottish practice were being considered between 1965 and 1976. Further, if Rabb's argument is accepted, the evolution of curricular policy-making in Scotland was not in the direction of giving more power to central agencies such as the SED. The CCC's broad over-arching brief as a curriculum-determining body could: ' . . . do little to maintain any general oversight of the curriculum as a whole, and (the CCC) worried aloud about this in its triennial reports' (Rabb 1981). Indeed, there were indications of decentralisation during the 1970s. Immediately prior to the Ruskin speech, the CCC was restructured with a membership independent of the Scottish Secretary of State, and it was anticipated that the chairman would no longer be designated by either the Secretary or the SED.

It should not, however, be overlooked that stronger parallels could be drawn on the issue of who the participants in curriculum policy-making should be. The Taylor Committee was aware that in Scotland there were newly established systems of broad community participation in the determining of curriculum at institutional levels, i.e., schools councils, (see Macbeth and Mackenzie 1976). According to Gatherer (1976), these bodies had given 'a recognition of the legitimate claims of parents', and accepted that curriculum development was a 'social process' which embraced the whole community served by the school. It is perhaps significant that the parties, if not the proportions of their representation recommended by Taylor, coincide with Scottish Schools Councils.

Overall there is limited evidence to support the 'blueprint' thesis, and on balance actual causal independence would seem to have been demonstrated in terms of curriculum trends between these two parts of the UK.

CONCLUSION

This paper has not completely explored the characteristics of Weick's model against the full range of material available on curriculum policy-making vis-à-vis the school sector.

Interplay between central departments, particularly the DES, MSC and the burgeoning intervention of other agencies, such as the Department of Trade and Industry, in the educational arena require further inquiry. The foregoing analysis has been confined to the macro level of policy-making when it could be argued that the most fruitful application of 'loose-coupling' occurs at institutional levels. Such issues must again await the attentions of future research. The 'school curriculum' has also become an increasingly fluid area of policy-making, especially at 16+. At the time of writing the Joint Board has just published its consultative document regarding the Certificate of Pre-Vocational Education and the Secretary of State has indicated an intention to move away from subject specialisation at GCE 'A' level with the introduction of Advanced Level Supplementary examinations. Any conclusions which may be drawn as to whether the 'linkages' between the partners in the curriculum process are being consolidated or weakened must remain illustrative rather than definitive.

Although it could be suggested that the school curriculum has been subject to increasing regulatory control from central government, indicated by the 'Training for Jobs' White Paper and the enactment of legislation to permit the DES to make specific grants and thus enhance its interventionist opportunities vis-à-vis local authorities, it would be difficult to argue that this trend has been uniform. The aftermath to Circular 6/81, for example, points to a drawing back from prescriptive control. Similarly, whilst Sir Keith Joseph may be credited with having made many more pronouncements on the school curriculum than previous incumbents, even his grasping of the nettle of 16+ examinations with the decision to go ahead with the GCSE can be seen, according to Dr Walter Roy, the NUT education committee chairman (*Education* 1984b), as only confirming what would have happened anyway. Christopher Price goes further in commenting on the conservatism of the change. 'The change is not nearly as dramatic as some have made out. I have no doubt that for many years to come, grades A, B and C of GCSE will continue to be described as 'O' level passes. Nor is there any guarantee that the actual 'O' level exam will cease to exist'. (*TES* 1984).

As other commentators have postulated (Boyd-Barrett 1982), legislation for curriculum control has been a 'weak guide to practice'. It may therefore be more appropriate to think of regulatory control as a cyclical issue, i.e. with trends towards greater central intervention evident between 1976 and 1981 but perhaps not being sustained thereafter.

There is evidence that postwar curriculum policy-making has supported Weick's concept of 'occasions when any one of several means can achieve the same end' and this is particularly true of the multiplicity of agencies now shaping the pre-vocational and vocational curriculum of 16-year-olds in full-time education. Thus, as Weick states, 'coupling imagery . . . suggests the idea of building blocks that can be grafted onto an organisation . . . with relatively little disturbance to either the blocks or the organisation'.

Co-ordination between central departments has often been suspect and there is every indication that this will continue — how will the Certificate of Pre-Vocational Education mesh with other initiatives such as TVEI, the curricular offerings of British Schools Technology and the Certificate of Extended Education? Sustained decentralisation and 'delegation of discretion' is more difficult to substantiate — particularly in relation to standards and the future of the examination system. As noted above, it is too early to judge how independently-minded the SEC and SCDC will prove to be. The frequency with which 'activities' within the curriculum arena have been 'inspected' has increased rather than diminished though both the comprehensiveness and efficiency of this development may be disputed. Thus it cannot be argued on the evidence presented that linkages throughout the framework of curriculum policy-making have been consistently tightened through time.

In conclusion, possibly the greatest asset of the loose-coupled model identified in this chapter has been the reminder that events with this and other policy-making processes can be causally independent. As Weick himself argued:

> The basic premise . . . is that concepts such as loose coupling serve as sensitising devices. They sensitise the observer to notice and question things that had previously been taken for granted.

Unstructured and ambivalent though loose-coupling may appear,[1] it offers considerable scope for describing both the evolution of the postwar school curriculum in England and Wales as well as delineating how the policy-making agencies have interacted.

NOTE

1. A valuable critical view of loose-coupling and its contribution to educational administration is given in Foster (1983).

REFERENCES

Auld, R. (1976) *William Tyndale Junior and Infant Schools: Public Inquiry*. London: ILEA.

Baldwin, R. W. (1975) *The Great Comprehensive Gamble*. London: Helios Press.

Becher, T. and Maclure, S. (1978) *The Politics of Curriculum Change*. London: Hutchinson.

Bernbaum, G. (ed.) (1979) *Schooling in Decline*. London: Macmillan Press.

Bolam, R., Smith, G. and Canter, H. (1978) 'Research Report: Local Education Authority Advisers and Educational Innovation'. *Educational Administration*, **6**(1) 19–31.

Boyd-Barrett, O. (1982) *The Control and Development of School Curriculum: External factors*. Unit 6 of E222: The Control of Education in Britain. Milton Keynes: Open University Press.

Brooksbank, K. and Revell, J. (1981) *School Governors*. Harlow: Councils and Education Press.

Bruce, G. (1969) *Secondary School Examinations — Facts and Commentary*. London: Pergamon.

Callaghan, J. (1976) 'Ruskin College Speech'. Quoted in *Education*, **148**(17) 332–3.

Cox, C. B. and Dyson, A. E. (ed.) (1969) *Fight for Education: A Black Paper*. London: Critical Quarterly Society.

Daft, R. L. and Becker, S. W. (1978) *Innovation in Organisations*. New York: Elsevir.

(DE) Department of Employment (1981) *A New Training Initiative: A Programme for Action*. London: HMSO.

Dennison, W. F. (1978) 'Research Report: The APU?'. *Durham and Newcastle Research Review*, **VIII**(40) 31–38.

(DE/DES) Department of Employment/Department of Education and Science (1984) *Training for Jobs*. London: HMSO.

(DES) Department of Education and Science (1964) *Report of a Working Party on Schools Curriculum and Examinations* (Lockwood Report). London: HMSO.

(DES) Department of Education and Science (1967) *Children and their Primary Schools: Report of the Central Advisory Council for Education (England)* (The Plowden Report). London: HMSO.

(DES) Department of Education and Science (1972) *Schools Regulations (Premises)*. London: HMSO.

(DES) Department of Education and Science (1975) *Report of the Committee of Inquiry appointed by the Secretary of State for Education and Science* (The Bullock Report). London: HMSO.

(DES) Department of Education and Science (1977a) *Educating Our Children: Four subjects for debate* (The Yellow Book). London: HMSO.

(DES) Department of Education and Science (1977b) *Education in Schools: A consultative document*. London: HMSO.

(DES) Department of Education and Science (1977c) *Curriculum 11–16*. London: HMSO.

(DES) Department of Education and Science (1977d) *A New Partnership for Our Schools* (Taylor Report). London: HMSO.

(DES) Department of Education and Science (1978a) *Primary Education in England: A survey by HMI*. London: HMSO.

(DES) Department of Education and Science (1978b) *School Examinations* (Waddell Report). 2 volumes. London: HMSO.

(DES) Department of Education and Science (1979a) *Local Authority Arrangements for the School Curriculum: Report on the Circular 14/77 Review*. London: HMSO.

(DES) Department of Education and Science (1979b) *Aspects of Secondary Education in England: A survey by HM Inspectors of Schools*. London: HMSO.

(DES) Department of Education and Science (1980a) *A Framework for the School Curriculum*. London: HMSO.

(DES) Department of Education and Science (1980b) *A View of the Curriculum*. London: HMSO.

(DES) Department of Education and Science (1980c) *Examinations 16–18. A Consultative Paper*. London: HMSO.

(DES) Department of Education and Science (1980d) *Education Act 1980*. London: HMSO.

(DES) Department of Education and Science (1981a) *Circular 6/81: The School Curriculum*. London: HMSO.

(DES) Department of Education and Science (1981b) *Curriculum 11–16. A review of progress: A Joint Study by HMI and five LEAs*. London: HMSO.

(DES) Department of Education and Science (1981c) *Review of the Schools Council* (The Trenaman Report). London: DES.

(DES) Department of Education and Science (1982) *17+. A New Qualification*. London: HMSO.

(DES) Department of Education and Science (1983a) *Circular 8/83. The School Curriculum*. London: HMSO.

(DES) Department of Education and Science (1983b) *Curriculum 11–16. Towards a statement of entitlement*. London: HMSO.

(DES) Department of Education and Science (1983c) *Records of Achievement for School Leavers*. London: DES (draft policy statement).

(DES) Department of Education and Science (1984) *The Organisation and Content of the 5–16 Curriculum: A Note by the Department of Education and Science and the Welsh Office*. London: DES, September.

(DES) Department of Education and Science (1985) *Better Schools*, Cmnd. 9469. London: HMSO.

Easton, D. (1957) 'An approach to the analysis of political systems'. *World Politics* **IX**, 383–400.

Easton, D. (1965) *A Systems Analysis of Political Life*. New York: Wiley.

Education (1977) 'Commons Debate on Youth Unemployment'. 3.6.1977, 386.

Education (1983) 'Skilbeck calls for new curriculum body'. **162**(24), 9.12.1983, 470.

Education (1984a) 'North of England 1984: A giant step to higher standards'. **163**(2), 13.1.1984, 28–29.

Education (1984b) 'GCSE: two into one will go' and 'Exams'. **163**(26), 29.6.84, 526 and 522–523.

Eggleston, J. (1973) 'Decision-making on the school curriculum: A conflict model'. *Sociology* (7), 377–94.

Eggleston, J. (1977) *The Sociology of the School Curriculum*. London: Routledge and Kegan Paul.

Educational Management Information Exchange (EMIE). Slough: NFER Various papers: see, for example:

'Curriculum based staffing of secondary schools: A working paper'. Humberside Education Department (1981).

'Falling rolls and secondary staffing'. Suffolk Education Department (1982).

'Secondary school staffing 1982/83: Form entry based curriculum-led staffing'. Birmingham Education Department (1982).

FEU Further Education Curriculum Review

and Development Unit (1979) *A Basis for Choice*. London: FEU.

Forrest, G. M. (1971) *Standards in Subjects at The Ordinary Level of the GCE, June 1970*. Manchester: Joint Matriculation Board.

Foster, W. (1983) *Loose Coupling Revisited. A Critical view of Weick's Contribution to Educational Administration*. Victoria, Australia: Deakin University.

Fowler, G., Morris, V. and Ozga, J. (1973) *Decision Making in British Education*. London: Heinemann.

Gatherer, W. A. (1976) 'Curriculum development in a regional context'. *Scottish Educational Studies*, **8**(2), 84 ff.

Gipps, G. and Wood, R. (1982) 'Evaluation of Testing in Schools Project'. *Primary Education Review*. Spring 1982 (13), 16.

Glassman, R. B. (1973) 'Persistence and Loose Coupling in Living Systems'. *Behavioural Science*, **18**, 83–98.

Gordon, P. and Lawton, O. (1978) *Curriculum Change in The Nineteenth and Twentieth Centuries*. London: Hodder and Stoughton.

Havelock, R. G. (1970) *Guide to Innovation in Education*. Ann Arbor, Michigan: University of Michigan.

Havelock, R. G. (1971) *Planning for Innovation*. Ann Arbor, Michigan: University of Michigan.

Heclo, H. (1972) 'Review Article: Policy Analysis'. *British Journal of Political Studies*, **2**, 84 ff.

Hopkins, A. (1978) *The School Debate*. Harmondsworth: Penguin.

Hopkinson, D. (ed.) (1978) *Standards and the School Curriculum: Analysis and Suggestions from HM Inspectorate*. London: Ward Lock.

Howell, D. A. (1981) 'Inside the Black Box'. *Research in Educational Management and Administration* (Proceedings of the 2nd BEMAS/SSRC Research Seminar). pp. 27–34.

(ILEA) Inner London Education Authority (1984) *Improving Secondary Schools*. Report of the Committee on the Curriculum and Organisation of Secondary Schools in ILEA, chaired by David H. Hargreaves. London: ILEA.

Jencks, C. et al (1974) *Inequality: A Reassessment of the Effect of Family and Schooling in America*. London: Allen Lane.

Joint Matriculation Board (1978) *Comparability in GCE*. Manchester: Joint Matriculation Board.

Kogan, M. (1966) *Central Development and Local Authorities*. London: George Allen and Unwin.

Kogan, M. (1971) *The Politics of Education*. Harmondsworth: Penguin.

Kogan, M. (1975) *Educational Policy-Making: A Study of Interest Groups and Parliament*. London: George Allen and Unwin.

Lawton, D. (1980) *The Politics of the School Curriculum*. London: Routledge and Kegan Paul.

Lawton, D. (1984) *The Tightening Grip: Growth of Central Control of the School Curriculum*. Bedford Way Papers 21: University of London Institute of Education.

Macbeth, A. and Mackenzie, M. (1976) 'Community participation and the Scottish School Councils'. *Scottish Educational Studies*, **8**(2), 106–12.

Mann, J. (1979) *Education*. London: Pitman.

Mann, J. (1982) 'Valedictory on the Schools Council'. *Education*, 23.7.1982, 59.

March, J. G. and Olsen, J. P. (1975) 'Choice situations in loosely coupled worlds'. Unpublished manuscript, Stanford University.

Meyer, J. W. (1975) 'Notes on the structure of educational organisations'. Unpublished manuscript, Stanford University.

Ministry of Education (1945) *Model Articles of Government*. Administrative Memorandum 25. London: HMSO.

Ministry of Education (1959) *Primary Education: Suggestions for the consideration of teachers and others concerned with the work of primary schools*. London: HMSO.

Ministry of Education (1959) *15–18: Report of the Central Advisory Council for Education (England)* (The Crowther Report). London: HMSO.

Ministry of Education (1959) Statutory Instrument: *Schools Regulations* (amended 1966). London: HMSO.

Ministry of Education (1963) *Half Our Future: A report of the Central Advisory Council (England)* (The Newsom Report). London: HMSO.

Nuttall, D. L. (1982) 'Prospects for a common system of examining at 16+'. *Forum*, **24** (3) 60–61.

Pedley, R. (1969) *The Comprehensive School*. Harmondsworth: Penguin.

Pile, W. (1979) *The Department of Education and Science*. London: Allen & Unwin.

Rabb, C. D. (1981) 'The changing machinery of Scottish educational policy-making'. *Scottish Educational Studies* **7**(1), 86–98.

Ross, J. M. et al (1972) *A Critical Appraisal of Comprehensive Education.* Slough: NFER.

Sallis, J. (1977) *School Managers and Governors: Taylor and After.* London: Ward Lock.

Schon, D. A. C. (1971) *Beyond the Stable State.* Harmondsworth: Penguin.

Schools Council (1975a) *Report of the Working Party on the Whole Curriculum of the Secondary School.* London: Schools Council.

Schools Council (1975b) *Examinations at 16+: Proposals for the future.* London: Methuen.

Schools Council Secondary Examinations Post-16 Working Party (1980) *A Programme of Improvement: Secondary examinations at 16+.* London: Schools Council.

Schools Council (1981) *The Practical Curriculum.* Schools Council Working Paper 70. London: Methuen.

Schools Council (1983) *Planning One Year 16–17 Courses.* London: Schools Council.

(SED) Scottish Education Department (1967) *Organization of Courses leading to SCE* (The Ruthven Report). Edinburgh: HMSO.

(SED) Scottish Education Department (1977a) *Assessment for All* (Dunning Report). Edinburgh: HMSO.

(SED) Scottish Education Department (1977b) *The structure of the curriculum in the third and fourth years of the Scottish Secondary School* (Munn Report). Edinburgh: HMSO.

Secondary School Examinations Council (1960) *Secondary Schools Examinations Other than GCE: Report of a Committee Appointed by the Secretary of the School Examinations Council* (Beloe Report). London: HMSO.

Select Committee (1976) *Public Expenditure to 1979–80.* London: HMSO.

Select Committee on Education and Science (1968) *Her Majesty's Inspectorate (England and Wales) Report, Part 1.* London: HMSO.

Select Committee (1976) *Public Expenditure to 1979–80.* London: HMSO.

Simon, J. (1979) 'What and Who is the APU?'. *Forum*, **22**(1), 7–11.

Skilbeck, M. (1983) 'Skilbeck calls for new curriculum body'. *Education* 9 December, **162**(24), 470.

Start, K. B. and Wells, B. K. (1972) *The Trend of Reading Standards.* Slough: NFER.

Stubbs, W. H. (1981) 'Pressures and the school curriculum'. *Curriculum*, (1), 15–20.

(TES) Times Educational Supplement (1968) Resumé of speech announcing Expenditure White Paper. *TES*, 16 February, 522.

(TES) Times Educational Supplement (1970a) 'Now Britain is strong — let's make it a great place to live' (Labour Manifesto). *TES*, 29 May, 6.

(TES) Times Educational Supplement (1970b) 'A Better Tomorrow' (Conservative Manifesto). *TES*, 29 May.

(TES) Times Educational Supplement (1973) 'Resumé of Circular 15/73'. *TES*, 21 December.

(TES) Times Educational Supplement (1974) 'Better Education' (Conservative Manifesto). *TES*, 15 February, 5.

(TES) Times Educational Supplement (1984) '"O" levels live on'. *TES*, 29 June (No. 3548), 88.

Weick, K. E. (1976) 'Educational organisations as loosely coupled systems'. *Administrative Science Quarterly*, **21**, 1–19.

West, J. (1980) *Children's Awareness of the Past.* Dudley Metropolitan Borough [Education Services].

West, J. (1981) *History 7–13: Guidelines, structures and resources.* Dudley Metropolitan Borough [Education Services].

Wilson, J. D. (1978) 'Information Paper 1: Curriculum development in Scotland — A new structure'. *Scottish Educational Review*, **10**(1), 50–53.

5

PROVISION, PROCESS AND PERFORMANCE IN COMPULSORY EDUCATION: AN ECONOMIC PERSPECTIVE ON CHANGING ENROLMENT

Hywel Thomas

INTRODUCTION: AN ECONOMIC FRAMEWORK

The coincidence of changing enrolments in the compulsory sector of education and the increased pressure on resources for education, caused by the UK economy's persistent difficulties, is the context within which education managers at system and institutional level must work. What are the consequences of these changes for the quality of educational provision, process and performance? It is the aim of this chapter to describe and analyse the key areas affected and the policies being adopted to manage the problem. The framework for the analysis is the input, process and output model of the economist.

Economists view education as a productive process in which the various human and physical resources, which they call inputs, are mixed together, or processed, in various ways. Out of these processing activities come educational outcomes or outputs, though no economist would suggest that these outputs are by any means as predictable and measurable as in more conventionally understood manufacturing processes. It is a framework which is, nevertheless, useful in several ways. First, by distinguishing inputs from process and outputs, it clarifies the differing nature and status of variables often discussed as though they were somehow the same. Second, this distinction assists any study of the interrelations between changing variables and it can, at best, lead to an examination of how changes in the availability of certain inputs affect process variables and how these in turn affect educational outcomes. Third, however, it also highlights the difficulties involved with any attempt to measure satisfactorily educational outcomes and the problems of evaluating the outcome effects of changes in selected input and process variables. Fourth, because the economist uses the framework to ask questions about efficiency in an educational world of scarce means and many wants, it is an analysis which may offer guidance for decision-makers on the resource allocations which are more likely to secure greater educational outcomes.

Appropriately, the next section describes and analyses the main changes to educational inputs linked to changing rolls but, concurrently and for reasons of clarity, will also examine some of the possible consequences of these changes for educational outputs. The subsequent section on the key school processes affected by changing rolls will similarly contain an analysis of the outcome effects. Thus the section on educational outcomes will give only a brief summary of these but will also include a discussion of the value and status of some process variables as possible decision criteria. The section will also discuss the policy implications of the problems explored in the chapter.

THE PATTERN OF EDUCATIONAL INPUTS

A distinction between human and physical resources provides a helpful first stage in the classification of educational inputs. Each of these needs sub-classifying and, for our purpose, the human resources will be considered in three categories, pupils, teachers, and ancillary and clerical staff. The physical resources will be considered in two categories, buildings, their maintenance and fittings, and educational books and equipment.

Pupil numbers and pupil needs

The 13-year decline in the number of births in England and Wales was reversed in 1978 signalling, for the relevant decision-makers, an increase in the number of five-year-olds entering primary schools in 1983 and also providing further evidence of the uncertainties of educational planning, which must attempt to anticipate population changes in order to make suitable provision.[1] The anticipated changes in primary pupil numbers after 1986 are summarised in Table 5.1[2], which also shows the scale of the earlier decline in numbers from 1973 to 1985.

The pattern of contraction followed by expansion shown by this data is a useful indicator of the future primary school pupil population for which provision will have to be made. However, its value has limitations since it does not show the detailed local pattern of demographic change which is of more immediate concern to a local authority. All regions and even local areas do not follow the same demographic trends. Local variations may even be counter to national trends and Gordon (1982) cites the example of East Anglia, a region which has not only experienced a recent increase in population but, moreover, is expected to follow this trend to 1990 and beyond. This pattern of local variation applies also to national trends in the secondary sector, also summarised in Table 5.1. Inevitably, because pupils transfer from primary to secondary schools the pattern is

Table 5.1 *Total population in the maintained schools sector in England and Wales, 1973–1995 (April figures in 000s).*

Year	Nursery and primary	Secondary	Total
1973	5253	3363	8616
1974	5273	3724	8996
1975	5242	3827	9069
1976	5215	3936	9151
1977	5138	4039	9176
1978	4895	4095	8990
1979	4760	4120	8880
1980	4595	4115	8710
1981	4405	4075	8480
1982	4195	4005	8200
1983	3995	3950	7945
1984	3865	3855	7720
1985	3820	3730	7550
1986	3840	3585	7425
1987	3885	3440	7325
1988	3970	3265	7235
1989	4100	3105	7205
1990	4200	3000	7200
1991	4300	2960	7260
1992	4400	2970	7370
1993	4500	3020	7520
1994	4600	3100	7700
1995	4700	3190	7890

Notes — Nursery and primary:
- Known school population ('actuals' up to 1980)
- Figures up to 1986 based on 'actuals' and known births
- 1986 shows upturn
- Figures up to 1992 based increasingly on estimates of future births
- From 1993 figures based entirely on estimates of future births

Notes — Secondary:
- 'Actuals' up to 1980
- Figures up to 1993 based on 'actuals' and known births
- 1992 shows upturn
- From 1994 figures incorporate estimates of future births

Notes — Total:
- 'Actuals' up to 1980
- Figures up to 1986 based on 'actuals' and known births
- Figures up to 1995 based increasingly on estimates of future births
- 1991 shows upturn

Source: ACSET (1981) *The Future of the Teacher Training System*, ACSET 81/24, London: DES.

similar, except that they are distributed over a different set of years, making the 1980s the decade of secondary contraction. Within this national pattern the local variations are again substantial, the case of East Anglia's growth contrasting with urban authorities such as Manchester and Birmingham having to adapt to a halving of their school rolls.

Table 5.1 also summarises the changing size of the *total population* in the maintained nursery, primary and secondary schools of England and Wales. They show that, taken as a whole, the 1980s is a decade of contracting rolls with an expected rise in school population occurring in 1991. The table also incorporates notes intended to guide the reader on the progressive unreliability of figures which must be increasingly based, as we move further into the future, on estimates of future births, a factor which affects the primary sector much earlier than the secondary sector. A key variable affecting the number of births is the fertility rate, and the DES's (1983b) principal projection assumes a recovery from the low levels of 1980–1982. However, the observed fertility rate up to the Spring of 1984 showed only a continuing decline.

Two changes in the input characteristics of pupils are particularly significant, the first of which is concerned with the changing size of the age groups progressing through the system. For the secondary sector Briault and Smith (1980b) discuss how managing the process of contraction creates difficulties which do not occur for existing small schools. One of these difficulties is the need to provide for the curricular needs of larger age groups at the older end of a school which is shrinking in its junior age groups. These difficulties become acute when specialist staff leave who cannot be replaced if the school is already above its staffing establishment. The problem differs in a primary sector which is expected to take half-a-million more children between 1986 and 1991; particularly in small two- and three-class schools increased numbers of the youngest pupils affects the balance of learner demands and activities, such that the classroom mix of children may have to be altered more than once as a child progresses through the school.

In both sectors one way of managing *falling* rolls is school closure, an option which has conventionally unmeasured effects on the input of time to learning. An expected consequence of school closure and the transfer of pupils elsewhere is that the journey time of pupils will increase, and may do so quite substantially in some cases. Longer journeys may have resource implications for local authorities in those circumstances where they are either obliged, or choose, to meet the cost of transport. Such costs may be calculated in evaluating closure options, but they may not be the most significant costs for pupils and their families for whom longer school journey times reduce time available not only for out-of-school learning but also for other non-school activities. In his discussion of the economics of small schools Simkins (1980) argues that 'It is difficult, if not impossible, to place a value on such costs . . . and it is doubtful whether the economist can say much that is useful about them'.[1] However, this is not the case. While economists may be unable to value non-budgetary costs and benefits, their training is an invaluable aid for simply identifying them. If they are not included as items in an analysis of costs and savings of closure options they might be assumed to be nonexistent. If they are included in such an analysis then the decision-makers are made aware of those unquantified factors which are affected by their choice.

Quantifiable change in pupil characteristics are somewhat easier to anticipate and manage than the likely qualitative changes in secondary pupils brought about by factors such as the high rate of youth unemployment, which is such a prominent feature of the UK economy's difficulties. The altering pattern of youth employment may contribute to significant changes in the preference of the 14–16 age group and their parents, who may become even more conscious of the value of certification in a more overtly instrumental curriculum package. In addition, others in the same age group who have less likelihood of securing suitable certification may become less content with the traditional curriculum. Simultaneously, schools must also adjust to the consequences for their pupils of the speed and nature of technological change. Life-long patterns of work, as well as the nature of work and leisure, are expected to change, requiring from the young higher grade skills and more flexibility. Despite its brevity this paragraph outlines what is the most important challenge facing the compulsory system of education, designing a curriculum suitable for pleasure and leisure, paid and non-paid work. Such a curriculum would be truly economic in that it would relate resource inputs and school processes to a broad range of post-school needs. This proposition will form a bench-mark for later analysis of performance and policy in which various curriculum proposals are examined for their economic value. Some of these proposals envisage considerable change, to which the teaching force must adapt while itself altering sharply in size, expectations and character.

The size and character of the teaching force

Despite the difficulties in precisely evaluating the effects of teachers on pupil learning there is, within education, a confident judgement that their contribution is very important. Even if this judgement is correct, it is unlikely that all teachers are equally effective agents of learning, so their changing quantitative and qualitative characteristics need to be examined and some attempt made to evaluate their effect on educational outcomes. The concept of human capital formation, introduced in Chapter 3, is a useful means of analysing these changes. Its view of people, as individuals who acquire and develop some of their skills by systematic investment (capital formation) in education, assists a coherent analysis of the internal training needs of the teaching force and analysis of the consequences of altering the skill composition and distribution of teachers. Drake (1973) comments that it:

> . . . offers a concept which provides a unifying principle for the investigation of many aspects of teacher education, off-the-job training and on-the-job training, teaching and learning, formal and informal, initial and in-service.

The logic of economic analysis then leads naturally to an evaluation of the consequences for educational outcomes (or quality) of the declining numbers and changing characteristics of the teaching force. Thus, following a descriptive section on changing size, it is within this human capital framework that this section analyses the three principal changes which we can expect among teachers in the coming decade: age and length of service, graduate composition and subject range.

Changing size

The total number of teachers employed by LEAs in England and Wales in January 1983 was 443 000 (HM Treasury 1984), a figure which, according to the same expenditure plans, is expected to fall to 414 000 by January 1987. By 1991, drawing upon DES (1983b) and

Welsh Office data, the expected number of teachers is expected to fall to 384 000. However, the 1987 and 1991 figures are estimates and it must be emphasised that the number of teachers in employment is particularly sensitive to alterations in government policy about staffing standards and a government's judgement about the perceived capacity of the economy to sustain any particular level of spending on education, as well as the levels of pay settlements for teachers. This difference between plans and outcomes is significant, because the evidence of recent expenditure plans is for improvement-by-drift in the level of PTR and the final numbers of teachers employed. Illustratively, when the expenditure *plan* for 1984 was first published in 1981 (HM Treasury 1981) it was expected that 386 000 teachers would be employed *in England* and the PTR would be 18.8. The *revised* plan for 1984, published in 1982 (HM Treasury 1982), showed a target of 390 000 teachers, which improved to 400 000 in the following year's revision (HM Treasury 1983). By the actual year, 408 000 teachers was the target for England (HM Treasury 1984) with a PTR of 18.0, an improvement-by-drift on teachers of 5.7 per cent over 1981 plans and 4.3 per cent on PTR.

These figures mask wide regional variations which are very important for a teaching force which is employed locally. Gordon (1982) illustrates this by showing that,

> . . . the anticipated fall in primary school population from 1976 to 1986 in the English northern metropolitan countries is 37 % (secondary — 22 %) while the figure for East Anglia is half of that at 18 % (secondary — 4 %).

This variation will mean that some LEAs will be more able than others to manage contraction with minimal redeployment and without redundancies.

The figures also need to be analysed by sector, although this means using the older ACSET (1981) data. It suggests that while the secondary sector may need to lose 60 000 teachers in the decade up to 1991, the primary sector's net drop will be around 10 000 teachers.

Age and length of service

The average age, length of service and cost of teachers will continue to rise as those recruited in the expansionary 1960s and 1970s progress along a service-related incremental scale. The change in the age structure will be considerable. Table 5.2 summarises the already substantial change in the age distribution up to 1980, as the recruits from the years of expansion grew older and, following the contraction of teacher training, were not followed by comparable numbers. Table 5.3 shows the effect of contraction in more detail: in 1971, 24.3 per cent of teachers were under 25, compared with only 8.2 per cent a decade later. Moreover, this contraction of the youngest age group of teachers is not yet complete, as is shown by the data on initial training in Table 3.2. The effect of this, and the higher wastage rate of teachers under 30, is that by the middle and late 1980s the numbers of under-30s in teaching will be much lower than the 28.6 per cent shown for 1980 in Table 5.2, DES (1983b) projections indicating less than 15 per cent from 1988 to 1991. And, while this is happening at one end of the age structure, the numbers of teachers over 55 will be falling because it is the members of this 'senior' age category, through a mixture of financial inducement and moral pressure, who are being encouraged into early retirement as a means of reducing teacher numbers without resorting to large scale redundancy. The

Table 5.2 *Full-time teachers in maintained nursery, primary and secondary schools (England and Wales) on 31 March (all figures in percentages): Age distribution in 'young, middle and senior' intervals.*

| | 1971 | 1975 | | | 1980 | | |
	All schools	Nursery and primary	Secondary	All schools	Nursery and primary	Secondary	All schools
Under 30	40.6	35.3	40.8	38.4	24.1	32.2	28.6
30–54	48.3	54.1	50.4	52.3	65.6	60.4	62.7
55 and over	11.1	10.6	8.8	9.6	10.3	7.4	8.7

Table 5.3 *Full-time teachers in maintained nursery, primary and secondary schools (England and Wales) on 31 March (all figures in percentages): Age distribution in five-year intervals.*

| | 1971 | 1975 | | | 1980 | | |
	All schools	Nursery and primary	Secondary	All schools	Nursery and primary	Secondary	All schools
Under 25	24.3	16.0	16.2	16.4	6.9	9.3	8.2
25–29	16.3	19.3	24.6	22.0	17.2	22.9	20.4
30–34	9.4	9.8	12.9	11.4	14.4	18.7	16.8
35–39	10.8	11.2	11.6	11.4	12.3	12.7	12.5
40–44	11.4	13.0	10.1	11.4	13.5	11.8	12.5
45–49	9.0	11.3	8.8	10.0	14.1	9.7	11.6
50–54	7.7	9.0	7.2	8.1	11.2	7.7	9.3
55–59	8.0	7.0	5.8	6.3	7.8	5.5	6.5
60–64	2.8	3.4	2.8	3.1	2.4	1.8	2.1
65 and over	0.3	0.2	0.2	0.2	0.1	0.1	0.1

Sources DES (1973, 1977, 1982a)

effect is to produce an age profile of teachers in primary and secondary schools which has a large middle-aged spread with disproportionately thin cohorts of younger and older teachers, with the secondary sector's profile becoming more sharply skewed because the primary sector will take a proportionately larger number of young teachers to meet the roll expansion beginning in 1986.

This more experienced, and therefore more expensive, teaching force of the next decade and more has not come about because policy-makers have acted as though they believed experience to be desirable but because the main emphasis in managing the numbers has been controlling access to initial training. But, in addition to its extra cost, does this experience count in any other way? Does a school staffed with teachers of 10 to 15 years' experience contribute more to effective learning by its pupils than a school staffed with teachers of 1 to 5 years' experience? It is a proposition which seems reasonable in human capital terms because it recognises that successful teaching requires the acquisition and development of a complex set of skills only some of which are learned formally during initial training, leaving others to be learned through a mixture of post-initial experiences. Empirical verification of the value of teacher experience is, however, difficult to demonstrate, and Hanushek's (1981) review of 104 North American studies which considered the effects of teacher experience on pupil achievement offers only modest encouragement. The survey found that 30 studies showed a statistically significant positive relationship between experience and pupil achievement, six studies showed a statistically significant inverse relationship and 68 showed no significant relationship.

This modest evidence of the apparent significance of teaching experience for improved pupil outcomes seems to offer some initial grounds for confidence as the compulsory sector contracts. But this should be a tempered optimism, partly because the empirical evidence is not all one way and possibly because the relationship between teacher experience and pupil learning may not always be positive. Does the initially trained teacher keep improving, though at a diminishing rate, or do returns become constant after a period of increasing returns with experience? Or, do returns eventually become negative as the human capital becomes obsolescent? If the first case of steady improvement is more generally true then it means that policies of early retirement entail offering some of the best teachers financial inducements to leave the job. Alternatively, if returns eventually become constant or even negative it suggests a need for in-service training to update or refit the human capital for the changing environment within which it works. And the 1980s may bring quite rapid alteration to the working environment if the curriculum preferences of pupils and parents alter as existing levels of youth unemployment persist and new patterns of work, training and leisure emerge. We also know little of the training relationship between new and experienced teachers. It may be that new teachers bring fresh ideas and new methods which are learned informally by more experienced teachers who, because of their time-related higher levels of competence, use these new ideas more productively than their still inexperienced colleagues. If some of the updating of skills occurs in this informal way then the smaller number of newly trained entrants reduce the learning opportunities of experienced teachers, which will have to be supplemented by more formal provision. The implications for in-service provision of the changing age/experience profile will be examined in the penultimate policy-related section of this chapter.

Graduate composition

There is no persuasive evidence which links the level of teacher qualifications to learner outcomes but, nevertheless, the altering graduate composition of the teaching force, because of its implications for teacher mobility, may be of significance if it leads to a filtering out of the profession those whose loss would be regretted. But first, let us consider the altering qualification profile of teachers as a group. The proportion of graduates in teaching increased from just over one fifth in 1971 to over one third in 1980. However, the inflow into teaching shows an even greater shift: while in 1970–71 less than a quarter were graduates, by 1979–80 the proportion was greater than half (DES 1982a). Perhaps more significantly, the proportion of initial training places provided for the one-year graduate training programme has increased at the expense of the BEd. (and the Certificate, before it ceased taking new entrants in 1983). While in 1970 only 21.5 per cent of admissions to initial training were taken by the PGCE and other one-year courses, by 1980 this had increased to 63.3 per cent (DES 1982a). And the planned intakes for 1983 to 1985 (Hansard 1982) show that the PGCE continues to take over half the places (see also Table 3.3). This growth in the proportion of young entrants to teaching who do not *only* have education-specific qualifications has implications for mobility because as Drake (1978) noted, they have not entered ' . . . an unbreakable servitude to teaching'. For these and for potential entrants to initial training courses one of the major problems ' . . . of contraction is to avoid the image of contracting opportunities in teaching, with a consequent reduction in the quality of new teachers' (Drake 1978). It is *not* being suggested here that PGCE-trained graduates make the best teachers but that this pattern of qualification enhances their mobility and, the greater the proportion of this group among all teachers, the higher is the potential mobility of teachers and the more sensitive the teaching force is to alterations in the relative position of teachers in the labour market. What *is* being suggested is that if effective teachers are those who also possess marketable skills elsewhere, the absence of adequate promotion opportunities in teaching may lead to their loss from teaching. This not only has an immediate effect on quality but also may have serious long-term consequences for schools because it is from recruits to teaching in the 1980s that the senior post-holders at the turn of the century will come. There is scope for using the Burnham process to counter these changes and they will also be examined in the penultimate policy-related section of this paper.

Subject range

The long-running failure of policies to secure a teaching force with a subject composition suitable for the curriculum preferences of schools is examined in Chapter 3. It should be noted that recent surveys by the DES (1983c) appear to show some improvements. Vacancies of mathematics posts in secondary schools in England and Wales fell from 466 in 1979 to 282 in 1983 and in physical sciences vacancies in England fell from 298 in 1981 to 187 in 1983. However, it must still be the case that much teaching continues to be done by teachers without significant qualifications in the subject. Moreover, there are reasons for believing that this will continue, partly because it is in this sector of the graduate employment market that job opportunities are most buoyant. In addition, it is quite likely that continuing pressures on public sector pay levels may cause the relative earnings of teachers to deteriorate by comparison with comparable occupations, though some feasible changes to the pay structure may give greater scope for paying more to teachers in shortage subject areas. Finally, it may be that pressures to provide more space for education in the use of computers or responses to MSC-inspired 'technology' curriculums may increase the relative demand for teachers in these chronic shortage areas. Thus a paradox of the 1980s will be a surplus of teachers for many areas of the curriculum while the shortage in some subjects may worsen, unless career opportunities for this group continue to be attractive. It is not only in subject shortage areas where problems occur. The major study of the management of falling rolls by Walsh et al (1984) indicates an increase in teachers teaching outside their specialist subjects. Their findings indicate a relationship between the level of mismatch and schools with higher levels of roll fall. One reason given for this is that taking on a new subject may be a means of avoiding redeployment, another example of unplanned outcomes from policies designed to moderate the impact of falling rolls on teachers.

The same study also notes the decline in subject specialists in primary schools, particularly in music and remedial work. In the case of the latter, the explanation appears to lie in the reduction of part-time teaching opportunities.

What implications this analysis of the changing character of the teaching force has for policy will be examined later in the chapter.

Ancillary and clerical staff

The expressed concern for maintaining teacher numbers as high as resources will permit has had its effect on LEAs. They have used their right to have different spending priorities from central government and have, for example, ' . . . an estimated 7000 extra teachers in post in 1981–82 compared with the planned number.' (HM Treasury 1982). This emphasis continues. Walsh et al (1984) draw on the evidence of the Expenditure Steering Group on Education (set up by the Consultative Council on Local Government Finance to contribute information to the public expenditure planning process) to comment that, 'There was a general tendency in LEAs to protect levels of teacher employment at the expense of non-teaching expenditure'. Less vocal is the concern to maintain numbers or ratios of secretarial, clerical and ancillary staff working in schools. However, such evidence as there is suggests little change in the proportion of total spending taken up by educational support and administrative staff. In secondary schools, for example, CIPFA statistics show 4.21 per cent of the total unit cost devoted to this item in 1978–79 (CIPFA 1980) while estimated expenditure on the item for 1983–84 was 4.25 per cent (CIPFA 1983). Whether this is an adequate proportion of the budget is another question. It is all too likely that teachers will continue to be paid to spend time on certain non-teaching tasks which could be done more cheaply and probably more efficiently by others. In what kind of environment and with what level of physical resources teaching will take place is considered next.

The buildings

School buildings, their maintenance and regular upkeep are expensive — absorbing about one sixth of all school running costs. Fowler (1979) notes that, of the quarter of the school budget committed to resources other than teachers' salaries some two thirds are on buildings and buildings-related resources. Simkins (1980) shows that since these types of costs are fixed, they do not fall proportionately with roll, so that only school closures could reduce this expenditure. Notwithstanding this, local authorities have been slow to take school places out of use, the plans published in 1982 (HM Treasury 1982) showing an assumption ' . . . that 470 000 temporary and permanent places will have been taken out of use between 1975 and 1983–84 (compared with 700 000 in Cmnd 8175) and 630 000 places by 1984–85'. Why local authorities have not conformed to these central government targets is an empirical question on which there is no direct evidence, though four factors may contribute to an explanation. Ultimately, a continuing process of taking school places out of use entails the closure of schools, a policy which is likely to generate opposition from teachers, because of the uncertainty and upheaval it visits upon them, and also from parents concerned about the continuity of their children's education, as well as other members of a community who might see a school as a focal point of community identity. But there is also a problem in defining space per pupil which, as the following examples illustrate, is by no means an unambiguous concept. Thus, allowing timetablers the capacity to place all science work in laboratories, or allowing all subjects to be taught in specialist rooms, or catering for half-year groups to be taught together on occasion, may all require more space per pupil than official criteria may allow. These factors assist us in recognising the breadth of the *opportunity costs* of school closures. While a closure decision might allow other educational activities to be supported from the budgetary savings it does so at the cost of alternative opportunities in the closing school and the possible preferences of parent and community groups. It is also necessary to be cautious about the level of savings obtainable from closure. This is partly because possible savings depend on the characteristics of the buildings in question. Briault (1979) points out that there is no direct relationship between the age of a building and maintenance costs because the specifications of new buildings have led to high maintenance charges. Fowler (1979) notes the danger that authorities may buy off parental hostility by subsidising transport, and it is also possible to envisage authorities maintaining premises for community use. Other issues related to buildings and school size are examined in a later section on school processes.

Educational books and equipment

The second category of physical resources is expenditure on educational books and equipment, an area in which prospects must be poor. Often expenditure on these items is on a *per capita* basis so that the amount available changes in proportion to the school roll, a process which is good news only for the primary sector, and that only after 1986. However, for local authorities searching for expenditure reductions this area offers a soft target since it does not attract the same interests in its defence as teacher employment levels or school closures. This may explain why authorities have not entirely reinstated the severe cuts made here in 1978–79 when only 1.28 per cent of the budget of secondary schools was allocated to educational books and equipment (CIPFA 1980). Whether this is a matter which should concern us depends on the importance we attach to materials for learning. Certainly, in proportion to spending on teachers, schools do not spend significantly on books and educational materials. Cummings's (1971) study analysed the proportion of classroom expenditure devoted to teacher costs and books and materials costs; he found that 95 per cent of expenditure was on the teacher, leaving only 5 per cent for educational books and equipment. The CIPFA (1975) estimates show a comparable figure, but the estimates for 1983–84 (CIPFA 1983) shows only 3.7 per cent allocated to this item. This relative concentration on teaching costs is unlikely to lessen as the teaching force becomes older and therefore more expensive and authorities continue to search for ways of controlling education spending.

SCHOOL PROCESSES

That school processes can generate desired outcomes is not only a belief widely held within the teaching force but is also one that is reinforced by the judgement of practice viewed by HMI in 'Ten Good Schools' (DES 1976) and by the type of empirical investigation reported by Rutter et al (1979). However, if we accept that school processes are not neutral and some are consistently beneficial, conclusive empirical verification of this is difficult to demonstrate. Here it is intended to identify those changes in school process which, in the opinion of this writer, are most significantly affected by changing rolls. These are: the age structure of institutions, school size, and the curriculum, including the class size in which it is offered.

The age structure of the schools

While Dean and Choppin (1977) note that one of the consequences of falling secondary rolls and the present economic climate is that an institutional break at 16 ' . . . represents a rationalization of resources which will increasingly recommend itself,' it would be a mistake to attribute pressures for a break solely to these factors. It is necessary to recognise that some of the growth in the number of sixth-form and tertiary colleges from 13 in 1970 to 117 by 1980 is because many believed that a separate institution better provides for the needs of the 16–19 age group. Because the colleges have more students they are better able to provide a wider range of courses than most sixth forms. Statistics drawn from the MacFarlane Report (1980) show that 65 per cent of sixth forms had 100 or fewer students, 50 per cent had 75 or fewer students, 35 per cent had no more than 50 students and 16 per cent no more than ten students. This relatively large proportion of small sixth forms is a consequence of comprehensive organisation because they are figures collected *before* falling rolls affected the 16–19 age range. However, their implication for some form of amalgamation is clear. The figure of 140 students is particularly important because, according to the DES (*TES* 1977), without that number teaching groups would be an uneconomic size, utilising resources inefficiently. However, this assumption of a correlation between efficiency and size of teaching group has only superficial plausibility. The size of a teaching group is not an indicator of efficiency. It is a process variable and not an educational performance measure. The circumstances of uncertainty in relation to the efficiency of alternative forms of provision are summed up by the MacFarlane Report (1980) which saw no ' . . . proven connection of universal validity between educational effectiveness and the size of the 16–19 age group in the individual institution.' Whether the 11–16 schools which are a corollary to an institutional break at 16 will increase the efficiency of the educational system is as speculative as the effect of the change on the 16–19 age group. While the 11–16 age range might no longer suffer from an in-school transfer of resources to the sixth form, the schools may find it difficult to attract sufficient numbers of staff of suitable quality in shortage areas such as maths and science. Other factors affecting input and process variables could be adduced in a debate about the relative merits for 11–16-year-olds of being in a school with a sixth form but the acid test of *output* effect is not known.

A discussion of the structural effects of changing rolls must not overlook its impact on middle schools because some of the re-organisation schemes submitted to the DES have changed three-tier structures of first, middle and high schools to a three-tier primary, 11–16 secondary and separate post-16 provision. The underlying decision criterion threatening middle schools is comparable to the issue of the range of curriculum affecting small sixth forms. The unit costs of maintaining the same range of subjects increases as school rolls fall and, in the present economic context, this may alter structural preferences. If the sixth forms in the high schools of the middle-school system are also small then the cost pressures are reinforced. Interviews reported by Walsh et al (1984) support these judgements. One county officer commented that, 'It's the middle schools that suffer most from falling rolls,' and an officer from another county comments that, 'The pressure to unscramble the middle schools is — in part — to sustain unviable high schools.' Walsh et al then note the apparent contradiction between these statements and the reality of an overall increase in the numbers of middle schools between 1977–78 and 1980–81. However, later statistics calculated by this writer from DES data (1984b) reveal the lag between the judgements on what needs to be done and the outcomes of policy decisions. January 1983 shows the first fall in the numbers of middle schools to 1405, from 1413 in January 1982. There is also a fractional drop in the percentage of all pupils attending middle schools, from an all-time high of 5.79 per cent in January 1982 to 5.75 per cent in January 1983. On this issue, as with others, it is probably reasonable to conjecture that considerations of cost minimisation have been more powerful factors than judgements of educational efficiency. Comparable considerations of cost arise when we consider how school size is affected by changing rolls.

School size

In 1978 some three quarters of 11–18 comprehensive schools had 800 pupils or more. According to the then Senior Chief HMI, within the decade from 1977, the most common size of comprehensive school will be from 450 to 700 pupils. In the same discussion Fiske (1979) usefully distinguishes rural areas where ' . . . the choice will often be between acceptance of that size or less and closure of the secondary school for that community . . . ' from urban areas, where there will be ' . . . a gradual shrinking over a period of some five years or more from around the current average of 900–1000 pupils towards . . . 600–700 pupils.' The choices available in using this extra space having been summarised by Gordon (1982) as, ' . . . (i) alternative use in public education, (ii) use by private education, (iii) non-educational public sector use, (iv) non-educational private sector use . . . [and] a fifth option, particularly given the expectation of increased future numbers in schools, might well be to "moth-ball" . . . ' . The proposed private sector use realises property and/or site values if buyers can be found, while the third choice fits with the often desirable objectives of ending split-site arrangements and taking out of educational use old, temporary or otherwise unsuitable buildings. Included in the first choice is the availability of more space which has the advantage, according to Briault and Smith (1980a), of providing more rooms for small groups, more play space per pupil and which means fewer pupils moving through corridors, examples which illustrate Fiske's (1979) observation, ' . . . that there is nothing magic about even the best of existing standards . . . ' . Selecting policies from Gordon's five categories of choice has cost implications. Fowler (1979), using highly aggregated statistics on non-teaching costs per child in the decade from 1966–67, shows a rise, in real terms, of 40 per cent in these costs for primary and 15 per cent in secondary. He suggests that ' . . . some of the rise in the primary sector was a consequence of falling numbers in primary schools over the last four years . . . ' and concludes ' . . . that avoiding school closures merely for the sake of avoiding them must lead to an increase in *unit costs*[3] per pupil.'

However, even if controlling local authority costs was the sole consideration, unit cost data are an inadequate basis for decisions on closure. Simkins (1980) clarifies the relevant cost concepts:

> Unit cost data, by definition, represent the *average* cost of provision in a particular situation. However, in costing alternative courses of action it is essential to identify those costs, and only those costs, which are affected by the decision itself. The relevant concept here is normally *marginal* cost . . . It is more likely that the marginal cost of making alternative provision for children whose school is to be closed will be lower than the average cost of provision in the schools which are closing. How much lower depends on the alternative being proposed . . .

Calculating these marginal costs entails a case-by-case approach because they will change with the alternatives being considered, though the degree of difference between cases will depend upon the proportion of school expenditure tied directly to pupil numbers, the higher this proportion the smaller the savings obtained from altering the pattern of provision.

These writers all recognise that evaluating the economics of closure requires also a consideration of the outcome effects of a decision. This must begin by examining the educational significance of school size. A review article by Smith (1980) considers the dubious evidence on which many judgements about school size are made, in that many are either input–input studies or, rather better, examine the effect of size on other school processes. The absence of conclusive judgements one way or the other does beg the question whether size is relevant because, if it is not, ' . . . there will be few grounds on which to resist a policy of large schools to reduce per pupil expenditure . . . [provided] . . . that all costs are considered: social, private and non-monetary'.

A principal explanation for higher per pupil expenditures in small schools is higher spending on staffing and the reason for this, according to the DES (1978), is to maintain a more generous pupil–teacher ratio in order to sustain a range of activities comparable with larger schools. Gordon (1982) stresses the linkage, ' . . . because the deployment of teachers is greatly affected by the size and number of schools, building policies also have implications for the school curriculum and manpower'. It is an issue which affects the primary and secondary sector and moves the analysis towards the curriculum implications of changing rolls.

The curriculum and class size

It is conventional practice to show, as above, that the staffing costs of comparable curriculums are greater the smaller the school. Rather overlooked is that this is true *only* if we are content to compare the range of subjects on offer and ignore the classroom context in which they are transmitted. However, to set aside this classroom context is to ignore factors which illuminate the superficiality of ostensibly comparable curriculums. Crucially, a comparable range of subjects in a smaller school is provided by extra staffing, which makes their average class sizes smaller and gives greater teacher access per pupil. It is suggested, then, that the curriculum as a process is more appropriately measured in ways which take account *also* of teacher resources per pupil. In this respect, the much-criticised PTR formula has greater merit, in that it does provide a measure of teacher resources committed to a school, than curriculum-led staffing formulae which are ostensibly designed to protect the range of subjects. These staffing formulae are, of course, *models* of reality and necessarily select from and simplify reality, and these alternatives select different aspects to emphasise. In particular, the PTR measures only teacher inputs, and only a crude quantification of that variable, and makes no judgement about the deployment of that resource in the curriculum process. By contrast, curriculum formulae measure a selected part of the curriculum process and inevitably make a judgement about which parts of the process to protect, also shifting the choice more towards the LEA and away from the school. The use of curriculum formulae as a way of staffing schools is a developing practice. However, Walsh et al (1984) note that 82 LEAs still use PTR as the basis of their staffing allocations.

Whichever model is selected as the basis for staffing, what is clear is that schools will *continue* to face choices over the deployment of their teacher resources. As Briault (1979) points out, ' . . . as schools shrink value judgements will have to be made in the curricular field about which subjects are sufficiently important to enjoy such protection as can be afforded and about the minimum size of option groups which can be sustained . . . '. A case study of a science department by ASE (1981) suggests choices which include: making science part of the core curriculum by having a science block in the options; allowing group sizes in years one to three to reach thirty periodically, mainly to sustain the range of middle-school and sixth-form options while their group size falls; as roll decline bites harder fifth and sixth form 'O' groups could be mixed to keep 'O' and 'C' separate. Some linkage of upper- and lower-sixth timetables might be introduced to allow whole sixth teaching in some non-science subjects and this pairing makes the options more rigid and requires the availability of two suitably qualified staff in each of the science subjects, a total of six out of the seven specialist staff. Some of these choices show how access to teacher resources is re-allocated as the roll falls, as pupils in years one to three lose in relation to the gains made with the smaller groups in the middle and sixth forms. The dominant factor is an acceptance of the normative judgement that a more extensive curriculum is desirable and to be preferred, at the margin, to maintaining lower school class sizes. And, undoubtedly, because of this preference, many class sizes will increase as secondary rolls fall even if PTR were only to remain constant but, it should be emphasised, this is because elsewhere in a school classes will be protected even as their numbers fall. This does not necessarily mean, as Clarke (1981) suggests, that 'It is inevitable that generally, standards will have to fall when class sizes rise or the level of provision of equipment and apparatus falls'. In fact the research message on the relationship between class size and student performance is that, as Cullen (1979) notes, ' . . . whatever other arguments there may be for reducing pupil/teacher ratios, no argument can safely be based on the existing empirical research on class sizes'. Some of the reasons which Kay (1980) cites for this lie with the complexity of a problem where pupil performance is not only affected by a wide range of factors outside the classroom, but performance itself is difficult to measure and, moreover, even the idea of a class is complex because a pupil's class may substantially vary in size over eleven years of schooling. What weight should be attached to the effect of changing rolls on curriculum choice and class size is but one further difficulty in evaluating the outcome effects of the change.

A further dimension is given to this problem by the wide regional variations in staffing standards, with its consequences for curriculum choice and class size. Revealing 'unpublished' DES statistics, The *Guardian* (1984) shows that despite the 'best ever' national PTR,

> . . . five LEAs have deteriorated to pre-1979 staffing levels across all three sectors of nursery, primary and secondary schooling. Thirteen have done so across two sectors, and a further 39 across one sector.

Moreover, variation also exists within LEAs. The study by Hough (1981) made comparisons of homogenous sub-groups of schools within each Authority and showed that in a number of cases twice or three times as much per pupil is spent at one school as at another. What policies are appropriate to respond to these circumstances is considered, with others, in the next section.[4]

PERFORMANCE AND POLICY

Up to this point the aim has been to identify the principal changes to input and process variables arising from changing rolls and their economic context and to seek to clarify the effects of each of these changes, all other things being equal, on educational outcomes. It is now appropriate to consider how important variables can be altered in order to attain specified educational ends. At the heart of this part of the analysis are pupil needs and the propositions advanced earlier that schools must adjust to the consequences for their pupils of the speed and nature of technological change; that schools in making effective provision must adapt to alterations in the nature and pattern of paid work, non-paid work, post-school education and leisure. Further, that schools may have also to accommodate demands by parents and pupils for a more overtly instrumental curriculum package. In summary, the bench-mark of the economics of changing rolls is the extent to which all school resources and processes can be better managed to attain these multiple, but not always harmonious, ends. To assist the analysis, two curriculums will be used as models. One of these is the more vocationally-oriented curriculum which may emerge as the influence on schools of the MSC's Technical and Vocational Educational Initiative

(TVEI) grows. The second model is the rather more general, and certainly non-vocational, curriculum advanced by the Hargreaves Committee for the ILEA (1984). It might appropriately be described as a comprehensive contemporary curriculum. While these will make different demands on teachers, they both appear to require substantial change in curriculum content and approaches to teaching. This similarity should be borne in mind in the discussion on training and career structure which follows; the differences between the models will inform the concluding discussion of the chapter.

In examining the relationship between school resources, processes and the changes in pupil needs, this section will be selective. From the previous two sections of the chapter a number of input and process variables will be selected and their implications for changing pupil needs will be examined; it will go on to consider appropriate policies by which these variables can better attain desired pupil needs. This will leave other variables unexamined and it is suggested that the reader may find it a useful exercise to examine the implications of these and to consider suitable policies for changing them and their consequences.

Consider first the changing age profile of teachers. Two aspects of this change, increasing average age and cutbacks in initial training are interrelated and of particular importance. As the average length of service of teachers increases, the question of the obsolescence of their initial training and skills becomes more acute. If teachers are expected to produce new curriculums to meet the changing needs of their pupils, some form of in-service training (INSET) would seem to be essential. However, one informal type of INSET, the process by which experienced teachers acquire fresh ideas and new methods from new teachers, is cut sharply by reductions in initial training. This still leaves a range of INSET, which can be classified according to degree of full-time commitment and level of formality.

The time commitment ranges from full-time secondment to staffroom discussions between colleagues during non-teaching periods, while the level of formality ranges from award-bearing courses to advice given by a colleague. However, information on the extent of even the most formal provision is limited and there is no useful information on the extent of the least formal. We do know the number of full-time secondments from the maintained sector, which was 1797 (0.42 per cent of the teaching force) in 1982, compared with 1588 (0.36 per cent) in 1979 (DES 1982a), although we do not know how many teachers take leave of absence to fund themselves privately. We also know the numbers attending full-time courses of four to fourteen days duration organised by the DES, which was 5975 in 1978–79 (DES 1981). We have very little information on the scale of provision of courses, and their take-up, as offered by LEAs or training institutions, let alone provision by subject and interest associations.

Apart from suggesting a need for more information to be collected on INSET, does this data suggest anything else? The information on secondments certainly offers a benchmark; if, for example, there was a judgement that teachers should receive at least one year of secondment if their careers might be expected to extend twenty years, it would be necessary not only to raise secondments to more than three times existing levels but also to concentrate on those with more than twenty years' service.[5] Of course, it may be that there is a sufficiency of part-time INSET to maintain teacher quality, though even here there is a subjective impression of cut-backs as schools become more restrictive in their policies for releasing staff to attend courses. The reason is a noble one. If, as rolls fall, schools wish to retain the same subject choices as earlier, this can be done by increasing the contact ratio but this, in turn, allows less non-teaching 'slack' in the school to cover the timetables of absent staff. However, a consequence of such policies may be to benefit existing pupils, while threatening the quality of provision to future year groups.

Another issue is the relationship between users and the training system. Consider an example concerned with retraining in a shortage subject. If teaching skills are subject-specific, courses need to include work on teaching methods as well as on the content of the subject. However, if teacher skills are largely transferable then only subject content needs attention and the course needed might vary in length and content according to the previous educational background of the teacher: thus biologists and chemists will have different needs if they wish to become teachers of physics. To what extent is the training system geared to these separate categories of need and to what extent is it offering diverse clients a uniform package? Moreover, to what extent are local authorities using their financial leverage (through control of secondment) to obtain suitably designed courses from the training institutions?

Given the scale of the curriculum changes faced by schools it would seem persuasive to devote more teacher time to INSET. This means, for example, that out of the total stock of teachers referred to earlier relatively more should be involved in some form of INSET and, by definition, fewer should be in a classroom. The first policy proposal to emerge is that LEAs should protect their INSET budgets and schools should maintain contact ratios at a level which enables staff to be released for short courses. LEAs would also be advised to use their financial leverage to adapt courses to their needs. The activity of central government has been contradictory on INSET resources. In its 1983 Expenditure Plans (HM Treasury 1983) it earmarked £7 million for selected priority areas, such as the training of heads, mathematics teaching and prevocational work in schools. A year later (HM Treasury 1984) £11 million was made available for this INSET. However, its plans for altering the criteria for approving initial teacher training courses (DES 1984a), signalled in the earlier White Paper (DES 1983a), militates against the development of INSET. The consequence of these plans will be to require the training institutions, and teachers in schools (who will be more involved in the student selection process), to spend more time on initial training work. Since no further resources will be forthcoming (DES 1984a) this will presumably be found from, among other things, time currently spent on INSET. Given the present nature of the teaching force and its expected changes, can this be a sensible allocation of resources?[6]

Another issue with implications for the characteristics of the teaching force is the salary structure, which has implications for its subject composition, its distribution between different schools and regions, and managerial structures within schools. It was argued in Chapter 3 that salary structures should be flexible, enabling LEAs and schools to adjust the salaries of teachers qualified in shortage subjects or teachers in selected schools (e.g. 'Social Priority Schools') in a way which recognises and adapts to the existence of the labour market for teachers. However, the structural rigidity of proposals emerging from the Burnham structure working party (*Education* 1984) fail to take account of this complex and segmented labour market. The emphasis of these proposals is on the creation of a 'professional grade', along which all teachers will progress to the top of what will be the equivalent of the existing scale 3 or 4, although there can be no guarantee that the real value of this relatively expensive change will be maintained in future salary reviews. Above this grade will be a small number (up to nine in the largest schools) of 'third-tier' posts and up to four 'assistant heads'. These proposals end the already limited flexibility of LEAs and head teachers to adapt to the realities of the labour market by paying teachers of shortage subjects relatively higher salaries. However, it should be emphasised that treating all teachers as though they are the same does not make them such or alter their differential ability to respond to more attractive opportunities in other occupations. Suggestions that the 'Social Priority Allowance' may be abolished is a further naive response to the surplus of teachers, because it rejects the possibility of using sensibly conceived salary differentials to improve the quality characteristics of staff in relatively unpopular schools (see Chapter 3). Set against these major weaknesses is the principal benefit and this is considered below.

These proposals reduce the disparity in promotion opportunities between the primary and secondary sector, for which there seemed no educational and equitable case. They also assist 11–16 schools as against 11–18 schools and sixth-form colleges. Earlier discussion notes that the output effects of a break at 16 are not known, although it does draw attention to the problems 11–16 schools may have in attracting sufficient numbers of suitably qualified staff in areas such as maths and science. The likely reduction in the number of 'promotion' opportunities with the introduction of the 'professional grade' reduces the disadvantage of 11–16 schools against those schools with 16–18 year olds. However, this change could have been introduced by altering the age-weighted unit total system (UTS) in favour of those who are 16 years and below[7] and would, thereby, have kept the greater managerial flexibility of the existing system of scale posts, examined below.

The proposals outlined here are also much more prescriptive than hitherto because, with regard to posts of extra responsibility, they leave heads with much less flexibility for devising management structures than under the existing scheme. Since schools vary in their needs, and the managerial solutions to those needs also differ, it seems inappropriate to sponsor a change which hinders the range of responses to these differing circumstances.

In sum these Burnham working party proposals are good in that they weaken inappropriate inequalities between the primary and secondary sector but, by treating equally all bar a few promoted teachers within each sector, they are likely to worsen existing inequalities in the provision of learning opportunities for pupils, and it is meeting their needs which should be the operating principle is guiding salary and other policies.[8]

Recognising the primacy of pupils needs, does this offer any guidance in policies towards buildings? Earlier it was noted and explained why space per pupil is not an unambiguous concept. Any of the curriculum variants proposed would seem to require more space per pupil, whether for machinery, information technology laboratories or drama and art studios. It would seem that the savings obtainable from closure of schools would not only have to be offset against extra provision for transferring pupils, but would also have to be increased to provide more space per pupil to provide for what are seen as the necessary curriculums of the 1980s.

Curriculum diversity emerges as an important dimension in discussions of school size although, as noted earlier, to use range of subjects as a satisfactory basis for comparing curriculums, ignoring even average class size, is to use a very restricted measuring device. Nevertheless, if the debate on school size offers us no conclusive evidence on the appropriate size of a school, the range of subjects available must inevitably be regarded as a persuasive decision rule. Differences betwen our two curriculum models are also relevant to this issue of diversity and range of subjects. Where the TVEI model seems to maintain a separation of the year groups, the Hargreaves proposals (ILEA 1984) suggest block timetabling and mixing fourth and fifth years, with pupils following a two-year modular course, where possible in mixed-ability groups; 62.5 per cent of their time would be in a compulsory curriculum. These proposals may enable smaller schools to be retained.

Some of these policies require substantial extra resources or a redistribution of more limited resources. In such circumstances who is to decide between competing wants? It is this question of choice which the last section briefly considers, together with some comments on an economic curriculum.

CONCLUSION

The previous section on 'Performance and Policy' was constructed on the premise that the bench-mark of the economics of changing rolls was the effectiveness of alternative curriculums in meeting pupil needs. There is considerable danger here for anyone concerned with identifying outputs, because the content of the curriculum to be offered is no more than a process variable. Only after pupils have engaged any curriculum do we begin to convert input and process variables into curriculum outputs. This is a critical event, not least because it is the stage at which pupils exercise choice. Learner choice is crucial in determining curriculum outcomes and these choices can include rejection (truancy), apathy (lack of attention in class), ineffective commitment (failure to comprehend) and effective commitment (successful completion of teacher-selected objectives).

The significance of learner choice for attaining desirable curriculum outcomes causes this writer to pose questions on the desirability of widening the choices of learners (and their parents), so that they are more involved in selecting what to learn and also where, when and how to do that learning (see Thomas 1983). This compares with most existing provision which leaves pupils only with the choice of attempting to learn what is being offered. This view assumes that there is no one curriculum which meets the needs of all pupils; rather that needs of individuals differ with regard to content, methods, time and place. Meeting those needs is likely to require more diversity from schools and more innovation from teachers. It may even require a re-appraisal of the length and nature of compulsory education, an issue which is not even on the education agenda. What is on the agenda, however, is a debate on the desirability of the school curriculum having a greater vocational orientation. My own view on this debate was signalled in an earlier section on the characteristics of an economic curriculum, where the importance of education for non-work time was mentioned. The dangers of a vocational curriculum are highlighted by Blaug's (1983) comments on 16–19 provision:

> There is, surely, a world of differences between creating jobs for which labour can be trained when it is recruited . . . and training people via special programmes for jobs which do not exist and may never exist.

What is needed is a curriculum which assists people to cope with a future which, while unknown, is expected to be very different from the present, '. . . and in this sense, there is a real economic merit in general, academic education as a hedge against technical dynamism' (Blaug 1983).

In summarising the economics of compulsory education it is worthwhile highlighting the main policy developments in relation to the major resources in the system, teachers and pupils. The emphasis for teachers needs to be on more INSET and a more flexible salary structure, enabling the use of differentials as appropriate. In practice, the policy of central government on INSET is contradictory, earmarking resources to fund selected secondment on the one hand, while forcing LEAs and the training institutions to direct more of their resources to initial training. On salary policy, where there are moves away from differentials and flexibility, the opportunities to respond to labour market differences will be fewer. For pupils and their curriculum the prospects are less clear. To the extent that parts of central government favour a more vocational curriculum (and use the MSC as its vehicle), it is supporting an expensive model for the curriculum which does not even have the merit of being economic. This seems an almost perverse stance for a government so concerned for value for money when there are educationists who, in advocating more comprehensive curriculum models, are supporting less costly proposals which are far more economic.

NOTES

1. Details of the subsequent fall in the number of births are given in note 2, Chapter 3. Births in the first four months of 1984 emphasise the unpredictability of population forecasts, showing a slight decline (203 232) against the same period in 1983 (206 380), (OPCS 1983 and 1984).
2. Those figures from ACSET (1981) have been retained because they show pupil projections for England *and* Wales. The more recent principal projection by the DES (1983b) is only for England and shows a downward adjustment from the ACSET figures and the earlier *Reports on Education* 97 (DES 1982c). The explanation for this lies in lower than expected number of births (see note 1) and more caution about the future fertility rate (see text, below).
3. My italics.
4. A theme of which we are likely to hear more concerns 'performance indicators'. CIPFA (1984) have produced a consultative document in this area and the Audit Commission have been exploring the non-teaching costs of secondary education with the purpose of producing audit-guides and value-for-money handbooks (see Audit Commission 1984; Esp 1984). Despite the use of terms like 'performance', 'efficiency' and 'value-for-money' these developments are essentially concerned with producing indicators of provision and do not relate resource use to the performance (outcomes) of the educational system.
5. This *rough estimate* is based on the existing levels of secondment from secondary schools (DES 1982b) and information on the length of service of staff in secondary schools (DES 1980).
6. More recently, the Government has decided to reduce still further LEA discretion on INSET. The proposals in *Better Schools* (DES 1985) envisage legislation, to increase central power to 'grant-aided in-service training' and extend central influence in determining priorities and provision.
7. The UTS determines the school score or its number of points and it is these points which determine the number of promoted posts. The last change was in 1974 when the scores were fixed at 2 for under-13 pupils, 2 for 13 and under-14, 3 for 14 and under-15, 4 for 15 and under-16, 6 for 16 and under-17, and 8 for 17 and over. For a fuller account see Saran (1982).
8. Discussions of revised salary structures have in practice become closely linked with questions of assessment and contract. The claims by teachers for 'properly rewarded' salary scales are being used by employers (LACSAB, 1984) as an opportunity to negotiate a more closely defined contract and some process of assessment at certain stages in a salary scale. The need for 'a more consistent and systematic approach' to teacher assessment was also strongly supported by the Secretary of State in his speech to the 1985 North of England Conference (Joseph, 1985). Given the outright rejection by the NUT of the LACSAB proposals, in November 1984, there is little doubt that disputes over these matters will be long and intractable.

REFERENCES

ACSET (1981) *The Future of the Teacher Training System: Initial Advice to the Secretaries of State*. ACSET 81/24, August: DES.

ASE (1981) Education (Co-ordinating) Committee of the Association for Science Education. 'The influence of the falling roll on one school science department'. *School Science Review*, **62**(220), 424–433.

Audit Commission (1984) Obtaining Better Value in Education: Aspects of Non-teaching Costs in Secondary Schools. London: HMSO.

Blaug, M. (1983) 'Where are we now in the Economics of Education?'. *Special Professorial Lecture*. London: University of London Institute of Education.

Briault, E. (1979) 'The Management of a Contracting Educational System'. *Educational Analysis*, **1**(2), 25–31.

Briault, E. and Smith, F. (1980a) *Falling Rolls in Secondary Schools, Part One*. Windsor: NFER.

Briault, E. and Smith, F. (1980b) *Falling Rolls in Secondary Schools, Part Two*. Windsor: NFER.

CIPFA (1975) *Education Statistics, 1975–76. Estimates*. London: CIPFA.

CIPFA (1980) *Education Statistics, 1978–79. Actuals*. London: CIPFA.

CIPFA (1983) *Education Statistics, 1983–84. Estimates*. London: CIPFA.

CIPFA (1984) *Performance Indicators in the Education Service. A Consultative Document*. London: CIPFA.

Clarke, Michael (1981) 'Class size and standards'. *Forum*, **23**(3), 64–5.

Cullen, B. D. (1979) 'Lessons from class-size research—an economist's perspective'. *Trends in Education* No. 4, Winter, 29–33.

Cumming, C. E. (1971) *Studies in Educational Costs*. Edinburgh: Scottish Academic Press.

Dean, J. and Choppin, B. (1977) *Educational Provision 16–19*. Windsor: NFER.

DES (1973) 'Teachers, England and Wales'. *Statistics of Education 1971*, **4**. London: HMSO.

DES (1976) *Ten Good Schools: A Secondary School Enquiry*. HMI Series: Matters for Discussion 1. London: HMSO.

DES (1977) 'Teachers, England and Wales'. *Statistics of Education 1975*, **4**. London: HMSO.

DES (1978) 'Falling Rolls 8: What the DES is planning on teacher numbers'. *Education*, **152**(23), 8 December, 549.

DES (1980) 'The Secondary School Staffing Survey'. *Statistical Bulletin 6/80*, July. London: DES.

DES (1981) 'Teachers, England and Wales'. *Statistics of Education 1979*, **4**. London: HMSO.

DES (1982a) *Statistics of Teachers in Service in England and Wales, 1980*. London: DES.

DES (1982b) 'Teachers in Service and Teacher Vacancies 1981–82'. *Statistical Bulletin 12/81*, November. London: DES.

DES (1982c) 'Pupils and school leavers: future numbers'. *DES Reports on Education No. 97*, May. London: DES.

DES (1983a) *Teaching Quality*. Cmnd. 8836, March. London: HMSO.

DES (1983b) 'Teacher Numbers—looking ahead to 1995'. *DES Reports on Education No. 98*, March. London: DES.

DES (1983c) 'Teachers in Service and Teacher Vacancies 1982–83'. *Statistical Bulletin 14/83*, September. London: DES.

DES (1984a) 'Initial Teaching Training: Approval of Courses'. *Circular No. 3/84*. London: DES.

DES (1984b) 'Statistics of Schools in England—January 1983'. *Statistical Bulletin 6/84*, April. London: DES.

DES (1985) *Better Schools*, Cmnd. 9469. London: HMSO.

Drake, K. (1973) 'The Economics of Teacher Education'. In Lomax, D. E. (ed) *The Education of Teachers in Britain*. London: John Wiley.

Drake, K. (1978) 'Falling Rolls 5: How Contraction will affect Quality'. *Education* **152**(7), 142–143.

Education (1984) 'The tape that holds the key to Burnham'. 11 May, **163**(19), 378: and 'Deputy Heads: new words for new ideas'. 8 June, **163**(23), 462.

Esp, D. (1984) 'The dirty dozen'. *Education* 25 May, **163**(21) 431.

Fiske, D. (1979) *Falling Numbers in Secondary Schools: Problems and Possibilities*. Sheffield Papers in Education Management (4): Sheffield City Polytechnic.

Fowler, G. (1979) 'Falling Rolls: Policy Options and their Resource Implications'. *Educational Analysis*, **1**(2), 33–45.

Gordon, A. (1982) 'Resource Redeployment in Education in the 1980s: problems and prospects'. *Educational Studies*, **8**(1), 55–77.

Guardian (1984) 'About the size of it'. 22 May, 13.

Hanushek, Eric A. (1981) 'Education Policy Research — An Industry Perspective'. *Economics of Education Review*, **1**(2), Spring, 193–223.

HM Treasury (1981) *The Government's Expenditure Plans, 1981–82 to 1983–84.* Cmnd. 8175, March. London: HMSO.

HM Treasury (1982) *The Government's Expenditure Plans 1982–83 to 1984–85.* Cmnd. 8494-II, March. London: HMSO.

HM Treasury (1983) *The Government's Expenditure Plans 1983–84 to 1985–86.* Cmnd. 8789-II, February. London: HMSO.

HM Treasury (1984) *The Government's Expenditure Plans, 1984–85 to 1986–87.* Cmnd. 9143-II, February. London: HMSO.

Hough, J. R. (1981) *A Study of School Costs.* Windsor: NFER.

ILEA (1984) *Improving Secondary Schools.* Report of the Committee on the Curriculum and Organisation of Secondary Schools in the Inner London Education Authority, chaired by Dr David H. Hargreaves, March. London: ILEA.

Joseph, Sir Keith (1985) 'Speech to 72nd Annual North of England Conference'. *Education*, **165**(2) 35–36.

Kay, B. (1980) 'Class Size?: the wrong question'. *Trends in Education* **2**, Summer, 39–45.

LACSAB (1984) *A New Remuneration Structure for Teachers — Proposals by the Employers.* Local Authorities Conditions of Service Advisory Board for the Burnham Management Panel, November.

MacFarlane Report, The (1980) *Education for 16–19 Year Olds.* London: CLEA/DES.

OPCS (1983) *OPCS Monitor*, WR 83/5, WR 83/8, WR 83/12, WR 83/15, WR 83/18 and WR 83/21. London: OPCS.

OPCS (1984) *OPCS Monitor*, WR 84/4, WR 84/7, WR 84/11, WR 84/14 and WR 84/18. London: OPCS.

Rutter, M., Maughan, B., Mortimore, P. and Duston, J. (1979) *Fifteen Thousand Hours; Secondary Schools and their effects on children.* London: Open Books.

Saran, R. (1982) *Reform of Teachers and Salary Structure.* University of Liverpool School of Education, Occasional Paper.

Simkins, T. (1980) 'The Economics of Smallness: the case of small primary schools'. *Educational Studies*, **6**(1), March, 79–91.

Smith, R. (1980) 'Comprehensive Schools: The Problem of Appropriate Size'. *Aspects of Education*, **80**(22) 29–44.

Thomas, H. (1983) 'Education and the maximization of welfare: a response to "curricular yogis and cost-benefit commissars"'. *Journal of Curriculum Studies*, **15**(1), 73–82.

Walsh, K., Dunne, R., Stewart, J. D. and Stoten, B. (1984) *Falling Rolls and the Management of the Teaching Profession.* Windsor: NFER.

6

COMPREHENSIVE SECONDARY REORGANISATION: A CASE OF LOCAL AUTHORITY POLICY-MAKING?

Peter Ribbins

APPROACHES TO THE STUDY OF POLICY-MAKING IN LOCAL GOVERNMENT

Given the long history and proud traditions of local government in this country, we know remarkably little about local authority policy-making. This is less surprising than it might seem, because the notion of a local authority as a significant governmental policy centre in its own right is of comparatively recent origin. Traditionally, policy-making (particularly on major issues) has been regarded as the proper prerogative of central government and the national political system. The history of comprehensive reorganisation in the postwar era fits uneasily into this tradition and suggests that local authorities have been more than the passive agents of policy determined elsewhere.

Thus, while DES statistics can be used to document the rise of the comprehensive school and the demise of the grammar and secondary modern, such figures may mask as much as they reveal. What are the 'facts'? Table 6.1 offers one kind of answer.

The most recent DES figures available at the time this chapter was written are for January 1983. They show that, at that time, state secondary schooling included 3340 comprehensives, 329 secondary moderns and only 175 grammar schools. Almost 90 per cent of pupils of secondary school age were experiencing comprehensive education and all 97 English local authorities possessed at least one comprehensive school. As against this, in 1982, over a third of these authorities also retained one or more grammar schools. The areas retaining the largest number of grammar schools were Kent (19), Lincolnshire (16), Buckinghamshire (14), Gloucestershire and Devon (11), Dorset (9), Essex, Liverpool and

Table 6.1 *Statistics of maintained secondary schooling 1955–1983[a].*

	Grammar		Secondary modern		Comprehensive	
Date	Schools	Pupils	Schools	Pupils	Schools	Pupils
1955	1180	528 455	3550	1 124 174	16	15 891
1957	1206	558 645	3719	1 424 041	43	42 416
1959	1252	641 044	3808	1 595 559	111	107 186
1961	1284	696 677	3872	1 698 379	138	141 899
1963	1295	722 492	3906	1 609 307	175	179 013
1964	1298	726 075	3906	1 640 549	195	199 245
1965	1286	718 705	3727	1 555 132	262	239 619
1966[b]	1179	660 463	3451	1 454 361	301	261 789
1970	1038	604 916	2691	1 226 619	1145	937 152
1974[c]	655	400 006	1469	836 968	2175	1 945 463
1976	459	284 977	971	573 689	2674	2 544 297
1978	305	195 526	639	385 672	3077	2 955 788
1979	254	162 993	536	328 090	3203	3 061 587
1980	218	142 588	433	261 524	3318	3 147 260
1981	200	130 849	382	228 648	3361	3 168 337
1982	185	123 944	357	211 367	3358	3 150 313
1983[d]	175	117 147	329	192 351	3340	3 128 793

[a] From the DES *Statistics of Schools*, HMSO.
[b] Figures before 1966 include Wales.
[c] Figures from 1974 are taken from DES (1984) *Statistics of Schools January 1983*. London: HMSO.
[d] Latest figures available at time of writing.

Trafford (8). Departmental figures also reveal that at their peak in 1964 there were 1298 grammar schools educating over 750 000 pupils. Over the next five years their numbers were reduced by over 250 to 1028 and during the years of Mrs Thatcher's administration they declined by over 380 more to 655. As Bayliss (1983) remarks 'the following Labour administration were responsible for the demise of 400 grammars' (p. 14), almost 50 more have been closed during Sir Keith Joseph's period in office, and further proposals to shut yet others continue to be sent to the Secretary of State for his judgement. What of the future? Pattison (1980) concludes that 'as we enter the 1980s the foreseeable future of selective schools seems secure . . . and a small but significant minority of LEAs (at least 11 and probably nearer 30) seem certain to retain selective systems' (p. 63). This suggests that, on this issue anyway, LEAs are not just the puppets of the central government.

To understand policy-making in local government it may well be necessary to consider the local authority both as a sub-system of a wider national political system, *and* as a political system in its own right. A problem with testing this proposition is the sheer lack of information we have about how policy is commonly made in local government. One of the few issues to have caught the attention of empirical researches has been secondary reorganisation. As, perhaps, the most contentious issue in the local and central government of education in the postwar era it ought to shed some light on the two sets of questions with which this chapter is centrally concerned. First, to what extent, by what means, and with what degree of success can the centre play a part in setting the boundaries or parameters (see Boaden 1971) within which local authorities operate in the making and implementing of policy? Second, if local government does exercise significant discretion over decision-making, who are the main groups and individuals involved in local policy-making and what roles do they play? Can any overall pattern be discerned? Which groups and individuals exercise the greatest influence and what methods do they use to secure that influence?

A major problem in attempting to answer these questions lies in the fact that the available literature, although extensive and growing, varies considerably both in scope and in depth. Furthermore, many of the case studies are primarily descriptive in character. Thus, although they usually make some attempt to analyse the case-study data, only comparatively rarely do these studies attempt to produce or to test propositions which might have applicability beyond the confines of their particular circumstances. Heclo (1972) has persuasively argued that this may be a characteristic feature of the majority of case studies of policy-making *whatever* their subject of attention resulting in the production of a series of 'isolated episodic descriptions . . . which are apparently thought to be of intrinsic interest' (p. 90).

Many of the studies of reorganisation are conducted with painstaking care and are often of considerable intrinsic historical interest, but they do not necessarily add very much to our understanding of policy-making. Generalisations within the field of policy-making in local government do not come easily but if they are not actively sought, it seems doubtful if they will come at all. Furthermore, it is not that researchers believe that generalisations are impossible in principle but they seem to assume that once some 'critical mass' of case studies is achieved such generalisations will appear as a matter of course.

Experience has shown this to be an unwarranted assumption. Rather it seems clear that if analytic variables are to be identified, and indications about their relative weight and likely direction of effect suggested (thus showing how patterns of interaction produce a collective outcome [Heclo 1972, p. 92]) and the general applicability of such analysis is established, future writers of case studies must actively pursue generalisations.

Another possible way forward, and one which has recently been adopted by a number of writers (James 1980; Pattison 1980; Ribbins and Brown 1979), is to use a *comparative review* of the available local and national case studies to identify the characteristic patterns of interaction between national and local government when engaged in initiating and implementing a major educational policy, and to describe, analyse and explain what happens.

EDUCATIONAL POLICY-MAKING AND THE EXTENT OF CENTRAL CONTROL

Dunsire (1981) sets out four familiar models which purport to depict the nature of central–local relations in this country. Each of these models follows from the 'facts' which different commentators choose to stress. One set of facts, which emphasise the sources of central power, sees central government at the apex of a hierarchic pyramid, the lower levels of which are occupied by the local authorities. In this *central control* or *top/down* model:

> the operative understanding is that the task of Local Authorities is to execute or implement national programmes suitably adapted to their localities, under the supervision and control of the departments of central government backed by a government with a majority and a mandate. (p. 174)

This model has wide currency in the literature of central–local government relations in general and is assumed in many of the studies of comprehensive reorganisation focusing on a national perspective. (See Pattison 1980, p. 63).

The other three models are less common, though all have their advocates. Thus some writers emphasise the relative independence of local government and advocate a *Local Autonomy Model*, and others stress the fact that neither central nor local government is monolithic. Rather, both are made up of a set of relatively interdependent agencies *each* with its own aims to pursue and its own axes to grind. This model entails:

> a sophisticated appreciation of central–local relations as essentially . . . inter-governmental . . . and an image of . . . a dense interconnected network . . . of units, with links of varying thickness in all directions with a federal centre and with one another. (Dunsire 1981, p. 175)

The last model emphasises that local authorities do not operate solely in a central–local context. They are also located within their own miniature political systems. The 'sovereignty' of this fact leads to the sort of *political systems model* used by several writers to study various aspects of educational policy-making (Brown 1977, 1978; Howell and Brown 1983; Field 1980; Howell 1976; Ribbins and Brown 1979).

Useful though these models are for the analysis of national–local relations, perhaps the most illuminating discussion of the characteristics of inter-governmental relations and the limitations of central control as it concerns the politics of comprehensive reorganisation, is to be found in a recent paper by Pattison (1980). Pattison contends that most studies of reorganisation, whether they have an essentially national or local focus, underestimate the significance and complexity of the structure and dynamics of inter-governmental relations. Studies that emphasise the role of the central government tend to assume the kind of 'top/down' model discussed above, and those that focus on local government commonly treat the role of the central government as an essentially exogenous influence. In attempting to depict the complex reality of the policy system within which decisions about secondary reorganisation are arrived at, Pattison (1980) draws heavily on Dunleavy's (1978; 1980) studies of policy-making on high rise housing. Since these ideas are considered at some length by Slater in Chapter 2, I shall not replicate that discussion here. Briefly, what Dunleavy suggests is that policy-making interactions involve more than a simple two-way flow of influence between central and local government. In particular, he stresses the key role of the *national local government system*, which is defined as 'the set of organizations and actors which together define the national role and state of opinion of local government as a whole' (p. 134). Dunleavy also emphasises the role of the *professionals* as a source of influence on inter-governmental policy-making. Complex as any model based on such an analysis is likely to be, Pattison (1980) persuasively argues that it needs to be even further elaborated if it is to do justice to the realities of policy-making in education:

> whereas high rise housing was a narrowly technical and governmental issue, in education there is a much wider field of expert opinion . . . Furthermore, high rise housing was a largely elite dominated issue little influenced by party politics or public opinion. In education this is clearly not so, as witnessed by the existence of pressure groups, media and intra-party organisations specializing in this field. (pp. 65–66)

Even this elaboration may not do justice to the complexity of inter-governmental relations in educational policy-making in that both the voluntary bodies (especially the churches) and governing bodies are not included.

Typically, accounts of secondary reorganisation have been structured around a small number of circulars, bills and acts; in which the historical narrative is divided up according to periods corresponding broadly to changes in party control of the central government (Benn and Simon 1972; Fenwick 1976; Kogan 1975; Saran 1979). Pattison (1980) claims that such an approach has a built-in tendency to exaggerate the part played by the central government and to obscure the role of other influences. However, his solution, which is to structure his own account into four periods corresponding to the main phases of comprehensive development at the LEA level might, in its turn, tend to overemphasise the role of local government. If, as Pattison (1980) persuasively argues, the history of policy-making on this issue is best analysed in terms of the fluctuating interactions and influence, over time, of several different groups, to write an account from the perspective of any *one* group is bound to be unsatisfactory. An alternative approach is to identify the key groups, and to describe and analyse the main phases of comprehensive reorganisation according to the attitudes, actions and influence of *each* of them.

Such a procedure would enable a 'history' of comprehensive reorganisation to be constructed which does not overemphasise the significance of any one group of participants. Furthermore, a comparison of the activities of the different groups and agencies involved might reveal a pattern which contrasts with that available from studies which take a more limited focus. A danger with adopting such a comparative approach is to assume that, because several groups are involved in the drama of policy-making on comprehensive reorganisation, they are all, somehow, equal players.

Were I attempting to offer a comprehensive account of all the factors and issues involved in shaping the course of secondary reorganisation, or seeking to allot precise quanta of influence to the diverse groups involved, then it would be necessary to base such a history on a detailed analysis of the activities of each of the main sets of participants involved. While such an attempt is clearly well beyond the scope of this chapter, what should be possible is to identify the main phases of local authority policy-making on comprehensive reorganisation, and to relate these, along the lines depicted in Table 6.2, to developments taking place amongst other significant groups and agencies. Thus *four* main phases in the history of local government policy-making on comprehensive reorganisation may be identified.

Phase I — from indifference to limited support: 1944–1957

In these years most local education authorities concentrated their efforts in providing secondary education for all along tripartite or bipartite lines. Some, like Cardiff, clung to their elementary schools into the 1950s, others considered ambitious plans for organising along comprehensive lines, and a few actually set up some experimental comprehensive schools. Fenwick's (1976) figures suggest that two counties and three county boroughs reorganised on comprehensive lines and some nine counties and eleven boroughs made proposals for one or more comprehensive schools. While Pattison (1980) has suggested that these figures are greatly exaggerated (p. 83), even they do not suggest any widespread enthusiasm for reorganisation along comprehensive lines. Such a lack of enthusiasm also characterised the attitudes of the central government, with ministers of both parties rejecting most of the comprehensive proposals they received. Those that were accepted tended to be from areas which did not pose threats to existing grammar schools,

Table 6.2 *A comparative approach to the study of policy making in comprehensive reorganisation*

Date	Comprehensive school pupils — Number (000s)	Percentage	Central government	National parties	Local government	Organised teachers	Expert opinion	Republic opinion
1944	0	0	Education Act 1944 *Phase I* (From overt hostility to guarded neutrality)	*Phase I* Qualified sceptical consensus	*Phase I* Mostly indifferent but a small number of LEAs experiment with reorganisation	*Phase I* Most teacher unions are studiously uncommitted or actively hostile	*Phase I* Mostly in favour of tripartite system — see influence of work of Burt	*Phase I* Mostly ignorant, sporadically hostile
1955	16	0.8						
1957	42	1.94		*Phase II* Tentative consensus supportive/open-minded			*Phase II* 11 + increasingly discredited, idea of wasted talent and link between education and social opportunity emphasized. Work of Vernon, Halsey, Floud, Vaizey, etc. in the ascendence — all favour the comprehensive option. Becomes 'conventional wisdom'	
1964	199	7.04	Education Act 1964 Circular 10/65		*Phase II* The comprehensive option becomes the prevailing orthodoxy but some LEAs continue to oppose the idea			*Phase II* Increasingly informed. Growing popular support but also emergence of a hostile minority. Opinion sometimes well-organised and often strident. Comprehensives usually get a 'good press'.
1965	240	8.5						
1966	262	11.1	Circular 10/66 *Phase II* (Increasingly determined support)			*Phase II* Increasing Polarisation amongst unions (NUT, NAS, etc.) Support for the setting-up of comprehensives and Joint 4 oppose the 'destruction' of selective schools		
1967	408	14.4						
1969	777	26.2		*Phase III* Growing conflict and the adoption of adversarial stances	*Phase III* The orthodoxy is increasingly questioned and some LEAs challenge the central government		*Phase III* Opponents of reorganisation raise the issue of declining standards.	
1970	937	32.0	Education Bill 1970 1970 Circular 10/70. *Phase III* (Conditional hostility)					
1974	1946	62.0	Circular 4/74		*Phase IV* A small core of LEAs actively oppose government policy and a larger number passively resist		First Black Paper in 1969. Strong and increasingly influential attack on the prevailing orthodoxy of the 1950s and 1960s	
1976	2544	75.6	Education Act 1976 *Phase IV* (Strong support)					
1978	2956	81.4						*Phase III* Growing doubts about the success of comprehensive education fuelled by less supportive media. Breakdown of 1960s, early 1970s consensus.
1979	3062	84.9	Education Act 1979 *Phase V* (Hostility)		*Phase V* A few LEAs attempt to extend section			
1980	3147	87.4						
1981	3168	88.2						
1982	3150	89.3						

Note. The various phases identified above are intended only to depict roughly distinct stages in the development of attitudes in each of the groups analysed.

or in which economic and demographic factors combined to create conditions particularly favourable to the aggregating of secondary provision. Saran (1979) concludes that 'Ministerial policy on comprehensive schools can be said to have done little more than move from aggressive to defensive neutrality between 1944–65.' (p. 29)

Over this period pro-comprehensive pressure groups worked away in a largely indifferent or even hostile environment to reverse the policy of the central government, to influence attitudes within the national political parties, to inform public opinion generally, and to support those few authorities which did wish to reorganise along comprehensive lines. From a comparative perspective, however, these years were dominated by the existence of a very widespread consensus in favour of the tripartite (or bipartite) organisation of secondary schooling, and of indifference or even hostility to the idea of a system organised along comprehensive lines. By 1957 only *five* LEAs out of 146 had more than two comprehensive schools and only *one* had organised more than a quarter of its secondary schools in this way.

Phase II—from limited support to orthodoxy: 1957–1967

During the next decade this impressive consensus in favour of the tripartite system, and against comprehensive reorganisation, disintegrated with astonishing swiftness. This was reflected in the activities of many local authorities, and not just those under more or less continuous Labour control. Thus by 1956, 35 out of 162 LEAs had set up two or more comprehensives and a further 6 had fully comprehensivised. Furthermore, there is evidence that many more authorities were considering setting up some comprehensive schools, a point emphasised by Crosland in the context of the debate around Circular 10/65 'Seventy-five per cent of secondary school children live in areas that have adopted, are adopting or are contemplating adopting comprehensive schemes' (*TES* 16.7.65). What had been very much the minority view in local government circles (sustained by the pioneering activities of a few local authorities) was already well on the way to becoming orthodox opinion at the level of the national local government system well before a Labour government came to power committed to proceed towards secondary reorganisation.

For some years expert opinion had been swinging against the 11 +, and the work of Floud, Halsey, Vaizey, Vernon and others was indicative of a growing consensus favouring comprehensive reform. Indeed, there even seemed to be a tentative consensus developing between the national political parties. In the years immediately before 1964 the central government, under Conservative control, showed some readiness to approve comprehensive proposals *even* in cases where these involved the reorganisation of a grammar school.

This growing consensus may have led the Labour Party, when it came to power in 1964, to resolve its long-standing internal debate on how reorganisation was to be achieved in favour of *co-operation* and against *compulsion*. Thus in July 1965 the DES issued Circular 10/65 'The Secretary of State accordingly *requests* local authorities, if they have not already done so, to prepare and submit to him plans for reorganizing secondary education in their area, on comprehensive lines' (my emphasis). LEAs were given a year in which to submit their plans.

Opinions are mixed on 10/65, both in terms of its effectiveness as a general political tactic and upon the extent to which it actually influenced the rate of reform in local government. Some have been very dismissive. Benn and Simon (1972) criticise the approach on the grounds that it was politically naive, demonstrated the lack of preparation of the Labour Party and the DES, and was influenced by too great a reverence for the idea that education should remain non-controversial. Pattison (1980) concludes that 'Central Government policy, expressed through the circular, was undoubtedly a strong influence on . . . the rate of change. Nevertheless . . . reform was under way and would certainly have continued and probably accelerated even without the circular.' (p. 69) We know that Crosland (Kogan 1971) believed that in the two years following the circular, comprehensive reform was progressing as fast as could reasonably be expected and certainly as fast as the limited resources of the DES could handle. Furthermore, in the following year the impact of the circular was increased by the issuing of another, 10/66, which announced that no capital allocations for school building would be made in future for proposals not designed to fit into a reorganisation plan. This did give some teeth to a process of 'government by circular', which Griffiths (1971) describes as a 'clear statement of national policy without the means to enforce it'. He concludes that:

> Basically the Labour Party is committed to a policy of piecemeal secondary reorganization, realizing the brute facts of politics, financial stringency and that the sheer magnitude of the endeavour precludes any simple or speedy solution. (p. 105)

Other writers stress that, whatever else the attempt to make policy by circular might have been, the one thing it was not, was politically unsophisticated. Buxton (1973) argues that the division of responsibility for policy-making between central and local government allows the former to be evasive about aspects of its policy that it does not want to reveal too closely. Furthermore, by making it appear that local authorities were expected to make their own minds up on key issues involved in reorganisation, it could be hoped that they would also assume the unpopularity for doing what the Labour government wanted anyway. Finally, since it was recognized that reorganisation would have to be achieved 'on the cheap', there would be advantages in keeping the public a little confused as to who was responsible for the policy.

Crosland always recognised that persuasion and encouragement might not be enough. Fenwick (1976) quotes him as concluding that 'if it came to confrontation . . . it would be quite proper to settle it by legislation'. Confrontation soon came. Although most LEAs during these years willingly accepted reorganisation, resistance also began 'as several authorities delayed, obstructed or completely rejected reform . . . (Furthermore) The decision to use a circular, and a weakly worded one at that, was crucial to the build up of resistance by local authorities.' (Pattison 1980, pp. 69–79)

While it may be true that the decision by the central government to attempt to make policy by persuasion rather than by legislation, may well have given reluctant LEAs time to stiffen their resolve and to learn the techniques of resistance, the explanation of the growing significance of such resistance in the later 1960s and beyond must be looked for elsewhere. One thing, at least, is clear. The mid-1960s represented the brief, high point of support for comprehensive reorganisation amongst politicians, the media and educationalists. What changed?

Up to 1967, much of local government was under Labour control but the Conservative victories of the late 1960s meant that 'It was the peculiar fate of the Circular 10/65 that it had to be implemented by local authorities who were in the majority of cases politically hostile to the Party who produced it.' (Griffiths 1971, p. 101). Cook, quoted in Kogan

(1973), develops this idea into a more general explanation of the pattern of inter-governmental conflict on this issue:

> On the political side, there is a change which seems to me to be significant. Over and over again now we are getting a national government of one party with a local government controlled by the opposition party. This has particularly affected the argument of going comprehensive. (p. 80)

Whatever the reasons, the period after 1967 witnessed the breakdown of the hegemony of the short-lived orthodoxy in favour of comprehensive reorganisation in local government circles and marked the beginning of a period of conflict between the central government and a growing number of local authorities.

Phase III — the retreat from orthodoxy: 1967–1974

In the two years immediately following 10/65, very few local authorities expressed an outright refusal to comply with the terms of the circular, but a much larger number of others began to resist in more subtle ways. By the end of 1967 some 40 LEAs out of 162 had still not produced acceptable schemes. But this analysis only presents a part of the picture. The figures attest that between 1967–1974 the pace of comprehensive reorganisation steadily continued to increase. Only 14.4 per cent of children in the maintained sector attended comprehensive schools in 1967 and 62.0 per cent did so by 1974 (see Table 6.1). James (1980) remarks that between 1970–1972 Mrs Thatcher used a variety of tactics which may have been designed, in part, to slow down the rate of reorganisation, but, in the event, the pace of comprehensivisation was little altered. What these figures do not reveal is that the great majority of the plans which became operational between 1970 and 1974 had been drawn up *before* 1970, when the pro-comprehensive tide was at its strongest, and *before* the Conservative victory at the 1970 election. As Pattison (1980) concludes: 'The period of Conservative government actually marked a clear deceleration in the number of reorganisations approved locally and a strengthening of opposition to reform from several authorities' (p. 71).

The years 1967 to 1969 represent a crucial divide in the history of policy-making on comprehensive reorganisation because it was during these years that the fragile consensus in favour of reform, in terms of intra-governmental and inter-governmental relations, began to disintegrate. The Conservative victories in the local government elections of 1966–67 effectively marked the end of any realistic expectation that reorganisation could be achieved universally by agreement. Growing pressure from local political parties seem to have played a significant part in terminating abruptly the tentative concordat of the Crosland-Boyle years and initiating the era of factional politics which exists to this day.

Initiatives from within local government sustained this conflict in a number of ways. Parkinson and Heidenheimer (1975) found that the vast majority of local authorities which had full comprehensive plans either accepted or implemented by 1970 had been under virtually uninterrupted Labour control. Conversely, almost all the authorities whose plans were rejected (16) or who had not submitted any (10) were controlled for almost all of the 1965–1970 period by the Conservatives. Furthermore, as Pattison (1980) notes:

> While local Labour Parties called for legislation against recalcitrant Tory authorities, those

authorities were demanding full support from the Conservative Party. The party conferences were one method of pressurizing the national leadership and . . . opponents of comprehensives achieved an amendment to the 1968 motion expressing clear support for resisting authorities. (p. 72)

It is possible that local influence also played a part in the appointment of both a minister (Edward Short) and a shadow minister (Margaret Thatcher) committed to the adoption of more openly adversarial styles than their predecessors had been. In 1970 both national parties signalled their conversions to harder line policies. The Labour Party first attempted compulsion by legislation in the form of the Education Bill of 1970, but passage of the bill was bungled at the Committee stage and, soon after, the Conservatives won the General Election. One of Thatcher's first acts as Secretary of State was to issue Circular 10/70, which revoked the earlier circulars and stated that: 'Where a particular pattern of organization is working well and commands general support the Secretary of State does not wish to cause further change without good reason'. Between 1970–1974 the minister approved the great majority of the proposals for change which were put to her but also used her substantial veto powers under s. 13 of the 1944 Act to protect the continued existence of over 300 schools, the great majority of which were grammar schools. The Conservative Party also espoused a policy of 'co-existence', which broadly seemed to mean the continued existence of grammar schools alongside comprehensives. While such a policy might have won some qualified support in Labour Party circles in the 1960s it did not in the 1970s. In opposition, Labour pledged itself to legislation when it returned to office.

Phase IV — conflict entrenched 1974–1984

The return to power of a Labour Government in 1974 re-established comprehensive reorganisation as the national policy. Circular 4/74 was issued reaffirming 10/65 and extending it to cover the voluntary sector.

Following local government reorganisation in 1974, ministers estimated that some 67 out of the 104 LEAs could be expected to have completed reorganisation by 1980. A further 31 were thought to have expressed a commitment in principle, although events were to demonstrate that a number of these pledges were bogus. Finally, some seven authorities had made it clear that they would not reorganise further unless forced to do so by law. (Bexley, Bucks, Essex, Kingston, Redbridge, Sutton and Trafford.) By 1976 they had been joined by an eighth, Tameside.

The lines of resistance had been clearly drawn. Education ministers made aggressive noises. Prentice was reported as having said to a Labour Party Conference: 'We shall be chasing up any laggards. We shall seek new legislative powers from Parliament if it proves necessary' (*TES* 17.1.75). It clearly was necessary and in 1976 an Education Act was passed which empowered the Secretary of State to require LEAs to submit detailed proposals for reorganisation. The Act was used quickly by Mrs Williams to require plans or partial plans from 34 authorities but she met with very limited success (Pattison 1980, p. 71). By this time, recalcitrant authorities had developed elaborate defensive tactics and considerable experience in practising the techniques of resistance. Some stalled, others asked for protracted consultation with the DES, and yet others put up partial or unsatisfactory plans. In this resistance they were much encouraged by the unequivocal support of the National Conservative Party and by a growing network of mutual support which developed amongst the resisters.

Furthermore, the Tameside (1976) decision strengthened the resolve of several authorities to challenge the Secretary of State to demonstrate in the courts that she really did have the power, under the terms of the 1976 Act to require them to reorganise (see Fenwick and McBride 1981, p. 22). Thus in 1978 and 1979 a series of court actions were brought by both sides broadly designed to test this issue. Only one case had been heard (North Yorkshire) in which the Secretary of State was successful, before the General Election of 1979. The victorious Conservatives lost no time in passing the 1979 Education Act which repealed those sections of the 1976 Act designed to coerce reluctant authorities to reorganise on comprehensive lines. This allowed LEAs, forced to make proposals under the previous act, to withdraw them.

Since 1979, debates on the organisation of secondary schooling have been dominated by the problem of declining numbers and this has tended to focus interest on a growing 'threat' to middle schools and a developing consensus in favour of some kind of reorganisation of provision for the 16–19 age group in separate institutions. During this period several authorities submitted proposals to the Secretary of State designed to extend their provision of comprehensive schooling. Some of these have been accepted, but although Sir Keith Joseph has presided over the closing of 50 or more grammar schools, he has vetoed proposals to do so which have involved areas as diverse as Avon, Gloucester, Halifax, Liverpool, Manchester, Whitehaven, Wolverhampton and Wiltshire, amongst others.

As Wilby (1984) has pointed out, what many of these authorities had in common was an attempt to tackle their problems of declining enrolment, in part, by closing grammar schools. He claims that 'Comprehensive schools could lose thousands of their brightest children to grammar schools over the next decade' (p. 7). This might happen in several ways. Three are discussed below, two of which may be the result of the activities of some LEAs and the third due to those of the Secretary of State.

First, through the activities of a number of Conservative LEAs who are engaged in attempts to bring back one or more grammar schools to their areas. The most publicised proposal has been Solihull but Mr Stuart Sexton, political adviser to Sir Keith Joseph, was quoted in the *TES* as telling the Chairman of the Education Committee 'that Solihull will meet no central political opposition to its plans . . . (and) that six Tory authorities divided evenly between the north and the south, boroughs and shires, had contacted him to say they were taking a keen interest in the proposals' (23.9.83). At the time of writing, as Passmore (1984) put it, 'The plan to reintroduce selection to the West Midlands Borough of Solihull, first reduced to two schools and then one, has now died completely. Members of the ruling Tory group decided by a large majority . . . not to pursue the plan, in view of the overwhelming opposition they encountered from local parents and schools . . . ' (p. 3).

Second, as a result of the policies which some authorities which retain one or more grammar schools are contemplating when faced with declining enrolment. These authorities seem to be of two kinds. On the one hand there are those who know they must either close schools or reduce their intakes but who know also that Sir Keith Joseph has blocked several proposals to close grammar schools for this reason: 'Since most grammar schools are too small to reduce their intakes sufficiently, the upshot is that councils have to fill empty places by increasing the proportion selected' (Wilby 1984, p. 7). On the other hand a number of Tory-controlled authorities 'have seized the opportunity to increase selection without any prompting from Joseph' (Wilby 1984). Wilby (1984) identifies these authorities as including Berkshire, Kingston-on-Thames and Redbridge, but Passmore (1984) documents the stiff resistance to their plans which all these authorities have encountered from local parents and teachers.

Third, through the activities of the Secretary of State in blocking the proposals of several authorities who had hoped to tackle their problems of falling numbers by closing grammar schools. Sir Keith Joseph, himself, has been careful to avoid public statements on these issues but both his political adviser, Stuart Sexton, and his Minister of State have been rather more forthcoming. Mr Robert Dunn told the Conference of the National Council for Educational Standards in London in 1983 that 'We have for too long ignored the very different needs of both the higher and lower academic ability children'. The Minister also remarked that 'it was in everybody's interest that the top 15 or 20 per cent should be given the best possible education . . . LEAs forced by falling rolls to rethink their secondary education might find it more economic to provide for the ablest in separate schools rather than by closing and amalgamating comprehensives to create viable 'O' level classes in subjects such as maths and physics' (Doe 1983, p. 13).

It may be that the 1980s represent a fifth phase in local authority policy-making characterised by a widespread increase in selection or even a return to a selective system. The issue of comprehensive reorganisation may not yet be as 'hors dè combat' as Hargreaves (1982) has suggested (p. 77).

ARE LEAs SIGNIFICANT EDUCATIONAL POLICY-MAKERS IN THEIR OWN RIGHT?

This brief account of policy-making on comprehensive reorganisation is designed to compare and contrast the relative impact of various groups on the processes of local authority policy-making. In particular, it attempts to test two propositions that have quite widespread currency. First, that the central government exercises the dominant control over policy-making in local government. Second, that when it comes to major policy-making, local authorities are little more than the *agents* of central government.

Neither proposition gets much support from the facts of secondary reorganisation. On the contrary, the analysis suggests that it was a small number of innovative LEAs which took the initiative in the late 1940s. At first they encountered much open hostility from the central government and an attitude of indifferent neutrality from the national local government system and other local authorities. Subsequently they became the vehicle for the rapid public dissemination of the growing hostility to the organisation of schooling on selective lines then becoming prevalent amongst the experts. They also began to influence the thinking of other local authorities, creating, as this took place, a kind of resonance or *multiplier effect* (see Pattison 1980, p. 73) which gave the process of innovation a momentum of its own, independent of any stimulus given by the activities of the central government. In the period after the issuing of Circular 10/65 there can be little doubt that the activities of the DES did greatly accelerate the momentum of reorganisation. However, even after the issuing of the circular, the initiative remained firmly with LEAs as Labour ministers tried first persuasion and then attempted compulsion to chase up the laggards. Similarly, whilst it was clearly true that Conservative ministers in the 1970s were able, with some success, to retard the momentum of reorganisation they were unable to do much about reversing the trend and Mrs Thatcher presided over the dissolution of more grammar schools than had her predecessor! Finally, the analysis illuminates the key role of the small number of LEAs who have been consistent in their opposition to demands that they reorganise. As with the original innovating authorities, they have exercised an influence greatly in excess of their initial small numbers. Their activities have also had a multiplier effect which diffused the process of resistance amongst a wider circle of authorities and beyond.

THE PROCESS OF LOCAL AUTHORITY POLICY-MAKING ON SECONDARY REORGANISATION: A POLITICAL SYSTEMS APPROACH

Clearly the central government and, for that matter, other groups and agencies have played a significant role in determining the parameters within which local authorities have sought to make and implement policy on secondary reorganisation. However, Regan (1977) is surely correct when he argues that although:

> LEAs of any political persuasion are disposed to follow a strong lead from the DES but where they feel unable to, even a determined Secretary of State has great difficulty in securing compliance. Despite the battery of financial and legal powers he possesses an adamant LEA is no mean opponent. (p. 53)

The evidence also suggests that no two local authorities have responded to pressures for reorganisation in exactly the same way. While it may be possible to categorise authorities as being more or less 'actively enthusiastic', 'cautiously sympathetic', 'reluctantly acquiescent', 'subtly resistant' or 'implacably hostile', it is also true that these attitudes can be expressed in very different ways. To explain these differences it is necessary to recognise both that LEAs are significant policy-making bodies in their own right, and that they operate within the context of an environment which is, in important respects, local. Given the number of more or less detailed case studies of secondary reorganisation now in existence (50 plus) it seems reasonable to hope that a comparative analysis might shed some light on some key questions about the structures and, especially, the processes of local authority policy-making.

This comparative review will attempt to offer answers to the questions about local authority policy-making raised earlier. It will also be used to test the explanatory power of an analytic perspective which relates the activity of policy-making to wider social and political processes based on a modified version of David Easton's political systems model. Howell and Brown (1983) offer a useful account of the main aspects of this model in the context of their studies of policy-making in London University and in the ILEA (pp. 13–33). The main elements of the model with which we shall be concerned are outlined briefly as follows.

Any social group (e.g. the local education service) has to make decisions about actions to be taken by, and on behalf of, the group if it is to survive. Furthermore, these decisions require the support of group members if they are to be effective. Theoretically, the functions of decision-making and support-seeking could be carried out by all group members. But in practice a division of labour takes place with the activities of politics being carried out by the political community (e.g. local interest and pressure groups, local media, local political parties, local legislators and administrators) and the actual final decisions by a set of authorities (to which, in this case, the LEA corresponds). The central activity of 'politics' is the process by which the *wants* of group members are converted into *demands* and subsequently 'reduced' into decisions and actions. A key objective is the processing of demands in such a way that the continued support of members is maintained at a level sufficient to ensure the continuing survival of the group. Decisions are monitored by various 'feedback' mechanisms.

Easton (1965) terms the process, seen as a whole, 'the political system'. For helpful diagrammatic representations of the actors involved and their interactions see Easton (1965, pp. 30, 74, 75, 374, 378), and Howell and Brown (1983, p. 25). Easton's (1965) dynamic response model of the political system 'consists of that set of interactions abstracted from the totality of social behaviour through which values are authoritatively allocated' (p. 57).

An 'allocation' is 'authoritative' in so far as the person to which it is directed considers it to be binding. Allocations may be seen as the *outputs* of the political system and characteristically take the form of authoritative policies, decisions and implementing actions. Demands, along with supports, form the main *inputs* into the system. Some demands arise out of the wants of group members. Others are raised directly by members of the political community (sometimes termed *withinputs*), yet others (with which I shall be particularly concerned in the rest of this chapter) follow from the processing of earlier demands ('breeder demands'). Is it possible to differentiate the notion of 'demand' further? Levin (1972) defines a 'decision' as: 'a deliberate act that generates commitment on the part of a decision-maker towards an envisaged course of action of some specificity' (p. 20). He depicts the policy-making process as one of increasing commitment on the part of the policy-maker to courses of action of increasing specificity: each successive decision on a policy issue marking an increase in one or both of these two variables. Combining these ideas with those of Easton discussed earlier suggests a framework for the analysis of the secondary reorganisation case studies which has three main aspects.

The first is the concept of the local authority as the focus of a local political system, the existence of which is attested by the presence of local political parties, interest groups, legislators, administrators, media and the like. The second is the idea that the central task of this system is to allocate values authoritatively for the local community and, more particularly, to process demands from local members of society about policies which might be adopted locally in areas like education, housing, social services, community health, etc. Finally, there is the notion that demands vary by specificity and that what is usually called 'policy-making' consists of a series of decisions arising from commitments to demands of increasing levels of concreteness.

The case studies of secondary reorganisation offer a good deal of evidence to support this idea. Thus, in the process of local authority policy-making on comprehensive reorganisation, it is possible to identify a sequence involving the processing of four levels of demand. First there is the demand that the local secondary system be reorganised. A successful outcome to this demand 'breeds' further demands about the type of reorganisation to be adopted (six possible types of acceptable schemes were outlined in Circular 10/65). Subsequently there are demands as to how the scheme adopted should be translated into a specific plan and what this means for the reorganisation of individual schools.

Finally, though there are remarkably few case studies dealing with this issue, there is the internal organization of the 'new' school. As my focus in this chapter is on the characteristics of LEA policy-making I shall restrict my remarks to the reduction of the first three levels of demand. The texts to which I shall refer, and the LEAs with which they deal, are as follows.

Texts concerned, in whole, or in part with a case study of comprehensive reorganisation

When Ribbins and Brown (1979) undertook this task in 1978 they identified the following studies: Batley et al (1970) Darlington and Gateshead; David (1977) 'Brownborough', 'Eastshire', 'Leanborough', 'Lightborough' and 'Westshire'; Eggleston (1966) Northamptonshire; Fenwick (1976) Coventry, Croydon, Leicestershire, Liverpool, Manchester, West Riding; Hampton (1970) Sheffield; Hewitson (1969) Norwich; Isaac-Henry (1970) Birmingham; Jones (1969) Wolverhampton; Lewin (1968) Merton and other outer London Boroughs; Newton (1976) Birmingham; Parkinson (1973) Birkenhead, Bootle, Wallasey and Liverpool; Pescheck and Brand (1966) Reading and West Ham; Rigby (1975) Crawley; Saran (1973) Middlesex; Stacey (1975) Banbury; Stern (1971) Manchester; Urwin (1965) Croydon; White (1975) Bath and Southampton; and Wood (1973) Bristol. There was also one useful unpublished, comparative summary of a large number of the case studies which has since been published: James (1980). Since 1978, further studies have appeared, including Fearn (1977) Doncaster, Chesterfield, Rotherham and Sheffield; Field (1980) Birmingham; Geen (1981) Cardiff; Pattison (1980) Sutton; Rhodes (1974) Oxford and Oxfordshire; and Saran (1979) Richmond.

The demand for reorganisation

In considering this demand we need to consider how it comes to be placed on the local political agenda and how it comes either to be rejected or to develop sufficient support to become local authority policy.

The evidence discussed earlier suggests that, although the initial demand for secondary reorganisation arose largely as a result of the initiatives of a small number of pioneering authorities, it was a series of policy actions taken by the central government which has forced the issue to the attention of most local political communities.

While it seems clear that central government pressure has forced some local authorities to reorganise which might not have done so otherwise (Cardiff, Richmond) and accelerated the process in others (Bath, Southampton, Tynemouth), it may actually have retarded its development in yet others (Croydon), and has been more or less successfully resisted by some (notably Kingston).

Focusing on local government, it is clear that in the great majority of cases the demand for reorganisation entered the system through the agency of the elected members of the ruling administration. There are also a number of cases where discussion seems to have been initiated by the Chief Education Officer (Bath, Coventry, Croydon, Devon, Kent,

Leicestershire and the West Riding). Other exceptions are much more difficult to find. For example, in Birkenhead and Reading the initiative seems to have come from non-elected party members, in Bootle from the local teacher's organisation and in Crawley from an elected member, but of the minority (Labour) group.

While this demand can reach the local political agenda by agencies other than the elected members of the ruling majority party, a successful outcome is unlikely without their active support. There are some exceptions to this rule. A few newly-elected Conservatives in the late 1960s and early 1970s found themselves having to accept reorganisation even though they were on record as determined to oppose it (Cardiff, Richmond, Southampton). Where the political will to reorganise existed in a ruling party that retained power for an extended term there seems to be no example of this being permanently thwarted by local agencies, although Fenwick (1976) suggests two examples of officers who seem, in very special circumstances, to have retarded its momentum through the system (Birkenhead, Liverpool).

Before moving on to the second demand, four points might be noted. First, as Pattison (1980) has pointed out, there are remarkably few case studies available of authorities which have determinedly and successfully resisted reorganisation. These relatively few recalcitrant authorities may have a significance which greatly exceeds their numbers. Having learnt the tactics of adversarial politics the hard way they could pass that knowledge on to their more timid counterparts. Pattison's study of Sutton, such limited information of Kingston as exists in the literature, and my own experience as a teacher and LEA administrator in Bexley, all point to the crucial influence of the elected members of the majority party in determining the outcome of this demand, both locally and in response to pressure exerted by the national political system.

Second, the case studies suggest that the argument that the pace and nature of decisions on reorganisation has been almost completely determined by the political colour of the controlling party locally needs to be used with some caution. This is not to deny that Conservative-controlled authorities were much more likely to oppose demands for reorganisation than were their Labour counterparts. Furthermore, not all Labour-controlled authorities demonstrated great enthusiasm for reorganisation even after 1965 (Birmingham, Luton, Sheffield). In some cases, e.g. Darlington in the 1950s, small numbers of powerful and senior members of the ruling Labour group, who had struggled to extend grammar school education and make it available to working-class children, were able to prevent reorganisation, sometimes for years. Conversely, by no means all Conservative controlled authorities have been opposed to reorganisation. This was particularly true of some shire counties (Shropshire, Leicestershire, Staffordshire) where the demographic and geographic advantages of comprehensive organised secondary schooling made it an especially attractive option. Nor should it be assumed that the comprehensive option appealed to ruling Conservatives only before 1965 and in rural counties — as the case of Merton shows.

Third, the case studies suggest that it can be very difficult to take reorganisation off the local political agenda, or to reverse decisions in favour of reorganisation once these have been taken (Southampton is the classic case). It can be done, even at the eleventh hour as in the case of Tameside. In some ways Bexley offers an even more interesting example, having managed the trick more than once!

Finally, it is worth remarking on the extent to which the policy-making process on this issue has been dominated by the activities, in most authorities, of a very small number of party members and others. James (1980) talks of the 'inner ring' that dominates LEA decision-making, in which the key people are Committee Chairman and Chief Officers generally and the Chairman of the Education Committee and the CEO in particular.

In this context, some recent studies have also emphasised the role of the Chairman of the Policy Committee as potentially particularly influential. More often than not the main efforts, in local party terms, have been made by a small number or even just one or two members on both sides as in Birmingham, Bristol, Crawley, Middlesex, Southampton and West Ham. In this respect educational policy-making may well differ little from other areas of local authority policy-making (Jones 1973; Self 1971).The reasons for this are easy to imagine. To be effective within the policy-making process it is necessary to work very hard at it. It may well be that secondary reorganisation is seen as a particularly complicated issue which, understandably, most elected members lack the background, experience, time or inclination to study closely and are only too grateful to leave the effort to the few party 'experts' with the desire to do so.

The type of reorganisation

In most of the case studies a report presented by the CEO is identified as forming the basis of the authority's final decision as to the form of reorganisation to be adopted. This certainly seems to have been the case where distinguished CEOs like Clegg and Mason were concerned but it also seems true of many who were much less eminent. In some cases the identification of the plan with the CEO was so great that it was even named after him as with the 'Peter Plan' in Darlington, where the Conservatives grumbled that the plan was 'the view of one man and one man alone' (Batley et al 1970, p. 47). Even on the comparatively rare occasions when it was members or others who took the public initiative in drawing up a plan the CEO has still normally played an active part in determining the outcome. James (1980) suggests that there are situations when CEOs lose the initiative 'and have to produce plans even for policies they would not themselves put forward' (p. 104), citing Middlesex and Gateshead as examples. But in Gateshead, the naming of the scheme after the Chairman and Vice Chairman of the Education Committee (the 'Luxton-Wheatley' Plan) disguised the significance of the part played by the CEO. Batley et al (1970) contend that his suggestions about the need for linkage between the proposed senior and junior schools and the proposal to abandon single-sex schools were just as vital to the scheme's success as the decision of the members to opt for a two-tier scheme.

Certainly, there are examples where CEOs have been required to provide simultaneously a variety of schemes for consideration (Bath) or where they have had to offer successively several schemes before one was found which was acceptable (Norwich). Other CEOs have had their schemes rejected altogether (Croydon, Devon). These examples are exceptional and there are numerous striking examples of officer control over this phase of demand reduction, including Barking, Birmingham, Crawley, Kent, Leicestershire, Luton, Reading, West Ham and the West Riding. Finally, in Birkenhead, a new CEO virtually coerced the Education Committee first to consider, and then to accept, a three-tier scheme when a two-tier scheme had been the local orthodoxy for a decade.

Is this impression of office-power exaggerated? Certainly a number of writers in the last few years have emphasised that we know remarkably little about the reality of officer–

member interaction and that much of what we believe may turn out to have been based on myth and misconception. Conversely, it is hard to deny that senior professional officers have at their disposal potentially significant sources of administrative, professional and political authority which they can use to exercise an influence over the processes of policy-making (Heclo 1969; Johnson 1965; Kogan 1973; Donnison and Chapman 1975; Pettigrew 1972; Hill 1974). James (1980) offers a useful summary of some of the reasons why the CEO is so often thought to be the 'real policy-maker':

> having at his disposal substantial sources of information and administrative experience, he also mediates between his authority and the DES and with local interest groups . . . Most requests, regulations and data are channelled through him (and) inherent in (this) position of information gatekeeper is the potential not only to control the flow of information to members but also to collect, combine and reformulate it. He has the necessary resources to formulate policies in detail and assess their feasibility . . . At the same time, (he is) likely to be aware of shortcoming in the (existing) system, of trends in educational thinking (and) more aware (than members) of the need to introduce changes to deal with deficiencies in existing policy. (pp. 102–103)

Many commentators share Donnison and Chapman's (1975) belief that it is the 'providers of services' (the officers), rather than 'the controllers of resources' (elected members) or 'clients', who usually initiate change. However, the exercise of such administrative initiative is qualified where the innovations under consideration either require significant additional resources (Donnison) or are regarded as politically sensitive (Saran 1973). In both cases members are likely to play a much more active role.

In this context, several writers believe that the critical variable is the degree of party political control that exists in an authority (Jones 1969; Jennings 1977; Saran 1973). There is certainly some evidence to be found for this view in the case studies. Lewin (1968) found that whilst 'Some CEOs have clearly played their role from the front . . . others have . . . let the decision-making process go ahead and (have acted) as technical advisers on the sidelines laying out alternative schemes as required' (pp. 146, 147). In Birmingham, in an early round of the struggle for reorganisation, the CEO has been described as a 'spectator', 'keeping a low profile' and 'faithfully reflecting changes in majority party opinion'. Other writers have attempted to demonstrate that the growth of disciplined party political control in local government over the last 10 to 15 years has tended to diminish the ability of officers to exercise the kind of influence over LEA policy-making that they were apparently able to exert in the past. Thus the history of events in Wolverhampton (Jones 1969), Middlesex (Saran 1973), Liverpool (Parkinson 1973), Cardiff (Geen 1981), amongst others, all document the processes by which administrators have tended to lose control over policy-making when faced with disciplined parties with clear ideas about what they wish to do. This 'truth' has also been demonstrated by comparative studies of reorganisation in the city and county of Oxford (Rhodes 1974) and of the four LEAs in the Sheffield area (Fearn 1977). James (1980) summarising the findings of the latter on this issue, concludes that:

> Where the parties are well organised and the majority party enjoys prolonged tenure of office the CEO's role is largely a subordinate one. In authorities where parties are less well organized and secure, the CEOs play a greater role though in no case did they emerge as major initiators of change. (p. 105)

There is some evidence to suggest that this much less 'heroic' conception of the policy-making role of the CEO would find quite widespread support amongst contemporary senior education officers. Neve (1977) found little evidence from his interviews with 80 CEOs and deputies that officers see themselves as dominant modifiers of the process of policy-making in education, particularly in highly politicised urban authorities. Rather they saw their role as concerned with humbler, although highly necessary, activities of 'facilitating', 'creating coalitions', 'negotiating', 'reconciling' and the like. These findings are not too surprising: civil servants of all kinds have long been adept at pleading how powerless they are. David (1977), also on the basis of a large number of interviews with officers, offers a rather more differentiated conception of administrator behaviour. She suggests that the key determinant of the role which senior education officers are likely to play in the process of policy-making is the sort of administrative *style* of influence they choose to adopt. Thus, in the case of comprehensive reorganisation, *conciliator* CEOs, who are primarily concerned to achieve a scheme which commands agreement, square rather well with Neve's (1977) analysis. However, David (1977), unlike Neve, also identifies the existence of *educator* CEOs, who are much more likely to give priority to specifically educational values in making judgements about the form of reorganisation appropriate for 'their' authority. They are much more likely than 'conciliators' to give some precedence to the views of the professionals who actually provide the service and to fight hard for their 'pet' scheme amongst members. 'Leanborough' provides an example of the former in action and 'Westshire' of the latter.

As things stand it seems doubtful if a truly authoritative statement on these issues is possible. In arriving at such a statement a more differentiated conception of policy-making than that which is adopted in many of the case studies will surely be necessary. Thus, for example, although the role of the elected member may be crucial in the initiation of policy (e.g. 'the demand for reorganisation') they may play a less significant part at the later stages of policy-making (such as the 'type of reorganisation' and its subsequent development into a 'detailed plan of implementation') (see Ribbins 1981).

Whatever qualifications one makes, the role of officers and members at both this, and the last, phase of policy-making on secondary reorganisation has clearly been powerful. By contrast, the influence of other groups, with one possible exception (the Catholic Church), seems to have been much more limited. This may be an appropriate place to refer to the processes of *participation* and *consultation* or, more accurately, to their absence. On the whole the secondary case studies bear out the conclusion of a survey quoted by Hill (1974):

> English local councils are secretive, content to consult only when required to by statute or ministerial direction. They have not gone out of their way to promote citizen involvement. (p. 156)

All too often the usual pattern of consultation, where it has existed, has been for the authority to decide what it is going to do first and to ask for comments afterwards. Thus in Birmingham in 1972, on the day after the Labour Party returned to power, the new Chairman of the Education Committee promised to hold public meetings before the end of the summer term after which 'we shall draw up a detailed plan and come back for a further series of meetings in the late autumn' (Sheila Wright quoted in the *Birmingham Evening Mail* 5.5.72). Field (1980) suggests that what actually seems to have happened was that two sets of consultation took place between the elections and 19 July! One of these consisted of five meetings of the Joint Consultative Committee with the teachers and it was at these discussions that the final plan based upon the idea of grouping schools into consortia was hammered out. The other took the form of 30 open meetings at which the views of the public were sought about possible types of reorganisation. Between 25 July and 6 September a detailed plan was produced, largely by the officers. Subsequently 29 further public meeting were held between 18 September and 13 October. Almost 60 public meetings looks like a good deal of consultation and indeed, these events did serve to inform the public and may have helped to sell the plan. However, the first set of public meetings seems to have had no influence on the actual plan adopted and very few changes were made to the details of the plan as a result of the second set of discussions. As far as the Outer London Boroughs were concerned, Lewin (1968) found that: 'the majority of authorities involved themselves in extensive consultation' (p. 172). The few that did not, tended to find themselves faced with a rather greater number of protests than those that did. However, the product in terms of public response where consultation did take place was usually negligible. He concludes that:

> It may be that the lesson of reorganization of schools in London is that the art of successful education administration of major policies may hinge upon pulling the public dragon's teeth by asking it . . . for its views . . . it may prove . . . that the mass of people may have no real views to express. (p. 173)

On a similar tack, James (1980) culls the available literature to demonstrate that the local electorate is largely both apathetic and ignorant, 'the reality is that for the great majority of people, politics is alien and remote' (p. 37). Both elected members and officials seemed largely satisfied with this situation although a few examples can be found in which consultation was taken seriously and the electorate did respond (Bath).

Birley (1970) argues that one group within the local community has been widely consulted the *teachers*, and he sees their support for particular reorganisation schemes as very valuable. But in practice the extent and character of consultation with teachers has varied very considerably and the extent to which teacher *pressure* has had a significant *effect* is debatable. In considering this issue Saran (1979) understandably plays it safe: 'was teachers' pressure at the local level effective . . . The answer is yes and no' (p. 34). Were teachers adequately consulted? Lewin concludes that no other group was so widely consulted and says that in Merton the CEO consulted the teachers even before he had put his plans before the schools sub-committee. In Bootle (where, unusually, the teachers first voiced the demand for reorganisation) it was a working party of teachers who drew up the organisation scheme. In Birmingham the incoming Labour administration secured agreement for a 'consortia' system with the two largest local teacher unions prior to 'open consultation' with the wider local public. 'Lightborough' also offers an interesting case, in that after 1965 the local authority set up a joint consultative committee which included councillors and teachers to advise on the future organisation of secondary education in the borough. However, 'the decision to reorganize secondary education took a long time since the teachers' representatives could not agree' (David 1977, p. 124). Perhaps the best example of teacher influence faced with an authority rather reluctant to consult them, is provided by the case of Norwich. Here the teachers were instrumental in defeating two different plans which had been recommended by the CEO and accepted by the Education Committee.

In many other authorities teachers have either not been consulted at all or they have been consulted late in the day or in a limited way. Thus in 'Eastshire', when an 'educator' CEO decided to attempt a limited experiment with comprehensive reorganisation, 'The

Education Officers formulated the policy and then the Education Committee took the decision in principle. The local community and teachers had not been consulted' (David 1977, p. 90). 'Brownborough' offers an even more salutory example. Like Birmingham, the incoming Labour administration pledged itself to get rid of selection 'within the year'. Officers discussed the merits of four possible schemes and did so in such a way that only one scheme was a serious contender. One of the schemes that had been turned down considered the virtues of the concept of the Sixth Form College. This had been rejected on the grounds that local teachers were hostile to the idea although there is little evidence that teachers had, in fact, been consulted!

> The choice of scheme was purely the idea of the officers: there had been no consultation with the major interest groups in the city . . . Although the teachers were very angry and worried about their personal prospects, there was nothing they could do. (pp. 72–73)

In Devon, Croydon and Middlesex, at various times, teachers were not consulted before the initial adoption of a proposed scheme, and in Crawley they found it very hard to find out what was happening when faced with a Chairman and CEO who believed that they had no legitimate role in anything that smacked of strategic policy-making. However, in all the authorities considered above, teachers were significantly involved in filling out the details. Finally, the case of a number of authorities (notably Barking and Croydon) shows the extent to which such consultations can be a form of officer patronage.

While a number of authorities were reluctant to consult their teachers, it is also clear that the object of the exercise in other instances was to solicit the public agreement (and therefore commitment) of local teachers, or else to show that teachers were divided (which they usually were) on the issues involved. In the latter case the authority could isolate and largely ignore the views of hostile groups of teachers (e.g. Gateshead).

It is perhaps not too surprising to find 'hostile' groups of teachers having so little influence, but a number of writers are doubtful if *any* teachers exert much real power. Geen (1981) contends that what his longitudinal study of policy-making in Cardiff between 1944–1970 demonstrates is:

> the impotence of the various pressure groups. During the immediate post war era the CEO remained unmoved at the constant requests of the teachers' organizations for Hadow reorganization. When further change was planned in the 1960s their views were again disregarded . . . (p. 102)

Parkinson's (1973) conclusions from his study of Merseyside are equally dismissive:

> In each case, reorganization represented a major challenge to the teachers' 'status quo'. In every case they took objection to the LEA's plans in detail, and in some cases in principle as well. But in no case, either in principle or in detail were the teachers successful. (p. 36)

While the influence which teachers have exercised over these phases of the policy-making process may have been less than is often thought, they have nevertheless exercised greater influence than have parents.

For their participation to mean much, parents normally have to be consulted at a relatively early state in the process of reorganisation, and given sufficient information, packaged in an appropriate form. The case studies suggest that few authorities tried hard to meet all these conditions and that many just went through the motions with little hope of finding the experience a helpful one. James (1980) emphasises that parents have usually been disparate, disunited and disorganised on this issue, and that both officers and members have often acted as 'frugal information gatekeepers'. None of the officers Kogan (1973) interviewed rated the part that parents could play highly and it seems that their views were fairly typical of both officers and members. While the rhetoric of liberal democracy stresses that one of the strengths of local government lies in its ability to facilitate intimate relationships between an authority and its electorate, in reality most tales of parental power are either exaggerated or based on myth. James (1980) remarks that most professionals and counsellors are content to have it so, and that the evidence suggests that professionals in education commonly seek to turn their customers into *clients* on the grounds that it is the expert who knows what is best. Furthermore, local government in general and elected members in particular are much less prepared than central government to accept that the activities of pressure groups are legitimate.

It is not hard to see why, in general, parents have been even less influential than teachers. The latter have some access to reliable sources of information not easily available to the LEA; a relatively high level of organisation; and their status both as professionals and as employees of the authority. Parents lack these advantages. Yet it is possible to paint too bleak a picture of parental impotence. There have been examples of well-organised, large scale and even partially successful parental revolts. Examples of this can be found in the case studies of Birmingham, Bristol, Ealing, Enfield, Liverpool, Middlesex, Richmond, Sheffield, Southampton amongst others. However, these are very much exceptions to the general rule and have usually been effective only by going outside the local political system and appealing to the minister or to the courts.

Birmingham and Liverpool offer examples of well organised, parent-led groups protesting against reorganisation schemes in their respective cities. In Birmingham, resistance was on a very large scale indeed as the 'Save our Schools' campaign struggled to prevent the reorganisation of the city's grammar schools. It used traditional methods of resistance, including the collection of the biggest petition protest on reorganisation that I know of, with some 1 500 000 signatures from 100 000 people (15 schools!). Field (1980) concludes that it had little or no influence on local policy-makers but may well have influenced the Secretary of State (Mrs Thatcher) to reject some three-fifths of the plan. Even this setback was only temporary, and once full approval had been given by a Labour Secretary of State in September 1976 organized parental opposition effectively collapsed. Sheffield, Southampton and Richmond provide examples where strong and evident parental support for reorganisation played a part in preventing incoming Conservative administrations from undoing the work of their predecessors. Saran (1979) briefly considers the history of reorganisation in Richmond and focuses especially on the role of organised and unorganised parental opinion. She concludes that parental opinion may have had a significant role in Richmond although the material she presents might as well be interpreted as a successful exercise of sustained central government pressure. Saran (1979) also notes 'that, where parents are concerned, it is potential, rather than actual, pressure that often exerts influence over policy' (p. 35). However, she offers little evidence to substantiate this interesting variant of the 'law of anticipated reaction'.

The case of Bath illustrates both what can be achieved where a tradition of consultation exists and officers and members are keen to sustain it, and the costs of serious consultation. Discussion on secondary reorganisation lasted nearly seven years and at one time the Education Committee found itself discussing the merits of no less than eleven different schemes of reorganisation.

Finally, the case studies do identify one highly effective non-governmental group — the

Roman Catholic Church. Sloman, in the wake of the present government's defeat on school transport in the House of Lords, suggests that, when they put their minds to it, the voluntary bodies are the most effective pressure group in English education (Brown 1981, pp. 114–115). The case studies offer a good deal of evidence to bear this out, although they do also seem to suggest that the Church of England may have been a rather less effective interest group on this issue than the Roman Catholic Church. In Darlington the decision to leave a Catholic school as the sole exception to an 11–18 all-through pattern was the only significant concession made to any pressure group. In Gateshead, where about one-sixth of the children in the area attended Catholic secondary schools, great care was taken to consult the Church. In Bexley, in the 1970s when the local Conservative administration was sternly resisting strong central government pressure, the Church was allowed to reorganise its only grammar school. In West Ham, Reading and Merseyside, there was substantial Catholic secondary provision and the Church played a major role in discussions on reorganisation. Curiously, Merseyside also provides one of the few cases in which Church pressure on an LEA was unsuccessful. There are a few other cases where the position of the Catholic schools were, at first, ignored (Barking), or where little attempt was made to consult the Church (Luton), or where such consultations as did take place were clearly inadequate (Crawley).

From scheme to plan: the reorganisation of individual schools

Few of the case studies go into anything like the same degree of detail in describing the processing of this demand as they do with the previous two. In practice, of course, there was often a good deal of overlap between this phase of the policy-making process and the last. Discussions about the relative merits of different possible schemes as part of a highly general and abstract debate are uncommon, although this did sometimes occur, particularly where an authority was looking for plausible ways to stall! More usually, where more than one scheme was being considered, officers would have been asked to sketch out the possible implementational implications of different schemes given the authorities' existing pattern of schools. Once a decision in favour of a particular scheme had been taken the 'sketch' was worked up into a detailed plan. In some LEAs, for example those that opted for 'consortia' type arrangements like Sheffield and Birmingham, the construction of a detailed plan seems to have entailed two fairly distinct phases — a division of the city into 'consortia' for reorganisation purposes, and the setting out of detailed proposals for each 'consortium'.

Who controlled this phase of the policy process? It seems safe to say that it is the professionals (administrators *and* teachers) who exercised the greatest influence, with elected members commonly adopting a general monitoring function and reserving their active interventions to defending the interests of their particular constituents and to resolving specific conflicts over the fate of individual schools. In Devon, officers took responsibility for the production and implementation of detailed plans but two committees were created to monitor their activities. These were a political committee — which was an ad hoc body of members of the Education Committee and largely concerned with issues like the timing of the various aspects of the scheme, and a planning (professional) committee — which dealt with issues like the 'staffing', 'internal organisation' and 'curriculums' of the reorganised schools.

Teachers have exercised influence over this phase of the policy-making process in a number of ways. Middlesex provides a classic instance of one kind of activity — the resisting of specific proposals within an overall plan. Here the teachers took the lead in 1948 in opposing a decision to incorporate a grammar school into a comprehensive school and eventually the plan was dropped. Teachers in Norwich, somewhat unusually, presented a united front when commenting on the plans produced by the CEO and were successful in achieving many revisions to his detailed proposals. Even in authorities which did not consult teachers much in the two earlier phases (Crawley, Kent, Barking) there was tendency to do so much more fully at this stage. In 'Eastshire' where the teachers (or anybody else in the local community) had not been consulted in formulating the policy and taking the decision, it was recognised by the members and officers that, 'They would be consulted over the details once the principle was established' (David 1977, p. 91).

In the event 'local teachers organized into one large local association' and made clear their 'fears and grievances'. As in many other cases the teachers were largely pacified by promises of salary safeguards and consultation on the working out of the detailed staffing implications of the scheme. However, teachers were not always consulted even in this phase of policy-making. In Sheffield, for example, the plans for the northern half of the city were drawn up in detail and agreed before the teachers were involved.

Finally, remarkably little evidence is to be found in the case studies that other groups within the local community were any more seriously involved at this phase of the policy-making process than they were at the others. There are occasional references to the fact that managers and governors were invited to express their views (Kent), and some examples of parents (or other groups) organising to defend the continued existence of 'their' particular schools, but these are rarely discussed at any length. In any case, as James (1980) remarks: 'It is . . . much easier to chronicle the extent of consultation than to assess the impact of such activity' (p. 63).

SECONDARY REORGANISATION AND POLICY-MAKING IN LOCAL GOVERNMENT: SOME CONCLUSIONS

Let us consider two questions. First, what can we learn of secondary reorganisation from the case studies? Second, what can we learn about the characteristics of local authority policy-making from a study of the case of secondary reorganisation?

As James (1980) has pointed out, much of the literature dealing with public policy making tends to portray governmental agencies as weak bodies located in strong environments dominated by the demands of various organised and unorganised pressure groups. Eckstein (1960) dismisses the role of formal decision-makers as serving as little more than cash-registers, more or less faithfully ringing up the demands and supports they receive from the powerful inhabitants of their environments. The secondary reorganisation case studies provide very little evidence which sustains such a view. Thus, although voluntary bodies, like the Catholic Church, have been influential occasionally, the part played by other groups within the local community has not often been significant. The role of parents, for example, has rarely been more than marginal. Rather more surprisingly, the case studies also seem to show that the influence of teachers may have been much more limited than has been popularly supposed, although they have been most effective in the processing of the third level of demand. Certainly few of the studies indicate much real enthusiasm for 'consultations', let alone 'participation', by many local authorities.

Conversely, these studies also suggest that on this issue the influence of local parties as major initiators of policy may have been underestimated in some of the literature. They also suggest that the 1974 local government reforms made it likely that an 'urban' rather than a 'rural' style of local party politics has become the norm — competitive, disciplined and policy oriented. Certainly the local political parties appear to have been the crucial agents in the initiation and reduction of the first type of demand, that for reorganisation. On the comparatively rare occasions when it was not the local majority party which first voiced this demand, its support was necessary if reorganisation was to take place. Similarly, majority party support was also necessary if subsequent demands were to be reduced successfully.

Thus it is possible to marshal a great deal of evidence from the case studies to demonstrate that the role of the two groups — officers and elected members (the 'authorities') — has usually been crucial. Not all members, of course. The prime initiators of policy seem to have been 'a small group of counsellors in the majority party, who typically exercise real decision making power' (James 1980, p. 99). This is an influence they have shared with senior officers and, in particular, with the CEO. It seems clear that, on a number of occasions, officers have played a significant role in voicing the demand for reorganisation or sustaining it in the face of less well-disposed regimes. Arguably, however, they have exercised much greater influence in the processing of subsequent demands. Some recent studies have suggested that the development of increasingly partisan politics in local government since the early 1970s has diminished the power of officers. Bush and Kogan (1982), while acknowledging that major changes have taken place in the contexts in which CEOs operate, also conclude that their backgrounds and attitudes have remained remarkably unaltered and that 'the CEO still has a powerful position within the local authority, widespread opportunities to influence objectives and relationships, and often considerable satisfaction from his work' (p. 67). In their attempts to redress the balance in the face of influential accounts which emphasise the power of officers as against members in the making of policy, some studies may have gone too far. If they have, this can be explained, in part, by the undifferentiated conception of 'policy-making' they sometimes employ and because they focus too much on initiation of policy and do not sufficiently consider the later stages of the policy-making process.

Finally, how far can what has been learnt from these case studies be seen as a reliable guide to patterns of local policy-making more generally? Arguably, in some ways, the case studies do not even provide a satisfactory guide to the processes of policy-making on secondary reorganisation. Although steadily growing in number, existing accounts do not cover all authorities or even a significant proportion. Few of them are really longitudinal and some cover rather short periods. Many focus on the period up to 1965 and comparatively few deal with the period after 1974. Furthermore, there seems some evidence that researchers have tended to turn their attention to areas where secondary reorganisation has attracted great political attention. Conversely there are remarkably few studies of the small group of authorities, largely under continuous Conservative control, which have led resistance to the policy initiatives of the central government in favour of reform. What is also surprising is the limited attention given to the internal dynamics of policy making in local parties, amongst different levels and types of officers, and, most seriously, of officer–member interaction. Finally, the question needs to be raised of how typical an issue within the local government of education (let alone local policy-making) secondary reorganisation really is? Brown (1981) suggests that:

> The short answer must be that we do not know . . . since no other subject has provoked anything like the same degree of interest amongst researchers. (p. 116)

Perhaps the most that can be said with any certainty, given our present state of knowledge, is that the secondary reorganisation case studies can be used to generate a number of tentative theories and hypotheses about local authority policy-making. But that before we can place much confidence in their validity it will be necessary to test them in the context of detailed case studies concerned with local authority policy-making on a wide variety of educational and non-educational issues with contemporary relevance (see Ribbins and Brown 1979, pp. 198–200).

SUMMARY AND CONCLUSION

The objective of this chapter has not been to attempt to offer a full account of the history of policy-making on comprehensive reorganisation, rather its purpose has been to try to answer the question, 'who controls local authority policy-making on secondary reorganisation?'. There is an influential literature that suggests that for purposes of the initiation and implementation of all kinds of policy, local authorities are best regarded as the *agents* of central government. In the first part of the chapter it was found that this proposition fitted rather poorly with the facts of policy-making on secondary reorganisation. On this issue at least, local government seems to have played the *proactive* part with the central government relegated to an intermittently effective, *reaction* role.

What also emerged from this discussion is that the structure of inter-governmental relations, and their location within the policy-making environment of education, conceived of as a whole, may be a good deal more complex than has often been assumed.

These considerations, and others, led to the view that to describe and explain policy-making in local government it is necessary, for analytic purposes, to regard individual local authorities as miniature administrative and political systems in their own right. This enables an attempt to be made at a comparative review of the many case studies now available on comprehensive reorganisation designed to distinguish characteristic patterns of LEA policy-making. Policy-making may be analysed as a process of decision-making which, in the case of secondary reorganisation, involves the reduction of demand at four levels, three of which are considered in the chapter. Evidence from the case studies strongly suggests that the role of two groups — senior officers and senior members — was usually crucial. The influence of other groups, with the possible exception of the Catholic Church, was much less significant. Few authorities have demonstrated any real enthusiasm for consultation, let alone participation, and the role of parents and, rather more surprisingly, teachers was not often more than marginal.

Finally, how far can generalisations derived from the case of secondary reorganisation be regarded as a reliable guide to the question of who controls local authority policy-making on other issues? The short answer is that we just do not know. Neither will we know till a sufficient number of 'in-depth' case studies become available on topics other than secondary reorganisation.

REFERENCES

Ashford, D. E. (1974) 'The Effects of Central Finance on the British Local Government System'. *British Journal of Political Science*, **4**(3).

Batley, R., O'Brien, O. and Parris, H. (1970) *Going Comprehensive*. London: Routledge and Kegan Paul.

Bayliss, S. (1983) 'Grammar school total drops to less than 200' *TES*, 26.3.83.

Benn, C. and Simon, B. (1972) *Half Way There*, 2nd edition. Harmondsworth: Penguin.

Birley, D. (1970) *The Education Officer and His World*. London: Routledge and Kegan Paul.

Boaden, N. (1971) *Urban Policy Making*. Cambridge: Cambridge University Press.

Brown, R. (1977) *Policy Making in F.E.* Unpublished PhD Thesis, University of London.

Brown, R. (1978) 'Research Report: Systems Analysis and Decision Making in the Local Government of F.E'. *Educational Administration*, **6**(2).

Brown, R. (1981) 'Review of *The Reorganization of Secondary Education* by James, P. (1980)' in *Educational Administration*, **9**(3).

Bush, T. and Kogan, M. (1982) *Directors of Education*. London: Allen and Unwin.

Buxton, R. (1973) 'Comprehensive Education: Central Government, Local Authorities and the Law'. In Fowler, G. et al (1973) *Decision Making in British Education*. London: Heinemann.

David, M. E. (1977) *Reform, Reaction and Resources*. Windsor: NFER.

Dearlove, J. (1973) *The Politics of Policy in Local Government*. Cambridge: Cambridge University Press.

DES (1984) *Statistics of Schools January 1983*. London: HMSO.

Donnison, D. V. and Chapman, V. (1975) *Social Policy and Administration Revisited*. London: Allen and Unwin.

Dunleavy, P. (1978) *The Politics of High Rise Housing in Britain*. Unpublished DPhil Thesis, University of Oxford.

Dunleavy, P. (1980) *Urban Political Analysis*. London: Macmillan.

Dunsire (1981) 'Central Control Over Local Authorities: A Cybernetic Approach' *Public Administration* Summer.

Doe, B. (1983) 'Practical plea for selective schools'. *TES*.

Easton, D. (1965a) *A Systems Analysis of Political Life*. New York and London: Wiley.

Easton, D. (1965b) *A Framework for Political Analysis*. New York and London: Wiley.

Eccles, P. R. (1974) 'Secondary Reorganization in Tynemouth 1962–1969'. *Journal of Educational Administration and History*, **6**(1).

Eckstein, H. (1960) *Pressure Group Politics*. London: Allen and Unwin.

Eggleston, S. J. (1966) 'Going Comprehensive'. *New Society*.

Fearn, E. (1977) *Role of Political Parties and Pressure Groups in Comprehensive Reorganization in Four Local Education Areas*. Unpublished PhD Thesis, University of Leeds.

Fenwick, I. G. K. (1976) *The Comprehensive School 1944–1970*. London: Methuen.

Fenwick, K. and McBride, P. (1981) *The Government of Education in Britain*. Oxford: Martin Robertson.

Field, D. (1980) *Secondary School Reorganization in Birmingham and the Development of the Consortia System*. Unpublished MEd Thesis, University of Birmingham.

Geen, A. G. (1981) 'Educational Policy Making in Cardiff, 1944–1970'. *Public Administration*, Spring.

Griffith, J. A. G. (1966) *Central Departments and Local Authorities*. London: Allen and Unwin.

Griffiths, A. (1971) *Secondary School Reorganization in England and Wales*. London: Routledge and Kegan Paul.

Hampton, W. (1970) *Democracy and Community*. Oxford: Oxford University Press.

Hargreaves, D. (1982) *The Challenge for the Comprehensive School*. London: Routledge and Kegan Paul.

Heclo, H. H. (1969) 'The Councillors' Job'. *Public Administration*, **47**, 185–202.

Heclo, H. H. (1972) 'Review Article: Policy Analysis'. *British Journal of Political Studies*, **2**(1).

Heidenheimer, H. and Parkinson, M. (1975) 'Equalizing Education Opportunity in Britain and the USA'. In *Tulane University Studies in Political Science*, **15**.

Hewitson, J. N. (1969) *The Grammar School Tradition in a Comprehensive World*. London: Routledge and Kegan Paul.

Hill, D. M. (1974) *Democratic Theory and Local Government*. London: Allen and Unwin.

Howell, D. A. (1976) 'Systems Analysis and Academic Decision-Making in Universities'. *Education Administration*, **4**(2).

Howell, D. and Brown, R. (1983) *Educational Policy Making: An Analysis*. London: Heinemann.

Issac-Henry, K. (1970) *The Politics of Comprehensive Education in Birmingham 1957–67*. Unpublished MSc Thesis, University of Birmingham.

James, P. H. (1980) *The Reorganization of Secondary Education*. Windsor: NFER.

Jennings, R. E. (1977) *Education and Politics: Policy Making in Local Education Authorities*. London: Batsford.

Johnson, N. (1965) 'Who Are the Policy Makers?'. *Public Administration*, Spring.

Jones, G. W. (1969) *Borough Politics*. London: Macmillan.

Jones, G. W. (1973) 'Political Leadership in Local Government'. *Local Government Studies*, **1**(2).

Kogan, M. (1971) *The Politics of Education*. Harmondsworth: Penguin.

Kogan, M. (1973) *County Hall*. Harmondsworth: Penguin.

Kogan, M. (1975) *Educational Policy Makers*. London: Allen and Unwin.

Levin, P. H. (1972) 'On Decisions and Decision-Making'. *Public Administration*, Spring.

Lewin, R. R. (1968) *Secondary School Reorganization in the Outer London Boroughs*. Unpublished MA Thesis, University of London.

Neve, B. (1977) 'Bureaucracy and Politics in Local Government: The Role of LEA Officers'. *Public Administration*, Autumn.

Newton, K. (1976) *Second City Politics*. Oxford: Oxford University Press.

Parkinson, M. (1970) *The Labour Party and the Organization of Secondary Education 1918–1965*. London: Routledge and Kegan Paul.

Parkinson, M. (1973) *Politics of Urban Education*. University of Liverpool.

Passmore, B. (1984) 'Parental opposition kills off Solihull selection scheme' *TES*, 2.3.84.

Pattison, M. (1980) 'Intergovernmental Relations and the Limitations of Central Control: Reconstructing the Politics of Comprehensive Education'. *Oxford Review of Education*, **6**(1).

Peschek, D. and Brand, J. A. (1966) *Policies and Politics in Secondary Education*. London School of Economics.

Pettigrew, A. M. (1972) Information Control as a Power Resource. *Sociology*, **6**.

Raison, T. (1975) *Local Government and Education*. London: Allen and Unwin.

Regan, D. E. (1977) *Local Government and Education*. London: Allen and Unwin.

Rhodes, R. A. W. (1974) *A Comparative Study of Decision Making Processes within Oxford City and Oxfordshire County Councils*. Unpublished BLitt Thesis, University of Oxford.

Ribbins, P. M. (1981) 'Review of "The Reorganization of Education", James, P. 1980)'. *Public Administration*, Summer.

Ribbins, P. M. and Brown, R. J. (1979) 'Policy Making in English Local Government: The Case of Secondary Reorganization'. *Public Administration*, Summer.

Rigby, B. (1975) *The Planning and Provision of Education in the Foundation and Development of a Post War New Town: Crawley*. Unpublished PhD Thesis, University of Southampton.

Saran, R. (1973) *Policy Making in Secondary Education*. Oxford: Oxford University Press.

Saran, R. (1979) 'The Politics of Education Policy Making: Pressures on Central and Local Government'. Unit 6 of Course E222:

The Control of Education in Britain. Milton Keynes: The Open University Press.

Self, P. (1971) 'Elected Representatives and Management in Local Government'. *Public Administration.*

Stacey, M. (1975) *Power, Persistence and Change: A Second Look at Banbury.* London: Routledge and Kegan Paul.

Stanyer, J. (1976) *Understanding Local Government.* London: Fontana.

Stern, M. A. (1971) *Policy Formation in the Reorganization of Secondary Schools in Manchester: 1957–67.* Unpublished Diploma in Public Administration, London School of Economics.

Urwin, K. (1975) 'Formulating a Policy of Secondary Education in Croydon'. In Donnison and Chapman (1975) *Social Policy and Administration Revisited.* London: Allen and Unwin.

White, P. T. (1975) *The Reorganization of Secondary Education in Bath and Bristol.* Unpublished MPhil Thesis, University of Southampton.

Wilby, P, (1984) 'Comprehensives lose more stars to grammars' *Sunday Times,* 11.3.84.

Wood, C. A. (1973) *Educational Policy in Bristol.* Unpublished MSc Thesis, University of Bristol.

7

SIXTEEN TO NINETEEN: TOWARDS A COHERENT POLICY?

Derek Slater

INTRODUCTION

This chapter is divided into two parts. The first part is an historical analysis, since 1944, of the issues which have played an important part in policy-making for 16–19s. Three issues have been identified which, for convenience, are treated separately: institutional issues; governmental issues; and curricular issues.

The second part is, up to a point, a palimpsest of the first, in that the issues are then re-interpreted in the context of Braybrooke and Lindblom's (1963) strategy of disjointed incrementalism as a model of decision-making, and some conclusions will be drawn on the usefulness of this model in this particular connection.

ISSUES IN POLICY-MAKING AS REGARDS 16–19s SINCE 1944

Institutional issues

These issues have centred on the most suitable types of institutional provision for 16–19s. From an acceptance of an essentially dual provision for this age range in both school sixth forms on the one hand, and technical colleges or colleges of further education on the other, there has developed a movement in favour of having an institutional break at 16, and incorporating all 16–19 educational provision into colleges, whether as sixth-form

177

colleges under secondary schools' regulations and dealing specifically for 16–19s, or as tertiary colleges, usually under further education regulations, and often dealing with the whole of the post-16 age range. This movement has been strongly resisted by supporters of school sixth forms.

Of the tripartite division of secondary education which formed the basis of many LEA schemes of reorganisation after the 1944 Act, it was envisaged that, of the three types of suggested schools—modern, technical and grammar—only the latter two would have post-16 (sixth-form) provision. In the event, relatively few LEAs opted for technical schools: in 1958, out of almost 6000 secondary schools, only 270 were technical schools, catering for about 100 000 pupils. And out of these, only 133 had sixth forms (Crowther 1959, Table 44). Of the rest, all but some 600 were either modern or grammar. This meant that, until the growth in the numbers of comprehensive schools,[1] nearly two-thirds of all 17-year-old pupils in the late 1950s were in maintained grammar schools (Crowther 1959, para. 329b). The sixth form was therefore the provision for the 'ablest boys and girls' (Crowther 1959 para. 329b), and as such provided for only a minority of the total 16–19 age range—and that from those who had already chosen to stay on an extra year into the fifth form when the school-leaving age was then 15. This provision for a relative minority was not materially altered by the decline in the numbers of grammar and modern schools in favour of comprehensive schools, or by the raising of the school-leaving age to 16 in 1972. Finally, as discussed in Chapter 13, another group of young people was being provided for in technical colleges or colleges of further education[2] in a variety of modes of attendance.[3]

As the modern school was supposed to be to the grammar school, so the further education college was supposed to be to the school sixth form: in the words of the Crowther Report, it was an 'alternative route' to 'the common goal' (Crowther 1959, para. 463). The new scheme of apprenticeships in a number of industries since 1945 had provided for apprentices to receive one day's release per week from work to attend courses at technical colleges to train them for a specific trade. Hence, the great area of growth in the 1950s and 1960s in technical colleges was in part-time day courses, the majority of which were day-release courses for apprentices (see Table 7.1; and also Crowther 1959, para. 475; Henniker-Heaton 1964, Appendix A, Tables 1(a) and 1(b)).

However, the two types of institution by no means covered the total population of young people under 18 or 19. There were many who entered industries not covered by apprenticeship schemes or who were not apprentices and received no day-release. These covered some 40 per cent or so of the young workers, 'many of them of limited intelligence' (Crowther 1959, para. 274; see also Table 7.1).

There was, however, provision under s. 44 of the 1944 Act for these young people: a network of county colleges of which existing technical colleges, with the creation of suitable courses, would become a part. This provision harked back to an abortive proposal in the Fisher Act of 1918 to establish compulsory part-time attendance at day continuation schools for most young people between the ages of 14 and 18; the proposal became permissive rather than mandatory, and these schools failed to take root. Similarly, after 1944, although under the County Colleges Order of 1947 it became the duty of every LEA to establish and maintain county colleges, no date for implementation was specified owing to scarcity of resources. When the Crowther Report resurrected this idea and urged that it be put into practice in the 1960s (Crowther 1959, para. 302), it was again ignored; while, more vaguely, the Henniker-Heaton Report argued that employers

Table 7.1 *Numbers in schools and non-advanced further education (NAFE) (all numbers subject to roundings).*

Year	Schools		All non-advanced further education (NAFE)		Part-time day (including day release) (NAFE)		Those receiving no further education or training	
	Numbers (000s)	Percentage of age range	Numbers (000s)	Percentage of age range	Numbers (000s)	Percentage of age range	Numbers (000s)	Percentage of age range
1956–7[a]	342.8	20.7	222.7	13.4	189.8	11.4	1091.0	65.9
1962–3[a]	634.6	28.4	351.0	15.5	272.9	12.0	1253.5	56.1
1973–4[b]	311.0	16.9	432.0	23.4	297.0	16.1	1054.4	57.3
1978–9[b]	368.0	17.6	500.0	24.0	288.0	13.8	1177.2	56.3

[a] From Henniker-Heaton (1964), Appendix A, Tables 1(a) and (b). Figures are for 15 to 17-year-olds.
[b] From Macfarlane (1980), Table 1. Figures are for 16 to 19-year-olds.
Note: Both sets of figures probably underestimate the numbers of students on part-time day courses by some 20 per cent. Because of the way figures are collected in the FE sector, some part-time day students are counted as full-time equivalents.

should pay attention to the further education needs of their young employees (Henniker-Heaton 1964, paras. 152–7) without making any institutional recommendations.

However, there was a further type of post-16 institution which Crowther recommended and which was given official endorsement in Circular 10/65. This was the 'junior college' which was a 'halfway house' between the school sixth form and the technical or further education college (Crowther 1959, para. 622). But few LEAs opted for junior sixth-form colleges in their plans for comprehensive reorganisation, preferring alternatives that kept sixth forms attached to individual schools: by 1968, only 20 of the then 162 LEAs had submitted plans which included sixth-form colleges in their proposals. (Corbett 1968, p. 15).

There may have been several reasons for this. First, Circular 10/65 was meagre in its endorsement of sixth-form colleges; it made it clear that options including sixth-form colleges were to be limited to a few experimental cases for which approval would be given. Second, there was an expectancy of both a growing school population[4] and an increasing staying-on rate[5] into the sixth form which would mean that most comprehensive schools could support a viable sixth form in terms of numbers. Third, there was pressure from the comprehensive school lobby itself for the prestige and points that the sixth form brought to the schools, giving them parity of esteem and status with grammar schools they replaced — or, sometimes, with whom they existed side-by-side. Fourth, there were ideological factors. Although the issue of sixth-form colleges did not completely overlie the party political divide, the sixth-form college, for many Labour-controlled LEAs, perpetuated at 16+ — whether overtly selective or not — the divide at 11+ that the comprehensive school was meant to do away with (Corbett 1968, p. 15). *Mutatis mutandis*, sixth-form colleges, if selective, did have their attractions for some Conservative-controlled LEAs who saw them as possible 'centres of excellence' to replace grammar school sixth forms.

Circular 10/65 made no mention of the further education sector, in its six possible model schemes of comprehensive secondary reorganisation. Again, a number of reasons may be posited. First, schools and further education were aiming at different markets: the FE sector was occupied with coping with the growth of part-time day education connected with employers and training, and for which the 1956 White Paper on Technical Education had envisaged a capital programme of £12 million to build and expand colleges. Schools, meanwhile, were busy coping with the growing school population. In these expanding markets, there was as yet little competition for clients. Second, financial resources were available for both sectors[6] even though some duplication was inevitable. Third, there was an educational divide which had long held that schools and colleges served different educational purposes — a divide which was reflected in the DES. Edward Boyle, Minister of Education from July 1962 to March 1964, characterised this divide as a 'dialectic' between what he termed the 'social justice' tradition and the 'technical college' tradition within the DES, and he perceived this division as 'quite sharp' (Kogan 1971, p. 24).

The result of this was parallel development in both sectors, with inevitable duplication and confusion, characterised by one interest group as 'a jungle' (ACFHE/APTI 1975, p. 4). At least one former minister of education — Edward Boyle — was arguing in 1971 for a new Education Act which would rationalise the framework for 16–19s (Raison 1976, p. 11). But in the event, the reverse occurred: not only was there no new Act to rationalise 16–19 provision, but also there was the total omission of any reference to '16–

19s' in the 1972 White Paper *A Framework for Expansion* (DES 1972) — supposedly the educational blueprint for a decade. When the OECD examiners criticised this omission (OECD 1975, p. 32), the DES defended itself by identifying a series of problems caused by the confusion: organisational complexity, lack of reliable data, changing adolescent attitudes to work and learning, and uncertainty about appropriate content as the reasons for the omission (OECD 1975, p. 55).

But, by the late 1970s, a new series of factors led to pressure for rationalisation of 16–19 provision. First, the chronic economic crises of the 1970s led governments to adopt a policy of cutting public expenditure: projected education expenditure was reduced from the mid-1970s (Fowler 1979, p. 58 ff.). This in turn led to an increasing concern with the more efficient and effective use of existing resources both in general and in the specific area of 16–19s. This theme runs through both Circular 10/75 — the first governmental circular since the ending of percentage grants in 1959 to suggest to LEAs where to make cuts — and the then Prime Minister's (James Callaghan's) Ruskin College speech in October 1976.

Second, there was the growing problem of falling school population, sequent upon the falling birth-rate for most years after 1965, and which would begin to bite hard into the secondary sector in the 1980s. More seriously for 16–19 provision in schools, the staying-on rate had risen hardly at all since 1972 (DES 1979, p. 2). Thus, at the beginning of 1977 both the then Secretary of State for Education (Shirley Williams) at the North of England conference in January (see summary in the *Times Educational Supplement*, 14 January 1977) and the then Permanent Secretary at the DES (James Hamilton) at the Society of Education Officers in February (Vaughan 1977) suggested not only that rationalisation of 16–19 provision was necessary, but also they both hinted broadly at the way this might be done: using the sixth-form college or the more novel concept of the tertiary college.

The tertiary college was a college that brought all 16–19 provision together in an area in one college under further education regulations, in an extension of the sixth-form college idea: some were primarily for 16–19s, while in others adult education was also contained within the college (for a discussion of tertiary colleges, see for example James and Miles 1978 or Cotterell and Heley 1981). The first one was opened in Exeter in 1970; by 1977 there were 12, and by 1980 there were 15 in operation (Macfarlane 1980, Table 4).[7] For a number of LEAs, tertiary colleges were a means of making financial savings by cutting out duplication. For others, particularly Labour-controlled LEAs, now that comprehensive secondary schools had become the norm, a break at 16 with all potential students in one college seemed the very obverse of a dozen years previously, sweeping away the divide at 16 between the 'elitist' sixth forms and further education colleges for the rest. By the early 1980s, a number of metropolitan, Labour-controlled LEAs were submitting tertiary college plans to the DES; and a tertiary system of colleges had become the policy of both the Labour Party and the SDP by 1982 (Labour Party 1982; Social Democratic Party 1982).

The growing debate on the institutional issue led the DES to set up a working party of local and central government representatives to produce a White Paper on the issue. With the change of government in May 1979, the working party was strengthened and a junior minister (Macfarlane) put in charge of it and its report was issued in December 1980 (Macfarlane 1980). It seems clear, from leaks in 1980, that the strength of the schools' interest groups,[8] led by two junior ministers (Dr Rhodes Boyson and Lady Young) was successful in preventing a report which appeared-to be heading for a recommendation of bringing 16–19-year-olds together in tertiary colleges. The final report carefully avoided any recommendation on institutional arrangements (Macfarlane 1980, para. 112) and instead opted for the exhortation that 16–19 provision needed to be looked at in totality with less emphasis on the division between schools and further education (Macfarlane 1980, para. 43).

In the event, the report was not followed by a White Paper; and Circular 4/82 (para. 4) made the point that the Secretary of State would not approve changes of use which would close sixth forms that 'have already proved their worth' (DES 1982b). In practice, the criteria of 'proven worth' appears to be that of large numbers in a particular sixth form, so that in a number of schemes for which approval has been given, tertiary or sixth-form colleges operate alongside sixth forms within an LEA.

Governmental issues

Institutional issues have been complicated by the intervention of governmental agencies other than the DES and LEAs. For convenience, the latter agencies and the national local government system in which they operate will be termed the 'education sub-government'.[9] This will be contrasted with the other agencies, notably the Department of Employment, its predecessor the Ministry of Labour and its sibling the Manpower Services Commission (MSC), which will be referred to as the 'training sub-government'.[10]

Although from 1945 to the mid-1960s it was generally left to employers to decide whether or not they sent their employees to be trained at colleges, by the end of the 1950s British economic and industrial performance was being compared unfavourably with that of our competitors. One of the problems identified as being a bottleneck in the economy was the shortage of skilled labour (e.g. ME 1956, para. 1; Crowther 1959, paras. 77, 83, 85, 91, 202e and 465; ME 1961, para. 67; ML 1962, para. 1). Furthermore, there was no uniform pattern of provision of courses in training (ME 1956, para. 26).

The education sub-government established a more coherent provision of courses for various categories of personnel: technologists, technicians, craftsmen and operatives (ME 1956; Crowther 1959; ME 1961). Meanwhile, the 1962 White Paper and the sequent 1964 Industrial Training Act were the first significant attempts by the Ministry of Labour to pressure employers as regards employee training. The Act established 29 Industrial Training Boards (ITBs) and a Central Training Council. The ITBs could 'fine' employers in the form of a levy of up to 4 per cent of any employer's wage bill (though in practice this never exceeded $2\frac{1}{2}$ per cent) if an employer failed to send employees to be trained; while they gave a grant to those employers who conformed to the Boards' requirements: the levy/grant system.

However, as they were based on individual industries, the Board system could not cope with a number of cross-sector manpower problems which arose from structural changes in the economy.[11] The response of governments was first to weaken the powers of the ITBs — for example, by making the raising of a levy permissive rather than mandatory — and then to restructure the whole system by the 1973 Employment and Training Act. This created the Manpower Services Commission (MSC) which subsumed the powers of the Central Training Council.[12] The MSC is a part of the Department of Employment Group,[13] but, unlike the Department, is not a ministry accountable to Parliament but only to the Secretary of State for Employment. Moreover, it has representation from outside the civil service — for example, trade union interests.

Though the main function of the MSC was initially to fund courses for adult retraining, the post-1974 recession soon shifted the bias of the MSC from retraining adults to the training of the unemployed — particularly the young unemployed. For though unemployment overall quadrupled between 1975 and 1982, unemployment amongst the under-18s went up five times over the same period (MSC 1982, para. 2.3). Moreover, unemployment was concentrated most heavily among the 300 000 or so school-leavers who had few or no educational qualifications (Fowler 1979, pp. 76–7). The MSC thus began a series of 'special' or temporary measures geared to providing this latter category with work preparation or work experience,[14] and some of these measures involved utilising the facilities of further education colleges.

This involvement of education facilities soon brought about tensions between the education and training sub-governments that were even guardedly referred to in the report of the House of Commons Expenditure Committee on policy-making at the DES (Tenth Report 1976, paras. 70 and 71). In this connection, there are several factors which may explain, in the words of the writer of an *Education Digest*,

> . . . the failure of politicians and bureaucrats to think broadly enough across the many strands . . . which affect the education and training of 16 to 19s, and to develop effective structures between the component parts (*Education Digest* 1981, p. ii).

The MSC was able to expand rapidly its role in financing training for the 16–19s because, unlike the DES, it could operate by means of specific grants. Within the context of the education sub-government, money had to be paid via the Rate Support Grant (RSG) to local authorities: there was no way that central government could ensure that local authorities would spend any monies put into the RSG for measures to help the young unemployed would be so spent; on the contrary, the evidence was that it would not.[15]

By contrast, the MSC could work outside the conventional structure of central–local relationships and the RSG by directly funding measures. The MSC could thus move at a much faster pace than the DES. For example, the MSC's ability to pay allowances directly to trainees without going through local authorities led the Secretary of State for Education (Shirley Williams) in 1977, to argue in cabinet that this was a disincentive to those staying on in full-time education, because Educational Maintenance Allowances (EMAs) — means tested and paid at LEA discretion — varied widely but did not average much more than £2 a week (Jackson 1977).[16] Her argument in cabinet was underpinned by research which suggested that even modest allowances would cause substantial numbers to stay on: it was calculated that an input of £64 million in EMAs would result in an extra 40 000 staying on (Stevens and Jackson 1977; Stevens 1980). But the Treasury argued against the provision of money in the RSG for EMAs as there was no guarantee that the money would be spent on them. So all that was obtained was permission for a pilot project in certain selected LEAs, but the government fell, in 1979, before it could be put into operation. Nevertheless, certain LEAs, notably ILEA and Sheffield, did introduce EMAs of £7 a week. By 1980, in both authorities, numbers staying on overall had risen substantially (Stevens 1980). But even this allowance compared unfavourably with the MSC trainee allowance, which by 1980 was £23.50 a week. Despite the actions of various pressure groups, such as the Child Poverty Action Group (see Burghes and Stagles 1983) no national scheme of EMAs had been put into operation at the time of writing.

A further factor which favoured the MSC was the growing political priority of measures to alleviate unemployment, particularly youth unemployment. This meant that while other government departments — including the DES — suffered retrenchment on their projected expenditure, the MSC's budget grew rapidly. By 1978–79, it had reached £643 million per year; by 1984–5, it was planned to rise to £2000 million; and then in 1985–6 to level off at £2400 million. The response of the education sub-government has been twofold. On the one hand, the DES has argued for the same facility of direct grant as the MSC has to fund specific projects.[17] On the other hand there has been some pressure for the splitting up of the MSC's functions. When the MSC's own Consultative Document (MSC 1981a) produced at least two responses (FEU 1981b and ACC 1981) which argued that the training functions of the MSC should become a part of the educational sub-government, perhaps in the form of a new Department of Education and Training, these were studiously ignored in the MSC's summary of responses (MSC 1981b). It is unlikely that other reports from a different angle (e.g. RSA 1982) suggesting the same thing will have much greater impact; while it remains to be seen, through the fortunes of the electoral process, whether party political commitments (Labour Party 1982; SDP 1982) to do something similar will have any success.

Another factor which has led to greater involvement of the training sub-government in 16–19 provision is in part curricular and will be dealt with later. It is sufficient to note here two features. First, policy-making has proceeded without any official distinction being made between the content of education and training. The House of Commons Expenditure Committee merely noted that no sharp distinction could be drawn between training and education, and that much vocational preparation must take place in the education system (Tenth Report 1976, para. 70). But if this gives the education sub-government a large claim to involvement in training, the converse is also true. And the reason for this lies in the second feature: the alleged failure of the education sub-government to cope adequately with the 40 per cent or so who left school with few or no qualifications, and who, by the mid-1970s, formed the core of the young unemployed. It was the failure to make suitable provision for, as it put it, 'the education of most disadvantaged children' that marked the starting point for the OECD report's criticism of the omission of 16–19 from the 1972 White Paper (OECD 1975, p. 36). There was a growing view that the training sub-government could make better provision as regards this cohort.

These factors all came together in 1978: this effectively marked the point when it was decided that the training sub-government would be the dominant partner in the provision for the young unemployed who were low achievers. The Holland Report in 1977 (Holland 1977) ushered in a five-year scheme, from April 1978 to March 1983, called the Youth Opportunities Programme (YOP) which would be the largest of three schemes dealing with unemployed 16–19s. It had an initial budget of £170 million per year, and was aimed at the one in ten of the most disadvantaged young people (about 23 000 a year). It was designed to give them primarily a six months' programme of work experience, with a limited commitment to additional education and training; but the education service clearly had a secondary role, with the emphasis firmly on the work experience element.

However, with the growth of youth unemployment, by 1980 the programme was already dealing with one in eight (234 000 leavers); by 1981, one in four (295 000 leavers). By 1982, half (550 000) of all school leavers passed through a YOP scheme (MSC 1982a, paras. 1.16 and 2.76). Over its five-year life, some 1.8 million young people passed through a YOP scheme. By the time the scheme ended, its original budget had been far exceeded: £1300 million had been spent on it in total, £750 million of that in 1982 alone. By 1980, fee income from the MSC for contracts to provide education and training, much of it for youngsters on YOP schemes, amounted to 6 per cent of total expenditure on non-advanced further education (Macfarlane 1980, para. 60). It is intended that the MSC should provide the funding for 25 per cent of work-related non-advanced further education by 1986–7 (DE/DES 1984, para. 46).[18] Moreover, under the second of its programmes — the Training for Skills Programme (TSPA), established in 1979 — the MSC indirectly contributed to the provision of part-time day students in colleges by its funding, through employers, of some 35 000 first-year apprentices in 1981–2 (MSC 1982, para. 2.70). The third programme — the Unified Vocational Preparation Programme (UVP) — was initially the brainchild of the DES in 1976, and was designed to improve the career prospects of young people in jobs with little or no prospect of further education. Problems both in finding the money and in paying the money directly to local authorities meant that, early in 1982, the MSC effectively took control of the whole programme; the DES's role was changed from a 'sharing' one with the MSC to a 'helping' one (DES 1982c, para. 5).

Thus, although the Macfarlane Report exhorted the education and training sub-governments to work 'harmoniously' together (Macfarlane 1980, para. 63), it is clear that the partnership is an unequal one, and remains so in the successor scheme to the YOPs — the Youth Training Scheme (YTS). The MSC remains the main training agency (DE 1981, para. 51), and the Director of the MSC reiterated to the Standing Conference of Regional Advisory Councils in 1982 that the role of the education service must be a support role, which, at best, would be that of a partner.[19] Since it is intended that the MSC sees the YTS as the first move towards a position where all young people under 18 will be able to choose full-time education or work experience and related training and education (MSC 1982, para. 1.4ii), it seems there will effectively be two patterns running side by side, each operated by a different sub-government in policy-making for 16–19s.

But, more than this, the MSC is now sponsoring the Training and Vocational Educational Initiative (TVEI). In 14 LEAs the MSC is funding provision for specialised vocational and technical education courses for 14–18-year-olds[20] and an additional 40 schemes in September 1984. It may well be that the alternative routes — to re-interpret Crowther's phrase — will begin at 14 rather than 16.

Finally, there is yet another governmental agency which is having an increasing interest in 16–19 provision. The Department of Industry (DoI) has taken over the Schools' Council Schools and Industry Project, and has proposed pilot schemes in schools; while, more specifically for 16–19s, 100 DoI-sponsored Information Technology Centres (ITECs) had, by the end of 1982, been opened in a number of towns[21] to train unemployed 16–19s in various computer skills, in co-operation with private industry. There may yet be a tripartite system for 16–19s.

Curricular issues

It has been noted earlier how policy-making has proceeded, and two sub-governments developed, without any attempt in policy-making documents to define the differences, in curricular terms, between education and training — though it is implicitly assumed that there is a distinction. Moreover, this partly overlies the curricular distinction for policy-making purposes within the education sub-government between 'general' and 'vocational' education. It has always been assumed that a part of training has involved 'vocational' education, which has, until recently, usually meant occupation-specific knowledge, combined with experience in a workplace. If training is characterised by anything in policy-making literature, it has been an emphasis on the skills required to do a job, rather than the personal development of the individual. Again, there is a further distinction used in the education sub-government at post-16 level: 'general' education has been equated with 'academic' education, which in turn has been seen as suitable for, as Crowther put it, the 'most able boys and girls'. On the other hand, 'vocational' education has been perceived as suitable for those less able to cope with an 'academic' education.

This, historically, has been translated into institutional terms. The school sixth form was the provision for the ablest with a number of hallmarks: a close link with the universities, specialisation, independent work, intellectual discipleship and social responsibility (Crowther 1959, paras. 330–37). Although Crowther complemented this view of sixth-form work by a broader view (Crowther 1959, paras. 447–60) of a sixth form to prepare pupils for entry to the professions, the essence of the sixth form was preparation for university entrance. Thus the curriculum of the grammar school, inherited from the public school and emulated by the comprehensive school was general in the sense that it was not geared to any specific vocation, and enshrined, after the ending in 1949 of the 'grouped' School Certificate, in Advanced Level GCE, a single-subject examination. This served — somewhat ambiguously in Crowther's view (Crowther 1959, para. 446) — both as a school leaving examination and a unversity entrance examination.

But the sixth-form curriculum, in Crowther's opinion, suffered from two major deficiencies. First, although 'general' in the sense that the subjects were not geared to any vocational area, it was too specialised and needed broadening. Second, there was the need to provide 'sixth forms with a difference' for the less academic pupils than those going to university or entering the professions.

As regards the first, Crowther suggested providing 'common' and 'complementary' studies (para. 419): literacy for science specialists (paras. 411–12) and numeracy for arts specialists (paras. 413–15) should be included in this programme. Since then this sort of pattern has acted as the basis for what is usually termed general studies, taught as well as GCE subjects in the curricula of sixth forms in most schools. But by the late 1960s, GCE 'A' Level itself was being questioned as being too specialised, and the 1970s saw a number of proposals, largely from the Schools' Council, most of which proposed to restructure totally the examinations system[22] for 16–19s in sixth forms, which would have had the curricular effect of reducing the degree of specialisation and depth and broadening the area of study: notably the 'Q' and 'F' levels and, less radically, the 'I' level, which would be complementary to Advanced level GCE.[23] While other proposals foundered, the 'I' level concept has reappeared in the decision to establish Advanced Supplementary (AS) level courses alongside 'A' level GCE courses, the new examination to begin in 1989 (DES 1985a). This will be a year later than the first General Certificate of Secondary Education (GCSE) examination (DES 1985b), which will implement the Secretary of State's previous acceptance in principle (DES 1982f) of the recommendations of the Waddell Report (Waddell 1978) to restructure Ordinary level GCE and combine it with the

Certificate of Secondary Education (CSE) into a common system of examination at 16+.

As regards the second deficiency — the lack of provision for the 'less academic' sixth former — Crowther did propose the beginnings of a move towards a more integrated, course-based curriculum of linked subjects (para. 456). But it was not until the growth in numbers of this type of sixth-former in the early 1970s — often termed the 'New Sixth' — that an experimental subject-based examination, the Certificate of Extended Education (CEE), was introduced from 1972. But this moved away from the course-based suggestions of Crowther, and had no practical bias towards, say, nursing or commerce as Crowther had suggested. Again, it was the increasing criticism of education's alleged failure to serve the 'less academic' pupil that prompted the Keohane Committee, set up to investigate the feasibility of the CEE, to recommend skewing the CEE more towards a vocational bias (Keohane 1979). But the CEE did not offer an alternative basis of general education that was not also academic. The sixth form thus continued to be dominated by GCE candidates (see Macfarlane 1980, Table 1); and the government did not approve the Keohane proposals.

It was from further education that an alternative conception of 'general' education emerged: the concept of vocational preparation.

In the 1950s, just as schools were the focus of 'general' education that was 'academic' for the 'ablest', it was in further education colleges that 'vocational' education took place, and, as such, students were much more instrumentally motivated (Crowther 1959, para. 484), and on a plethora of courses (Crowther 1959, para. 464). The problem, therefore, was twofold. First, there was a need to rationalise provision and courses by level of skill: technologist, technician, craftsman, operative (ME 1956, paras. 56–80; Crowther 1959, paras. 479–83 and Appendices A and B to Chapter 29; ME 1961, paras. 21–40), together with 'general' (diagnostic) courses for school leavers who might be suited to being either craftsmen or technicians (ME 1961, paras. 41–3). Further, there was concern with the high wastage rates on courses and with measures, like better selection procedures, to reduce them (ME 1956, paras. 81–85; Crowther 1959, paras. 505–33; ME 1961, paras. 37; 45–51; 56–62). Although the 1961 White Paper urged the need to develop courses specifically for technicians, where there was then a gap (ME 1961, paras. 5 and 30–33), it was not until 1969 that the Haslegrave Committee, set up in 1967, recommended a set of new modular-based courses run by two new examining bodies — the Technician Education Council (TEC) and the Business Education Council (BEC)[24] with 'bridging' courses between craft and technician levels. And the system was not properly under way until a decade later.

The second problem was in part bound up with the first and similiar to that in the school sixth form: how to broaden the courses. Although the 1956 White Paper stated that a place would always have to be found for what it termed 'liberal education' in technical studies, the Crowther Report refined and extended this idea, in that it recommended that, at least in county colleges, the basis of the curriculum should be personal development rather than vocational education (Crowther 1959, para. 274). This was an attempt to define a concept of general education that was not also academic. Further, in existing further education colleges, Crowther wished to see both a full-time induction period for new students to assess their capabilities (paras. 541–46) and the development of a tutorial system (paras. 547; 549).

In the event, the county college recommendations were lost, and there was no systematic attempt to put into operation the recommendations on induction and tutorial provision either. What remained was a concept of general education which in practice meant adding the subject of 'general studies'[25] to the curriculum of most technical courses in colleges, even if the aims and content of general studies have remained an issue of hot debate ever since, and general studies consequently had great problems in establishing its credibility.[26] Expressive notions of personal development, as represented by general studies, sat uneasily in the instrumental curriculum of the colleges, dominated as they were at this time by the need to produce product skills in their students for particular industries.

However, the concept of vocational preparation offered a new attempt to develop a curriculum of general education that was not also academic.[27] This concept emerged from a section of the education sub-government: the Further Education Review and Development Unit (FEU), set up in 1977 as an advisory, intelligence and development unit for further education (DES 1982d, p. 45; DES 1982e, pp. 10–11).[28] While purveyed in the language of training — that is, as the development of skills — in conception, vocational preparation is a process of personal development (FEU 1981a, paras. 32–64). As such, it has proved attractive to the MSC as it seems a way of producing a flexible workforce with process skills, such as planning and diagnostic skills, that can easily be transferred as the context of work changes in the economy (MSC 1982, paras. 2.5c and 410f), unlike the product skills produced by the occupation-specific training encouraged by the single-industry ITBs. Hence vocational preparation is the basis of the Youth Training Scheme, the 48 week training and work-experience programme for all unemployed school leavers. The main elements of the YTS are clearly laid down in the 1981 White Paper: induction and assessment; basic skills; occupationally relevant education and training; guidance and counselling; record and review of progress (DE 1981, para. 26). In all this, there is more than a whiff of Crowther revisited. Paradoxically, the expressive has now also become the instrumental: the notion of personal development has been transformed, through the medium of vocational preparation, into that of personal skills.

This same concept of vocational preparation is being applied within the education sub-government. Again, the FEU played a key part. The Mansell Committee[29] was set up to examine pre-employment courses for young people in further education (Mansell 1979, para. 1). Its recommendations — the setting-up of one-year vocational preparation courses made up of a basic core of general education plus vocational studies — were accepted by the government instead of the Keohane proposals, to form the basis of the '17 +' — the Certificate of Pre-Vocational Education (CPVE), to be available to schools as well as further education colleges. It is meant to be the education sub-government's equivalent of the YTS and close co-operation is envisaged between those engaged in teaching both YTS and CPVE programmes (DES 1982a, paras. 9 and 10; 1985a, p. 36).

However, the co-operation is most likely to be within further education colleges; for it is not intended that schools should have any direct[30] part in the YTS itself (DE 1981, para. 29), which may increase the concentration of schools on their traditional, if declining, 'A' level GCE market in the sixth forms (Watts 1982, p. 2), especially if 'high quality' YTS courses are developed as a foundation year for students wishing to enter the professions and who have hitherto taken 'A' levels. A former Senior Chief Inspector, Sheila Browne, has even suggested that the MSC's 14–18 TVEI project will take pupils away from 'A' level subjects, reducing the numbers and making some 'A' level subject groups unviable. It may well be that there will be a new curricular divide between the subject-based curriculum of the sixth form as a preparation for university, and the system-based vocational preparation of the rest.[31]

AN APPLICATION OF DISJOINTED INCREMENTALISM AS A MODEL OF POLICY-MAKING AS REGARDS 16–19 PROVISION

This part of the chapter will be given over to a re-interpretation of the earlier survey of issues in terms of Braybrooke and Lindblom's (1963) strategy of disjointed incrementalism (see also Lindblom 1959; 1979). The essence of the strategy is that policy-making is is assumed to take place in an indefinite and exploratory series of small or incremental steps in response to particular, and frequently recurring, problems. It is the antithesis of comprehensive and synoptic approaches to planning and policy making, and is basically pragmatic: ' . . . it reveals both man's limited capacities to understand and solve complex problems and an unsettled, shifting compromise of conflicting values' (Braybrooke and Lindblom 1963, p. 71). As such, the strategy contains a number of practices or features which ' . . . taken together as a mutually reinforcing set of adaptations . . . constitute a systematic and defensible strategy' (Braybrooke and Lindblom 1963, p. 82). Therefore, in the remainder of this chapter, each of the features which together form elements of the strategy will be applied to the development of 16–19 provision.[32]

Margin-dependent choice

This feature is in many ways the basis of the strategy, for it assumes that policy-makers will consider policies whose results differ only incrementally from what already exists. Questions of ultimate principle will be avoided to minimise conflict (Braybrooke and Lindblom 1963, pp. 74; 85–7).

As regards 16–19 provision, this feature perhaps best explains why there has been no attempt, in institutional, governmental or curricular terms, to undertake a radical reconstruction of provision for 16–19s. In institutional terms, provision in schools and colleges has been allowed to grow in both, with marginal adjustments — the emergence of the sixth-form and tertiary colleges, experiments with consortia of schools — but with both systems remaining side by side. In governmental terms, rather than restructure provision, the distinction between education and training has been institutionalised in two different sub-governments. In curricular terms, there has been a marked reluctance at a public level for policy makers to explore either the purposes and aims of education in any great detail, or its relationship to training; while the development of the concept of vocational preparation is an evolution of the earlier Crowther ideas as to the curriculum of county colleges.

Restricted variety of policy alternatives considered

Braybrooke and Lindblom (1963) argue that if attention is given only to those policies which differ incrementally from the status quo, then many potential policies with more radical consequences will be omitted from consideration (Braybrooke and Lindblom 1963, p. 88).

In institutional terms as regards 16–19s, the policy of instituting county colleges, with all the resource implications, as advocated in both the 1944 Education Act and the 1959 Crowther Report, was ignored as a policy option. Similarly, the omission of the 16–19s from the proposed educational agenda of the 1972 White Paper was, in the words of the OECD report ' . . . a more or less unconscious decision resulting from the concentration on apparent priorities at that time' (OECD 1975, p. 37). In governmental terms, pressure to conflate the education and training sub-governments at central level into a new Department of Education and Training has so far been ignored. In curricular terms, none of the committees which have sat on various aspects of the examinations' structure for 16–19s — Haslegrave (1969), Waddell (1978), Keohane (1979), Mansell (1979) — was given a remit that would allow them to recommend wholesale restructuring of both the schools and further education examination system. Moreover, the emergence of the YTS has not in itself restructured all courses across all levels of skill (from operative through to technician) away from product and towards process skills; so that any developments in this direction will be gradual — if the YTS is extended to become a common foundation year for all levels.

Restricted number of consequences considered for any given policy

Just as certain policy options are ignored, so, Braybrooke and Lindblom (1963) argue, a number of the consequences of those policies which are either considered or adopted are also omitted from consideration (1963 pp. 90, 93).

The duplication of provision in schools and further education as regards 16–19 was ignored until rationalisation of resource provision became a pressing issue in the late 1970s. The increasing involvement of the MSC in 16–19 provision has ignored the consequences for the education sub-government: it was only after the announcement of the YTS that the DES belatedly inquired, in Circular 6/82, as to how the education service proposed to cope (DES 1982c, para. 9). Moreover, the YTS, by concentrating on training, ignores the consequences for trainees when they have taken the programme. Experience of the YOP scheme suggests that trainees will have difficulty in finding jobs afterwards (Banks, Mullings and Jackson 1983; Bedeman and Courtenay 1982; Dawes, Bedeman and Harvey 1982). This is linked to curricular issues: the concept of vocational preparation is one of preparation for work. The consequence, in terms of motivating trainees, if vocational preparation is to be re-orientated as a programme which is intrinsically valuable in itself, is again ignored.

Adjustment of objectives to policies

This feature is characterised by the mutual adjustment of means and ends, rather than the establishment of ends and then a search for a means to obtain those ends. Thus, objectives are never stabilised but are constantly being adjusted; while the means to achieve them are themselves liable to change as the objectives change (Braybrooke and Lindblom 1963, pp. 94 and 97).

On institutional issues, objectives which were pursued were governed by the means to achieve them. The existence of school sixth forms and further education colleges side by side has meant that the objective of rationalising 16–19 provision has had to take into account the physical and human investment in each sector; while the existence of 16–19 provision in each sector has in turn influenced the degree to which rationalisation of 16–19 provision has been feasible. On governmental issues, the same is true: objectives in 16–19 provision are to a great extent conditioned by the existence of an education and a training sub-government, so that, for example, the aim of vocational preparation is achieved by different means within each sub-government. In curricular issues, interest groups have tailored their objectives to fit existing policy themes. On the one hand, given the developing thrust towards relating general and vocational education much more closely, Keohane attempted to skew the CEE towards a more vocational bias, and Mansell — given a much clearer signal in its terms of reference — produced proposals which involved new vocational preparation courses. Again, the MSC's Consultative Document on the New Training Initiative (MSC 1981a) and its sequent Agenda for Action (MSC 1981b) put forward proposals broadly, though not totally, in line with that which the government in its White Paper (DE 1981) showed to be its policy, and with costs which were acceptable.

Reconstructive treatment of data

Braybrooke and Lindblom (1963) suggest that policy-makers restructure fact-systems as new fact-systems are discovered; which in turn leads to the redesigning of policy proposals as new views of the facts are adopted. Both of these in their turn cause shifts in the values deemed relevant to settling the questions at hand (Braybrooke and Lindblom 1963, p. 98). For example, fact-systems have been restructured to remove school leaver unemployment from the political agenda, via the YTS: 'The YTS is not about youth unemployment' (MSC 1982, para. 1.1) The YTS thus removes the MSC's 'policy off' projections of more than 50 per cent school leaver unemployment (MSC 1982, para. 2.3; and Annex 2) from the 'facts'.

By presenting the YTS as a solely economic policy intervention to ensure a supply of suitably trained labour (e.g. MSC 1981a, paras. 5–15; MSC 1981b, paras. 3–15; DE 1981, paras. 1–3; MSC 1982, paras. 1.3–1.18), the extent to which it is also a social policy intervention, (as with the previous YOP) as a policy of social order and social control (see, for example, Stern 1982, p. 28) is ignored.

Moreover, the whole issue of training an adaptable workforce to meet changing industrial or economic needs has certainly been put forward as *a priori* justification of government intervention on the training side (see below); but it can also be interpreted as an *ex post facto* justification for that same intervention.

Serial and remedial orientation of analysis

On the one hand, Braybrooke and Lindblom (1963) identify a feature which they characterise as 'remedial' in that policy-makers react to problems: they define their aims largely in terms of moving away from observed ills rather than towards some other aim

(1963, p. 102). Moreover, they contend that these problems are 'serial' in the sense that many of them are recurrent, so that policy-makers constantly return to the same problems (p. 100).

In this respect, it is possible to interpret policy-making for 16–19s as a series of responses to problems, a number of which are recurrent. One such problem has been that of the unfavourable comparison of the UK performance in education/training, the economy/industry with that of our competitors, and the bottleneck of a shortage of the right type of skilled labour (DE 1972, Annex 2; MSC 1981a, para. 15; MSC 1981b, paras. 4 and 5; DE 1981, paras. 5 and 6; MSC 1982, paras. 1.3, 1.10, and 1.11). Closely allied to this has been the perceived need to create a flexible and adaptable work force with the skills to cope with change (see earlier; ME 1956, para. 8; Crowther 1959, paras. 79 and 80; ME 1961, para. 5; MSC 1981b, para. 7; DE 1981, para. 5; MSC 1982, para. 4.3c). Similarly, the problem of high wastage rates on many courses in technical colleges is a problem to which the literature of policy-making constantly returns (e.g. ME 1956, paras. 81 and 82; Crowther 1959, paras. 513–17, Table 65 and Chart no 19; ME 1961, paras. 12 and 62; Haslegrave 1969, paras. 38 and 119).

On the other hand, new problems which have emerged severally have been, notably, the problem of falling school population and a staying-on rate which has not increased very much since 1972, and which has led to a questioning about the duplication of 16–19 provision; and the issue of unemployment. It is doubtful that, without the problem of high youth unemployment, the YOP or TYS programmes would have ever been mooted.

Social fragmentation of analysis and evaluation

It is this feature which, in Braybrooke and Lindblom's (1963) analysis, is the main reason for the additon of the adjective 'disjointed' to a description of the strategy: they argue that analysis and evaluation of different aspects of a problem are often carried out in a large number of centres with frequently little co-ordination between them (pp. 104 and 105–6).

This feature explains much of the paradox and even contradiction in policy-making in the 16–19 area, notably the negotiative tension between the education and training sub-governments. Moreover, within each respective sub-government there are different centres of analysis. Within the education sub-government, the development of groups who have argued for a break at 16 has been opposed by a number of groups in favour of maintaining a sixth-form presence in secondary schools, and — as has been shown — both have been involved in decision-making in that area. Within the training sub-government, the MSC may be interpreted as a centre of analysis which has gained increasing influence in 16–19 provision.

An evaluation of the usefulness of disjointed incrementalism as an explanation of policy-making for 16–19s

As a strategy of policy-making, incrementalism has, from a theoretical standpoint, been subjected to important criticisms.[33] Among them are the arguments that the strategy is conservative and does not cope easily with policy innovation; that incremental decisions are taken within the context of more fundamental decisions about which the strategy has little to say; and that the strategy is unclear on the question of what is meant by rationality.

Despite these theoretical deficiencies, however, there is some evidence from empirical studies of various social agencies that an incremental strategy of decision-making is one that is extensively used (e.g. Booth 1978; Jansson and Taylor 1978). Education in this country, with its complex relationships of checks and balances[34] is perhaps one of the services most amenable to an incremental model in seeking to explain and describe the dynamics of policy-making; and that, too, is the opinion of a number of policy-makers and policy analysts[35] of this area (e.g. Butler 1971, p. 25; OECD 1975, pp. 49–50; Kogan and Bowden 1975, p. 238; Fowler 1979, pp. 54–5).

Smith and May (1980, p. 159) have suggested, in the light of evidence that incrementalism is widely practised, that whereas rationalist models perform a prescriptive function in advocating what ought to happen in policy-making, incrementalist models perform an explanatory function in describing what actually happens in the making of policy. Lindblom (1979), however, argues that synoptic models, positing as they do perfect knowledge, can do more harm than good:

> The choice between synopsis and disjointed incrementalism . . . is simply between ill-considered, often accidental incompleteness on one hand, and deliberate, designed incompleteness on the other (p. 519).

Moreover, Lindblom (1979) has also developed the related analysis of partisan mutual adjustment[36] in connection with policy analysis. He argues that in all political systems, decision-taking is fragmented or decentralised, to a greater or lesser degree; and that the mutual adjustments (e.g. by bargaining) that each of the participants make with others actually achieves a co-ordination superior to any attempt at central co-ordination (pp. 522–3). In this connection, the notions of policy 'communities' or 'networks', which process issues and problems to the satisfaction of participants (Richardson and Stringer 1981, p. 54) are similar. Policy happens because competing elements in the decision-making process make mutual accommodations endlessly in order that the political process may continue.

Despite its considerable influence elsewhere, the incrementalist approach is rarely applied to the explanation of policy making in specifically educational contexts. Even in such fine exemplifications of incrementalism in action as are to be found in Lodge and Blackstone's (1982) examination of *Educational Policy and Educational Inequality* little attempt is made to make use of ideas and concepts drawn explicitly from the incrementalist model.

It is not easy to explain why so little attention has been given to the incrementalist model as a whole, as opposed to some of its concepts in particular, in the analysis and interrogation of cases of policy making in education. Taking the case of policy making for the 16–19 age group, it would seem that 'incrementalism' (and 'partisan mutual adjustment') offers a persuasive approach to the explanation of how competing participants — DES and MSC, schools and colleges, opponents and supporters of concepts of 'general' and 'vocational' education, 'academic' and 'non-academic' courses, involving a range of alternative rationalities — have, for better or worse, made the areas of 16–19 provision what it is today.

NOTES

1. See above, Chapter 6.
2. The terms 'technical college' and 'further education college' are here used synonymously for convenience, although the latter term only came into common use in the 1960s.
3. Unlike schools, where full-time attendance is mandatory, under the 1944 Education Act, on all those registered as school pupils.
4. In England and Wales, the total school population grew from 5 million in 1946 to a peak of 9 million in 1977 (DES 1979, p. 1).
5. The staying-on rate increased steadily: by 1972, 25 per cent of the secondary school population stayed on in the sixth form for one year, and 16 per cent for two years (DES 1979, p. 2; Boyson 1980).
6. From 1955–64, educational expenditure grew faster than both national income and expenditure in other areas of the public sector; and, though it no longer grew as fast as other areas of public expenditure after 1965, it still continued to rise (see Coates 1972, pp. 37–8).
7. At the time of writing, there were 20 tertiary colleges in operation and a further 13 approved by the Secretary of State.
8. For the case for the retention of sixth forms in some schools, particularly the 'mushroom' sixth form—a number of 11–16 schools feeding in to the sixth form of an 11–18 school—see Naylor (1981).
9. See above, Chapter 2.
10. The distinction between the two sub-governments is heuristic rather than empirical: it is accepted that the interface between them is in practice blurred. Acting together, they form a 'policy network' or 'policy community'. See Richardson and Stringer (1981) and above, p.193.
11. For an analysis of the weaknesses of the ITB structure, see DE (1972) especially paras. 37–42, 103–123, and Annex 1, para. 35.
12. For a critical analysis of the MSC, see Gray (1980) and *Education Digest* (1983).
13. The Department of Employment replaced the Ministry of Labour in 1965.
14. For more detailed discussion of aspects of measures to assist the young unemployed, see Rees and Atkinson (1983).
15. See above, Chapter 2.
16. Burghes and Stagles' 1983 survey of LEAs found that the average EMA paid in 1981–2 was £5.25 a week and the average maximum award was £7.60. In only 8 of 33 LEAs did more than 10 per cent of the previous year's fifth form receive assistance to continue their education, whether in schools or further education. For total spending on EMAs by each LEA in 1981–2, see ESA (1983, pp. 144–6).
17. This argument has met with mixed response both inside and outside the education sub-government: the local authority associations in particular are against the extension of specific grants, which would reduce their autonomy over local expenditure. See above, Chapter 2, for details of ESGs.
18. See also Chapter 2.
19. Speech reported in the *Times Educational Supplement* (17 September 1982).
20. For details of the 14 schemes, see ESAC (1983) pp. 129–43; and Haxby (1983).
21. In October 1982, it was announced in Parliament that a further 50 ITECs were to be set up. It is intended that there will eventually be a total of 175 ITECs (DE/DES 1984, para. 21).
22. One strand of these proposals, however, called only for a merger of 'O' levels and CSE, it was first formally proposed by the Schools' Council in 1970, and formally recommended to the then Education Secretary in 1976, who, in turn, set up the Waddell Committee to investigate its feasibility in 1977.
23. For a full account of these developments, see Schools Council Working Papers, 45, 46, 47 and 60.
24. These councils merged in October 1983 to become the Business and Technician Education Council (B/TEC).
25. Sometimes termed, among others, 'liberal', 'complementary' or 'contrasting' studies. Circular

323 from the Ministry of Education in 1957 officially recognised the need for general studies in technical courses. See also ME 1962.
26. See Blythe (1982, pp. 21–3) for a brief but succinct summary of the main issues in the debate.
27. For some of the organisational and curricular issues this raises, see Woollard et al (1983).
28. For a critical analysis of the FEU, see Ebbutt (1982). From January 1983, the FEU became an independent limited company with charitable basis; though it remains based at the DES.
29. Its chairman was Director of the FEU.
30. Administrative arrangements involving further education regulations may give some schools an input into the YTS.
31. See FEU (1982), which argues that unless there is the possibility of progression to more advanced education/training, vocational preparation will become increasingly identified with the less able unemployed young person (para. 26).
32. An attempt to apply incrementalism to training policy in Britain from 1964–1980 has been made by Richardson and Stringer (1981), though they do not use the features outlined by Braybrooke and Lindblom (1963).
33. See, for example, Smith and May (1980, pp. 151–2) for a survey of these criticisms.
34. See above, Chapter 2.
35. Lindblom (1979) distinguishes between incrementalism as a political pattern, and incrementalism as policy analysis.
36. This concept and one of the features of disjointed incrementalism — social fragmentation of analysis and evaluation — are cognate. Partisan mutual adjustment is seen by Lindblom (1979) as a separate but, in practice, closely linked analysis to incrementalism.

REFERENCES

(ACC) Association of County Councils (1981) *Response to the MSC New Training Initiative — A Consultative Document.* London: ACC.

(ACFHE/APTI) Association of Colleges for Further and Higher Education/Association of Principals of Technical Institutions (1975) *After 16.* London: ACFHE.

Banks, M. H., Mullings, C. and Jackson, E. J. (1983) 'A bench-mark for Youth Opportunities'. *Employment Gazette*, **91**(3), March, 91–5.

Bedeman T. and Courtenay, G. (1982) 'Taking the Opportunity' *Employment Gazette*, **90**(10), October, 44–43.

Blythe, J. (1982) 'Social Education and social and life skills in post-16 education and training'. In A. G. Watts (ed.) *Schools YOP and the New Training Initiative*, pp. 21–23. Cambridge: CRAC Publications.

Booth, T. (1978) 'Finding Alternatives to Residential Care — The Problem of Innovation in the Personal Social Services' *Local Government Studies*, **9**, 3–14.

Boyson, R. (1980) Reply to a question from J. Marshall M.P. in the House of Commons on 28th July, reported in *Education*, 8 August, 151.

Braybrooke, D. and Lindblom, C. E. (1963) *A Strategy of Decision-Policy Evaluation as a Social Process.* New York: The Free Press.

Burghes, L. and Stagles, R. (1983) *No Choice at 16 — a study of educational maintenance allowances.* London: Child Poverty Action Group.

Butler, R. A. (1971) *The Art of the Possible.* London: Hamish Hamilton. Reprinted in part as 'The Politics of the 1944 Education Act'. In G. Fowler et al (1973) *Decision Making in British Education.* London: Heinemann.

Coates, R. D. (1972) *Teachers Unions and Interest Group Politics.* London: Cambridge University Press.

Corbett, A. (1968) 'Sixth-Form Colleges'. *New Society*, 28 March. Reprinted in *Education — A New Society Social Studies Reader* pp. 15–17. First edition. London: IPC Magazines.

Cotterell, A. B. and Heley, E. W. (ed.) (1981) *Tertiary — a radical approach to post-compulsory education.* Cheltenham: Stanley Thornes Publishers.

Crowther, G. (1959) *15 to 18 — Report of the Central Advisory Council for Education (England) Vol I.* London: HMSO.

Dawes, L., Bedeman, T. and Harvey, J. (1982) 'What happens after YOP—a longer term view'. *Employment Gazette*, **90**(1), January, 12–14.

(DE) Department of Employment (1972) *Training for the future—a plan for discussion*. London: HMSO.

(DE) Department of Employment (1981) *A New Teaching Initiative—A Programme for Action*. Cmnd 8455. London: HMSO.

(DES) Department of Education and Science (1972) *A Framework for Expansion*, Cmnd. 5174. London: HMSO (White Paper).

(DE/DES) Department of Employment/Department of Education and Science (1984) *Training for Jobs*. Cmnd 9135. London: HMSO.

(DES) Department of Education and Science (1979) *Report on Education No. 96 — Trends in School Population*. London: DES.

(DES) Department of Education and Science et al (1981) *The Legal Basis of Further Education*. London: DES.

(DES) Department of Education and Science (1982a) *17 + A New Qualification*. London: HMSO.

(DES) Department of Education and Science (1982b) *Circular 4/82—Statutory Proposals for Secondary Schools and Falling Rolls*. London: DES.

(DES) Department of Education and Science (1982c) *Circular 6/82—The Youth Training Scheme: Implications for the Education Service*. London: DES.

(DES) Department of Education and Science (1982d) *The Educational System of England and Wales*. London: DES.

(DES) Department of Education and Science (1982e) *The Department of Education and Science—a brief guide*. London: DES.

(DES) Department of Education and Science (1982f) *Examination at 16 plus: A statement of policy*. London: HMSO.

(DES) Department of Education and Science (1985a) *Better Schools* (White Paper). London: HMSO.

(DES) Department of Education and Science (1985b) *General Certificate of Secondary Education: A General Introduction*. London: HMSO.

Ebbutt, K. (1982) 'The FEU—the first four years'. *Higher Education Review*, **14**(2), 65–79.

Education Digest (1981) '16 to 19'. *Education*, 24 April.

Education Digest (1983) 'MSC: the first decade'. *Education*, 15 July.

(ESAC) Education, Science and Arts Committee of the House of Commons (1983) *Education and Training, 14 to 19 year Olds. Minutes of Evidence together with Appendices*. London: HMSO.

(FEU) Further Education Review and Development Unit (1981a) *Vocational Preparation*. London: HMSO.

(FEU) Further Education Review and Development Unit (1981b) *Response to MSC New Training Initiative—A Consultative Document*. London: FEU.

(FEU) Further Education Review and Development Unit (1982) *Progressing from vocational preparation*. London: FEU.

Fowler, G. (1979) 'The Politics of Education'. In G. Bernbaum (ed.) *Schooling in Decline*, pp. 47–90. London: Macmillan.

Gray, L. (1980) 'The Manpower Services Commission'. In I. Waitt (ed.) *College Administration—A Handbook*, pp. 207–17. London: NATFHE.

Haslegrave, H. L. (1969) *Report of the Committee on Technician Courses and Examinations*. London: HMSO.

Haxby, P. (ed.) (1983) *Technical and Vocational Education Initiative for 14–18 Year Olds*. Coombe Lodge Report **16**(5). Bristol: Further Education Staff College.

Henniker-Heaton, C. (1964) *Day Release*. London: HMSO.

Holland, G. (1977) *Young People and Work. A Report on the feasibility of a new programme of opportunities for unemployed young people*. London: HMSO.

Jackson, M. (1977) 'Mrs. Williams insists on local action to stem unemployment'. *Times Educational Supplement*, 6 May.

James, F. and Miles, J. (1978) *Tertiary Colleges*. Tertiary College Panel.

Jansson, D. S. and Taylor, S. H. (1978) 'Search Activity in Social Agencies: Institutional Factors that Influence Policy Analysis'. *Social Services Review*, **52**, 189–201.

Keohane, K. (1979) *Proposals for a Certificate of Extended Education*, Cmnd 7755. London: HMSO.

Kogan, M. (ed.) (1971) *The Politics of Education: conversations with Edward Boyle and Anthony Crosland*. Harmondsworth: Penguin.

Kogan, M. and Bowden, K. (1975)

Educational Policy-Making. A Study of Interest Groups and Parliament. London: Allen and Unwin.

Labour Party (1982) *16–19— Learning for Life.* London: Labour Party.

Lindblom, C. E. (1959) 'The Science of "Muddling Through"'. *Public Administration Review,* **19,** Spring, 79–88.

Lindblom, C. E. (1979) 'Still Muddling, Not Yet Through'. *Public Administration Review,* **39**(6) November/December, 517–26.

Lodge, P. and Blackstone, T. (1982) *Educational Policy and Educational Inequality.* Oxford: Martin Robertson.

Macfarlane, N. (1980) *Education for 16–19 Year Olds.* London: HMSO.

Mansell, J. (1979) *A Basis for Choice— Report of a Study Group on Post-16 Pre-Employment Courses.* London: FEU.

(ME) Ministry of Education (1956) *Technical Education.* Cmnd 9703. London: HMSO.

(ME) Ministry of Education (1961) *Better Opportunities in Technical Education.* Cmnd 1254. London: HMSO.

(ME) Ministry of Education (1962) *General Studies in Technical Colleges.* London: HMSO.

(ML) Ministry of Labour (1962) *Industrial Training: Government Proposals.* Cmnd. 1892. London: HMSO.

(MSC) Manpower Services Commission (1981a) *A New Training Initiative— A Consultative Document.* London: MSC.

(MSC) Manpower Services Commission (1981b) *A New Training Initiative— An Agenda for Action.* London: MSC.

(MSC) Manpower Services Commission (1982) *Youth Task Group Report.* London: HMSO.

Naylor, F. (1981) *Crisis in the Sixth Form.* London: Centre for Policy Studies.

(OECD) Organisation for Economic Co-operation and Development (1975) *Reviews of national policies for education: educational development strategy in England and Wales.* Paris: OECD.

Raison, T. (1976) *The Act and the Partnership; an essay on educational administration in England.* London: Bedford Square Press.

Rees, T. L. and Atkinson, P. (ed.) (1983) *Youth Unemployment and State Intervention.* London: Routledge and Kegan Paul.

Richardson, J. J. and Stringer, J. K. (1981) 'The Politics of Change, with special reference to the Politics of Industrial Training Policy 1964–1980'. *Industrial and Commercial Training,* February, 54–61.

(RSA) Royal Society of Arts (1982) *Foundations for the Future: An Education and Training Policy.* London: SDP.

Smith, G. and May, D. (1980) 'The Artificial Debate between Rationalist and Incrementalist models of decision making'. *Policy and Politics,* **8**(2) 14–161.

Social Democratic Party (1982) *Foundations for the Future: An Education and Training Policy.* London: SDP.

Stern, E. (1982) 'Learning through work experience in YOP'. A. G. Watts (ed.) (1982) *Schools YOP and the New Training Initiative,* 28–30. Cambridge: CRAC Publications.

Stevens, A. (1980) 'It pays to stay on at school'. *Observer* 12 July, 26.

Stevens, A. and Jackson, M. (1977) 'Mrs. Williams's shaky ground in Cabinet fight for 16–19s'. In *Times Educational Supplement* 24 June.

Tenth Report (1976) *Policy-making in the Department of Education and Science: Tenth Report of the Expenditure Committee.* HC Paper 621. London: HMSO.

Vaughan, M. (1977) 'DES Chief puts his weight behind sixth-form colleges'. *Times Educational Supplement,* 4 February.

Waddell, J. (1978) *School Examinations.* Cmnd. 7281. London: HMSO.

Watts, A. G. (1982) 'Introduction and Overview'. In A. G. Watts (ed.) (1982) *Schools YOP and the New Training Initiative,* 2–5. Cambridge: CRAC Publications.

Wollard, A. et al (1983) 'The "New" F.E.'. *Coombe Lodge Report,* **16**(3). Bristol: Further Education Staff College.

8

HIGHER EDUCATION: TOWARDS A TRANS-BINARY POLICY?

David Elliott

INTRODUCTION

'Apart from electronics and natural gas, higher education has probably expanded faster than any other major industry in the 1960s' (Layard and King 1968, p. 227). These words were written towards the end of a momentous decade, now regarded as something of a golden age by nostalgic academics. Consider what it covered:

1. The Robbins Report (1963) with its enunciation of the famous Robbins 'Principles'.
2. The promotion of the colleges of advanced technology (CATs) into full university status.
3. The Woolwich speech by Anthony Crosland (1965) and the Lancaster speech by the same politician (1967), which officially launched the binary policy.
4. The 1966 White Paper on Polytechnics which gave substance to the principles enunciated at Woolwich and which were to be elaborated and developed at Lancaster.
5. The 1966 Weaver Report on the government of colleges of education which liberated the maintained colleges to some extent from tight local authority control.
6. The designation of the first polytechnics, beginning in May 1968 with 16 schemes approved, subject to modification, and the first admission of students to such institutions from September 1968.
7. Planning Paper No. 2 (October 1970) with its clear indication of the intention of the Department of Education and Science (DES) of expanding the public sector of higher education during the 1970s.

The whole could be said to have culminated in the 1972 White Paper in which resources were to be concentrated in developing the public sector of higher education at the expense of both the universities and the remainder of the further education system. The situation seems very different now (1985). Beginning in the mid-1970s, higher education seems to have been under attack and on the retreat (see Kogan and Kogan 1983). Look at the following:

1. The wholesale 'slaughter' of the colleges of education from 1975 onwards.
2. The 1979 Expenditure White Paper which cut education spending as a whole by nearly 5 per cent, most of the savings to come from the public sector.
3. The 'capping' of the Advanced Further Education (AFE) Pool in 1980 which, it has been argued, was 'a long step towards complete central control of higher education'. (Matterson 1981, p. 189).
4. The University Grants Committee (UGC) administered cuts to the universities in July 1981, with the misery being unequally shared, and with some of the new technological universities such as Salford and Aston suffering most heavily. In March 1985 the UGC Chairman warned of further severe cuts in the latter half of the decade.
5. The establishment of the National Advisory Body (NAB) in 1982, and its extension in 1985 to include the voluntary colleges, to oversee a rationalisation of public sector higher education, which would at the same time reduce overall costs by at least 10 per cent.

To a system reeling from the demographic shocks that had been progressively administered throughout the 1970s, aware that much public opinion was apathetic or even hostile, rationalisation came to be seen as synonymous with cuts. All sectors of higher education seemed to face common difficulties. The 'glad, confident morning' of the 1960s had been replaced by the 'melancholy, long withdrawing roar' of the 1980s.

It is in such a changing context that this paper seeks to examine the apparent determination to abandon the binary policy which has underpinned higher education policy for the best part of 20 years and the trend towards a trans-binary policy that some have detected as emerging into greater prominence over the past few years. In doing so, it attempts to look at four major aspects, which can be expressed in the form of four questions:

1. Has there ever been a binary policy?
2. What is the binary policy?
3. Has the binary policy failed?
4. Is a trans-binary policy emerging?

HAS THERE EVER BEEN A BINARY POLICY?

This question needs to be asked. For a policy to exist there must be: a coherent set of statements expressing the intention to do certain things to achieve certain ends; and a set of actions clearly designed to translate those statements of intent into reality. Does the belief that higher education in England and Wales has been shaped since the mid 1960s by a binary policy satisfy these tests? I believe that, on balance, it does. The Woolwich and Lancaster speeches, together with the 1966 White Paper do add up to a coherent set of policy statements, and the designation and establishment of the polytechnics, and the growing public sector of higher education were clearly designed to translate the rhetoric into reality.

WHAT IS THE BINARY POLICY?

In a nutshell, as Peter Scott puts it (1983, p. 166), 'so far as we have in Britain any policy for higher education, it is the binary policy', a policy evolved by Anthony Crosland and Sir Toby Weaver in the mid-1960s to cope with the issues raised in the Robbins Report and the upsurge of entrants into higher education anticipated in the later 1960s. Such an answer is only partly accurate and over-simplified, and it does not get us very far. Scott goes further and suggests that the policy has a dual nature; it is at one and the same time a conception of how higher education in the United Kingdom ought to be developed and a set of administrative and financial arrangements intended to implement the convictions embodied in the political view. Because of this, he argues, debate about the binary policy is inherently likely to be confused and ambiguous unless the protagonists make it abundantly clear in which sense they are using the term. There is, he says, 'no natural congruence between the two aspects of the binary policy' (p. 166).

Does the purported origin of the policy in the mid-1960s help us to become any clearer as to its meaning? I think it does. The Robbins Report (1963) had presented proposals for expanding the existing system of higher education to meet the increased demand expected, in the process enunciating the famous, much-quoted and, by now, much-criticised 'Robbins Principle', that places should be provided for all young people 'able to satisfy suitable entrance requirements for higher education and who wished to be admitted.' (1963, p. 268). Fowler (1983) claims that this was the only part of the Report to be fully accepted and that 'many of the other recommendations were rejected or quietly forgotten' (p. 266). Robbins assumed that higher education provision was synonymous with university education and suggested a number of changes to strengthen and extend the university sector. The process of rejection was begun by Michael Stewart who has some claim to be recognised as the founding father of the binary policy, a view upheld by Richard Crossman (see Fowler 1983, p. 266). At this point, the desire to maintain close local authority (and DES) control over part of the higher education system was already an issue of some significance.

Crosland is usually given the credit of being the architect of the binary policy and his Woolwich speech in April 1965 is its classic statement. Kogan (1971) reports him as, in private, much less confident than he appeared in public, and inclined to be critical of the civil servants whom he felt had rushed him into a premature disclosure (p. 52). It did reveal the way a power struggle within DES had progressed, for Crosland, in taking the stance he did, had adopted the policy advocated by Sir Toby Weaver, who held that the universities were not sufficiently 'socially responsive', nor under 'social control'. The alternative policy, advocated by Sir Anthony Part, favoured the Robbins approach 'that higher education meant the universities and that in consequence work which existed outside them should be brought under their aegis as far as possible' (Fowler 1983, p. 266).

What then did Crosland do at Woolwich and why did he do it? First, he was proposing to reject further claims from institutions outside the university sector to be transferred to that sector. Second, to try and offset the natural disappointment, he set out to paint a glowing picture of an alternative scenario in which institutions remaining in the public sector (i.e. under local authority control) would become equal but different members of the higher education system, which seems a somewhat curious argument to be put forward by the minister who in Circular 10/65 was rejecting a very similar argument put forward in defence of the existing system within secondary education.

In plumping for this solution, Crosland was clearly rejecting a number of possible alternative models for higher education, such as a unitary system (as Robbins had suggested), a ladder model (which many public sector institutions may have preferred) or an undifferentiated model (which would have essentially left things as they were). Crosland defended his decision with four main arguments (see Pratt and Burgess 1974, p. 204):

(a)   the need for vocational, professional and industrially-based courses could not be fully met by the universities;

(b)   the temptation to many institutions to seek university status would distort their development and depress the standards and morale of the remainder of the further education sector;

(c)   the need to retain substantial elements of higher education 'under social control and directly responsive to social needs';

(d)   the ruinous effect of down-grading the non-university professional and technical sectors.

His claim was that the overriding need was for a pluralist rather than a unitary system.

At Lancaster University in January 1967 Crosland entered into a more carefully reasoned defence of the policy he had adopted, and to which, by now, he had given greater substance in the 1966 White Paper on polytechnics. He argued that the binary policy was already in existence prior to Robbins, indeed that over 40 per cent of students in full-time higher education were outside the universities.

> The plain fact is that we did not start off tabula rasa; we started off with a given historical situation. A plural system already existed. (Pratt and Burgess 1974, p. 208)

Crosland also suggested that such a policy would provide valuable opportunities for educational and social mobility by encouraging working-class young people to undertake degree studies, and that the local authorities ought to be deeply involved in higher education. He asserted that:

> at a time of rapid expansion and changing ideas we want not a monopoly situation in higher education but a variety of institutions under different control — a unitary system would surely imply an omniscience which we do not possess. (Quoted Pratt and Burgess 1974, p. 209)

In conclusion he commented:

> I hope I have said enough to make it clear that I do not want any rigid dividing line between the different sectors — quite the contrary. I think these fears partly arose because 'binary' is possibly not the best word to describe the system of higher education that we have in this country ... we have a strikingly varied, plural and diverse system ... I think this variety and diversity is thoroughly healthy and we should seek to preserve it. (p. 213)

So what was the binary policy? It was the policy publicised and elaborated by Crosland, which legitimised and restated the policies previously followed of developing higher education in two major sectors, an 'autonomous' sector, consisting mainly of universities but containing a number of institutions controlled by the voluntary bodies, and a 'public' sector, under local authority control. Scott 1983, p. 167 supports Crosland's opinion that such a policy was inevitable: 'the effective question has always been not whether a binary line should be drawn but where it should be drawn'. Kogan reports Crosland as arguing more pragmatically that any alternative would have to face up to the major resource problems of tooling-up an indefinite number of institutions to university levels of building, residential accommodation, library facilities and so forth. Others have seen more discreditable motives at work.

J. R. Lukes (1975) claims that the policy was formulated to enable DES to develop higher education more cheaply and retain control of the developments, and that this was the reality that underlay the rhetoric of Woolwich, Lancaster and the 1966 White Paper. Fowler (1983) also feels that it was a means of having higher education on the cheap:

> binarism (is) less the rejection of elitist ideology than the provision of the same number of higher education places in similar subjects at lower cost — or higher education on the cheap. (p. 268)

To writers such as these the real issue in 1965–67 was the struggle for power over the developing higher education system and the DES determination to deny any further drift into autonomy. In this context the binary policy was the validating ideology that underlay the dynamic of change and the impending restructuring of the system (Salter and Tapper 1981). It was based on the triple pillars of equality, efficiency and equity (see *THES* 26.8.83, p. 24) and was 'most obviously expressed through improved access and faster expansion'.

There has been some confusion about what the binary policy was supposed to be doing. Eric Robinson has argued (1968) that it should have been more radical and produced a much more comprehensive system of higher education and some have agreed with him. Pedley, for example, proposed that a hundred comprehensive collegiate universities should be established (see Hoggart: *THES* 28.10.83, p. 9). However, Robinson, Pedley and others were arguing for a different kind of policy altogether, what Scott has called (p. 168) 'the binary policy that might have been'. Those who have suggested that the policy, as enunciated, hindered the natural development of polytechnics and colleges into quasi-university institutions are equally guilty of misunderstanding Crosland's object-ives. There is also confusion in that some have tended to equate binarism with polytechnics, but it is important to remember that the binary policy is not just a polytechnic policy; in a very real sense it is a policy relating to the totality of higher education and 'embodies a particular view of the correct balance of types of institution and of the styles of higher education which they represent within the total system' (p. 168). It is thus a policy relating to colleges of education, to voluntary colleges, to polytechnics and to universities. Unwittingly, however, it has come to be regarded as a policy relating to two sectors, university and polytechnics, autonomous and public sector.

There is one final source of confusion and this is a very important one. It is easy but quite wrong to treat the terms 'binary policy' and 'binary system' as virtually synonymous. That a binary policy was adopted in the mid-1960s is undeniable; that a binary system exists, which is the implementation of that policy, is open to question. As

Scott argues (p. 169), the use of the term 'binary system' implies that there are two relatively homogeneous sectors, an 'autonomous' sector containing mainly universities, and a 'public' sector containing mainly polytechnics. The assumption is that within the two sectors the institutions are very similar. As a description of the system it was not accurate in 1965, let alone in 1985. The non-university sector is extremely heterogeneous, covering voluntary colleges, polytechnics, colleges and institutions of higher education, liberal arts colleges, monotechnic colleges of education, and colleges of further education with advanced courses. The universities, although fewer in number, are also very diverse. Among the universities the appearance of homogeneity tends to dissolve the more closely it is examined: ' . . . to talk of a binary system of higher education is a nonsense . . . The most accurate formula is to talk of a binary policy within a plural system' (Scott 1983, p. 179).

Having considered at some length the genesis and nature of the binary policy, one is bound to ask, 20 years later and facing moves towards a trans-binary policy, if binarism has been a success or failure, and this takes us to the third major issue under consideration in this paper.

HAS THE BINARY POLICY FAILED?

Criticism of the binary policy

Clearly the policy as enunciated by Crosland did not escape criticism at the time and it is informative to examine briefly the nature of these early criticisms.

1. There were those who argued that Crosland was fundamentally mistaken and that the pool of ability was too finite to make it worth expanding higher education outside the universities. The proposals would merely serve to dilute the system.
2. The Labour Party's Taylor Committee in 1963 had argued strongly for a large and undifferentiated higher education system as more in keeping with the party's basic egalitarian philosophy. This point was echoed by Eric Robinson with his conception of the 'peoples' universities' and is still the philosophy of a section of the Labour Party who regard the binary policy as perpetuating an elitist system.
3. Some felt that Crosland had unjustly treated the universities in implying that they were unduly expensive, uninterested in applied studies and insufficiently socially responsive (see Layard and King 1963, p. 247). In their view Crosland should have accepted the Robbins proposals, recognised that the universities conferred high status on applied studies and avoided dissipating resources.
4. Local authority involvement in higher education to the extent apparently envisaged by Crosland filled many with dismay. There were views that LEAs were not up to it and would hamstring development by petty-minded policies. This was to remain a serious point of contention (but see Pratt and Burgess for a contrary view). Government policy towards local authority involvement was itself ambiguous. On the one hand, it insisted that the authorities must be involved and that the new

polytechnics must remain within the public sector. On the other hand, the powers of the authorities were circumscribed quite tightly in the post-Weaver governing bodies established both for polytechnics and colleges of education, a case of giving with one hand and taking away with the other.

One can see in these criticisms the mixture of prejudice and serious worries that one might expect when finding a development of this kind made as explicit as Crosland made binarism explicit in the period 1965–67. The government, however, admitted to few doubts about the correctness of its policies and moved ahead, designating polytechnics and developing the public sector at great speed. In the 1966 White Paper, it nailed its colours to the mast in the trenchant statement 'The Government believes that the best results will be achieved by developing higher education on polytechnic lines wherever possible' (p. 5). A binary policy did imply a binary divide between the universities on the one hand and public sector institutions offering advanced further education (AFE), principally the polytechnics, on the other. How did the institutions on either side of the divide differ? A succinct summary was offered by Sir Peter Swinnerton-Dyer in December 1983 (see *THES* 16.12.83, p. 4). He saw five components to the binary divide:

1. Style and dignity. Universities had all the paraphernalia of charters, chancellors and powers to award their own degrees. Public sector institutions had none of these.
2. Clientele. Universities mainly catered for the 18 + group, studying for first degrees at honours level, while polytechnics also catered for a wide range of part-time, mature and post-experience students, many engaged on sub-degree work.
3. Research. This was seen as a major element of university activity but only peripheral to the main aims of public sector institutions, though this is changing rapidly at the present time.
4. External influences. Universities were seen as largely free from external academic influences while polytechnics served a wide range of professional bodies as well as CNAA.
5. Self-government. Universities were seen as autonomous whereas most public sector institutions were maintained by local authorities.

Although it is possible to disagree in detail with the five points, there is little doubt in my mind that they formed the basis of the public image of the two sides of the binary divide, the realisation of the binary policy.

But did the binary policy work? Or, to put it another way, has it failed? Scott argues that this is, in one sense, the wrong question to ask since, in his view, a binary policy is inescapable. The real question is: has *this* binary policy failed i.e. have the particular administrative, economic and political arrangements set up in the late 1960s to develop higher education in Britain failed? To answer that question, one really needs to identify the goals established in 1965–67 and examine to what extent these have been achieved in the sense intended by Crosland, Weaver et al. It is to that task that I now wish to address myself and in doing so to adopt the basic formula of analysis used by Peter Scott in his Leverhulme Seminar paper on this issue in which he identified five main objectives of the binary policy (Scott 1983).

Five objectives

To prevent the total domination of the higher education system by the universities

Robbins had recommended a university-controlled system for higher education.In addition to making the CATs into universities, there had been proposals for the creation of six new universities and the virtual absorption of the training colleges into the university system. Whatever else the binary policy did or did not set out to achieve, it determined to reject these recommendations. There were to be no more new universities for at least a decade, and the colleges of education (as the teacher-training colleges were renamed) were to remain under LEA or voluntary body control. In this respect the colleges, linked to the universities for validation purposes but not allowed to merge with them or enter into any organic relationship, uneasily straddled the binary divide as a number of them still do, in spite of the developments of the late 1970s. In this way, the government produced a policy that was 'both radical and conservative' (Scott 1983, p. 171), radical in that it made explicit the view that 'the university was not the only conceivable model for a fully mature institution of higher education' (p. 171), but conservative in that it sought to maintain a balance between types of institution that existed in the early 1960s and that Robbins had proposed to alter. Robbins had gone in for university empire-building on a grand scale and Crosland was preventing this from happening by developing the AFE sector as a respectable counterweight. Thus Crosland's policy was radical in its conceptions but conservative in its administrative arrangements.

This objective was largely accomplished. The university sector was prevented from expanding and the figures show the balance remained quite close.

1962/63   60 per cent of full-time students in universities (130 000 out of 216 000)
1980/81   58 per cent of full-time students in universities (297 200 out of 516 300)

Thus in global terms, in spite of considerable changes to the system, the number of students in non-university institutions on full-time courses as a percentage of the whole has hardly changed. If the objective itself was a valid one in 1965, then it has certainly been accomplished.

To encourage the development of vocational or 'relevant' courses in higher education

This view was clearly expressed by Crosland in his Woolwich speech (quoted Pratt and Burgess 1974, p. 204), with the implication that the universities either could not or would not devote time and effort in developing such programmes. By the time of his Lancaster speech Crosland would seem to be back tracking on this objective because there is no major reference to it in that speech. Did he now reject his former view? Or did he feel that it had been too crudely put, had aroused too much unnecessary antagonism? Scott believes that there are signs that the objective was still around in sections of the 1972 White Paper (see p. 9) and in the generally-held view that polytechnics were intended to offer a more 'relevant' form of higher education (Fowler 1982, p. 131).

What, after all, were 'relevant' courses in higher education? Quite clearly, in the context of the 1965–67 debate, they were courses of advanced technological education with an overt vocational emphasis. There was the widely-held belief that the universities were concerned with 'ivory tower' education; that if they ever got involved with science and technology, it was on the level of 'pure' rather than 'applied' studies. Ignoring the point that these assumptions were never really subjected to detailed analysis, the fact remains that many people believed them to be true, and this led to the understanding that the new public-sector higher education institutions would remedy the alleged deficiency.

Crosland claimed that the institutions he proposed to develop would similarly be vocationally-orientated 'with opportunities for learning comparable with those of the universities, and giving a first-class professional training' (Quoted Pratt and Burgess p. 204).

Scott claims that this argument went underground after the Woolwich speech, but its influence remained (p. 173). It ignored the fact that Robbins had made proposals to develop technological education (see *THES* 5.8.83, p. 24 and 12.8.83, p. 32) and that the universities had made heroic efforts to develop courses in applied sciences, engineering, metallurgy and other vocational and 'relevant' areas of study, only being held up by lack of appropriately-qualified students (see Fowler 1982, p. 124). Unlike the first objective, this second objective contained within itself a number of untested assumptions and socio-philosophical assertions that were never examined with sufficient intellectual rigour at the time of its formulation.

In seeking to establish whether or not this objective has been achieved one runs into major problems of definition. What are more vocational or 'relevant' courses anyway? As Fowler says (1982, p. 131) 'vocationalism is, in part, like beauty, in the eye of the beholder'. How does one measure 'relevance'? Is it to do with the inputs, the through-put, or the outcomes? Do the polytechnics offer significantly different portfolios of courses from the universities, or significantly more vocationally relevant courses? In spite of the obvious difficulties and ambiguities inherent in this objective, one can suggest some tests by which claims to 'relevance' can be measured. Scott suggests three, namely:

(a)   the characteristics and perception of students — inputs;
(b)   the balance of subjects, modes of study and methods of teaching — the through-put;
(c)   the employment to which students go on completion of their courses — the outcomes.

In relation to the first, Donaldson (1975) found that on most key issues students saw little or no distinction between the two sectors. The second test is more complex. As far as balance of subjects is concerned, there seems little difference; the most rapid growth in polytechnics has been in subject areas more akin to university courses than traditionally important FE programmes. In modes of study, polytechnics have tended to be more adventurous, developing modular degrees and sustaining sandwich courses more fully than the universities. The evidence in relation to the third test is also ambiguous; there seems little real difference in patterns of employment of university and AFE graduates. However, Scott's analysis of the employment patterns of graduates in biological sciences, management and business studies, and mechanical engineering (p. 181) seems to suggest that employment of polytechnic graduates tends 'to be at the "sharp" end of industry and commerce, in production rather than R and D, in marketing rather than in financial control' (p. 181). The tests then, such as they are, would seem to suggest that this objective, in spite of its ambiguity, is reaching a measure of achievement.

To sustain full-time sub-degree courses and part-time advanced courses

This particular objective seems quite clear-cut, occurring as it does in both the Woolwich and Lancaster speeches and receiving emphasis in both. It was maintained at the forefront of ministerial activity. Public sector higher education, unlike the universities, was to treat sub-degree courses and part-time advanced courses as equally important as full-time degree programmes. However, the policy was devised to concentrate full-time courses as far as possible in the polytechnics, which would also have a substantial share of sub-degree and part-time advanced courses. Other institutions in the public sector could offer sub-degree and part-time advanced courses, but the latter only if there were already full-time degree courses being taught, or in association with an institution, such as a polytechnic, that was offering such courses. Thus there were a number of ambiguities in that the implications of the policy in relation to concentration or wider dispersal of sub-degree and part-time advanced courses were never fully spelled out and practice obscured rather than clarified the issue. However, the general thrust of this objective seemed clear.

Critics of polytechnics have mounted a major onslaught on their alleged failure to achieve this objective. The polytechnics have been condemned for academic 'drift', for aping the universities, for seeking university status by the back door (Robinson 1968; Pratt and Burgess 1974), for abandoning sub-degree courses, and for restricting part-time advanced courses. Yet, as Scott argues (pp. 181–182), 'the record is rather more ambiguous'. The climate has generally been hostile to the development of sub-degree and part-time courses. The way Burnham FE graded levels of work, the mandatory grants system with its built-in bias towards full-time degree courses, the increasing scepticism among employers about the value of day-release for their employees, and the growing demand for professional qualifications at degree level have all contributed to 'the virtual stagnation in the number of part-time students whether studying during the day or the evening' (Scott p. 181). There has instead been 'an explosive growth of degree students in polytechnics and colleges', although this may well have been exceptional in soaking up the existing surplus. Government policies, such as phasing out all sub-degree work in teacher training for example, have contributed to this phenomenon. Scott shows (p. 182) that about one-third of enrolments in polytechnics in 1973 were for part-time courses and the figure had hardly changed by 1978. There is little evidence to support the charge that the polytechnics have abandoned part-time courses wholesale.

To keep a substantial part of higher education 'under social control and directly responsive to social needs'

In some respects this was the most contentious and politically most significant of the objectives laid down by Crosland. In his Woolwich speech he used the terms quoted in the heading, but at Lancaster denied that this meant that the universities were not socially responsive. What he meant can be deduced from the examples he quoted in the Lancaster speech. Clearly, within DES, as Lukes argues, there was the major fear that institutions would drift towards university status and, in achieving this, become 'autonomous' i.e. less directly responsive to detailed administrative control. There is no doubt that this is what lay behind the refusal to accept the Robbins proposals in relation to the teacher training colleges and the subsequent policy in relation to polytechnics. 'Social control' was, as

Scott argues, essentially 'a rather limited and even negative concept'. It was based on fear of losing control of a rapidly expanding system; anarchy could only be kept at bay by the establishment of a firm battery of administrative controls.

That this was the basic reason can be seen when one turns to look at the companion objective of LEA involvement. In spite of the rhetoric of Woolwich and Lancaster, all the arrangements for the government and academic organisation of the polytechnics restricted local authority involvement (Locke 1975). The local authorities were to ensure good financial husbandry and to guarantee pluralism, yet their real powers were limited. There was thus a basic lack of clarity at the heart of the whole policy. No-one ever made it clear what the social needs were or who would identify them in the future. The form of government developed for the polytechnics effectively precluded any forms of direction from outside, and certainly during the late 1960s and for most of the 1970s there was no attempt to engage in any sort of direction either on the part of local authority or central government. Presumably, the polytechnics themselves were to identify the 'social' needs and then respond by proposing appropriate courses which the administrative machinery could process. There was, however, no evidence that the academic or managerial staff of the institutions concerned possessed such prescience. The system of course approval that was established forced the institutions to concentrate their attention on meeting established demands rather than generating new, maybe more socially responsive, but possibly less popular, courses. (See Cadbury's article 'The Challenges of a Changing World', *THES* 25.11.83, p. 18 for a view supporting the basic argument of this paragraph.)

In so far as the policy set up a machinery to maintain 'social control' in the sense outlined above it has been very successful. The machinery has remained largely unchanged, although applied with a fair measure of freedom in the heady days of expansion. DES has rigidly controlled the teacher-training system, largely through a manpower planning model that has been consistently inaccurate, being based on shifting presuppositions (See Chapter 3). The regional machinery became increasingly harsh in the later 1970s, basing its decisions ever more clearly on projected or anticipated student demand. In this respect the stated NAB intention of steering the system towards programme rather than course approval, perhaps ultimately approval of a whole institution with its complete portfolio of courses, is an acknowledgement from the centre that the machinery set up to deal with this policy objective is no longer adequate.

The role of the local authority in higher education has been very difficult to determine. There is no doubt that many LEAs have generously supported their institutions of higher education until recently. There is also no doubt that others have been less generous, more restrictive. Increasing demands for greater freedom from local authority control were heard during the 1970s from the Committee of Directors of Polytechnics (CDP) and others, even to the extent of seeking chartered status (i.e. to become universities); and in 1981 the government actually proposed to remove all major institutions of higher education from local authority control (DES 1981). In spite of the horror stories, there is little evidence of general LEA interference in the academic development of polytechnics. Within the polytechnics, strong central management has emerged, over whom local authorities exercise fitful and often marginal control. In fact, Crosland never clearly showed why 'social control' had to mean 'local' control (Fowler 1982, p. 129) and in reality, as already suggested, it has meant central control with a veneer of local influence.

To develop the potential of public sector institutions to attract working class students and other 'disadvantaged' groups

In Scott's view this was 'only half an objective' (p. 44). Certainly it did not crop up in the Woolwich speech and occurred only in an oblique way in the Lancaster speech. The prevailing belief was that:

(a) the universities were inescapably and irredeemably middle class in terms of their social constituency;

(b) a great pool of untapped talent lay available which the nation needed, and that an institutional framework ought to be devised to enable it to come forward.

In this respect, many saw the polytechnics and other AFE institutions as a solution; the young working-class student would attend the local technical college although he/she might be frightened off a conventional university education. Crosland placed great emphasis on this at Lancaster where, as Scott argues, there appeared 'the strongest official statement of the "egalitarian" objectives of the binary policy' (p. 15) that was made. Crosland identified the groups that he anticipated would be particularly assisted by the policy he was proposing, namely

(a) under-achievers at school who for one reason or another had failed to make the university system;

(b) those who left school at the close of compulsory education and gained qualifications in non-advanced FE;

(c) mature students anxious to make up later in life for education missed at 18+ ;

(d) first-generation students socially or psychologically averse to entering the university sector.

How linked these groups actually are to social class is a matter of debate but it certainly became part of the received wisdom. As Donaldson (1975) pointed out:

> This argument is so credible that it is still quite widely believed (in 1975), notwithstanding the papers and articles which have been published showing evidence to the contrary. (p. 19)

Crosland also appeared to believe that the only alternative to his policy would be to follow the Robbins recommendations which, he felt, would create a truly binary divide of horrendous proportions. The universities would secure the vast majority of degree courses and all other institutions would be confined to sub-degree or part-time work. In his view, this would be educationally and socially divisive. From this point of view the public sector institutions must be comprehensive, covering degree, sub-degree and part-time courses, to enable a genuinely comprehensive system of higher education to emerge.

To what extent has this objective been achieved? It is undeniable that where a comparison across the binary divide is possible, polytechnics students generally have a poorer 'A' level profile than university students (DES 1982, p. 5). More polytechnic students begin degree courses with other than conventional 'A' level qualifications. A much higher percentage of such students are 25 or over (in 1978 20 per cent of full-time and sandwich course students in polytechnics compared to 7 per cent of university students). A larger number are of working-class origins (36 per cent as against 27 per cent). In spite of the qualifications one can attach to all these points, Scott believes that there is some substance to the view that this objective, whether consciously formulated by

Crosland or not, has gone some way to achievement. However, Hoggart claims that the socially privileged character of higher education has hardly been challenged. 'The great body of working-class people have been left almost untouched' (*THES* 28.10.83, p. 11), and in another *THES* article (18.11.83, p. 13), Gareth Williams reports on a study which shows that the relative position of working-class and middle-class participation in higher education had hardly changed between 1961 and the late 1970s. As Williams remarks:

> This suggests that unless there have been dramatic changes since 1961 in the distribution of intellectual ability among social classes, the pool of untapped ability defined in Robbins' terms remains at least as large as it was then.

The evidence then appears somewhat ambiguous.

Success or failure?

In thus reviewing these objectives and the extent to which they have been achieved, can one say that the binary policy has been successful bearing in mind the ambiguities and reservations identified? It is quite possible for the binary policy as formulated by Crosland and Weaver to have achieved its objectives, yet for those objectives to have been misconceived or stated in unduly restricted terms. It is certainly no indication that the binary policy has been a success. There are a number of weaknesses to which one has to draw attention.

Peter Scott claims (pp. 187–192) that there were five major flaws in the implementation of the binary policy such that, in his view, the present structure no longer provides the best environment in which to pursue its goals. These flaws are:

1. All the emphasis and attention has been on the public sector so that, in fact, there was only half a policy until very recently.
2. The binary policy enabled the universities to escape much needed reforms in the middle and late 1960s.
3. The original policy was implemented by trying to concentrate most of the advanced courses in too limited a number of large, comprehensive institutions, the polytechnics.
4. The policy of concentration failed because of the problems of teacher education and the emergence of a large and vociferous 'third force' in colleges and institutions of higher education.
5. It remains unclear whether 'its centrifugal administrative intention has been powerful enough to overcome centripetal forces by disciplines' (p. 191).

Of these points, the first two and the second two are linked together very closely and seem undeniable. The fifth I find difficult to understand and am not even sure that were it to be true it would constitute a definite weakness in the binary policy. Perhaps the most important is the fourth point, because government policy over the mid to late 1970s has produced a complicating factor in the reorganising of the colleges of education and the transformation of many of them into liberal arts colleges, often still retaining residual teacher training functions, thus blurring the distinctions within the public sector without necessarily adding to its logic.

In concluding this section, I find myself driven into believing that the binary policy cannot be said to have failed, because it is difficult to establish with any clarity exactly what the binary policy was intended to achieve. We can identify to some extent what Crosland hoped to achieve (or said he hoped to achieve) and see how far those objectives were accomplished. Yet that does not really answer the question on which this section was based. The meaning of any policy tends to change over time especially when implemented by individuals other than those who initially conceived it. In addition, there are ambiguities at the heart of most far-reaching policies of this kind — deceptively simple in formulation, fiendishly difficult to work out in practice — and such ambiguities reveal themselves over time. What is certain is that many influential figures in the world of higher education, not least in the DES, have become convinced that the binary policy is no longer serving the system as it was intended and needs to be replaced. This leads me to the final question.

IS A TRANS-BINARY POLICY EMERGING?

In the later 1970s the binary policy began to come under increasing criticism. The polytechnics, or at least some of their directors, hankered after crossing the binary divide into university status. While that remained out of reach, the existing system and its machinery was attacked as ponderous and anachronistic. Academics and politicians alike saw the binary divide as unwelcome and in need of blurring.

It is important at this stage to remind ourselves that the binary policy, both as formulated by Crosland and as maintained by successive Secretaries of State since, was an ideological statement. It reflected a set of judgements and beliefs and was used to underpin or validate a particular set of 'constitutional, administrative and financial arrangements'. To some extent, we have seen how these were established and validated. It must follow that if the binary policy *itself* is undergoing serious criticism, rather than just the current ways in which it is implemented, then the whole ideological underpinning of the present system is under attack. If it is to disappear, then two consequences are likely, namely the emergence of a new ideology and, concurrently, the development of new structures which the new ideology will validate. Some readers will no doubt recognise the influence of the Salter and Tapper model of political change on the above, a three-phase model that will serve as a useful tool for interpreting the changes that can be detected in the higher education system since at least 1974.

Towards trans-binary change? Interpreting the making of policy using the Salter and Tapper Model

The dynamic of change

According to the Salter and Tapper (1981) thesis, the initiatory stage is one where pressures for change begin to mount. Such pressures may be political, educational, economic, financial or social, but they contribute to a complex set of demands for change to the existing system, in this case the higher education system. Therefore we need to identify such pressures in the period 1974–83 and seek to assess their strength and significance.

First, one can detect a number of factors which combined to produce a growing disillusionment with higher education in the country as a whole. Student disturbances in many institutions in the early 1970s although minimal when compared with what went on in Europe and USA, led to considerable doubts about student motivation and the purpose of higher education (see Carter 1980). There were disturbing signs of graduate unemployment which seemed to suggest to many that perhaps there were too many students anyway. Furthermore an OECD study on the economies of some 23 advanced countries revealed no firm evidence of a correlation between production of graduates and economic performance (Lukes 1975, p. 69).

By itself, this disillusionment need not have led to major difficulties, but it coincided with the growing economic difficulties which faced the U.K., not least among which was the problem of rising inflation. As Lukes points, out, there was bipartisan agreement on the need to reduce public expenditure, both at central and local level. The costs of public sector higher education had been rising rapidly just at the time that costs, and control of costs, became a major preoccupation of DES (as an organ of central government) and of local authorities (under strong pressure to reduce expenditure and keep down the rates). The Pooling Committee sought to contain costs by applying ever harsher interpretations of the Delaney Rules on staff–student ratios (SSRs) in polytechnics. Departments and faculties were pressed to operate nearer and nearer to the top of the SSR bands. The pooling system itself was constantly under attack, particularly from local authorities with no institution of higher education of their own to maintain. Higher education was increasingly seen as prodigal of resources and in urgent need of rationalisation, which to government was synonymous with reducing expenditure. Ultimately the government took positive steps to control expenditure on higher education first by 'capping' the pool in 1980 and later by 'capping' the rates, thus controlling the wishes of some local authorities to 'top up' the pool allocation from the rates.

Concurrently with this, Salter and Tapper detect a distinct change in DES policy, a more aggressive interventionist stance, particularly, but not solely, towards public sector higher education. Some have seen this as concomitant with the appointment of Sir James Hamilton as Permanent Secretary at the Department. The DES had traditionally left local authorities to manage the system, being content to provide central policy guidelines but leaving detailed control to the authorities. In the late 1970s, this policy changed. The Department became prepared to take on the local authorities because it was disillusioned with the constant haggling over the pooling system and with the local authority unwillingness to consider seriously the proposals contained in the Oakes Report. The Oakes Committee had been set up in February 1977 and reported in March 1978. Its central objective was an attempt to give the public sector AFE institutions greater freedom whilst retaining a substantial measure of local authority control. This attempt to square the circle ran into serious criticism, both in relation to the composition and powers of the proposed National Body and in relation to the arrangements devised for funding higher education outside the universities.

> There was also a fear that LEA influence on the National Body might enforce a greater interest in tight financial control and too little an interest in educational planning or innovation. (Matterson 1981, p. 186)

The DES also took exception to the way the LEAs had used the in-service grants provided by Shirley Williams in 1977 and was very unhappy at its loss of influence over the 16–19 sector because of its demonstrable inability to control the LEAs. As a result the central state bureaucracy departed 'publicly from its customary posture of passively aggregating group interest in the formation of policy . . . and adopted an explicit leadership role' (Salter and Tapper 1981, p. 228).

How did this show itself? There were two main indicators in relation to public sector higher education. The first was the 1981 Green Paper 'Higher Education in England Outside the Universities' (DES 1981), which boldly proposed to remove some 90 institutions (30 polytechnics and 60 other colleges) from local authority control and put them under a central planning body to distribute grants and co-ordinate courses. Although, after meeting a great deal of fairly predictable opposition, the proposals in that form were retracted and another paper was produced, containing two alternatives, one similar to the original suggestion and the other maintaining substantial LEA controls, the point had been made and the DES emerged with greater influence. The second indicator was the establishment of NAB, a national body charged with planning public sector higher education, containing LEA representatives but under direct DES control, a sharper, more rigorous version of the national body proposed by Oakes. The creation of NAB to oversee the whole of public sector higher education was a distinct reversal of previous DES policies, which had been to resist proposals to set up such a central co-ordinating body. Its emergence generated the capacity to co-ordinate all higher education by linking the new body with the UGC. UGC itself was forced to take an increasingly interventionist stance, first exemplified in the financial arrangements for the universities published in 1981. The greater emphasis on earmarking funds has given it more intrusive powers and the growth of special funds is all part of the general drift away from individual university decision-making (see *THES* 22.7.83, p. 8).

The 1981 UGC financial allocation had not spread the misery equally and NAB early declared its intention to adopt a similar posture. From the outset, it was made clear that some institutions would probably be earmarked for closure as a result of NAB deliberations. In August 1983 all public sector institutions were given a provisional breakdown of student numbers by programme, an indication of the degree and sub-degree components of those numbers, and a statement in relation to the financial implications. They were given a short time in which to reply, after which NAB considered all the representations, made what adjustments were considered necessary and reported to the Secretary of State who in December 1983 accepted all their recommendations. There is little doubt that NAB will be retained and used more widely as a DES-inspired agent of change within the system.

The ideology of change

Salter and Tapper argue that when the pressures for change become too strong to be disregarded or diverted, a validating ideology has to emerge. This legitimises the change that will come if the system is to be restructured in any radical way. The binary policy which was validating ideology for higher education in the period 1965–77, as we have seen, is coming increasingly under attack. Given the pressures for change that we have discussed above, the next question must be: what ideology, if any, is emerging in the present situation?

I would argue that an ideology is emerging which is a combination of three factors. First, there is an 'economic' ideology for higher education which is replacing the old ideology of a liberal education — courses in the humanities and the social sciences are widely regarded as less useful to society than courses in science and technology. The underlying view is that 'Education is fundamentally an economic resource which should be employed in a way which maximises its contribution to the development of Britain as an industrial nation' (Salter and Tapper p. 149). Of course in one important sense, this is not a new ideology. In a very real way, it was present in the Robbins Report which 'paid far more attention to the "economic" case than many of its critics have been prepared to concede' (*THES* 5.8.83, p. 24). It put forward the view that there was an economic demand for higher education that was partly for theoretical knowledge which could be productively deployed and partly for highly skilled labour. As Hoggart put it (*THES* 28.10.83, p. 11), 'more higher education would "pump-prime" a more sophisticated economy'. Yet, as Sir Charles Carter argues, (*THES*, 4.11.83, p. 11), the assumptions 'about the necessity of more higher education for the creation of wealth . . . were in fact woolly and confused'. The argument from economic needs should lead not to overall expansion but to a selective expansion based on staffing forecasts and manpower planning models that Robbins explicitly rejected.

In the years of expansion, much of the world of higher education either resisted or ignored the 'economic' ideology. Now that hard times are upon everyone, it matters a great deal. Higher education, it is claimed , has to be responsive to 'social need' and ensure that it is 'socially relevant' in what it is seeking to accomplish. A classic statement of the case can be seen in the letter sent by Sir Keith Joseph (Secretary of State for Education and Science) to Sir Edward Parkes (then Chairman of UGC) entitled 'Development of a Strategy for Higher Education', dated 1 September 1983 and published in *THES* (16.9.83, p. 5). *Inter alia*, the Secretary of State writes:

> The Government would like to see a shift towards technological, scientific and engineering courses *and to other vocationally relevant forms of study* throughout higher education . . . I hope that the Committee will consider what measures might be taken to increase the resources devoted to fundamental scientific research, and to applied research and development, and to encourage their most effective use, for the sake of the quality of our science and *for its contribution to the economy*. (My emphasis)

One would find it difficult to discover a clearer statement of the resurgence of this ideology.

Linked with this is the second factor, that of rationalisation. As we have already seen, the whole apparatus of administrative controls set up by DES in the 1960s did not really help to produce a rational system, in the sense of a system of which every part had a role to play in ensuring sufficient and comprehensive provision. Instead, the system of course approvals was allowed to operate in a fairly haphazard way. DES however has increasingly adopted the view that rationalisation is a vital necessity, to eliminate wasteful duplication and cut out courses that are only of marginal value, as measured by the criteria of 'social relevance', although it is still seeking to resolve the problems created by the desire to maintain both regional provision and existing courses of proven quality, wherever these exist (see the discussion on town planning courses in *THES* 2.12.83, p. 32). Hence the establishment of NAB to carry out this task in relation to the public sector in the first instance, with heavy hints that this is a trial run for a more extensive operation later on which will involve the universities. Richard Bird, then Deputy Secretary responsible for higher education at DES, said in 1981 that NAB and UGC could 'be merged under a single umbrella committee or through some other collaborative machinery' (quoted in Salter and Tapper 1981, p. 229). Such a merger would include financial and academic planning (particularly course distribution) and rationalisation of regional links. Thus, out of an ideology of rationalisation could emerge a trans-binary policy. Already there are a number of signs of this taking place.

The third factor is really a re-emphasising of Crosland's earlier argument of 'social control', now operating under the guise of public accountability. As we have seen, 'social control' meant a set of administrative and financial arrangements which maintained strong central control over a major sector of higher education. This element has been strengthened over the past decade. The realities of UGC dependence on DES have been emphasised recently, as the *THES* put it (16.12.83, p. 24), 'In one sense the UGC is merely a branch of the DES'. It is important to realise just how dependent universities are on government-supplied finance and how fragile, therefore, their 'autonomy' is. As Robbins said in 1964:

> There is no absolute safeguard against interference with the distribution of grants to universities. It is a convention that government abstains. But it cannot bind its successors; nor is its agreement likely to imply abstention in the face of major difficulties. (Quoted in Salter and Tapper 1981, p. 229).

Recent experience has shown how prophetic these words were. Institutions in receipt of large sums of public money have to be accountable for the way they use such income. Recent DES attitudes have equated this with cost-effectiveness and rationalisation. Indeed the whole issue of quality assurance in higher education, about which both UGC and NAB are so concerned, is really a debate about value for money.

It seems, therefore, that one can detect the emergence of a new ideology, unashamedly economic in character, based on the twin pillars of rationalisation and public account-ability. It assumes the need for strong central direction and this role will be exercised by DES, acting through subordinate bodies, currently UGC and NAB, maybe later a Higher Education Commission.

The new structures

Salter and Tapper argue that the third stage in their model of educational change is the emergence of new or radically revised structures which embody the new ideology. If, as I have argued above, a new ideology is emerging, can such new structures or a new structural system be identified?

At the moment, the situation is far from clear, although this is perhaps only to be expected. There is, however, some evidence of a definite trans-binary policy emerging which should eventually result in appropriate structural arrangements; and signs of these can already be detected. Thus, DES intentions of ending the binary policy and its accompanying structures may be presaged in the reorganisation of branches within DES in 1980 in which HFE1, previously responsible for non-university higher and further education, was merged with HFE3, previously responsible for the universities, to form a new super-branch FHE1. One senses here a clear intention to co-ordinate planning across the binary divide, to restrict the traditional university independence within DES and to allow DES to 'push ahead more purposively with its policy of course rationalisation on a broad trans-binary front, and to implement any "broad-steer" to subject balance which manpower forecasts might suggest' (*THES* 23.5.80).

In asserting that there is some evidence of the emergence of a trans-binary policy, one ought to indicate briefly in what sense one is using the term. The concept of 'trans-binary' implies the blurring rather than the elimination of the binary policy and its accompanying system. Essentially the binary policy will be modified and adapted to allow for greater crossover between the autonomous and the public sectors. As Scott argued in *THES* (18.10.83, p. 9) the message is that the binary line should not stand in the way of sensible rationalisation. 'With money short today and possibly students short tomorrow, the case for streamlining higher education is stronger than ever'. If such streamlining involves breaching the binary divide, so much the worse for the binary divide. Such a development would be wholly consonant with British traditions of pragmatism.

One widely heralded piece of evidence of the emergence of trans-binary solutions is the sudden interest in university-public sector institution mergers, the so-called 'polyversities'. There appear to be two major motives behind these developments, one being the need for rationalisation, the other being a reviving interest in the establishment of more comprehensive institutions to cater for all, or almost all, post-18 students. With the impending dearth of 18-year-olds by the end of the decade, many institutions may well look with greater favour on this idea and be more ready to incorporate students at all levels and studying in a variety of modes. Of course there are difficulties in the way, but these are not insuperable (see *THES* 28.10.83 for Scott's views on how they can be overcome), and only time will tell whether or not 'polyversities' are a will o' the wisp, but the idea is firmly on the agenda for the time being.

In March 1982 the Government announced its intention to merge the New University of Ulster (NUU) with Ulster Polytechnic, to operate as a university (to be known as the University of Ulster), thus removing the binary divide from Northern Ireland and establishing the first genuine trans-binary institution in the kingdom. In England, at least three different sets of discussions were initiated during 1983: (a) between City University, City of London Polytechnic and Polytechnic of Central London (PCL); (b) between Thames Polytechnic, Avery Hill College, City University and two colleges of London University, Goldsmith's and Queen Mary's; (c) between Westfield College of London University and the Central School of Speech and Drama. Scotland is the third area where moves of this kind seem to be afoot. Two proposals became public knowledge in 1983. The first came from the court of Aberdeen University suggesting an inquiry into a merger of the university, Robert Gordon's Institute of Technology and Aberdeen College of Education, while the second was from the Principals of Stirling University and Paisley College of Technology, supported by their respective academic councils.

Another straw in the wind may be seen in the debates which have been taking place involving several polytechnics in 1984 and 1985 on the possibility of a change of name to university (Middlesex, NELP, Plymouth and Portsmouth). The issues involved are discussed in a leader in the *THES* entitled 'What's in a name?' (12.10.84, p. 35).

One indication of the changed climate was the appearance of a joint statement by the Committee of Vice Chancellors and Principals and CDP on collaboration between their institutions (reported *THES* 1.7.83, p. 1). What was said was pretty unremarkable and there was no hint of new national machinery being considered but the very fact that 'the two groups had considered the subject worthy of their first ever joint venture shows that the evolutionary change . . . ' (*THES* 4.11.83, p. 9) hoped for by many could well be under way.

There are also signs that government policy is pressing ever more strongly in the direction of trans-binary policies — or perhaps one should say towards the blurring, if not elimination, of the binary divide. Thus, for example, the terms of reference for the Committee for Local Authority Higher Education (parent body of NAB) include one for contributing

to a co-ordinated approach to provision, as necessary in relevant academic fields, between the local authorities and the university, voluntary and direct-grant sectors of higher education.

NAB has been directed to establish effective liaison with the university sector and has set about doing just that. Limited cross representation exists between the UGC and the NAB board, and trans-binary working parties have been established to examine provision in agriculture, architecture and pharmacy. In another context a trans-binary Committee for the Accreditation of Teacher Education courses which will give the seal of approval to initial teacher training courses in both universities and public sector institutions has been established. Already the Secretary of State has moved to implement the proposals. Both the NAB document inviting public sector institutions to respond to a series of questions about the nature of higher education until the year 2000 and the 28 questions sent by UGC to the universities late in 1983 refer to similar issues, many of which cannot be settled by either sector in isolation.

What sort of administrative and financial arrangements may then emerge to replace the present system? This is not easy to say but one may hazard the view that university autonomy will be much reduced as UGC is brought to operate more like NAB, (consider the tone of the letter sent by Sir Keith Joseph to Sir Edward Parkes on 1 September 1983 'However polite its phrasing, its tone is of a master addressing his servant' — *THES* 16.9.83, p. 28), while the public sector higher education institutions which survive the traumas of the next few years may secure greater freedom of action than they have hitherto enjoyed. Neither UGC nor NAB needs to disappear although it would be tidier if they did and were replaced by a Higher Education Commission, but a powerful liaison committee would probably work equally well.

However, the major inquiries into higher education in the last four years — the House of Commons Select Committee on Education, Science and the Arts and the Leverhulme inquiry — have been ambivalent, not opposing the idea in principle but suggesting that the time is not ripe for it. Some authorities, like Lord Crowther-Hunt, strongly advocated a merger of the NAB and UGC but the Leverhulme inquiry in the end decided on an 'over-arching body' which would co-ordinate but not interfere' (p. 25). Local authority 'control' in public sector higher education does not have to be totally eliminated although it might be easier if it were. What seems very likely is much tighter central control of the higher education system as a whole and more central planning for all higher education institutions, with regional links being forged with increasing importance as finance remains tight and numbers of students dwindle.

However, predicting the future in educational policy making is a notoriously hazardous endeavour: a number of different scenarios seem possible. The one outlined

above sees more central planning for all higher education institutions, increasingly significant regional links, with finance restricted and student
numbers reduced as a result of declining rolls and the wholesale abandonment of the Robbins principles. Greater control may be exercised in one or more
of several ways. One possible instrument of central control would be increasingly direct
management of higher education by the DES. Given recent history, what may be more
likely is that such control would be exercised indirectly through the UGC and NAB (or
something like the Higher Education Commission discussed above). If this is the route
taken by those who wish to centralize the system, much will depend on how compliant the
NAB and the UGC or their successors, prove to be. On this issue the evidence is unclear.
Until quite recently neither body has been seen in higher education as significant sources
of resistance. But things may change and the 'servants' of the Minister may turn out to be
less amenable to DES control than, at one time, seemed likely. Should this happen then
another scenario seems more credible: one in which further attempts at the central control
of higher education meet increasingly severe resistance.

It may be possible to discern the first significant public signs of such resistance in a joint
statement issued by the NAB and the UGC 'Adapting to a changing world' reported in
the *THES* towards the end of 1984 (14 September). In this statement, the two bodies
expressed their firm commitment to the four objectives essential to the higher education
system identified by Robbins more than twenty years ago: 'instruction in skills;
promotion of the general powers of the mind; the advancement of learning; and the
transmission of a common culture and common standards of citizenship' (Robbins 1963,
p. i). Each of these objectives is reinterpreted to make sense to today's circumstances and a
fifth objective is proposed: 'This we would define as the provision of continuing education
in order to facilitate adjustment to technological, economic and social development'
(UGC and NAB 1984). In such proposals, and in their hostility to the idea that plans
should be made for a decline in student numbers for higher education, the NAB and UGC
seem to offer a serious challenge to the 'economic ideology' discussed earlier in this
chapter. This is not to say that the authors of the joint statement are not prepared to
countenance some reworking of the central Robbins axiom: 'that courses of higher
education should be available for all those who are qualified by ability and attainment to
pursue them and who wish to do so' into such a statement as 'courses of higher education
should be available for all those who are able to benefit from them and who wish to do so'
(UGC and NAB 1984). In many ways, this draws the parameters of those who would
qualify for higher education even more liberally than the Robbins Committee.

Finally, the value of higher education to society in general and to the individual in
particular is unequivocally expressed, as well as the assumption that some kind of binary
divide can and should be sustained in the future 'a longer-term strategy must build on the
strengths of the two sectors of higher education and must maintain the present diversity of
provision' (NAB and UGC 1984). In whatever way this and much of the rest of the joint
statement may be interpreted it does seem to represent a serious challenge to any narrowly
'economic' justification of higher education. And the statement goes some way to suggest
that the UGC and NAB, as constituted at present, represent uncertain instruments
for the development of further central control of the system of higher education.

However, some evidence suggests that DES officials may take a different view. In this
context, as in many others, the much postponed Green Paper on Higher Education may
reveal governmental thinking. Karen Gold (*THES* 22 December 1984) in a paper entitled
'Green Paper may strengthen UGC', suggests that the government is 'considering

strengthening the powers of the University Grants Committee in order to switch student places from arts to science and experiment with a two-year degree' (p. 1). What is envisaged within the DES is that 'the UGC should take a leaf out of the book of NAB and set target numbers for particular fields' (Gold 1984). If a university chose not to deliver its targets within the specified areas then those places would not be funded. Officials within the DES could claim that the merits of such a system would be that 'Universities would be free to reject the UGC targets, and the Government would have looked after the taxpayer's interests' (Gold 1984).

What seems clear is that on the issue of the ways in which they allocate funds to individual universities, the UGC are 'under considerable pressure from ministers to demonstrate that they believe in selectivity and that they can more quickly implement such a policy' (Marsland 1984, p. 2). In this respect the UGC's (1984) circular letter to all vice chancellors, 'Planning for The Late 1980s', which announced their decision 'that it is time to embark upon a review of the present baseline distribution of resources and an examination of universities' plans for the rest of the decade' (p. 1), may be a portent of things to come.

As an instrument of central control much would depend on how pliable the UGC proved to be in practice. Much would also depend on how amenable to change higher education actually is. In a recent leader, 'Two Faces of Change' the *THES* (11 December 1984) considered this issue and concluded that 'The difficulty for higher education is that the system has to cope with two quite different patterns and paces of change which are superimposed'. Change in its deep underlying structures is very slow whereas change within its culture is highly volatile. This being so the writer welcomes the 'modesty' of the forthcoming Green Paper and warns that the government 'should be realistic about its ability to remake higher education after its own image. That is not going to happen any more than the 1960s enthusiasm for the white heat of the technological revolution could reform higher education . . . by an effort of rhetorical will'.

CONCLUSION

What then can be said about the likely future of higher education in general and the binary 'system' in particular? Clearly political or economic factors, unnoticed or misinterpreted by the writer or the forthcoming Green Paper, could falsify the predictions made here. Yet, in spite of this, it does seem as if new policies are being followed, based on an ideology rather different from that which is represented by binarism, and that these policies will be driven home to their logical conclusion. If Salter and Tapper's model has any validity, and I believe that it does, then we may well see new structures come into existence before the end of the 1980s. The binary policy, after all, has no divine right to exist. In spite of all the things said about it at the time, Crosland formulated it explicitly to meet a particular set of circumstances and to operate within certain parameters.

When those circumstances have changed and the parameters have been drawn in different places, then logically new policies have to be devised. Just as Crosland argued that in the circumstances of the mid-1960s what the country needed was a plural system of higher education with a substantial public sector to balance the autonomous sector, so Sir Keith Joseph and his advisers could argue that what the country needs in the mid-1980s is a more rationally planned and financed system, under much tighter central control, in which previous boundaries will disappear because the assumptions which supported them have been discarded. The logic of binarism in the 1960s will thus be replaced by the logic of trans-binarism in the 1980s. This is not to say that binarism was wrong in conception or that it has not served the higher education system well, but that times have changed, perceived needs have changed and policies must perforce change with them. *Autre temps, autres moeurs.*

REFERENCES

Carter, C. (1980) *Higher Education for the Future.* Oxford: Blackwell.

DES (1966) *A Plan for Polytechnics and Other Colleges: Higher Education in the Further Education System.* Cmnd. 3006. London: HMSO.

DES (1972) *Education: a Framework for Expansion.* Cmnd. 5174. London: HMSO.

DES (1981) *Higher Education in England outside the Universities: Policy, Funding and Management.* A Consultative Document. London: HMSO.

DES (1982) *Statistics of Education School Leavers CSE & GCE 1982.* London: HMSO (see especially tables C11 [III] and C12 [VII]).

DES (1983) *Degree Courses in the Public Sector of Higher Education: an HMI Commentary.* London: Department of Education and Science.

Donaldson, L. (1975) *Policy and the Polytechnics.* London: Saxon House.

Fowler, G. (1982) 'May a Thousand Flowers Bloom: the Evolution of the Higher Education System and of Institutions within it'. *New University Quarterly*, **36**(2) Spring Term.

Fowler, G. (1984) 'Policy Formulation and Administration: A Critique'. In Alexander, R. J., Craft, M. and Lynch, J. (ed.) *Change in Teacher Education: Context and Provision Since Robbins.* Eastbourne: Holt, Rinehart and Winston.

Fowler, G. and Houghton, V. (1974) 'Unit 14. Decision Making in Post School Education'. *E221: Decision Making in British Education Systems.* Milton Keynes: Open University Press.

Kogan, M. (1971) *The Politics of Education.* London: Penguin.

Kogan, M. and Kogan, D. (1983) *The attack on Higher Education.* London: Kogan Page.

Layard, R. and King, J. (1968) 'The Impact of Robbins'. *Higher Education Review.*

Locke, M. (1975) 'Government of Polytechnics'. In Dobson, L., Gear, T. and Westoby, A. (1975) *Management in Education: some techniques and systems.* London: Ward Lock Educational.

Lukes, J. R. (1975) 'Government Policy over Higher Education'. *Aspects of Education No.18 — Higher Education.* University of Hull.

Marsland, E. (1984) 'Reading the UGC tea-leaves'. *University of Birmingham Bulletin* **501**(10) 12.

Matterson A. (1981) *Polytechnics and Colleges.* New York: Longman.

Pratt, J. and Burgess, T. (1974) *Polytechnics: a report.* London: Pitman.

Robbins Report (1963) *Higher Education: a report of the Committee appointed by the Prime Minister under the Chairmanship of Lord Robbins.* Cmnd 2154. London: HMSO.

Robinson, E. E. (1968) *The New Polytechnics.* London: Cornmarket Press.

Salter, B. and Tapper, T. (1981) *Education, Politics and the State.* London: Grant McIntyre.

Scott, P. (1983) 'Has the Binary Policy Failed?'. In Shattock, M. (ed.) *The Structure and Governance of Higher Education.* Guildford: Society for Research into Higher Education.

SRHE (1983) *Excellence in Diversity: Towards a New Strategy for Higher Education.* Guildford: Society for Research into Higher Education.

UGC and NAB (1984) 'Adapting to a changing world (A Joint Statement from the University Grants Committee and the National Advisory Board)'. *The Times Higher Education Supplement*, 14 September.

UGC (1984) *Planning for the late 1980s.* London: University Grants Committee (Circular Letter 17/84).

MANAGING THE INSTITUTION

9

ORGANISATION THEORY AND THE STUDY OF EDUCATIONAL INSTITUTIONS

Peter Ribbins

INTRODUCTION

If there is to be a profession of educational management[1] there must be a body of relevant knowledge in which its practitioners are superior to non-managers. One area in which such a claim might be sustained is a knowledge of organisations. Hodgkinson (1978) advances just such a claim. Thus he defines 'organisations' as 'those goal seeking collectives which give rise to administration' (p. 3) and 'administration' as 'that general form of human behaviour which defines and achieves ends through organisations' (p. 7). It follows that:

> 'a serious administrative aspirant, whether amateur or professional, would be moved to gain familiarity with whatever body of knowledge or principle the social sciences could present in the general form of organization theory, and to deepen his insight and practical skills in the arts of decision making and policy formulation' (p. 80).

As far as it goes, this is a persuasive argument. But what is also true is that contemporary organisation theory is anything but monolithic in character. Students of educational management who turn to organisational theory for guidance in their attempt to understand and manage educational institutions will find not a single, universally-applicable theory but a multiplicity of theoretical approaches each jealously guarded by its particular epistemic community. Griffiths (1979; 1982) depicts organisation theory as giving the impression of being in a state of considerable confusion, even chaos, and Perrow (1974), in a paper aptly entitled *Zoo Story*, describes organisation theorists as rather like children in a sandpit indulging in what Piaget might describe as a 'collective monologue'!

Keeping these salutory warnings in mind, this chapter will attempt to do *four* main things. First, to consider the school[2] as an institution and to identify the *five* basic elements of which any such institution may be said to be composed, and from this basis to distinguish the ways in which different theorists 'see' the relationship between these five basic elements and to explain how these alternative perceptions entail different theories of organisation. Second, to locate this discussion within a framework of more fundamental paradigms[3] within the social sciences based upon contending epistemological perspectives and upon the different explanations given to the existence and persistence of order in social relationships. From this analysis *three* main sets of organisational perspectives or approaches will be identified according to a continuum with *chaos* at one polar extreme, and *harmony* at the other. In the third part of the chapter these perspectives will be outlined and considered briefly. An attempt will be made to illustrate this discussion with material drawn from a composite case study based upon the author's researches into different aspects of the comprehensive school. Finally, some attention will be given to the dangers of overemphasising any particular perspective, and to the advantages for those engaged in the management of educational institutions at whatever level to make use of apparently conflicting models of the school or college as an organisation.

THE SCHOOL AS AN INSTITUTION: FIVE BASIC ELEMENTS

Schools are institutions, and like all institutions can be said to consist of *five* basic elements:

1. A structure of *formal roles* or 'statuses' into which expectations regarding appropriate behaviour ('role performance') are built.
2. A collection of individual human beings whose behaviour is related to a greater or lesser extent to the roles they fill in the role structure.
3. Between the formal structures and the individuals are what might be called *informal* or *micro-political* structures and processes 'characterized more by coalitions than by departments, by strategies rather than rules, by influence rather than power and by knowledge rather than status' (Hoyle 1982, p. 88).
4. A set of more or less related aims, values, beliefs, attitudes, ideas, etc., which may be thought of as the *culture* or, perhaps, *sub-culture* of the institution, which are manifested in the perspectives which individuals adopt to the institution and to their own and others' positions and actions within it.
5. A set of interactions of varying intensity and continuity between members of the institution and the individuals and groups which, taken collectively, may be said to constitute its *environment*.

Most organisational theorists and, it might be suggested, most administrators as well, implicitly assume this kind of a model of the school but the way in which they 'see' the relationships between these elements varies very greatly. The result has been the development of competing paradigms based essentially upon the priority given to the system or structure on the one hand (as in systems theory and the structural/functional model of social life) and to the individual actor (as in action theory and the interpretive model of social life) on the other. More recently some authors have stressed the extent to which both these forms of organisational theory *decontextualise* social life and underestimate the part which educational institutions in general and schools in particular play in producing and reproducing existing patterns of social and economic control. Dialectical approaches, they suggest, avoid these errors and possess the further advantage of stressing the essentially conflictive character of social life and the role of *power* and *dominance* in the construction of social order.

Given all this, is it possible to make some sense of the confusion into which the study of organisations has fallen? Many answers to this question have been suggested, of which we shall be able to consider only four. First, to plump boldly for one approach and to reject all others. Second, to take an eclectic approach and to ignore epistemological and other problems associated with such attempts to 'sit on philosophical fences' (Ahier 1976). Third, to construct a new dominating paradigm as Hage (1980) has attempted to do through what one influential reviewer (Benson 1982) has called a 'great synthesis'. Such a synthesis, given the current state of the field, seems premature and Benson concludes that, despite his prodigious efforts, Hage's (1980) attempt to reconcile the opposing theories largely fails. Finally, to produce a 'map' or 'maps' of organisational theory. Several attempts have been made to produce such maps and these maps are usually based on still more fundamental attempts to provide frameworks for the analysis of the social sciences in general and sociology in particular.

FRAMEWORKS FOR THE ANALYSIS OF COMPETING ORGANISATIONAL THEORIES AND THEIR ROOTS WITHIN THE FUNDAMENTAL PARADIGMS OF SOCIAL SCIENCE

As Best (1977) has put it:

> Contemporary sociology may be seen as characterized by competing paradigms, each of which embodies a set of fundamental assumptions about the nature of man and his world, a definition of what counts as a 'puzzle' to be solved and a research methodology for its solution (p. 69).

Where Best is discussing sociology in general, Burrell and Morgan (1979) make much the same point about organisational theory in particular in their contention that 'all theories of organization are based upon a philosophy of science and a theory of society' (p. x). However, while it is widely recognised in the literature that any comprehensive 'map' of sociology (and *parri passu* of organisation theory) will focus on theories of society and theories as to how social phenomena should be studied, there is much less agreement as to what this entails. For both types of theory, a number of apparently conflicting, dichotomous categories have been canvassed in the literature. For example, with regard to theories of society we can identify 'system versus action', 'normative versus interpretive', 'conflictive versus consensual', 'structural versus phenomenological', etc. and in the case of theories as to how social phenomena should be studied we can detect, 'subjective versus objective', 'individualistic versus holistic', 'relativistic versus absolutistic', etc. (Best 1977; Burrell and Morgan 1979; Dawe 1970; Fletcher 1974; Horton 1966).

For Burrell and Morgan (1979) the dichotomy dealing with the 'nature of social science' is represented in terms of the 'subjective–objective' divide and that focusing on the 'nature of society' distinguishes between the 'sociology of regulation' and the 'sociology of radical change'. Taken together these two dimensions form the four main paradigms of social theory from which the main schools of organisational analysis can be derived as follows:

The sociology of radical change

The sociology of regulation

Figure 9.1 *Four paradigms for the analysis of social theory. Source: Burrell, G. and Morgan, G. (1980) Sociological Paradigms and Organizational Analysis, p. 22. London: Heinemann. (Reproduced with the permission of Gower, and of Heinemann Educational Books, Inc., for the USA and Canada.)*

Best (undated) employs a basically similar approach although he identifies different dimensions for his matrix analysis. Prescription for the way in which social phenomena should be studied are divided into the paradigms of 'individualism' and 'holism' which are:

> defined by the degree to which theories concentrate on the individual actor, on the social group or society as a whole, and the degree to which they are willing to accept the assertion that all statements about social 'wholes' are reducible to statements about the individuals who comprise them. (p. 2)

For his second dimension, Best considers the merits of two alternative sets of dichotomies. The first identifies the 'action'/'system' dichotomy which 'divides most of social theory into two main camps' (p. 3). Thus the 'holistic' paradigm can be sub-divided into 'theories like structural functionalism that assume consensus as the essential feature of society on the one hand, and the dialectical theories like Marxism which assume conflict to be typical, on the other' (p. 2). A similar distinction can be made between the several sub-schools of the individualistic paradigm. To take the case of symbolic interactionist theories, it is possible to distinguish between their various formulations according to the degree to which the *self* is emphasised as a relatively passive object of social creation (e.g. as in the work of Mead) or as a comparatively active subject of social interaction (as in some of Goffman's writings and as in the work of Turner).

In the second of his formulations on this dimension, Best suggests that the paradigms of 'absolutism' and 'relativism' might replace those of 'system' and 'action'. In this schema:

> Structural functionalism . . . is characterized as Absolutist, tending as it does to view right and wrong as things on which, given societal definitions, we can be positive, and meaning as something which can be objectively determined. Marxism is characterised as Relativistic

because it accepts that truth, belief, meaning, etc., are subjective and may vary according to the individual's experiences, position in society, etc. (p. 3)

Interactionist theories, although they all share an individualistic orientation, also vary according to the degree to which they tend to make absolutistic assumptions (e.g. Mead) or to assume a more relativistic stance (e.g. Jock Young, Laing, etc.)

	Individualistic	Holistic	
System	1. Interactionist Mead Goffman	3. Structural functionalist Parsons	Absolutistic
Action	2. Interactionist Peterson Turner Young Laing	4. Dialectical Marx	Relativistic

Figure 9.2 *Four more paradigms for the analysis of social theory. After Best (undated) A Critical Analysis of Symbolic Interactionism as Theory and Paradigm.*

Whatever its limitations, what such an analysis demonstrates is the danger of exaggerating the degree of homogeneity of apparently distinct schools of sociological theory. This may be illustrated by the case of symbolic interaction which is commonly taken to include the work of Mead on the one hand and Turner on the other. Thus, while they both share an 'individualistic' orientation, Mead's work may be characterised as 'systemic' and 'absolutistic' whilst Turner's ideas are essentially 'relativistic' and take an 'action' approach (see Best pp. 5–8).

The models for the analysis of social theory discussed thus far have laid considerable stress on dichotomous paradigms. This approach has been challenged by several writers who have argued in favour of using three competing paradigms rather than a matrix composed of two sets of dichotomised paradigms. Such attempts commonly adopt a typology of three approaches based upon considerations of *epistemology* (Culbertson 1981; Fletcher 1974), assumptions about the roots of *social order* (Best 1977; Hoyle 1982), or of some combination of both (Bates 1982; Griffiths 1982).

Culbertson (1981) offers a useful and brief example of the first of these approaches in a paper entitled 'Three Epistemologies and the Study of Educational Administration'. Following Susman and Evered (1978), he suggests that the field of organisational theory faces a crisis which is essentially epistemological (related 'to questions about the nature and validity of knowledge', p. 1) in character. Within this ferment 'three scholarly traditions, which reflect relatively distinct epistemologies, are now contending for the allegiance of social science scholars and professors of educational administration. These are: logical positivism, hermeneutics, and critical theory' (p. 1). Each of the three approaches is briefly analysed and some attempt is made to 'illuminate their critical epistemological presuppositions and to describe how knowledge developed through the use of the different approaches is linked to practice' (pp. 1, 2). The contrasting features of each of these approaches in terms of their original disciplinary links, major authors, central purposes, significant outcomes, modes of generalisations, presumed relation between researchers and researched, assumptions about knowledge, and criteria of validity are all usefully summarised in diagramatic form (p. 6) in the context of an account which depicts the relationships between knowledge and practice for logical positivism as 'technical' ('practice impacted through newly developed means to achieve established ends'), for hermeneutics as 'practical' ('policy and practice informed through understandings and interpretations of past events and contexts'), and for critical theory as 'emancipatory' ('policy and practice changed through critique and through liberating theories of human potential') (p. 6).

In an article commenting on Culbertson's paper Burnett (1981) offers a number of reasons why most philosophers of education 'disdain' such attempts 'to generate insights for educational administration from three epistemologies of recent vintage' (p. 6). The reasons discussed include first that:

> 'epistemologies of the types which Culbertson cites are "school epistemologies", the distillations of thinkers each of which is considerably more complex than the distilled, composite version effected of their views. Second, profound contradictions are often discovered when one analyses the thoughts of one as opposed to another, of the thinkers within a given, composite view. Third, insofar as the epistemologies *are* primarily philosophical, they are couched in terms which indeed do apply universally, but they say little about the particulars of specific endeavours (such as education, schooling, administration)'. (pp. 6–7)

Finally, as Burnett also points out, 'why just *these* three epistemologies . . . Culbertson proffers no defense of the three he presents except they are recent . . . ' (p. 7). These are important criticisms, and although they are made specifically of Culbertson's analysis, many of them would apply equally to any other approach based similarly on such generalised typologies.

This notwithstanding, the conception of sociology as characterised by a number of competing paradigms is both deeply rooted in contemporary thinking and may offer an illuminating way of tackling the task of exploring the contribution which the social sciences may make to the study of the school as an organisation. In this context the writers who stress the epistemological distinctions of different approaches offer one alternative. Another approach, and one which informs much of the rest of this chapter, begins with the proposition that a central purpose of sociology in general and of organisation theory in particular, is to describe, analyse and explain the existence and persistence of order in social relations. This is a problem which has exercised most of the great founding fathers of the social sciences as they have attempted to grapple with Hobbs' famous question which asks why 'war of all against all' is not the normal human condition?

To tackle this question let us first construct a continuum of possible answers. At one polar extreme is *chaos*, a condition of total disorder, conflict, and discord. At the other polar extreme is *harmony*, a condition of order, consensus, and co-operation. Between these poles are conditions characterised by greater or lesser order or disorder, conflict or consensus, discord or co-operation. As suggested earlier, a number of writers have used this approach to distinguish three sets of theories or competing paradigms: that which tends to assume consensus, that which tends to assume conflict, and that for which the resolution of conflict is an essentially empirical matter. Since I wish to illustrate the strengths and limitations of each of these paradigms by applying them to the interpretation of a particular school, this seems an appropriate place to say something about the school and its history.

MALLORY STREET SCHOOL

Mallory Street School[4] (Mallory) is now an 11–18, mixed comprehensive school of rather over 1200 pupils. Over the last 30 years or so it has changed in a number of ways. We shall be concerned with the period from the late 1950s to the early 1970s during which time it is possible to distinguish two main phases.

Phase I: from the early 1950s to the early 1960s: an indulgency pattern

The school's origins can be traced back to its days as a senior elementary school. By the early 1950s it had been reorganised as a small (400), mixed secondary modern characterised by its working-class clientele and by its mainly poorly qualified teachers with low hopes of advancement, low expectations as to the kind of academic performance that might reasonably be expected of their pupils and a level of achievement to match. The climate of the school for both staff and pupils seems to have been friendly, undemanding and unchallenging. The head and several of his most senior colleagues were nearing retirement and were reluctant to support any proposals for change. Only towards the end of this period, as the school faced the prospect of comprehensive reorganisation, was any pressure for reform exerted either by those within the school or by parents, the LEA, governors or anyone else. In short, it seems that senior ('administrative') staff and other staff on the whole shared very similar attitudes about goals, standards, processes, etc. within the school. Furthermore, the existing regime was challenged by few pupils and even fewer parents. On the contrary the school and its teachers seem to have been well thought of by its local community.

While the status of staff did depend to some degree upon their occupational position it was also clear that relationships and friendship patterns cut fairly freely across formal organisational hierarchies. During these early years Gouldner's (1965) term *indulgency pattern* seems as apt a description of life at Mallory as any. 'Management' did not attempt to supervise other staff too closely. Rather staff at all levels were allowed a great deal of discretion as to what they did, how they did it and at what pace. Existing rules for staff promulgated by the LEA were frequently flouted but rarely in any outrageous way. The situation seemed to suit almost all concerned with the exception of a few new staff, pupils and parents. A small number of unusually energetic and persistent staff did try to get things changed but were usually frustrated by hostile or lethargic colleagues.

To summarise, during these years most staff, pupils and parents seemed satisfied with things as they were. From the point of view of junior staff the work was undemanding and social relationships were pleasant. Senior staff were also largely content — there was little tension within the school, other staff were loyal, pupils were tractable, parents were amenable, and friendly, easy-going relationships were the norm.

Phase II: from the middle 1960s to early 1970s; comprehensive reorganisation

The relatively stable situation that characterised life at Mallory was shattered in the middle of the 1960s as the LEA went about the task of comprehensive secondary reorganisation. It soon became clear that members of the LEA (both councillors and officers) were less satisfied with Mallory's 'achievements' and character than were the staff. These were egalitarian, optimistic and thrusting times and Mallory was clearly out of step. Furthermore, reorganisation as planned meant a considerable increase in the size of the school and significant changes in its catchment area. The new catchment area planned for Mallory meant that, for the first time, it would recruit significant numbers of children from middle-class areas and it was unlikely that their parents would be as acquiescent as those with whom the staff had dealt with in the past.

Given their attachment to existing conditions it was not surprising that many staff viewed the changes proposed with mounting alarm. With the retirement of the head the authority took the opportunity to put in a man much more sympathetic to the trend of contemporary educational thinking. Clearly, he was appointed to 'tighten things up' and quickly acted to replace the indulgency pattern with a much more demanding and tightly organised system. In undertaking this task he was helped by the fact that he was able to offer a number of appointments at senior and key middle management levels to people who shared his 'vision'. Few of these appointments, during the first year at least, went to existing staff.

Faced with such a threat to the indulgency pattern it might have been anticipated that there would be considerable dissatisfaction and even some open opposition from those staff who survived the 'carnage of reorganisation', particularly as several of them had been demoted in terms of status, albeit on protected salaries. Resistance might also have been expected from pupils facing a regime which was both more demanding of them in academic terms *and* which would exercise much closer control over them. Although some pupils were hostile, and vestigial elements of this hostility survived into the early 1970s, the new regime was helped by the fact that reorganisation was planned to take five years at the school.

It might have seemed likely that conflict, when it arose, would focus on the indulgency pattern itself. As far as the pupils were concerned, this did, to some extent, happen. With the staff things were rather more complicated. In an important sense both 'sides' (the 'new' and the 'old') recognised both that the indulgency pattern was the major point at issue *and* that its doubtful legitimacy made it difficult to negotiate overtly. The struggle, when it came, apparently took place over a quite different set of issues. It focused in particular, on the kinds of goals and processes for which the new regime was pressing — for example, giving up streaming, introducing more integrated work, the setting of much more homework, an emphasis on success in public examinations and sporting competitions — and on the demands of the 'old guard' that new responsibilities and more work should be accompanied by extra pay.

For some months the situation at Mallory was very tense and quite minor disagreements frequently became serious conflicts. However, things gradually settled down as the ideas of the new regime came to be accepted by a growing majority of staff and pupils. Exactly how this happened is not entirely clear but a number of explanations might be offered. First, during the reorganisation and shortly afterwards several of the staff moved on to other posts including some of those most committed to the old regime. Second, it soon transpired that although many of the secondary modern staff were happy enough to go along with the indulgency pattern, only a few were really deeply committed to it. Third, the head was able to bring in several, often quite senior, staff who had not experienced the indulgency era, and who were, in any case, selected largely because they shared the new head's ideas. Fourth, the kinds of things which the new regime was pressing for were beginning to win widespread approval in educational circles outside the school.

To achieve the changes they wanted, the head and his supporters used a variety of strategies. Following Chin and Benne (1974), three main types of strategies may be identified as follows:

1. *Empirical–Rational* strategies which involve demonstrating to members that a particular situation or procedure makes sense under the circumstances, and is in any case in members' own interests;
2. *Normative–Re-educative* strategies in which sociocultural values are invoked to legitimate a situation or course of action in order to gain members commitment to it. Appeals to wider values and ideals and an affective as well as rational response are characteristic of such strategies;
3. *Power–Coercive* strategies in which the compliance of those with less power to the plans of those with greater power is achieved by more or less naked, more or less manipulative, direction and leadership from above" (Best et al 1983, pp. 220—221)

For the kinds of reasons discussed above, the new head and his supporters were able to make an appeal on moral grounds for greater commitment by the staff. More rarely, he was prepared to use other tactics of an empirical–rational or, even, of a power–coercive kind to buy the support of some staff and force the acquiescence of others. But it was essentially the head's ability to use normative–re-educative tactics which won over the majority of staff to his own ideas and, once this was done, it was a relatively simple matter to turn the school into a place characterised by its ambitious goals and high expectations, which made heavy demands on both its teachers and its pupils to the satisfaction of its increasingly middle-class parents. A new balance was achieved.

In the analysis which follows, this brief sketch of some twenty years in the life of Mallory will be used to illustrate aspects of the three organisational paradigms discussed below.

CONSENSUS-BASED APPROACHES

From the rise of the 'theory movement' in the USA in the early 1950s, consensus-based approaches have constituted the dominant paradigm for the study of educational administration. Broadly, the approaches that make up this paradigm usually attempt to construct a scientific theory of educational organisations and adopt a structural–functional conception of social life which finds its purest expression in systems theory.

Hodgkinson (1978) points out that, 'the temptation to analogise between organizations and organisms is long standing' (p. 35) and he describes theorists such as Michels and Parsons as talking 'throughout of the organizational "natural whole" as a living, responsive organism' (p. 38). In fact 'the idea of organizations as systems with needs existing within environments and making adaptive changes for survival . . . can be traced back to Plato' (p. 38). The elements involved in general systems theory as applied to organisations are frequently represented diagrammatically, sometimes sophisticatedly (see Thomason 1974, 'The Input-Output Model' p. 42), more often simply, as follows:

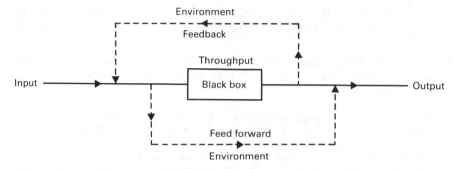

Figure 9.3 *Organisations as systems: a cybernetic approach.*

As Hodgkinson (1978) puts it 'The form of a general system consists of energic input, throughput and output which is self directing according to its targeting and feedback mechanism' (p. 49). In an analysis which focuses on the organisation as a system within an environment Greenfield (1983) identifies a set of propositions which, he argues, taken together summarise the systems conception of organisation and the postualtes of managerial action such a conception entails:

1. Organizations are real entities that . . . are bounded, structured and goal oriented.
2. Organizations exist in environments that are just as real as the organizations they encompass. They challenge, stimulate, and support organizations, but ultimately they judge them against . . . the great test that permits only the fittest to survive.
3. The alternative to adaptation and conformity to environmental demands is extinction . . .
4. Organizations that survive have read aright their environment and its great law . . .
5. The administrator's task is to assist in the adjustment of the organization to its environment. In this work, the administrator will be helped by a knowledge of organizational theory, but the process of adjustment is natural. (p. 8).

Now Greenfield, as was noted in Chapter 1, is a fierce critic of the systems/functionalist approach and, to some extent, what he does is to construct a 'straw man' designed to be torn apart in much of the rest of his paper. Notwithstanding this, the account quoted above is fair as far as it goes and offers a useful point of departure in our attempt to cash the metaphor of the organisation as organism.

For this purpose, organisms may be depicted as entities which have needs which are derived from the demands of the environment in which they are located, from the exigencies of their own purposes, and from the interaction of environmental demand and internal purpose. To meet these needs organisms learn or are taught knowledge, skills, practices, attitudes and the like which add up to a more or less coherent, more or less integrated, more or less effective *design for living*. In order to carry out this 'design for living' organisms act and do so by mobilising such resources as are available to them from their environments and by using such intellectual and physical capacities as they command.

Much the same analysis can be made of organisations. They may be said to have needs and purposes derived also from the demands of their environments, from the imperatives of their internal purposes, and from the interaction of the two. To meet these needs, organisations develop and sustain a design for living ('culture') through a process of learning and teaching ('socialisation'). To carry out their design for living organisations *act* and do so by mobilising the resources they can get from their environments and by employing the physical and intellectual capacities they possess ('roles' and 'role structures') in ways which are more or less functional and efficient to their needs. Finally, just as organisms which respond inappropriately to the demands of their environment do not prosper and may, ultimately, not survive, much the same can be said of organisations. For both organisms and organisations a kind of *environmental determinism* may be said to apply in which the form and fate of each is largely externally determined. Greenfield (1983) goes even further and argues that most organisational theorists are not just environmental determinists but are also social Darwinians, moralists and optimists:

> Organizational theorists are Darwinian because they see in the struggle of organizations against their environments the dynamic of an upward spiralling evolution. They are moralists because they are concerned both for the health of the organization and for their right adjustment to environmental demands. They believe also in an evolutionary spiral in organizational morality. It is not just that the fittest survive, but they do so after a contest that involves the struggle between good and evil, between death and life, between extinction and survival. (pp. 9–10)

How far have these and associated ideas been applied to the school as an organisation within an environment? It must be said that the literature dealing explicitly with this theme is not rich. Sugarman (1969) expresses surprise 'that the analysis of the school as a social system has attracted so little attention from scholars, especially since the sociology of education and organization theory are two of the most highly developed areas of the social sciences today' (p. 15). Writing some years later, Bell (1980) points out a rather different problem. Following Hoyle (1973) he argues that the most significant organisational studies of the late 1960s and early 1970s 'such as Hargreaves (1967), King (1969) and Lacey (1970) have been more concerned with the pupil world than the staff world and therefore tell us little about how schools operate and how decisions are made' (p. 183). This is an observation which would apply equally to many such studies written since then, for example in the work of Willis (1977) and, more especially, in Turner's (1983) interactionist research into pupil orientation and adaption to school. For this, and for other reasons, he suggests that:

> The development of the study of schools as organizations thus appears to have been inhibited by the selective nature of the application of organizational analysis to schools and by a failure to take account of the major conceptual difficulties which exist within much of the literature of organizational theory. This has led to the development, albeit embryonic, of a view of schools as organizations which may be, at best, inappropriate and, at worst, misleading. (Bell 1980, pp. 183–184)

He is, in particular, concerned with the need to develop a sociology of the school, 'which not only embraces the recognition of . . . anarchic tendencies but which does not place undue emphasis on order, stability, practicability and rationality and which can provide practical guidelines for those working in schools' (p. 191).

Bell (1980) also quotes Davies (1970) as arguing that 'We lack anything like an adequate sociology of the school and that one aspect of that lack is in terms of our knowledge of schools as organizations' (p. 250). Returning to this theme some ten years later Davies (1981) speculated that 'The arrival of a decent sociology of school organization has now been so long delayed that we must suspect that it has come already without our noticing it, or that there is something wrong with the news delivery system' (p. 47). He suspects that 'In the study of schools, organizational analysis has often been "done", or at least its basis provided for, without its recognition as such'. This may well be so but what is certainly true is that few of the most distinguished of the functionalist/systems theorists have given much attention to the school. For example, 'Parsons' theory of school organization is a small part of his writings . . . and Parsonian concepts are seldom used in empirical studies of the organization of the school. What we usually have are exercises where . . . the attempt has been made to fit what we know, or think we know, about school processes into the Parsonian schema' (King 1983, pp. 18, 20). Parsons (1951) has himself made some attempt to do just this in the context of an essay on 'The School Class as a Social System'.

Parsons, as we have said, has written little which focuses explicitly on the school. For all his influence, he has written scarcely more on the organisation as such. Rather, he offers a model of society conceptualised as a social system and then seeks to apply this to the study of organisations in two papers published in *Administrative Science Quarterly* in 1956 (Clegg and Dunkerley 1980, p. 173). In these papers Parsons proposes that the basic problems which face organisations are the same as those which are encountered by *all* social systems. He also suggests that although organisations can be said to be composed of sub-units (such as individual members) and can themselves be said to be sub-units of wider social systems, it is also useful to analyse them as systems in their own right. Schools are organisations, what would be involved in analysing them as systems?

In such an analysis there is an emphasis upon the way in which the action and interaction of the parts of the school are structured and determined by the needs of the school as a whole to achieve its ends and satisfy its wants. Such a view entails conceiving of the school as a purposive entity which can organise itself to act in order to satisfy its needs. The idea that organisations have needs is central to systems thinking and has been worked out at some length by Parsons (1956). Every social system, he argues, must solve *four* basic problems ('meet four functional imperatives') if it is to survive and prosper. Clegg and Dunkerley (1980) divide these into two categories. First, there are the problems associated with the way in which a system relates to its *environment* ('adaptation' and 'goal attainment'). Second, there are the problems associated with the *internal needs* of the system for *efficiency* ('integration') and with its *stability* ('pattern maintenance') (p. 176).

Shipman (1968) dons a functionalist guise in attempting to apply these ideas to the school:

> A successful school has solved two sets of problems. First it has achieved the goals for which it was set up, or which have emerged since, and has continually adapted to extreme demands as these have changed. Secondly, it has integrated staff and pupils into a community in which there is a minimum tension. Goal achievement, adaptation to external changes, tension management within and integration of its members are all related fields, all necessary in this success. (Quoted in King 1983, p. 21)

What these 'problems' might entail for a school and how it could respond to them can be illustrated by the case of Mallory's attempts at *goal attainment* and at *latency*.

'Goal attainment' deals with the ways in which organisations make decisions about what their goals should be *and* with what those decisions are. In the context of the school this focuses attention both on its decision-making regime and on the decisions which that regime makes. Mallory offers a revealing example of the 'polity' of a school in action. During the 'indulgency' phase, senior staff led by a head nearing retirement pressed for goals designed, in practice, to make the school a convivial, well-ordered, caring but academically undemanding place. These goals were widely shared amongst teachers at all levels and by the majority of pupils, and the dominant regime worked actively to isolate and discourage the few staff or students who threatened this comfortable equilibrium. During the reorganisation phase, and subsequently, a new regime with very different aims and managerial practices was set up. This was facilitated by the retirement or departure of many of the senior staff and of other staff with long service within the school. The managerial cadre who replaced them had little experience of the indulgency pattern and less sympathy with its objectives and practices. Much more demanding goals were set, particularly in so far as these were concerned with the academic activities of the school, and the organization of management was increasingly bureaucraticised. After a surprisingly brief, if intense, period of struggle and adjustment Mallory settled down once again to a new and, for both staff and pupils, much more demanding equilibrium.

'Latency' is concerned with the ways in which social systems resolve the tensions which are generated by their efforts at 'adaptation' (make the best use of the resources available to them to meet the demands imposed by their environment), at 'integration' (structure and integrate their parts), and at 'goal attainment'. In the wider society, Parsons identifies the *family* as the most effective vehicle for the 'latency function' due to its ability to provide the individual with both support (moral, emotional, physical, etc.) and a secure place to relax ('to let off steam', 'to be off guard', 'to be off stage', etc.). Like all schools, Mallory tried to provide contexts and to create opportunities for support and relaxation. Support, for pupils, was mediated primarily through the school's pastoral care system ('tutor groups', 'houses', 'tutors', 'house heads', etc.) which might be usefully, regarded in this context, as attempts to construct surrogate families. Mallory also provided contexts within which both pupils and staff could relax, such as playgrounds, playing fields, sixth-form common rooms, staff rooms, departmental staff rooms and the like.

Such an analysis tells us something about the needs of the school as an organisation and offers some clues about how these needs are met. What has still to be explained is how the school can respond as a whole to its needs and what makes this response possible? In structural–functional theory, solutions to these questions are offered which entail regarding the school as a system composed of a set of parts (the 'role structure') in which each part (each 'role') performs tasks for every other part ('role') and, therefore, for the school as a whole in such a way that the whole is greater than the sum of its parts. In this model of the school, then, social relationships are not conceptualised as taking place between persons acting severally and together but rather as between the differentiated parts of the collective role structure, and the active social unit is not the individual person but the player of a role. The concept of 'role' is examined in a later chapter.[5] For the present it may be sufficient to define it both as a position or status within a structure *and* the associated behaviours which relevant others ('role set') expect of the role holder ('role incumbent'). Adherents of the structural–functionalist perspective perceive, for example, the role of the teacher in terms of publicly agreed expectations of behaviour on a whole range of functions — instructor, disciplinarian, carer, etc. — each with a high degree of prescription. Systems theorists looking at Mallory would draw attention to the extent to which the different players involved share similar ideas about what might be expected of, for example, subject teachers, tutors, heads of house, and would emphasise the extent to which the behaviour of individual role incumbents was predictable. They would also point to the ways in which sets of particular roles (maths teacher, head of maths, director of studies, etc.) concerned with a differentiated aspect of the work of the school (its academic purposes) can interact in coherent and integrated ways (subject department) to produce role structures in which the whole is greater than the sum of its parts. Finally, systems theorists would also stress that roles have to be learned, and the term they use to describe such processes of learning is 'socialisation'.

Since the concept of 'socialisation' represents the *fourth* key element in the pantheon of systems thinking it warrants further attention. In some of his writings, Parsons identifies the fourth 'functional imperative' as pattern maintenance and the main method for its achievement as socialisation. For our purposes 'socialisation' can be defined as the ways in which its teachers and its pupils learn and assimilate both the 'culture' of a school and their parts (roles) within its structure. Shipman (1968) suggests that schools normally employ four main methods of socialisation, all of which were used at Mallory:

(a)   clear definitions of appropriate behaviour;
(b)   maximum exposure of new members to the culture of the organization;
(c)   rewards for culturally approved behaviour; and
(d)   punishment for culturally disapproved behaviour (pp. 61, 62).

Furthermore, responsibility for undertaking such socialisation is commonly designated to particular role holders within schools. At Mallory one of the deputy heads had the specific responsibility for the induction of new members of staff and the head of the lower school for that of incoming first-year pupils. However, some formal responsibility for socialisation was a feature of a wide variety of the institutionalised roles within the school. Finally, socialisation should not be regarded as either a 'one-off' process or as necessarily restricted to the formal aspects of schooling. On the contrary it is very much a part of the continuing experience of pupils and teachers as they struggle to refine their knowledge of what is expected of them; a great deal of it takes place informally.

In this brief discussion of socialisation, its function as a means of enabling members of the school to learn their place within its role structure and its culture has been stressed. The concept of culture is the fifth, and last, of the key elements of a systems view of the school to which attention will be drawn in this chapter. Do different schools have different cultures? If so, what follows from this?

These, and similar questions, are considered in a report of a study undertaken by Charles Handy (1984). This study was informed by the hope 'that someone who knew something of organisational theory but little of schools would be able to shed some useful light on schools as organisations' (p. 7). Handy acknowledges that every organisation is different from every other organisation and that every school is different from every other school, and that 'It was the recognition of the essential rightness of differences that led to the development of the idea of organisational cultures' (p. 9).

On the basis of some ideas originally outlined by Harrison (1972), Handy offers a fourfold classification of cultural types 'with indications of when and where each culture might be expected to thrive and how the four cultural types blend together to form each individual organisation's cultural mix' (pp. 9, 10). Although these cultural types were derived from business contexts, Handy found they applied readily to schools as well. The four cultures are:

1.   *The Club Culture*
     The 'organisational idea' . . . is that the organisation is there to extend the person of

the head . . . the organisation should be an extension of themselves, acting on their behalf, a club of like minded people. (p. 10)

2. *The Role Culture*

    The underlying 'organisational idea' is that organizations are sets of *roles* or job boxes, joined together in a logical and orderly fashion so that together they discharge the work of the organisation. (p. 11)

3. *The Task Culture*

    The 'organisational idea' of this culture is that a group or team of talents and resources should be applied to a project, problem or task. In that way each task gets the treatment it requires . . . and the groups can be changed, disbanded or increased as the task changes. (p. 12)

4. *The Person Culture*

    The 'organisational idea' behind this culture is that the individual talent is all-important and must be serviced by some sort of minimal organisation. (p. 13)

In a sense, these four represent ideal types. Handy stresses that most organisations will contain more than one and often all four: 'What makes organisations different is the mix they choose. What makes them successful is, often, getting the right mix at the right time' (p. 13). What of schools?

Handy suggests that 'Teachers, with few exceptions, saw themselves as task culture aficionados' (p. 15). However, when teachers look at their schools as organisations a rather different picture emerges: 'The Primary schools were scored . . . as almost pure task culture, although observation would suggest that in some cases a benevolent club culture would have been a more appropriate description . . . Secondary schools on the other hand were scored with a predominance of the role culture' (p. 15). For secondary schools, this can give rise to a kind of organisational schizophrenia. 'It is not easy, perhaps not possible, to run a role culture stuffed full of person-culture professionals. Primary schools do not try. They remain task or club cultures, which tolerate professionals as long as they are not outrageously independent' (p. 16).

Handy concludes that schools, just as much as any other organisations, face conflicting demands from each of these cultural values. This being so: 'It is the task of management to gather the cultural forces together, using the strengths of each in the right places. It is no easy task. It would be foolish to ignore the lessons one can learn from other organisations' (pp. 116, 117). In much of the rest of his analysis Handy examines the four ways in which schools are different from other organisations and the ways in which they are similar. In tackling the latter issue, Handy asks 'What is it that good organisations have in common?' and offers seven recipes for excellence which are identified by Peters and Waterman (1983) in their examination of the most successful business organisations in the USA. Handy interprets these for schools as:

1. A bias for action
2. Close to the customer
3. Autonomy and enterpreneurship
4. Productivity through people
5. Hands-on, value driven
6. Stick to the knitting
7. Simple form, lean staff

and concludes that 'Schools are not *that* different, or they need not be' (p. 33). Fortunately, schools can change. To achieve this it will be necessary, Handy argues, to take them more seriously as organisations. To do so is to ask the question 'Why are schools run as they all too often are?' In tackling this question, Handy proposes five alternatives

1. Distinguish between leadership and administration
2. Separating policy and execution
3. Turn teachers into managers
4. Comprehensive federalism
5. Find more faces for success (pp. 35–41)

This is to say that schools can be more effective and successful than they sometimes are but to achieve this those given the task of running them will need to think much more urgently and imaginatively about their cultures and structures as organisations.

The significance of 'culture' and 'structure' as important aspects of an analysis of the school as an organisation is widely acknowledged in the literature. Shipman (1968) taking, once again, the part of a functionalist, emphasises both and the links between them as an essential part of any analysis of the school as a system. He defines the culture of a school as 'the total of material objects, values, knowledge and techniques which persist while waves of individuals pass through' (p. 25). Different schools, he suggests, have different cultures:

> Each school would seem to have its own distinct climate or ethos and its own way of organising its group life. These two aspects, culture and structure, are convenient concepts for the analysis of any social organisation . . . Underlying this model is the assumption that individuals involved in the same culture come to share the same values and that social structure dovetails individuals into an integrated system (pp. 23, 24)

In this context then:

> A culture is a way of life, which when learnt, defines the situation for all who share it, so that they can communicate and respond to one another. But individuals do not just learn common values and norms; they learn those which apply to the particular positions they occupy (p. 42)

Such an analysis has much relevance to the case of Mallory. Not only is it possible to distinguish the school's underlying culture (or rather, during successive periods in the career of the school, its *two* cultures — the 'indulgency pattern' and the 'post-reorganisation bureaucraticisation') but also to trace the influence of the prevailing culture on the norms and role expectations of its teachers and pupils. How then can conflict be accounted for?

Systems theorists can account for conflict in various ways but they stress that such conflict is peripheral and untypical. Rather, they contend that the existence of a common culture and a shared set of values, a coherent role structure and effective methods of socialisation ensures that all role players will know what to expect of each other when they interact and that this tends to make for harmonious social relations. But why should this be so?

To answer this question it is necessary to return once more to the idea that organisations have needs and to the biological analogy upon which the very notion of a social system rests. The parts of an organism, or at least, of a stable and healthy one, are not structured haphazardly; rather they are related functionally. Thus to ask why the parts of an organism behave as they do amounts to asking what contribution they make by doing so to the needs of the organism regarded as a whole. Much the same analysis can be made of the school as an organisation viewed as a system. As such, it can, like an organism, be viewed as a structure of parts in which each part is related to every other part in predictable patterns of behaviour which are functional to the needs of the school as a whole. For this to take place three further conditions must be met. First, there must be a high level of shared values amongst the members of the school (both staff and pupils) and they must share a common culture. For such coherence to be sustained the school must, second, possess and employ powerful mechanisms for the socialisation of new members and resocialisation of those who, for whatever reason, attempt to behave in ways which may be regarded as dys-functional. Third, the school must also, at some minimal level at least, be meeting the demands and expectations of the environment in which it is located and that environment itself must be relatively stable.

Within such a model, the presence of some degree of deviance and conflict within a school can be accommodated and accounted for in various ways, including imperfect socialisation, inadequate specifications of individual roles, flaws within the role structure, and changes in the pattern and nature of environmental demands or supports. From a functionalist perspective, such conflict is regarded as a temporary and peripheral phenomenon. Consensus is the normal condition of social life and so is solved the Hobbesian problem of order!

What are the implications of such an analysis for the activities of managers in schools? Greenfield (1983) proposes that the logic of the systems/functionalist approach is to view the administrator as an agent not just of the organisation, but of the organisation within its environment:

> The task of the administrator is to maintain the integrity of the organization — its purposes and its structures — in the face of environmental pressure and challenge. To succeed in this task, they must work not so much *against* the unrelenting discipline of the environment but rather in harmony with that discipline (p. 9)

Something like this seems to have happened at Mallory. During both the phases identified, senior staff made little attempt to resist the discipline of the environment. Rather, the school resembled quite closely a model of a system in equilibrium, responding to accommodate changes originating from its environment. In this response senior staff (although, of course, different sets of senior staff at different times) took very much the leading role in ensuring that the school took a realistic view of its 'real' needs within its environment. They also made sure that its culture and role structure facilitated action designed to achieve those needs, and did so by using remarkably effective methods of socialisation.

While this may well be the case, what is also true is that during the 20 years in question, Mallory experienced some change and a good deal of conflict. Critics of the systems/functionalist approach sometimes suggest that it has no satisfactory explanation to offer for these phenomena. It is not possible to do justice to this proposition here, but a number of points can be made which might give some idea of the issues involved. First, functionalists do not, normally, deny that organisations experience conflict and change. What they do suggest, however, is that most conflict is temporary and peripheral and that most change is caused by external factors. Several explanations which would account for temporary conflict have already been suggested and these include (a) environmental change, (b) cultural ambiguity, (c) structural inadequacy, and (d) the fact that:

Socialisation is never strong enough to produce individuals perfectly tailored to fit into a social structure, even with an adequate system there will never be completely harmonious relationships nor complete consensus over values. (Shipman 1968, p. 67)

Longer-term and more serious conflict presents a greater problem for the functionalist. Where it is seen to exist it is either said to be functional to the needs of the organisation in some way which is, as yet, unclear, and/or characterised as due to deviance and tackled as such. Under certain circumstances, as Durkheim (1957; 1964) has recognised, a major breakdown can occur in the norms and values of a social system and this condition of norm conflict he has termed *anomie*. So much for conflict, what of change?

Clegg and Dunkerley (1980) conclude that, although functionalists recognise both *endogenous* and *exogenous* factors, for Parsons:

Normally . . . the source of change in organizations is exogenous, a consequence of environmental change, especially from the viewpoint of changes in society's central value system . . . if there is a change in the value system, this will necessitate a change in organization goals which, in turn, will produce changes within the structure and process of the organization . . . the organization will adapt in such a way as to arrive at a new equilibrium . . . *vis à vis* the environment. (p. 179)

Amongst the things which this analysis points up is that, while it may be illuminating to focus on the school in its own right, it is necessary to recognise that schools are also located within wider social systems which may profoundly influence their behaviour. Once again, Clegg and Dunkerley (1980) offer a useful summary of Parsonian thinking on this issue:

The legitimacy of organisational goals arises from the contribution that can be made to the functional requirements of the wider social system (society). In this way, the organisation is enabled to place its goals above the goals of the sub-systems comprising the organisation. Furthermore, the organisations' goals are integrated into those of the wider social system (p. 175)

Such an analysis has many implications for the school as a social system; we shall consider just three. First, it stresses, as Shipman (1968) has put it, that 'Schools are part of a wider culture and share its values' (p. 34). Second, it emphasises that schools may be regarded as performing a variety of functions for the wider social system (society). Parsons argues that organisations can be classified according to the contribution they make to the four 'functional imperatives' of society regarded as a superordinate system. In this typology schools are classified as *pattern maintenance* organisations in so far as their primary function is with the socialisation of the young into the values and norms of society. Finally, it calls attention to the fact that schools are not isolated from society. One example must suffice. Bernstein (1967), in a paper entitled 'Open Schools, Open Society?', makes the point that:

There has been much talk among sociologists concerned with education about the possibility of analysing the school as a complex organisation. The approach to current changes in the structure of the contemporary school system, which I attempt in this paper, was initially set out by Durkheim over 70 years ago in his book *The Division of Labour*. I shall interpret the changes in terms of a shift of emphasis in the principles of social integration — from 'mechanical' to 'organic' solidarity. Such changes in social integration within schools are linked to fundamental changes in the character of the British education system: a change from education in depth to education in breadth (p. 359)

Structural-functionalist and associated theories constitute the dominating paradigm within the study of educational management but it is a paradigm increasingly under attack. As Griffiths (1979) has put it 'if educational administration is not in a state of intellectual turmoil, it should be, because its parent, the field of organisation theory certainly is' (p. 43). He goes on to argue that 'criticisms of the prevailing paradigm range from the profound to the petty'. Seven such criticisms are considered briefly below.

First, as Griffiths (1979) recognised, too much theorising about organisation has been based on the perspective of the top executives (p. 46) and this explains 'the disregard for the plight of women and minorities by organisational theorists and the existence of unions' (p. 46).

Second, there is a tendency among functional theorists to treat organisations, or for that matter their environments (see Greenfield, 1983), as if they were real — known as the problem of *reification*.

> we speak of organisations as if they were real, 'serve functions', 'adapt to their environment', 'clarify their goals', 'act to implement policy'. What it is that serves, adapts, clarifies or acts seldom comes into question. Underlying widely accepted notions about organisations, therefore, stands the apparent assumption that organisations are not only real but also distinct from the actions, feelings and purposes of people (Greenfield 1975, p. 71)

Griffiths (1977) challenges this view: 'To me, New York University is "real", the Salvation Army is "real", British Airways is "real", and the Catholic Church is "real" ' (p. 6). However, it should be noted that even Griffiths is constrained to put his use of the term 'real' in parenthesis implying, presumably, something other than normal usage.

Third is the use functionalists tend to make of the crucial concept of 'function'. If, as they hold, the existence and persistence of any part of a system is to be explained in terms of the contribution it makes (its 'function') to the needs of the system as a whole, how can such a theory cope with persistent deviance? What explanation can be given of Willis' (1977), 'Lads' or Woods (1979) 'divided school'? As Best (1977) points out:

> this highlights a fundamental weakness in the systems or functionalist paradigm: there is a circularity here . . . For there appears to be no way in which we can refute the account it gives of society: to cite instances of persistent and apparently dysfunctional phenomena is merely to invite the answer that, if it persists, it must be functional and the only puzzle is to establish the exact nature of the function. (p. 72)

He goes on to remark that 'ignorance (Moore and Tumin 1949), social inequality (Davis and Moore 1967) and crime (Erikson 1964) have all been explained as functional' in so far as, in the final analysis, they all contribute to social cohesion.

For a recent and fundamental re-examination of the place of the notion of 'functional requirements' within functional theory, the reader could scarcely do better than to follow the debate which has been taking place between Willower (1980; 1983) and Hills (1982; 1983) in the pages of *Educational Administration Quarterly*. This began with Willower's (1980) quotation, apparently favourably, of Merton's remark that this concept was 'one of the cloudiest and empirically debatable concepts in functional theory'. For his part Hills (1982) has sought to resist the assignment of this notion 'to the category of dubious ideas' (p. 36), and does so in the context of an argument in which 'the concept of system' is seen as 'fundamental to the theory of action' (p. 37). The debate continues!

Fourth, this is not the only circularity in functionalist thinking. As Silverman (1970) observes:

> If we analyse organizations in terms of their needs then, except teleologically, we are hardly in

a position to consider the causes, as distinct from the consequences, of action; for the basic cause of any act can only be that the needs of the system made it necessary. (p. 53)

Fifth, as Silverman (1970) also points out, functionalists tend to confuse 'ought' and 'is' propositions:

one is never quite sure whether what is being attempted is a description of how organizations actually work or an abstract discussion of the conditions necessary for their stable functioning. (p. 121)

Sixth, as Clegg and Dunkerley (1980) suggest, 'perhaps the most noticeable feature of systems theory is its almost total neglect of history and social change' (p. 211). For many others its most serious weakness is a profound lack of interest in the meaning of action and the subjective reality of its members.

Finally, the use functionalists make of the concept of 'consensus' has been said to suffer from many of the same limitations as their use of 'function'. As Van den Berghe (1973) puts it:

Most complex societies (and organizations) show considerable dissension, and that there are alternative bases of integration to consensus (e.g. economic interdependence and political coercion). Consensus, then, is a major dimension of social reality, but so is dissension and conflict. (p. 46)

THEORIES THAT ASSUME ORDER TO BE EMPIRICALLY CONTINGENT

For over a decade Greenfield and his allies have mounted a sustained attack on traditional organisational theory as applied to the study of educational administration. The corpus of his writings and the response of his principal 'opponents' (Griffiths and Willower) have been usefully summarized by Gronn (1983) who identifies 12 articles and papers by Greenfield and some 46 publications in all that have some bearing on the issues involved. Much of the debate has centred on Greenfield's (1975) challenge that an examination of the assumptions underlying orthodox theories about educational administration was long overdue.

Such an examination is not only appropriate but essential in the face of an alternative view which sees organizations not as structures subject to universal laws but as cultural artifacts dependent upon the specific meaning and intention of people within them (p. 74)

How this alternative view is to be labelled is less clear. Gronn (1983) argues that it is inappropriate to think of Greenfield as a 'phenomenologist':

In fact, the two writers most frequently drawn upon by Greenfield are the sociologist Max Weber and the psychiatrist R. D. Laing. The non-functional or *Verstehen* side of Weber's writing, usually known as interpretive or social action theory is referred to throughout Greenfield's work, while Laing, first cited in 1976, appears in most of the writings from then on. Weber was not a phenomenologist and Laing is normally seen to be an existentialist cum Marxist. (p. 4)

In this chapter attention will be focused on the Weberian tradition and its contribution to what might be termed as the *Interpretive* or *Action* approach to organisational theory.

Central to this tradition is the notion of man as an active producer of his world rather than as a passive product of it. Hence, unlike the approaches discussed earlier, satisfactory explanations of social phenomena have to be adequate at the level of the individual person, to avoid reification, to reject positivism, and to make no assumptions about consensus as the necessary basis of social order. In analysing this paradigm and in thinking about its relevance to the study of educational management three things will be attempted. First, to consider the implications of regarding social phenomena as cultural artefacts and to tease out what such an analysis entails for concepts like 'role' and 'structure'. Second, to outline a particular action-based framework suggested by Silverman (1970) which emphasises the processes rather than the structures of organisations, and to apply this model to interpret the case of Mallory. Finally, to review some of the problems and limitations of this approach and of its constitutive paradigm.

Social phenomena as cultural artefacts: a role for structure?

The *action* approach to the study of social life takes a variety of forms. Hammersley and Woods (1976) identify three principal sub-schools. In their account, the symbolic interactionist is concerned mainly with the processes through which people come to construe their actions, the phenomenological sociologist seeks to provide a description of what people think they know, with, that is, their meanings, and the ethnomethodologist explores the rules of social interaction (see Burton and Walker 1981, pp. 227–228). Whatever their differences all these approaches draw more or less heavily upon the ideas of Weber and of Schutz and all share broadly similar reasons for the rejection of functionalist explanations of social life.

Action theorists owe a great deal to the ideas of Max Weber. It is not possible here to do much more than suggest the extent and some aspects of this debt and to do so by reference to Best, Ribbins and Jarvis' (1980; 1983) interpretive study of pastoral care at 'Rivendell'.

Much of action theory derives from a number of crucial distinctions Weber (1964) made between 'behaviour', 'action' and 'social action'. In particular that 'action' was to be distinguished from 'behaviour' by the fact that individual actors attribute subjective meanings to their actions. As Greenfield (1983) has recognised, for Weber (1947) the study of individual actors and their subjective interpretations of reality is the 'foundation block' of his theory of organisations and of his methodology for studying them, and both individual action and organisational reality are to be understood from this perspective (Greenfield 1983, p. 36).

> In 'action' is included all human behaviour when and in so far as the acting individual attaches a subjective meaning to it . . . Action is social action in so far as, by virtue of the subjective meaning attached to it by the acting individual (or individuals), it takes account of the behaviour of others and is thereby oriented in its course . . . It may be convenient or even indispensable to treat social collectives . . . as if they were individual persons . . . But for the subjective interpretation of action in sociological work the collectives must be treated as solely the resultant . . . of the particular acts of individual persons, since these alone can be treated as agents in a course of subjectively understandable action. (Weber 1947, p. 101, quoted in Greenfield 1983)

Following Weber, action theorists of all kinds share the view that any explanation of a social phenomenon has to take account of how the actors involved construe their actions, and of the contexts in which these actions are effected. Actions become social actions when individual actors take account of the possible actions of 'relevant others' when formulating their own. Social action is most fully exemplified in the kind of interpersonal relations in which a number of actors over time negotiate reality in the light of the perceived meanings which 'significant others' come to attach to the situation. In their study of Rivendell, Best et al (1980) argue that viewed from the perspective of individual actors any social situation in which they are involved entails at least three dimensions:

    (i)   There is the actor himself, who exists as a subjective consciousness, making sense of the situation, and seeking to make the situation manageable as he goes about the rational accomplishment of certain actions and the pursuit of certain goals.

   (ii)   There are other actors, who, although 'other' for the actor and therefore part of the objective reality which confronts him, are apprehended as other subjective consciousnesses like himself.

  (iii)   There is the objective reality which all actors agree to exist as external to themselves and whose objectivity resides in their nature as the objectification of inter-personal constructs (p. 253)

If this is so, for any particular actors, then their actions must be formulated and take place in the context of social situations whose meanings are in part negotiable but which are as well, for them, socially constructed objective realities within which others are also pursuing their planned actions and, in doing so, expect certain sorts of actions from them. We should now be in a position to say something about the processes by which social actors make their interpersonal reality manageable in organisations. To do this it is necessary to describe, analyse and explain how more or less shared patterns of meanings and of actions are both constructed and sustained *and* contested and changed.

Gronn (1983, pp. 12–19) offers a useful summary of the ways in which action theorists use the term 'meaning' and discusses the debate between Weber (1947, p. 88) and Schutz (1972, pp. 3–44) over the question of 'What is meaning?' Greenfield (1975, p. 90; 1973, p. 556; 1976, pp. 7, 8), Gronn (1983, p. 14) argues, uses the term in at least three different ways. What is clear is that Greenfield's (1979) vision of an alternative conception of organisations:

Recognizes the placing of meaning upon experience as a bedrock upon which human life is built. Some people invent ideas which give shape and meaning to experience; others borrow these ideas to understand themselves; and many have no choice as others' ideas are forced upon them . . . This context of ideas by which we understand our experience defines organisation. In this sense, organisation exists whenever people accept sets of ideas as fit and proper guides for their own behaviour and that of others. (pp. 4–5)

So, not all actors are equal in the process through which interpersonal meanings are constructed and sustained but what can we say of the process itself? This question is at the heart of much of what Best et al (1983) have to say about Rivendell. They argue that, typically, actors construct interpersonal meanings by identifying characteristics of situations as coming under certain generalised categories, with each new situation interpreted, partly at least, in terms of categories made in earlier interactions. Indeed it would be hard to see in what way social interaction would be possible if the actors involved could not share such categories. Rather, social life must be lived through the sets of typifications which make reality intelligible and shareable by those involved. Schutz (see Schutz and Luckman 1974) suggests that it is in terms of such typifications that actors make their actions in context rationally accountable both to themselves and to others.

Given this, the identification of key categories in the accounts which actors give of their actions is an important means of detecting the perspectives which they adopt for various aspects of their social life. The problems such an approach raise for the researcher are discussed at length in Ribbins et al (1981). From their research at Rivendell they conclude that:

> Teacher perspectives in terms of the kind of emphasis they give to different aspects of the school and of the teacher's roles are many and varied . . . the school is not the same 'reality' for all its teachers. (p. 81)

In a sense, then, there are as many 'realities' of the school as there are teachers (or pupils). For all that, it may be possible to understand something about the 'deeper structures' that underlie these 'realities'. In their attempt to do this, Best et al (1983) employed Weber's notion of the ideal type[6] to identify five perspectives (child-centred, pupil-centred, discipline-centred, administrator-centred, and subject-centred) which underlay the accounts which teachers offered of their activities within the school (see 'Teacher Perspectives' pp. 56–82). What place, if any, have the notions of 'role' and of 'structure' in all this?

Greenfield (1975) points out that an action 'view leads to the concept of organisations as "invented social reality" . . . and to the paradox that, having invented such a reality, man is perfectly capable of responding to it as though it were not his own invention' (p. 81). An important feature of the invented yet shared reality of social actors in an institutionalised setting such as a school, is the framework of expectations objectified as the roles and role structures of the institution within which they have to act. So far as this goes such an account shares some of the ideas and much of the language of the functionalist. Action theorists, however, stress that such roles and structures exist in a real sense only in so far as the actors involved agree they exist and accept their prescriptions for their actions. Even formally designated roles (e.g. Head of House, Tutor) and structures of roles (Houses, Tutor Groups) are therefore constantly being produced and reproduced by the teachers and pupils who 'work' them and work within them. To fail to take account of the way in which roles and structures are perceived and interpreted by those who fill them or interact with them is to reduce these to little more than formal positions in a formalised structure. As Best et al (1983) stress, what existed at Rivendell was a reality in which each role incumbent was:

> Active in constructing the role he 'plays', and in the interpersonal negotiation which characterizes interaction between roles. To some extent, this is a question of the *interpretation* of formal role expectations such that it is possible to talk of the *style* with which the individual meets them, but it may also be a matter of intentional variation and redefinition of the formal role by the actor himself . . . it is thus perfectly possible, indeed inevitable, that there will be differences between formal designations of roles within an institution and the way in which these roles are actually perceived and 'played'. (p. 54)

These and related issues are considered by Best et al (1983) in an analysis dealing with 'Roles, Styles and Ideologies' (pp. 82–110). The way in which teachers at all levels at Rivendell responded to the relationship between personal fulfilment and formal role expectations and the varying degrees of 'attachment' and 'commitment' (see Goffman 1977) which characterised their role play is illustrated by reference to four pairs of teachers facing broadly similar problems in 'Identities' (pp. 139–188) and to an account of the regimes of its three headteachers (pp. 213–251). This last section also includes a framework for the analysis of the management of continuity and change in schools using an action-based approach.

Silverman's action framework: towards a Geisteswissenschaften approach?

Clegg and Dunkerley (1980, pp. 275–297) offer an excellent and brief account of Silverman's (1968; 1970; 1975) ideas about the action frame of reference. Silverman (1970) attempts to present an 'ideal–typical action theory' (p. 126) and couches this in the form of seven propositions which are axiomatic to his account (p. 127). Clegg and Dunkerley (1980) summarise these as follows:

> The familiar phenomenological distinction between natural science and social science is stated; sociology, as a social science, does not just observe behaviour . . . but understands action. Action is meaningful and meaning defines social reality. Meaning is institutionalized in society and continually reproduced and changed through the routine actions of everyday life . . . explanations of human actions must take account of the meanings which those concerned assign to their acts; the manner in which the everyday world is socially constructed yet perceived as real and routine becomes a crucial concern of sociological analysis. (p. 275)

Or, to put it more briefly, it stresses the need for a cultural science approach to the study of organisations rather than upon a model of social life derived from the natural sciences.

Silverman acknowledges that the approach he adopts does not provide a theory of organisations as such. Rather, 'it is best understood as a method of analysing social relations within organizations' (p. 147). The path along which such an analysis should proceed involves looking at six interrelated areas in the following sequence:

1. The nature of the role system, the history of its development and the extent to which it represents the shared values of its members.
2. The orientation and involvement of ideal–typical actors and the way in which these derive from their experiences inside and outside the organisation.
3. The actors' present definitions of their situations within the organisation and their expectations of the likely actions of others.
4. The typical actions of different actors and the meanings they attach to their actions.
5. The consequences (intended and unintended), in terms of actions and patterns of interaction, for the organisational 'rules of the game' which constrain action and meaning. The 'rules of the game' are those definitions of situations which take the form of widely shared and accepted 'institutionalized expectations about the likely action of others without which social life cannot proceed' (p. 152). These persist 'not because it serves the interests of a dominant class, coalition or group to make them do so, but because all groups tend to accept them for the time being' (Clegg and Dunkerley 1980, p. 278).
6. The sources of change, both endogenous and exogenous (p. 154).

Silverman (1970) uses this model to reinterpret Gouldner's (1965) famous case study 'Wildcat Strike'. It can also be used to interpret the events at Mallory described earlier.

The 'Indulgency Pattern'

Role system	Characterised by consensus derived from and sustained by the shared values (mainly of an axiological[7] nature) of most teachers and pupils — the 'indulgency pattern'.

Involvements	Both managerial and other staff shared similar normative orientations and involvements.
Definitions of present situation	Largely favourable with moral persuasion as the major shared strategy but also some coercion.
Actions	Strongly influenced by widespread acceptance of the prevailing role system and its 'rules of the game'.
Consequences	The *intended* consequences were that most of those involved were prepared to settle for things as they were. The *unintended* consequence was that the stability of the regime was to be more fragile than it seemed.
Sources of change	The LEA increasingly questioned the values upon which the indulgency pattern was based. An opportunity for intervention was presented by a decision to reorganise the school on comprehensive lines.

During the years of reorganisation at Mallory two sub-phases can be identified. The first was characterised by instability and struggle and the second by the development of renewed stability albeit on very different lines from the indulgency pattern.

The Struggle for Reorganisation

Role system	Characterised by conflicting expectations. Existing staff wished to perpetuate the indulgency pattern but the new regime sought to 'tighten things up' and to evoke a much more demanding commitment from teachers and pupils.
Involvements	The new regime was deeply morally orientated and pressed for deontological[7] values and closer managerial control. The orientation of other staff became increasingly fragmented. Some were hostile and alientatively involved, others were won over by promotion and calculatively involved and yet others were either won over to share the moral commitments of the new regime or were recruited to the school as it grew because they were perceived to hold such views.
Definition of present situation	Regarded as unacceptable by all parties.
Action	Struggle to impose conflicting values and definitions of the situation.
Consequences	The intended consequence was widespread discussion and debate and the unintended consequences was a good deal of initial confusion and some destructive conflict.
Source of change	Essentially internal and the result of the activities of the new regime and the widespread recognition that the struggle that was taking place needed to be resolved.

The reader may find it a useful exercise to undertake a similar interpretation of the second of the sub-phases identified earlier.

Criticisms of the action paradigm

Many criticisms of the action approach to the study of organisations are to be found in the literature, we shall consider just five.

First, it is argued that much that is written from the perspective of this paradigm is highly theoretical and abstract and that few studies of educational institutions using such an approach have been published (Burrell and Morgan 1980; Griffiths 1982). There is some justification for both these criticisms although a number of studies using an action perspective have been undertaken including Tipton's (1973) excellent early account of a technical college and, more recently, the studies of comprehensive schools by Best et al (1983) and Burgess (1983). Furthermore, much of the recent sociology of the school draws significantly on interactionist ideas (e.g. Ball, 1981; Hammersley 1983; Hargreaves 1967; Lacey 1970; Woods 1979).

Perhaps the most useful introduction to the interactionist approach to the study of the schools is to be found in Woods' (1983) book on this theme. His opening chapter contains a brief yet comprehensive summary of the key concepts of the interactionist method and in subsequent chapters each of the following concepts — 'context', 'perspectives', 'cultures', 'strategies', 'negotiation', and 'careers' — are examined in some depth.

In his final chapter Woods (1983) attempts to summarise the contribution which interactionist studies might make to the improvement of schooling, which he lists as:

> . . . (1) better teaching; (2) less conflict in schools, less deviance, and hence a better situation for teaching; (3) better understanding of one's own career and those of others, possibly leading to better satisfaction in teaching; and (4) better understanding about how school and society are inextricably riddled with inequalities, and how they are reproduced, and an appreciation of how the heavy constraints that surround the teacher's job are acted out and in part created by the school, thus providing a sounder base for institutional and curriculum reform. (p. 175)

As one reviewer remarks 'Woods goes on to point out that interactionism not only induces reflexivity and analysis of one's own thought, action and motive, but also draws attention to all participants in a situation and can hence lead to greater self awareness and awareness of others. Perhaps this kind of intangible contribution is interactionism's major contribution to practicing teachers' (Fielding 1984, p. 90).

Second, a number of serious questions have been asked about the philosophical antecedents of phenomenologically – based social theories particularly in so far as these have been said to be related to the work of Husserl as it has been reformulated by Schutz (see Bauman 1973; Best 1975; Gorman 1975; Hindness 1972).

Third, the essentially micro-sociological concerns of this approach have been variously criticised by macro-sociologists on grounds that include the fact that it is ' (1) idealistic; (2) trivial; (3) causally contingent; (4) reductionist' (Collins 1981, p. 88). The issues involved in this debate are comprehensively discussed in the series of papers brought together by Knorr-Cetina and Cicourel (1981).

Fourth, it is argued that such approaches do not give sufficient attention to the link between micro-level studies and broader macro-social structural considerations. Fielding (1984) identifies a number of possible stances one may take within the sociology of education. One such approach includes what Whitty (1974) has described as the 'analytic/possibilitarian' dichotomy:

While the former approach attempts to understand social processes, the latter approach has an explicit concern with social change, characterized particularly in structural-conflict, neo-Marxist approaches to education. Whitty (1974) describes the analytic stance as one which does not seek to challenge the mundane experience of the everyday world and the possibilitarian stance as one which sees in sociology the possibility of transcending just those experienced realities and hence actively contributing towards change. (Fielding 1984, p. 90)

Some interactionists have attempted to discuss this linkage (e.g. Barton and Meighan 1978) and in Woods' (1983) study some attempt is made to emphasise its importance:

interactionists need to go further. Much of their work . . . has been descriptive and empirical . . . We need . . . to give more though to 'formal' theory . . . (to) discover more fundamental processes with more general applicability . . . Macro theories can be reinforced by sound ethnographic data. But micro situations can only be understood properly if it is realized that there are sinews and filaments in it that reach out into the wider world. (p. 179)

As Fielding (1984) remarks 'Woods notes several instances where specific concepts have been used to explore the interface between macro and micro perspectives. He lists "teacher's occupational culture", "coping strategies", "group perspectives" and "pupil cultures" as cases in point' (p. 90). However, Fielding also expresses some surprise that Woods and other interactionists such as Turner (1983) make so little mention of the concept of the 'hidden curriculum' in this context.

While it is possible to argue that micro-sociologists of the school have not given sufficient attention to micro–macro linkages in their studies this may, in part, be explained by an understandable fear of appearing to 'hammer reality into shape'.

Finally, there are those who argue that micro-sociologists underestimate the extent to which the patterns of behaviour they study are the result of macro-patterns (Collins 1981, p. 87) and also that such theories underestimate the role of conflict in social phenomena of all kinds. Such criticisms have led some writers to adopt what Perrow (1979) has described as an ethno-Marxist approach which involves seeing 'organizations as finding ways to gather in resources; to legitimate themselves with mantles of myth and ceremony, and to cope with external controls imposed by governments in dominant monopolies' (p. 244). An example of such an approach to the study of the school is to be found in the work of Sharp and Green (1975). What of conflict-based approaches more generally?

CONFLICT-BASED APPROACHES

Despite their influence within sociology in general and the study of organisations in particular (see Clegg and Dunkerley 1980, Chapters 9–13 for a useful summary) conflict-based approaches have made little impact within the study of educational administration until comparatively recently.

Nevertheless, it may be that these and other radical approaches will be more influential in the future. To a significant extent the impetus for such a development may well be due to the series of texts which form part of the 'Theory and Practice in Educational Administration Course' at Deakin University, Australia. As Richard Bates remarks in his introduction to the series 'The sudden politicization of the context and conduct of education has raised issues of immediate import that cannot be dealt with by functionalist analysis or behavioural science. The collapse of these theoretical traditions in educational administration has produced a vacuum into which a very haphazard collection of intellectual bric-à-brac has been sucked'. While the exact content of this 'bric-à-brac' is not identified, what is stressed is that each of the volumes of the series is based upon an attempt to explore an intellectual tradition that has 'until now been largely ignored or dismissed by educational administrators'. What the texts have in common 'is a rejection of a purely technical, functionalist approach to educational administration, and a commitment to a critical and reflexive consideration of educational practice'. This being the case it is not surprising to find that many of the books consider the applicability of Marxist ideas in general and those of critical theory in particular to the theory and practice of educational administration (Bates 1983; Codd 1984; Giroux 1983; Watkins 1983).

While all conflict theories ultimately draw much of their inspiration and many of their central ideas from the various writings of Marx, it is possible to identify several different versions of the Marxist critique. These include 'traditional Marxism', 'ethno-Marxism', 'neo-Marxism' and the various schools of critical theory. I shall restrict my remarks to a brief treatment of four topics, as follows:

A Marxist approach to the interpretation of social life and its implications for schooling

Griffiths (1982) suggests that 'The Marxist view interprets organizational life in terms of power, conflict, contradictions, crises, dialectics and class, and this type of interpretation is the basic thrust of the Marxist critique of traditional organizational theory' (pp. 18, 19). In Marxist analysis society is regarded as consisting of a set of individuals, each pursuing his or her own interests and purposes and, in doing so, interacting with other individuals similarly engaged. However, since humankind's wants are pretty well unlimited and since their resources (particularly their economic resources) are not unlimited, some level of competition and conflict is inevitable. In this competition, actors who seek similar goals will tend to make alliances. What begins as limited alliances for particular purposes tend with the passage of time, to develop into more comprehensive and permanent coalitions competing over the distribution of the economic resources of their society. This struggle finally leads to the development of classes and the establishment of order based upon the dominance of the class which owns and controls the means of production. What implications has all this for the way in which Marxists approach the explanation of schooling and the school?

One thing, at least, is clear. Any explanation which detaches the school from its social, historical and economic context must be misleading. Best (1977), in his attempt to describe how a Marxist might approach an explanation of art, offers an analysis which we may readily reinterpret to the case of schooling. Four of the central themes of Marxist social theory are identified as follows:

1. All social phenomena are located within a 'cultural superstructure' which is itself based upon and the product of the 'mode of production'.
2. In so far as the consciousness of individuals and groups are determined by their position in the productive process, there will be different and competing versions of

'reality' which reflect different class ideologies. The cultural superstructure will be dominated by the ideology of the ruling class.

3. The development of mankind and their 'social, political, cultural, etc. structures (are) part of an ongoing historical pattern called the 'dialectic' . . . the contradictions in any one epoch are the motors of change . . . '.

4. That, until a communistic mode of production is achieved man will be alienated from 'his labour, his fellow-men and himself' (p. 76) and 'deviance' is a legitimate and rational response to the realities of the social existence of the exploited classes.

The characteristic puzzles of this paradigm 'include the identification and education of the agents of social control which sustain the position of the ruling class, and the acquiescence of the inferior class to its exploitation ("false consciousness")'.

Explanations of education and of schooling from such a perspective will include the following three tasks:

1. To establish the meanings which individual teachers and pupils attach to their actions 'within the social and historical context in which they function . . . the significance we attach to their meanings must be located within the framework of the sort of themes . . . outlined above'. In particular, to grasp the meanings of the actions of individual and groups of teachers and pupils it will be necessary, in part at least, to interpret these in terms of their social class.

2. To distinguish the different forms of education and schooling and to explain the social and economic purposes they serve. If different classes exist within society, with different interests and ideologies, it follows that there will be more than one form of education and, therefore, more than one form of schooling. It ought to be possible to distinguish the characteristics of the schooling provided for the 'bourgeoisie', the 'petit bourgeoisie' and the 'proletariat' and to explain the contribution which these different forms of schooling make to the reproduction of the existing social order and how they serve the interests of the ruling elite.

3. It follows that if the ruling classes' definition of education is dominant, the conceptions of education held by other classes will be discounted. There is a good deal of evidence that working-class notions about the purposes and processes of schooling have normally been neglected. It might also be observed that although only the remnants of the post war tripartite system remain, that, in this country at least, the public schools are still what they have always been, the places where the ruling classes educate their young and, as such, serve to perpetuate their privileged positions.

These, and similar issues, are discussed at some length in Bowles and Gintis' (1976) classic, 'Schooling in Capitalist America'.

Although the sort of dialectical approach outlined briefly above emphasises the historical socio-economic context of education as a key aspect of any explanation of schooling it does not deny the possibility that micro studies of particular schools can illuminate the mechanisms of social reproduction (e.g. Sharp and Green 1975; Willis 1977).

The applicability of a conflict approach to the school as an organisation

Shipman (1968) suggests a number of reasons why a conflict approach to the study of a school may be illuminating. He stresses that in every school there are likely to be individuals who deviate from the norms of the school, furthermore 'Individuals rarely adopt deviant roles in isolation. Innovators and rebels become leaders of groups pressing for change, opposing authority and resisting official influences . . . all organisations contain groups that are in conflict with harmony' (p. 79). Waller (1965) goes even further: 'to understand the political structure of the school we must know that the school is organized on the authority principle and that that authority is constantly threatened' (p. 10). Some traditional schools maximise this threat by emphasising goals that are clearly relevant to only a minority. Conversely, as Shipman (1968) points out 'Progressive schools regard it as essential . . . that regulation should be minimal' (p. 83). However, even this may not be enough and Willis (1978) suggests that as one source of conflict is removed so it will be replaced by another: 'as school uniforms cease to be the most obvious cause of conflict in schools as more liberal regimes develop, we may expect drinking to become the next major area where the battle lines are drawn' (p. 22). Waller (1965) too, makes use of the idea of 'battle lines' with teachers and pupils as the principal antagonists, 'it is not enough to point out that the school is a despotism. It is a despotism in a state of perilous equilibrium' (p. 10). While Shipman (1968) contends that such a view under-estimates 'the strong normative pressures to be orderly that pervades most schools' (p. 86) he does acknowledge that 'there will inevitably be domination and subjection' (p. 83) and recognises that 'Waller's view of the school as a despotism' carries some conviction 'because, however well the children have absorbed the school's values, they still comply when their interests are really challenged because they know that they will be forced to and falling into line is more pleasant' (p. 116). Mallory illustrates that such an analysis may also apply to subordinate groups of teachers who comply with the demands of their more powerful colleagues even when their own interests appear to be threatened. Some may remain alienated but others may come to embrace the ideology of their 'oppressors'.

It is for this kind of reason that Watkins (1983) claims that in

> the study of any organization, an understanding of the employment relations is crucial in revealing why and how organizational controls eventuate, and why and how these controls are sometimes challenged and contested . . . This relationship is best understood as a class relationship . . . Moreover, teachers as well as being subject to overt control techniques, are also, as intellectuals subject to more covert ideological methods of control especially via the concepts of 'professionalism' and 'a good teacher'. (p. 8)

Following a discussion of these ideas and a case study of their relevance to a battle for control over the conditions of teaching in Victorian high schools over a 12-year period between teachers and their employers, Watkins attempts to draw out the implications of his analysis for a theory of educational administration. The lessons to be drawn, it is suggested are:

> First, that if one is to really understand how organizations operate and the relationship between people in organizations, a clear idea of class relationships is vital. Second, it should be realized that controls are never iron-clad or monolithic, there is always contestation, albeit in varying degrees. To be successful the administrator must recognize these factors and incorporate this recognition into an administrative process . . . In essence, the administrators should ensure progressive planning by democratizing the organizational planning process. (p. 26)

The way to do this Watkins (1983) claims, would be by following the ideas of Habermas (1971; 1976; 1979), implementing a critical theory of organisations and their adminis-tration 'which would unmask much of what is accepted as "rationality"' (p. 26). As

Habermas (1971) has claimed, an approach to organisation based on the ideas of critical theory would lead to:

> a decreasing degree of repressiveness . . . a decreasing degree of rigidity . . . , an approxima-
> tion to a type of behavioural control that would allow role distance and the flexible
> application of norms that while well-internalized, would be accessible to reflection. (p. 119)

Thus Watkins (1983) is led to suggest that such:

> a critical approach to the study of the administration of educational organizations would
> provide a clearer insight into the way organizations actually operate. Not only would the
> dialectic process of organizational formation be revealed but also the structures of
> domination. Through such a process, organizations may become more democratic and their
> members emancipated. (p. 28)

If even only a part of these claims can be substantiated, the claims of a critical approach to the study and the practice of educational administration need to be taken seriously.

A note on critical theory and its role in the study and practice of educational administration

While mainstream Marxist theorising has had little impact on the study of educational administration, the case in favour of an approach utilising ideas drawn from critical theory has received growing attention. Tipton (1977) raises the issue in the context of a valuable paper analysing 'The Tense Relationship of Sociology and Educational Administration' and Culbertson (1981) offers a brief account of the history and some of the ideas of critical theory. More recently a number of writers on educational administration have pressed for the merits of an approach based upon critical theory in general and have called attention to the work of one or more particular critical theorist. Thus Watkins (1983) and Bates (1982) have focused on the work of Habermas, while Codd (1984) has emphasised the work of Gramsci, and, in perhaps the fullest analysis of the relevance of critical theory to the study of educational administration, Giroux (1983) considers the work of Adorno, Horkheimer and Marcuse. This last study contains discussions of a number of concepts central to an understanding of the ideas of the Frankfurt school including such topics as 'rationality', 'theory', 'culture', and 'theory of consciousness'.

It is not possible to do justice here to the issues involved in such attempts to apply the tenets of critical theory to the theory and practice of educational administration, and, in any case, given its comparatively recent emergence in this field, any such attempt may be somewhat premature. This is not to say that the assumptions and various formulations of critical theory have gone unchallenged. On the contrary, Lane (1983), in the context of a critical response to Bates's (1982) paper, goes so far as to question whether critical theory is really all that critical. For a much more fundamental and comprehensive, yet eminently readable, critique of the ideas of critical theory and of the main critical theorists (especially Horkheimer, Adorno, Marcuse, Fromm and Habermas) the reader might turn to the third volume of Leszek Kolakowski's (1981) 'Main Currents in Marxism: The Breakdown' (pp. 341–421).

Some final thoughts on the conflict paradigm

Criticisms of ideas drawn from the conflict paradigm normally rest upon critiques of the various formulations of Marxism which represent its fullest expression within the social sciences. There is a problem with attempting to adopt such an approach in the context of the practice and the study of educational management. Because, although Nash (1984) can plausibly claim that currently, the British sociology of education is dominated by Marxist perspectives (p. 19), until very recently such perspectives have made little impact upon the field of educational management and administration. Although a number of students of educational management, and especially Bates and his colleagues at Deakin University, Victoria, have been actively engaged in the 1980s in developing what may yet turn out to be an influential approach to educational management, this project has only just begun and has, as yet, had little impact on contemporary thinking about the field. This being the case, any attempt at a comprehensive critique seems premature, although when it does become necessary it will, no doubt, take account of such criticisms of aspects of Marxist sociology of education as are to be found in recent papers by Hargreaves (1982) and Hickox (1982).

SUMMARY AND CONCLUSIONS

Rather than attempt a detailed recapitulation it might be helpful if the arguments discussed are summarised in the form of a table (see Table 9.1).

Finally, why is it useful for the student and the practitioner of educational management to be able to think about the school as an organisation in so many different ways? Tipton (1977), discussing an associated issue, comments that:

> It is tempting for the outsider to want to pass this all off as the not unusual battle for place in the academic hierarchy. The point is, however, that the content of ideas in the debate is not trivial. They are about the very nature of social reality — what is meant by it, how we establish it. (p. 47)

Much of this chapter has been concerned with an attempt to distinguish between three competing paradigms and their implications for the way in which the school might be viewed. No claim is made that all these paradigms have been equally influential in the study and practice of educational management. This would be far from the case. Rather, it seems that the paradigm (based on a consensus approach to the problem of order) which has dominated the field for the last 30 years has come under increasingly insistent attack from an alternative paradigm (in which answers to the problem of order are taken to be essentially empirical). Yet more recently a third paradigm (based upon a conflict approach) has just begun to make an impact. While the possible future importance of this last approach may be considerable, for the moment it has only been partly worked out and its influence is very limited. At this time the aspiring professional manager might understandably focus his efforts on achieving an understanding of both of the more developed paradigms. A grasp of both is necessary as there are dangers in overemphasising either. A preoccupation with system and formal structures can lead to a model of the school in

Table 9.1 *Three paradigms for the analysis of organisational theory.*

	Consensus assumed	Order as empirically contingent	Conflict assumed
1. Principal theories	Systems theory 'open', 'closed', 'loosely coupled'	Action theory 'social phenomenology' 'ethnomethodology', 'symbolic interactionism'	Marxist theory, critical theory
2. Model of social life	Functionalist	Interpretive	Dialectic
3. Concerns	Culture, role structure, role, socialisation, role play, role set, role conflict, system order, functional imperatives, functional behaviour, anomie, environment, integration	Interest, meaning, interaction, intersubjective life — its character and the process of its creation, rules of the game and the maintenance of social life, perspectives, style, negotiation, social interaction, typification	Ideology, class structure, dominance, power, conflict of interests, control, class struggle, false consciousness, cultural superstructure as product of economic arrangements of society, alienation, identification of agents and process of social control, acquiescence of those exploited, ideology
4. Social unit at the micro level	Role player	Actor	Class protagonist
5. Character of social relations at the micro level	Role play	Interaction	Praxis
6. Research approach and type of explanation aimed at	Scientific, logical positivist, neutral — seeks causal explanation, positivistic	Tends to be subjectivist, neutral, seeks understanding	Varies according to type of theory — tends to be committed, expository and emancipatory

which the individual teacher or pupil comes to be regarded very much as the player of certain given roles which he or she happens to fill and to behave in ways determined by his or her socialisation into the culture and role-structure of the school. Conversely, a preoccupation with the teacher or pupil as individual actor, while properly emphasising that all schools are ultimately produced and reproduced through the actions of their members, can underestimate the extent to which institutions have a sort of life of their own and, as such, are resistant to change (either internally or externally sought) and may also underestimate the degree to which schools can and do constrain and mould the activities of those within them.

The importance attached to the third element (informal and micro-political structures and processes) and the way in which the fourth and fifth elements of an institution like a school (the set of ideas, aims, beliefs, attitudes and values that constitute its culture, and the set of physical, personal, normative and other interactions with things outside that make up its environment) are perceived depend very much on the emphasis given to the other two. Where the system or structure is taken as the prime dimension there is a tendency to see the culture of the school as a more or less coherent set of aims, values, etc. which are more or less uniformly understood and embraced by its members, and through which orderly and consensual pursuit of institutional goals is effected. Where the emphasis is placed on the individuals and their goals, interests and motives, then the notion of culture is reduced to little more than a set of more or less shared meanings and attitudes, while on significant issues various competing ideologies and perspectives can be anticipated. Much the same account can be offered with regard to the notion of environment. Where the idea is accepted that schools as social systems are real and exist within environments which are equally real then there is a tendency to see the environment as the ultimate source of the needs of the school and the dominant determinant of its culture, role structure and, ultimately, of the behaviour of its members. Where the emphasis is on the individual actor then there is less temptation to think of the social environment of the school as real. Rather it is 'simply other people in other organizations — or, most simply, other people' (Greenfield 1983, p. 35) or a source of 'stocks of knowledge', 'finite provinces of meaning' and 'definitions of situations' as they are subjectively constituted (Silverman 1970, p. 148).

The reality of most schools is probably best regarded as a combination of both models although, of course, some schools will be more like one model than the other. Thus most schools as institutions will consist of a hierarchial system, with some division of labour, located in an environment which more or less shapes its behaviour and the actions and attitudes of its members, and with something of an established and shared culture. But it will also be true that individual definitions, motives and meanings will vary more or less significantly and a variety of quite distinct and separate perspectives and styles will be adopted by different teachers and pupils, and groups of teachers and pupils, to the various aspects of life in the school.

To be able to conceptualise schools as organisations in a variety of ways is not an esoteric luxury for the student and the manager. Rather it is to be liberated from the embrace of a particular vision which probably obscures as much as it reveals and constrains as much as it enables.

NOTES

1. In this chapter the terms 'management' and 'administration' are used interchangeably. It is acknowledged that a more comprehensive review would need to take some account of the distinctions which Hodgkinson (1978) has proposed (see Introduction p. xii).
2. Although this analysis focuses on the school, much of the argument it contains is just as applicable to other kinds of educational institutions.
3. The answers we give to the question 'What must the world be like in order that man may know it?' is what Kuhn (1962) calls a 'paradigm of thought', or, more commonly, simply a 'paradigm'. Masterman (1970) argues that Kuhn uses the term in several different and sometimes ambiguous ways, in the context of a paper which Ford (1975) has dismissed as 'rather pedantic' (p. 186). Paradigms, she argues, 'are conglomerations of exemplary thoughts . . . they consist of thoughts wrapped up in thoughts about thoughts. And these devices serve as patterns both for knowledge itself, and for the acquisition of knowledge' (p. 2). Any particular paradigm will be analysable into four constituent elements which include 'Basic Beliefs', 'Figuration of Facts', 'Rules of Reasonableness' and 'Kept Knowledge' (p. 25). These ideas are worked out at some length by Ford (1975) in *Paradigms and Fairy Tales* in an introduction to the epistemology and practice of social science research which is lucid and always entertaining.
4. Mallory Street School is a somewhat fictionalised account based largely on the author's researches into a number of comprehensive schools over the last decade.
5. See Chapter 14.
6. The concept of 'ideal type' is crucial to Weber's thinking and is used several times in this book. For both these reasons it needs some clarification. Clegg and Dunkerley (1980) suggest that, following Weber (1948) himself, any such attempt should begin with a discussion of what an ideal type is not. '1. It is not a type in the sense of being an average . . . . 2. It is not a logical class or more usual type' (p. 137). Nor is it, '3. an extreme type'. Neither, by 'ideal' was Weber 'suggesting that the content of the type is in any way desirable' (p. 38). Furthermore, as Parsons has observed, it is not a hypothesis, a thing, a process, or a collection of common characteristics. Mouzelis (1967) suggests that one way in which an 'ideal type' may be distinguished from a model or a theory is to identify what is involved in its construction. This entails '1. Selecting empirical date and then conceptualizing them (which) may involve an inductive process of considering real phenomena. 2. The selected features are then exaggerated to their logical extreme . . . 3. The selection and exaggeration of these features is done in such a way that the complete construct has an inter-connected logical consistency' (Clegg and Dunkerley p. 138). For an example of such an analysis in the context of the school see Best et al's (1983) construction of teacher perspectives, styles and ideologies (pp. 56–109).
7. Hodgkinson (1978) offers a useful model (p. 111) for the analysis of the value problems administrators encounter. In this model a key distinction is made in the concept of value between 'its two components of the "right" and the "good". This is the difference between the "desirable" and the "desired" (see Kant . . . .) and is technically known as the distinction between the axiological (good) and the deontological (right). The former refers to what is enjoyable, likeable, pleasurable; the latter to what is proper, "moral", dutybound, or simply what "*ought* to be"' (p. 110).

REFERENCES

Ahier, J. (1976) 'Sitting on Philosophical Fences'. *Radical Education*, Summer.

Ball, S. (1981) *Beechside Comprehensive*. Cambridge: Cambridge University Press.

Barton, L. and Meighan, R. (1978) *Sociological Interpretations of Schooling and Classrooms: A Reappraisal*. Driffield: Nafferton.

Bates, R. (1982) 'Towards a Critical Practice of Educational Administration'. *Studies in*

Educational Administration CCEA **27**, September.

Bates R. (1983) *Educational Administration and the Management of Knowledge.* Victoria, Australia: Deakin University.

Bauman, Z. (1973) 'On the Philosophical Status of Ethnomethodology'. *Sociological Review*, **21**(1).

Bell, L. (1980) 'The School as an Organization: a re-appraisal'. *British Journal of Sociology of Education*, **1**(2).

Benson, J. (1977) 'Organizations: A Dialectical View'. *Administrative Science Quarterly*, **22**(1).

Benson, K. (1982) 'Review of Hage (1980) Theories of Organizations: Form, Process and Transformation'. *Administrative Science Quarterly*, **27**(1).

Berger, P. and Luckman, T. (1966) *The Social Construction of Reality*. New York: Doubleday.

Bernstein, B. (1967) 'Open Schools, Open Society?'. *New Society*, 14 September, 351–53.

Best, R. (undated) *A Critical Analysis of Symbolic Interactionism as Theory and Paradigm.* Unpublished paper.

Best, R. (1975) 'New Directions in Sociological Theory?'. *British Journal of Sociology*, **26**.

Best, R. (1977) 'Sketch for a Sociology of Art'. *British Journal of Aesthetics*, **17**(1).

Best, R., Jarvis, C. and Ribbins, P. (1980) *Perspectives on Pastoral Care.* London: Heinemann.

Best, R., Ribbins, P., Jarvis, C. and Oddy, D. (1983) *Education and Care.* London: Heinemann.

Bowles, S. and Gintis, H. (1976) *Schooling in Capitalist America.* New York: Basic Books.

Burgess, R. (1983) *Experiencing Comprehensive Education.* London: Methuen.

Burnett, J. (1981) 'On the use of epistemologies for guiding educational administration'. *UCEA Review*, **XXII**(1).

Burrell, G. and Morgan, G. (1980) *Sociological Paradigms and Organizational Analysis.* London: Heinemann.

Burton, L. and Walker, S. (1981) 'Part 4 Sociological Perspectives and the Study of Education'. In Meighan, R. (1981) *A Sociology of Educating.* London: Holt, Rinehart and Winston.

Chin, R. and Benne, K. (1974) 'General strategies for effecting change in human systems'. In Bennis, W., Benne, K. and Chin, R. (1974) *Planning of Change.* London: Holt, Rinehart and Winston.

Clegg, S. and Dunkerley, D. (1980) *Organization, Class and Control.* London: Routledge and Kegan Paul.

Codd, J. (1984) *Philosophy, common sense, and action in educational administration.* Victoria, Australia: Deakin University.

Collins, R. (1981) 'Micro-translation as a theory-building strategy'. In Knorr-Cetina, K. and Cicourel, A. (1981) *Towards an Integration of Micro- and Macro-Sociologies* (pp. 81–109). London: Routledge and Kegan Paul.

Culbertson, J. (1981) 'Three Epistemologies and the Study of Educational Administration'. *UCEA Review*, **22**(1).

Culbertson, J. (1982) *Educational Administration and Planning at the Crossroads.* Paper given at the 5th IIP of the CCEA in Nigeria (mimeo).

Davies, B. (1970) 'Organizational analysis of educational institutions'. In Brown, R. (ed) (1973) *Knowledge, Education and Culture Change.* London: Tavistock.

Davies, B. (1981) 'Schools as Organizations and the Organization of Schooling'. *Educational Analysis*, **3**(1).

Davis, K. and Moore, W. (1967) 'Some Principles of Stratification'. In Bendix, R. and Lipset, S. (ed.), *Class Status and Power.* London: Routledge and Kegan Paul.

Dawe, A. (1970) 'The Two Sociologies'. *British Journal of Sociology*, **27**.

Durkheim, E. (1957) *Professional Ethics and Civic Morals.* London: Routledge and Kegan Paul.

Durkheim, E. (1964) *The Division of Labour in Society.* New York: Free Press.

Erikson, K. (1964) 'Notes on the Sociology of Deviance'. In Becker, H. (ed.) (1964) *The Other Side.* New York: Free Press.

Fielding, R. (1984) 'Interactionist Sociology of Education'. *British Journal of Sociology of Education*, **5**(1).

Fletcher, C. (1974) *Beneath the Surface.* London: Routledge and Kegan Paul.

Ford, J. (1975) *Paradigms and Fairy Tales.* London: Routledge and Kegan Paul.

Giroux, H. (1983) *Critical Theory and Educational Practice.* Victoria, Australia: Deakin University.

Goffman, E. (1977) *Encounters*. London: Allen Lane.

Gorman, R. (1975) 'The phenomenological "humanization" of social science — a critique'. *British Journal of Sociology*, 26(4).

Gouldner, A. (1965) *Wildcat Strike*. New York: Harper.

Greenfield, T. (1973) 'Organizations as social inventions: rethinking assumptions about change'. *Journal of Applied Behavioural Science*, 9(5), 551–74.

Greenfield, T. (1975) 'Theory about organization: a new perspective and its implications for schools'. In Hughes, M. (ed) *Administering Education: International Challenge*. London: Athlone.

Greenfield, T. (1976) 'Theory about what? Some thoughts about theory in educational administration'. *UCEA Review*, 17(2), 4–9.

Greenfield, T. (1979) 'Organization Theory as Ideology'. *Curriculum Inquiry*, 9(2).

Greenfield, T. (1983) *Environment as Subjective Reality*. Paper presented to the Conference of the American Educational Research Association, April 1983 (mimeo).

Griffiths, D. (1977) 'The individual in organization: a theoretical perspective'. *Educational Administration Quarterly*, 13(2).

Griffiths, D. (1979) 'Intellectual turmoil in educational administration'. *Educational Administration Quarterly*, 15(3).

Griffiths, D. (1982) *Theories: Past, Present and Future*. Paper given at the 5th IIP of the CCEA in Nigeria (mimeo).

Gronn, P. (1983) *Rethinking educational administration: T. A. Greenfield and his critics*. Victoria, Australia: Deakin University.

Habermas, J. (1971) *Knowledge and Human Interests*. Boston: Beacon Press.

Habermas, J. (1976) *Legitimation Crisis*. London: Heinemann.

Habermas, J. (1979) *Communication and the Evolution of Society*. Boston: Beacon Press.

Hage, J. (1980) *Theories of Organizations: Form, Process and Transformation*. New York: John Wiley.

Hammersley, M. (ed) (1983) *The Ethnography of Schooling*. Driffield: Nafferton.

Hammersley, M. and Woods, P. (1976) *The Process of Schooling*. London: Routledge and Kegan Paul.

Handy, C. (1984) *Taken for Granted? Understanding Schools as Organisations*. London: Longmans for Schools Council.

Hargreaves, A. (1982) 'Resistance and relative autonomy theories: problems of distortion and incoherence in recent Marxist theories of education'. *British Journal of Sociology of Education*, 3(2).

Hargreaves, D. (1967) *Social Relations in a Secondary School*. London: Routledge and Kegan Paul.

Harrison, R. (1972) 'How to describe your organization'. *Harvard Business Review*, September–October.

Hickox, M. (1982) 'The Marxist sociology of education: a critique'. *British Journal of Sociology*, 33(4).

Hills, R. (1982) 'Functional Requirements and the Theory of Action'. *Educational Administration Quarterly*, 18 (4).

Hills, J. (1983) 'The Intellectual Status of the Functional Imperatives: A Rejoinder to Donald Willower'. *Educational Administration Quarterly*, 19(2).

Hindness, B. (1972) 'The "Phenemonological" Sociology of Alfred Schutz'. *Economy and Society*, 1(1).

Hodgkinson, C. (1978) *Towards a Philosophy of Administration*. Oxford: Blackwell.

Horton, J. (1966) 'Order and Conflict Theories of Social Problems as Competency Ideologies'. *American Journal of Sociology*, 71, 701–13.

Houghton, V., McHugh, R. and Morgan, C. (ed.) (1973) *Management in Education: The Management of Organizations and Individuals*. London: Ward Lock.

Hoyle, E. (1973) 'The Study of Schools as Organizations'. In Houghton, V., McHugh, R. and Morgan, C. (ed.) (1973) *Management in Education: The Management of Organizations and Individuals*. (1973) London: Ward Lock.

Hoyle, E. (1982) 'Micropolitics of educational organizations'. *Educational Management and Administration*, 10(2).

King, R. (1969) *Values and Involvement in a Grammar School*. London: Routledge and Kegan Paul.

King, R. (1983) *The Sociology of School Organization*. London: Methuen.

King, R. (1984) 'School Management and the Sociology of Education'. *Educational Management and Administration*, 12(1).

Knorr-Cetina, K. and Cicourel, A. (1981) *Towards an Integration of Micro- and Macro-Sociologies*. London: Routledge and Kegan Paul.

Kolakowski, L. (1981) *Main Currents in Marxism: 3 The Breakdown*. Oxford: Oxford University Press.

Kuhn, T. (1962) *The Structure of Scientific Revolutions.* Chicago: University of Chicago Press.

Lacey, C. (1970) *Hightown Grammar: The School as a Social System.* Manchester: University Press.

Lane, T. (1983) 'How Critical is Critical Theory?'. *Studies in Educational Administration, CCEA* **32**, December.

Masterman, M. (1969) 'The Nature of a Paradigm'. In Lacktos, I. and Musgrave, A. (ed.) *Criticism and the Growth of Knowledge.* Cambridge: Cambridge University Press.

Moore, W. and Tumin, M. (1949) 'Some Social Functions of Ignorance'. *American Journal of Sociology*, December.

Mouzelis, N. (1967) *Organization and Bureaucracy.* London: Routledge and Kegan Paul.

Nash, R. (1984) 'On Two Critiques of the Marxist Sociology of Education'. *British Journal of Sociology of Education*, **5**(1).

Parsons, T. (1951) *The Social System.* Chicago: Free Press.

Parsons, T. (1956) 'Suggestions for a Sociological Approach to the Theory of Organizations'. *Administrative Science Quarterly*, **1**(1) and **1**(3).

Parsons, T. (1959) 'The school class as a social system'. *Harvard Educational Review*, **29**(4).

Perrow, C. (1979) *Complex Organizations.* Illinois: Scott, Foresman.

Peters, T. and Waterman, R. (1983) *In Search of Excellence.* London: Harper and Row.

Ribbins, P., Best, R., Jarvis, C. and Oddy, D. (1981) 'Meanings and Contexts: The Problem of Interpretation in the Study of a School'. In Ribbins and Thomas (ed.) (1981) *Research in Educational Management and Administration.* Coombe Lodge: BEMAS.

Ribbins, P. and Thomas, H. (1981) (ed.) *Research in Educational Management and Administration.* Coombe Lodge: BEMAS.

Schutz, A. (1972) *The Phenomenology of the Social World.* London: Heinemann.

Schutz, A. and Luckman, T. (1974) *The Structure of the Life-World.* London: Heinemann.

Sharp, R. and Green, A. (1975) *Education and Social Control.* London: Routledge and Kegan Paul.

Shipman, M. (1968) *The Sociology of the School.* London: Longman.

Silverman, D. (1968) 'Formal Organizations or Industrial Sociology: Towards a Social Action Analysis of Organizations'. *Sociology*, **2**.

Silverman, D. (1970) *The Theory of Organizations.* London: Heinemann.

Silverman, D. (1975) 'Accounts of organisations'. In McKinlay (ed.) *Processing People: Cases in Organizational Behaviour.* London: Holt, Rinehart and Winston.

Sugarman, B. (1969) 'The school as a social system'. *Moral Education*, **1**(2).

Susman, G. and Evered, R. (1978) 'An Assessment of the Merits of the Action Research'. *Administrative Science Quarterly*, **23**.

Thomason, G. (1974) 'Organization and Management' (especially pp. 41–53 'The Input–Output Model'). In Hughes, M. (1974) *Secondary School Administration.* Oxford: Pergamon.

Tipton, B. (1973) *Conflict and Change in a Technical College.* London: Hutchinson.

Tipton, B. (1977) 'The Tense Relationship of Sociology and Educational Administration'. *Educational Administration*, **5**(2).

Turner, G. (1983) *The Social World of the Comprehensive School.* London: Croom Helm.

Van Der Berghe, V. (1973) 'Dialectic and Functionalism'. In Chambliss, W. (ed.) (1973) *Sociological Readings in the Conflict Perspective.* Reading, Mass: Addison-Wesley.

Waller, W. (1965) *The Sociology of Teaching.* New York: Wiley.

Watkins, P. (1983) *Class, Control and Contestation in Educational Organizations.* Victoria, Australia: Deakin University.

Weber, M. (1947) *From Max Weber: Essays in Sociology.* London: Routledge and Kegan Paul.

Weber, M. (1964) *The Theory of Social and Economic Organization.* New York: Free Press.

Whitty, G. (1974) 'Sociology and the problem of radical educational change'. In Flude, M. and Ahier, J. (eds) *Educability, Schools and Ideology.* London: Croom Helm.

Willis, P. (1977) *Learning to Labour.* London: Saxon House.

Willis, P. (1978) *Profane Culture.* London: Routledge and Kegan Paul.

Willmott, H. (1981) 'The Structure of Organizational Structure: A Note'. *Administrative Science Quarterly*, **26**(3).

Willower, D. (1980) 'Contemporary Issues in

Theory in Educational Administration'. *Educational Administration Quarterly*, **16**(3).

Willower, D. (1982) 'School Organizations: Perspectives in Juxtaposition'. *Educational Administration Quarterly*, **18**(3).

Willower, D. (1983) 'Analogies Gone Awry: Replies to Hills and Gronn'. *Educational Administration Quarterly*, **19**(1).

Woods, P. (1979) *The Divided School.* London: Routledge and Kegan Paul.

Woods, P. (1983) *Sociology and the School: An Interactionist Viewpoint.* London: Routledge and Kegan Paul.

10

LEADERSHIP IN PROFESSIONALLY STAFFED ORGANISATIONS

Meredydd Hughes

INTRODUCTION

Leadership and profession are terms of wide application which conjure up a variety of interpretations. At different times they have both given rise to controversy in public discussion, each having many overtones, both positive and negative. Both concepts have generated a formidable social science literature.

The first two sections of the chapter will provide, in turn, an inevitably brief survey of the concepts of leadership and professionalism, giving attention in particular to studies in an organisational context. The leadership of professionals in organisational settings, which will be considered in the third and final section, has been comparatively neglected in the general literature. It will be considered mainly in the specific context of the leadership of educational institutions, but will draw as appropriate on relevant ideas and research of a more general kind which is described in the earlier sections.

The issues involved are somewhat complex, but are of importance in the management of education and more widely. Many of the approaches discussed are firmly grounded within the system/functionalist paradigm as considered in the preceding chapter, but attention is also given to contemporary challenges to traditional concepts of leadership and profession. A micro-political viewpoint is finally advocated.

APPROACHES TO LEADERSHIP IN ORGANISATIONS

For over half a century leadership has been studied by social scientists from a variety of perspectives. Many of the studies, particularly those of industrial psychologists, had one or other of the practical aims of improving the selection processes for posts involving leadership responsibilities or of improving the leadership behaviour of those already in post. Resulting publications have been comprehensively reviewed on a number of occasions (Stogdill 1948; Gibb 1954; Hemphill 1964; Stogdill 1974). Some of the studies have been in an educational context, and a survey of the field by Hoy and Miskel (1978 p. 176) led them to describe leadership as 'an elusive but fascinating topic of continuing interest among students of administration'. According to Everard (1984, p. 5), leadership qualities 'are indispensable to the effective manager, since he holds responsibility for motivating the people in his charge'.

Handy (1981) chose leadership as one of the seven basic concepts to be studied in understanding organisations, but did so almost apologetically. This was because 'it implies setting one man up above another, raises spectres of elites and privileged classes'. After expressing such doubts he continued: 'Yet, call him chairman or co-ordinator, representative or organiser, there is a need in all organisations for individual linking-pins who will bind groups together and as members of other groups represent their groups elsewhere in the organisation' (p. 87).

Definitions of leadership often assume that it can be taken for granted that there is general agreement in the organisation or group on common goals and preferred outcomes. Thus Newall (1978 p. 222) used leadership as a generic term 'which refers to processes characterised by interrelationships among people as they work together in the formulation and achievement of common goals'. Cartwright and Zander (1953 p. 538), in their treatise on group dynamics, viewed leadership as 'the performance of those acts which help the group achieve its objectives', and noted that 'such acts may be termed group functions'. It is thus a paradox that, while early studies focused almost exclusively on discovering the distinctive leadership qualities of great men and women, the consensual assumptions concerning goals of the prevailing structural-functional paradigm tended to diminish the significance of the leadership concept. If there is general accord on aims and objectives, all that may be required of the formal leader is a public relations exercise to inspire the troops.

Later studies, as will be noted, have sought to take account more directly of the actual situations in which leadership acts are performed and of the reality of power and authority in organisations.

Traits and styles

The assumption of the trait theorists was that leadership can be explained in terms of the innate, personal characteristics of particular individuals. They sought to identify common personality traits which are believed to distinguish leaders from non-leaders, regardless of circumstances or organisational setting. As demonstrated by Stogdill (1948) and Gibb (1954) such studies proved disappointingly unproductive, leading to some unremarkable findings. Leaders, it would seem, tend on the whole to be of above average intelligence, dependability, social participation and socio-economic status, but many exceptions could be cited under each heading. Stogdill concluded as follows: 'A person does not become a leader by virtue of some combination of traits, but the pattern of personal characteristics of the leader must bear some relationship to the characteristics, activities and goals of the followers' (p. 64).

Attempts to define the distinctive characteristics of leadership gave way to approaches which sought to identify contrasting leadership styles, the crucial issue being the relationship between leader and followers. A classic study of adolescent groups by Lewin, Lippitt and White (1939) distinguished between *autocratic* and *democratic* leadership. An intermediate category, laissez-faire leadership, was interposed, and a host of studies made use of the resulting classification, which was naturally seen to have a critical value-laden significance at the time of the Second World War. Some of the studies assumed a linear leadership dimension from autocratic to democratic, particular leadership styles being regarded with approval in so far as they tended towards the democratic end of the continuum.

A study of leadership in twenty research establishments (Baumgartel 1957), which was based on the Lewin typology, has relevance to the leadership of professional staff, which will be specifically considered later in the chapter. Baumgartel identified three leadership styles, *directive*, *laissez-faire* and *participatory*. With directive leadership decisions were made by the laboratory director, following some subordinate involvement. With laissez-faire leadership there was little interaction or involvement, many decisions being left to subordinates. Participatory leadership signified high interaction and involvement of the director with subordinates, and extensive reliance on joint decision-making. The least favourable attitudes among the scientists occurred, as anticipated, under directive leadership. More noteworthy, the scores for participatory leadership were consistently higher than for laissez-faire leadership. The scientists wanted their research director to be involved; they did not work so well, apparently, under a director who granted autonomy but kept his distance and evinced little interest in the outcome.

Within education the Getzels–Guba model described in Chapter 1, which distinguished between an institutional (or nomothetic) and a personal (or ideographic) aspect of a social system, also led to a corresponding differentiation between leadership styles. The perceived contrast was between a nomothetic style which emphasised institutional goals, rules and regulations, and an ideographic style which stressed the individuality of people and the quality of personal relationships with subordinates. Again a third, intermediate, transactional style was identified by Moser (1957), in a study of the leadership patterns of school superintendents and principals. The transactional leader was in this instance regarded as the one meriting approval, judiciously combining a stress on goal accomplishment with provision for individual need fulfilment.

Leadership studies in a number of different contexts have led to polar differentiation between two kinds of emphasis. Cartwright and Zander (1953, p. 541) differentiated between 'goal achievement' and 'group maintenance' activities within groups, while Bales (1958) contrasted 'task direction' and 'socioemotional support'. Etzioni (1965, p. 690), in developing a theory of dual leadership involving a positional leader and his or her deputy, distinguished between 'instrumental' and 'expressive' leadership, a distinction also used by Burnham (1968) in comparing the respective roles of head teacher and deputy head in a school.

Perhaps the most notable of the dichotomies which may be taken to imply either a *system* or a *person* orientation (Brown 1967, p. 68) on the part of the leader of an enterprise was formulated by McGregor (1960) in terms of his Theory X and Theory Y. According to Theory X the average human being avoids work and responsibility if this is possible, dislikes change, prefers to be directed, and only responds to coercion and control. This is a convenient theory for an organisational leader exclusively concerned with control structures. Theory Y in contrast represents a more optimistic view of human motivation; it asserts that people will direct and control themselves in the service of objectives to which they are committed. From such a view it is up to management to create conditions 'such that the members of the organisation can achieve their own goals best by directing their efforts towards the success of the enterprise' (McGregor 1960, p. 49). The two theories may be assumed to result in very different leadership styles.

Identifying contrasting leadership styles may be an advance on the monolithic 'great man' assumptions of trait theory, but — even when conceptualised as a continuum rather than a dichotomy — it does not go very far in recognising the dynamic complexity of leadership behaviour in real life. A further step forward took place with the appreciation that more than a single dimension is required in understanding and assessing leadership behaviour.

Dimensions of leadership

In the course of studies in the USA, conducted independently at about the same time in the Universities of Michigan and Ohio State, it was clearly demonstrated that leadership behaviour cannot adequately be mapped on a single dimension. In both cases two independent dimensions were identified.

In early studies at the University of Michigan two contrasting styles of leadership were proposed, on the lines of those already described. The two types were designated 'production-centred' and 'employee-centred' (Katz, Maccoby and Morse 1950). It was initially assumed that a simple, inverse relationship would apply, i.e. that a high emphasis on production was a safe predictor of low regard for employees, and vice versa. It was found on the contrary that the same person could be high on both orientations, on one only or on neither. Two distinct dimensions appeared to be involved, which were almost entirely independent of each other.

The studies at Ohio State University resulted in the development of a leader behaviour description questionnaire (LBDQ), which has had educational applications. The LBDQ has been used to assess the leadership behaviour and ideology of a wide range of subjects: aircraft commanders, factory supervisors, liberal arts college departmental heads, school superintendents and school principals (Hemphill and Coons 1950; Halpin 1955). The two basic dimensions, which were consistently identified in repeated factor analysis of data from different sources, were given the names, *initiating structure* and *consideration*. They were defined as follows:

> *Initiating structure* refers to the leader's behaviour in delineating the relationship between himself and members of the work group, and in endeavouring to establish well-defined patterns of organisation, channels of communication, and methods of procedure.
> *Consideration* refers to behaviour indicative of friendship, mutual trust, respect, and warmth in the relationship between the leader and the members of his staff. (Halpin 1966, p. 86)

Perceptions of leadership behaviour were ascertained from the questionnaire responses of work-group members, and the corresponding leadership ideology by asking the leader how one *should* act in the context of the same LBDQ items.

Studies in different contexts showed that leaders who scored highly on both dimensions were those considered by others to be most effective. In a comparative study of educational administrators and aircraft commanders, Halpin (1955) found that the administrators who were not outstanding on both dimensions tended, in terms both of ideology and reported behaviour, to be strong on 'consideration' and weak on 'initiating structure'. The less effective aircraft commanders, on the other hand, tended to be strong on 'initiating structure' but weak on 'consideration'. In each group only a small number were weak in both dimensions. Halpin related these contrasting patterns to differences in organisational setting. While refraining from drawing any implications for the training of aircraft commanders, he suggested that the then predominant 'human relations' emphasis in the educational literature should be re-examined.

Like Halpin's later organisational climate questionnaire, OCDQ, already discussed in Chapter 1, the LBDQ has been widely used as a measure of leader behaviour. It has also been subjected to criticism — some items, according to Erickson (1977, p. 459), 'eliciting more information about the respondents than about the administrators whose perform-ance purportedly is being described'. That the instrument does have partial validity, if circumspectly used, is suggested by an interesting small-scale observational study of the speech patterns of elementary school principals (Lucietto 1970), as Erickson himself also concedes (1977 pp. 459–61).

The implication in the LBDQ literature that there is an identifiable leadership style, with a high score in both 'initiating structure' and 'consideration', which is the most effective in all situations, has been challenged by Reddin (1970 pp. 35–38) and by Hersey and Blanchard (1977 pp. 129–30). In both cases leader effectiveness was proposed as a separate dimension, to permit empirical investigation of the circumstances in which different combinations of 'initiating structure' and 'consideration' are most effective.

A different three-dimensional model has also been proposed by Yukl (1971), who noted that the Hemphill-Halpin formulation does not take account of the significant issue of the extent of the subordinate participation associated with the leadership behaviour, a question highlighted in the autocratic — laissez-faire — democratic conceptualisation of Lewin and his associates. Yukl explored this aspect by adding a centralisation–decen-tralisation dimension to the initiating structure and consideration dimensions as previously defined. In the following chapter Keith Lloyd describes his use of this model in a study of primary school heads.

Situational approaches

The felt need to introduce three and possibly more dimensions to describe leadership behaviour is symptomatic of a more general unease about approaches that seek to identify a leadership style or combination of styles appropriate under all circumstances. Whereas conventionally it had been assumed that there is an optimum leadership style which universally achieves maximum worker satisfaction and productivity, Filley and House (1969), in their review of leadership research, showed that variation in leadership style may be of only marginal significance as compared with basic situational differences in influencing important variables such as worker satisfaction and productivity. More emphasis on 'consideration' may not always be the answer.

It is of interest that some of the foremost advocates of a human relations leadership style modified their own views as a result of unhappy personal experiences in difficult circumstances. Thus Handy (1981 p. 91) has quoted McGregor, inventor of the Theory *X*–Theory *Y* construct, ruefully reflecting on his period of office as a college president:

> I thought that maybe I could operate so that everyone would like me — that 'good human relations' would eliminate all discord and disagreement. I couldn't have been more wrong. It took a couple of years, but I finally began to realise that a leader cannot avoid the exercise of authority any more than he can avoid the responsibility for what happens to his organisation.

Similarly Hoyle (1975, p. 39) has noted the chastening experience for Bennis who, as a university administrator, had to face acute student problems. Confronted with this practical challenge, Bennis (1973) reported that he felt like the character in W. H. Auden's poem, 'who lectured on navigation as the ship was going down'.

Consequent recognition of the situationally contingent nature of leadership has been associated with an appreciation that 'the concept of leadership is really a composite of power, authority and influence phenomena' (Hemphill 1968, p. 6). This accorded with Etzioni's (1965, p. 690) definition of leadership as 'the ability, based on the personal qualities of the leader, to elicit the followers' voluntary *compliance* in a broad range of matters' (my emphasis). Similarly Hall (1982, p. 159) remarked that 'leadership is closely related to power, but involves more than simply the power allocated to a position in the organisation . . . '

A significant advance towards developing a coherent and well integrated situational model of leadership was taken by Fiedler (1967) as a result of his extensive studies of work group members' perceptions of each other. Fiedler's contingency model made what was regarded at the time as a very radical assumption, i.e. that different types of situation require different kinds of leadership. He identified three major factors which determine the 'favourableness' of the situation for the leader:

(a) the leader's position power, determined by his ability to reward and punish subordinates with organisational backing;
(b) the task structure, i.e. the extent to which the work to be done is clearly defined;
(c) the inter-personal relationships of leader and subordinates.

His findings suggested that, when the task is well-defined and the inter-personal relationships are good, a directing type of leadership is expected, but that if the task is unclear but the inter-personal relationships are good, a more participative approach is appropriate. If the task is ambiguous and the inter-personal relationships are bad, a directive approach may offer the only hope. It may be noted that most of Fiedler's work was done in an industrial context and did not involve professional workers.

An extension of Fiedler's model, which has been proposed by Handy (1981, p. 96), may be called the 'best fit' approach. It suggests four sets of factors to be considered:

(a) the leader's personal characteristics and preferred style;
(b) the subordinates' preferred leadership style in that situation;
(c) the task, taking account of objectives and technology;
(d) the environment, taking account among other factors of the power position of the leader and relationship to the group.

The object is then to achieve the best fit among the first three sets of factors, assessed on a scale from 'tight' to 'flexible', taking account of the environmental requirements.

The leader as model and representative

Further complexities in the leadership role have also been noted by Handy (pp. 105–6) which may be of particular importance in the leadership of professional staff. Because of his or her position, the leader is inevitably a model for the group, whether in terms of attitudes and behaviours to be imitated or to be avoided. The leader is also an ambassador or representative of the group, whether to those of higher rank in the organisation or to those in related organisations. Not surprisingly, positive consequences follow when subordinates find that their leader has influence with his or her superiors in matters such as promotion (Pelz 1951) and in the interchange of information (Graen 1977). The importance for internal relationships of the leader's ability to be an effective representative of the organisation externally has also been demonstrated (Hills 1963).

Leadership and power in organisations

Leaders are sometimes 'seen as powerful agents for change' (Campbell, Corbally and Ramseyer 1966, p. 164) in contrast to administrators, who are perceived as 'concerned primarily with maintaining, rather than changing, established structures, procedures or goals' (Lipham 1964, p. 122). Such differentiation is not realistic in practice, because opportunities and expectations of leadership are associated with high ranking in the hierarchy. The study of leaders in organisation has in fact been mainly concerned with leaders who have the power of organisational position rather than the 'emergent' power of leaders of informal groups.

It should not be assumed, however, that senior managers are always in a position to provide potent leadership, envisaged in heroic terms (Bridges 1977, pp. 204–6). Hall (1982, p. 158) has argued that for most organisations in most circumstances positional leadership is heavily constrained, so that 'changing leadership is little more than a cosmetic treatment', the important factors being 'organisational structure, power coalitions and environmental conditions'. Given some flexibility, however, in the organisational structure, the positional leader's own resources of power are far from negligible, and it is of interest that Hall's own review of leadership research in organisations later leads him to concede that 'in organisations with relatively loose structures and where the leadership is expected to have a great deal to do with what goes on in the organisation, leadership behaviour will have a large impact' (p. 173).

Hall's two conditions are significant: *loose structure* and a *leadership closely involved* in the organisational task. Schools and other educational institutions readily come to mind as such institutions, which are 'loosely coupled', to use Weick's phrase (see Chapter 1), and in which positional leaders, as well as the teaching staff, would claim to be educational professionals. It is therefore appropriate that consideration in some detail is given in the next section to the concept of professionalism and the role of the professional in an organisation.

PROFESSIONALISM AND THE MANAGEMENT OF ORGANISATIONS

In this section consideration will first be given to the different views which have been expressed concerning the nature of professionalism, earlier assumptions concerning essential characteristics of professions being more recently questioned. The implications for organisational management of employing a professional work force will then be considered, including the potential for conflict and how such conflict can be resolved or avoided.

The concept of professionalism

Profession, like leadership, is an elusive concept and is a word with variations of meaning in the social science literature and even more so in general usage. Millerson (1964, p. 5) noted 23 distinct traits which have been included in various definitions of the term profession. According to Goode (1960), many of the characteristics that have been proposed are derivative, the two core characteristics in his view being a lengthy period of training in a body of abstract knowledge and a strong service orientation. Elsewhere he described the characteristics of a professional community as a sense of identity associated with shared values, an agreed role definition, a common technical language, and a recognition that the professional group has power over its members (Goode 1957, pp. 194–209). His work may be cited as an example of sociological studies which tended to accept, somewhat uncritically, the rhetoric of prominent professional groups and their unduly idealistic self-definitions of their special characteristics. As Johnson (1972, p. 25) has aptly observed, 'while the service ethic may be an important part of the ideology of many professional groups, it is not so clear that practitioners are necessarily so motivated'.

In contrast to the 'trait' approach adopted, though in a compressed form, by Goode, Barbar (1963) looked for characteristics of professionalism which might be regarded as having functional relevance for the relationship of professional to client or for society generally. He identified four such characteristics: a high degree of systematic knowledge, orientation to community interest, control through a code of ethics emanating from a voluntary association, and a system of rewards which is 'primarily a set of symbols of work achievement' (p. 672). The underlying assumption that there is a universally recognised community interest, which is distinctively served by highly qualified occupational groups whose members are expected to place symbolic rewards above monetary gain, and generally do so, is one which may understandably give rise to scepticism, as Jackson (1970, p. 8) has noted. In a later definition of professional behaviour Barber (1978, p. 601) essentially retained the first three characteristics but made no reference to symbolic rewards.

A consistent advocate of a more critical approach to professionalism has been Everett Hughes, who cogently argued that the available evidence indicated that 'the concept "professional" in all societies is not so much a descriptive term as one of value and prestige' (Hughes 1958, p. 44). He later proposed that attention should be given to the empirical question of how professionalised certain occupations are at a particular time, rather than seeking to determine whether they are professions in some absolute sense (Hughes 1963). He was followed by Ben-David (1963–64), who analysed professions in relation to the class system of different societies, and Prandy (1965), who examined professional associations as status bodies which bestow a qualification and seek to maintain and enhance its prestige. Oleson and Whitaker (1970, p. 184), in a review of studies of professional socialisation, conclude that there is a tendency 'to overlook major discrepancies between the symbol of profession and the everyday human realities on which it rests'. In a similar realistic vein, Larson (1977, p. XVI) saw professionalisation as 'the process by which producers of special services sought to constitute *and control* a market for their expertise'.

Hall (1969) followed up his previous study of the elements of bureaucracy (noted in Chapter 1) by a similar dimensional approach to professionalism. He examined the structural aspects of 27 professions and the attitudes expressed by their members, and found significant discrepancies between structural and attitudinal scores (pp. 87–8, Table 4.2). Professionalised occupations structurally did not rank as highly as some others in terms of belief in service to the public or of sense of calling to the field. They invariably had the highest ranks, however, in terms of belief in self-regulation and the use of the professional organisation as a reference group.

The structures and procedures within professions which ensure a substantial measure of professional autonomy and control are increasingly being vigorously challenged by those who use professional services, as Barber (1978) and Wirt (1981) have clearly shown. Wirt has provided an instructive developmental model of political conflict between professionals and non-professionals, i.e. 'the laity'. He distinguishes five phases as follows: *quiescence*, which entails professional dominance; *issue emergence*, involving a growing number of random individual complaints by clients; *turbulence*, characterised by strong challenges and militant pressure groups, and in some cases by the emergence of 'inside agitators' within the professional ranks; *resolution*, the phase in which both the professional and lay representatives are engaged in vigorous debate and action, and which may also involve government as mediator or adjudicator; and finally *closure*, signifying the reduction of conflict as the professionals typically accept some redefinition of professional services, whether voluntarily or as a result of legally imposed constraints. Wirt's illustrative examples relate mainly to medical and legal services in the USA, but he also includes apposite references to parental concern and governmental intervention in education in both the USA and the UK. The resulting involvement of professionals in external political activity, both at a micro level and at group level, albeit in a non-party sense in most cases, is well documented in Wirt's paper.

This brief review may be summed up with the observation that the early phases of Wirt's developmental model appear to be relevant to the concept of professionalism itself. The period up to about 1960 was largely one of quiescence, when the self perceptions of the professionals themselves, reinforced by their professional associations, were largely accepted not only by the relevant client groups but also by most social scientists. The 1960s and early 1970s may be regarded as a period of issue emergence, when the rhetoric of the professions began to be questioned, first by social science academics and then, in more robust terms, by individual clients and client groups. Since the mid-1970s there has clearly been a period of turbulence when the challenges are stronger and more co-ordinated, and some of the professional groups are themselves more active and vociferous in defending their interests, younger professionals themselves sometimes schizophrenically challenging established practice. Politicking flourishes, and there is little sign as yet of an abatement of conflict between the seemingly elitist aspirations of professionals and a widespread populist revolt which receives encouragement from radicals of both the political left and the political right. At the general level under consideration it appears that Wirt's final categories, resolution and closure, are difficult to envisage, being quite remote from the practical politics of life today.

Factors conducive to conflict within organisations

Professionals employed in organisations are liable to have difficulties from time to time in their relationships, not only with their clients or the public at large, but also with those in authority in their employing organisation. Professionals, it has been claimed, are unreasonably resistant to administrative control (Abrahamson 1967). Studies of scientists in research establishments (Hall and Lawler 1970), studies of doctors and nurses in hospitals and clinics (Engel 1970; Corwin 1961), studies of social workers in local authority departments (Jordan 1979; Glastonbury and Cooper 1982), studies of accountants in large commercial firms (Sorenson and Sorenson 1974), studies of teachers and lecturers in schools and colleges (Corwin 1965; Noble and Pym 1970) all share a common characteristic. They display similar patterns of latent or actual conflict between the occupational group and organisational requirements which cannot be simply explained away in terms of the recalcitrance of awkward individuals. The real issue, it appears, in the ubiquitous strain between professions and organisations is the relationship 'between two institutions, not merely between organisations and individuals' (Kornhauser 1963, p. 8).

Areas of conflict have been comprehensively reviewed on a number of occasions (Scott 1966; Etzioni 1969; Harries-Jenkins 1970; Rotondi 1975; Larson 1977). Many aspects have been discussed, Etzioni for instance suggesting that teachers, social workers and nurses might appropriately be regarded as semi-professionals on the two assumptions that they are more amenable than other professionals to bureaucratisation and that a higher proportion of them are women. The suggestion that these two assumptions are interconnected has been vigorously challenged (Neuse 1978, p. 440), and the concept of semi-professionalism has largely been discarded, having proved to be even more elusive than that of professionalism itself.

Returning to the main theme, one can broadly distinguish in the literature between problems related to the professional's claim to autonomy within the organisation, and problems arising as a result of his or her external orientation and affiliations.

The professional's claim to autonomy

Because of their specialised training, professionals expect to be accorded a large measure of discretion in dealing with matters considered to be within their area of expertise. It is argued that it is by using their trained judgement in professional matters that they can best contribute to the objectives of their employing organisation. If they are employed in a highly structured, tight bureaucracy, a certain level of endemic conflict, erupting from time to time in major incidents, appears to be an almost inevitable consequence, as evidenced by research in different contexts.

A comprehensive study by Hall (1968) provides support for the proposition that the professional's quest for autonomy is the professional value which causes most difficulty in organisations. The research included doctors, nurses, lawyers, accountants, social workers and teachers. Bureaucratisation scales were developed for the organisational units within which the various professionals worked, and measures were obtained of attitudes towards professional values such as service to the public and sense of autonomy. Whereas other relationships proved to be relatively weak, Hall found a strong negative relationship between 'feeling of autonomy' and each of his five bureaucratic dimensions, namely, hierarchy of authority, division of labour, rules, procedures, and impersonality. He concluded that increased bureaucratisation threatens professional autonomy. The strong professional drive for autonomy, he noted, 'may come into direct conflict with organisationally based job requirements. At the same time the organisation may be threatened by strong professional desires on the part of at least some of its members' (Hall 1968, pp. 102–3).

A related issue is the professional's reluctance to accept without qualification the legitimacy of a hierarchy of authority. Professionals are well aware that technical expertise does not necessarily increase with position in the formal hierarchy. The extent of resistance to hierarchical control varies according to circumstances, as will be noted later, the availability of appeal and consultative procedures being a significant factor. The quality of the professional commitment at the different organisational levels seems also to make a difference. Thus Scott (1965) found that social workers who regarded their supervisors as professionally oriented were less hostile to routine supervision than those who designated their supervisors as less professional, the supervision being acceptable when seen as an opportunity for helpful guidance by a senior colleague. On the other hand it was the more professionally oriented workers who were generally more critical of the control system than their less professionally motivated colleagues. A similar polarisation of attitude has been found among teachers and lecturers, identified by Corwin (1965) as a difference between *professional* and *employee* orientations, which is of relevance to the discussion of leadership in education later in the chapter.

The professional's external orientation

The second basic factor which tends to create problems is that the ideal stereotype of a professional establishes him or her as an incorrigible cosmopolitan. In a study of professionals in public agencies, Reissman (1949, p. 309) found that, in contrast to other employees, the professionals had a strong tendency 'to face outwards and away from the bureaucratic structure of their organisation'. With the accelerating increase of knowledge in all specialisms, the external aspect of professionalism has steadily increased in importance, familiarity with current professional literature and contact with colleagues across organisational boundaries being essential for the maintenance of standards and the further development of expertise. By such means professional credibility is retained and renewed, but this may sometimes be at the expense of the immediate organisational task. It is not surprising that frustrated, locally based administrators, who have to be concerned with the mundane task of organisation maintenance, become sceptical about the priorities and organisational loyalty of professional staff. Such differences of perspective are commonplace, for instance, in universities and polytechnics.

A notable pioneering study in this area was carried out by Gouldner (1957), who studied three aspects of the role orientation of the staff of a liberal arts college. He found that a high commitment to professional skills was positively related to an outside reference group orientation, and that both were negatively related to loyalty to the employing organisation as indicated by a wish to remain indefinitely in the organisation. Adopting a distinction drawn by Merton (1957) between *cosmopolitan* and *local* community leaders, Gouldner defined as 'cosmopolitan' the members of an organisation high in commitment to specialist skills and strongly oriented to outside reference groups, but low in organisational loyalty. The 'locals' were opposite in each respect. There is tension, Gouldner concluded, between an organisation's instrumental need for expertise which is provided by the cosmopolitans and its social need for loyalty which is provided by the locals.

Whereas the idea of a single cosmopolitan–local continuum of role orientations has had a powerful influence on later writers, Gouldner's assumption that his three variables, professional commitment, reference group orientation and organisational commitment, were so highly associated that they formed a single continuum was only partially supported by his research findings. Subsequent research has clearly demonstrated that the cosmopolitan–local typology is an over-simplification (Grimes and Berger 1970) and that at the very least one must consider two independent dimensions, related respectively to professional commitment (or cosmopolitan orientation) and to organisational commitment (or local orientation). In addition to Gouldner's 'cosmopolitans' and 'locals', a two-dimensional model thus envisages two further categories, the 'cosmopolitan–locals' (i.e. those high on both dimensions), and the 'indifferents' (i.e. those low on both dimensions). That many persons do in fact manage to combine loyalty to their profession and to their organisation has been repeatedly shown in empirical research (Blau and Scott 1963; Corwin 1965; Thornton 1970; Goldberg 1976; Jauch, et al 1978). Goldberg showed, additionally, that commitment to organisational goals could be an incentive to professionals to increase their professional expertise.

While recent research has thus shown that it is misleading and unhelpful to automatically equate professionalism with disloyalty to the organisation, it is equally important not to lose sight of the fact that the insight of Reissman and Gouldner retains at least partial validity. It has to be accepted that, if professional expertise is to be credible and relevant in the modern world, a cosmopolitan, outward-looking stance is an essential element in the role orientation of professionals in organisations. Like the claim to autonomy, however, it is liable to give rise to tensions and problems in organisations which employ professionals.

Modes of organisational accommodation

In spite of the rhetoric which flies around when conflict erupts, it may be noted that although strains and tension do arise between professional and organisational loyalties they seldom lead to major confrontation, accommodation being nearly always somehow achieved. A major reason for this, according to Blau and Scott (1963 pp. 60–3), is that bureaucracies and professions have many things in common.

In their classic contribution on this topic Blau and Scott suggest that, in spite of differences between bureaucratic and professional perspectives, there are important common elements. Both are concerned to establish and uphold general standards of performance which can be rationally defended. They are similar in studiously avoiding exaggerated claims: professional expertise is specific and limited, bureaucratic authority is explicitly defined and circumscribed. For both the professional and the bureaucrat, relationships with clients are expected to be psychologically detached, avoiding emotional involvement. Professional recognition and advancement is the result of specific achievement as assessed by the colleague group; similarly bureaucratic advancement is expected to be determined by objective criteria rather than by personal considerations. In view of these common characteristics it is not surprising that at least some professionals find little difficulty in adapting to organisational life.

Research by Blau and others tends to support this kind of interpretation. Blau (1968) found that the presence of a clear hierarchy is welcomed by the professionals if it is perceived to facilitate effective two-way communication with senior management. La Porte (1965 p. 37) found that a hierarchical structure is acceptable if it 'acts as a filter of organisational uncertainty', making it possible for the work of the professionals to proceed without extensive bureaucratic interference. Hall (1982 p. 109), in a later comment on his own research, previously mentioned, observed that a strong negative relationship between professional attitudes and hierarchy of authority was only established in the case of attitude to autonomy (Hall 1968, p. 102). 'The presence of a relatively rigid hierarchy', he concluded, 'may not adversely affect the work of professionals if the hierarchy is recognised as legitimate.'

Focusing on another bureaucratic characteristic, Organ and Greene (1981) examined the extent to which formalisation, defined as 'the control of job activities by administrative rules and procedures' (p. 238), results in conflict between administrative imperatives and professional norms. They found that conflict 'is neither omnipresent nor inevitable' (p. 251). To some extent formalisation did increase role conflict for professionals, but this was more than offset by its effect in reducing role ambiguity and in enhancing identification with the organisation. The organisation might become more meaningful to the professional, they suggested, 'by providing a Gestalt within which he can define more reassuringly the nature of his own contribution to the larger enterprise' (p. 250).

An entirely different perspective on factors to be considered in achieving harmonious working relationships has been provided by Tuma and Grimes (1981). Though their research interest was focused on role conceptions, they concluded from their study of academic and administrative staff at a large research-oriented university that 'the organisational and professional settings are as important as a person's role orientations in determining how the person performs professional and organisational roles' (p. 187). Their study considered separately the three dimensions originally proposed in Gouldner's (1957) study, namely *professional commitment, external or reference group orientation* and *local orientation* as indicated by intended organisational immobility. They added another measure of organisational commitment, *commitment to organisational goals*, on the grounds that it cannot be assumed, when employment opportunities are diminishing, that a wish to continue in an organisation necessarily implies such a commitment. A further refinement was their recognition of the importance of another role dimension, *concern with advancement*, which relates to the basic human desire to get on, whether this is achieved through the profession or the organisation.

Tuma and Grimes found that there was some association between the five conceptually distinct aspects of role orientation which they had identified. In explaining such relationships, they conceded that cognitive congruence, as proposed by Gouldner, operated to some extent, but suggested that two organisationally related mechanisms were also likely to be influential. These are:

(a) the recruiting policies which determine the criteria whereby organisational members are appointed;

(b) the behavioural feedback by means of which role aspirations within the organisation may adapt to the career opportunities available.

The latter mechanism, and the related recognition of 'concern for advancement' as a significant variable that over-rides the idealised professional–organisational dichotomy, brings a note of realism into the literature, which is in accord with the critical political analysis provided by commentators such as Johnson (1972) and Wirt (1981).

From the accounts which have been given of recent research in different contexts and from different standpoints, it may be concluded that some oversimplification was inevitably involved in our separate discussion of factors conducive to conflict and accommodation in the management of professionally staffed organisations. Neither internally, in relation to formalisation and control structures, nor externally, in relation to the recognised cosmopolitan orientation of professionals, is the situation as clear-cut as some of the earlier literature might suggest. Hierarchy, for instance, can be seen either as an impediment to professionals or as facilitating professional input into organisational decision-making. Conflict and accommodation are intertwined, and it is evident that, as Tuma and Grimes observed, the organisational and professional settings are of crucial importance in achieving co-operation rather than disharmony.

A considerable challenge is thus presented to those in leadership positions in professional organisations, i.e. in organisations which are largely staffed by professionals and have a recognised professional function such as healing the sick or providing education. As the cited research suggests, the challenge is partly that posed by the subtle and fascinating internal complexity of professionally staffed organisations which may be recognised as revealing a hitherto largely neglected arena of micro-political activity. There is also the challenge to professional authority and control posed by powerful external forces, which is of increasing importance and again has a political dimension in the non-party sense, at both micro and macro levels.

The implications of this double challenge for the leadership of professionally staffed organisations will now be considered. Without neglecting issues applicable to professional organisations generally, the discussion will be focused specifically on the role of leadership in the management of educational institutions.

LEADERSHIP ROLES IN EDUCATIONAL INSTITUTIONS

In general, those who have managerial and leadership responsibilities in educational institutions would claim to be educational professionals. This gives rise to ambiguities as well as to opportunities. The strains and tensions which have to be accommodated will include those which are personal to the individual concerned, who may conveniently be referred to in this context as the professional-as-administrator. The scope of the discussion is widened as it is recognised that *all* teachers have managerial, as well as academic, responsibilities.

A dual role model is proposed which seeks to take account of the situation that arises when the *chief executive* of a professionally staffed organisation may also be considered to be its *leading professional*. An essential element in the model is the close interdependency of the two aspects. This is demonstrated in relation to school headship, but is equally applicable at other levels and in different types of educational organisation.

The chapter ends by considering some of the challenging tasks which face the educational professional-as-administrator in three domains of professional leadership. The first two domains are concerned respectively with instrumental and expressive aspects of the internal activities of the organisation, the third being concerned with external aspects and the extent to which the professional-as-administrator may be able to develop a positive, pro-active, representative role.

The professional-as-administrator

In professionally staffed organisations it is usual for institutional heads to be appointed who have a strong professional background in the relevant area of expertise. Such appointments may be regarded as co-opting devices designed to defuse tensions between practising professionals and their managers. As noted by Moore (1970, p. 211), ' . . . the manager who has some basis for understanding the problems intrinsic to the professional role and its organisational setting is likely to elicit somewhat greater confidence than would be accorded a mere layman'. Moore also observed that there is a representative as well as an internal co-ordinating function to be performed and that a similar point applies: representation by 'one of their own kind' is more acceptable to professionals than 'by anyone viewed as an outsider'. The role of the *professional-as-administrator* may thus be presented, in structural-functional terms, as the ultimate accommodating technique: it legitimises hierarchy, helps to ensure that bureaucratic formalisation does not restrict professional autonomy, and provides external representation which expresses a professional standpoint. Whether it works like that in practice is another matter. The implication that, in terminology first introduced in relation to secondary school headship, the leading professional of the organisation is simultaneously its chief executive (Hughes 1972) is an attractive concept, but ultimately depends for its justification on the extent to which a leadership style is adopted which elicits the co-operation of the professional group.

That the appointment to high office of committed and inspired professionals does not necessarily ensure a collegial style of leadership is easily demonstrated by considering some of the familiar names that might grace a pantheon of educational leaders. Moody and Eustace (1974), in their well-known chapter on university vice-chancellors, singled out Hetherington of Liverpool, and then of Glasgow, and Irvine of St. Andrews for special mention as outstanding leaders. A later principal of St. Andrews wrote about Irvine twenty years after his death, 'I have been told that professors trembled when called before him. I have also been told that they felt that this was only right and proper' (Moody and Eustace 1974, p. 149). There was a similar tradition of directive autocratic leadership in further education, as Pat Twyman shows in Chapter 13.

Arnold of Rugby and Thring of Uppingham, doyens of what has been called the 'headmaster tradition' of the English public schools (Baron 1975), would also, it may be assumed, have an honoured place in the pantheon. On the one hand they were certainly leading professionals, and on the other they fitted Norwood's description, quoted by

Baron, of the headmaster as 'an autocrat of autocrats', so that 'the very mention of the title conjures up in the minds of most people a figure before whom they trembled in their youth, and with which they have never felt quite comfortable even in mature life' (Norwood and Hope 1909, p. 213).

It would be unwise to draw general conclusions, particularly as it has been noted that little reliance can be placed on a trait or 'great man' theory of leadership. There is, however, at least one significant characteristic which is common to Hetherington, Irvine, Arnold and Thring: each had a strong commitment to the education of those in their charge, and not simply to carrying out the managerial duties of their office. They each illustrate Hall's dictum, quoted earlier, that one of the conditions necessary for the leader's behaviour to have a large impact is that 'the leadership is expected to have a great deal to do with what goes on in the organisation' (Hall 1982, p. 173). Because of their acknowledged wisdom as educational experts in their particular field, they were able to exert influence also externally on behalf of their institutions. It is on record that much of the funding of St. Andrews University and of Rugby School depended during their periods of office, on the personal initiative and effort of Irvine and Arnold respectively.

The strong professional commitment of such archetypal father figures is a quality shared to varying extents by the heads and other senior staff in schools, colleges, and universities. Those with leadership responsibilities at different levels in educational institutions, ranging from the small primary school to the large university or polytechnic, aspire to professional authority as educators as much as to positional authority as managers of organisations. A similar reliance on professional, as well as on organisational, authority may be attributed to inspectors and advisers, as noted in Chapter 16, and applies to considerable extent also to local education officers (Bush and Kogan 1982, pp. 9–12).

Though it is at the school level that the co-existence of professional and organisational authority systems has been given most attention (e.g. Thomason 1974), it has also been recognised in higher and further education. In discussing leadership in higher education, Becher and Kogan (1980, p. 64) refer to 'the dual system of hierarchy and collegium running through the system', which is epitomised in the Janus-like role of university vice-chancellors, polytechnic directors and college principals. For vice-chancellors this view is confirmed in studies by Szreter (1968; 1979) and by Moody and Eustace (1974, p. 127) who observe of vice-chancellors that 'although their day to day activities within the university may conveniently be described as "administrative", they are expected to be, and in fact often are, academic in purpose and outlook'.[1] The description of 'chief academic and administrative officer', used of vice-chancellors in university charters since 1948, was significantly adopted in describing college principals in DES Circular 7/70. The duality is recognised in a NATFHE college administration handbook in a chapter (Edwards and Easton 1980) which recognised both that 'in administrative matters the principal may be regarded as a manager acting on behalf of the LEA' (p. 148) and that 'clearly, within the college, the principal has responsibility for being an educational initiator, either by introducing new ideas or encouraging others to bring forward ideas' (p. 146).

The four chapters which immediately follow discuss some of the specifics of the consequent involvement in 'what goes on in the organisation' in relation to leadership at different levels in primary and secondary schools and in further education. The concern is not simply with structures and processes but also with educational outcomes, i.e. with pupils and students learning and understanding, gaining skills and changing attitudes.

Hence the emphasis on curriculum change, on student welfare through pastoral care and on the development of coping strategies in adverse environments. Such specific preoccupations are in accord with Paula Silver's (1983) call, in her discussion of professionalism in educational administration, for an emphasis 'on the practical problems encountered by administrators *in their efforts to enhance student learning outcomes* as the appropriate focus of attention for the emerging profession of educational administration' (p. 14, my italics).

It may be concluded that, with some difference of emphasis, the professional-as-administrator is an ever present phenomenon in the educational system, in each sector and at every level. The strain involved in the occupancy of such positions is not always fully recognised, external accommodation being often achieved at the expense of internal conflict. The potential clash of loyalties is similar to that experienced by the scientist involved in both research and research administration. 'As an administrator, he must make decisions that are in the organisation's interest. As a scientist he has scientific values and peers in the scientific community whose approval and support he desires. What happens when organisational and interests diverge . . . ?' (Lambright and Teich 1978, p. 135). A related discussion by Feldman (1978) of the administration of the mental health service is of particular interest because of the similar professional ideology of mental health and education. An initial reluctance to be involved in the exercise of power and control was noted, but Feldman concluded that 'the mental health professional in government who is able to blend the use of power with an understanding of human needs is likely to be an extremely effective administrator' (p. 142).

The dual (leading professional–chief executive) role model

In order to examine more closely the professional-as-administrator phenomenon at the headship level, it has been conceptualised (Hughes 1972) as the simultaneous activation of two sub-roles which deeply inter-penetrate each other: the role of *leading professional* (LP) and the role of *chief executive* (CE). As a tentative first approximation one can then visualise the two sub-roles as distinct entities. This involves differentiating between activities which are *prima facie* professional and those which are *prima facie* executive (managerial), while also explicitly recognising that there are internal and external aspects to both role conceptions. The resulting dual (LP–CE) role model of headship is shown in Figure 10.1 below as applied to secondary school headship (Hughes 1976), but could easily be formulated for use in other contexts.

The inter-relationships of elements of the model will be explained by briefly describing aspects of the empirical research in which it was used, which involved interviews with the heads of 72 schools and with a stratified sample of teaching staff and school governors.

The research first revealed significant inter-relationships between internal and external aspects of each of the two sub-roles. Within the LP sub-role, heads who were strong in their external professional orientation (i.e. cosmopolitans, in Gouldner's classification) tended to—and were expected by staff to—take an innovatory stance in their internal professional role, i.e. they were pre-eminently the heads who encouraged colleagues to try out new ideas and media. Within the CE sub-role, heads granted recognition and autonomy by external authority were more likely than those not so recognised to take initiatives themselves internally in executive matters and to delegate effectively to

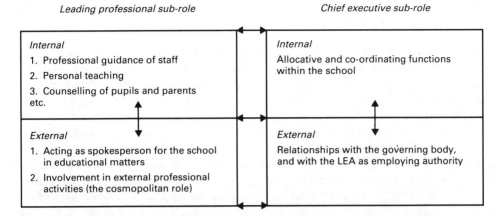

Figure 10.1 *The dual (leading professional–chief executive) role model.*

members of staff. Within both sub-roles internal and external aspects were inter-related.

More significantly it was found that elements of the two sub-roles were related to each other so that, as suspected, the notional separation into distinct sub-roles proves to be no more than a convenient heuristic device. Matters related to teaching by the head, for instance, (e.g. whether the head should teach, how much, which classes and at what level) were mainly considered by heads and by others not in terms of their professional implication for the head as teacher and for the pupils taught, but in terms of the implications of the head's teaching for the school as an organisation. Conversely the head's supervision of staff in the interest of the school as an organisation (an aspect of the CE sub-role) was more acceptable when it could be regarded by both heads and staff as an opportunity for providing professional guidance to inexperienced staff (an aspect of the LP sub-role).

The research identified areas in which the LP and CE sub-roles were supportive, those in which they appeared not to relate, and those in which there was potential conflict. There were two aspects of the CE sub-role, one internal and one external, for which the head's claims to be a leading professional appeared particularly relevant:

(a) allocating resources;
(b) presenting and interpreting to the governing body and the LEA information concerning the school's academic achievement.

In general the research confirmed a substantial inter-penetration of the two sub-roles. It seems that the professional-as-administrator does not act in some matters as a leading professional and in others as a chief executive. Professional knowledge, skills and attitudes are likely to have a profound effect on the whole range of tasks undertaken by the head of a professional organisation.

It may be noted that Morgan, Hall and Mackay (1983, p. 13) have recently referred to the LP–CE conceptualisation as helpful in their categorisation of the managerial tasks of the secondary school head. They also drew on Robert Katz's (1974) analysis of administrative skills as *technical, human* and *conceptual*, the latter referring to the ability to see the enterprise as a whole. Designating task categories to match the three types of skill, they added a fourth category of *external management* tasks, and this four-fold structure provides a convenient framework for Don Field's discussion of secondary headship in Chapter 12.

It must be added, however, as the issue is of some importance, that Morgan, Hall and Mackay appear not to have recognised the integrative significance of the professional-as-administrator concept. They assume a close relationship between the LP sub-role and their technical (i.e. educational) task category, but only apparently at the expense of regarding the human, conceptual and external management task categories as exclusively within the CE sub-role (p. 13). Subsequently, when those with whom the head interacts are identified, the dichotomy is formulated differently, internal school management generally being designated as 'the professional domain' and the school's external management as 'the public domain' (p. 16, Table 2). Either way the implied separation, though useful in generating a job description, does not appear to take account of the complexity of the linkages between professional and executive elements. The sharp professional/executive differentiation of heads' tasks, proposed by Morgan and colleagues, might appear to be taken a step further by Handy (1984) who argues that schools should have both leaders (senior professionals) and administrators (lay bursars), 'To combine the two roles in one person', he observes, 'is an invitation to stress' (p. 23). Handy is, however, using the term 'administration' to refer solely to subordinate, regulatory activities, as is common usage in commercial management, whereas 'leadership' for him 'includes the "direction" of the institution, the setting of its vision and its standards, and the oversight of its working' (Handy 1984, p. 35), i.e. it effectively includes both the LP and the CE sub-roles, as conceptualised in the dual role model.

An implicit assumption in regarding these two sub-roles as separate and mutually exclusive, as Ouston (1984) has observed, is that 'the head-as-professional can be left to the educational theorists, whereas the head-as-executive is a management issue' (p. 54). This is a view which has, in fact, been put forward in relation to headteacher training and development (Everard 1984, p. 52). Such a division, Ouston considers, would be 'artificial and possibly dangerous', a comment with which I fully agree. It may therefore be permissible in concluding this section to recall the unequivocal standpoint adopted under the sub-heading 'Towards a unified role model of headship', in the original formulation of the construct:

> Though they are useful as analytical and heuristic devices, it has to be recognised that our (LP-CE) role models are but abstractious, which only partially reflect the reality. In seeking to develop a more unified role model it is therefore salutory to recall that many heads to some extent, and some heads to a great extent, succeed in simultaneously activating and integrating the contrasting and potentially conflicting aspects of their total role. (Hughes 1976, p. 59)

In applying the dual role model at other levels in educational organisations, a similarly integrative approach would be appropriate.

The domains of professional leadership

Drawing on the earlier discussion of approaches to leadership in organisations, it is appropriate finally to consider three broad areas in each of which the professional-as-administrator has a significant part to play. Professional leadership, as has been shown, is concerned with task achievement, with group maintenance and development, and with the external, representative aspects of the role. These are considered in turn.

Task achievement

Only in the small school is the direct contribution to task achievement of the professional leader, such as through personal teaching, likely to be unavoidable. Many secondary as well as primary school heads would, however, regard being involved in some personal teaching as having substantial symbolic significance. This would not be so likely in further education, even at head of department level. Heads of department in universities, more perhaps than in polytechnics, would attach importance to their teaching role as a form of leadership by example. This would not normally apply, however, to university vice-chancellors or to polytechnic directors.

The most significant professional contribution of the positional leader to task achievement will be indirect. The opportunities for leader participation may conveniently be expressed in terms of a classical management cycle, as applied to education in a number of management by objectives formulations (e.g. Davies 1975). The leader is likely to be involved in:

(a)   any attempt that is made to identify aims and objectives for the organisation;
(b)   the broad formulation of means by which the resulting decisions are to be implemented;
(c)   the measures adopted, whether formally or informally, to judge the extent to which agreed objectives are being achieved;
(d)   any further action which is taken as a result of the assessments made.

It will be noted that though the above are unmistakably elements of the management process, the crucial decisions which have to be made at each stage are essentially professional, involving value judgements which would often benefit from explicit philosophical analysis.

The kind of leader participation will vary. It may involve contributing personally some of the new ideas relating to goal identification, policies for implementation, and outcome appraisal. This would be more likely to occur on a substantial scale in a school than in the more complex situation of a university or polytechnic. Even at the school level, however, it may be argued that the head should primarily be a facilitator or convener of organisational problem-solving rather than attempting to solve all problems personally (Schmuck and Nelson 1977; John 1980).

Additionally or alternatively, therefore, the leader inevitably will be involved in a critical appraisal of the contributions of others and in the use of professional and political judgement in co-ordinating, reconciling and integrating those contributions. Such processes can be formalised, as happened in 1984 at the University of Birmingham, where the vice-chancellor took the initiative, against a background of diminishing resources, in establishing an Advisory Planning Committee, under his chairmanship, to develop new academic initiatives, which will then be more widely considered through the normal channels of academic decision-making.

It is, of course, not only at the summit of the organisational hierarchy that the professional-as-administrator concept is relevant to task achievement. The initiation of structure within universities, polytechnics and colleges by deans of faculties, heads of department and individual lecturers, gives rise to issues of both professional and organisational significance, the consideration of which typically takes place within a well developed committee structure, as discussed in later chapters. Similarly in schools, though the formal structures may be less elaborate, there is room for a concept which differentiates between curricular and interpersonal management skills in considering task achievement at every level and not simply in relation to the role of the head (Campbell 1984).

Group maintenance and development

The appointment of professional persons as heads of professionally staffed organisations has mainly been advocated, not in terms of their contribution to task achievement but on the grounds that such persons are well placed to have the confidence, and to elicit the co-operation, of professional staff. Etzioni (1964 p. 82), for instance, observed that having a professional at the head of the authority structure will mean that 'the needs of professionals will be more likely to receive sympathetic attention'. Similar views have been expressed by Abrahamson (1967, p. 83), by Moore (1970, p. 211) and by Cyert (1978, p. 345). It is not simply that, because of a shared commitment to professional values, the professional staff will expect to find the organisational head sympathetic to their viewpoint and welfare, but that for the same reason professional influence will also flow in reverse, the views and wishes of the professional head being more likely to be heeded, other things being equal, than those of a lay manager.

Human relations theorists have shown that a rigid hierarchial emphasis can make the achievement of a genuine colleague relationship very difficult. Thus Bennis (1959) discussed the hierarchical superior as 'an instrument and arm of reality, a man with power over the subordinate', who is also potentially an agent of growth, 'a helper, trainer, consultant and co-ordinator'. The two aspects, he concluded, are liable to be in conflict, and 'a commitment to maturity' is required on both sides to activate the two roles simultaneously.

In practice the situation is likely to be even more complicated, for the extent to which there is a significant commitment to professional values will vary within the subordinate group, as it will among the positional leaders themselves (Corwin 1965). Hoyle (1975 p. 37) has usefully differentiated within the teacher group between restricted professionality, confined to work in the classroom, and extended professionality which additionally includes an awareness of wider dimensions. Sensitivity to such differences of attitude is clearly advisable for heads of department who wish to obtain the co-operation of their colleagues in planning for change and in working together to achieve it (Watts 1977).

Innovative school heads, it has been reported (Hughes 1975), are particularly aware that informal contacts with staff colleagues, such as over a cup of coffee in the common room, are highly political occasions, providing opportunities for collegial influence to be exerted in both directions, through 'dropping hints', 'sowing the seed', 'deliberate kite flying', and the most subtle manipulative activity of all, 'making it appear that the new idea has come from someone else'. There is clearly scope for more detailed study of such informal occasions, using the methods of symbolic interactionists and ethnomethodologists.

A parallel case study of teacher-principal interaction in American schools (Hanson 1976) reported examples of manipulative behavioural management by both teachers and principals, both parties relying on a common commitment to professional values. Democratic procedures and informal bargaining served as conflict reduction mechanisms, and principals, through their control of the reward structures of teachers, had an additional powerful organisational resource at their disposal.

Both studies thus provide examples in the domain of group maintenance and development of the inter-penetration of the LP and CE sub-roles, as previously described:

> The innovating head, it appears, relies partly on exerting influence on staff colleagues as a fellow professional; equally, however, he accepts his position as chief executive, and uses the organisational controls which are available to him to get things moving. Professional and executive considerations reinforce each other as complementary aspects of a coherent and unified strategy. (Hughes 1976, p. 58)

The use of professional, executive (i.e. managerial) and democratic strategies for achieving change will be discussed by Derek Slater in Chapter 19. Formal staff participation, which has long been a familiar feature of university government and is now a recognised part of the management of further education and, to a lesser extent, of schools, may be seen as the institutionalisation of the informal collegial interaction of positional leader and professional group which was described in the Hughes and Hanson studies. Whether it occurs formally or informally, staff participation is liable to come into conflict with interpretations of organisational accountability which are currently strongly supported, as will be shown by John Thorp in Chapter 17. The professional-as-administrator then has a particularly difficult role in achieving a balance, if not a reconciliation, between the conflicting demands, which is accentuated as a national assessment scheme to monitor teacher performance becomes a matter of public debate.

Implicit in the above is the idea of a close connection between the task achievement and the group maintenance and development domains. In a useful discussion of the management of higher education institutions in a period of contraction and uncertainty, Davies and Morgan (1983) discuss policy formation in terms of four successive phases: an *ambiguous* stage, a *political* stage, a *collegial* stage and an *executive* stage. Davies and Morgan suggest that 'to miss any phase, or to allow insufficient time for it, is to invite problems subsequently . . . ' (p. 172). They refer to the significant role of the university head in creating communication links and dialogues between parties who may have the capability to develop new perspectives. 'At its most sophisticated, the vice-chancellor's or administrator's role involves coalition building between potentially like-minded groups' (Davies and Morgan 1983, p. 173).

The encouragement of systematic, institution-wide staff development, which is discussed by Michael Matthewman in Chapter 18, may thus be seen as one of the leadership tasks of the senior professional-as-administrator, who, in virtue of his or her formal position, has some control over organisational resources. Tom Bone (1982, p. 277) has suggested that the best forms of staff development are side-effects of participative management, and institutional heads are thus especially well placed to contribute to the development of members of their senior management team, encouraging them in turn to assist in the professional development of their colleagues generally.

A fruitful concept at each level is 'action-centred leadership' (Adair 1973), which seeks to achieve a balance among the overlapping requirements of the *task*, the *individual* and the *team*, the term 'team' significantly replacing the impersonal 'setting' of the familiar 'tri-dimensional concept' of job, person and setting (Ostrander and Dethy 1968, p. 384). Action-centred leadership can be further accommodated within the comprehensive framework of organisation (or human resources) development (OD/HRD), the essential principle of which is to involve organisational members themselves 'in the diagnosis, transformation and evaluation of their own social system' (Schmuck 1982).

Experiental learning in a group setting is an important ingredient in OD-type collaborative problem-solving, task-related information being fully and frankly shared. The approach has been shown to work well when the participants perceive themselves as the 'owners' of the programme and its outcome (Milstein 1982), but the exercise quickly becomes sterile when the members consider themselves manipulated (Wolcott 1977) or to be under threat in a situation of contracting resources (Cyert 1978). The challenging, but sometimes unenviable, nature of the professional-as-administrator's leadership responsibility for maintaining and developing the group becomes very apparent (Taylor 1980; Bone 1982).

The external domain

In discussing the problems facing professions in the public service, Mosher (1978) mentioned a number of major social changes which significantly add to the complexity of the role of professional leadership. He drew attention particularly to the erosion of the line conventionally drawn between the roles of the professional expert and the politician acting as the people's representative, which he coupled with a growing demand for public involvement in making and executing domestic policy. Other significant factors, he suggested, were the greater concern within society for equal rights and opportunities, wherever disadvantage could be perceived, and the growing strength and militancy of unions in the public service, including those of the professionals themselves.

Mosher was writing of public service professions in the USA, but his words have a familiar ring in a UK context, and particularly in relation to education. Marten Shipman (1984, p. 5), in a book on education as a public service, sees the education service as a net, which depends for its shape on the various pressure groups pulling away at the corners. On the one hand there are administrative influences through national and local government and the voluntary bodies; on the other hand there are varied professional and academic pressures. Development, he suggests, is the result of interaction between these two groups of factors *within* the education service, but taking account also of pressures from a disparate set of other influences, the *external* forces. Among these he includes not only other government departments, the Manpower Services Commission, the Racial Equality and Equal Opportunities Commissions, etc., but also parents, employers, trade unions and others 'acting through interest groups both to affect the legal and financial basis of the service and to influence professional practices' (p. 6). It was these latter groups which Lord Morris (1975) had in mind when he referred to a new kind of politics, which would mean that 'the new Machiavelli can no longer make up his mind what he wants to do, and then bring the people round to putting up with it' (p. 14). 'All sections of the community', he added, 'divided up and organising themselves in very crisscross ways, are going to speak up for themselves without apology and if necessary with vigour' (p. 18). Several chapters in the present volume present a similar picture.

Given the turbulent environmental uncertainties with which educational institutions are faced, it is evident that there is an important external aspect to the professional leadership expected of the professional-as-administrator, which accords with Handy's insistence, noted earlier, on the representative or ambassadorial role of the leader. It is also noteworthy that authority as a leading professional and not simply as a chief executive is frequently required in relationships with clients and their parents, with the community and with governmental and other agencies. The professional leader also has the complementary task of making visible and interpreting to the professional group the concerns and interests of increasingly influential external groups and authorities.

In recently expressing a personal view on the changing nature of headship skills and public confidence, Ken Lambert (1984) quotes Yukl's view that school heads will need to spend more time in external activities such as shaping community expectations, soliciting co-operation and support and conducting public relations activities. Declining enrolments and economic stringency are factors which tend to strengthen the pressure for such involvement. Similar issues also arise in relation to further and higher education, as Tom Bone (1982) has shown.

The need for professional leaders to cultivate a sensitive political awareness, already mentioned in the internal institutional context, becomes even more evident in relation to the external domain. This had been foreseen by Lord Morris (1975, p. 18) in his forecast that administration in education, as in the other public services, would move towards the activities of politics, not in the party sense but in fundamental approach. Its practitioners would have to show more of the arts and skills of politics. Essentially the same message was expressed in a more radical guise in a volume, *Professions for the People: The Politics of Skill* (Gerstl and Jacobs 1976), which includes a sustained critique of education as a professional activity (Wenger 1976).

Earlier in the chapter Wirt's (1981) developmental model of dynamic political interaction between professions and their environment was described. The model has become particularly applicable to education. The phases of *issue emergence* and *turbulence* have become very familiar, and the idea of government involvement, whether as mediator or adjudicator, in a subsequent *resolution* phase can be recognised as more than a possibility. Though Wirt does not refer specifically to the part played by the professional leader in the achievement of *resolution* and *closure*, his analysis provides convincing confirmation of the importance for the external aspect of the professional-as-administrator role of political skill combined with a recognised integrity of purpose, recognised both by external groups and by the leader's professional colleagues.

CONCLUSION

In seeking to understand the nature of leadership in educational institutions, regarded as professionally staffed organisations, much ground has been covered, and an attempt has been made to uncover similarities and inter-relationships at various levels.

The various attempts which have been made to clarify the concept of leadership were discussed in the first section. It was shown that formulations in terms of traits, styles and dimensions, though valuable to some extent, have needed to be supplemented by approaches which recognise both the situationally contingent nature of leadership and its representative aspect.

In the second section the considerable literature on professionalism and on professionals in organisations was drawn on to discuss aspects of the professional's internal and external orientation which are liable to result in conflict between professionals and the ever increasing constraints of their employing organisation. Ways in which accommodation is achieved were considered, bearing in mind particularly recent research findings which have relevance to educational organisations.

In the final section of the chapter the challenging but equivocal leadership role of the professional-as-administrator at different organisational levels has been considered, a dual role model being outlined which incorporates both a *leading professional* and a *chief executive* sub-role. The inter-penetration of these two aspects was emphasised as a necessary step towards achieving a more unified concept of the professional leadership role in the final part of the section. This was considered in action-centred leadership terms in relation to task achievement, group maintenance and development, and the external domain. The need for professional commitment to be balanced by political awareness and skill has been a dominant theme in the latter part of the discussion, as account has been taken of internal and external pressures. It is appropriate to end by quoting yet again from Lord Morris (1975, p. 19), who, referring to the educational administrator, wrote as follows:

> . . . it is his task to present an *acceptable* scheme; for today only acceptable schemes are operable. In all parts of the world this is a task which is likely to prove a formidable and exciting challenge to the educational administrator in the years ahead.

NOTES

1. The same duality is recognised, but with a significant difference of emphasis, in the Jarratt Report (Jarratt 1985):

    No one can doubt the need for the Vice-Chancellor to be recognised as the academic leader of his institution and in no way should other responsibilities be seen as diminishing this. But to enable the institution at least to survive and to seize the opportunities open to it in the future, the Vice-Chancellor will have to adopt a clear role as the executive leader as well — and have the necessary authority to carry it out (p. 26).

REFERENCES

Abrahamson, M. (1967) *The Professional in the Organisation*. Chicago: Rand McNally.

Adair, J. (1973) *Action Centred Leadership*. New York: McGraw-Hill.

Barber, B. (1963) 'Some problems in the sociology of the professions'. *Daedalus*, **92**, 669–88.

Barber, B. (1978) 'Control and responsibility in the powerful professions'. *Political Science Quarterly*, **93**, 599–615.

Baron, G. (1975) 'Some aspects of the "Headmaster Tradition"'. In Houghton, V., McHugh, R. and Morgan, C. (ed.) *Management in Education, Reader 1: The Management of Organisations and Individuals*. London: Ward Lock Educational.

Baumgartel, H. (1957) 'Leadership style as a variable in research administration'. *Administrative Science Quarterly*, **2**, 344–60.

Becher, T. and Kogan, M. (1980) *Process and Structure in Higher Education*. London: Heinemann.

Ben-David, J. (1963–64) 'Professions in the class system of present-day societies: a trend report and bibliography'. *Current Sociology*, **12**, 247–330.

Bennis, W. G. (1959) 'Leadership theory and administrative behaviour: the problem of authority'. *Administrative Science Quarterly*, **4**, 259–301.

Bennis, W. G. (1973) *The Leaning Ivory Tower*. New York: Jossey-Bass.

Blau, P. M. (1968) 'The hierarchy of authority in organisations'. *American Journal of Sociology*, **73**(4) 453–67.

Blau, P. M. and Scott, W. R. (1963) *Formal Organisations: A Comparative Approach*. London: Routledge and Kegan Paul.

Bone, T. (1982) 'Problems of institutional management in a period of contraction'. In Gray, H. L. (ed.) *The Management of Educational Institutions*. Barcombe, Lewes: Falmer Press.

Bridges, E. M. (1977) 'The nature of leadership'. In Cunningham, L. L., Hack, W. G. and Nystrand, R. O. (ed.) *Educational Administration: The Developing Decades*. Berkeley, California: McCutchan.

Brown, A. F. (1967) 'Reactions to leadership'. *Educational Administration Quarterly*, **3**(1), 62–73.

Burnham, P. S. (1968) 'The deputy head'. In Allen, B. (ed.) *Headship in the 1970's*. Oxford: Blackwell.

Bush, T. and Kogan, M. (1982) *Directors of Education*. London: Allen and Unwin.

Campbell, R. J. (1984) 'In-school development: the role of the curriculum post-holder'. *School Organisation*, **4**(4) 345–57.

Campbell, R. F., Corbally, J. E. and Ramseyer, J. A. (1966) *Introduction to Educational Administration, 3rd edition*. Boston: Allyn and Bacon.

Cartwright, O. and Zander, A. (ed.) (1953) *Group Dynamics: Research and Theory*. Evanston, Illinois: Row, Peterson and Co.

Corwin, R. G. (1961) 'The professional employee: a study of conflict in nursing roles'. *American Journal of Sociology*, **66**, 604–15.

Corwin, R. G. (1965) 'Militant professionalism, initiative and compliance in public education'. *Sociology of Education*, **38**, 310–31.

Cyert, R. M. (1978) 'The management of universities of constant or decreasing size'. *Public Administration Review*, **38**(4) 344–9.

Davies, J. (1975) 'A discussion of the use of PPBS and MBO in educational planning and administration'. In Dobson, L., Gear, T. and Westoby, A. (ed.) *Management in Education, Reader 2: Some Techniques and Systems*. London: Ward Lock Educational.

Davies, J. L. and Morgan, A. W. (1983) 'Management of higher education institutions, in a period of contraction and uncertainty. In Boyd-Barrett, O. et al (ed.) *Approaches to Post-School Management*. London: Harper and Row.

Department of Education and Science (1970) 'Government and conduct of establishments of further education'. London: DES Circular 7/70.

Edwards, D. B. and Easton, W. A. G. (1980) 'The role of the principal'. In Waitt, I. (ed.) *College Administration: A Handbook*. London: National Association of Teachers in Further and Higher Education.

Engel, G. V. (1970) 'Professional autonomy and bureaucratic organisation'. *Administrative Science Quarterly*, **51**, 50–60.

Erickson, D. A. (ed.) (1977) *Educational Organisation and Administration*. Berkeley, California: McCutchan.

Etzioni, A. (1964) *Modern Organisations*. Englewood Cliffs, New Jersey: Prentice-Hall.

Etzioni, A. (1965) 'Dual leadership in complex organisations'. *American Sociological Review*, **30**, 688–98.

Etzioni, A. (ed.) (1969) *The Semi-Professions and their Organisation*. New York: The Free Press.

Everard, K. B. (1984) *Management in Comprehensive Schools—What can be Learned from Industry?* 2nd edition. University of York: Centre for the Study of Comprehensive Schools.

Feldman, S. (1978) 'Conflict and convergence: the mental health professional in government'. *Public Administration Review*, **38**(2) 139–44.

Fiedler, F. A. (1967) *A Theory of Leadership Effectiveness*. New York: McGraw-Hill.

Filley, A. C. and House, R. J. (1969) *Managerial Process and Organisational Behaviour*. Glenview, Illinois: Scott, Foresman.

Gerstl, J. and Jacobs, G. (ed.) (1976) *Professions for the People: The Politics of Skill*. Cambridge, Massachusetts:

Schenkman Publishing.

Gibb, C. A. (1954) 'Leadership'. In Lindzey, G. (ed.) *Handbook of Social Psychology Vol. II*. Cambridge, Massachusetts: Addision-Wesley.

Glastonbury, B. and Cooper, D. M. (1982) 'Case studies of bureaucratisation'. In Glastonbury, B. et al. *Social Work in Conflict*. London: British Association of Social Workers.

Goldberg, A. I. (1976) 'The relevance of cosmopolitan/local orientations to professional values and behaviour'. *Sociology of Work and Occupations*, **3**, 331–56.

Goode, W. J. (1957) 'Community within a community: the profession'. *American Sociological Review*, **22**, 194–200.

Goode, W. J. (1960) 'Encroachment, charlatanism and the emerging professions: psychology, sociology and medicine'. *American Sociological Review*, **25**, 902–13.

Gouldner, A. W. (1957) 'Cosmopolitans and locals: towards an analysis of latent social roles: I and II. *Administrative Science Quarterly*, **2**, 281–306 and 444–80.

Graen, G. (1977) 'Effects of linking-pin quality on the quality of working life of lower participants'. *Administrative Science Quarterly*, **22**, 491–504.

Grimes, A. J. and Berger, P. K. (1970) 'Cosmopolitan-local: evaluation of the construct'. *Administrative Science Quarterly*, **15**, 407–16.

Hall, D. T. and Lawler, E. E. (1970) 'Job characteristics and pressures and the organisational integration of professionals'. *Administrative Science Quarterly*, **12**, 461–78.

Hall, R. H. (1968) 'Professionalisation and bureaucratisation'. *American Sociological Review*, **33**(1) 92–104.

Hall, R. H. (1969) *Occupations and the Social Structure*. Englewood Cliffs, New Jersey: Prentice-Hall.

Hall, R. H. (1982) *Organisations: Structure and Process*, 3rd edition. Englewood Cliffs, New Jersey: Prentice-Hall.

Halpin, A. W. (1955) 'The leader behaviour and leadership ideology of educational administrators and aircraft commanders'. *Harvard Educational Review*, **25**, 18–32.

Halpin, A. W. (1966) *Theory and Research in Education*. New York: Macmillan.

Handy, C. B. (1981) *Understanding Organisations*, 2nd edition. Harmondsworth, Middlesex: Penguin.

Handy, C. B. (1984) *Taken for Granted? Understanding Schools as Organisations*. London: Longman.

Hanson, E. M. (1976) 'The professional/bureaucratic interface: a case study'. *Urban Education*, **11**(3) 313–32.

Harries-Jenkins, G. (1970) 'Professionals in organisations'. In Jackson, J. A. (ed.) *Professions and Professionalisation*. London: Cambridge University Press.

Hemphill, H. D. (1968) 'What is leadership?'. *The Canadian Administrator*, **8**(2) 5–8.

Hemphill, J. K. (1964) 'Personal variables and administrative styles'. In Griffiths, D. E. (ed.) *Behavioural Science and Educational Administration*. Chicago: University of Chicago Press.

Hemphill, J. K. and Coons, A. E. (1950) *Leader Behaviour Description*. Columbus, Ohio: Ohio State University.

Hersey, P. and Blanchard, K. H. (1977) *Management of Organisational Behaviour*, 3rd edition. Englewood Cliffs, New Jersey: Prentice-Hall.

Hoy, W. K. and Miskel, C. G. (1978) *Educational Administration: Theory, Research and Practice*. New York: Random House.

Hoyle, E. (1975) 'Leadership and decision-making in education'. In Hughes, M. G. (ed.) *Administering Education: International Challenge*. London: Athlone.

Hughes, E. C. (1958) *Men and their Work*. Glencoe, Illinois: The Free Press.

Hughes, E. C. (1963) 'Professions'. *Daedalus*, **92**, 655–68.

Hughes, M. G. (1972) *The Role of the Secondary School Head*. Ph.D. thesis, University of Wales (University College, Cardiff).

Hughes, M. G. (1975) 'The innovating school head: autocratic initiator or catalyst of co-operation?'. *Educational Administration*, **4**(1) 29–47.

Hughes, M. G. (ed.) (1975) *Administering Education: International Challenge*. London: Athlone.

Hughes, M. G. (1976) 'The professional-as-administrator: the case of the secondary school head'. In Peters, R. S. (ed.) *The Role of the Head*. London: Routledge and Kegan Paul.

Hughes, M. G. (1977) 'Consensus and conflict about the role of the secondary school head'. *British Journal of Educational Studies*, **25**(1) 32–49.

Jackson, J. A. (ed.) (1970) *Professions and Professionalization*. London: Cambridge University Press.

Jarratt, Sir A. (Chairman) (1985) *Report on the Steering Committee for Efficiency Studies in Universities*. London: Committee of Vice-Chancellors and Principals.

Jauch, L. R., Glueck, W. F. and Osborn, R. N. (1978) 'Organisational loyalty, professional commitment and academic research productivity'. *Academy of Management Journal*, **21**, 84–92.

John, D. (1980) *Leadership in Schools*. London: Heinemann.

Johnson, T. J. (1972) *Professions and Power*. London: Macmillan.

Jordan, B. (1979) *Helping in Social Work*. London: Routledge and Kegan Paul.

Katz, D., Maccoby, N. and Morse, N. (1950) *Productivity, Supervision and Morale in an Office Situation*. Detroit: Darel.

Kornhauser, W. (1963) *Scientists in Industry: Conflict and Accommodation*. Berkeley: University of California Press.

La Porte, T. A. (1965) 'Conditions of strain and accommodation in industrial research organisations'. *Administrative Science Quarterly*, **10**, 21–38.

Lambert, K. (1984) 'The changing nature of headship skills and public confidence: a personal view'. *Educational Management and Administration*, **12**(2) 123–126.

Lambright, W. H. and Teich, A. H. (1978) 'Scientists and government: a case of professional ambivalence'. *Public Administration Review*, **38**(2) 133–9.

Larson, M. S. (1977) *The Rise of Professionalism*. Berkeley: University of California Press.

Lewin, K., Lippitt, R. and White, R. K. (1939) 'Patterns of aggressive behaviour in experimentally created "social climates"'. *Journal of Social Psychology*, **10**, 271–99.

Lipham, J. M. (1964) 'Leadership and administration'. In NSSE *Behavioural Science and Educational Administration*. Chicago: University of Chicago Press.

Lord Morris of Grasmere (1975) 'Acceptability: the new emphasis in educational administration'. In Hughes, M. G. (ed.) *Administering Education: International Challenge*. London: Athlone.

Lucietto, L. L. (1970) 'Speech patterns of administrators'. *Administrator's Notebook*, **18**, 1–4.

McGregor, D. (1960) *The Human Side of Enterprise*. New York: McGraw-Hill.

Merton, R. K. (1957) *Social Theory and Social Structure, revised edition*. Glencoe, Illinois: The Free Press.

Millerson, G. (1964) *The Qualifying Associations: a Study in Professionalisation*. London: Routledge and Kegan Paul.

Milstein, M. M. (1982) 'Training internal change agents for schools'. In Gray, H. L. (ed.) *The Management of Educational Institutions*. Barcombe, Lewes: Falmer Press.

Moodie, G. C. and Eustace, R. (1974) *Power and Authority in British Universities*. London: Allen and Unwin.

Moore, W. E. (1970) *The Professions: Roles and Rules*. New York: Russell Sage Foundation.

Morgan, C., Hall, V. and Mackay, H. (1983) *The Selection of Secondary School Headteachers*. Milton Keynes: Open University Press.

Moser, R. F. (1957) 'The leadership patterns of school superintendents and school principals'. *Administrator's Notebook*, **6**(1) 1–4.

Mosher, F. C. (1978) 'Professions in public service'. *Public Administration Review*. **38**(2) 144–50.

Neuse, S. M. (1978) 'Professionalism and authority: women in public service, *Public Administration Review*, **38**(5) 436–41.

Newall, C. A. (1978) *Human Behaviour in Educational Administration*. Englewood Cliffs, New Jersey: Prentice-Hall.

Noble, T. and Pym, B. (1970) 'Collegial authority and the receding locus of power'. *British Journal of Sociology*, **21**, 431–45.

Norwood, C. and Hope, A. H. (1909) *The Higher Education of Boys in England*.

Oleson, V. and Whitaker, E. W. (1970) 'Critical notes on sociological studies of professional socialisation'. In Jackson, J. A. (ed.) *Professions and Professionalisation*. London: Cambridge University Press.

Organ, D. W. and Greene, C. N. (1981) 'The effects of formalisation on professional involvement: a compensatory process approach'. *Administrative Science Quarterly*, **26**(2) 237–252.

Ostrander, R. H. and Dethy, R. C. (1968) *A Values Approach to Educational Administration*. New York: American Book Company.

Ouston, J. (1984) 'The role of the secondary school head'. In White, J. (ed.) *Education plc?*. Bedford Way Papers 20, London: University of London Institute of Education.

Pelz, D. C. (1951) 'Leadership within a hierarchical organisation'. *Journal of Social Issues*, **7**, 49–55.

Prandy, K. (1965) *Professional Employees: a Study of Scientists and Engineers*. London: Faber.

Reddin, W. J. (1970) *Managerial Effectiveness*. New York: McGraw-Hill.

Reissman, L. (1949) 'A Study of role conceptions in bureaucracy'. *Social Forces*, **27**, 305–10.

Rotondi, T. (1975) 'Organisational identification: issues and implications'. *Organisational Behaviour and Human Performance*, **13**, 95–109.

Schmuck, R. A. (1982) 'Organisation development for the 1980s'. In Gray, H. L. (ed.) *The Management of Educational Institutions*. Barcombe, Lewes: Falmer Press.

Schmuck, R. and Nelson, J. (1977) 'The principal as convener of organisational problem solving'. In Schmuck, R. A. et al *The Second Handbook of Organisation Development in Schools*. Palo Alto, California: Mayfield.

Scott, W.R. (1965) 'Reactions to supervision in a heterogeneous professional organisation'. *Administrative Science Quarterly*, **10**, 65–81.

Scott, W. R. (1966) 'Professionals in bureaucracies — areas of conflict'. In Vollmer, H. M. and Mills, D. L. (ed.) *Professionalisation*. Englewood Cliffs, New Jersey: Prentice-Hall.

Shipman, M. (1984) *Education as a Public Service*. London: Harper and Row.

Silver, P. F. (1983) *Professionalism in Educational Administration*. Victoria, Australia: Deakin University.

Sorensen, J. E. and Sorensen, T. L. (1974) 'The conflict of professionals in bureaucratic organisations'. *Administrative Science Quarterly*, **19**, 98–106.

Stewart, J. D. (1974) 'Corporate management and the education service'. *Educational Administration Bulletin*, **3**(1) 1–9.

Stogdill, R. M. (1948) 'Personal factors associated with leadership: a survey of the literature'. *Journal of Psychology*, **25**, 35–71.

Stogdill, R. M. (1974) *Handbook of Leadership: A Survey of Theory and Research*. New York: Free Press.

Szreter, R. (1968) 'An academic patriciate — vice-chancellors 1966–7'. *Universities Quarterly*, **23**(1) 17–45.

Szreter, R. (1979) 'The committee of vice-chancellors revisited: the pattern ten years later'. *Educational Studies*, **5**(1) 1–6.

Taylor, W. (1980) 'Managing contraction'. In Farquhar, R. H. and Housego, I. E. (ed.) *Canadian and Comparative Educational Administration*. Vancouver: University of British Columbia.

Thomason, G. F. (1974) 'Organisation and Management'. In Hughes, M. G. (ed.) *Secondary School Administration: A Management Approach*, 2nd edition. Oxford: Pergamon.

Thornton, R. (1970) 'Organisational involvement and commitment to organisation and profession'. *Administrative Science Quarterly*, **15**, 417–26.

Tuma, N. B. and Grimes, A. J. (1981) 'A comparison of models of role orientations of professionals in a research-oriented university'. *Administrative Science Quarterly*, **26**(2) 187–206.

Vollmer, H. M. and Mills, D. L. (ed.) (1966) *Professionalisation*. Englewood Cliffs, New Jersey: Prentice-Hall.

Watts, J. (ed.) (1977) *The Countesthorpe Experience: The First Five Years*. London: Allen and Unwin.

Wenger, M. G. (1976) 'The case of academia: demythologisation in a non-profession'. In Gerstl, J. and Jacobs, G. (ed.) *Professions for the People: The Politics of Skill*. Cambridge, Massachusetts: Schenkman Publishing.

Wiles, D. K., Wiles, J. and Bondi, J. (1981) *Practical Politics for School Administrators*. Boston: Allyn and Bacon.

Wirt, F. (1981) 'Professionalism and political conflict: a developmental model'. *Journal of Public Policy*, **1**(1) 61–93.

Wolcott, H. F. (1977) *Teachers Versus Technocrats*. Eugene: University of Oregon Centre for Educational Policy and Management.

Yukl, G. (1971) 'Toward a Behavioural Theory of Leadership'. *Organisational Behaviour and Human Performance*, **6**, 414–40. Also in Houghton, V., McHugh, R. and Morgan, C. (1975) *Management in Education Reader 1*. London: Ward Lock.

11

MANAGEMENT AND LEADERSHIP IN THE PRIMARY SCHOOL

Keith Lloyd

INTRODUCTION

Primary schools operate today in circumstances which are more rapidly changing and complex than they have ever been in the past, dominated by the hard facts of contraction and faced with such issues as increasing public accountability and the demands of value for money within comparatively meagre budget levels. Curriculum expectations have grown and expanded into new and previously unexplored areas of science and technology, while at the same time the teaching force experiences depressed career-mobility and becomes progressively more dominated numerically by its older rather than younger members. Few would disagree with the view of the NAHT (1979) that 'the Head's task of administering the school is a great deal more complicated and time-consuming and, it is important to add, more stressful'.

The aims of this chapter are two-fold. First, within the broad context of primary education today, it seeks to explore the concepts of management and leadership — initially at a general level, and then more specifically in relation to three substantive issues which exert a strong influence on the quality of life and work in our schools, namely, curriculum, accountability and staff involvement. Second, by drawing on recent empirical research which examined the leadership role perceptions of primary heads, the characteristics and effectiveness of six headship types will be discussed, with special reference to the issues and ideas expressed in the first part of the chapter.

CLARIFYING CONCEPTS IN THE PRIMARY SCHOOL CONTEXT

The process of management

It is proposed to discuss the process of management in terms of a three stage model (Hughes 1981), while recognising that there will be some overlap in practice between the three stages:

1. *Planning* — problem identification, search for and choice of solutions.
2. *Organising for implementation* — including communicating, delegating, consulting and co-ordinating.
3. *Exercising control* — including evaluation and effecting change.

Planning

The dominant characteristic of this first stage in the management process is that of uncertainty. Major sources of uncertainty stem from fluctuating numbers on roll, changing fashions in curriculum content and philosophy, and the disparate expectations which are expressed by groups which make up the school's external domain.

Changes in numbers on roll, whether they are the substantial reductions which many primary schools have experienced in recent years or the modest expansion expected in the late 1980s, make organisational and curriculum planning a complex task (see also Chapter 5). This happens, in part, because staffing allocations for a new school year may be significantly affected by the movement of quite small numbers of children either into or away from the school, depending on the LEA's policy of teacher allocation and the individual school's position within its framework. Associated factors are the distortions of year-group numbers as different sized intakes work their way through the school, and the difficulties experienced in arranging options in relation to the age-groupings of each class. Such circumstances sometimes involve changes to mixed age groupings for the first time, or large differences in the size of classes across the school as a whole. Failure to achieve acceptable solutions to resulting problems is likely to result in a narrowing of curriculum opportunities, and may also lead to a loss of confidence in the school among parents and the community, governors, and in some cases the LEA. It may also lead to a lowering of staff morale.

Staff attitudes towards the school's aims and objectives are likely to vary from open enthusiasm for new ideas and plans to a reluctance to move away from traditional, well-tried approaches. The head's philosophy of education and professional leadership will undoubtedly be tested as he or she has to decide both on levels of staff involvement at the planning stage and on how much ground he or she is prepared to give in what is essentially a process of negotiation:

> For the head the task of curriculum planning is essentially one of relating what is theoretically desirable to what is practically possible. (Whitaker 1983)

In searching for solutions many schools have made positive gains which might not otherwise have occurred. School-focused in-service training, for example, the involvement of people from outside the school, and greater co-operation among groups of schools which look to each other for mutual support — these serve to illustrate a response which can add a valuable external dimension to the planning process, as well as developing greater levels of resourcefulness and initiative than would, in more stable times, have been necessary to make a successful primary school.

Organisation for implementation

Primary schools are relatively small organisations compared with the average secondary school, and their internal authority structure is much less complex in character. The primary head, as Coulson (1980, p. 282) observes, 'has no tradition of delegation, and the "flat", class-based structure of most of the schools encourages teacher independence rather than teacher inter-dependence.'

These characteristics exert a strong influence on this stage of the management process; communication ought to be much simpler in a small organisation, but in the primary school only the head has the time and relative freedom which is required, and even this is not available to the full-time teaching head. Co-ordination, which aims to promote continuity and consistency within the school, may often meet with resistance from teachers who have strong feelings of professional autonomy, their relative isolation may weaken the desire for co-operation, and the flatness of the authority structure may lead many to reject the initiatives of anyone except the head.

It is against this background that primary schools translate their plans into action, pursuing curricular aims which are widely acknowledged to be more complex and demanding than before within a situation in which the expectations of groups external to the school — parents, governors, the LEA and central government — are becoming increasingly explicit and not always in unison with one another. Let us consider, for instance, the situation in a school which has lost a member of staff due to falling rolls and in which, in consequence, it has been agreed to break with tradition and reorganise some of the classes as mixed year groups.

In this case, the process of communication assumes a crucial role for both the head and class teachers, particularly in relation to allaying the anxieties of parents, which are an inevitable consequence of almost any organisational change in the primary school. This is described by Morgan and Hall (1982) as:

> the capacity to communicate with the non-professionals . . . whose views of reality and vocabularies supporting their views may differ markedly from those of the groups residing in the head's professional domain.

If we set this alongside Whitaker's (1983, p. 2) view that 'heads and teachers now find that they are having to respond more consciously to higher and more vociferous parental expectations', it becomes clear that the example of reorganisation to mixed age groupings contains much potential for conflict if the head's skills of communication, and to a lesser extent those of individual teachers, are weak and inadequate.

The implications within the school in these circumstances will also be significant, with concentration on staff capacity to adapt their teaching styles and classroom organisation to the new demands of a much wider age and ability range. Inevitably, the head will be the focus of attention from both within and beyond the school during this critical period, resolving conflicts and ambiguity, negotiating, articulating, and reacting on behalf of the school as a whole. There is little scope for delegation in these circumstances, which emphasises perhaps most acutely the head's exposed and sometimes rather lonely position.

Exercising control

If we continue with the example which was used to illustrate 'organising for implementation', this third stage of the management cycle involves an on-going assessment of the new mixed-age groupings, with particular attention being paid to the effectiveness of classroom organisation and learning strategies. The process of evaluation will need to include careful observation of classroom practice alongside an agreed system for monitoring the progress of individual children, and the extent of the head's involvement is likely to vary from school to school, depending to a large extent on time available to observe other colleagues at work, as well as his or her perceptions of the legitimacy of this activity.

The gathering of information is, however, only a part of the process of control since, unless its findings are used so as to influence or modify practice, it can hardly be considered to be a worthwhile activity. The issue of effecting change in this way is one which Anning (1983) describes as the 'Beechers Brook' of headship, the uncomfortable and conflict-generating consequences of which she suggests cause 'many headteachers to lose their nerve, drop the reins and dismount'.

In terms of the reorganisation of class age groupings therefore, the head may conclude at the end of the first term that one of the teachers concerned has continued to operate on much the same lines as before, using a teaching style which is inappropriate for, say, a class of 7–9-year-olds. The gap between the teacher's perception of what is happening and the reality of the situation may be very wide, and the head who has reached this conclusion faces a challenge which will be a rigorous test of the quality of his or her professional leadership.

Leadership

Over the last few decades concepts and theories of leadership have undergone substantial modification and refinement, as was shown in the previous chapter. While a dimensional approach will be adopted in the latter part of this chapter, it is also appropriate briefly to consider changing leadership styles in primary schools, and to note the relevance of situational considerations.

The traditional view, supported by research from the 1960s and 1970s, perceived the primary school head as a benevolent autocrat, whose paternal style of leadership thrived during comparatively stable times within an internal authority structure which concentrated virtually all power into the one pair of hands. These were men and women whom Coulson (1980) describes as having an 'ego identification' with the school, causing them to think of it as their own and 'therefore to feel a deep sense of personal responsibility for everything and everyone in it'.

The extent to which this style of leadership is in the process of being replaced in primary schools by one which is more participative or collaborative in character is the subject of much debate today. Recent research by Nias (1980) makes a useful contribution in identifying three leadership types — 'passive', 'positive' and 'bourbon' — and exploring the attitudes of class teachers towards them. This suggests that there are limits as to how far class teachers wish to be involved in decision-making, although they are quick to complain if opportunities to do so are withdrawn completely, as in the case of the 'bourbon' head, who may be characterised as an aloof, inefficient autocrat. 'Positive' leaders were those most favoured, who had 'high standards of personal commitment and professional competence', gave 'support and encouragement to individuals', and took initiatives to establish a 'sense of cohesion within the school as a whole'. Nias concluded that 'educational commentators place a higher value on complete freedom of judgement and decision-making for teachers than the latter themselves do' (p. 272).

Sensitivity by the leader to situational differences and their implications for leadership style is, of course, helpful. Newell (1978) observed that, in contrast to dealing in a directive manner with routine matters, leadership in professional tasks emphasises assistance and support. Thus in primary schools decisions relating, for example, to class time allocation in the school hall might well be taken by the head and/or the deputy head alone. Few primary heads, however, would attempt to introduce new curricular policies without at the very least consulting all members of staff and taking their views into account. Essentially this is a contingency approach to leadership.

Management and leadership as related concepts

It will be evident from the above that management and leadership are closely related, conceptually and practically. This is well illustrated in the example of the school which, in response to a declining roll and reduction of staff, took the step of reorganising classes on a mixed-age basis for the first time. In these circumstances, and particularly at the 'organising for implementation' stage of the management process, the inter-dependence of leadership and management is very great indeed at every level of the authority structure of the school. The interplay of professional leadership skills, with an emphasis on support and encouragement for staff who lack confidence with the new system of organisation, together with the management-oriented tasks of communicating, co-ordinating and consulting, becomes so complex that several of these activities will occur simultaneously, each having an influence on the effectiveness of the other. At the same time, the school must also be responding to the demands of external groups such as parents, governors and the LEA who, at such times, will tend to relate especially to the head teacher. Many parents may, for example, be anxious about effects on their children's learning, or will not understand why their child has seemingly stayed 'down' this year with the younger children. Responsibility for replying to such questions will fall heavily on the head teacher, who must also interpret and feed back to staff the general feelings and opinions which are channelled through him. The innovation of moving to mixed age classes therefore involves the whole spectrum of management and leadership functions, and illustrates how, from the head's viewpoint in particular, the two processes can be mutually supportive.

We may conclude, therefore, that it no longer seems appropriate to think of primary school management in terms of unproblematic maintenance functions, operating independently alongside those associated with leadership. Successful management today embraces change rather than stability, requires adaptation as opposed to a reliance on what has gone before, and includes a level of creative thinking which in all begins to assume many of the characteristics which have traditionally been associated with leadership.

SUBSTANTIVE ISSUES IN PRIMARY SCHOOL MANAGEMENT

The curriculum

The concept of the curriculum as a 'moving target' seems a particularly appropriate way of conveying the on-going, continuous process of curriculum development and appraisal which is a central feature of our best primary schools today. Their work takes place against a canvas of continuing change, which makes searching demands on the time, energy and skills of everyone involved.

Recognising the formidable challenge to the professional knowledge and skills of the individual class teacher, Norman Thomas (1984), former HM Chief Inspector for Primary Education, observed that it is not reasonable 'to expect primary school teachers today to be confident and knowledgeable in all aspects of the curriculum unless they have close support' (p. 108). 'The support must come', he concluded, 'from the expertise, latent and current, that exists among teachers now in schools'. The dilemma which then faces school management is how to make optimum use of specialist knowledge and skills without damaging the wholeness of the learning process and close pupil–teacher relationships, which are among the strengths of the class-teacher system.

It appears that a much more flexible and creative approach to the management of staff and resources has to be adopted if the notion of a professional team is to become a reality. In particular, a high level of mutual trust and confidence between head and staff is necessary if the traditionally very personal and autonomous area of classroom organisation and teaching style is to be opened up. Implications for leadership and management will clearly include a need for collaboration, explicit programmes for collective professional development, and a headship style based on close knowledge of, and involvement with, the day-to-day work of every classroom. Management of the curriculum in primary schools today thus demands a degree of professional leadership with which it has not traditionally been associated.

The curricular role of the primary school head also has an external aspect, for schools cannot ignore the fact that they have become much more open institutions than ever before, with many voices to be heard in the national and local education debate. With a wide spectrum of views being expressed and discussion documents and research reports emanating from the DES, the local authorities and the universities, the primary head needs to be well-informed, and this involves a substantial professional commitment in terms of reading and listening, and involvement in the meetings and conferences of professional bodies. There can be little doubt, however, that schools and their heads can no longer afford to insulate themselves from the lively and continuing debate which surrounds the school curriculum today.

The trend towards accountability

Discussing the effects of the increasing emphasis on accountability, Bush (1981, p. 71) argues that this has 'particular significance for the head, who is often seen as the personification of the school. The school's accountability is essentially the head's accountability'. We could interpret this as something of a mixed blessing for the head, since on the one hand the increased level of exposure offers opportunities to enhance prestige and professional respect within the school and the wider community, while at the same time holding the potential to reveal shortcomings which might previously have been known only to those working within the confines of the school.

Heads will consequently find themselves fulfilling a role which places them in a forum described by Tomlinson (1982) as 'the flashpoint between professional practice and public concern', requiring a number of skills which have only recently begun to be reflected in the content of school management and leadership training. Apart from the more obvious skills of diplomacy, negotiation, articulation, and the capacity to resolve conflicting arguments or ambiguity, the most critical determinant of a head's success in this external domain relates to the ability to convince parents, governors and other groups external to the school of the value of his or her own educational philosophy and policies in straightforward, jargon-free terms.

Success in resolving the conflicting expectations which are often generated by circumstances of this kind thus enhances the head's authority and influence within the wider context of the school, giving opportunities to interpret what Bush (1981, p. 71) describes as the 'various pressures', in order to 'give them differing emphasis and to use them in furtherance of his own policies for the school and its future'. Where political skills of this kind are not within the head's capability however, he or she may become a source of frustration and embarrassment for colleagues as well as governors and parents, fulfilling not so much the role of the 'leading professional' as that of the 'leading obstruction'.

In the final analysis, the success of the school's relationships in its external domain depends on the willingness of head and staff to identify and engage those groups beyond its boundaries which have either an interest in, or influence over, its professional activities and affairs. Bush (1980, p. 467) describes this process as 'marketing' and his comments are an appropriate way of concluding this discussion:

> In a period of falling demand, marketing must become an essential component of a school's management strategy. Schools must project themselves to their community . . . they must explain curriculum change and seek and respond to parental opinion. If schools don't respond to their views, parents may vote with their feet and send their children elsewhere.

Staff involvement

As new subject matter and technology are introduced into the schools, and as knowledge and skills in these and existing areas are constantly developing, it becomes increasingly likely that individual teachers will possess greater knowledge and expertise in specific curriculum areas than the head teacher, which, although not automatically leading to increased teacher participation, holds the potential to alter the balance of professional authority within the school. The HMI survey, 'Education 5 to 9' (1982), suggests that this is already well established in many primary schools:

> Most heads made sure that their teachers played a part in the formulation of school policy.
> Many delegated responsibility for at least some areas of the curriculum to members of staff.

My own research (Lloyd 1981) showed that the majority of heads interviewed (84 per cent) perceive this involvement in terms of consultation, rather than delegation where others are empowered to make decisions in the head's name. Only 8 per cent of heads come into this latter category, although it should be added that in most cases where consultation prevailed, this involved extensive opportunities for staff to influence decisions, and heads took their views very carefully into account.

A related issue in this context concerns the role of the scale post-holder, which received substantial criticism in the HMI Primary Survey (1978) for a widespread failure to influence the work of other teachers in the schools. It was recognised that the successful fulfilment of this middle management role involves many of the functions of leadership and management — organising, co-ordinating, communicating and creating for example — and the conclusions which HMI reached in 1978 stimulated a great deal of activity among local authorities in attempting to improve the effectiveness of their scale post-holders.

Concentrating on those posts which are potentially able to influence the professional activities of others, and leaving aside those which simply fulfil a service function, there are three sources of constraint which help to explain the very low incidence of successful practice. The first concerns uncertainty and confusion among staff and post-holders themselves in relation to the responsibilities which have been delegated; the second stems from the relatively horizontal authority structure of the primary school, which accords only low status to intervening levels of management, and leads to a reluctance on the part of many class teachers to accept the authority of anyone but the head; and the third constraint is the difficulty of releasing staff during the day from a full-time responsibility for their own class of children — although some tasks can be carried out at other times, there are those, such as working alongside colleagues, which cannot take place out of school hours, and this exerts a strong limitation on the activities of the post-holder.

Improved effectiveness consequently lies partly with the teachers themselves, whose leadership and management skills must be developed through in-service training and regular appraisal within the school as proposed in the GRIDS project (McMahon et al 1984); it must also depend on more precise and clear role definition which will be understood and accepted by the staff generally; it may also suggest the desirability of considering some modification of the present system of promotion in the direction of Fiske's (1979) suggestion that within an adequately remunerated career salary grade, scale posts 'could be recognised instead by a reduction of timetable and teaching loads'.

Discussion by Hunter and Heighway (1980) of decreased staff mobility in middle schools, due to contraction of the service, also has relevance to primary schools. They suggest that where morale and motivation are low, there is a need for 'creative turbulence to be engendered or facilitated, while recognising that it is possible for too much turbulence to be demotivating' (p. 484).

The key to the success of this creative process must initially be in the hands of the head teacher, who, unless he or she also has reached the stage referred to by Hunter and Heighway as a 'situational adjustment', is in a unique position to initiate a programme of staff development within the school, to motivate teachers through the sharing of meaningful responsibility, and to seek persistently for the means to increase levels of job satisfaction for everyone.

Much therefore depends on the individual head's perceptions and value system. These will themselves be coloured or influenced by a variety of factors — level of trust in the competence of staff, anxiety related to having ultimate responsibility in an increasingly accountable service, and the degree of confidence shown by the hierarchy of authority beyond the head, in his or her ability to make sound judgements and good decisions with a minimum of interference. The future growth of staff involvement in the primary school is consequently finely balanced, with the conspicuously sound arguments offering benefits for the school and everyone associated with it on the one hand, and the highly susceptible idiosyncrasies of the individual head teacher, on which everything must ultimately still depend, on the other.

There is perhaps no better illustration of this issue than that offered by studies of the role of the deputy head in the primary school, which are unanimous in supporting Coulson's (1974) view that 'the deputy's role is dependent on the head's capacity and inclination for delegation; if he has none, the role scarcely exists' (p. 4). Burnham (1968) also argues that the deputy's duties 'vary immensely and there seems to be little consistency between school and school' (p. 177). In the context of the argument for greater staff involvement, therefore, a number of interesting developments suggest themselves. If the head's philosophy *is* predisposed towards increased participation for teachers, the authority structure of the school may become even more horizontal, reducing still further the need for an 'intervening' level of management and leadership (i.e. that of the deputy) between the head and the staff. If, on the other hand, the head maintained a firm control over all aspects of the management and leadership process, it seems unlikely that this would result in a meaningful role for the deputy either, over and above that of a class teacher, since delegation would not be a strong feature of such a leadership style (Waters 1983).

As well as emphasising the ambiguities which surround the role of the deputy, these examples also emphasise the vulnerability of every management role in the primary school other than that of the head himself or herself. The strength or absence of a perspective which values the notion of personal and professional fulfilment for every member of staff, through the level and quality of their involvement with the life of the school as a whole, is thus likely to be a powerful influence in determining the leadership style of the primary head, the subject of which occupies the final section of this chapter.

THE LEADERSHIP ROLE OF THE HEAD: A RESEARCH STUDY

The research described

The changing context of primary school headship and the new approaches to the head's leadership role which are currently emerging have been considered in the earlier part of the chapter, but without as yet offering any empirical evidence as to how the heads themselves perceive their role. The purpose of this final section therefore is to summarise the conclusions of a research study (Lloyd 1981) which examined the role-perceptions of

50 primary heads, highlighting in particular their differences. A typology of headship is proposed which enables us to discuss the likely effectiveness of each of the types identified, but bearing in mind the inevitable limitation that reported role-perceptions and actual behaviour may not in all cases be in full accord.

The research, which took place in three LEAs, focused on the role perceptions of head teachers in four major areas: their relationships with staff; influencing teachers and initiating change; supervising and evaluating the work of class teachers; and involving staff in the process of decision-making.

The theoretical framework for analysis of the data is based on Yukl's (1975) three-dimensional theory of leader behaviour, which adopts the two dimensions of the Ohio State Leadership Studies (Hemphill and Coons 1954) — 'consideration' and 'initiating-structure' — and adds a third dimension of its own which Yukl describes as 'decision-centralisation'. This latter refers to the extent to which a leader allows subordinates to influence and take part in the making of decisions, and, since this will vary from one decision to another, the term indicates the 'average degree of participation which can be computed for any specified set of typical decisions' (p. 163). However, for present purposes it is more convenient to have regard to decision-*de*centralisation, so that a *high* score indicates a *high* level of staff involvement in decision-making and goal-setting, and vice versa.

The broad criteria by which individual heads were rated are as follows.

1. Initiating structure:
    (a)   encourages staff to try out new ideas and media;
    (b)   lets staff know what is expected of them and criticises poor work;
    (c)   ensures that teachers work to capacity and maintains definite standards of performance;
    (d)   provides on-the-job instruction for teachers and is aware of the need for their professional development.

2. Consideration:
    (a)   is friendly and approachable with minimal social distance;
    (b)   shows concern for the personal welfare of staff.
    (c)   shows respect for staff and listens to their views;
    (d)   mixes freely with staff, treating them as equals.

3. Decision-decentralisation. Perceptions were analysed using the following continuum:

(a) Head decides then informs staff;	(b) Head listens to staff views, then makes up own mind;	(c) Head states willingness to accept staff consensus decision.

Low rating . . . . High rating

Areas of activity which were found to be of particular significance with regard to decision decentralisation included: organisational issues, such as the planning of class age groupings, or arrangements for giving parents information about their children's progress; curriculum issues, such as changes in the teaching of reading, or the adoption of a new approach to handwriting; resource allocation and the spending of the school allowance; and administrative decisions such as staff-duty rotas or timetables for the use of a hall.

The large quantity of data obtained through structured interviews with head teachers produced a wide range of characteristics in terms of leadership perceptions, to an extent that no single existing typology could adequately account for them all. For this reason I adopted elements of three typologies: Lewin (1944), 'paternal' and 'coercive'; Hughes (1975), 'extended professional'; and Nias (1980), 'passive'. To these I added two of my own: the 'nominal' and the 'familiar' headship types.

On the basis of the criteria outlined above for each of the three dimensions of leader behaviour, individual head teachers were therefore rated as above or below average rating, the combinations of which produced the model in Figure 11.1.

It will be noted that although the model has the potential to generate a total of eight leadership types, the research data suggests the existence of only six. The absence of examples at position (7) indicates that the existence of good relationships is dependent in some degree on the job satisfaction of the staff, obtained either through being able to take on responsibility and influence policies and planning themselves ('decision-decentralisation') or through operating within a well-defined and positively directed school organisation ('initiating structure').

The absence of examples at position (8) is also interesting, since this headship type suggests a manipulative approach to leadership in which the rationale for the involvement of staff in decision-making would be based not on a perception of the positive benefits for the professional and personal development of the staff, but rather on a one-sided belief that its 'pseudo-democratic' procedures, conducted in a climate of poor relationships, would provide the head with the justification to proceed with his or her own policies. The study indicates therefore that 'manipulators' of this kind are rare or non-existent in the primary school, where heads either genuinely involve their teachers in decision-making for positive reasons, or not at all.

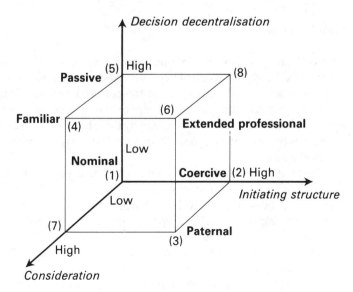

Figure 11.1

The headship types—characteristics

The 'nominal' headship type

Only one head perceived his role in terms which were characteristic of this type. In his relationships with staff this head felt insecure, lacking in trust, and showed little respect for the teachers, whom he described as 'neurotic, emotional and immature'. The lack of trust and respect gave rise to an unwillingness to allow staff any involvement in decision-making, this head being in fact the only one from the sample who, although doing little to initiate structure himself, did not feel comfortable about this being undertaken by others. Efforts to encourage staff to try out new ideas were minimal, but any criticism of the staff was considered to be 'bad for morale'. This type of head, as the name suggests, is a leader in name only.

The 'coercive' headship type

This group of four heads, 8 per cent of the sample, was characterised by low levels of staff involvement, and relationships which, although friendly up to a point, were more formal and reflected low levels of trust and professional respect. Attitudes towards organisation and supervision reflected a strong 'task' orientation, with the greatest emphasis on a supervisory as opposed to an innovatory role, and little concern for the professional development of staff. All four gave examples of having imposed decisions arbitrarily without any prior involvement or consultation of staff, and even on those occasions when teachers had been invited to give their views, it appeared to be against a background in which the head had already made up his mind.

The 'paternal' headship type

This large group of heads, 30 per cent of the sample, was one of the more clearly recognisable of the six headship types. They perceived themselves as friendly and approachable figures in school, who cared about the personal welfare of teachers, and were concerned that they should be given support and encouragement in their professional activities. Staff were held in high regard by these heads, who in some ways felt very protective towards their teachers, especially in relation to external influences such as parents and the local authority.

Ratings for initiating structure were high, the paternal heads perceiving themselves as active and fairly dominant influences in their schools. They had high expectations of staff, were not reluctant to criticise work which they considered was unsatisfactory, and frequently referred to the importance of leading by example, which generally involved as much personal teaching as possible. Perceptions of decision-decentralisation revealed a fairly dominant approach to goal-setting and decision-making, and although many consulted their teachers and did involve them in the discussion of aims and objectives, it was clear from their responses that for the most part they would only be prepared to accept outcomes with matched their own strongly-held views.

The 'familiar' headship type

The overall philosophy among this group of heads, who represented 14 per cent of the sample, was essentially to maintain a happy, family atmosphere with a minimum of conflict and stress. 'Consideration' behaviour scores were high, their relationships with staff being perceived as warm, friendly and informal. Ratings for decision-decentralisation were high also, with perceptions based either on belief in the value of staff being involved for the benefit both of themselves and of the school, or on the belief that the head's own professional knowledge and skills were inferior to those of the teachers, 'Lots of the staff are better at the job than me, and I don't presume to know better than they do.'

Ratings for 'initiating structure' were low, there being evidence of strong respect for the autonomy of the class teacher, in addition to a reluctance to disturb the harmonious atmosphere in the school. Levels of evaluation and supervision were consequently low, and this group of heads was prepared to intervene in the work of class teachers only if things went drastically wrong. Curriculum guidelines were deliberately vague, and there was little or no involvement with the professional development of staff.

It was interesting that four of the seven heads in this group were shortly due to retire, and that they talked about their approach to headship in their earlier years in very different terms. Remarks such as: 'Ten years ago most ideas came from me — I made all the big changes', suggest that some heads may become more relaxed in their approach to leadership as time goes by, which confirms the views of Waters (1979) — 'After ten years the old magic fades' — and Craig-Wilson (1978), who suggests the existence of a cycle of leadership: the 'power-triangle'. This involves a personally creative initial stage, a shared planning stage, and a third 'position' stage which is accompanied by 'an inert maturity characterised by a sense of security, complacency and conformity'. It may be that, for many heads who have reached this latter stage in the cycle, the 'costs' of overcoming the routine by initiating another creative stage may be too high in terms of its effect on the social harmony of the school. In these circumstances, Craig-Wilson suggests, the school must 'await the advent of another charismatic leader once again to begin generating new and potentially revolutionary plans'.

The 'passive' headship type

Only two heads in the sample were placed in this category, some of their characteristics being similar to those of the familiar heads — which is predictable in as much as they are both examples of decentralised 'non-initiators' — but they differed in terms of their relationships with staff. These were much more formal accompanied by greater social distance and low levels of respect for the teachers. Neither head spent any time in his staffroom. The overall impression which they conveyed was one of remoteness and isolation, in which initiatives for change or development depended largely on the staff themselves, with little or no involvement from the head.

The 'extended professional' headship type

This formed the largest single group among the six types (42 per cent), but there were variations within it which were significant enough to suggest that two sub-groups may be identified. I have called these the 'average' and 'high' rating extended professionals, but it should be emphasised that the differences between them were far less pronounced than those which existed between the six main types themselves.

Although the heads in this category had above-average ratings on all three dimensions, over half the group were rated as only marginally so in one or more, particularly in the case of decision-decentralisation. This suggests that the combination of initiating structure with high levels of decision-decentralisation is a difficult one to achieve, there being a strong likelihood that enthusiasm for the activities associated with initiating structure leads to a style in which the head plays a more dominant role, and which consequently begins to assume the characteristics of the paternal approach to leadership.

The small number (5) who did perceive themselves as successfully combining high ratings for these two dimensions regarded their schools as joint professional enterprises in which staff involvement was not only desirable but was an essential feature of the shared approach to decision-making — 'If something isn't going well, the whole school must share in getting it right'. One head was prepared to abide by a majority staff decision, but did add that he would then 'monitor whatever had been decided very closely indeed', while another felt for example that 'together we can come to a better solution than the original idea'. Several believed that only through staff participation would they reduce the likelihood of superficial change — 'If we move by the head's edict, the staff will conform but their thinking won't have changed' — their collaborative approach being influenced considerably by a commitment towards the professional development of their teachers.

Levels of evaluation and classroom supervision were relatively high, with a strong emphasis on being in the classrooms, and they set high personal standards of expectation in their schools. At the same time, however, these heads perceived their relationships with staff as friendly and informal, apparently reconciling the task and the social-emotional aspects of leadership successfully and without detriment to the effectiveness of one or the other.

The headship types — conclusions

Although the primary school head clearly remains a potentially influential and powerful figure, with the capacity to impose a very personal and egotistical regime in the school, this is no longer perceived desirable by over half the heads in this sample. The evidence suggests that the paternal and coercive headship types, which may once have been the most common approaches to primary school leadership, are now in decline, and that the trend away from the 'head-centred' approach has in the case of 18 per cent of the sample ('familiar' and 'passive' types) moved to the opposite extreme. It can be argued that the dominant styles of the paternal and coercive heads inhibit the professional growth of the teacher and place an excess of power and influence in the hands of one individual. By contrast, the familiar and passive types *under*estimate the importance of their leadership roles, leaving a vacuum of initiative which may or may not be filled by their teachers, and which may in any case result in diffuse and unco-ordinated centres of decision-making.

Evidence also suggests that the task of combining genuine involvement of staff in goal-setting and decision-making, with the responsibility for ensuring that the school continues to move towards its educational objectives, presents a difficult challenge for most primary heads. Nevertheless, 60 per cent of heads in the sample were rated as above average in terms of decision-decentralisation, which suggests that there may indeed be a firm trend towards increased teacher-participation in the primary school. Overall, above-average ratings for consideration (86 per cent) and initiating-structure (80 per cent) do however indicate that establishing good relationships with staff, and ensuring that tasks are carried out and goals achieved, remain firmly established in the leadership perceptions of the primary school head.

It may be noted that the 'nominal', 'passive' and 'familiar' heads all had low ratings on initiating structure. With the 'nominal' and 'passive' headship types, there were indications also of poor relationships with staff, leading to disorganised schools which lacked clear direction and provided few opportunities for staff development. In the case of the 'familiar' headship type, the onus was again on the staff themselves to introduce change and appraise their own effectiveness. Though the heads in these schools perceived a 'happy family atmosphere', there was evidence from the research which suggests that the absence of initiating structure on the part of the head becomes a cause of job-dissatisfaction, many teachers preferring less autonomy and desiring more positive leadership behaviour.

'Coercive' and 'paternal' heads both show a high level on initiating structure, with a low level of staff involvement. Arguments have previously been advanced in favour of encouraging and developing the professional skills of teaching staff, and it may be argued that few individuals can effectively manage and lead a primary school today without significant help and support from their teacher colleagues.

It thus appears that the sixth headship category, the 'extended professional', is likely to prove to be the most effective of the six types which have been identified, a view which receives strong support from the earlier discussion of the changing role-demands of primary school leadership and management today. A summary of these points makes an appropriate conclusion to the chapter as a whole.

1. In periods of organisational uncertainty, and within a climate of conflicting expectations, effective leadership in the primary school requires a sound, confident philosophy of education, supported by a background of relevant and wide experience.
2. The head's 'role-set' includes a broad spectrum of interested groups within and beyond the school, many of whom will respond positively to effective communication and good personal relationships. The ability to be articulate and diplomatic, and to negotiate skilfully, become valuable qualities for successful leadership, especially in the school's external domain.
3. The concept of the head as 'leading professional' is of crucial significance today, given the complexity and scope of today's primary curriculum, and for this reason professional credibility becomes an important factor in the process of influencing the work of colleagues. A background of excellence as a class teacher, giving the head the authority of the 'master craftsman', makes the 'Beecher's Brook' of headship less daunting and formidable, and increases the likelihood that it will be negotiated successfully.

4. The inter-relationship of the management and leadership processes has been discussed, putting forward the suggestion that, in today's circumstances, management requires a creative and imaginative approach which assumes many of the characteristics of leadership. The important point however is that effective primary headship depends very much on the ability successfully to combine the 'chief executive' and 'leading professional' concepts, so that they become mutually supportive and complementary elements of the same process.

5. The involvement of staff, argued from the school's point of view as well as from that of the individual teacher's, has assumed considerable importance in several areas of this chapter. The evidence suggests that while teachers expect to be given opportunities to influence school policies and decision-making generally, their job satisfaction also depends heavily upon a sense of cohesion in the school, brought about by the positive initiatives of the head. Maintaining the desired equilibrium between these two potentially conflicting processes requires high levels of self-confidence and professional conviction on the part of the head, for whom this may represent the most difficult of all challenges.

The concept of the joint professional enterprise becomes a reality, however, under action-centred leadership of this kind, where collaboration both promotes individual growth and self esteem, and also takes the school as a whole forward towards jointly-defined and consequently jointly-shared goals.

REFERENCES

Anning, A. (1983) 'The Three Year Itch'. *Times Educational Supplement* 24 June 1983.

Burnham, P. S. (1968) 'The Deputy Head'. In Allen, J. B. (ed.) *Headship in the 1970's*. Oxford: Blackwell.

Bush, T. (1980) 'Contracting Schools: Problems & Opportunities'. In Bush, T. et al (ed.) *Approaches to School Management*. London: Harper & Row.

Bush, T. (1981) 'The Role of the Head'. In *Block 4, Pt. 3, Policy-Making, Organisation & Leadership in Schools*. Open University E323: Management and the School. Milton Keynes: Oxford University Press.

Coulson, A. A. (1974) '*The Deputy Head in the Primary School*', M.Ed. Thesis, Hull University.

Coulson, A. A. (1980) 'The Role of the Primary Head'. In Bush et al (ed.) *Approaches to School Management*. London: Harper & Row.

Craig-Wilson, L. (1978) *School Leadership Today*. Boston: Allyn & Bacon.

Department of Education & Science (1978) *Primary Education in England*. London: HMSO.

Department of Education & Science (1982) *Education 5 to 9. An Illustrative Survey of 80 First Schools in England*. London: HMSO.

Fiske, D. (1979) *Falling Numbers in Secondary Schools — Problems & Possibilities*. Paper delivered at North of England Education Conference 1979.

Hemphill, J. and Coons, A. (1954) *Leader Behaviour Description*. Columbus, Ohio: Personnel Research Board, Ohio State University.

Hughes, M. G. (1975) 'The Professional as Administrator: The Case of the Secondary School Head'. In Houghton, V. et al (ed.) *The Management of Organizations & Individuals*. London: Ward Lock Educational.

Hughes, M. G. (1981) *Leadership in the Management of Education*. London: Commonwealth Secretariat, Education Division.

Hunter, C. & Heighway, P. (1980) 'Morale, Motivation & Management in Middle

Schools'. In Bush, T. et al (ed.) *Approaches to School Management*. London: Harper and Row.

Lewin, K. (1944) 'The Dynamics of Group Action'. *Educational Leadership*, **1**, 195–200.

Lloyd, K. (1981) *'Primary School Headship Types — A Study of the Primary Head's Leadership Role Perceptions'*. M.Ed. Thesis, University of Birmingham.

McMahon, A., Bolam, R., Abbott, R. and Holly, P. (1984) *Guidelines for Internal Review and Development in Schools: Primary School Handbook*. London: Longman.

Morgan, C. & Hall, V. (1982) 'What is the Job of the Secondary School Head'. *Supplement to Education*, 18 June 1982.

NAHT (1981) 'Evidence to Clegg Commission 1979'. In *When Breaking Point Comes to a Head. Times Educational Supplement*, 20 November, 15.

Newell, C. (1978) *Human Behaviour in Educational Administration*. New Jersey: Prentice-Hall.

Nias, J. (1980) 'Leadership Styles & Job Satisfaction in Primary Schools'. In Bush, T. et al (ed.) *Approaches to School Management*. London: Harper & Row.

Thomas, N. (1984) 'The primary school curriculum — building on the past to make a better future'. *Educational Management and Administration*, **12**(2) 105–10.

Tomlinson, J. (1982) 'Make the Professionals More Responsible'. *Education*, 17 December, 479.

Waters, D. (1979) *Management & Headship in the Primary School*. London: Ward Lock.

Waters, D. (1983) *Responsibility and Promotion in the Primary School*. London: Heinemann.

Whitaker, P. (1983) *The Primary Head*. London: Heinemann Educational.

12

HEADSHIP IN THE SECONDARY SCHOOL

Don Field

INTRODUCTION

The secondary school head in England and Wales, like the primary school head, is formally charged with control of 'the internal organisation, management and discipline of the school', to use the wording usually found in articles of government, and is universally regarded by governors, the local education authority, parents, the general public and the Secretary of State for Education and Science as bearing direct and personal responsibility for the school. The head thus occupies a key position which has been variously depicted as being at the boundary between the school and those outside who have contact with it (Richardson 1973), at the centre of the school organisation (Judge 1973; Jones 1974) or in the neck of an hour glass and subject to internal forces from one section and external ones from the other (Packwood 1981). Though the success of a school clearly depends on many factors, including the skill and dedication of the staff and the support of parents and other members of the community, there is widespread support for the view that the most significant factor is the quality of leadership provided by the head (DES 1977a; HMSO 1983).

Studies of the head's role have focused on traditional aspects (Baron 1968; Taylor 1968; Bernbaum 1976), the relationship between role conception and school size (Cohen 1970; Bates 1973), or the need for a managerial approach (Davis 1974; Gray 1974; Trethowen 1981; Everard 1984). Others have been written from a sociological perspective (King 1968; Musgrove 1971; Bennett 1974; Hughes 1976; Packwood 1977; Ouston 1984).

The tasks of secondary headship have been examined by Thomason (1974) and more extensively by Lyons (1976). Both studes showed the variety of events crowded into a normal school day, these being frequently of short duration, unconnected and often interrupting each other. There have also been a number of accounts from a practitioner viewpoint, partly descriptive and partly prescriptive (Allen 1968; Goodwin 1968; Jennings 1977).

A formal job specification is unusual. Morgan, Hall and Mackay (1983), reporting on the POST Project (Project on the selection of secondary headteachers), noted that only one of the 85 local education authorities surveyed could provide a written job specification for secondary heads. The researchers therefore compiled their own, organising the tasks in four categories, as noted in Chapter 10. These four broad categories — technical, conceptual, human relations and external management tasks — provide convenient headings for the discussion of headship in the present chapter, though the interpretation of the terms will not coincide precisely.

EDUCATIONAL (TECHNICAL) MANAGEMENT TASKS

These tasks are technical in the sense that they are specific to the primary purpose of the school organisation, namely educating pupils. We will consider in particular the part played by the head in relation to curriculum change and pastoral care.

Curriculum change

The management of curriculum changes makes demands both upon the head's professionalism as a teacher and upon his skills as a manager and negotiator (Mitchell 1984). Changes in the curriculum may also be regarded as the proper concern of the staff, parents, pupils, governors and the LEA so that that the time required for discussion and dissemination of information may be considerable.

If one accepts the view expressed by Sir Keith Joseph that 'there is now no serious dispute that the school curriculum is a proper concern not only of teachers but also of parents, governing bodies, LEAs and the government' (*Education* 13.1.84) then the head's boundary role as an advocate must be crucial to the successful introduction of innovations. The introduction of courses which might include controversial topics, or which have been traditionally linked with a particular age range or sex, or changes in the 'rules' governing freedom of choice in subject option schemes are examples of changes which require careful preparation with all the interested groups. This is an area in which the more clearly defined functions proposed for governing bodies in a government Green Paper (HMSO 1984), and elaborated in its White Paper (HMSO 1985a), are clearly a relevant factor.

Except in very large schools, option schemes which permit pupil choice are likely to produce a dilemma, which experience shows is difficult to resolve without mixed ability groups in many subjects. This is a situation which colleagues without timetabling experience find it difficult to accept if they prefer grouping by ability. Developments in the external examination system, including the widely welcomed introduction of a single examination at 16+, the General Certificate of Secondary Education, are likely to be influential in resolving these and related problems. Both educational and managerial considerations are involved, which require significant leadership from the head and senior colleagues, as well as the wider involvement of staff generally.

Another innovatory development of considerable significance has been the launching of the New Technical and Vocational Education Initiative (TVEI), under the auspices of the Manpower Services Commission, as noted in Chapter 7, which involved 58 local authorities from September 1984. For the initial 14 LEAs selected to operate approved schemes from September 1983, this introduced an entirely new dimension to the scene, detailed contracts being negotiated between the LEAs and the MSC, which is under the Department of Employment rather than the Department of Education and Science. The LEAs appointed directors or co-ordinators for TVEI, thus creating another branch of the authority with which heads of the schools concerned needed to negotiate. The boundary role of each of these heads was thus substantially extended.

In this writer's LEA the TVEI director heads a team which includes advisory teachers, a careers adviser and teachers with responsibility for schools-industry links, all team members also having other responsibilities. Each TVEI centre, which may be an individual school or a pair of adjoining schools, has a co-ordinator with responsibility for monitoring and developing TVEI work within the centre and for maintaining links with the director, colleges of further education and local industry. The grafting-on to the school's internal organisation and to its relationships with the LEA of the TVEI organisation raised numerous questions about the roles of all the staff concerned, not least because of the very short time which elapsed between acceptance of outline proposals and implementation.

Perhaps the most dramatic change resulting from TVEI is the inclusion of the MSC in the interested parties now concerned with the curriculum. Not only is it able to bring to bear the persuasive power of separate funding but its emphasis on vocational subjects and the resulting reduction in time available for other aspects of the curriculum represents a change in direction for schools which had heeded more broadly based advice from the DES and from HMI (DES 1977b; 1979; 1980; 1981). Managing the curriculum, never an easy matter when there is general unease about what it is appropriate to teach and with no clear consensus about long-term needs, is further complicated when the piper has a new paymaster with very forthright views about the tune.

Pastoral care

One of the most striking developments in schools has been the growth of pastoral care structures which have been depicted as a response to the non-academic needs of children and to potential problems, especially the proliferation of choice, arising in large comprehensive schools (Best, Jarvis and Ribbins 1980).

A problem facing heads of shrinking schools is the extent to which it is practicable to maintain pastoral hierarchies, as there are fewer staff and points for promoted posts. While reduction in size may alleviate some pastoral problems, others, such as general supervision in existing buildings, may not reduce in scale and constriction on the curriculum may affect behaviour when it is not possible to meet pupil and parental expectation. Inexorably external factors such as widespread unemployment not only affect pupils' motivation in school but also reduce incentives to attend school (Jones 1983). Further, there is a continuing tendency to expect schools to solve current problems by extending the guidance available.

One solution to the difficulty of providing individual counselling is to establish a guidance programme for form periods which attempts to establish concepts, attitudes, facts and skills which are helpful to all. Marland (1980) makes the useful distinction between helping individuals in this way and the very time-consuming process of giving individual help. Other topics may be included in the syllabuses of compulsory subjects at an appropriate stage; health education topics may be part of a biology or a home economics syllabus, for example.

The unfamiliarity of some topics and the sacrifice of time from other curriculum areas may well cause apprehension for some teachers involved and the introduction of a guidance programme is clearly demanding both on the head's managerial skills and upon his or her experience as a teacher. Full consultation with colleagues, governors and parents is a *sine qua non* for such an innovation and teachers may welcome support from other agencies such as the careers service and the health service as well as opportunities for appropriate in-service training.

A matter which needs very careful advance consideration is the extent to which pupils should be involved in discussion of school policy or in decision-making. The inclusion in the pastoral programme of discussions on topics such as school rules, acceptable conduct or school uniform must produce critical comments and could lead to negative responses if pupils feel impotent to influence policy. Conversely, experience with an elected school council and with pupil governors suggests that pupil involvement in decision-making tends to be limited by discontinuity of representation, the difficulty of achieving a consensus view, the complex nature of some apparently simple problems and a natural tendency to concentrate on short-term or relatively trivial issues which are more readily capable of resolution.

Although the establishment of appropriate structures and procedures to maintain good standards of pastoral care is clearly one of the head's executive tasks his or her credibility with colleagues, parents, pupils and other agencies largely depends upon their perception of the head's leading professional role. Furthermore, although other professionals and parents may accept that delegation of pastoral responsibility is essential and that others may have more detailed knowledge of individual pupils there are inevitably situations, especially if they are very serious or delicate, where the head must be directly involved. Similarly, problems which arise internally and prove to be incapable of resolution at other levels in the system eventually reach the head. Faced with the most intractable problems it is not easy for the head to maintain a balanced view, particularly where pupil behaviour is concerned, unless a representative sample of pupils are seen through personal teaching and by creating other opportunities such as seeing pupils whose work and conduct merit congratulation or by making opportunities to be in contact with pupils when they are moving about the school or engaged in lessons and extra-curricular activities.

The establishment of specific posts for pastoral responsibility may encourage other colleagues to regard the holders as experts whereas the quality of care available to individual pupils depends upon the concern of all staff. The creation of an appropriate climate and the development of good relationships, however, stems from the head and his or her relationships with pupils and colleagues.

CONCEPTUAL AND OPERATIONAL MANAGEMENT TASKS

This category includes those tasks which are directly concerned with the running and controlling of the organisation (Katz 1974) and are regarded as generic to senior management whatever the enterprise. Morgan, Hall and Mackay (1983) included in this group the deployment of staff and the production of job descriptions, but placed the selection and appointment of staff in the educational or technical category. To a practising head it seems that the two aspects are better considered together under the present heading, since appointments are usually made with a particular deployment in mind. Decisions about appointments and the allocation of tasks and responsibilities both, in fact, require a combination of professional experience and managerial skill. Similarly, the distribution of the resources available to the school seem appropriately considered as part of the process of running the school, although decisions about allocation again call for the exercise of professional judgement and are based upon different criteria from those which may be applied in other enterprises. The inseparability of professional and executive aspects of the role becomes increasingly apparent.

The appointment and deployment of staff

Although the selection of staff, their deployment and the measures available to deal with unsatisfactory performance are vital to the success of any organisation the power given to heads varies extensively. While some have considerable autonomy, others require approval from inspectors for even junior appointments and in some authorities senior staff may be appointed by panels on which the head has no voting power. Some assistant teachers argue for the presence of a local authority representative at every interview and for a code of practice to control the questions which may be asked at interview (NAS/UWT 1983). Procedures for dealing with weak or incompetent teachers are often complex, lengthy and difficult to operate especially since it would be difficult to find an agreed description of a 'weak' teacher (Hatfield 1984) or argue on criteria for action. Thus the head often lacks the authority to appoint and dismiss staff which is awarded to the managers of other enterprises of similar size and this is possibly the most significant example of the underpowering of heads in relation to the goals they attempt to attain (Musgrove 1971).

As falling rolls and economic pressures have resulted in a dramatic reduction in staff mobility, it follows that careful selection of staff, who may remain in the school for a considerable time, is vital and is best shared with senior colleagues such as deputies or heads of department, depending on the type of post to be filled.

Candidates need full information about the school and the particular post in order to reduce possible dissatisfactions after appointment, and shrinking schools may need to indicate possible requirements for teachers to offer subjects other than their main specialism. Despite the disapproval of some bodies, heads often consider the contribution which candidates may be able to make to school activities (NAS/UWT 1983) and certainly need to take into account the personal qualities of candidates as they may relate to colleagues and, in some cases, to parents.

Occasionally a deliberate decision may be taken to appoint someone who seems likely to initiate change or whose views appear to be very different from those of other members of the group but such a potentially disruptive course needs to be undertaken after careful analysis of possible outcomes. It is only rarely that the irritant in the oyster produces a pearl. Further, experience suggests that an attempt to compensate for the shortcomings of individual teachers, such as a head of department, by appointing promising subordinates is more likely to produce frustration and dissatisfaction than bring on improvement.

Increasing specialisation and the rate of change in syllabuses and subject aims and objectives make it difficult for a head to assess a candidate's suitability as a subject specialist, so the advice of a head of department or an inspector can be most helpful. In addition, the latter will be aware of standards throughout the authority and possibly nationally, but will not necessarily have detailed knowledge of the school and its particular needs. In some authorities references are obtained by officers or inspectors rather than by the appointing head, and while these may avoid the bias, whether for or against the candidate which one finds occasionally, they are often of such a general nature as to be of little value.

In some schools, an unwelcome addition to the head's tasks has been to manage a reduction in the number of staff by transfer or redeployment because of falling rolls or reduced resources. Having carried out a curriculum analysis to identify the subject areas in which the number of staff could be reduced the dilemma is to choose the most appropriate time at which to nominate individuals. If this is done at an early stage uncertainty is removed and those nominated are in a position to look for other posts, but conversely the need for redeployment may not arise if other staff find posts elsewhere in the normal way and the nominated staff may feel that they have been subjected to unnecessary stress. Redeployment is particularly difficult when it involves long-serving teachers and those in relatively senior positions, for whom the opportunities of finding an equivalent post are likely to be more limited.

The identification of colleagues for transfer or redeployment is an unpleasant task which requires the establishment of clear criteria in advance, full consultation with staff before implementation and definition of the roles of those concerned, both in the school and outside. Such a sensitive issue again makes demands upon the head's skill as a negotiator and manager and upon the head's credibility and understanding as a fellow professional.

Most heads are appointed to schools which already have a staff of varying competence and experience, and one of their first tasks must be to attempt a realistic assessment of their colleagues. There is increasing concern in relation to various aspects of teacher assessment, and heads will wish to devise strategies which maximise the strengths of colleagues and reduce the consequences of weaknesses, including their own.

The extensive delegation of tasks within the bureaucratic and hierarchical structure of a large school creates a need for clear statements about responsibilities and the establishment of lines of communication. Although job descriptions may be regarded with suspicion by some teachers, they are now to be found in most schools. Interestingly in one authority which, in common with most others has no job description for its head (Morgan, Hall and Mackay 1983), the first task given to the heads of reorganised schools was to prepare job descriptions for all staff. Only when these were complete were applications for the new posts invited. In established schools the identification of tasks, particularly when this is a shared exercise, provides the individual with the security of clearly defined areas of responsibility and also enables shortcomings in the organisation to be more readily recognised. The school organisation still has to respond to change, however, so job descriptions cannot be permanent and sacrosanct. For some teachers, adapting to an organic and evolving institution can be a painful experience which undermines their security but perhaps this is less so if there is scope for them to be involved in the formulation of policy.

Although reference has been made only to teachers, similar considerations apply to the appointment of non-teaching staff, except that the head's responsibilities are often less clear. Some, such as the caretaker or school meals manageress, may report both to the head and to a superior within their own branch of the service so that lines of communication are not always clearly defined and confusion can occur, particularly at times of stress.

The allocation of resources

The extent to which heads have control over the expenditure involved in running schools varies and in some areas is the subject of experiment (Humphrey and Thomas 1983) but there is normally an annual allocation, based on the number of pupils, for equipment, books and materials (Knight 1983). Heads may have complete freedom to distribute resources, or the allocations may be assigned for specific purposes such as books, telephones, etc., or there may be restrictions on the purchase of items costing more than a designated amount. As it is not normally possible to carry official funds forward from one financial year to another the timing of expenditure is difficult both in individual schools and, with the imposition of strict cash limits, within the authority. It is therefore useful to maintain lists of readily available items, especially those which are regularly required, to facilitate late spending and some suppliers will agree to spread the cost of more expensive items over two payments in consecutive financial years.

The growth in size and complexity of schools and the adoption of a more participatory style of management have led to changes in the methods by which most schools allocate their resources. In the 1960s practice varied from the traditional control by the head, with heads of department pleading their particular needs, to the adoption of a formula based on factors such as the number of pupils and lessons, and the needs for particular materials (Benn and Simon 1970). After a detailed investigation of 16 schools (Lyons 1974) it was suggested that distribution should be discussed at meetings of heads of department and that student hours with weighting for special materials should form the basis for distribution (Lyons 1976). Such meetings provide heads of department with an opportunity to argue their own case, and also to appreciate the needs of others and the difficulty of arriving at a fair allocation. It follows that the use of resources within a department needs to be discussed with all the staff concerned before the head of department makes a final decision. Apparently fair procedures based on the use of an agreed formula can lead to difficulty when there is in-built flexibility. For example, an annually repeated pattern of distribution may inhibit major innovations (Barry and Tye 1975) and small departments could find the purchase of major items impossible unless the system includes provision for development or special expenditure. The use of increasingly sophisticated equipment also requires careful investigation of maintenance and running costs which create a commitment to future expenditure and which may be of greater significance than the cost of purchase.

The management of funds raised by the school is usually subject to fewer external constraints but can lead to dissatisfaction and a lack of commitment to fund-raising unless an open approach is adopted. In large schools particularly there may be considerable sums involved and a great deal of work for which neither the head nor any other staff may be trained (Handy 1984).

The management of resources, both 'official' and 'private', clearly calls for technical expertise and administrative skill. It also involves judgement about priorities, which depends upon the head's experience as a teacher and is more likely to be acceptable to colleagues if they regard him or her as the leading professional as well as the chief executive of the school.

Buildings and facilities

Changes in school size, teaching methods and the curriculum have created demands for changes in buildings and facilities which are unlikely to be met except for specific projects such as TVEI. The problem in most schools is to make the best use of existing ones but it is inevitable that the curriculum and timetabling will be constrained by the availability of specialist facilities. Other aspects of school organisation are also affected by the design and location of buildings. For example, supervision of movement depends upon the size of circulation areas, distances between buildings and the grouping of specialist rooms. The development of a sense of community is affected by the size of assembly halls and the provision of play and social areas, while the availability of suitable accommodation is clearly a factor in the provision of extra-curricular activities.

Local authority policy on maintenance is diverse, and is dependent on the way in which corporate management is interpreted in the authority. The head's boundary role becomes particularly uncomfortable when there are severe economic restrictions. Teachers wrestling with problems arising from poor maintenance or inadequate facilities may naturally see the head as a target for their frustration, while heads are unable either to initiate remedial action or obtain an adequate response from officers, who may themselves only be able to pass requests on to other departments.

Greater freedom of action for heads would therefore have its attractions, though it would create additional administrative work and the need for new skills. In one such experiment, as already noted, new financial arrangements were instituted, and it was found possible to respond more rapidly to needs (Humphrey and Thomas 1983).

HUMAN MANAGEMENT TASKS

One of the most marked changes in the head's role in the second half of this century has been the rejection of an autocratic style of leadership (Nockels 1981) and the aspirations of teaching and non-teaching staff to play a greater part in policy-making. Pupils and their parents also reflect society's reluctance to accept authoritarianism. Thus, although these groups will usually accept the head's leadership role, the ability to negotiate, communicate and consult become increasingly significant, as has been indicated in Chapter 10.

Communication, participation and delegation

It is characteristic of professionals that they prefer to regard themselves as members of a team, each having independent responsibility and being answerable to a co-ordinator rather than to a supervisor (Drucker 1952). The tension which may be created by a hierarchical structure for teachers who value classroom autonomy (Watson 1969) may well be exacerbated by increasingly insistent demands for assessment and closer supervision of teachers. It has been suggested that staff co-operation may be enhanced by participation in decision-making if this is within their capacity to respond and supported by 'an adequate programme for development through in-service training' (Hughes 1980, p. 247) but most heads will have encountered colleagues who resist efforts to involve them in policy-making or training.

In addition to size, factors such as the arrangement of buildings and the provision of offices, telephones, etc. influence the effectiveness of communications and it is difficult to see how a head whose room doubles as the school office, as revealed in one survey (Weeks 1983), can develop good personal contacts with colleagues. While the need for formal channels of communication is self-evident the development of the head's understanding of colleagues and opportunities for them to raise individual matters is also important, but there is likely to be conflict between such a time-consuming activity, possibly regarded by some as a readiness to deal with trivia, and other tasks which might appear to be of greater moment.

Most teachers have ambivalent feelings about meetings, having on the one hand a desire to participate in planning and policy-making and a reluctance to give up valuable time and, possibly, to accept the responsibility which accompanies group decisions on the other. Rutter et al (1979) reported better pupil attendance and less delinquency in schools where joint planning resulted in better co-ordination and where there was more guidance and supervision. The development of an agreed policy by discussion can be applied to almost every aspect of a school's activities but it is a *sine qua non* that once policy has been formulated after the consultative process, it should be implemented by all, whether it had their support in debate or not.

It is useful to distinguish between consultation, which implies that the head seeks the views of colleagues and may then modify proposals, and negotiation, which leads to a compromise acceptable to all. If the former is to be taken seriously by colleagues it is essential for the head to be prepared to respond and to accept change to proposals but it is not always easy to choose between a less attractive policy which has a better chance of implementation because it has strong support and risking lack of staff commitment by selecting a alternative, or refusing to accept modification.

Like all compromises, negotiated policies could be the worst of all possibilities although most participants in schools will be anxious to avoid this. Care is essential when selecting issues for negotiation since the establishment of a precedent would make it difficult to adopt a different approach to similar issues in the future.

Especially in large schools, where senior staff are often called upon to communicate and interpret school policy and adjudicate on controversial issues, regular meetings of a senior management team are essential. Additionally, they enable the group to become aware of the repercussions on the work of others of decisions taken within individual areas of responsibility, to acquire a more accurate overview of the school and to share and gain expertise.

As well as a hierarchical consultative structure the establishment of *ad hoc* groups can make a useful contribution if they report on specific issues or manage particular activities. Not only may such groups pool the best available expertise but they can also play an important part in the professional development of colleagues.

The growth in the influence of the teacher unions, particularly during disputes, has made consultation and negotiation with school representatives essential in order to develop a *modus vivendi*. Some legislation, such as the Health and Safety at Work Act (1974), and local agreements have developed the role of union representative and involve the head in the industrial aspects of management in which, unless they are themselves active in union affairs, they are likely to be inexperienced (Stenning 1979). A head who is a member of a union which also includes assistant teachers may experience role conflict when called upon to implement union sanctions during a dispute, and occupies a 'no-win' situation when he is regarded by staff as a representative of 'management' and by his authority as an employee. When staff belong to different unions which are rarely united on policy or sanctions, an important factor to consider is the effect of decisions upon long-term relationships. Sadly, however, it is rarely possible to return to the previous situation after a dispute, even though the origins are outside the school, and there is usually some loss of non-contractual activities.

The size of secondary schools, the complexity of their organisation and subject specialism make delegation imperative and indeed 'any head must delegate or disintegrate' (Watts 1980, p. 293). The choice of staff for particular tasks requires great care, especially if related to a salary grade which could make the decision irreversible. Delegates then need the opportunity to work without undue restriction and with the maximum scope for initiative, not only for the benefit of the school but also to promote job satisfaction and opportunities for professional development, as is further discussed in Chapter 18. Having delegated tasks it is then essential for the head to accept responsibility if colleagues make mistakes, whatever he or she may say to them privately, and also to resist the temptation to claim the credit for their successes.

Finally it may be noted that one inevitable consequence of the hierarchical organisation is that it can lead to the head being mainly occupied with those tasks or problems which have proved too difficult for others. In order to avoid a situation where the head has little opportunity to achieve success or maintain a balanced overview of the school, it is therefore desirable to ensure that there are also opportunities to see staff and pupils who are not involved with problems.

The head's responsibilities for staff development

The reduction in teacher mobility, resulting from falling rolls and the contraction of the education service, has focused attention upon the need for planned staff development. When the supply of teachers was failing to meet the demand appointments were largely based upon the candidates' potential as perceived by the selectors, but recent experience suggests that for some years ahead candidates will be expected to have had experience of the tasks to be undertaken or training suitable for the new post. Teachers in post may well find that they have to respond to changes in organisation or curriculum as their schools become smaller and, in order to avoid stagnation, may need the stimulation of exposure to new concepts and techniques or opportunities to take on new responsibilities. If problems arising from the relationships between salary and responsibilities can be resolved, heads may wish to consider rotation of tasks to broaden the skills of colleagues and to provide variety of experience. Thus there is a need for teachers to evaluate their present knowledge and skills and to participate in appropriate additional training. The head's attitude, both explicit and implied, is critical in the development of a climate in which staff development can flourish.

Although both formal and informal evaluation of the work of colleagues are not new, especially for the preparation of references, proposals involving assessment of professional colleagues are now appearing (McMahon et al 1984). There is a natural tendency to look upon them with suspicion although such procedures are established in parts of the public sector such as the Civil Service, Health Service and Police (Morgan, Hall and Mackay 1983) and in some commercial undertakings. There are indications that both teacher unions and local authorities are coming to regard evaluation of some kind as legitimate, but the nature and purpose of such evaluation are differently perceived and are currently matters of hot dispute.

In addition to courses available elsewhere it is useful for the head to encourage school-based in-service training, which can be planned to meet the special needs of the staff and avoid time-consuming and tiring travel. Although such occasions cannot provide the valuable exchange of ideas with colleagues from other establishments which is a feature of good courses, by careful choice of visiting speakers or group leaders it is possible to stimulate and invigorate participants and ensure that the activity is relevant to the specific needs of the school and its staff. This topic is taken further in Chapter 18.

Personal relationships

The relationships between pupils, parents and staff are crucial to the effectiveness and harmonious functioning of the school. Adolescents and young adults can place great demands on the ability of the staff to achieve a balance between clear and firm standards of conduct combined with good attitudes to work, and the caring relationships which are more difficult to maintain than the more distant attitudes which used to obtain in schools. Committed teachers, anxious to see pupils do well or concerned about aspects of school life of which they disapprove, can be abrasive with pupils and with each other, and an arbiter is often required to resolve disputes. Even when staff are in agreement on broad issues, minor matters may be potential sources of conflict when staff are under pressure.

The head and senior colleagues have a continuing responsibility for identifying possible sources of tension, for seeking ways of avoiding conflict and for resolving it, should it occur. Deputies and other senior staff can alert the head to potential dispute so that either preventive action can be taken or it can be taken into account when policy is being developed. In meetings and group discussions, the structure of the agenda, advance preparation and good chairmanship can contribute to ensuring that vigorous argument does not degenerate into conflict.

When disputes involving pupils arise, the most difficult issues to resolve occur when careful investigation leads the head to the view that a teacher was in the wrong and that natural justice demands that the pupil should be exonerated, albeit in a way which does not undermine the status of the teacher. By accepting responsibility in such cases, the head can indicate his concern to all those involved and may be wise to admit that the school was in error, except where legal action is likely. In most cases where a teacher's actions are unacceptable the matter can be dealt with internally, but serious cases may involve the use of the authority's disciplinary procedures. Particularly where this is a possibility careful written records are essential from the beginning.

If the head's pastoral role with colleagues is to be effective it is helpful to develop informal as well as formal contacts with them but responsibility for evaluation, the patronage exerted though the control of internal promotions and the preparation of references are among the factors which tend to establish a barrier in relationships with colleagues (Bacon 1980). Inevitably, since it is easier to develop friendly relationships with some colleagues than others, the risk of charges of favouritism or prejudice are considerable. As human relations theorists have recognised, it is difficult to maintain a proper distinction, which is clear to all, between working relationships and the less formal ones which are appropriate in the context of extra-curricular or social activities. This applies particularly if it becomes necessary to criticise a colleague.

Similar problems can also occur in relationships with members of the head's role set outside the school. Although heads are no longer the authority figures they used to be they can become distanced, because of the positions they occupy, from other members of the community.

EXTERNAL MANAGEMENT TASKS

Although deputy heads, pastoral heads and other staff may regularly have contact with groups outside the school, the head occupies the key boundary role, receiving or controlling the input of information to the school and determining the way in which it is presented to parents, governors, the local authority and others. The intervention by such groups, and especially their demands for accountability, have increased and become a more significant factor in school management.

Central government policy and school management

The increasing influence of central government policy on the management of education at system level has been discussed in Part 2 of this volume. Cumulatively the effect on the schools has been substantial, in both curricular matters and the control of resources (Dennison 1984).

For secondary schools and their heads the impact of government policy often has been indirect and the result of the rigorous control of local authority expenditure which has affected staffing, capitation, maintenance, school meals and cleaning. Apart from difficulties created directly such changes lead to uncertainty about future provision, resulting in a reluctance to embark on new long-term developments. Furthermore, reductions in resources and staffing tend to lower staff morale and the head's task of stimulating development is correspondingly more difficult. In reporting on the effects on schools of local authority expenditure cuts, HMI have reminded us that what is important for the pupils is what is actually offered at present and that 'perceptions of what is necessary and desirable were being restricted by what was immediately possible' (DES 1983a). Such observations would be strongly supported by heads and their staff.

Legislation on general matters has also resulted in government policy having a direct impact upon schools. The Health and Safety at Work Act 1974, established lines of responsibility and liability, but, while inspection by staff representatives is an effective way of identifying potential hazards, schools do not usually have authority to take direct remedial action. Procedures for staff appointments and the curriculum have had to be examined in the light of the Sex Discrimination Act 1975, while the Race Relations Act 1976, creates a need to consider all aspects of school life with action to ensure 'equality of opportunity and good relations between persons of different racial groups', a point strongly re-emphasised in the Swann Report (HMSO 1985b).

Accountability to the local authority and to the governors

The relationship between the head and the local authority is affected by a variety of factors including the geography of the area, the extent of political involvement and the management style of the Chief Education Officer. As a professional leader with respect for the autonomy of institutions (Brooksbank 1980) the latter may make arrangements to consult regularly with groups of heads or with individuals, since the isolation of individual schools may create a need for understanding support and evidence of a personal interest by the chief officer. Much of the information required by the authority is collected on standard or *ad hoc* forms and most heads would support the view that demands for information, and therefore time devoted to administrative paper work, have increased, while most schools lack adequate ancillary help. While most officers have teaching experience, usually limited in time and variety, there are relatively few with personal experience of headship or senior management in schools, and misunderstandings and frustrating procedures can lead to tension unless there is adequate consultation before the implementation of changes.

Inspectors and advisers, experts in their subject who have the advantage of also visiting schools and meeting teachers on courses, form an important link between schools and the authority. Their advice on subjects in the curriculum for which the head lacks specialist knowledge can be helpful both in the resolution of problems and in formulating new policy.

Governing bodies, required by the Education Act 1944 to be responsible for 'the general direction of the conduct and curriculum of the school' (HMSO 1977, p. 7), were often ineffective due to grouping of schools, political imbalance, and controlled agendas with minimal reports and minutes (HMSO 1977; Corbett 1978). The recommendations of the Taylor Committee (HMSO 1977), especially that each school should have its own governors representing the authority, the staff, parents and the local community, although still not fully implemented, has generally led to the appointment of more committed and active governing bodies. Some heads had reservations, but it is relevant to note that, after five years' experience in Sheffield, which established such governing bodies in 1971, most of the heads felt that the new arrangements strengthened, rather than weakened, their position, gave protection from controversy and left them feeling isolated (Bacon 1978; 1980). My personal experience would support this view and further suggests that the complexity of the school's organisation and activities places the head in a strong position *vis à vis* lay governors. Further development will largely be influenced by recently announced government decisions concerning increased parental representation and a more closely defined role for governing bodies (HMSO 1985a).

Relationships with parents

In secondary schools, one of the frustrations for those who seek the full support and co-operation of parents is that in areas where great interest is shown at the primary stage, or where any proposal to change or close a school results in a vociferous reaction, there is a tendency for apparent parental interest to decline as pupils become older. No doubt this reflects increasing adolescent independence and, when pupils are in trouble, a sense of embarrassment. The first meeting is crucial since it can establish a relationship which may help to make visits less daunting and is an opportunity to explain the importance of regular contact even when there are apparently no problems. When pupils are admitted it is usually possible to persuade or coerce almost all parents to visit and thereafter, by following up non-attendance at formal parents evenings, to maintain a programme of regular consultation.

In addition to group consultations it is usually helpful and often essential to meet some parents individually. While an appointments system is less disruptive and enables the staff to be fully briefed, a school's public declarations about its caring role quickly lose credibility if inflexible procedures inhibit contacts when parents need to raise a matter of concern. Difficult situations are more easily resolved if dealt with promptly and, especially in large schools, it is usually possible to ensure that one of the senior staff team is available. A parents' association is a valuable support in developing positive attitudes towards the school and, in addition to the usual fund-raising functions, it can offer support and sometimes mediation.

CONCLUSION

Among the stimulating and yet paradoxically frustrating characteristics of headship are the variety, unpredictability and pace of events, as the head simultaneously fulfils the leading professional and chief executive aspects of the total role. After the relatively ordered existence of a post such as head of department most heads will also have had experience as deputies in dealing with urgent disciplinary matters, staff crises and deputising for the head in dealings with parents and others. Nevertheless this usually proves to be less than adequate preparation for the bombardment of events, telephone calls, visits and correspondence which require the head to respond urgently, which interrupt each other and which are not conducive to the forward planning and careful consideration of alternative policies, which the role also requires.

New heads are not always prepared for the isolation which accompanies ultimate responsibility. This loneliness may be mitigated if there is a supportive senior management team (Weeks 1983), but new heads with a different style of management from their predecessor sometimes find that deputies do not provide the supportive or critical responses they need (Weindling and Early 1984). Additionally there are areas of responsibility, such as the management of school accounts and relationships with the local authority, for which the head may not have received training or the opportunity to gain experience. Particularly when dealing with matters for which responsibility is not clearly defined, heads often lack the authority to initiate action or take decisions and are under-powered in relation to the tasks and goals which they are set (Musgrove 1971).

Given the multiplicity of tasks, the allocation of time becomes a major problem and decisions on priorities are difficult. Most heads wish to retain some teaching, and there is evidence that this is generally welcomed by colleagues, but if it interferes with efficient management and organisation it may be counterproductive (Hughes 1980; Nias 1980). The absorbing nature of day-to-day activities restricts opportunities for reflection and personal study but if a head is to be an 'extended professional', open to external influences and ready to innovate, rather than a 'restricted professional' (Hoyle 1975) it is essential to find some time for reading, attendance at courses and for meeting other heads. Finally, in order to avoid total preoccupation with work it is helpful to maintain interest in other activities, however limited the time available.

As the tasks performed by all those with management responsibility in a secondary school become more complex, the need for specific management preparation for heads is increasingly appreciated (Esp 1982; Hegarty 1983) and has received official recognition (DES 1983b) with the consequent creation of a three-tier structure of basic courses, one-term training opportunities and a National Development Centre (NDC) at Bristol University. The NDC was established to evaluate existing courses, develop new materials and act as an advisory centre. It has switched its emphasis, according to its Autumn 1984 Newsletter, from management training to management development which focuses on 'finding ways of improving performance on the job itself' and may involve 'various forms of consultancy and support'. The NDC is also working with a number of LEAs 'to help them plan, implement and evaluate a management development policy and programme for heads and senior staff in schools'.

The recent White Paper (HMSO 1985a, p. 56) recognises the strong influence that headteachers exercise over the quality of education provided in schools, but does not pursue a previous suggestion, which has attracted little support, of a probationary period for all new heads. This is to be welcomed, as the resulting career uncertainty would have deterred good candidates while newly appointed heads would have been tempted to play for safety.

Secondary school headship, it may be concluded, involves great responsibility, anxiety and frustration and requires stamina, versatility and mental agility. It also provides unusual but satisfying opportunities to contribute to the quality of teaching and learning in schools.

REFERENCES

Allen, B. (ed.) (1968) *Headship in the 1970s.* Oxford: Blackwell.

Bacon, W. (1978) *Public Accountability and the School System: A Sociology of School Board Democracy.* London: Harper and Row.

Bacon, W. (1980) 'Headteachers and School

Governors'. In Bush, T. et al (ed.) (1980) *Approaches to School Management*. London: Harper and Row.

Baron, G. (1968) 'An Overview'. In Allen, B. (1968) *Headship in the 1970s*. Oxford: Blackwell.

Barry, C. H. and Tye, F. (1975) *Running a School*. London: Temple Smith.

Bates, A. (1973) 'The Planning of the Curriculum'. In Fowler, G. et al (ed.) (1973) *Decision-making in British Education*. London: Heinemann.

Benn, C. and Simon, B. (1970) *Half Way There*. Maidenhead: McGraw Hill.

Bennett, S. J. (1974) *The School: An Organizational Analysis*. London: Blackie.

Bernbaum, G. (1976) 'The role of the head'. In Peters, R. (ed.) (1976) *The Role of the Head*. London: Routledge and Kegan Paul.

Best, R., Jarvis, C. and Ribbins, P. (ed.) (1980) *Perspectives on Pastoral Care*. London: Heinemann.

Brooksbank, K. (ed.) (1980) *Educational Administration*. London: Longman.

Bush, T. et al (ed.) (1980) *Approaches to School Management*. London: Harper and Row.

Bush, T. (1981) 'Key Roles in School Management'. *Open University, Management and the School (E323), Block 4, Policy-making; Organisation and Leadership in Schools*. Milton Keynes: Oxford University Press.

Cohen, L. (1970) 'School Size and Headteachers' Bureaucratic Role Conceptions'. *Educational Review*, **23**, 50–56.

Corbett, A. (1978) *Much To Do About Education*. London: Macmillan.

Davis, M. J. (1974) 'Delegation and Internal Communication in a Large School'. In Hughes, M. G. (ed.) (1974) *Secondary School Administration, 2nd edition*. Oxford: Pergamon.

Dennison, W. F. (1984) *Educational Finance and Resources*. London: Croom Helm.

DES (1977a) *Ten Good Schools: A Secondary School Enquiry*. London: HMSO.

DES (1977b) *Curriculum 11–16*. London: DES.

DES (1979) *Aspects of Secondary Education in England*. London: HMSO.

DES (1980) *A View of the Curriculum*. London: HMSO.

DES (1981) *The School Curriculum*. London: HMSO.

DES (1983a) *Report by Her Majesty's Inspectors on the Effects of Local Authority Expenditure Policies on the Education Service in England in 1982*. London: DES.

DES (1983b) *The In-service Teacher Training Grants Scheme: Circular 3/83*. London: DES.

Drucker, P. F. (1952) *Harvard Business Review*. **30**, 84–90.

Esp, D. (ed.) (1982) *Training for Heads in Europe*. Haywards Heath, Sussex: NAHT (with ATEE).

Everard, K. B. (1984) *Management in Comprehensive Schools — What can be Learned from Industry?* 2nd edition. University of York: Centre for the Study of Comprehensive Schools.

Fowler, G. et al (ed.) (1973) *Decision-making in British Education*. London: Heinemann.

Goodwin, F. J. (1968) *The Art of the Headmaster*. London: Ward Lock.

Gray, H. L. (1974) 'The Head as Manager'. *Education 3–13*, **2**(2) 81–84.

Handy, C. B. (1984) *Taken for Granted? Understanding Schools as Organisations*. London: Longman.

Hatfield, D. (1984) 'Problems Caused by Weak Teachers'. *Education*, **163**, 7.

Hegarty, S. (ed.) (1983) *Training for Management in Schools*. Windsor: NFER-Nelson.

HMSO (1977) *A New Partnership For Our Schools* (Taylor Report). London: HMSO.

HMSO (1983) *Teaching Quality*. London: HMSO.

HMSO (1984) *Parental Influence at School: a new framework for school government in England and Wales*. Discussion Document (Green Paper), Cmnd. 9242. London: HMSO.

HMSO (1985a) *Better Schools* (White Paper), Cmnd. 9469. London: HMSO.

HMSO (1985b) *Education for All* (Swann Report), Cmnd. 9453. London: HMSO.

Hoyle, E. (1975) 'Leadership and Decision-making in Education'. In Hughes, M. G. (ed.) (1975) *Administering Education: International Challenge*. London: Athlone.

Hughes, M. G. (ed.) (1974) *Secondary School Administration 2nd Edition*. Oxford: Pergamon.

Hughes, M. G. (ed.) (1975) *Administering Education: International Challenge*. London: Athlone.

Hughes, M. G. (1976) 'The Professional-as-Adminstrator: The Case of the Secondary School Head'. *Educational Administration Bulletin*, **2**, 1973; and Peters, R. S. (ed.) (1976) *The Role of the Head*. London:

Routledge and Kegan Paul.

Hughes, M. G. (1980) 'Reconciling Professional and Administrative Concerns'. In Bush, T. et al (ed.) (1980) *Approaches to School Management*. London: Harper and Row.

Humphrey, C. and Thomas, H. (1983) 'Financial Delegation to Schools'. Part 1 *Education*, **162**, 7; Part 2, *Education*, **162**, 8.

Jennings, A. (ed.) (1977) *Management and Headship in the Secondary School*. London: Ward Lock.

Jones, P. (1983) 'The First Destination of School and College Leavers 1982'. Unpublished report.

Jones, R. (1974) 'The Application of Management Principles in Schools'. In Hughes, M. G. (ed.) (1974) *Secondary School Administration, 2nd edition*. Oxford: Pergamon.

Judge, H. G. (1973) 'Headmasters'. *Education*, **141**, 2.

Katz, R. L. (1974) 'Skills of an Effective Administrator'. *Harvard Business Review*, **52**, 90–102.

King, R. (1968) 'The Headteacher and his Authority'. In Allen, B. (ed.) (1968) and Fowler, G. T. (ed.) (1973) *Decision-making in British Education*. London: Heinemann.

Knight, B. A. A. (1983) *Managing School Finance*. London: Heinemann.

Lyons, G. (1974) 'Administrative Tasks of Head and Senior Teachers in Large Secondary Schools'. University of Bristol, 1974.

Lyons, G. (1976) *A Handbook of Secondary School Administration*. London: NFER.

McMahon, A., Bolam, R., Abbott, R. and Holly, P. (1984) *Guidelines for Review and Internal Development in Schools: Secondary School Handbook*. London: Longman.

Marland, M. (1980) 'The Pastoral Curriculum'. In Best, R., Jarvis, C. and Ribbins, P. (ed.) (1980) *Perspectives on Pastoral Care*. London: Heinemann.

Mitchell, P. (1984) 'The headteacher's role as curriculum manager'. In White, J. (ed.) *Education, plc?*. Bedford Way Papers 20, London: University of London Institute of Education.

Morgan, C., Hall, V. and Mackay, H. (1983) *The Selection of Secondary School Headteachers*. Milton Keynes: Open University Press.

Musgrove, F. (1971) *Patterns of Power and Authority in English Education*. London: Methuen.

NAS/UWT (1983) *Interviews — A Code of Fair Practice*. Birmingham: NAS/UWT.

Nias, J. (1980) 'Leadership Styles and Job-satisfaction in Primary Schools'. In Bush, T. et al (ed.) (1980) *Approaches to School Management*. London: Harper and Row.

Ouston, J. (1984) 'The role of the secondary school head'. In White, J. (ed.) *Education, plc?*. Bedford Way Papers 20, London: University of London Institute of Education.

Packwood, T. (1977) 'The School as a Hierarchy'. *Educational Administration*, **5**, 2; and in Bush, T. et al (ed.) (1980) *Approaches to School Management*. London: Harper and Row.

Packwood, T. (1981) 'Policy-making and organization in the school'. *Open University: Management and the School (E323) Block 4*. Milton Keynes: Open University Press.

Peters, R. S. (ed.) (1976) *The Role of the Head*. London: Routledge and Kegan Paul.

Richardson, E. (1973) *The Teacher, the School and the Task of Management*. London: Heinemann.

Rutter, M. et al (1979) *Fifteen Thousand Hours*. London: Open Books.

Stenning, R. (1979) 'The Changing Nature of Employment Relations in Secondary Schools'. *Educational Administration*, **7**, 2.

Taylor, W. (1968) 'Training the Head'. In Allen, B. (ed.) *Headship in the 1970s*. Oxford: Blackwell.

Thomason, G. F. (1974) 'Organization and Management'. In Hughes, M. G. (ed.) (1974) *Secondary School Administration, 2nd edition*. Oxford: Pergamon.

Trethowen, D. (1981) 'The Missing Link: Managing the head'. *The Head*, **5**, 22.

Watson, L. E. (1969) 'Office and Expertise in the Secondary School'. *Educational Research*, **11**, 2; also in Fowler et al (1973) *Decision-making in British Education* (London: Heinemann) and Bush, T. et al (ed.) (1980) *Approaches to School Management* (London: Harper and Row).

Watts, J. (1980) 'Sharing it out: The Role of the Head in Participatory Government'. In Bush, T. et al (ed.) (1980) *Approaches to School Management*. London: Harper and Row.

Weeks, J. C. S. (1983) *The Professional Development of Secondary Heads*. Bristol: County of Avon.

Weindling, R. and Earley, P. (1984) 'Honeymoons and Headaches'. *Education*, **162**(1).

13

MANAGEMENT AND LEADERSHIP IN FURTHER EDUCATION

Patricia Twyman

INTRODUCTION

Further education (FE) provision in Britain has, since the last war, been characterised by a high degree of turbulence, complexity and change. Fowler (1973), writing more than a decade ago, put the point succinctly:

> If the virtue of FE is that it is as flexible as a rubber hose, and highly sensitive to social demand, the corresponding vice is that it is also a maze, through which only the old and experienced are likely to find their way without error. (p. 183)

There is little evidence to suggest that FE is any less complex today than it was at the turn of the 1970s. Quite the contrary, in so far as the years since then have seen a number of developments which have made the exercise of leadership and management in FE even more difficult than it was a decade ago. Thus to understand the role of leadership and management within FE it is necessary to be clear about the changing context within which such managers operate. Much of the first part of this chapter will seek to offer a brief and, necessarily, schematic account of the structure and context of FE as it has developed over the last decade or so and as it exists now. It will be argued that these developments have been accompanied by significant shifts in attitudes amongst college staff and amongst their political and administrative 'masters' towards the nature of what constitutes effective and acceptable relations of power and control *within* the contemporary college of FE and in terms of its interactions with the various *external* governmental and other bodies with which it is involved. In the penultimate section of the chapter the implications

325

which all these developments have for the nature and character of the internal structure of management and organisation of the college of FE in the 1980s and, in particular, for the roles of managers at various levels in its structural hierarchy — the principal, the head of department — will be explored briefly. Finally, some attention will be given to the implications of this analysis for the management training needs of the FE sector.

STRUCTURE AND CONTEXT

To an extent any definition of 'FE' is likely to be unsatisfactory. The statutory basis for the provision of FE by LEAs in England and Wales is sec. 41 of the 1944 Act, which has been amended several times over the last 40 years. Section 41 laid upon authorities the duty of securing:

> the provision for their area of adequate facilities for further education, that is to say: (a) full-time and part-time education for persons over compulsory school age; and (b) leisure time occupation, in such organised cultural, training and recreative activities as are suited to their requirements, for any persons over compulsory school age who are able and willing to profit by the facilities provided for that purpose.

By this definition FE overlaps with schools at one end and with higher education at the other and, as Fowler (1973) remarks, may 'be held to embrace the youth service on the one hand and much of adult education on the other together with activities as disparate as those conducted in play centres or at recreational complexes' (p. 181).

As Farmer (1982) puts it 'It is easier to define what further education is not, than to state what it is' and he goes on to argue that much of FE provision is 'for the most part technically illegitimate' (p. 18). This problem was recognised by the Government when it announced that it was consulting with the Local Authority Associations with the aim of setting in hand an appropriate study. This resulted in a joint working party comprising officers from the DES, the Welsh Office and from the local authorities. The group's report (Thompson 1981), on 'The Legal Basis of Further Education', offers a useful resumé of the law as it stands, a case for change which emphasises the inadequacies of existing legislation, and a proposal which could constitute a basis for a revised legal fabric. The clarity of its analysis has not prevented most of its recommendations being largely ignored.

The uncertainty of aspects of the legal basis of FE has had little apparent effect on its growth and development. As Fowler (1973) remarks 'no area of British education has expanded so explosively since the war as full-time further education' (p. 181). A statistical bulletin from the DES, *Statistics of FE Students in England*, published in November 1983, offers useful tables (FI) which document the growth of FE in England and Wales between 1900–1980, and in England between 1970–1982 (November).

What was true when Fowler was writing largely remained true of the next decade as well and even of the last few years. Thus, for example, the DES (1983) confirms that: 'Total enrolments on full-time and sandwich courses in major establishments of FE in England were 573 000 in November 1982, 41 000 more than a year earlier. This increase of 8 per cent followed a 10 per cent increase in the previous year' (p. 1).

For the purposes of this chapter a more restricted definition and one which, perhaps,

Table 13.1 *Course enrolment in maintained, assisted and grant-aided establishments in England and Wales since 1951 (in 000s).*

Year	All	Full-time and sandwich initial teacher training (included in 'All')	Part-time Day	Part-time Evening	Adult education centres	Total
1951	71	25	298	550	993	1912
1956	93	26	422	635	781	1931
1961	166	34	556	784	963	2469
1966	287	85	712	803	1374	3175
1971	398	113	718	746	1519	3382
1976	501	84	703	718	1797	3719
1980	509	30	733	635	1645	3522

The figures for England in November 1982 are shown in Table 13.2.

Table 13.2 *Numbers of students by type of establishment and the level of course.*

	Polytechnics	Other major establishments	Grant-aided establishments	Adult education	Total
Advanced courses	203 072	146 019	32 438	—	381 525
Non-advanced courses	17 715	1 397 296	4 098	1 533 544	2 952 653
All	220 787	1 543 315	36 532	1 533 544	3 334 178
Number of establishments	29	450	33	3 958	4 470

Both Table 13.1 and Table 13.2 are derived from DES (1983) *Statistics of FE Students in England* HMSO.

accords more with conventional usage, might be useful: thus little further mention will be made of the up to 90 institutions whose primary purpose is the provision of 'HE', i.e. those institutions which are concerned mainly with courses rated as post-'A' level or its equivalent. Neither will much more be said about the 4000 or so centres of adult education. Rather we shall focus more on the 400 or so institutions often known as 'colleges of FE' or 'technical colleges' which are mainly concerned with the provision of all kinds of non-advanced work and which have more recently been the focus of much MSC-sponsored training. As Table 13. 1 shows, this area has experienced a steady rise in numbers over the last 20 years. This has been rather less spectacular in part-time than in full-time courses, although it may be that MSC initiatives will reverse this trend.

What is all this provision for? Waven (1972) catches some of the dreams and idealism which informed the 1944 Act in a paper entitled *A Philosophy of Technical Education*. He wrote:

> Can we now convert and transform that which has grown up as a means of 'instruction in technology' to a system of 'total education for a technological era?' For a rapidly increasing proportion of the population, some form of technical, commercial and other vocational education provides their last contact with formal education; it must, therefore, be their 'finishing school', not only technically but educationally, giving them not only the 'means' of earning their living, but saying something also of the 'ends' to which that living should aspire. (p. 1)

Whatever the merits of this vision, what is clear is that to many observers the FE college of the early 1970s was hardly an 'educational' institution in its own right. Leech (1982) suggests that its activities were far more orientated towards training for, and a general subservience to, industry (p. 24). The expansion of activities for Industrial Training Boards (some of which are now defunct, such as the Food, Drink and Tobacco ITB) and the Manpower Services Commission, both referring to their students as 'trainees', all served to emphasise such subservience. As against this, Venables (1967) stressed the need for the philosophy to change to one of partnership; in which industry keeps the training role in context and FE colleges achieve more influence in shaping the curriculum.

King (1976) emphasised that the FE tradition is based on two principles: voluntarism and consumerism. Voluntary bodies in the nineteenth century were the earliest agencies for the education of adults outside the universities. Voluntarism of provision was matched by voluntarism of attendance. A strong link existed in FE between voluntarism and consumerism. This orientation towards their consumers, potential students and potential sponsoring employers was expressed in the entrepreneurial character of much of the work of college principals and heads of department, sounding out local demands and matching them with proposed courses (p. 98). However the principal, cited by Bristow (1970), who said: 'A technical college exists primarily to serve the needs of industry, commerce and the professions', seems by 1984 to have been contradicted by events with, for example, the relative decline of day-release studies over the last few years. Against this, King (1976) examines 'The flight to the college', and he describes the rapid expansion in the 1970s of the number of day students following FT courses in FE colleges as an illustration of the consumerism capacity of the colleges to adapt to new demands. Having briefly considered the structure and organisation of FE in the early 1970s, let us turn to an examination of some of the forces of change.

The DES Circular 7/70 had particular significance for FE. It gave guidance on instruments and articles of government for FE colleges; these were based on the recommendations of the Robbins (1963) and Weaver (1966) Reports and the 1968 Education (Number 2) Act. The Weaver Reform proposed a division of responsibility between the governors, the LEA, the principal and the academic board — the last being a new feature for many colleges.

The LEA, in consultation with the governors, is now responsible for determining the general educational character of a college and its function in the local education system. The governors give a college its legal status since it is through the instrument of government which establishes the governing body and its composition, that the college is an entity at law. Responsibility for the internal organisation, management and discipline of the college is delegated to the principal. The academic board is responsible for (or advises on) the planning, co-ordination, development and overseeing of the academic work of the college.

While there may be doubts about the legitimacy of much further education, the legal antecedents and impact of some of the newcomers in the field are clear. The Manpower Services Commission was established in 1974 under the provisions of the 1973 Employment and Training Act, with a remit to run the public employment and training services. Its aims were:

(a)   to contribute to efforts to raise employment and reduce unemployment;
(b)   to help assist manpower resources to be developed and contribute to economic well-being;

(c)   to help secure for each worker the opportunities and services he or she needs in order to lead a more satisfying working life;

(d)   to improve the quality of decisions affecting manpower;

(e)   to improve the efficiency and effectiveness of the commission.

By 1980–81 the MSC was providing about 6 per cent of expenditure on non-advanced further education. By the end of 1983 this had risen to about 10 per cent. In January 1984 the Government White Paper 'Training for Jobs' announced steps that would lead to the MSC being responsible for 25 per cent of non-advanced further education: the additional MSC funds would come from a cut in the provision for FE in the rate-support grant. In its leader the *Times Education Supplement* (3.2.84) described this move as ' . . . a giant's stride towards the nationalisation of further education' (p. 2). While describing the White Paper as another move to centralise power in education and to exclude any other than purely instrumental considerations relating to economic functions, the article predicted local authorities becoming mere agents of a quango responsible to the Department of Employment.

Given this background of management and control mechanisms likely to operate in the later part of the 1980s, it is perhaps helpful to consider some of the issues that came to the fore in the late 1970s and early 1980s that may influence the development of FE. Rising unemployment in both the 16–19-year-old age group and among adults, the decline of traditional engineering and manufacturing, the growth in the service industries, have all had an influence. Against this national economic backdrop and the MSC's pragmatism, educational philosophy has focused primarily on provision for many young people who would not under normal circumstances have been involved in further education, and this in turn has led to the polarisation of the 'education' versus 'training' issue (see Chapter 7). Farmer (1982) wrote: 'The educational response to employment uncertainty and rapid technological change has been to argue the need for training to be underpinned by opportunities for personal development and further education related to adult life in general as well as the particular demands of the world of work' (p. 58). Professionals in the education service have become cautious in their contacts with the MSC, a relatively well-resourced agency linked to the Department of Employment. A dichotomy has arisen between civil service guidelines and their emphasis on skills development in obtaining and retaining jobs and the educationalists' emphasis on the needs of young people in a rapidly changing environment.

Farmer's (1982) work on 'The Impact of the New F.E.' and Parkes' (1982) on 'The Changing Face of F.E.' provide a detailed analysis and account of the forces of change at work in the last seven to ten years. Farmer in particular emphasises the various Government papers and responses to them in terms of new educational and training philosophies towards post-16 young people in FE, from the Youth Opportunities Programme (YOP) to the Youth Training Scheme (YTS) and the Technical and Vocational Education Initiative (TVEI). Certain common threads may be discerned in many of the developments Farmer identifies: the desire on the part of many 16-year-old school-leavers to continue a broad-based general education with a vocational bias; a feeling that a further year of full-time education and training would enhance opportunities in the range and level of jobs available; the view that planned work experience combined with work-related training and education may be preferable and more relevant than the traditional one or two years' full-time FE provision characteristic of the 1970s.

The present picture is, in the main, one of fragmentation, confusion, complexity and competition; Pratley (1980) talks of 'the tangle of pre-employment courses' although she does acknowledge the moves to produce at least a common curriculum core. Farmer (1982) concludes: 'Despite the clear intentions of the Butler Act the realization of a freely accessible, progressive and comprehensive range of educational opportunities for those over 16 is the challenge of the 1980s' (p. 73).

Having examined some of the forces of change, let us now examine, in brief outline only, a variety of technical aspects of FE within which these changes will operate.

Remuneration of staff in FE is determined by the Burnham FE Committee. While this is relatively straightforward, conditions of service for FE staff are particularly complex. In *College Administration: A Handbook* (Waitt 1980) this aspect of further education occupies over 80 pages of detailed information. It includes: contracts of employment; notice; discrimination; TU membership; maternity regulations; suspension; disablement; dismissal and redundancy.

FE teachers' pay and other conditions of service are determined separately. Salaries are established under statute, while conditions of service are determined by negotiation. A 1973 agreement established what might best be called conditions of tenure, while the most far-reaching agreement was one made in 1975 concerning day-to-day conditions of service. This agreement, given the multi-sessional and extended year character of further education, seeks to ensure that FE teachers should have conditions of service not less favourable than those of their colleagues elsewhere in the education service.

No less complex are the FE mechanisms of course approval, control and validation. In addition to validating regulations laid down by individual external examining bodies, e.g. RSA, CGLI, BTech, GCE, CSE and numerous other industrial/commercial/training agencies, colleges have to work within guidelines and regulations laid down by both local authorities and regional advisory councils (RAC). Similarly they are subject to inspection by both local authority advisors/inspectors and by Her Majesty's Inspectors (HMI).

The functions of the RACs are numerous but in the main they are concerned with providing a forum between further and higher education, industry and commerce and with advising on the provision of further education in their area. They make recommendations with respect to the location of advanced courses, invariably with DES support via a regional staff inspector (RSI). Some RACs have a machinery concerned with the location of non-advanced courses. In addition, local authorities may exercise control over the location of courses in particular colleges; such controls have become more rigorous in a time of financial constraints, as has the attention paid to minimum class sizes for viability. Minimum course numbers relate primarily to the category (Burnham) of work, depending on whether it is primarily classroom or workshop based. Local authorities are empowered to close courses at short notice if they are numerically non-viable.

Finally, the typical college structure within which future change will take place merits some discussion. Ferguson (1980) wrote: 'During the last few years there has been a relatively small but nonetheless significant move in further education to find alternatives to the traditional hierarchical structure based on departments' (p. 1).

Ferguson (p. 2) identified the basic principles of the hierarchical organisational structure as:

(a)   task specialisation — the range of the organisation's activities, the services of special skills;
(b)   scalar principles — the chain of command;
(c)   unity of command — only one direct superior;

(d)   span of control — a superior can direct the operation of only a limited number of subordinates.

Application of these principles has led to the classic organisation chart, or 'tree structure' or 'pyramid', where the mode of working is essentially vertical. Such a structure includes principal and vice principal(s) and between four and six heads of department in the average FE College. Each head will usually have a principal or senior lecturer deputy depending on the size of the department. Within each department specific areas will be managed by senior lecturers/lecturer grade IIs. Within each area will be a number of lecturer Is. Staff below the grade of head of department will be responsible to the head; similarly the head will be responsible for all staff, students and courses within the department. The senior management team in such a college generally includes deputy heads of department and ranks above.

In the mid-1960s views began to emerge that different structures might be explored to meet changing needs in further education. In particular, the matrix scheme was advocated. Ferguson describes the matrix management structure thus:

> In this arrangement the academic staff was to be organised into academic groups around cognate subject areas with direct access to the academic board. Originally these groups were called divisions and a number of divisions would be attached to schools for administrative purposes. Thus the normal line management was replaced by a two way system cross-cutting in a matrix with one direction being essentially administrative and the other being essentially academic. (p. 4)

Advocates of the matrix emphasise that it facilitates the horizontal flows of information and work as well as the vertical ones. A number of colleges, including some but by no means all of the new tertiary colleges, were quick to adopt the matrix system and extensive research has been done on alternative structures by Ferguson, Cuthbert (1979) and others.

Ferguson's summary of the advantages, and disadvantages of both the hierarchical and matrix systems is, perhaps, the most concise account published (pp. 33–34).

For *traditional hierarchical departmental structures* the advantages he lists include:

(a)   the fact that empire building can and may give rise to excellence and can thus attract students and good staff;
(b)   the fact that identification with a discipline will produce professionalism with its attendant advantages;
(c)   the inculcation of team spirit and;
(d)   clear lines of authority and communication.

Its possible disadvantages include:

(a)   possible problems of adjusting to changing demands;
(b)   difficulties of developing inter-disciplinary work;
(c)   a tendency to 'empire building';
(d)   over-identification with a subject discipline;
(e)   demarcation disputes;
(f)   problems caused by a difficult or inadequate head of department.

The advantages for an alternative *matrix structure* include:

(a)   the creation of permanent aspects of temporary projects (courses) that do not necessarily conflict;

(b)   minimisation of inter-disciplinary problems;

(c)   internal communication facilitated;

(d)   diminishing the consequences of 'bad' senior staff;

(e)   possible reduction of 'empire building' and

(f)   allowance for great flexibility.

Some of the disadvantages of such a structure are said to be:

(a)   both staff and students are responsible to two or more leaders with the problems this can cause;

(b)   a lack of the feeling of identity and security that can come from membership of a department;

(c)   the apparent structural complexity of matrix structures; and

(d)   problems due to the primacy of the course leader over the subject leader leading to frustration and conflict.

It is not suggested that these items of advantage and disadvantage are of equal weight. Furthermore, to attempt any final balance of advantage between the 'department' and 'matrix' structures would surely be premature. What is clear, however, is that many colleges reorganised on non-departmental lines over the last few years and have adopted a matrix or some other kind of structure. What of these 'other' structures?

A third alternative for colleges is the 'mixed' structure. Ferguson believes that one can find more mixed structures than pure structures when analysing organisational structure (p. 11). Many FE college principals have long recognised that the best features of the hierarchical structure may successfully be combined with the optimum features of the more radical matrix. Their strategies are varied. It is possible to transcend departmentalism by the establishment of a wide variety of college academic board, boards of study, working parties and ad hoc groups with clear agenda and accountability; representation on all would be cross-college, thus endowing a vertical structure with a horizontal network. Alternatively it is possible to ensure that heads of department have an individual cross-college responsibility, while deputies acquire an increasing responsibility for departmental management.

In a sense the general environment of FE and the internal structural arrangement of the institutions of which it is comprised constitute contexts of power and power relationships within which the exercise of leadership and management takes place. What can we say of this issue?

POWER RELATIONS AND MANAGEMENT AND LEADERSHIP IN FE

Where power lies in a college of further education, and what relationships exist between the constitutent parts who exercise, or who are believed to exercise, power in the context of college management and leadership are questions that have attracted considerable research in recent years.

Empirical evidence from two published case studies of FE colleges, where the evidence was obtained prior to Circular 7/70, shed light on college government that is still relevant today. Both Charlton, Gent and Scammells (1971) and Tipton (1973) concluded:

(a)   that the role of the governors is mainly to act as a 'rubber stamp' on decisions taken elsewhere;

(b)   that the dominant role in policy-making is played by the senior academic staff.

A senior college administrator interviewed by Tipton said 'The real policy-making is done before the governors ever meet. That's why they only deal with minor points at meetings . . . The real issues escape discussion'. Similarly Charlton et al report a principal as saying 'The governing body has little influence — most matters of importance are agreed with the officials (of the LEA) before the meetings'. Among the reasons suggested for this ineffectiveness were that governors were too old or too busy or too involved with other competing interests. Charlton et al were of the view that power in colleges lay in the hands of the principal and that it was he or she who determined a college's development. Tipton, however, felt that it was senior staff more broadly conceived who played the major role in shaping a college's future although she acknowledged that a principal with charismatic personality could occupy the central role.

These are issues explored more recently by Ebbutt and Brown (1978). Ebbutt's study concerned the effects of the introduction of academic boards. Brown investigated the ILEA's reorganisation of 33 area and local colleges following a review of the authority's post-school educational provision.

Brown's work bears out the suggestion that the governors' role is primarily that of a 'rubber stamp'. At only one of the colleges involved did the governors fail to endorse the report of the academic staff to the authority's proposals as reported to them (p. 7). If the governing body is not a major power source, does the academic board occupy this role? Brown's research suggests not. On the contrary the academic boards he considered emerged as an arena for competing interests, bargaining and adjustment (p. 8). Like Charlton et al, Brown's research led him to the view that the real centre of power is the principal although he also stressed the influence of the union branch.

Brown suggests four sources of power implicit in the office of principal (p. 9):

1.   He has greater contact with the chairperson of the governing body than has any other member of staff, and he is usually the one source of information for the chairperson.
2.   In the majority of FE colleges the principal is not only chairman of the academic board but also regarded as its 'representative' on the governing body.
3.   The principal is the prime college representative with a very wide range of organisations outside college, in particular with the local education authority.
4.   Since the principal spends a good deal of time outside college he can best judge opinions outside the college and effects of outside events upon the college.

Ebbutt's research shed light on heads of department as sources of power, especially in larger, multi-site colleges. This independence was explained by one head: 'The Principal relies on the heads of department for all communication . . . . He is often out of college, on other business, and not often seen. It is a compliment that he seldom interferes' (p. 11). Ebbutt's findings did not reveal any major change in power distribution in colleges visited as a result of the institution of academic boards. At most the boards tended to modify relations between principals and heads of department.

Ebbutt and Brown discerned a slight shift in power relations in that they noted a tendency to increase the proportion of NATFHE-backed teaching staff on academic boards to the extent of outvoting the principal and heads on occasions. This in turn has led to new senior management tactics: production of documents supporting a case, the use of detailed knowledge and information sometimes privy only to senior management in advance, careful canvassing before board meetings and a casuistic evaluation of the likely outcome of an issue before deciding whether to put it on an agenda.

In general, the introduction of governing bodies and academic boards may have led to some decentralisation of power within colleges. Governing bodies are certainly not loci of power nor are academic boards in their own right. Power appears to be shared between principal and heads of department. In those colleges where staff have acquired more participation in the decision-making process this appears to have taken place at the expense of the power of heads, not the principal. The college's union branch, NATFHE, may also be a power centre depending largely on the strength and activity of its membership, which varies considerably between colleges.

Cavanagh (1983) when writing on manipulation as a tactic in FE colleges refers to defence mechanisms used by staff. 'Staff can conceal individual responsibility by maintaining a united front, while management can lose their responsibility in an "involuted hierarchy". This term . . . describes how the locus of power appears to recede both when examined from above ("we governors only rubber-stamp decisions taken elsewhere") and below ("As Principal I fully agree, but the governors/Academic Board/L.E.A. won't like it.")' (p. 33). And Noble and Pym, having argued in their seminal article 'Collegial authority and the Receding Locus of Power', that the existence of a large number of professionals in an institution leads to a structure resembling 'collegiality' conclude that a complex committee structure may conceal where policy is made. They identify three areas necessary to decision-making and implementation that sustain the influence of powerful individuals within the organisation: specialist knowledge/expertise; control of plant, equipment and funds; and membership of important committees.

Billingham (1982) set out to test some of the ideas of Noble and Pym using empirical evidence obtained from a large college of FE. He found that either the principal or vice principal attended all committees and that the chief administrative officer and heads of department attended most. Membership of such committees gave senior staff specialist knowledge and opportunities to develop political skills, competence in committee procedure and expertise in the presentation of documentation. The same senior staff group dominated curricular and advisory groups and had the greatest contact with external agencies such as the LEA. Such contact reinforced the power base of the senior executive in the college. Billingham found that control of plant rested firmly with the principal and heads. Academic board had not led to any real intervention in budgetary procedure which, given increasingly tight LEA controls, remained with the principal and chief administrative officer. Departmentalism in the college reinforced the power of heads of department, and even those who had adopted a participatory style did so in such a way that they were left with a substantial residue of power. Billingham concluded that: 'The hierarchy has responded by absorbing the new intruders, sharpening their political skills and moving to a committee system where the receding locus of power operates'. While the committee system protects the powerful few from responsibility and accountability, senior management in FE dominate the committee structure. Thus this situation is supportive of the survival, in another form, of the old hierarchy. Paradoxically a democratic committee structure, evolving from the introduction of academic boards, has produced a centralised oligarchy.

Cavanagh (1983) lays emphasis on a rather different dimension — the power of the LEA and power relationships between the LEA and the principal. She writes: 'The Principal is likely to be keenly aware of the sanctioning power of the LEA and its effect on the internal management of the college, especially in times of cutbacks in LEA spending' (p. 10).

Cavanagh also emphasises another relatively new aspect of power relations: the relationships between the college and outside agencies such as BTEC and the Manpower Services Commission. Accountability to outsiders such as MSC is likely to increase, particularly if such an organisation's 'control' over FE increases towards the projected 25 per cent. Similarly the growth in FE in recent years of self-financing or externally funded economic courses, as opposed to the traditional, rate-borne FE provision, is leading to a greater degree of accountability to outsiders.

Cavanagh counsels FE staff to be aware of the danger of over-simplification *vis à vis* the concept of authority in colleges. If the college hierarchy is seen as the expression of all legitimate power relations within a college, staff lower down the hierarchy are more likely to see power as coercive and to feel entitled to perform to minimum standards only. She argues that if the survival of FE colleges depends on their capacity to negotiate change with their environment, an effective college staff and management need to be aware of factors which limit flexibility. Much emphasis is laid on the complexity of resources and the multiplicity of resource providers. A search for resources which relies on the principal alone, or on one member of the senior staff, is unlikely to be as successful as a network search carried out by many different sections of the college and co-ordinated by the principal. Insularity and defence of narrow departmental interests are inadvisable; management has a responsibility to demonstrate that power is expandable and that, for example, the growth of the department can mean enhanced status for the college as a whole. In turn, it is suggested, smaller departments can gain much from the growth of the large department in that courses could be transferred from the larger to the smaller to achieve a more equitable balance.

Power and power relations in terms of the management and leadership in FE colleges is now an area of complexity. A variety of fairly new forces have entered into an arena that was once (prior to 1970) comparatively simple and straightforward. It is encumbent upon FE colleges that wish to maintain their valued place in a rapidly changing society to be aware of these new forces and their implications for management and leadership, and to devise varying strategies to keep pace with the changes that such forces imply.

SOME LEADERSHIP ROLES IN THE COLLEGE OF FE

Limitations of space mean that this discussion of leadership in FE will be restricted to an examination of the roles of the principal and the head of department.

Stoddart (1972) described colleges as being run by 'benevolent autocrats'. A decade later Richmond (1983) writes that: 'The days of the entrepreneurial, autocratic principal, single-handedly directing a complex institution with inadequate lines of communication and management structure, have long since disappeared and neither will, nor should, re-emerge' (p. 387). Hicks (1975) adds: 'The days of "free enterprise" building Principals have perhaps gone for ever'. Richmond outlines the forces of change that have led to such changes. The period from the 1950s to the early 1980s has been one of unprecedented expansion in the number of institutions, in their size and their importance to the nation. Expenditure on further education has greatly increased. The management and leadership of even so-called small colleges has become a significant managerial task, involving not only constant review of management tasks but also the necessary training of existing and future principals. Since the early 1970s, successive governments of both political parties have sought reductions in expenditure while maintaining and increasing output. This increased emphasis on efficiency and productivity has placed, and will continue to place, immense tasks on principals who are often served by insufficient support staff. Richmond emphasises: 'The resulting pressures and expectations have placed a growing burden of work and responsibility on principals and make it more than ever essential for principals to be fit for their tasks — mentally, intellectually and indeed physically' (p. 387).

When once the entrepreneurial benevolence of the autocrat-principal sufficed, now a new type of enterprise is essential for successful management and leadership. This enterprise requires the establishment and constant evolution of trust and effective personal relationships between senior management and staff; between senior management and officers and members of the LEA; between senior management and governors and other outside bodies. The term 'senior management' rather than 'principal' has been used deliberately. Such is the diverse and complex task of principal in the 1980s, that a growing tendency can be discerned to delegate to vice-principal(s) and heads of department executive responsibility for defined areas which were, fifteen years ago, the sole prerogative of the principal. Such a development, which frees the principal to become 'the general manager', has led to increasing emphasis within the college on the executive or senior management team as a corporate managing body for the institution within which the principal becomes *primus inter pares*.

Richmond also advises that the growing accountability of colleges operating in the public sector is a measure of that sector's strength and should be looked upon as such rather than as a chore to be reluctantly accepted. In this context, Birchenough's (1982) paper, which 'describes an experiment in institutional self-assessment which is taking place in ILEA colleges' (p. 189) offers a useful example of a management audit which might have relevance outside London.

A recent indication of the rich variety and contemporary range of responsibilities attached to the post of principal is given in the index of 'The Role of the College Principal' (Coombe Lodge Report 1983). While it does not claim to define all the manifold responsibilities of principals it does include such tasks as:

(a) representation on external bodies;
(b) research and consultancy;
(c) the impact of the Youth Opportunities Programme on one college;
(d) allocation and control of resources;
(e) curriculum and staff development;
(f) the appointment of staff;
(g) liaison with the Local Education Authority;
(h) pastoral care of students;
(i) the impossibility of being a principal — a plea for understanding; and
(j) a critical look at management systems.

One may compare this list of responsibilities in 1983 and a list of the four major functions of a principal as described in 1975 by Hicks (1975): responsibility for finance; liaison with external bodies; acquaintance, but not deep knowledge, of academic disciplines and vocational courses in departments; effective use of resources. Such a comparison is in itself a commentary on the changed role of the FE principal.

As with the principal's role, so too the role of head of department (HOD) has developed changes in recent years, but there is less evidence of fundamental change. Stoddart (1972), commenting on the period before Circular 7/70, described the HOD as having little academic role; the main concern for the HOD was an administrative/supervisory task; the HOD handed out syllabuses generally externally designed and externally marked, controlled staff timetables, checked student registers, monitored attendance and bought equipment. There was in the main no need for course appraisal or evaluation, course development, course assessment or discussions on educational policy issues. During such an era it was not uncommon to find that a HOD's staff resources consisted of less than half-a-dozen full-time posts together with a very large number of visiting teachers (i.e. part-time). Few concessions were made to democracy or participation and, indeed, the preponderance of visiting teachers, whose contract was solely to teach, ensured that participation was limited. Rather like principals, HODs were all-wise and all-powerful and FE's inherited traditions from schools were perpetuated.

Against this historical background, Webb (1981) engaged in research on 'The Role of the Head of Department in FE'. Essentially Webb's research included an analysis of the role-based empirical evidence obtained from a number of HODs in two very different FE colleges. Using a systems approach to the HOD's role Webb arrived at a number of conclusions:

(a)   that there is descending expectation about the role as one moves down the college hierarchy, with principals expecting the HOD to do much more than departmental staff expect, and indeed more than the HODs themselves expect to do;

(b)   that the teaching staff emphasised the HODs' institutional activities, i.e. maintenance of relationships, developing of morale and becoming a focus for departmental identity;

(c)   that a notable lack of enthusiasm emerged for the HOD becoming too involved in pedagogic or academic activities;

(d)   that a clear managerial role existed for heads;

(e)   that the management of change closely involved heads;

(f)   that a gap existed between the HODs' perception of their role and their staff's perceptions of their role.

Webb concluded on this evidence that the HOD's role is seen as being primarily administrative, supportive and managerial, including morale building, motivating and liaising.

In another study, Oxtoby (1983) considered the 'Problems facing Heads of Department' in colleges of FE. His analysis led him to the question of whether and to what extent heads of departments can and ought to play the roles of academic, administrator and manager. Summarising his findings, Oxtoby remarks that:

> HODs seem to be preoccupied with day-to-day problems that are more closely allied to checking and routine maintenance functions than to monitoring and future planning. The great majority of these problems are raised by sub-ordinate staff and students rather than by peers or superiors . . . What the survey . . . does not do is to tell us whether HODs are really concentrating on the sorts of problem which they ought to be concentrating on; whether, to

use Tolley's words, they are 'over busy rather than over worked' . . . What the survey does is illustrate that the job of an HOD is much less tidy, straightforward and easily defined than might be supposed simply by looking at specimen job descriptions. (p. 243)

The idea that the role of the HOD defies easy generalisation is widely recognised in the literature but a number of writers have attempted to identify key functions. Webb (1981) lists four major functions as follows: they are a major force for cohesion in a college; they are administrators responsible for various forms of bureaucratic control; they are facilitators, clearing the way through the college's processes and using resources efficiently and effectively; they engage in a wide range of liaison work inside and outside the college. These findings reflect work done at Coombe Lodge, the FE staff college, where a questionnaire given to all HODs attending courses at the college since 1970 has revealed that HODs spend much more time on formal and informal meetings with staff than on academic or pedagogic pursuits. It also seems that they deal much more with staff than with students. Finally, many of these findings are confirmed in a study by Turner (1977) who questions, as others have, whether the most highly-paid member of a department should be so involved in routine administration. Others have made the same point about more senior staff and even of the role of the principal. To an extent this has led to questions about the training needs of management staff at all levels within FE.

IDENTIFYING AND MEETING MANAGEMENT TRAINING NEEDS IN FE

During the last decade a number of social and economic changes have made the identification and meeting of management training needs in FE a complex problem. Williets' (1982) research of these changes categorises the following six as particularly significant:

1. Economic stringency has led to greater stress on the management of contraction and the need for managers to cope with personnel problems and with the retraining of staff. Senior staff have also been forced to spend more time dealing with the finances of the college.
2. Staff immobility means fewer promotions and less job mobility and calls for more in-service training and greater in-house opportunities.
3. Rapid technological change and decline of manufacturing employment entails a rapid change in the pattern of FE provision and requires different kinds of equipment and changing staff skills.
4. Falling school rolls and the demographic decline of the 16–19s from a peak 841 000 in 1981, and a decline in the number of 16-year-olds by 1993 by 34 per cent.
5. Growing unemployment among school-leavers and others has already had a major impact on FE, not least through the activities of MSC's Youth Training Scheme. The complexities of MSC funding has led to its management becoming a major task for senior staff.
6. Radical curriculum developments have taken place, many sponsored by the work of the Further Education Curriculum and Development Unit (FEU). Senior and middle

managers in FE face the challenge of enabling staff to cope with innovations such as the introduction of close linkage between on-the-job and off-the-job training and the college–agency liaison involved, the emphasis on social and life skills, intergrated learning packages, etc.

Williets' research identified the following areas of training for all FE managers:

(a) inter-personal relationships;
(b) college administration;
(c) specific 'administrative' skills;
(d) philosophy and vision;
(e) course organisation and design;
(f) staffing;
(g) FE and the educational system;
(h) the political dimension.

His other findings included an identification of the three most important elements for effective management training as: discussions, seminars and exchanges of views; members drawn from different colleges; lectures/talks by experts. Less important, but still important were: projects related to one's work; placements or visits to other colleges; studying or observing management in action; placements or visits to industry/commerce; cross-section of staff grades among 'course' members.

In the provision of such training, Coombe Lodge, located at Blagdon near Bristol, is unique as the Further Education Staff College. Assisted by a £100 000 grant from industry, the college was founded in 1960 and courses began in 1963. The aim of Coombe Lodge has been described as: 'to provide a place where members can learn and think effectively. That effectiveness comes from a totality of activity—meeting together, listening to lectures, studying papers, considering cases, confronting experts, questioning witnesses, working in groups of various sizes or making visits' (Waitt 1980, p. 156). The College's extensive information bank is available to anyone in further education; it contains more than 3000 papers, case studies and reports on virtually every aspect of FE. In additon, Coombe Lodge provides an advisory service to colleges and to individuals in FE.

A variety of qualifications in educational management and administration are available in universities, and Waitt (1980) offers a useful summary (pp. 135–138). Likewise, Williets provides details of CNAA courses and institutions offering the Diploma in Management Studies (pp. 180–183). A particularly significant feature in recent years has been the provision and use of MSC 'Robertson shilling' finance for training staff teaching on YOP courses; training which it previously financed will be taken over by MSC-funded accredited centres with reference to YTS work.

Finally, as Hollyhock (1982) has written: ' . . . the hard problems of management in a changing environment must be forced back at the home college . . . An understanding of . . . management and function is essential for all teaching staff to appreciate that decisions are not made in a vacuum . . . The management of continuing change may well be the major priority in the job specification . . . now and in the future' (p. 56). The identification and meeting of management training needs will be of fundamental importance for further education in the foreseeable future. This is a view also taken in a report of the Education Management Working Group of the Further Education Teachers

Sub-Committee of ACSET (1984). The group was set up in 1982 with the object of producing 'A document of advice on the development of training for educational management in FE . . . ' (p. 1). Its report emphasises the complexity of the context within which management in FE must operate and the consequent 'need for management training at almost all levels in FE' (p. 13). The Working Group makes six main sets of recommendations for the future shape and character of such management training provision (pp. 17–21) and stresses, in particular, the need 'to develop more and better "home grown" provision and the assistance and information needed to make it effective' (p. 17).

SUMMARY AND CONCLUSION

The virtues and vices of FE as seen by Fowler in 1973 still have some relevance for FE in the 1980s, but with certain qualifications. The maze to which Fowler referred has grown in both size and complexity. Not least among the factors responsible was the announcement in Parliament in April 1984 that, despite the recommendations in the review 'The Legal Basis of Further Education', ministers have said that they have no plans to reform the legal basis of further education. Perhaps a more significant factor is that although some traditional FE areas have experienced a decline, e.g. engineering, the growth in new work especially in the area of externally funded provision has been so great that it has brought about dramatic changes in many FE colleges. Even Fowler's 'old and experienced' are no longer necessarily finding their way through these new dimensions to the maze without error.

Whether FE remains 'as flexible as a rubber hose' is debatable. Colleges and their staff found it easy to be flexible during a time of growth and expansion. It was equally easy to be highly sensitive and responsive to social demand in an era when local authorities were able to fund new educational ventures without difficulty. Colleges in the 1980s are no less sensitive to social demand than they were in the early 1970s but their ability to respond is necessarily constrained by strict budgetary control at college, local authority and national levels. The analogy of the rubber hose is no longer so appropriate; a less malleable material containing a metallic content might be more indicative of the contemporary constraints on FE.

Parkes (1982) summarises changes in FE in the decade 1972–1982: ' . . . change has taken place: change in the role of the lecturer, in his place of work, in the courses he teaches, in the students he relates to. Change, too, in the organisation, the climate and ethos of the College — the way in which the Principal is seen' (p. 3). He concludes that FE is now essentially reactive rather than proactive and that being so it might accommodate present changes as it has absorbed past ones. The critical question he poses is whether the 1980s will be a watershed rather than a small change in direction.

Indicators during the two years 1982–1984 point to a watershed; evidence of this may well lie in the Government's comments: ' . . . and taking account of other measures now in hand to promote efficiency and effectiveness in further education, the Government has decided not to introduce new legislation on further education at present'. Passmore identified these 'other measures' as including the switch of funding and control of one quarter of all non-advanced, work-related courses to the MSC (*TES* 20.4.84).

While it is easy and often very pleasant to reminisce about the good old days of entrepreneuralism and expansionist policies in further education, it would perhaps be wiser to adopt a harder and more realistic attitude towards FE in the 1980s and 1990s. The changes referred to throughout this chapter are likely to be permanent in that there will be no reversal to FE as it was in the 1960s and early 1970s. FE may well face a statistical decline unless with ingenuity and determination it can expand in new ways, e.g. open learning and adult retraining. Controls upon FE are likely to become yet stronger, especially economic and financial controls with a concomitant decline in colleges' power that in the past stemmed from considerable independence. It is perhaps more positive to recognise that while power may be lost, influence from within FE may increase; if staff prove equal to the demands that will be made upon them both as educationalists and realists who recognise that whatever their views, both personally and as professionals, the survival of FE may well depend on their efficiency and effectiveness individually and corporately.

NOTES

1. On this topic, as upon many others the reader will find Watson, L. (1981) (ed.) *The Management of the Further Education College: An Annotated Bibliography*, Sheffield Papers in Education Management, particularly useful. This bibliography contains references to over 400 items drawn from the literature dealing specifically with 'colleges of further education or technical colleges' (p. 8). Some idea of the scope of this bibliography may be gathered by the fact that it contains no less than 14 items dealing with the topic of the academic board.

REFERENCES

ACSET (1984) *Further Education Teachers Sub-committee: Report of the Education Management Working Group*. London: DES.

Billingham, R. (1982) *The Establishment of Academic Boards in Colleges of F.E.*. MEd Dissertation (Unpublished), University of Birmingham.

Birchenough, M. (1982) 'Keeping the College under Review'. *Educational Management and Administration*, **10**(3).

Boyd-Barrett, O., Bush, T., Goodey, J., McNay, I. and Preedy, M. (ed.) (1983) *Approaches to Post-School Management*. London: Harper & Row.

Bristow, A. (1970) *Inside Colleges of F.E.*. London: HMSO.

Cavanagh, D. (1983) *Power Relations in the F.E. College*. Sheffield City Polytechnic: Studies in Educational Management.

Charlton, D., Gent, W. and Scammells, B. (1971) *The Administration of Technical Colleges*. Manchester: Manchester University Press.

Cuthbert, R. (1979) *Matrix Management Structures in H.E.*. Blagdon: Coombe Lodge.

DES (1983) *Statistics of F.E. Students in England*. London: HMSO.

Ebbutt, K. and Brown, R. (1978) 'The Structure of Power in the F.E. College'. *Journal of Further and Higher Education*, **2**(3).

Farmer, C. (1982) 'The Impact of the New

F.E'. In Parkes (1982) *The Changing Face of F.E.*. FEU: DES.

Ferguson, C. (1980) *Alternative Organisational Structures in H. and F.E.*. Blagdon: Coombe Lodge.

Fowler, G. (1973) 'Further Education'. In Bell, R., Fowler, G. and Little, K. (ed.) *Education in Great Britain and Ireland*. London: Routledge and Kegan Paul.

Hicks, J. (1975) 'College Principals and Vice Principals and the Administration of British Colleges'. *Educational Administration*, 4(1).

Hollyhock, R. (1982) 'Middle Management'. In Parkes, D. (ed.) (1982) *The Changing Face of F.E.*. FEU: DES.

Leech, M. (1982) 'The College and its Environment'. In Parkes, D. (1982) *The Changing Face of F.E.*. FEU: DES.

King, R. (1976) *School and College: Studies of Post-16 Education*. London: Routledge and Kegan Paul.

Noble, T. and Pym, B. (1970) 'Collegial Authority and the Receding Locus of Power'. *British Journal of Sociology*, 21(4).

Oxtoby, R. (1983) 'Problems Facing Heads of Department'. In Boyd-Barrett, O. et al (ed.) (1983) *Approaches to Post-School Management*. London: Harper and Row.

Parkes, D. (ed.) (1982) *The Changing Face of F.E.*. FEU: DES.

Pratley, B. (1980) *Signposts*. FEU: DES.

Richmond, A. (1983) '"Foreword" to the Role of the College Principal'. *Coombe Lodge Reports*, 15(10).

Robbins Report (1963) *Higher Education: A Report of the Committee Appointed by the Prime Minister, 1961–63*. London: HMSO.

Stoddart, J. (1972) 'The Head of Department and the Academic Board'. *Academic Boards in F.E.*. *Coombe Lodge Reports*, 5(17).

Thompson, N. (1981) *The Legal Basis of F.E.*. London: DES.

Tipton, B. (1973) *Conflict and Change in a Technical College*. London: Hutchinson.

Turner, C. (1977) *How the Head of Department Structures His Time — Simulation Case Study*. Blagdon: Coombe Lodge.

Venables, E. (1967) *The Young Worker at College*. London: Faber.

Waitt, I. (ed.) (1980) *College Administration: A Handbook*. London: NATFHE.

Waven, H. (1972) *A Philosophy of Technical Education*. Paper to ACHFE.

Weaver Report (1966) *The Government of Colleges of Education*. London: HMSO.

Webb, C. (1981) *The Role of the Head of Department in F.E.*. M.Ed. Dissertation (Unpublished), University of Birmingham.

Williets, D. (1982) *Management Training Needs in Further and Adult Education*. Department of Social and Administrative Studies in Education: University of Birmingham.

14

THE ROLE OF THE MIDDLE MANAGER IN THE SECONDARY SCHOOL

Peter Ribbins

INTRODUCTION

Marland (1974) coined the term 'single order school pattern' to depict the organisational structure of the small secondary school of the past. In such a school 'the headmaster and classroom teachers were . . . the key figures' (Siddle 1978, p. 1) within a simple structural hierarchy of communication and control, with the head and his deputy at the apex and all other teachers at the base. Richardson (1973) makes the point that in schools like this the head

> could regard each form teacher as a kind of extension of himself into each class of thirty or so children. Generally speaking it was the head himself who stood behind each form teacher to give support whenever it was needed. (p. 107)

But in a comprehensive of over a thousand,

> one man cannot pretend that he will be able to contain this enormous flock. 'Pastoral care' must be delegated to senior colleagues who, it may be supposed, will become like 'mini-headteachers' in relation to the pupils and to those who tutor the pupils in their sections of the school. (p. 108)

To some extent this development was formalised and reinforced by the Burnham salary agreement of 1956 which made it possible for extra payments to be made to teachers carrying additional responsibilities. However, during the years following 1956, 'no attempt appeared to be made by any LEA to give clear and precise definitions to the specific duties or responsibilities to be discharged by heads of department . . . Houghton

(1974) suggests that fundamentally the position of the head of department is as vague as in 1956: "Although there are five levels of assistant teacher, they do not imply the chain of command found in most industrial and administrative organisations" . . . ' (Siddle 1978, p. 3).

It is the purpose of this chapter first to offer an account of the growth and functioning of the complex systems to be found within the contemporary secondary school, and second to locate and analyse the role of middle managers within them.

STRUCTURES AND SYSTEMS WITHIN THE CONTEMPORARY COMPREHENSIVE SCHOOL: THE CASE OF 'RIVENDELL'

> Schools are expected not only to 'care' for children but also to contain, assess, select and train children, as well as to meet the more general and hard to define requirement of educating them. Teachers thus play complex and diffuse roles as instructors, disciplinarians, administrators and so on . . . (Best et al 1983, p. 30)

To undertake these diverse responsibilities and to support teachers in the various roles they have to play, comprehensive schools usually create some kind of 'pastoral' and 'curricular' structure designed, it seems, to institutionalise their 'caring', 'disciplinary' and 'academic' functions. Such structures may be thought of as sets of related roles, and as the organisational expression of the kinds of differentiation of task and division of labour deemed necessary in almost all secondary schools today.

In order to account for and justify the existence of middle managers within the secondary school it is necessary both to locate them within the kinds of structures identified above *and* to justify the structures themselves. The issues involved in any such attempt may be identified and examined with reference to the case of 'Rivendell' — a fairly large (1300 +), mixed, 11 –18, comprehensive school located in the South East of England (see Figure 14.1).

Two main sets of differentiations seem particularly significant — the *horizontal* and the *vertical*.

Horizontal divisions of labour are used by schools to undertake their substantive functions and these are exemplified by the academic ('curricular') and pastoral ('non-curricular') systems institutionalised at Rivendell. For functional purposes, each of these systems is further divided. At Rivendell the *pastoral* structure includes a 'house' structure (concerned with the caring needs of children), a 'year' structure (intended to monitor the academic progress of pupils), and a 'schools within schools' system (dealing with the maintenance of discipline and with the school's administrative needs). Each of these sub-systems is divided, into five 'year' groupings, four 'houses', and three 'years within years'. The same kind of differentiation exists in the *academic* system which is composed of eight 'faculties' and their constituent subject departments.

At Rivendell, as in most secondary schools, these structures consist of sets of related roles which embody a vertical as well as a horizontal division of labour:

> It is usual in any institutionalized system for each role to stand in a position of superiority, inferiority or equivalence to others, not only in the social and material rewards accruing to it,

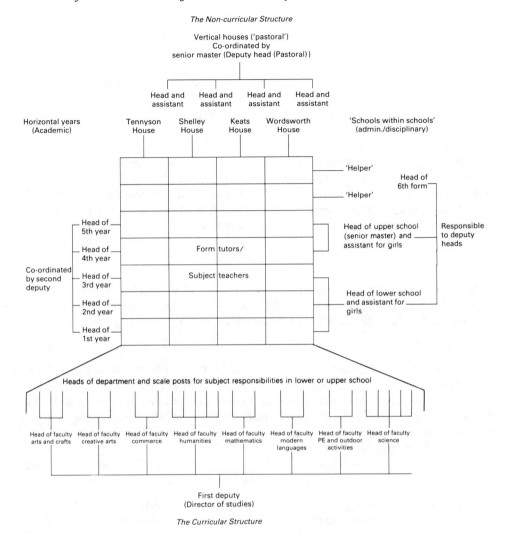

Figure 14.1 *Vertical and horizontal divisions of task at Rivendell.*

but also in the power and influence it carries, and in the scale of domain over which it is responsible for and for which it is accountable. (Best et al 1983, p. 31)

That is to say that the academic and pastoral systems are not merely 'jobs of work' 'purporting to represent the "caring" (or the "instructional") dimension of the teacher's service to his pupils, but also more or less rigid and stratified structures of management and authority . . . the structure is invariably *hierarchical*, embodying some "chain of command"' (p. 32) in which three main levels may be distinguished. At the apex are the 'senior managers' who carry responsibilities school-wide and beyond for its curricular and non-curricular activities. Below them are the group labelled 'middle managers' who are answerable for particular, horizontally defined aspects of the pastoral or academic work of the school. They are accountable to senior staff and carry a managerial and professional responsibility for the work of the staff allocated to them. Finally, there are 'other staff' who are answerable initially to designated middle managers, and beyond them to the senior staff. Most staff, of course, make a contribution to more than one aspect of the work of the school and some carry responsibility at more than one level. For example, at Rivendell, the director of studies is also a member of the maths faculty and the head of science is a form tutor within the sixth form. In one respect, the structure of responsibility at Rivendell is a little unusual in that several staff carry middle-management responsibilities within *both* the academic and the pastoral structures (e.g. the head of English is also a head of house).

Such complex, and expensive, managerial and professional structures are usually justified on the grounds that they are necessary if schools are to meet the diverse needs of their pupils today. They are, that is to say, functional. Much the same might be said of the role or roles of middle managers. How and why this should be so has received little attention in the literature of educational management.

ACCOUNTING FOR THE DEVELOPMENT OF VERTICAL AND HORIZONTAL DIVISIONS OF LABOUR AS THE BASIS OF STRUCTURE IN THE COMPREHENSIVE SCHOOL

How might the roles of the different kinds of middle manager be treated as problematic? To do this, it is necessary to consider both the structures within which they are located *and* the divisions of labour and task from which those structures are said to be derived as phenomena which need explanation and justification. To ask why the secondary school is differentiated internally along *horizontal* lines is to ask for a justification for the kinds of pastoral and academic sub-structures which have become the norm.

From a review of the literature on pastoral care, Best et al (1977; 1980; 1983; 1985) suggest that a 'conventional wisdom' emerges which includes the following ideas:

(a)   that schools are not just engaged in the imparting of knowledge, they are also concerned with the personal, social, and emotional welfare and development of children;

(b)   that this is a concern shared by most teachers;

(c)   that, for a variety of reasons, children face more problems than they used to;

(d)   that the resolution of these problems cannot be left to chance;

(e)   that the institutionalisation of such caring provision is in the form of pastoral systems which are a characteristic feature of the comprehensive school;

(f)   that teachers as tutors find the leadership and support they need at the level of middle management in the head of house/year etc. 'who are very important as leaders of teams, and as such, vital to the school' (Marland 1974, p. 74).

(g)   that pastoral care systems perform a number of essential functions for society at large;

(h)   that, as a matter of fact, the pastoral arrangements in most schools are fairly successful in achieving their aims.

This view presents a very attractive conception of the origins and practice of pastoral care and, as such, offers a powerful justification for the existence of pastoral structures of roles. While sharing many of the prescriptions of this conception of pastoral care, Best et al question whether it offers an accurate account of its development and functioning. They suggest an alternative explanation which includes some of the following propositions:

(a) that the aims, purposes and practices of pastoral care are all too often not clearly worked out in schools;

(b) that much of the time and resource allocated to pastoral care is either wasted or spent on activities which have little to do with publicly expressed aims;

(c) that pastoral structures are often primarily administrative and disciplinary conveniences and a response to the growing size and complexity of comprehensive schools;

(d) that teachers at all levels within pastoral systems lack opportunities to develop the knowledge and skills they need to undertake their duties as effectively as they might. That, in particular, little initial or in-service training focuses explicitly on pastoral care;

(e) that the origins of institutionalised pastoral care had as much to do with the problems educational administrators faced over comprehensive reorganisation, and from union and other demands for a better career structure, as they did with developing conceptions of the needs of pupils;

(f) that not all teachers are child-centred. Rather, different teachers attach different meanings to 'pastoral care' expressed in the way they think and in the things they do;

(g) that some teachers emphasise their own interests as instructors, disciplinarians and administrators and this shapes the attitudes they adopt towards pastoral systems and practices;

(h) that many of the limitations of existing pastoral structures and systems are related to the problem of attempting to institutionalise something which has quite different meanings for different teachers and groups of teachers within the same school. This has considerable significance for the role of the pastoral middle manager.

While not all their research findings support this 'alternative' view of the origins and practice of pastoral care (see Best and Ribbins 1985), the case of Rivendell did suggest that although many of the school's official documents and public statements of senior staff were couched in the language of the conventional wisdom what was said and what took place in other contexts could be very different given that:

1. Only two of the four houses and heads of house worked effectively.

2. The role of year head was nowhere clearly specified and few teachers were clear as to what should be expected of them.

3. Teachers were frequently uncertain about to whom they were responsible, to whom they should go for support, and to whom they should refer children with problems. Problems of protocol abounded.

4. Despite all this many teachers used the system for passing on their own problems, and as a means for buttressing their own discipline.

5. Teachers frequently evaluated the system as an unsatisfactory use of scarce establishment points, an administrative nightmare, and an ineffectual disciplinary instrument.

6. When the system was finally drastically simplified and 'rationalised', the rationale for

that reorganisation seemed to have little to do with the advantages and disadvantages of alternative systems and structures for *the care of children.*

No doubt some of these problems were particular to Rivendell although there is a growing literature of 'critique' which focuses on pastoral care (see Ribbins and Best 1985) which suggests that Rivendell is not unique.

The critique presented above it not intended to suggest that pastoral care has no place in contemporary comprehensive schooling. Far from it, but what it has attempted to do is to examine critically the idea that pastoral systems *necessarily* serve the interests of children. As Best et al (1983) conclude:

> The Rivendell experience shows clearly that without a substantial degree of consensus about what it is that people and structures are supposed to be doing the opportunities for inefficiency, misunderstanding, tension, conflict, and personal antagonism are enormous. Once there is some agreement about what you want to happen, its happenings cannot be left to chance. It must be institutionalised in structures which are appropriate to the aim in view. (p. 282)

If pastoral structures are to be functional for the needs of children, it is necessary for those responsible to strive to achieve both common understandings amongst staff *and* suitable managerial and organisational arrangements. How far is this true of the subject department?

Let us begin by asking the question 'Why do we need subject departments?'. Falk (1980), writing in the context of higher education in the USA, offers an answer which may be relevant to the UK secondary school. As higher education has grown, the importance of the academic department has also increased:

> This is believed to be so because the increased specialisation of knowledge has made it imperative that faculty members identify with that unit of university life from whence their discipline derives all its resources, that is, the department. (But) it can be argued that specialisation of knowledge is not the cause of departmentalism but the effect. Thus, some say that 'departmentalism erodes the unity of knowledge' and that, in addition, departments actually prevent the growth of new areas of endeavour because 'established' faculty fear that new ideas could threaten their control over funds and students. (p. 79)

Could it be that the contemporary patterns of 'subjects' to be found in the secondary school are more the consequence than the cause of existing patterns of subject department organisation? To consider this question, we might take up Musgrove's (1968) suggestion that researchers should:

> Examine subjects both within the school and the nation at large as social systems sustained by communication networks, material endowments and ideologies. Within a school and within a wider society subjects as communities of people competing and collaborating with one another, defining and defending their boundaries, demanding allegiance from their member and conferring a sense of identity upon them . . . even innovation which appears to be essentially intellectual in character can usefully be examined as the outcome of social interaction. (quoted in Goodson 1981, p. 163)

Such a sociological conception stands in contrast to more philosophically based views which inform, for example, the work of Hirst and Peters who argue that:

> 'the central objectives of education are the development of mind' and that such objectives are best pursued by the development of 'forms of knowledge' (a definition later broadened to include 'fields of knowledge'). From these forms and fields of knowledge so defined, school

subjects are themselves derived and organized. Hence what is implied is that an intellectual discipline is created and systematically defined by a community of scholars, normally working in a university department and is then 'translated' for use as a school subject. (Goodson 1981, pp. 165, 166)

This view of the school subject as derived from fundamental intellectual disciplines (however defined) is widely shared amongst teachers but it has been challenged on a number of grounds. One influential set of criticisms follows from Bernstein's (1971) proposition that: 'How a society selects, classifies, distributes, transmits and evaluates the educational knowledge it considers to be public, reflects both the distribution of power and the principles of social control' (p. 47). As Young (1971) puts it:

Academic curricula in this country involve assumptions that some kinds of areas of knowledge are much more 'worthwhile' than others: that as soon as possible all knowledge should become specialized and with minimum explicit emphasis on the relations between the subjects are themselves derived and organized. Hence what is implied is that an intellectual therefore, to view curricular changes as involving changing definitions of knowledge along one or more dimensions towards less or more specialized and open organisation of knowledge. Furthermore, that as we assume some patterns of social relations associated with any curriculum, these changes will be resisted in so far as they are perceived to undermine the value, relative power and privileges of the dominant groups involved. (p. 34)

Given this, he criticises the kind of philosophical view identified above as based upon 'an absolutist conception of a set of distinct forms of knowledge which correspond closely to the traditional areas of the academic curriculum and thus justify, rather than examine, what are no more than socio-historical constructs of a particular time' (p. 23)

John White and Michael Young (1975; 1976) have debated these issues. White acknowledges that 'one of the benefits of the recent onslaught of "new direction" sociology on the place of the forms of knowledge in the curriculum has been that it has raised the question of their justification' but questions whether 'going into the question of curriculum content', involving as it does 'all kinds of value judgement and their rationale', is to 'be doing sociology of education?' (p. 51)

Goodson (1981), although sharing many of its ideas, also claims that, despite appearances, Young's thesis is as unhistorical as those which he sets out to criticise. In this damaging criticism, Goodson argues that: 'To view subjects as "no more than socio-historical constructs of a particular time" while correct at one level hardly serves to clarify the part played by those groups involved in their continuance and promotion over time' (p. 165). For a more fruitful way 'to question the consensus view that school subjects derive from intellectual "disciplines" or "forms of knowledge" it is important to focus on the historical process through which school subjects arise' (p. 166). Such an analysis would focus on accounts of how 'new' disciplines and their associated school subjects evolve. A number of such studies have been attempted and these include: Layton's (1973) investigation of the evolution of science (which offers a tentative model for the evolution of a school subject); Goodson's (1981) study of the way in which geography began in schools and then, successfully, developed as a university discipline; and Goodson's (1983) account of the development of biology as a university discipline sponsored by groups within the parent disciplines of zoology and botany. This study also contains a fascinating description of the tactics used by geographers and, to a lesser extent, biologists within higher education and within schools to block the development of environmental studies.

There are also studies which either warn of the dangers of assuming that either parent disciplines or school-based subjects are necessarily monolithic in character, or seek to explain how 'new' subjects 'succeed' or 'fail' within particular schools. In Richardson's (1973) study of Nailsea, attempts to create a new humanities course in the lower school are shown to have encountered great resistance and little success. Conversely, at Rivendell, Best et al (1983) describe the tactics used by senior staff to ensure the acceptance of an ambitious mixed ability, intergrated humanities course for years one to five. In the words of a humanities team leader:

> Barber (the head) set up the system year by year. He, Jarrett (deputy head) and Waddell (head of humanities) began the first year, designed the worksheets and when they had worked through the year they left Joan Rayner in charge and moved on to the second year. When they had devised the second year work and worked through that for a year they left Roslyn Parker in charge and moved on to the third year . . . (p. 231)

Studies which examine the diverse and problematic character of subjects and disciplines include Ball's (1982) and Ball and Lacey's (1980) accounts of the competing conceptions of 'English' to be found in schools and in higher education, Goodson's (1981) study of 'geography', and Cooper's (1983) analysis of how and why changes occur in the legitimacy of particular definitions of secondary school maths and science.

In Goodson's (1983) account of school subjects and curriculum change during this century, the 'pursuit of material interests (in terms of status, resources and careers) is (seen as) a major explanatory factor' (p. 403). Thus he argues that: first, the broad structure of school subjects which make up the curriculum emerged in 1904–1917; 'The 1904 Regulations defined the subjects suitable for the secondary grammar schools. These were largely academic subjects and they were subsequently enshrined in the School Certificate exams launched in 1917. From then on these exam subjects inherited the priority treatment on finance and resources . . .' (p. 403). Second, this structure has 'effectively survived the ensuing changes in the education system' (p. 403). Third, 'the material interests of teachers — their pay, promotion and conditions — are broadly interlinked with the fate of their specialist subject communities'. Hence, fourth, in the secondary school 'the self-interest of the subject teachers is closely connected with the status of the subject in terms of its examinable knowledge' (p. 404).

While there are powerful forces within and beyond the school making for what appears to be a high level of continuity with respect to the structure of the curriculum as expressed in a set of subjects, it is also true that this continuity is under fairly constant threat. This threat takes at least *three* main forms: pressures in favour of new disciplines and for their associated school subjects (on which see Goodson 1981; 1983); the decline of hitherto powerful disciplines and subjects (e.g. classics); and the continuing struggle between competing groups to define and redefine existing disciplines and their attendant school subjects (for this see Ball and Lacey 1980; Cooper 1983; Goodson 1984).

What implications does all this have for the way in which we might view the subject department in the secondary school? Ball and Lacey (1980) summarise the issues:

> The subject department provides a set of constraints that should not be confused with subject disciplines (as epistemic communities). In the secondary school . . . the department . . . provides the basis for political action and as such demands allegiance from its members. The rewards of cohesion are tangible and immediate in such fields as the time-table, teaching of desirable and undesirable pupils, accommodation, . . . and secure academic status. Cohesion, therefore, demands strategic compliance from actors on a whole range of issues that contain within them differences of importance when viewed from the

perspective of the subject discipline. In other words, differentiation of the epistemic community is normally suppressed in favour of organisational and status gains. (p.150)

So much for the horizontal division of labour, what of the vertical? Three key issues might be identified — 'managing professionals', 'hierarchy' and 'bureaucracy'.

Bayne-Jardine and Hanham (1972) suggest that the role of head of department, as we understand it now, is a phenomenon of the post-war era. Its origins, they claim, can be traced back to the lasting impression which service within the hierarchic and bureaucratically structured armed forces made upon many returning teachers and administrators. However, as a number of writers have pointed out, the existence of a structure of posts does not necessarily entail any real hierarchy of management let alone of bureaucracy. Westwood (1967) makes the point:

> The increase in the hierarchy of positions within the school due to the system of responsibility allowances and graded posts, may not of itself mean that they have become in any real sense bureaucracies. It is necessary to find out what duties and authority are invested in these offices, what rights and obligations they carry, before any judgements can be made. It is possible they are minimal or non-existent. (p. 25)

Watson (1975) takes a rather different view. While stressing the tensions that exist between hierarchial structures and the attitudes of teachers as professionals, he yet holds that:

> It is clear that there are many bureaucratic elements in the secondary school, and many bureaucratic pressures. Offices, such as those of headmaster, head of department and assistant master, are ranked in order, with the superordinate to a large degree responsible for the actions of his subordinate. Salaries are paid according to fixed scales and tenure is according to stated contractual obligations. There is at least some attempt to ensure that the most competent are promoted to higher positions. Similarly, there are considerable pressures towards standardisation of the system. (p. 119)

This may be so, but some researchers have found little evidence of such bureaucratisation in practice. Heycock (1970), for example, argues that many of the heads of department he studied seemed to exercise little real responsibility for anything. Lacey (1970), also suggests that the 'bureaucracy' at Hightown Grammar was more apparent than real:

> The main task of the school, teaching, was performed equally by heads of departments, heads of houses and assistant masters. For some purposes the staff are best looked upon as a professional group, differentiated on the basis of seniority, whose activities are controlled by professional and traditional norms . . . The 'allowance' system, with its graded posts of responsibility allowances, was more a formal recognition of seniority and qualification (status confirming) than the authority structure. (pp. 160, 161, 162)

If, as it seems, there is some doubt as to whether the creation of structures of posts of responsibility within schools necessarily results in structures which are *hierarchic* in any real sense, there has also been some conflict of opinion as to whether they ought to be. This issue has been debated in *Educational Administration*, a debate initiated by Packwood's (1977) attempt to defend 'hierarchy' in schools against its critics as a 'time honoured form of organisation for getting work done' (p. 1). Turner (1977) challenges this view: 'For some kinds of organisation in some kinds of settings and at the right time of development, I have no doubt that hierarchic systems have much to commend them. My belief is that these criteria do not apply to schools or colleges' (p. 13). Drawing upon the work of Cohen, March and Olsen (1972) he argues that schools 'are by the nature of their enterprise, anarchic, and . . . attempts to retain predictability by strong boundary maintenance are irrelevant, since unpredictability is built into the organisation' (p. 11). Lambert (1977) dismisses Turner's paper as 'an interesting academic exercise' and claims that 'its assumptions can be challenged both on academic and pragmatic grounds, the challenge coming particularly from those practising educational administration in schools themselves' (p. 102), and suggests that as far as the structures of schools are concerned Turner simply underestimates the advantages of some degree of hierarchy and bureaucracy.

But are schools *bureaucracies*? Should they be? Certainly a number of studies have treated schools as if they are (Anderson 1968; Corwin 1970; King 1973). This may be so, but Musgrove (1971), in the context of a powerful defence of bureaucracy, stresses that 'to talk in terms of the bureaucratic ideal type is not adequate' (p. 89) given that subsequent critical scrutiny and empirical examination have refined and elaborated the dimensions of bureaucracy as originally defined by Max Weber. Of particular significance:

> . . . are the clear indications in recent research that the various aspects of bureaucracy are relatively independent . . . thus research into contemporary organisation is important not least because it enables us to look realistically at bureaucratisation as a historical development. We need not expect to find all aspects of bureaucracy changing together and in union . . . a close examination of changes in the organisation of the education service in general and of schools in particular over the past hundred years shows these bureaucratic features in complete disarray; while some march forward steadily, others retreat.

In short, it makes sense to talk of schools as more or less bureaucratic in terms of particular dimensions as well as whole sets of dimensions.

Although Musgrove (1971) does deal with issues of rationality and efficiency, much of his discussion challenges various aspects of what he describes as the 'tragic view of bureaucracy' (p. 105) as it applies to educational institutions. In this view the bureaucratisation of schools is seen as diminishing the dignity of the individual, associated with low levels of satisfaction and power, and as a source of alienation. As against this, Musgrove claims that:

> The development of bureaucracy over the past century has made us a less servile people. It has helped to make jobs secure and has based appointments and promotions on qualifications rather than personal connections. It has regulated activity through rules; but obedience to rules is probably less humiliating than submission to persons. The whim and caprice of superiors at work have been constrained. The advantages of these bureaucratic advances are nowhere more evident than in education. (p. 85)

Bell (1980) expresses doubts about such a conception of the school, arguing that it rests on a 'view of organisations which attributes to them orderliness and rationality (which) may be extremely attractive especially to those working in schools. It promises consistency, productability and a stable and secure framework within which to work' (p. 186). But it may be simplistic and misleading:

> There is . . . increasing evidence that at least some organisations are not always like this. Cyert and March (1963) suggest that the overall rational pattern of behaviour in organisations based on a set of commonly held goals was frequently modified by a large number of departmental, rather than organisational, interests. Experience in schools leads to the belief that this is equally true of departments and groups in schools. (p. 186)

As a result of these and other kinds of factors, schools may be organisationally 'more complex, less stable and less understandable' than has often been assumed. Schools thus display many of the characteristic features of organised anarchies as discussed in Chapter 1.

Bell (1980) stresses that this should not be taken to imply that they are 'formless' or composed of 'unpredictable collections of individuals'. Rather, the school is 'anarchic in the sense that the relationship between goals, members and technology is not as clearly functional as conventional organisation theory suggests that it will be' (p.187). Thus in their 'garbage can' model of choice and decision-making. Cohen et al (1972) 'suggest that much organisational activity can best be understood as being characterised by unclear goals, unclear technology and fluid membership since such characteristics . . . may be instrumental in creating a set of internal responses to perceived ambiguities' (Bell 1980, p.187).

Where such characteristics are to be found, then the predominant ethos of the school as an organisation is one of unpredictability. In such a case 'traditional forms of organisational analysis will . . . tend to confuse rather than clarify and conceal more than they reveal' (p. 189). To see the school as an organised anarchy, it is claimed, is to regard it 'as an unpredictable organisation existing within a turbulent environment' in which the:

> individual must be highly adaptive, creative and flexible in order to react to constantly changing situations which cannot be predicted. He will need to have discretion and full delegated powers from his superiors in order to cope with such situations. It is likely that the decisions made by such an individual will be short term and made in an attempt to respond to immediate demands and, as such, may be subject to rapid modification. For such responses to be understood the traditional notion of the school as a hierarchial decision-making structure with a horizontal division into departments and a vertical division into authority levels needs to be abandoned. (pp. 189–190)

Dennison (1985) also makes the point that it is not just individuals that need to be adaptable and flexible but structures as well if schools are to respond effectively to the contemporary needs of their pupils. To achieve this he advocates a structure based upon a multi-dimensional matrix in place of the kind of framework currently prevalent in schools based upon their pastoral and curricular dimensions.

Thus far we have discussed the vertical and horizontal contexts within which middle management in the secondary school is located. What of the role of the middle manager? This is a topic which has attracted increasing attention much of which treats the concepts of 'role' and 'role structure' as taken for granted.

THE CONCEPTS OF 'ROLE' AND 'ROLE STRUCTURE'

As Morgan and Turner (1976) have put it, 'the way in which people should and do behave in organisations, is frequently explained by role theory . . . the concept of role has been a pervasive one in administrative theory. There is a plethora of papers and also some severe critics' (p. 8). A major problem lies in the fact that the meaning given to 'role' and 'role structure' varies according to the sociological paradigm (see Chapter 9) within which they are located.

In commonsense usage, the term 'role' is often taken to mean a designated *position* (e.g. 'head of house') within a *structure* of positions (e.g. 'house'). For the organisational theorist a role is more than just a position in a structure; it is the behaviours associated with it which those in other positions expect the role incumbent to engage in. Roles are therefore defined in the relationships between positions in a structure expressed in the behaviours considered appropriate rather than merely in the designated positions themselves.

Adherents of the functionalist perspective (see Chapters 1 and 9) tend to emphasise the needs of the organisation as determining its role structure and therefore the behaviour of its members. From such a perspective, the organised, consensual character of the school is stressed, with particular teacher or pupil roles being reduced to a network of inter-related, articulated and coherent set of behaviours maintained by shared norms and by publicly agreed expectations involving high levels of prescription.

All this would seem to leave little room for conflict. Yet some degree of role strain and conflict appears to be a pervasive part of everyday life within all kinds of social groups. How is this to be explained? First, what is 'role strain' and 'role conflict'? Briefly, role strain may be thought of as the tensions which an individual role incumbent experiences as a result of some form of role conflict. Both concepts are closely tied to the notion of 'expectation' and, it must be said, are often used as if they were interchangeable. Thus Peeke (1983) suggests that: 'Role strain occurs when expectations are contradicted or actors do not hold expectations in common' (p. 226) and Morgan and Turner (1976) argue that: 'Role conflict refers to the incompatibility in the demands and expectations a role incumbent faces' (p. 8).

Hargreaves (1972) identifies eight sources of role conflict which Peeke (1983) lists as follows:

1. Where an actor simultaneously occupies two positions whose roles are incompatible.
2. Where there is a lack of consensus amongst the occupants of a position about the content of a role.
3. Where there is a lack of consensus amongst the occupants of one of the complementary role positions.
4. Where an actor's conception of his role conflicts with the expectations of a role partner.
5. Where various role partners have conflicting expectations.
6. Where a single role partner has incompatible expectations.
7. Where role expectations are unclear.
8. Where an actor lacks basic qualities required for adequate role performance. (p. 226)

Since Hargreaves was writing from an essentially interactionist perspective we might well expect the notion of role conflict to play a significant part in any account of interpersonal relations which he offers. However, some level of role conflict, may also be explained within a functionalist approach. It must be remembered that the model of social life upon which it is based is essentially an 'ideal type'. In practice some degree of variation always exists in the ways in which people play the roles they are allotted. Possible reasons for such variation include: imperfections within the culture, structure and methods of socialisation which exist within organisations; the fact that individuals within organisations perceive the expectations as to the particular roles they are filling with a greater or lesser degree of accuracy; because, as Morgan and Turner (1976) argue, 'Freedom of individual action is partly preserved by the large degree of latitude to many roles, where the powerful expectations are of prohibition rather than prescription' (p. 7). The idea of 'continuums of 'compulsion' are further developed by Silverman (1970), who distinguishes between 'must', 'should' and 'could' prescriptions, and by Schein (1965) who differentiates between the 'pivotal', 'relevant' and 'peripheral' norms or attributes relevant to a particular role.

Morgan and Turner (1976) identify three main forms of role conflict: conflict between roles; conflict within a role; and conflict within a *role set*. Woodland (1979) distinguishes two levels at which an individual may experience role conflict 'first, within his own body of roles, and second between his own roles and those of other actors' (p. 161). Two examples of the former are identified. First, if there is a discrepancy between ego's perception of his role and his perception of his actual behaviour, this could have harmful effects on his self image' (p. 161). Best et al (1983) discuss just such a case in their account of the conflicts experienced by Mrs Chalmers during her probationary year at Rivendell (pp. 142–147). Second, conflict can also occur when an individual 'perceives some incompatibility between performing certain prescriptions of one of his roles and carrying out those of another of his roles' (Woodland 1979, p. 161). Once again, Mrs Chalmers offers a case in point as she struggled to meet what she saw as the conflicting demands of her role as a tutor with those of her role as a teacher.

Conflict, as Woodland (1979) argues, 'may arise at a second level when the way ego perceives his role differs from the definition of his role by the occupants in counter positions' (p. 161). This form of conflict was the subject of research by Gross et al (1958) whose work 'represents a major attempt to measure how the actor actually defines his role and the extent of consensus in such role definitions between different role occupants' (Woodland 1979, p. 162). This study of the role of the school superintendent is concerned with both *intrapositional* consensus (agreement on role definition between holders of similar roles) and *interpositional* consensus (agreement on role definition between different positions within the role set). Gross also offers an analysis of the means of resolving role conflict in which the player of a particular role 'chooses, avoids or compromises between conflicting expectations of other actors in terms of how legitimate he perceives these expectations to be, how strong he perceives the sanctions against his nonconformity to these expectations to be, and whether he gives priority to the sanctions or the legitimacy of the expectations, or compromises between the two'.

Morgan and Turner (1976) take 'an essentially *structural* conception of role, which asserts that individuals occupy organisational offices and social positions, to which are attached constraining expectations and demands' (however) 'in spite of the pervasive influence of other people's expectations, the role player retains substantial opportunity for choice in his role performance . . . Role theory in our view does not of necessity provide a deterministic and conforming view of behaviour . . .' (p. 13). As regards the usefulness of 'role theory', they suggest that;

(a) Role theory offers a useful tool of analysis through which to identify the set of expectations associated with a particular status position;

(b) It also conceptualizes the elements, systematic and personal, which constitute a status position;

(c) In its deployment of role conflict, it incorporates the 'problem' of lack of consensus among varying expectations of the holder of a particular status position.

The relevance of these ideas to the study and practice of educational management is the specific concern of a paper by Burnham (1969). Although a brief reference is made to the interactionist ideas of Turner (1969), in his analysis Burnham also adopts a functionalist approach. In this analysis 'the concepts of role and role expectation provide one way of thinking about administrative behaviour. In this sense, administration can be seen as the process of defining, allocating and integrating roles and personnel to maximise the probability of achieving the goals of the organisations' (p. 202). As applied to the head of a contemporary comprehensive school:

The genius of administration, according to Nolte (1966) lies in this endless process of diagnosing, defining, classifying and interpreting roles, in the context of an intimate knowledge of the personalities of a large and varied staff. It is a competency which requires to be based in a clear understanding of the social and educational goals of the institution, a thorough analysis of the jobs to be done, and a perceptive awareness of the interests, skills and idiosyncrasies of the staff, (p. 204).

Much the same may be said of the middle manager.

Best et al (1983) discuss the attractions of an alternative conception of role which is based on an *interactionist* perspective. They stress that the formal structure of roles that exist in schools such as Rivendell may be viewed both as a 'social fact', with an objective reality over and above any individual teacher's perception of it, and, in an important sense, as existing only in the conceptions which teachers hold of it and in the recognition they give to it. To fail to take account of this is 'to ignore the dynamic aspect of role-play as teachers negotiate the complexities of their professional and personal lives on a day-to-day basis' (p. 53). Role incumbents do not just 'step into' a role. Rather:

> as Symbolic Interactionists have been at pains to point out, roles are also . . . the product of interaction between social actors. Each 'role incumbent' is active in construing the roles he 'plays', and in the interpersonal negotiation which characterises interaction between roles. To some extent this is a question of the *interpretation* of formal role expectations such that it is possible to talk of the *style* with which the individual meets them, but it may also be a matter of intentional variation and redefinition of the formal role by the actor himself. (Best et al 1983)

As Turner (1969) points out, social actors do not merely 'take' roles as they are presented to them, but actively 'make' them what they are. Furthermore, even if an actor does appear to 'take on' a role, this does not explain why he does so. Functionalists would point to the 'fact' that such behaviours are 'functional' to the needs of the organisation but other explanations may be equally plausible. For example, Goffman (1977) argues that adequate role-play often requires an actor to 'present a front' and for his fellow actors collectively to 'sustain a front'. But such an actor may meet the formal requirements of the role he is playing in two ways. Thus, Goffman distinguishes between *role commitment* (a situation in which he accepts the formal requirements of the role as ones he must meet but in which he does not much value his role performance as a person) and *role-attachment* (a situation in which he identifies his role performance with his own values and his own needs as a person). Goffman uses the term 'role distance' to describe the situation in which an actor plays the role adequately but in a more-or-less offhand manner.

For all these reasons there will be differences between the formal designation of roles within an organisation and the way in which those roles are actually perceived and 'played'. Moreover, as Hargreaves (1972) has shown, the officially designated roles are by no means the only roles to be found in schools. On the contrary, there are a host of ascribed, achieved or confirmed *informal roles* which are an important part of the social structure of the school. As Best et al (1983) conclude, 'the structure of officially designated roles is one thing, but the reality in practice may be something else altogether' (p. 54).

But Best et al (1983) also recognise that:

> it is tempting to exaggerate the degree of freedom which the individual can exercise over the shape of his role. This is especially true where roles are institutionalised in formal organisations like the school . . . The reality is of a dynamic, complex and often tense relationship between the free and rational actor on the one hand and the formal structure of role expectations on the other. (p. 54)

From this perspective a satisfactory explanation of the academic, the pastoral, etc. provision of a school must approach its caring or curricular systems as both social facts external to, and constraining the role incumbent's behaviour, and as the subjective interpretation and negotiation of role which individual actors make. It must also be seen as the product of an ongoing interaction between *both* these sets of 'realities'. Best et al (1983) illustrate this point with reference to an account of three successive regimes of heads at Rivendell (Chapter 8) and also by examining the ways in which different pairs of teachers played what were ostensibly the same role. In doing so they explore,

> how different teachers responded in very different ways to the relationship between personal fulfilment and formal role expectation and the varying degrees of 'attachment' and 'commitment' which characterized their role play . . . how role-performance is to some extent dependent upon the 'perspectives' which teachers adopt on their sub-roles and the ideologies which seem to underlie them or which they are in the process of constructing as they work out the more or less tense encounters which make up their daily life. (p. 142)

With these theoretical frameworks in mind, what can we learn from the literature of the role of the academic and pastoral middle manager?

THE ROLE OF THE PASTORAL AND ACADEMIC MIDDLE MANAGER

No attempt will be made to offer a comprehensive review of the growing literature dealing with the role of the middle manager within the secondary school. Rather, a number of topics will be identified and discussed which might serve to illustrate the scope and character of 'what we know' on this topic.

Marland (1981), who has done as much as any writer to shape our thinking about the role of the middle manager within the comprehensive school, argues that 'their function is unique to this country, and is a clear practical demonstration of the philosophy of the devolved system of educational responsibility in Britain' (p. 1). The way this devolution has effected the nature of the school can be summed up as follows:

1. The U.K. school is largely autonomous, and therefore its structure, procedure, curriculum and counselling can be devised within the school . . .
2. The professional career structure and additional payments see promotion clearly as related to further *responsibility* . . .
3. Administration and pedagogy are fused . . .
4. The head of department (or of house etc.) is regarded as a senior member of the overall leadership and planning of the school. (p. 1)

We should, he holds, relish such a system. But, if we cannot make good use of the opportunities it allows, then perhaps we would be better off 'with an educational system that retains all significant decision making outside the school' (p. 2).

In this context, several writers suggest that how these 'opportunities' might be construed is subject, in part at least, to interpretations which have varied over time. Before turning to this issue it might be helpful to be clear about what is entailed, logically, by the notion of a department and of a head of department. Bailey (1981) is one of the few to attempt to do this. He holds that:

> In principle, a department begins to exist (1) when two or more teachers begin to teach a

subject formerly taught by one; (2) when those teachers begin to co-ordinate their work so that together they can perform tasks which no one of them could perform singly; and (3) when, however informally, one teacher begins to lead and another to follow. (p. 106)

Departments, then, may be said to exist only where deliberate *collaboration* takes place, enabling an exchange of ideas and knowledge and facilitating some specialisation of task through various divisions of labour. By such criteria, the 'departments' and 'heads of department' of the pre-comprehensive era hardly qualify. As Bayne-Jardine and Hanham (1972) point out, the circumstances of these schools differed greatly from that of the modern comprehensive and in the subject departments which developed within them there was little emphasis on the notion of the 'team'. Heads of department tended to be appointed for their seniority and their skills as a subject teacher, and not for any perceived managerial skills or aptitudes. Holt (1981) argues that while 'all this is far removed from the assumptions of the contemporary comprehensive school . . . yet . . . however noble our curriculum intentions might be, the formal structure of the typical comprehensive school curriculum bears more than a passing resemblance to that of the grammar school from which it was derived . . . (and it is) still possible for the insular-minded department head to follow historical precedent, to run his own show, and leave the members of his department to run theirs'. As Best et al (1983) show, much the same kind of comment can be made of the pastoral head.

Bayne-Jardine (1981) stresses the necessity of analysing the ways in which heads of department have responded to 'match their *historical* role with changes in both organisations of schools and subject matter' (p. 38). He describes a number of *pathologies*, first identified by Hoyle (1969), which 'give an interesting insight into the way that the working of a subject department and curriculum development can be rendered difficult by the unquestioning acceptance of an ill-defined or inappropriate role'. These pathologies include the 'ritualist' (who hides behind detail), the 'neurotic' (who worries ineffectually about problems of carrying theory into practice), and the 'robber baron' (who is mainly concerned with 'increasing his territory', creating an image of efficiency and innovation, and achieving promotion rather than in developing the members of his 'team').

A number of attempts have also been made to present a history of pastoral care (Lang 1984; Ribbins and Best 1985) and Blackburn (1983b) identifies three main phases which he caricatures as follows:

> In phase 1 concern was for developing minds in healthy bodies . . . phase 2 was concerned with providing individual guidance to pupils as they passed through the system and with mopping up the casualties . . . phase 3 is concerned with involving pupils in a range of learning processes within groups designed to enable them to cope more effectively. (p. 20)

In attempting to meet this growing list of responsibilities:

> so the possibility of the pastoral head becoming the chief carer . . . has become unrealistic. He has to work through the team of tutors. From 'super tutor' he has to move to the role of managing the work of the members of his team. This transition has to take place very often without anyone declaring that there has been a change in expectations of what is to be achieved and without any in-service training being offered to help the pastoral head identify the skills and methods that he will now have to acquire for success.

In *Head of House, Head of Year*, Blackburn (1983a) offers a number of examples of the roles and responsibilities that particular schools (Altwood, Crown Woods, North Westminster, Sidney Stringer and Stantonbury) expect of their pastoral teams and pastoral heads which demonstrates just how wide-ranging and complex are the tasks and skills involved. He also quotes a list of *18* duties of a head of house or year taken from an advisory document produced by the Lancashire County Council. This formidable catalogue includes such tasks as:

> 4. To co-ordinate supervisory responsibility of staff and pupils on duty. 5. To know pupils in the year as well as possible, and to become accepted as a person to whom they can turn for guidance . . . 6. To have a watching brief over the academic progress of pupils . . . 7. To co-ordinate the keeping of written records of individual children . . . 10. To arrange meetings with parents . . . 11. To liaise closely with other services . . . (p. 18)

Finally, Blackburn (1983a) offers a useful diagrammatic representation of what he sees as the six main areas of responsibility to be exercised by the pastoral head (aims and roles; planning, organisation and evaluation; the pastoral curriculum; casework; parents; staff support) and the six main methods he or she must learn to use (one-to-one contact; staff meetings; induction; in-service training; record-keeping; work with pupils) in which 'each "area" interlocks with each "method"' (pp. 39, 40).

Such intimidating catalogues of responsibility are not restricted to the pastoral task. The prescriptive literature dealing with the subject department and the head of department fully reflects Dunham's (1978) judgement that 'when a school is reorganised into the comprehensive system the role (of the head of department) is changed so much that it is probably misleading to retain the same name for it' (p. 11). This change was recognised by HMI in the early 1960s. What was taking place, they suggested, was a 'new concept of relationship' between heads and heads of department and between members of a department. These changes entailed a wide range of duties for the head of department which they listed under the following five headings: curriculum; supervision of staff; organisation of the department; communications; and finance (discussed in Siddle 1978). Siddle takes the view that:

> Although written for the guidance of HMIs during the 1960s, the general job specifications provided under the five headings appear from the observations of the author to be relevant today. (p. 6)

Many of these functions do, in fact, appear in more recent accounts. Hall and Thomas (1977) suggest a classification of the functions of the head of department under the headings of 'managerial' (related to the management and control of all aspects of the work of the department), 'representative' (the school to the department and the department to the school), and 'academic' (all aspects of teaching the subject). Ogilvie and Bartlett (1979), in the context of a comparison between departmental heads in Australia and England, suggest that despite superficial differences:

> Bailey's (1973) grouping of the traditional functions of the subject master is very similar to Hall and Thomas and might usefully be modified to: (a) academic (to know his subject, to keep himself up to date) (b) representative (to represent his subject in the school) and (c) managerial (to plan, teach and resource courses and evaluate pupils). (p. 3)

Bailey (1973) goes on to argue that the growth of the large comprehensive school has meant that heads of department have had to take on further responsibilities under the following *four* headings: staff control; pupil control; resource control; and communication.

The report by Hall and Thomas (1977) focuses primarily on the role of the head of the maths department and, as such, is one of a number of such studies which are concerned with the role of heads of particular subjects. Examples of these are Siddle's (1978) wide-ranging monograph on the role of the head of science and Raleigh's (1983) book on the English department which, although 'addressed to every member of the English department . . . will be most useful to the new or inexperienced heads of department' (David 1983 p. 25). Yet other studies, although not focusing on the role of the head of department as such, have useful things to say about it. A notable example of this is the Cockcroft Report (1982) on the teaching of maths. In this report the role of the head of maths is given great significance:

> We consider that, among heads of department, the head of mathematics has a task which can be especially difficult and demanding . . . Unless he or she provides positive and sustained leadership and direction for the maths department it will not operate as effectively as it might do and the pupils will be correspondingly disadvantaged. (p. 154)

The list of duties for which the head of maths should take responsibility includes:

> the production and up-dating of suitable schemes of work;
> the organisation of the department and its teaching resources;
> the monitoring of the teaching within the department and of the work and assessment of pupils;
> playing a full part in the professional development and in-service training of those who teach maths;
> liaison with other departments in the school and with other schools and colleges in the area. (p. 154)

Finally, there are studies of the role of the head of department which, although they do not focus explicitly on a particular subject do, as a matter of fact, tend to offer examples drawn particularly from one subject. Perhaps the best example of this is to be found in Marland's (1971) early study of *The Head of Department*, in which the writer makes good use of his experience as a head of English in two large comprehensive schools.

Marland (1971; 1974; 1981; 1983) has written extensively on the role of both the pastoral and academic middle manager. To do justice to the range of his ideas is beyond the scope of this chapter, but since he offers his own summary of the *ten* tasks which may be expected of a head of department, we may quote that instead:

1. Structure a departmental team . . . to create a cogent internal structure
2. Take a major part in appointing teachers
3. Deploy teachers . . . consistent with their strengths and weaknesses and their career development — as well as fulfilling the needs of the school
4. Monitor teacher's work
5. Assist the development of teachers' professional skills . . .
6. Contribute to the initial training of student teachers
7. Take a part in the planning of the school's overall curriculum, and lead the planning of the curriculum within the department
8. Oversee the work of pupils . . .
9. Manage the finances, physical resources and learning methods efficiently
10. Assist in the overall leadership of the school. (Marland 1981, p. 2).

Although the kind of view of the role of the middle manager discussed thus far has been very influential, it has not gone unchallenged. For a number of years Best et al (1977; 1980; 1983) have questioned whether such accounts too often tend to confuse what ought to happen with what does, in that despite the growth of interest in the topic, far too little systematic, empirical or theoretical research has taken place. Thus, in particular, there are very few ethnographies which focus on the activities of the middle manager in the context of particular schools. Other critics have suggested that we do not really know much about what expectations middle managers have of their roles or what others in schools expect of them (Lambert 1975). Yet others have argued that the kinds of expectations to be found in much of the literature are utopian and/or involve a conception of the middle manager as 'paragon' (Thomas 1983). To be fair, many of the accounts discussed thus far do contain reservations that acknowledge that things may not always be as they ought to be. What do these reservations amount to?

As long ago as the early 1960s, HMI recognised that 'there are wide variations in the extent to which department heads are exercising their responsibilities. In some cases inadequate action is the result of failure to appreciate the extent to which responsibilities have multiplied and increased in importance but this is often accompanied by a traditional reluctance to interfere with the professional work of one's colleagues' (quoted in Siddle 1978, p. 4). Many commentators emphasise the importance of control, supervision and the monitoring of the work of departmental staff as a key, even *the* key, function of the middle manager (Bailey 1973; Blackburn 1983 a and b; Marland 1981). This view is expressed particularly forcefully in Cockcroft (1982):

> We regard it as an essential part of the work of the head of department to be aware of the quality of teaching which is going on within the department . . . In our view it should be the normal practice for the head of department to visit lessons given by other members of department.

This may well be correct, but it is almost equally widely recognised that this is an aspect of their work which causes many heads of department great role strain. Bailey (1973) comments that heads of department 'have often to be persuaded to take charge of their departments', and Siddle (1978) concludes that:

> Heads of science are generally reluctant to supervise their departmental colleagues by assigning tasks, supervising their performance, recognising good performance and criticizing poor performance, correcting mistakes or resolving difficulties in the fashion of a good quality controller . . . They much preferred to adopt a laissez-faire attitude. (p. 13)

The evidence available suggests that such attitudes are commonly shared by heads of other subject departments (Hall and Thomas 1977) and by pastoral heads (Best et al 1983). While this is an important source of role conflict, there are others as well.

Dunham's (1978) survey of 92 heads of department suggests that the middle managers of today face a greater possibility of stress and role conflict than did their historical predecessors. In a chapter in his latest book dealing with *Stress in Teaching*, Dunham (1984) considers the pressures on middle managers in the contemporary secondary school as compared with those experienced by their predecessors:

> One major change has resulted in departmental heads becoming involved in management responsibilities . . . while still being required to carry a heavy teaching load . . . (and of) the pressures on Pastoral Care heads arising from their wide range of duties . . . as well as having to teach for some of the week. (p. 75)

The result was that some of his sample spoke of frustration leading to indifference, to depression, to demoralisation and to a withdrawal from responsibility, and others expressed real anxiety associated with considerable role confusion. The consequences of these stresses were manifest in tiredness, physical ailments, psychosomatic illness and sickness (Dunham 1978, p. 46). Bloomer (1980) summarises the findings of three series of workshops of teachers and others drawn from a wide range of institutions to investigate 'what sort of functions a head of department should have' (p. 1). Four sets of reasons why departmental organisation in schools is less efficient than it might be are distinguished as follows:

1. The organisational problems have become greater in the last twenty years . . .
2. Modern democratic styles . . . While they may well lead to an enrichment of school work also call for greater skills and adaptability in heads of department.
3. There is ambiguity as to the definition of the role of heads of department. Detailed contracts are rare, and most heads of department learn their role 'on the job' through their perceptions of what other heads of department do and the expectations of head teachers.
4. Training for the work of management in schools . . . is comparatively rare . . . (pp. 2–3)

While Bloomer (1980) found a 'considerable degree of consensus amongst workshop members', he also acknowledges that Lambert's (1975) research paints a different picture. Lambert set out to examine 'what heads of department and Heads saw as the role functions of heads of department, and to see if there was any evidence of potential role conflict between the perceptions of heads of department and the role expectations of heads' (p. 29). A four-fold typology of role functions is employed, based upon a division between *instrumental* (task-centred) and *expressive* (person-centred) functions and a second division between *academic* and *institutional* functions:

1. 'Instrumental–academic' (e.g. the development and carrying out of school policy; the formulation of departmental policy; curriculum development).
2. 'Instrumental–institutional' (e.g. choice of text books, deployment of staff).
3. 'Expressive–institutional' (e.g. links with outside agencies and with parents; extra-curricular activities; departmental report for the head).
4. 'Expressive–academic' (e.g. assisting new staff; supervising and monitoring staff).

Lambert (1975), summarises his findings on each of these role functions as in Table 14.1

Only on the 'instrumental–academic' is there a high level of agreement between heads of department, between heads, and between the heads of department and heads. The overall index of agreement is particularly low on the set of items dealing with 'expressive–academic' functions but even these low figures mask the reluctance of heads of department to supervise and monitor their colleagues as against the high level of expectations shared amongst heads that this was a function that heads of department should perform. These findings are supported in a more recent piece of research by Howson and Woolnough (1982) in which it is reported that, when heads of department and heads were asked to rank in order of importance 15 representative tasks, heads of department placed 'assessing the teaching competence of staff in the department as low as 13th whereas heads ranked it 7th'.

Table 14.1 *Summary of the Four Role-Functional Areas (from Lambert 1975, p. 36).*

Area	Heads of Dept	Heads	Indices of Agreement
Instrumental–academic	85%	92%	0.93
Instrumental–institutional	66%	80%	0.82
Expressive–institutional	50%	62%	0.81
Expressive–academic	67%	89%	0.75

Lambert (1975) concludes that 'the expressive-academic area would seem to be the area which was likely to be the source of possible role conflict . . . that the expressive areas are the danger areas . . . In present practice there appears to be an assumption of a consensus of opinion on the role-functions of the head of department which the survey did not seem to justify' (p. 37). In commenting on these findings, Marland (1975) remarks that 'the conflict is not only between the Head and the head of department, but also between the subject teachers and their supposed leaders' (p. 38). He also suggests that 'by the early 1970s the expected duties of the holder of such a post were fairly well known, even if not always met' (p. 38).

Amongst the solutions to the problems which middle managers face, two are widely canvassed. First, that there 'is a need for an element of clearer role-definition within schools' (Lambert 1975, p. 37) from which it follows that 'every school must draw up an agreed job specification' (Marland 1975, p. 39) for its middle managers, a view shared by the Committee on the Curriculum and Organisation of Secondary Schools of the ILEA, in its report on *Improving Secondary Schools* (the Hargreaves Report, ILEA 1984). In the section dealing with the head of department two recommendations are made, one of which is that '*Headteachers* ensure that all heads of departments have clear job specifications' (p. 103). Ogilvie and Bartlett (1979) warn that although the potential for role conflict exists, necessitating clear role-definition, 'this might be achieved by more detailed job descriptions but is more likely to be achieved through regular professional discussions . . . so that expectations are clarified and consensus reached regarding these expectations' (p. 6). Second, that more attention should be given to the training needs of middle managers who have all too often in the past, had to learn 'on the job' or by 'trial and error'. Some areas such as the ILEA have faced special problems. Thus the Hargreaves Report comments that while 'most heads were unstinting in their praise of their effective heads of department . . . not all heads of departments were carrying out their functions as well as they should be.' This weakness at the level of middle management 'dates mainly from the early and mid-1970s when the steep rise in house prices and the near impossibility of obtaining adequate reasonably priced rented accommodation' drove aspiring young potential middle managers out of London and discouraged experienced teachers from coming to London. This meant that 'there are schools which are still suffering the effects of unsuitable appointments made at the time' (p. 102). Part of the solution is to offer more training opportunities:

> Since 1980 the ILEA has taken active steps to mitigate this state of affairs by offering a wide range of courses in management training. During 1982–83 115 teachers (from 79 schools) attended these courses, 74 of whom were heads of departments and 41 were pastoral heads. The course agendas now relate closely to the work of schools, and include school visits, the exchange of ideas and experiences between course participants, and practical work. (pp. 102, 103)

The training opportunities for teachers holding posts of middle-management responsibility have significantly increased over the last few years and there are now some very impressive short courses to be found, such as the DES Regional Course 'Middle Management in the Secondary School' run at the University of Nottingham with Derbyshire, Lincolnshire and Nottinghamshire. However, while there has clearly been some improvement in the training opportunities available it must still be said that, given the number of teachers who carry middle-management responsibilities, this has only just begun to scratch the surface of what is necessary. Such provision as is available is also unevenly distributed in various ways. Marland (1983) summarising the available evidence, suggests that as far as training opportunities are concerned, the pastoral head may be even worse off than the subject head:

> Whereas the aspiring head of department has had an initial training in the appropriate specialism, and usually had some inservice support or further training in the specialism, the aspiring head of house/year had usually been expected to 'pick it up' as she or he goes along. (p. 25).

Just how limited are the training opportunities available to those with pastoral responsibilities is confirmed by Maher and Best (1984). However, in his paper 'Preparing for Promotion in Pastoral Care', Marland (1983) does make a number of suggestions as to the kinds of knowledge and skills that the aspiring pastoral middle manager should seek to acquire and how to go about obtaining them.

Since the beginning of the 1970s the role of the middle manager within the secondary school has received increasing attention and we know a good deal more than we did about the kinds of conflicting expectations and ambiguities of role which confront those who take up such responsibilities. What we still know very little about is what middle managers actually do, how they account for their actions, and how they interact with 'relevant others' within particular schools. To explore these kinds of issues a quite different approach to the study of such middle management is necessary: one which adopts an interactionist conception of role and a broadly ethnographic methodology.

This is not to say that there have been no interactionist studies which have touched upon the activities of middle managers in the secondary school. Both Hargreaves (1967; 1972) and, especially, Lacey (1970) do consider this topic, and not all they have had to say is particularly reassuring. Lacey (1970), for example, suggests that many heads of department at Hightown regarded their duties as 'chores' or as stepping stones to further advancement. Like the work of Lacey and Hargreaves, Richardson's (1973) study of Nailsea is based on long and painstaking field research. As Siddle (1978) acknowledges, an issue such as, for example how far a head of department is free to make decisions without seeking the approval of a superior 'is impossible to assess without embarking upon the type of investigation undertaken by Richardson . . . ' (p. 10). Certainly we can learn much from Richardson's report about the extent and nature of the power of different departments and heads of department and of the ways in which they act and interact. Her account of the modern languages, and especially the science, departments as 'the "giant" departments able to make their own conditions regardless of changes elsewhere in the system — almost, at times, to be holding the staff to ransom' (p. 90) is particularly revealing.

More recently, two in-depth case studies of comprehensive schools located in the South-East ('Rivendell' by Best et al 1983) and in the Midlands ('Bishop McGregor' by Burgess 1983) represent a welcome return to the traditions of the approach used so tellingly in the study of 'Lumley Secondary Modern' (Hargreaves 1967) and 'Hightown Grammar' (Lacey 1970) in the late 1960s. None of these studies focus primarily on the role of the middle manager, but they all examine the roles of various middle managers both in the context of the institutionalised sets of prescriptions and expectations that, taken as a whole, make up the formal structure of the school and also in terms of the interpersonal interactions of the individuals who sustain these structures. For as McGuiness (1984) recognises, such 'systems are not cold, clinical machines. The human beings who operate within them can make an inadequate system surprisingly effective — equally, the uncommitted or the incompetent can foul up the best of systems' (p. 152). What these studies also have in common, is a desire to offer detailed explanations of the various ways in which the patterns of the perception and actions of middle managers holding a variety of roles are determined by their personal needs and are shaped by the interactions of those who fill them with senior staff, other middle managers, and other staff.

In the nature of things it is difficult to offer brief illustrations of the kinds of insights into the role of the middle manager which such an approach provides, as the researcher focuses on 'the way in which the school *actually* worked in contrast to the ways in which different teachers thought it *should* work' (Burgess 1983, p. 84). Best et al (1983) too, seek to explore a 'serious mismatch between *theory* and *reality* at a number of levels' with respect to the provision of care at Rivendell:

> at the level of what the 'conventional wisdom' says pastoral care is/ought to be and what is actually happening in schools; at the level of the school's official pronouncements about pupils' welfare and what a school actually does about it; and at the level of what teachers claim to mean by 'pastoral care' and the day-to-day practices in which they actually engage. (p. 29).

In both Bishop McGregor and Rivendell the researchers found major differences in the ways in which different houses and subject departments operated. As Burgess (1983) comments of Bishop McGregor, 'each house and department held a position within the school which had initially been defined by the headmaster. However, the staff in these houses and departments quickly established their own patterns of activity, their own characteristics, and their own relationships with each other and with their pupils'. These differences are explored at some length in Burgess's description of the 'Newsom' department and of the struggle for power that took place within it as its teachers attempted to operate with no formally designated head but with 'an "unofficial, self-appointed head of department" and at least two major competitors for the role' (pp. 182–190). Burgess also stresses the extent to which the houses at McGregor were different and the degree to which such differences were explicable in terms of the attitudes and practices of their heads of house:

> individual house heads defined the school's activities in different ways. When the school opened house heads had taken the opportunity to establish their own distinctive pattern of work and routine. In letters that were sent out to parents, house heads . . . indicated differences in their aims, objectives and activities . . . In Westminster house, the aim was simply to form a link between the home and the school . . . in Southwark house, it was emphasised there would be social, educational and fund-raising activities . . . In Arundel there were to be regular house masses together with a variety of clubs and societies for house pupils . . . in Hexham . . . it was intended that direct links should be established with (the) diocese of Hexham. (p. 58)

In these, and many other, ways each house 'developed a distinct set of aims, routines, practices and activities' (pp. 57–60).

Best et al's (1983) study of Rivendell explores largely similar issues. Thus, much of a long chapter on 'Identities' (pp. 139–187) looks closely 'at the *styles* with which teachers interpreted their roles . . . and at some of the sorts of role-conflict which they experienced' (p. 142). In doing this, attention is focused mainly on the way in which three pairs of middle managers interpreted their roles and at the sorts of role-conflict they met. This analysis tries to show how different teachers respond 'in very different ways to the relationship between personal fulfilment and formal role-expectations, and the varying degrees of "attachment" and "commitment" which characterises their role play' (p. 142).

The study also seeks to show:

> how role performance is to some extent dependent upon the 'perspectives' which teachers
> adopt on their sub roles and the ideologies which seem to underlie them or which they are in
> the process of constructing as they work out the more or less tense encounters which make up
> their daily life.

It is in such a description of 'the various ways in which particular individuals sought to come to terms with such tensions and work them out in their interaction with other members of staff in a way which was institutionally acceptable and personally meaningful and rewarding' (p. 186) that it is possible to convey something of the flavour of what role play for the middle manager can mean.

As McGuiness (1984) remarks, studies such as these 'journey into a world of great interest and enormous complexity' (p. 151) in which the perceptions and actions of those involved are subjected to close and sustained examination over considerable periods of time using a case-study approach. Not that such an approach is free of difficulty. Amongst its 'problems' are the fact that it is very time-consuming and, inevitably, limited to a very restricted number of settings. This calls into question the typicality of the generalisations that are identified. This is certainly a serious problem, but Bassey (1981) suggests that what he terms 'open generalisations' which offer reliable predictions beyond the particular case although 'obviously useful . . . are also scarce in number and . . . once these few have been mastered . . . they appear obvious and no longer valuable'. For the teacher 'closed generalisations can stimulate his thinking about possible lines of action and can alert him to possible consequences; it can also assist him in deciding what to do, but it cannot tell him' (p. 84). This being so, 'an important criterion for judging the merit of a case-study is the extent to which the details are sufficient and appropriate for a teacher working in a similar situation to relate his decision making to that described in the case-study. The reliability of a case-study is more important than its generalisability' (p. 85).

By the kinds of criteria entailed in the sort of enriched conception of role outlined above, most published studies of the role of the middle manager (and of the head as well) are seriously deficient in so far as they *decontextualise* role. This decontextualisation takes two main forms, which can be illustrated using the case of the middle manager. First, such roles are decontextualised in so far as they are considered in isolation from the whole set of managerial and other roles with which they commonly interact and which shape and constrain what is possible or desirable for those who fill them. Second, these roles are decontextualised in so far as they are considered out of the context of the particular institutions within which they are, in practice, enacted. Whatever the merits of approaches which decontextualise in this way, there is a strong case for the use of an in-depth, comprehensive, case-study approach to the study of middle management in the secondary school. As far as I know no such studies have been published to date and no funded research project using such an approach is taking place at present.

SUMMARY AND CONCLUSIONS

Limitations of space have necessitated some hard choices as to the issues which could be considered in this chapter. A fuller treatment would have given attention to a number of themes not discussed here including, for example, the growing debate over whether comprehensive schools need, or can afford, both a pastoral and an academic structure and heads of house/year as well as heads of department (see Best and Ribbins 1983 for a discussion of the arguments involved in the debate on the 'pastoral/academic split').

What has been emphasised is an attempt to identify aspects of the role of middle management within the contemporary school which are often taken for granted in much of the literature and to treat some of these aspects as problematic in themselves. Thus the 'horizontal' and 'vertical' divisions of labour and of task, which constitute the usual settings within which the role of the departmental head and the pastoral head are located and accounted for, are examined critically. Some attempt has also been made to treat the concepts of 'role' and 'role structure' in the same sceptical way and much of this critique focuses upon the two main alternative conceptions of role derived respectively from 'functionalist' and 'interactionist' frames of reference. Finally, the literature dealing with the role of the pastoral and the academic middle manager is reviewed briefly and a case made out in favour of subjecting these roles to a more interactionist approach than has been the norm to date. It is suggested that, whatever the limitations of such an approach, it would have the merit of avoiding the kind of 'decontextualising' assumptions implicit in traditional studies.

Finally, are schools over-complex and over-managed? And is the role of the middle manager really necessary? HM Inspectorate have had something to say on both these issues. Thus the Welsh Inspectorate suggest that 'The status of heads of department in Welsh secondary schools has diminished in recent years at the same time as their responsibilities have increased' (Lodge 1984, p. 9). The report also concludes that 'Whether a pupil achieves or underachieves is largely dependent on the quality of planning, execution, and evaluation that takes place within individual departments' (HMI (Wales) 1984). There is little reason to suppose that what is true of Wales and the subject head of department is not also true of England and of the pastoral head. HMI (1979) are also on record as taking the view that: 'No institution which seriously tried to respond to differences of need, capacity and interest among large numbers of adolescents could be other than complex. It is still possible to question whether the existing complexities fulfil their purpose; whether complexity is often greater than it need be . . . ' (p. 267). Their answer is unequivocal and might serve as an authoritative coda to this chapter:

> There is little evidence to suggest that schools of any kind of size are overmanaged or that teachers spend too much time outside the classroom. On the contrary, the indications are that they may need to give more time to a necessary range of non-teaching duties, particularly those of planning, consultation and assessment. Heads of department and teachers with guidance and pastoral responsibilities are often particularly short of time. (p. 267).

REFERENCES

Anderson, J. (1968) *Bureaucracy in Education*. Johns Hopkins Press.

Bailey, P. (1973) 'The Functions of Heads of Departments in Comprehensive Schools'.

Journal of Educational Administration and History, **V**(1).

Bailey, P. (1981) 'Appraising the Performance of Departments in Maintained Secondary

Schools: Concepts and Approaches'. In Ribbins, P. and Thomas, H. (ed.) *Research in Educational Management and Administration*, 106–114. Coombe Lodge: BEMAS.

Ball, S. (1982) 'Competition and conflict in the teaching of English: a socio-historical analysis'. *Journal of Curriculum Studies*, **14**, 1–28.

Ball, S. and Lacey, C. (1980) 'Subject Disciplines as the Opportunity for Group Action: A measured Critique of Subject Sub-cultures'. In Woods, P. (ed) *Teacher Strategies*. London: Croom Helm.

Bassey, M. (1981) 'Pedagogic Research: on the relative merits of search for generalisations and study of single events'. *Oxford Review of Education*, **7**(1), 73–94.

Bayne-Jardine, C. (1981) 'The Qualities of a Good Head of Department'. In Marland and Hill (ed.) (1981) *Departmental Management*. London: Heinemann.

Bayne-Jardine, C. and Hanham, C. (1972) 'Heads of Department'. *Forum* **15**(1).

Bell, L. (1980) 'The School as an Organisation: a re-appraisal'. *British Journal of Sociology in Education*, **1**(2), 183–193.

Bernstein, B. (1971) 'On the Classification and Framing of Educational Knowledge'. In Young, M. (ed.) *Knowledge and Control*. London: Macmillan.

Best, R., Jarvis, C. and Ribbins, P. (1977) 'Pastoral Care: Concept and Process'. *British Journal of Educational Studies*, **XXV**(2), 124–135.

Best, R., Jarvis, C. and Ribbins, P. (1980) *Perspectives on Pastoral Care*. London: Heinemann.

Best, R., Ribbins, P. Jarvis, C. with Oddy, D. (1983) *Education and Care*. London: Heinemann.

Best, R. and Ribbins, P. (1983) 'Rethinking the Pastoral Academic Split'. *Pastoral Care in Education*, **1**(1), 11–18.

Best, R. and Ribbins, P. (1985) 'Researching the Secondary School: The case of pastoral care'. Paper presented at the BEMAS Research Seminar on Management in the Secondary School. Sheffield Polytechnic.

Blackburn, K. (1983a) *Head of House, Head of Year*. London: Heinemann.

Blackburn, K. (1983b) 'The Pastoral Head: a developing role'. *Pastoral Care in Education*, **1**(1), 18–24.

Bloomer, K. (1980) 'The Role of the Head of Department: Some Questions and Answers'. *Educational Research*, **22**(3), 83–97.

Burgess, R. (1983) *Experiencing Comprehensive Education*. London: Methuen.

Burnham, P. (1969) 'Role Theory and Educational Administration'. In Houghton, V. et al (ed.) *Management in Education*. London: Ward Lock.

Cockcroft, W. (1982) *Mathematics Counts*. London: HMSO.

Cohen, M., March, J. and Olsen, J. (1972) 'A garbage can model of organisational choice'. *Administrative Science Quarterly*, **17**(1), 1–25.

Cooper, B. (1983) 'On Explaining Change in School Subjects'. *British Journal of the Sociology of Education*, **4**(3), 206–222.

Corwin, R. (1970) *Militant Professionalism. A Study of Organisational Conflict in High School*. London: Appleton.

Cyert, R. and March, J. (1963) *A Behavioural Theory of the Firm*. Englewood Cliffs, NJ: Prentice Hall.

David, H. (1983) 'Team Spirit'. *Times Educational Supplement*, 28 January, 215.

Dennison, W. (1985) 'Flexible structures and secondary schools'. *Educational Management and Administration*, **13**(1), 29–37.

Dunham, J. (1978) 'Change and stress in the head of department's role'. *Educational Research*, **21**(1), 44–48.

Dunham, J. (1984) *Stress in Teaching*. Beckenham: Croom Helm.

Falk, G. (1980) 'The Academic Department and Role Conflict'. *Improving College and University Teaching*, **27**(2), 78–86.

Goffman, E. (1977) *Encounters*. London: Allen Lane.

Goodson, I. (1981) 'Becoming an Academic Subject: patterns of explanation and evolution'. *British Journal of Sociology of Education*, **2**(2), 162–179.

Goodson, I. (1983) 'Subjects for Study: Aspects of a Social History of Curriculum'. *Journal of Curriculum Studies*, **15**(4), 390–408.

Goodson, I. (1984) 'Beyond the Subject Monolith: Subject Traditions and Subcultures'. In Harling, P. (ed.) *New Directions in Educational Leadership*. London: Falmer.

Gross, N., Mason, W., and McEachern, A. (1958) *Explorations in Role Analysis*. New York: Wiley.

Hall, J. and Thomas, J. (1977) 'Research

Report: mathematics departmental headship in secondary schools'. *Educational Administration*, **5**(2), 30–37.

Hargreaves, D. (1967) *Social Relations in a Secondary School*. London: Routledge and Kegan Paul.

Hargreaves, D. (1972) *Interpersonal Relations and Education*. London: Routledge and Kegan Paul.

Heycock, C. (1970) *A Study of Some Aspects of Internal Organisation and Management*. Penarth: Pulin Publishing.

HMI (1979) *Aspects of Secondary Education*. London: HMSO.

HMI (Wales) (1984) *Departmental Organisation in Secondary Schools*. Welsh Office: HMSO.

Holt, J. (1981) 'The head of department and the whole curriculum'. In Marland, M. and Hill, S. (ed.) (1981) *Departmental Management*. London: Heinemann. 9–25.

Houghton, Lord (1974) Report of the Committee of Inquiry into the Pay of Non-university Teachers. London: HMSO.

Houghton, V., McHugh, R. and Morgan, C. (ed.) (1975) Management in Education: The Management of Organisations and Individuals. London: Ward Lock.

Howson, J. and Woolnough, B. (1982) 'Head of Department — dictator or democrat'. *Educational Management and Administration*, **10**(1), 37–45.

Hoyle, E. (1969) *The Role of the Teacher*. London: Routledge and Kegan Paul.

(ILEA) Inner London Education Authority (1984) *Improving Secondary Schools*. Report of the Committee on the Curriculum and Organisation of Secondary Schools in ILEA, chaired by David H. Hargreaves. London: ILEA.

King, R. (1973) 'The Head Teacher and his Authority'. In Fowler, G., Morris, V. Ozga, J. (eds.) (1973) *Decision Making in British Education*. London: Heinemann.

Lacey, C. (1970) *Hightown Grammar: The School as a Social System*. Manchester: Manchester University Press.

Lambert, K. (1975) 'Research Report: the role of head of department in schools'. *Educational Administration*, **3**(2), 27–39.

Lambert, K. (1977) 'Organising Education Institutions as Anarchies'. *Educational Administration*, **6**(1), 101–112.

Lang, P. (1984) 'Pastoral Care: Some Reflections on Possible Influences'. *Pastoral Care in Education*, **2**(2), 136–146.

Layton (1973) *Science for the People*. London: Allen and Unwin.

Lodge, B. (1984) 'Department heads' drop in status'. *Times Educational Supplement*, 11 May, 9.

Maher, P. and Best, R. (1984) *Training and Support for Pastoral Care*. London: National Association of Pastoral Care in Education.

Marland, M. (1971) *Head of Department*. London: Heinemann.

Marland, M. (1974) *Pastoral Care*. London: Heinemann.

Marland, M. (1975) 'Comment on Lambert (1975) "Research Report: the role of head of department in schools"'. *Educational Administration*, **3**(2).

Marland, M. (1983) 'Preparing for Promotion in Pastoral Care'. *Pastoral Care in Education*, **1**(1), 24–36.

Marland, M. and Hill, S. (ed.) (1981) *Departmental Management*. London: Heinemann.

McGuiness, J. (1984) 'Review Article: Education and Care'. *Pastoral Care in Education*, **2**(2), 151–155.

Merton, R. (1957) 'The Role-Set: Problems in Sociological Theory'. *British Journal of Sociology*, **8**.

Morgan, C. and Turner, L. (1976) 'Role, the Education Manager and the Individual in the Organisation'. *Unit 14 Management in Education (E321)*. Milton Keynes: Open University Press.

Musgrove, F. (1968) 'The contribution of sociology to the study of the curriculum'. In Kerr, J. (ed.) *Changing the Curriculum*. London: University of London Press.

Musgrove, F. (1971) *Patterns of Power and Authority in English Education*. London: Methuen.

Nolte, M. (ed.) (1966) An Introduction to School Administration: Selected Readings. London: Macmillan.

Ogilvie, D. and Bartlett, V. (1979) 'Departmental Heads in England and Australia: Some Comparisons'. *Studies in Educational Administration*, CCEA, **15**.

Packwood, T. (1977) 'The School as a Hierarchy'. *Educational Administration*, **5**(2), 1–6 and 12–13.

Peeke, G. (1983) 'Role Strain in the Further Education College'. In Boyd-Barrett, O. et al (ed.) *Approaches to Post School*

Management. London: Harper and Row.

Raleigh, M. (ed) (1983) *The English Department Book.* London: ILEA English Centre.

Ribbins, P. and Best, R. (1985) 'Pastoral Care: Theory, Practice and the Role of Research'. In Lang, P. and Marland, M. (ed.) *New Directions in Pastoral Care in Education.* Oxford: Blackwell.

Richardson, E. (1973) *The Teacher, The School and The Task of Management.* London: Heinemann.

Schein, E. (1965) *Organizational Psychology.* New York: Prentice Hall.

Siddle, J. (1978) *The Head of Science and the Task of Management.* Herts: The Association for Science Education.

Silverman, D. (1970) *The Theory of Organizations.* London: Heinemann.

Thomas, H. (1983) 'Review of Marland and Hill (1981) "*Departmental Management.* (London: Heinemann)"'. *Pastoral Care in Education,* **2**(1), 144–147.

Turner, C. (1977) 'Organizing Educational Institutions as Anarchies'. *Educational Administration,* **5**(2), 6–12 and 13–15.

Turner, R. (1969) 'Role-taking: process versus conformity'. In Lindesmith, A. and Strauss, A. (ed.) *Readings in Social Psychology.* New York: Holt Rinehart and Winston.

Watson, L. (1973) 'Office and expertise in the secondary school'. In Fowler et al (ed.) *Decision Making in British Education.* London: Heinemann.

Westwood, L. (1967) 'The Role of the Teacher'. *Educational Research,* **10**, 21–37.

White, J. and Young, M. (1975) 'The Sociology of Knowledge'. *Education for Teaching,* **98**, 4–14.

Woodland, D. (1979) 'Role; social role; role taking; role conflict'. In Mitchell, G. (1979) *A New Dictionary of Sociology.* London: Routledge and Kegan Paul.

Young, M. (ed.) (1971) *Knowledge and Control.* London: Macmillan.

Young, M. and White, J. (1976) 'The Sociology of Knowledge—Part 2 of a Dialogue'. *Education for Teaching,* **99**, 50–59.

PART FOUR

THE MANAGEMENT OF EVALUATION AND CHANGE

15

PERSPECTIVES ON EVALUATION[1]

Hywel Thomas

INTRODUCTION

Evaluation is a well-established and accepted activity within education, engaged in by teachers not only when considering the performance of their pupils or students but also in making judgements about their own work and that of their colleagues. Yet evaluation is also viewed as a major innovation to educational practice, often treated by the same teachers with a mixture of hostility, scepticism and caution. How is it that ostensibly the same activity is viewed in such different ways? Evidently evaluation is a complex concept and process, with diverse meanings and practices, some of which are more widely accepted than others by educationists. It is the purpose of the following sections of the chapter to examine this complexity and, in so doing, attempt to identify the reasons for the mixed response to evaluation by educationists.

The chapter begins with a section which attempts to define evaluation and is followed by an account of the purposes of evaluation. Concerned as these two sections are with questions of what evaluation is and why evaluation occurs, the discussion reveals not only the multiple meanings of and motives for evaluation but also the range of groups with an interest in its practice and outcomes. Logically then, the third section, titled 'The Theatre of Evaluation', describes and analyses the structures of relationships between evaluators and evaluated as well as the modes of conduct within those relationships. This leads to the fourth section which examines techniques of evaluation and the various dimensions along

[1] I wish to thank Peter Ribbins for his illuminating comments on the first draft of this chapter. As a consequence of our discussions the model analysing structural relationships in evaluation was altered to include the third parameter, which considers *for whom* evaluations are carried out. It is a change which adds substantially to the analytical power of the model.

373

which evaluation procedures can vary, the selection from which is normally predicated upon particular structures and conducts within the evaluation relationships. The concluding section summarises the principal elements of the chapter and emphasises the importance of who controls evaluation. It also considers reasons why teachers may find it valuable to react positively to more public and systematic evaluations.

The location of this chapter in the text is important for three reasons. First, because evaluation is such a commonplace activity for educational managers, its analysis provides a retrospective illumination for the earlier chapters on 'Managing the Institution'. Second, since the theme of Part Four is 'The Management of Evaluation and Change', it is appropriate to begin with a discussion of evaluation. As an activity it precedes any change which may be sought by an education manager, who must first *evaluate* whether a change is necessary or desirable. Evaluation also occurs in parallel with a change and at its end, as part of a process of monitoring progress and drawing conclusions about outcomes. In these respects the chapter provides a framework for issues considered in Chapters 18 and 19, by Michael Matthewman and Derek Slater respectively. The focus of this chapter upon the relationship between evaluators and evaluated is also relevant to the discussion of 'Accountability versus Participation?' in Chapter 17, much of which examines relationships between teachers and some of their external evaluators, particularly the role of governing bodies. Related to their role as external evaluators, governing bodies can also act as agents representing community views on the need for continuity or change from educational institutions. Finally, the third reason for the location of the chapter is that the analytical framework which is proposed here is used for examining, in the next chapter, selected cases of evaluation relationships. The most prominent of these cases are the national and local inspectorates, agencies which often use their evaluation activity to contribute to the management of change.

WHAT IS EVALUATION?

The essence of evaluation is a process of measurement, although it is rarely precise and the only measuring scale which might readily be used would be ordinal. With regard to an educational decision, it includes the whole process of information gathering, analysis of and reflection about this information, the weighing of alternatives and making a final judgement of their relative worth. It is the process which precedes the point of decision, which is the act of choice. It is a widespread activity. It includes the evaluation process undertaken by teachers, examining the range of materials, before choosing how to introduce new topics to classes; the processes followed by governing bodies when they select new head teachers; course appraisal and validation by the CNAA. It could be used to describe the process of policy appraisal by a Secretary of State before issuing a new circular on teacher training. The extent of its presence within educational institutions is captured by Adelman and Alexander (1982 p. 286):

> An educational institution's inhabitants are engaged in a more or less constant process of evaluation: every decision demands it, from matters of overall policy to a teacher's decision about what to say or do at a particular point in time in the process of classroom events and relationships.

It is important to emphasise the link between evaluation and decision and also to clarify the meaning attached to a 'decision'. Events occur in schools, as in everyday life, which may only have the outward appearance of a decision. Consider the head teacher who 'knows' that all ideas which come from young teachers are bad and must be rejected. Such 'knowledge' is used when the head rejects a young teacher's proposal for some change in school practice. Since this event is not a product of weighing alternatives but is a reflex action it is, ' . . . by definition, of no interest in decision analysis. If no alternative action is perceived, no choice is possible.' (Drake 1979, p. 82) Following Shackle (1969, p. 2), 'Decision, therefore, is choice in face of bounded certainty.' And since choice entails the selection from alternatives, so evaluation describes the process of measuring or weighing these alternatives against each other. Moreover, as decision entails evaluation so also does evaluation entail decision. The process of collecting data, for example on the numbers enrolled on particular courses, is not itself evaluative activity. However, if it was collected to make judgements about the continuation of courses it is part of an evaluation process. The final outcome of evaluation, the event by which we recognise it as having occurred, is the expression of a preference, the act of choice again. This need not only be an executive action in the sense of a decision about minimum numbers to be enrolled on courses but can include a final report on a curriculum project, which has no immediate consequence beyond affecting the perceptions and judgements of those to whom it is addressed.

The definition of evaluation proposed is wide-ranging and is no less than ' . . . an extension into the everyday work of educators of those continuous appraisals of conditions and events on the basis of which humans act and interrelate' (Adelman and Alexander 1982, p. 286). The value of this broad definition is that it includes much of the informal, private and idiosyncratic processes which incorporate most of the evaluation which takes place ' . . . and as far as the quality of educational experiences available to the student is concerned, this level of evaluation is probably the most potent' (Adelman and Alexander 1982, p. 286). Since it is a working definition eschewed by some writers it requires some defence.

Harlen, for example, insists that evaluation be defined as occurring only when criteria are made explicit (1980 p. 53) and 'It is the insistence on explicitness about criteria which distinguishes evaluation as used here from the "everyday" use of the term' (1980, p. 57). Such explicitness is somewhat obscured when we learn that the criteria ' . . . will not be found neatly listed and agreed by all concerned; they will instead have to be inferred from people's writings, actions and speech' (p. 53). Moreover, the evaluator has to select when there is a lack of consistency ' . . . between the criteria which can be inferred from what people do and what people say' (p. 54). This need to judge between actions and expressed purpose appears to place the evaluator in the position of arbiter of criteria and it is this which seems to be the crux of the distinction drawn between Harlen's definition of evaluation and the everyday use of the term.

Having given the broad definition of evaluation, and one with which this writer agrees, Adelman and Alexander (1982) actually write about a narrower form of evaluation. This is a perfectly proper exercise but it involves making a distinction which is not wholly persuasive. They distinguish between 'formal' and 'informal' evaluation, the latter including the 'idiosyncratic and private' (p. 286) while the 'formal' means:

> . . . the making of judgements of the worth and effectiveness of educational endeavours at a *public* level, sometimes as a matter of *deliberate institutional policy*. These judgements are ostensibly informed by criteria and methods which are to some degree open to scrutiny and appraisal in order that judgements may reasonably claim to be valid and fair. (p. 287)

They would include evaluation programmes deliberately set up within institutions for specified purposes and the validation processes of the CNAA. However, they would apparently not include as a formal evaluation the UGC decisions of 1981 (see Chapter 8) because criteria and methods were not open to scrutiny. Similarly, the recommendations which the UGC made following the 'great debate' of 1983/84 would not be counted as a formal evaluation. Yet both events are highly formal in the sense of apparently following an elaborate procedure, while there may be other evaluations which are much less elaborate but are more open to scrutiny.

Since the criteria for classifying evaluation is examined more fully in later sections this will not be developed further here. However, the case for retaining and using a broad definition of evaluation remains to be completed. First, since the informal, private processes of evaluation are the most common they need to be retained in the analysis as a reminder of their widespread presence. Second, since the informal may also be the most potent in their effect on educational experiences, their importance requires their inclusion. Third, it must not be taken for granted that more formal (in the sense of 'elaborate procedure') evaluation is necessarily better than the informal variety. Whether more formal processes are always better than more intuitive and informal processes is problematic. It is certainly important to guard against formal processes in which inappropriate criteria are used and, by considering only formal evaluation, there is the danger that they come to be regarded as the best. Fourth, formal evaluations are probably more time-consuming than the informal and the costs of formality have to be assessed. It is certainly the case that this broad definition of evaluation begins to explain the contradiction noted in the first paragraph of this chapter which is apparent in the diversity of response which the concept attracts from educationists.

Having argued for retaining a broad definition of evaluation, the specific concern of this chapter will be with evaluation in and of educational institutions such as schools, colleges and universities. It is not directly concerned with approaches to and problems of evaluation in institutions which have a primarily non-educational task (e.g. the prison service) or with agencies which service educational institutions (e.g. the DES or the education offices of local authorities).

Finally, with regard to questions of definition, it is appropriate to offer a personal definition of assessment in order to distinguish it from evaluation. If evaluation is the whole process of weighing alternatives, assessment might be regarded as the more narrowly focused task of considering the merits and de-merits of a particular option. For example, when heads have a number of promotion posts available for distribution, they may assess the personal merits of individual candidates but in arriving at decisions they must not only assess these candidates against one another but take into account issues such as the subjects they teach (e.g. shortage subject or not) and other perceived needs of the school which are viewed as relevant criteria. Why heads and others must evaluate is the next question which needs to be examined.

WHY EVALUATE?

Why those involved in education engage in evaluation is a deceptively straightforward question which needs to be broken down into a number of more particular themes to assist the analysis and explanation. Three are suggested, the first of which is concerned with the reasons why teachers evaluate their own work and that of their colleagues. The second is related to those involved in education who are not teachers but, nevertheless, are interested in evaluating educational activity; they are sometimes called 'stakeholders'. The third deals briefly with the changing climate of education and its consequence for evaluation.

Why do teachers evaluate?

Teachers are frequently presented with circumstances which require decisions and, because of this and the definition of a 'decision' given earlier, it is inevitable that evaluation is a regular part of their activity. However, this is no more than saying that life involves evaluation and provides no special category for life in education as lived by educators and this may overlook some rather special characteristics of education. These are considered by Straughan and Wrigley (1980) who argue that evaluation is embodied in education in three important ways. First, it is a fact that education embodies evaluation; ' . . . education is pretty well all about evaluation when one considers the amount of time teachers put into testing . . . ' (p. 4). Second, there is a moral obligation on teachers to evaluate. Given a belief in the importance of educational activity and its powerful influence, ' . . . it is the duty of educators to monitor the effects of that influence . . . ' (p. 4). Third, it is argued that there is a logical and conceptual link between evaluation and education such that:

> . . . one cannot claim to be sincerely engaged in the business of teaching unless one is concerned about how successful one is being in trying to ensure that others master items of knowledge . . . So it might be claimed that one cannot attempt to educate a child without constantly monitoring his progress to evaluate whether his understanding is indeed developing. (p. 5)

These aspects of evaluation as fact, moral obligation and logical construct are considered in a somewhat different way by Black and Broadfoot (1982), but are embedded in their discussion of the teachers' assessment role, with its concern for reporting, diagnosis and guidance. Reporting involves giving information about a pupil's progress through the school, an activity illustrating clearly evaluation as a fact of school life (pp. 7–11). Evaluation as a moral obligation and logical construct is evident in the Black and Broadfoot account of diagnosis and guidance, the former designed to give information on areas and activities which a pupil has not mastered (pp. 11–12) and the latter to assist a pupil to come to a ' . . . better understanding of his own strengths, weaknesses and interests and allow the teacher to become better acquainted with the needs of individual pupils' (p. 12).

These two accounts emphasise the closeness of evaluation to pupils and students, but Harlen (1980) introduces an element of distance between some forms of evaluation and the learners in reminding the reader of other motives for teachers engaging in evaluation. Sometimes the purpose is to fulfil ' . . . an obligation to "evaluate" some sponsored innovation' (p. 59). Other evaluations are carried out ' . . . in response to dissatisfaction felt either within the school or by parents or more generally in the community' (p. 59). Harlen also draws attention to ' . . . so-called evaluations . . . carried out for the purposes of advancing the status or qualifications of individuals . . . (and) the activities of evaluation "bandwagoners" . . . ' (p. 60). Finally, there is evaluation arising from research which Harlen distinguishes from her normal view of evaluation because the researcher has greater freedom in selecting the areas of inquiry (p. 63).

This account of why teachers evaluate indicates that it is a legitimate, indeed essential, activity for teachers. But it also mentions evaluations undertaken in response to parental and community anxieties, and this brings our attention to the interests of non-teachers in these activities.

Why do non-teachers evaluate?

Evaluation is not the sole concern of teachers. Other parties, not least pupils and parents, have legitimate and profound interests in the provision, process and performance of educational institutions because they carry the long-term consequences of the quality of education available. This is an interest which teachers recognise, at least in part, by preparing and sending home reports on individual children. The link between evaluation by teachers and the accountability to non-teachers is made by Black and Broadfoot (1982, p. 86):

> . . . just as it is the legitimate and vital concern of the teacher to keep careful track of his pupils, so it can be argued that his progress . . . is the legitimate concern of many other interested parties . . . the assessment of (pupil) achievement may form the basis of the accountability of a teacher, or of a school, or of the system as a whole to its various customers.

Hoyle (1980, p. 161) also views evaluation as part of the process of accountability to outside interests, although it is also part of the internal management processes of the school, suggesting that different modes of evaluation are suitable depending on the balance between accountability and internal management activity. In his account, the assessment of effectiveness is the critical factor and 'Broadly speaking effectiveness is the degree to which an organization approximates to achieving its goals' (p. 160).

Two other observations by Hoyle are of particular importance. First, despite the intractability of assessing effectiveness it must be recognised as a legitimate demand, although it is right that attempts should be made to alter the views of those who have simplistic notions about this (p. 161). Second, other comments alert us to the diversity of interests concerned with evaluation and the sometimes competing criteria of these interests. He notes that ' . . . the lack of consensus about educational goals means that a whole range of criteria may be considered by different groups' (p. 163).

This lack of consensus is based upon fundamental differences about the purposes of education, which might manifest themselves in different conceptions about an appropriate curriculum. Differences also exist in teaching styles, pastoral care and school organisation, and these would all generate different criteria for evaluating effectiveness. Pateman (1978) classifies this diversity into five different sets of values about the orientation of the education system which should, depending upon the particular dominant value system, focus upon one of the following:

> . . . a) respond to parental preferences; (b) use public resources efficiently; (c) allow teachers professional freedom; (d) meet the requirements of society and (e) satisfy children's needs. (p. 61)

Pateman recognises that people do not normally hold value positions which fit neatly into a single category and that in practice beliefs about the purposes of education are more complicated. But even this classification leaves no room for doubt about the potential for tension and conflict between those with diverse views about the purposes of education. Such disputes lead immediately to disagreements about appropriate criteria for use in evaluations because the choice of criteria used for measurement reflect the presumed purposes or goals of an institution or a system. In these respects there is an inescapable political nature to evaluation (House 1973, p. 3 and Lawton 1980, p. 109).

Conflict and tensions over criteria and purposes make evaluation a battleground between the several groups with an interest in education, whether they are teachers, pupils and parents, employers, the LEA, the DES, the churches or the MSC, to name but a few. The relationships between these groups in the theatre of evaluation is the subject of the next section of the chapter, but it is important to include a brief note about the changed climate in which evaluation is taking place.

Changing climate?

Despite the question mark in the title there is little doubt about the changed climate in which evaluation occurs. Several chapters of this book refer to the more hostile climate within which education must survive and there is no purpose in further examining here the reasons for those changes; instead the reader's attention is drawn particularly to the discussions in Chapters 2 and 4.

However, it is important to recognise that demands for more overt evaluation, which is an underlying theme of the Government White Paper, *Better Schools* (DES 1985), are a product of this general decline in public confidence in education. A more overt and systematic approach to evaluation is seen as a way of reconstructing public confidence. Shipman (1979) noted this relationship:

> All who educate are under pressure to assess their effectiveness and to make the assessment public. You can label that accountability . . . The right to autonomy rests on a duty to evaluate (pp. ix and x)

while Sockett (1980), writing about accountability, catches the mood of public scepticism about education:

> . . . the main point on which all its (accountability) advocates would agree is that it is an attempt to *improve* the quality of education, and, it is sometimes added, to *prove* that this is being done. (p. 10)

If evaluation is one way of proving that something is being done about educational quality, how do the evaluators and the evaluated relate to each other?

THE THEATRE OF EVALUATION

Introduction

Theatre is an appropriate metaphor to consider the relationship between the many interested parties who are actually engaged in educational evaluation. As a metaphor it creates the imagery of the stage, its actors and audiences, but it also creates the imagery of battle and its competing armies. Relationships between evaluators and evaluated within this theatre are complex and it is the purpose of the following sub-section to identify the principal features of their structure, leaving it to the subsequent sub-section to consider the way in which the relationships are conducted within their structure. A final sub-section examines the implications of climate for these relationships and their conduct.

Structural relationships in evaluations

There is no simple dichotomy between evaluators and evaluated. Pupils are the most evaluated people in education but they are also evaluators, often making judgements about their own teachers. Teachers also occupy both roles and, when engaged in self-evaluation, act on themselves as evaluators. In order to narrow the scope of the rest of this section, only the position of individual teachers in relation to evaluation will be discussed. This focus upon the *individual teacher* is to be distinguished from an alternative analysis which could be based upon the *institution* as the focus for an evaluation. In this respect the model is adaptable, able to be applied to individuals, or ostensibly cohesive groups (e.g. departments or faculties) and also whole institutions. This flexibility as to whom or what is regarded as the evaluated is demonstrated in the next chapter, which treats the institution as the focus of attention in the analysis of the inspectorate, while the subject department is the focus in the analysis of a school-based evaluation scheme. The third section, in examining LEA schemes of self-assessment, directly raises the problem of defining the evaluated 'self' in such documents.

   Three sets of parameters are suggested as boundaries structuring evaluation relationships and all are briefly introduced here before being examined in more detail in the following paragraphs. The first parameter is that of an orientation in the evaluation relationship towards autonomy or control. The second is concerned with whether or not those who actually undertake the evaluation are internal or external to the institution, while the third is concerned with whether or not the *results* of an evaluation are principally *for* those being evaluated (i.e. 'internal' to the individual or group being evaluated) or for others (i.e. 'external' to the individual or group being evaluated). In the case of the application of the analysis to the individual teacher, where the results are for others than those being evaluated (i.e. 'external'), these *others* may be physically located inside or outside the institution in which the evaluated works. By comparison, in the application of the analysis to the inspectorate in Chapter 16, where a whole institution is treated as the focus of the evaluation, if the *results* of the evaluation are not *for* the institution (that is, it is for an 'external' interest) then it is, necessarily, for an interest physically located outside the institution.

   The earlier section on 'Why do non-teachers evaluate?' noted the tensions which can arise from conflicting views about the purposes of education. Where the views of non-teachers differ from teachers, but are still pressed, the autonomy of teachers is threatened. Hoyle (1980, p. 173) describes the issue of 'control versus autonomy in the teaching profession' as ' . . . the perennial problem . . . generated yet again by the question of evaluation'. Too much emphasis on control, he argues, ' . . . would lead eventually to the de-professionalization of teachers,' who ' . . . like other professionals, need a degree of autonomy if they are to be effective' (p. 173). But teacher autonomy is not only affected by non-teachers. Several chapters in Part Three of this book examine the role of teachers as managers of other teachers and Chapter 10, in particular, examines some of the difficulties which can arise in those relationships. Given these other chapters, enough has been said here to explain that the tension between control and autonomy, and the continuum between those opposites, must be borne in mind when analysing the relationships between evaluators and evaluated. In the account which follows, the characteristic of an autonomous relationship is that evaluators and evaluated are free to enter or leave the process. In the control relationship the evaluated are obliged to accept the evaluative activity of others upon them because those others control certain sanctions or rewards which are needed by the evaluated.

The second parameter is concerned with who does an evaluation, and distinguishes between evaluations which are carried out by members of an institution from those carried out by external evaluators. Such a distinction is seen to be helpful on the basis that whoever is being evaluated will feel rather differently if it is done by someone within the institution, whom they know and with whom they are likely to have fairly regular contact, as against an outsider who has less obvious identification with the institution and the evaluated. This internal/external distinction is helpful in structuring an answer to the question, *by whom* is the evaluation made, but it does not offer any guidance in examining the question, *for whom* is the evaluation carried out. For this dimension of the proposed model we need to consider the third parameter.

The third parameter structures the relationships according to whether the results of an evaluation are principally for those being evaluated or for others. It is a distinction which could be of great importance in explaining differences in the response of the evaluated to an evaluation and a brief example may be helpful in illustrating these differences. Consultants are normally external to institutions, but the response which they receive is likely to be very different if their report is sent only to the institution and is for its own use, as against a report which is prepared for a body, such as the LEA, which is outside the institution. The knowledge that a wider public than the staff of the evaluated institution will receive the document is likely to affect the view those being evaluated take of the whole process.

Figure 15.1 attempts to show the structures of relationships which can exist between evaluators and evaluated within these three parameters. Along the top of Figure 15.1 is the

Authority — By whom	Autonomy	Control	Authority — For whom
Internal	(1) Personal evaluation	(3) Internal assessment	Internal
Internal	(2) Presentational review	(4) Public audit	External
External	(5) Consultancy	(7) Advice	Internal
External	(6) Research	(8) Inspection	External

Figure 15.1 *Relationships in evaluation.*

authority distinction of autonomy/control which is concerned with the freedom to enter or leave the relationship. On the left of the figure is introduced the internal/external distinction as related to the question, *by whom* is the evaluation done. On the right is introduced the second internal/external distinction, which is in relation to the question, *for whom* is the evaluation done. These three parameters combine to form eight possible sets of relationships and these, with cases as examples, are considered below.

Personal evaluation

This is the most common form of structural relationship, partly because it includes those cases where teachers, privately and often idiosyncratically maybe, judge their own performance normally for their own professional purposes. In this form it impinges not at all on autonomy because the whole activity is internal to the individual. Included here also is an evaluation relationship involving a group of teachers. An example here would be where teachers in a secondary school, who choose to act as a team in preparing a syllabus and its materials, may also engage in team teaching. The evaluation of the materials, the qualitative judgements of process and performance, are all shared activities. These are circumstances where a teacher's classroom autonomy has been altered, but it has been replaced not by control but by an essentially voluntary and team approach to self-evaluation. A university example would be the system of course review. University teachers have a high level of autonomy in designing courses and determining their content. Once a course has been validated (see the account in the internal assessment model), the control of assessment gives its tutors great freedom in determining methods and content. Underlying this autonomy is an ideology which has ' . . . a view of the individual . . . as professionally competent over the full range of activities he undertakes, and this competence includes the necessary knowledge and skills to make or seek insightful and valid appraisals of his work and to act on these appraisals' (Adelman and Alexander 1982, p. 297).

The importance of this personal evaluation is underlined by comments on public sector higher education from Sheila Browne, the former senior chief HMI, who has argued that academic standards are largely guaranteed by staff and not by external pressures, largely because 'We talk an enormous amount about standards in England, but we don't do a great deal about them'. The role of validating bodies and HMI were seen as providing only a somewhat negative guarantee of minimum standards (*THES* 1984, p. 5).

This form of evaluation engaged in by choice and carried out by the evaluator(s) for the evaluated is part of the normally private activity of any teacher wishing to improve practice. Less private, but still engaged in voluntarily, is the category of evaluation relationship described as presentational review.

Presentational review

The characteristics of this form of relationship is that teachers are free to accept or reject the evaluation process, that it is carried out either by the evaluated themselves or another member of the institution, and that the immediate outcome of the evaluation is for others than those being evaluated. It is an important and common form of evaluation relationship, as the examples should illustrate. If teachers want more resources to support new activities, one way of persuading superordinates is to invite them into the classroom and show them what is already being done, as a means of convincing them that the proposed new activities are well worth supporting. It is an evaluation, voluntarily entered into by the evaluated, where the superordinates who are invited to make the judgement are internal to the institution but, on the 'for whom?' parameter of the model, are external to the evaluated.

Beyond the level of the individual teacher, this form of evaluation relationship exists when a department volunteers a presentation of its work to parents, an example where the evaluation is for a group normally located outside the institution. Motives for such activity may be numerous, but they could include the purpose of raising the status of a subject area in order to gain more parental support when pupils make subject choices at 14 +. This voluntary aspect to evaluation does not occur in the next two sets of relationships.

Internal assessment

The underlying ideology of the internal assessment relationship is 'managerial', where superordinates in a hierarchy have a right and an obligation to monitor and judge the work of subordinates. The approach of universities to course approval is an intriguing example of this internal assessment relationship, particularly as the 'managerial' ideology clashes with the importance universities attach to an ideology of professional autonomy. There is a problem in generalising about universities because they are autonomous institutions and there has been little research into their styles of course approval and validation. Church (1983, p. 61) cites a number of commentators in this description,

> The way in which universities handle their curriculum has been denounced as elitist . . . , as amateurish and managerially diffuse . . . and bereft of clear objectives. . . . As a result, it is sometimes said courses can be launched without due thought, put together in any old how and monitored, if at all, by external examiners rather than by proper self-scrutiny.

Church's own research suggests a complex range of different approaches which entails scrutiny which, ' . . . many respondents insist, is not to be regarded as merely a rubber stamp' (p. 62). Some universities, and Surrey is given as an example, introduce external representatives to the procedure and reference is made to a number which have Faculty Development Committees with evaluative responsibilities for new proposals. Set against these observations is that in their replies to this survey only a ' . . . quarter of the universities circulated specifically addressed themselves to this problem, and it appears that the norm is for consideration of courses to be handled by the normal channels of academic governance rather than by special bodies' (p. 61). Such an approach might be expected given an ideology of professional autonomy, which is likely to mean that sanctions embodied in control mechanisms are used very reluctantly. Applying the three parameters of the model, what is clear about this example is that staff who wish to introduce a new course must submit the proposals to certain bodies and these alone have authority to *control* approval of new courses. The process is normally carried out internally to the institution, while the commentaries made and judgement given seem essentially for the information and guidance of those who made the proposal, the evaluated of this particular example.

However, there is a case to be made for locating this process of course approval within the next form of evaluation relationship, if it is argued that the *principal* purpose guiding decisions are concerns about the interests of students and the larger community which a university serves. This raises two important principles. First, it may be that the results of evaluations are intended for more than one party and that it is, therefore, necessary to identify the *principal* party for whom it is prepared. Related to this is the fact that there may be cases where an evaluation is only for one party but that it may be, quite incidentally, useful for others. The second principle is concerned with a distinction between theory and practice. An evaluation structure such as university course approval may in theory be concerned to produce an evaluation *for* students and the community but in practice, because of the conflict with notions of professional autonomy, the process of managerial control is so weak that the evaluation is effectively for the support and guidance of those who make the submissions. This last aspect contrasts with the next form of evaluation relationship.

Public audit

The substantive difference between this and the earlier relationship is that the results of the evaluation are principally for someone other than those being evaluated. Thus, the assessments of several teachers carried out by a head teacher before making a decision as to an internal promotion is done for the managerial purposes of the head and not with a supportive, staff development purpose in mind. A second example would be those cases of school-based self-evaluation schemes, where the principal purpose was to demonstrate to a sceptical public outside the school that it is working hard at improving performance. This particular relationship is examined further in the next chapter, in the sections which consider 'Departmental review' and 'LEA self-assessment schemes'.

Consultancy

The principal features of a consultancy relationship are that the evaluated teacher, department or institution enters the relationship voluntarily, and that the evaluator is external to the institution but its results are for the evaluated. Normally then, we might expect an externally located professional, often a teacher or former teacher, doing evaluative work within an institution which is in the position of having invited in the evaluator, is able to ask the evaluator to leave and, ultimately, is able to reject or ignore the evaluator's conclusions. It may be a relatively uncommon model, perhaps particularly at the level of a teacher and possibly a department, but its use is growing at the level of the institution. Within the field of education management in the UK the intention of BEMAS, the relevant professional association, to develop a register of consultants may encourage the growth of this form of evaluation relationship.

Research

Research undertaken by academics is an appropriate example of this type of relationship. It is voluntarily entered into and the researchers are not only external but also direct their results to an external audience. A study like that of Rutter et al (1979) on the performance of schools is a clear example of this type of relationship. When the outcomes are known, they may be of value to those who were the subject of study, but that is essentially incidental to the investigation where the aim was to inform a wider audience.

Advice

The categories of advice and inspection are particularly important forms of external evaluation and they will also be examined in the next chapter in relation to the work of the inspectorate and LEA self-assessment schemes. Accordingly, these two sections will outline briefly the characteristics of the relationships and consider examples different from those which follow in Chapter 16.

In the case of the advice relationship, the evaluated must accept the intervention of the evaluator who is normally located outside the institution, while the purpose of the evaluation is principally for those being evaluated. The role of LEA advisers in assisting poor teachers is an example of this relationship, where a head asks an adviser to assist a poor teacher. The teacher may have no choice as to whether or not the adviser is brought in, but the purpose is essentially one of support and guidance, the giving of advice.

Inspection

Much of the work of HMI falls into this relationship. They are external to the institution and can insist on entry, while the purpose of their evaluation is principally for others than those being evaluated. Since their role, and that of LEA inspectors and advisers, will be considered in Chapter 16, they will not be discussed further here. Instead, the role of CNAA course-approval teams in public-sector higher education will be considered. It fits the inspection relationship since members are external and have a control relationship to those who wish to introduce or continue courses, and their evaluation is principally for the CNAA and not for the relevant teaching staff. McNay et al (1982) give an account of CNAA course validation in public-sector higher education and the account lists the criteria which must be used when judging courses (pp. 43–4). The judgement decides whether a course may be introduced, altered, continued or stopped. However, the authoritativeness of this judgement is doubted by many participants. One regular member of a CNAA visiting panel commented, 'It's terribly difficult to make a judgement — the team could just have had an off day. If we'd gone the previous week, may be the decision would have been different' (McNay et al 1982, p. 49) and a course-team member's view shows the anxieties which can exist over the criteria being used, 'I can design you a course now, get it through the panel and recruit for next year. That's because I know what they want. But it's not what I want' (p. 48).

Some of these doubts, particularly within the institutions, can be traced back to the ideology of professional competence discussed earlier and the belief that many polytechnics and colleges of higher education have the capacity, like the universities, to be self-validating. This goes some way to explain the setting up of the committee of inquiry, chaired by Sir Norman Lindop, into the validation of degree courses in the public sector and which is due to report in the early summer of 1985 (*Education* 1984, p. 320).

The choice of the CNAA as an example was deliberate because the changing nature of its approach to evaluation shows that describing the structure of the relationship is not enough. It is necessary to recognise that the way in which a relationship is conducted has important implications for the quality of the interaction between evaluators and evaluated. The next sub-section considers this aspect.

Conduct within evaluation relationships

Two parameters are suggested which appear to guide conduct within already structured evaluation relationships; one is concerned with the setting of criteria and the other with the judgements of outcomes.

Figure 15.2 makes it possible to differentiate between alternative models of conduct. The first parameter concerns the setting of criteria for evaluation, an activity which can range from the evaluated negotiating, or setting, their own criteria, to the evaluated having to accept criteria imposed by others. Imposition may give rise to criteria being set which do not match the desired objectives of the evaluated and Harlen (1980, p. 57) dismisses evaluation on inappropriate criteria as not being legitimate. If she means by this that the evaluated may not welcome criteria which are inappropriate to their objectives she is undoubtedly correct, but if she means that evaluators must only set criteria with which the evaluated concur, she is not correct. Criteria reflect objectives and are selected as a means of helping evaluators decide whether their objectives are being achieved. They must be

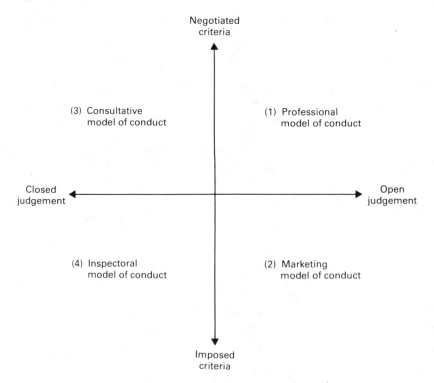

Figure 15.2 *Conduct within evaluation relationships.*

recognised as weapons in the struggle over who controls evaluation. Adopting criteria which reflect the preferences of evaluators can be seen as a means of forcing the evaluated to alter their practices and purposes, so that they more closely match those of the evaluators.

The second parameter is about controlling the outcomes of evaluation and is along a range from closed judgement to open judgement. By a closed judgement is meant that those being evaluated have no part in preparing the final evaluation statement. By an open judgement, the evaluated have influence over the preparation and even the content of the final statement. These distinctions are clarified in the examples which follow.

The 'professional conduct' model gives the evaluated most freedom. They are not only able to negotiate the criteria which will govern the evaluation but may also be able to prepare the final report. Teachers evaluating themselves fit into this category but so also might external evaluators working to the type of evaluation proposed by Parlett (1974). The 'marketing conduct' model is given that name because it is intended to give the impression of some flexibility in the relationship between evaluators and evaluated. The 1980 Education Act is an intriguing example of this model of conduct. While it requires schools to publish their exam results, the school is left to present those results in the form it feels most appropriate. Some approaches to research may fit this model in that the researchers adopt certain criteria, for measurement, but might discuss their judgements with, and be influenced by, the schools. The 'inspectoral model' would certainly include the HMI reports of today, although over a decade ago they would have probably fitted the 'professional model'. This changing emphasis is examined more fully in the subsequent chapter. Finally there is the 'consultative model' of conduct, where criteria are negotiated but the final judgement is not. Here the evaluators agree, with those being evaluated, the criteria which would properly judge an event, but the evaluators, who could be outside consultants, make their own judgements. Dean (1979, p. 148) gives the example of LEA advisers who need to be sensitive to ' . . . frames of reference of those involved and arrive at some common view of what is being assessed and how the assessments are to be judged'. This last clause suggests an openness on judgement, but since Dean goes on to explain that the adviser must also take account of the aims of the Authority and the community, the final judgement must incorporate these factors and be that of the adviser, not the institution.

Not included in these examples are the plethora of evaluation documents which have now been produced by LEAs. They do not fit into a single category because it turns on how they are used. The Solihull documents (1979; 1980), for example, appear to fit the 'professional model' because it is apparently left to the schools to decide whether and how to use them. The Oxford document (1979), on the other hand, could fit more than one category, depending upon how governing bodies in the county interpret their role and how they interact with the heads, a reservation which echoes some of the issues to be examined in Chapter 17 in relation to the study of governing bodies, by Bacon (1978), in Sheffield. This question of interpretation also informs the last part of this section on 'The Theatre of Evaluation'.

Relationships, conduct and climate

The structures of relationships and modes of conduct examined here raise fundamental questions about the relative independence of individual teachers and institutions.

Differing relationships and conducts affect the capacity of teachers and educational institutions to determine their purposes and to control judgements of their performance. The relationships and conduct which dominate evaluative practice are, at any time, mediated by the climate in which education must work. It has already been noted that the education service finds itself in a more hostile climate, weak in public confidence and support. Its consequence is that we would expect less emphasis on autonomy and more on control relationships, with increased activity by external evaluators. Also, modes of conducting evaluation would move towards imposed criteria and closed judgements. Moreover, these changes should also be reflected in the techniques of evaluation which are adopted, and this provides the focus of the next section.

TECHNIQUES OF EVALUATION

Introduction

Writing on the subject of accountability, Nisbet (1978, Chapter 4) lists five different methods of assessment, four of which apply also to evaluation. They are standardised tests, conventional examinations, inspection and self-assessment by schools. The use of each of these for purposes of evaluation has altered and/or grown in recent years. It should also be realised that while some of these can be used on their own for an evaluation, it is more likely that evaluators may draw on a range of procedures. In the same chapter, Nisbet cites the eight dimensions on which, Stake (1976) suggests, evaluation procedures may vary. These dimensions are:

(a)   formative ————————— summative;
(b)   informal ————————— formal;
(c)   case particular ————————— generalization;
(d)   process ————————— product;
(e)   descriptive ————————— judgemental;
(f)   responsive ————————— preordinate;
(g)   holistic ————————— analytic;
(h)   internal ————————— external;

and will be used illustratively in the following discussion of the four different methods of assessment already mentioned.

Standardised tests

Nisbet (1978, pp. 102–104) refers to the '. . . wealth of experience in the construction, use and analysis of tests to assess national and regional standards . . .' but also to the scepticism towards testing by some of those who recall the 11 +. Such scepticism has not prevented the Assessment of Performance Unit (APU) attempting to develop item banks for testing different areas of the curriculum, with the consequence of providing evaluators of the system at the national level with an extra source of data for informing their judgements on the performance of the education system. Standardised tests can also be used locally, as in the case of an LEA in the north-west which each year sent to its primary school heads a letter giving two pieces of information from an authority-wide reading test; one was the average performance of the tested age group in the whole authority, and the other the average performance of the same age group in the particular school. The aim was to stimulate those schools performing below the average to improve the performance of their pupils.[1]

The use of standardised tests in the ways described here fits best the right hand side of the dimensions listed from Stake (1976) above. They are formal evaluations in the sense defined earlier in the chapter, more concerned with generalisation than with understanding the particular circumstances of individual pupils and institutions, product oriented, judgemental and external. They are also preordinate in that criteria have already been set, and analytic in that they examine parts of provision, process and performance and do not attempt to place parts in the context of the whole. The formative/summative dimension does not easily fit this kind of evaluation activity, possibly because it seems to describe individual projects and not long-term programmes of evaluation. Formative evaluation, according to Eraut et al (1975, p. 13) is where the ' . . . audience is the development team and the purpose is to guide further development work' and summative evaluation is where the ' . . . audience is the decision-makers and the purpose is to guide their decisions'. It leads to ' . . . a final report which seeks to brief all those who may participate in decisions about the adopting or implementation of the project's proposal . . . ' (p. 19).

The use of standardised tests by an LEA in the way described here is open to the same criticisms as are levelled against using conventional examination results for evaluating school performance and these are described in the next section.

Conventional examinations

Gray (1979) summarises the crudeness of an approach which assumes that it is possible to judge:

> . . . how well a school is doing for the pupils and community it serves by selecting a few statistics and comparing them with the national average. In practice, this would appear to mean *one* statistic: the number of examination passes. (pp. 23–24)

It is an approach which, at the very least, ignores the quality of intake and any outcomes other than examination achievement. However, as a consequence of the 1980 Education Act, schools are now required to publish their exam results; a development, like that of the APU, of a movement towards making evaluation processes more controlled than professionally autonomous and imposing criteria for judgements which will inevitably affect school processes.

The use of exam results in this way also fits the right-hand side of Stake's eight dimensions, although on this occasion it might also be appropriate to see their use as fitting the right side of the formative/summative dimension, especially in relation to their publication as a guide to parents making school choices for their children.

Inspection

Inspection as conceived by Nisbet (1978, pp. 104–105) is a particularly complicated style of assessment because it includes so much, from ' . . . old-style formal inspection . . . ' to 'consultancy', although by this he seems to mean an assessment process which fits the Advice and Inspection relationships described earlier (see Figure 15.1), because the cases cited do not suggest the voluntaryism necessary to fit the consultancy evaluation relationship. Because of this breadth of category, Nisbet suggests an alternative title ' . . . for "inspection", read "external assessment by respected (or respectable) agencies" . . . ' and in this form ' . . . is capable of development into a wide range of techniques'.

In relation to Stake's eight dimensions of evaluation procedures, this inspection style occupies the external end of the internal/external dimension. As for the seven other dimensions, all that can be said is that it depends upon the particular inspection activity. For example, an inspection of a school or college by HMI would tend to the right on some dimensions, being summative, formal and judgemental, but on the left of others, being case particular, process oriented and holistic. An inspection might be located in the centre of the responsive/preordinate dimension because HMI are by no means unresponsive to the particular goals of schools, a proposition supported by an examination of some recent reports.

If the inspection category as defined by Nisbet is about external evaluators, the last style of assessment is concerned with internal evaluation.

Self-assessment

The self-assessment procedure outlined by Nisbet (1978, p. 107) involves a ' . . . formal underpinning and an explicit structure; it is based on a process of self-study by the school . . . '. This is very similar to the 'formal' evaluations defined by Adelman and Alexander (1982, p. 287) and cited earlier. However, in accord with the definition of evaluation given in this chapter the definition of self-assessment used here is broader and includes those often private and informal ways in which teachers judge their own performance.

The boundaries of self-assessment suggest that they are internal, but can reflect either peer-evaluation relationships or internal control relationships. In practice, where consultants are invited in on terms of collaborative evaluation, it is possible to see an external dimension to this self-assessment. Moreover, as many self-assessment schemes seem to begin with local authority initiatives, the degree of institutional autonomy must be taken to be problematic. Indeed, they might be viewed as a means of increasing external control, a proposition all too likely given the changing climate to which reference has been made.

A section in Chapter 16 is devoted to examining LEA-sponsored schemes of self-assessment. However, it should be noted here that to explore the meanings and understandings attached to these schemes by those involved in their use would require empirical investigations along the lines described for 'Rivendell' in Chapter 14. Such a research methodology is echoed in Chapter 19 where Derek Slater draws attention to the need to examine the context of educational change. These caveats on the need for research to clarify the use of the evaluation schemes make it impossible convincingly to locate them on Stake's eight dimensions along which evaluation procedures may vary. However, it is appropriate to note that since 13 of the 21 schemes examined by G. Elliott et al (1981) have formal or informal links with LEA inspectors, and 16 use a detailed objectives model, there is a strong likelihood that these *ostensibly* 'self-evaluation' schemes incorporate a shift to a greater involvement of external evaluators and a move to relationships of advice and inspection.

The shift suggested here is what would be expected given the changed climate in which education operates. It is in the same direction as the resurgence in the use of standardised tests by APU, the requirement for schools to publish examination results, the increase in formal inspections and the publication of HMI reports. That the interpretation of methods and techniques of evaluation seem increasingly in the direction of control is the logical consequence of the changing structure of relationships between evaluators and evaluated.

CONCLUSION

This chapter began by asking how it is that evaluation is simultaneously a well-established and accepted activity within education and also an innovation treated with a mixture of hostility, scepticism and caution. It has been the purpose of the chapter to describe, analyse and explain this apparent contradiction. It began by describing evaluation as the process of information gathering, analysis and calculation leading up to a decision. This broad definition offers no obvious explanation why it should be suspected by teachers. However, the next question, on motives for evaluation, begins to offer an explanation. Evaluation as practiced by non-teachers and also by some teachers involves making judgements about the work of teachers and the performance of educational institutions. When this is examined more closely in 'The Theatre of Evaluation', it becomes clear that evaluation is about power and control in education and that there is increasing emphasis on those evaluation relationships which mean greater control over teachers. Consequently, when techniques of evaluation are examined, we find an increasing emphasis on interpreting techniques in ways which reflect the preferences of controller evaluators.

It is because some forms of evaluation are seen as methods of increasing control on teachers that they are often greeted with hostility and caution. At worst, they may be treated with open hostility and endeavours to reject new forms of evaluation out of hand. There are several reasons why such a response would be mistaken.

First, evaluation at the more public and systematic level which is emerging is one way by which teachers can demonstrate to a sceptical public that they are using their best efforts to improve the quality of education. Second, moves to schemes where teachers respond more openly to evaluators can serve as opportunities for teachers to explain the complexities of education process and product, thereby educating their evaluators who may sometimes have conceptions of education which are simplistic. Third, teachers do not have a monopoly of wisdom on educational purposes and a more public approach to evaluation may lead to teachers learning more about the educational purposes of their evaluators, as in the John Elliott et al (1981, Chapter 3) Cambridge Accountability Project. His account illuminates the interest of many parents in the quality of school process rather than only in the product, adopting an humanistic perspective on schooling, where concerns about happiness and the quality of relationships predominate. Fourth, a more formal and open process of in-school evaluation enables teachers to learn from each other. Private and idiosyncratic approaches are not always the best. Fifth, since nothing can prevent the 'stake-holders' from evaluating education, a more open and public system gives teachers a better opportunity for negotiating and influencing the criteria to be used.

Finally, it is useful to remind ourselves again of the theatrical metaphor adopted earlier, and of teachers as the actors. Even if the lines of the play were to be written increasingly by members of the audience, teachers like actors are still left with immense opportunities of interpretation. However, such a comparison is surely too weak a view of the influence of teachers, and Peston (1980, p. 120) is probably closer to the mark:

> . . . education in the United Kingdom is producer-dominated in several senses. Decisions as to curriculum, syllabus, and pedagogic method are taken largely by teachers. They are subject to external pressure in the form of examinations (although these too are essentially the business of teachers), and to a moderate degree by Her Majesty's Inspectorate. (At the higher level there is the CNAA for the public sector, but virtually no external control for the universities.) Teachers are limited by the resources made available to them by officials and politicians, and there is a minimum performance requirement to do with actually turning up and doing the job in a nominally correct fashion.

The last sentence draws attention to resources and there is a crucial link to evaluation. How well teachers respond to an increasingly formal and public process of evaluation may be crucial for the level of resources available and all that may mean for educational quality.

NOTES

1. Information supplied informally by the Chief Education Officer of the Authority.

REFERENCES

Adelman, C. and Alexander, R. (1982) *The Self-Evaluating Institution*. Reprinted as 'Evaluation, Validation and Accountability' in Boyd-Barrett, O. et al (ed.) (1983) *Approaches to Post-School Management*. London: Harper and Row.

Bacon, W. (1978) *Public Accountability and the Schooling System*. London: Harper and Row.

Black, H. and Broadfoot, P. (1982) *Keeping Track of Teaching*. London: Routledge and Kegan Paul.

Church, C. H. (1983) 'Course Control in the University Sector'. In Church, C. H. (1983) *Practice and Perspective in Validation*. Guildford: Society for Research into Higher Education.

Dean, J. (1979) 'Evaluation and Advisers'. Paper presented at the annual conference of the British Educational Research Association, Brunel University, September.

(DES) Department of Education and Science (1985) *Better Schools* (White Paper), Cmnd. 9469. London: HMSO.

Drake, K. (1979) 'Decision-making in the classroom: a microeconomic analysis'. In

Eggleston, S. J. (ed) (1979) *Teacher decision-making in the classroom; a collection of papers*, 82–92. London: Routledge and Kegan Paul.

Education (1984) 'A new committee to examine validation', **163**(16), 20 April.

Elliott, G. et al (1981) *Self Evaluation and the Teacher: An Annotated Bibliography and Report on Current Practice, 1980, Part 2.* University of Hull/Schools Council.

Elliott, J. et al (1981) *School Accountability.* Grant McIntyre.

Eraut, M., Goad, L. and Smith, G. (1975) *The Analysis of Curriculum Materials.* University of Sussex Education Area, Occasional Paper No 2.

Gray, J. (1979) 'The Statistics of Accountability: Two approaches to improving information for LEA decision-making'. In *Educational Policy Bulletin* 7(1), Spring, 23–42.

Harlen, W. (1980) 'Evaluation in Education'. In Straughan, R. and Wrigley, J. (ed.) *Values and Evaluation in Education.* London: Harper and Row.

House, E. (1973) (ed.) *School Evaluation: The Politics and Process.* Berkeley. California: McCutchan.

Hoyle, E. (1980) 'Evaluation of the Effectiveness of Educational Institutions'. *Educational Administration*, **8**(2), 159–178.

Lawton, D. (1980) *The Politics of the School Curriculum.* London: Routledge and Kegan Paul.

McNay, J., McCormick, R. with Torode, P. (1982) 'Case Study 3, The CNAA Educational Studies "A Third Level Course".' *Curriculum Evaluation and Assessment in Educational Institutions E364.* Milton Keynes: The Open University Press.

Nisbet, J. (1978) 'Procedures for Assessment'. In Becher, T. and Maclure (ed.) *Accountability in Education.* Windsor: NFER.

Oxfordshire, C. C. (1979) *Starting Points in Self Evaluation.* Education Department.

Parlett, M. (1974) 'The New Evaluation'. *Trends in Education*, **34**, 13–18, July.

Pateman, T. (1978) 'Accountability, Values and Schooling'. In Becher, T. and Maclure, S. (ed) *Accountability in Education.* Windsor: NFER.

Peston, M. (1980) 'Economic Aspects of Accountability'. *Education Policy Bulletin*, **8**(2), Autumn, 115–126.

Rutter, M., Maughan, B., Mortimore, P. and Ouston, J. (1979) *Fifteen Thousand Hours — Secondary Schools and their effects on Children.* London: Open Books.

Shackle, G. L. S. (1969) *Decision, Order and Time in Human Affairs*, 2nd edition. Cambridge: Cambridge University Press.

Shipman, M. D. (1979) *In-School Evaluation.* London: Heinemann.

Sockett, H. (ed) (1980) *Accountability in the English Education System.* Sevenoaks: Hodder and Stoughton.

Solihull (1979) *Evaluating the School: A Guide for Secondary Schools in the Metropolitan Borough of Solihull.* Solihull.

Solihull (1980) *Evaluating the Primary School: A Guide for Primary Schools in the Metropolitan Borough of Solihull.* Solihull.

Stake, R. E. (1976) *Evaluating Educational Programmes: the Need and the Response.* Paris: OECD/CERI.

Straughan, R. and Wrigley, J. (ed.) (1980) *Values and Evaluation in Education.* London: Harper and Row.

THES (1984) 'Staff "guarantee standards"'. Times Higher Education Supplement. 6 April, (596) p. 5.

16

THE PRACTICE OF EVALUATION

Ken Lambert, Peter Ribbins and Hywel Thomas

INTRODUCTION

The previous chapter proposed two models, one for analysing the structures of relationships between evaluators and evaluated (Figure 15.1) and the second for analysing the modes of conduct within those relationships (Figure 15.2). This chapter will apply those models in an analysis of three important approaches to evaluative activity in education. The case to be examined first, and at greatest length, in view of the significance of their position, is the relationship and conduct with educational institutions of HMI and LEA advisers and inspectors. They offer an example of evaluators who are clearly external to the institution and normally in a control relationship. But the question of 'for whom' they carry out their evaluations is more problematic and much of this part of the chapter will focus on this issue. This will be followed by an analysis of departmental review at Great Barr School, Birmingham, interesting because of the way it has sought to make more formal, systematic and open the informal processes of evaluation of staff typically carried out by senior management in schools and colleges. This is a case where the evaluators are internal and in a control relationship. Issues to be examined further include the problems — for whom is the evaluation carried out and how is it conducted? Finally, the use of evaluation documents produced by LEAs will be considered, representing as they do an important initiative towards institutional self-evaluation. This section discusses the problems of the definition of 'self' and also analyses the difficulties of locating the relationship structures which exist in each of these schemes.

INSPECTORS AND ADVISERS AS EVALUATORS

Introduction

Inspectors are to be found within most educational systems although what they do remains a matter of considerable confusion and misunderstanding, particularly in the UK. In the previous chapter Hywel Thomas offered a comprehensive heuristic model for the analysis of evaluation in educational contexts which focuses on structures of relationships, modes of conduct, possible techniques and the influence of changing political and educational climates. If this account is justified it ought to have explanatory value in an examination of the role of inspector as evaluator. A full interrogation of Thomas's model, let alone of all aspects of the work of inspectors in different countries, is well beyond the scope of this chapter. This analysis will focus instead upon the narrower issue of how inspectors as evaluators relate and interact with those whom they evaluate and with those for whom they evaluate in the particular context of England and Wales. First, what is 'inspection' and how does it relate to the concept of 'evaluation'?

'Inspection', 'assessment' and 'evaluation'

In the last chapter 'evaluation' was seen as entailing some process of appraisal designed to lead to a choice of action. To 'appraise' is to estimate the amount or worth of something. 'Inspection' occurs when an appraisal takes the form of a careful scrutiny or close examination and an 'inspector' is ' . . . an officer appointed to examine into . . . and report upon, the working of some department or institution, or the due observance of certain laws and regulations . . . ' (*Shorter Oxford English Dictionary*). It might be noted that such a definition makes no mention of 'for whom' an inspection is made and offers no advice as 'to whom' any report should be made. What it does stress is that inspection may be usefully thought of as an aspect of evaluation and that the inspector is a particular kind of evaluator. Paradoxically, while educational inspectors in this country and elsewhere do many things other than evaluate, yet evaluation of some kind is at the heart of all they do.

Structures of relationships in evaluation in education

Metaphors such as theatre or arena seem appropriate in thinking about the structures and patterns of relationships between those concerned with evaluation in education. In analysing these relationships Thomas calls attention to three key parameters derived from the possible answers which may be given to the following three questions—'who evaluates?', 'who controls whether an evaluation is to take place?' and 'for whom is the evaluation undertaken?'. As applied to the particular case of the inspectorate the first two questions raise relatively few problems but the third does.

'Who evaluates' and 'who decides if an evaluation is to take place?'

In England and Wales, unlike in many other countries, there is *both* a national inspectorate (usually known as Her Majesty's Inspectorate) *and* a local inspectorate (sometimes known as the local advisory service).[1] Rayner (1982), in the context of an examination of HMI as one of a series of studies being carried out in each department of the Civil Service under the co-ordination of Sir Derek Rayner, offers an authoritative attempt to distinguish between the two services:

> HMI work nationally. Local advisers work for the authority which employs them. HMI report to the Secretary of State and the Department (DES) in the context of central government responsibilities and using national yardsticks. Local advisers report only to their LEA and within the context of local policies and standards.

Inspection, then, is clearly a form of *external* evaluation in the sense that it is carried out by a cadre of officials who are appointed for the purpose and who are not members of the educational institutions which may be the subject of their examination. What of the issue of who controls whether an evaluation should take place?

In analysing this question, Thomas distinguishes between 'autonomous' relationships (in which it is those who are the possible subject of an evaluation who determine if and when it will take place) and 'control' relationships (in which it is those who evaluate who make such decisions). Although teachers do sometimes attempt to frustrate, with varying levels of success, the efforts of inspectors to scrutinise what they do, the latter's right to inspect is well established by historical precedent, by custom, and by law. This view, as it applies to HMI, is bluntly expressed in a recent DES (1983a) policy statement: 'The Inspectorate has an unfettered right of access to any institution it may inspect' (p. 2). The historical antecedents of such a claim date back to the origins of the National Inspectorate in 1839 and to one of the first statements made by the newly constituted Committee of Education of the Privy Council: 'The Committee recommend that no further grant be made now or hereafter for the establishment of a normal school or of any other school unless the right of inspection be maintained'. Over time this right has been refined and strengthened in various ways and: 'The present statutory base for the inspectorate's work is section 77 of the Education Act of 1944. This requires the Secretary of State to cause inspections to be made of primary, secondary, special and independent schools, establishments of further and higher education and of teacher training and adult education' (DES 1983a, p. 2).

In a sense, then, the 'right' has become a 'duty'. But this should not be taken to mean that the Secretary of State is under an obligation to ensure that every educational institution is the subject of an annual review or even that there should be a regular programmed cycle of such inspections. As another DES (1983b) booklet, designed to explain the work of HMI to parents, points out 'there are over 32 000 schools and more than 5000 further education establishments in England and Wales . . . With a maximum of 490 HMIs, the inspectorate cannot hope to carry out regular inspections of each institution . . . ' (p. 4). Rayner (1982) confirms that: 'Although it may have been the case in the last century that all schools in receipt of a grant from central government were inspected formally on an annual basis, that this was no longer true by 1902 . . . (by) the first world war, the cycle of full inspections of secondary . . . schools was envisaged as every five years . . . had become ten years by 1922 and effectively got longer and longer . . . ' and was finally abandoned in 1968 (p. 12). Not that HMI has ever given up inspections, although, as Rayner (1982) shows, the extent of full inspections (defined as 'inspections resulting in written reports to the schools concerned' (p. 100) conducted by HMI are subject to considerable fluctuations in the numbers undertaken. Between 1970–1980 the numbers of inspections varied in primary schools from 4 (1977) to 82 (1979), of secondary schools 6 (1977) to 78 (1980), and of FE and HE establishments between 15 (1977) and 46 (1980) (see Appendix B, pp. 99–100). The DES (1983b) now stresses the numbers of visits and inspections that HMI undertake: 'In any year the overall programme of inspectors' visits is likely to involve almost all secondary schools and FE colleges and nearly 5000 of the 28 000 primary schools . . . Each year perhaps 20 institutions, mainly schools, have a formal inspection because the Secretary of State or HMI or the LEA believe this sort of help necessary. The other 250 or so institutions formally inspected each year are either chosen to illustrate particular aspects of education or ways of doing this, or are suggested by the computer as part of a sample' (p. 5). What is clear from all this is that as far as HMI is concerned, those chosen for evaluation have little choice in the matter. Is this true also of the local inspectorate?

Although the duty of the LEA to cause such inspections as it deems necessary is less clearly stated in law than is that of the Secretary of State, its right to do so has an equally unambiguous statutory base — a point emphasised in an *Education Digest* (1976) on the 'Advisory Service' which quotes s. 77(3) of the 1944 Act: 'Any local authority may cause an inspection to be made of any establishment maintained by the authority; and such inspections shall be made by officers appointed by the LEA' (p. i). Thus while some LEAs, some teachers and even some local authority advisers are reluctant to see the adviser as an inspector, the statutory right of an LEA to use its advisers as inspectors is clear. Teachers, as some of the teachers at William Tyndale discovered to their costs, have no general legal right to refuse to be inspected by a properly constituted local inspectorate (see Auld 1975). Conversely, not all LEAs and by no means all advisers succeed in exercising this right and some choose not to claim it.[2]

All advisers and inspectors are external but while most LEA advisers and all HMI exercise control over whether an evaluation is to take place some local advisers (for example teacher advisers with limited subject responsibility paid under Burnham) do not. It may be helpful to think of the relationship of the former with schools as 'controller evaluation' and of the latter as 'collaborative evaluation'. Thus far the analysis has been straightforward — it becomes much more problematic when attention is given to the question of 'for whom' an evaluation takes place.

'For whom' is the evaluation conducted?

A key issue in determining the attitudes of both evaluators and evaluated to an evaluation is 'for whom' it is seen as being conducted. The notion of 'for whom' in this context is capable of being used in two related but very different senses. In the first sense attention is focused upon the 'audience' to which the evaluation is directed and in the second sense there is the idea of 'in whose interest'. Both senses may be seen as having an internal or an external dimension. The implications of this analysis may be illustrated by taking the case of 'controller evaluation' which may take one or other of two forms — 'advice' and 'inspection' (see Figure 16.1).

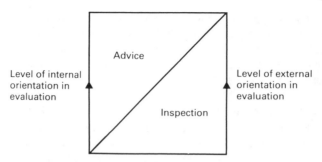

Figure 16.1 *Forms of 'controller evaluation'.*

Those working in educational institutions are much happier if their evaluators adopt an advisory rather than an inspectoral posture. The former is seen as evaluation 'for' those who work within schools and colleges, while the latter is seen as essentially serving the needs of others. Finally, as Figure 16.1 implies, it is possible for evaluators to conduct their evaluations in such a way that they are aimed at both an internal and an external audience and which serves both internal and external interests. This may, in part, explain why not all externally orientated evaluators seem equally threatening to those in the institutions they evaluate. Rayner (1982) makes the point in a chapter dealing with the relationship between HMI and the local advisory service:

> We have received much evidence from teachers on the value they place on local advisers as facilitators of change . . . the extension of this role in the direction of inspection is, however, questioned and regarded as less acceptable. This view stems from a perception of the local advisers as being part of a local administration involved with teachers' prospects and seemingly at one and the same time author and critic. (p. 35)

Winkley (1982) traces this problem back to the origins of the local advisory service in London (1872) and Birmingham (1876). As local 'administration' and 'inspection' evolved as separate branches of the same local service, 'and the inspectorates increasingly came under the umbrella of an administrative hierarchy', the local inspector faced 'the dilemma of being expected to be both a "highly qualified snooper" (to use Edmonds' (1962) phrase), and also, increasingly, to advise teachers at a sophisticated professional level, which required gaining their close confidence and co-operation' (p. 121). Since Callaghan's Ruskin speech of 1976 'a number of LEAs have restyled their "advisory services" as "inspectorates" (often to the dismay of advisers themselves) and, where they can overcome or ignore teacher opposition, have instituted more formal inspections of school . . . ' (Winkley 1982, p. 132). This may be true, but it remains the case that some LEAs and many advisers do not see themselves as in the business of inspecting. For example Rayner (1982) remarks that 'unlike many advisers in England, local authority advisers in Wales are not in general seen to have an inspectoral role' (p. 77). And Bolam (1978), in attempting to quantify the kinds of activities advisers engage in, found that the most common (93 per cent of his sample claimed to spend *some* time on in-service education and 85 per cent claimed to spend some time on advising individual staff) had little to do with evaluation, let alone inspection. Furthermore, while some 66 per cent of his sample were engaged in the evaluation of teachers and 50 per cent in carrying out general inspection, these were also the activities which they wished to give less time to.

It may be that, for whatever reason, teachers are reluctant to acknowledge the legitimacy of any evaluation that smacks of inspection, but we still need to explain why inspection by HMI seems to be so much more acceptable than inspection by local advisers. Various explanations have been offered for this, including the higher status, greater experience, etc. of HMI. Perhaps a more plausible line of argument stresses the extent to which: 'Whether they like it or not, advisory services have tended to become instruments of purpose defined by administrators, and are in danger of being absorbed into the administrative will' (Winkley 1982, p. 135). The corollary of this is that not only are local advisers increasingly seen as taking an inspectoral role but also a significant administrative one as well. As Rayner (1982) puts it, 'local advisers are involved to a greater extent with the appointment and promotion of teachers, supervision of probationers . . . the allocation of resources to individual schools . . . increasingly advisers have also been spending considerable time on the redeployment of individual teachers as school rolls fall' (pp. 34, 35). Whereas, from the teachers point of view, 'HMI is seen to have the inestimable advantage of being independent of the LEA and, therefore, impartial'. Furthermore, other than their powers to inspect and report 'They have no powers. They have to earn attention by what they are and what they do. Their effectiveness depends on relationships which have to be worked at. Perhaps their most significant characteristics are their professional independence from Government, local authorities and teachers . . . ' (DES 1983b, p. 3).

Although Fiske (1977) envisages a role for local advisers as 'keepers of the conscience of the CEO', there seems little reason to believe that this is the way they are thought of by teachers. As advisers are seen to perform a growing number of administrative functions their status as independent professional advisers may be eroded in the eyes of many teachers who then view attempts by such advisers to inspect as confirming their fears. Advisers as inspectors, then, may expect increasing resistance from teachers, not so much because they are seen to undertake such inspections for an external audience but because they do so for those who employ teachers and, apparently, as the obedient servants of the LEA. Since HMIs are widely regarded amongst teachers as 'independent' and since they are clearly not the servants of the LEA, this may explain, in part anyway, why their engagement in inspectoral activities arouses less suspicion and hostility amongst teachers. But how real is their independence and, as Rogers (1983) asks 'whose servants are they?'.

It may not be doing much violence to Rayner's (1982) argument to caricature it as proposing that HMI are servants by statute and independent by profession. Certainly, Rayner believes that the meaning and limitations of their independence is widely misunderstood and the report attempts to put the record straight.

> HMI does not have a constitutional independence . . . the duty of causing inspections to be made in the maintained sector rests with the Secretary of State and inspections are carried out on his behalf. Moreover, the Permanent Secretary is responsible to the Secretary of State for the management of the work of the whole Department and, as accounting officer, is accountable to Parliament for the expenditure on the Inspectorate as well as the rest of the Department. (p. 10)

Rayner also stresses that although the 1944 Act lays the duty of causing inspections to be made: 'Neither the purpose nor the nature of such inspections are defined and the implication is that the inspections are to be such as the Secretary of State thinks fit. Indeed HMI has no function independent of that of the Secretary of State . . . the purposes of inspection derive from the Secretary of State's functions and needs and are directed towards assisting him in the discharge of his statutory responsibilities' (pp. 7, 9).

Within these limitations, Rayner acknowledges that HMI does enjoy a degree of professional independence and, indeed, must do so if it is to retain its credibility within the educational system as a whole. The report identifies three strands of this professional independence based upon: first, the right of direct access of the Senior Chief Inspector to the Secretary of State; second, the long established 'right' that anything that is published will be as the Inspector involved wrote it given that 'the duty of the inspectorate is to report what they see and not what others would wish them to see' (p. 10). Kogan (1971) stresses that 'No administration dare change an HMI report' and neither, it would appear, does even the Secretary of State. Furthermore, 'Since January 1983 the Secretary of State . . . has published all the reports made to him by HMI following formal inspections of schools, colleges and other educational provision in England' (DES 1984, Preface); and third, the fact that it is for the inspectorate 'to decide how to go about the business of inspection and what to inspect' (Rayner 1982, p. 10). However, this apparently unqualified precept did not prevent the writers of the report from making a number of critical observations about the way in which the FHE Inspectorate went about the business of inspection or from offering a number of specific recommendations as to how they ought to do it (pp. 20–21).

Rayner's propositions that HMI first does have and ought to have a significant degree of professional independence, and, second, does not possess and ought not to exercise constitutional independence of a more fundamental kind, can both be challenged on a variety of grounds.

There are those who question whether HMI exercises any real independence. Rogers (1983) reports Fowler, a former junior Minister of Education, as accusing 'HMI of caving in to Govenment pressure to endorse and promote "traditional values" in schools (and) instanced the highly critical HMI report on Madeley Court Community School . . . The implication was that the Government saw community schools as reflecting unsavoury modern methods of schooling, and so the Inspectorate was leaned on to produce a report backing the Government's view'. These remarks, made at a teachers' conference on community schools, were vigorously denied by an HMI attending the conference: 'The Inspectorate had never been leaned on in that way — and would reject any attempt to do so. The report was critical because Madeley Court was not operating as well as it should — not because it was a community school' (Rogers 1983, p. 8).

This may well be true but it is also possible that the process of 'leaning on' is rather more subtle and there are those who suggest that the appearance of independence which HMI gives is very much in the interests of the DES. As Rogers (1983) conjectures: 'It may well be that the Inspectorate has successfully maintained an impartial and non-political stance throughout the last few years. But such impartiality seems to drift into passivity and a vulnerability to being used (or abused) in a political way' (p.13). Two cases in which this may have happened are discussed. In the first, Rogers returns to the case of Madeley Court and speculates that this may be an example in which an LEA can 'use' HMI: 'It is alleged that the LEA wanted to get rid of the school's head and felt that a critical report by the Inspectorate would do the job for it. It did'. Philip Toogood (1984), the head who resigned following the HMI report on his school, has now told his side of the story and, while he attempts a detailed rebuttal of many of the criticisms made by HMI, his own criticisms are directed much more at the LEA (Shropshire) than at the Inspectorate. In the second example, Rogers considers Leslie Stratta's dispute with Hereford and Worcester over the staffing levels at St. Barnabas, his son's school. It is suggested that an 'HMI inspection, carried out because of a reorganization proposal, was used by the DES to reject Stratta's complaint even though the inspection did not really tackle the issues complained of'. Stratta claims that when invited to discuss his concerns with HMI as they prepared themselves to undertake their inspection it soon became 'clear to me that the team of HMI would not probe some of the important questions which the DES was failing to probe . . . After the meeting it occurred to me that one way of interpreting the DES use of HMI was that it was quite a clever move on their part'.

Salter and Tapper (1981) make much the same point in the context of their thesis — that the DES is seeking a shift in the balance of power as part of their attempt to exercise greater central control over educational policy-making (see Chapter 2). This, they claim, has entailed a tightening of relationships between HMI and the DES in which it becomes increasingly difficult to know 'How far HMI can be regarded as the willing tool of the DES in its attempts to impose central definitions of desirable policy shifts, and how far is HMI an independent body with its own opinions and values of its own' (p. 109). In either case it is very much in the interests of the DES to sustain 'the myth of autonomy . . . since it enhances the supposed objectivity of the information on which the Department rests its policy proposals'. Thus, while Salter and Tapper seriously question the validity of claims that HMI are more than the servants of the DES, they do not doubt that: 'Should the distinction between the Inspectorate and the DES become blurred in the eyes of the public, the role of HMI as the organic intellectuals weaving the appropriate ideological blanket to legitimate future DES policy will be seriously endangered' (p. 234).

If there are those who are sceptical as to whether HMI really do exercise significant professional autonomy, there are others who argue that they retain, if only to a vestigial extent, an element of constitutional independence due to their designation as 'Her Majesty's Inspectorate' and to their appointment by the 'Queen in Council'. Not all commentators have been impressed by this as the comments of two former senior officials of the DES may illustrate. Weaver (1979), while acknowledging that HMI are, indeed, appointed by the Queen through an order of her Privy Council, yet takes the view that 'In everything but formal procedure, the Department appoints HMIs and it is possible that their independence in educational matters derives from their history rather than their mode of appointment' (p. 50). Kogan (1971) adds that 'their later promotions within the inspectorate come through the Secretary of State so that their independence, while considerable, is to that extent trammelled' (p. 21). Finally, when a Parliamentary Select Committee for Education and Science undertook a major review of HMI in 1967–68 they concluded that: 'We do not consider appointment by the Queen in Council to be of any great significance, although we recognise that it delights the people who enjoy it . . . The DES and the Inspectorate are a very integrated body'.

This may be so, but it might also be true that HMI would be a very different sort of body if it were to be clearly redesignated as the DES inspectorate. This issue was raised in a more recent meeting of the House of Commons' Education, Arts and Science Committee (1981) by a number of members who felt that the independence of HMI was under threat from what they saw as the centralising tendencies of the Department. A member of the Committee asked the then Senior Chief Inspector (Sheila Browne) what would be the consequences if the Inspectorate were in the future 'appointed by the DES and no longer by the Queen in Council'. Her reply seems worth quoting fairly fully:

We would only, I think, be able to do a different job; because that change vis-a-vis the Department would totally change our relationship with the system and the system's perception of our functions . . . If we were the Department's inspectors, I think that we could not have a freedom of professional judgement to recommend anything at all, and I would take it that we would have to work only within areas of defined policy . . . I think we would therefore be remarkably suspect in institutions because we would no longer be neutral. (House of Commons 1981, p. 100)

While it is unclear in what sense, or even from whom, HMI are neutral, what this analysis seems to suggest is that if inspectors appear to become the creatures of the administration or even if they are seen to exercise significant managerial functions, then their credibility with those they evaluate will be called into question. On the whole HM Inspectorate seem to have understood this well, while some local advisory services, pressed into service as inspectors, have not. Kogan (1974) stresses that the kinds of tasks which local and national advisers undertake may be broadly defined as 'advisory', 'inspectoral' and 'administrative' and the fact that many are called upon to perform all three can lead to role conflict and ambiguity. Two issues then arise: first, if these ambiguities matter, can they be corrected? Second, are all three functions necessary? Kogan recognises that it is difficult to believe that the education service could afford to provide separate inspectoral and advisory services but that it is very doubtful whether inspectors and advisors should act as managers.

It would seem that Rayner (1982) also takes this view. Thus they comment 'that most FE inspectors are involved to some extent in the operation of the course approval system, a quasi-administrative function which is quite different from inspection. In our view, HMI's involvement in course approval over many years has led to a distortion of its role because it has limited its capacity to inspect . . . ' (p. 20). Such a view was also shared by a number of the bodies who presented evidence to Rayner. For example, the Standing Conference of Principals and Directors of Colleges and Institutions of HE argued that 'the hostility which has been aroused in institutions to the course approval system has inevitably rubbed off on the inspectorate operating through RSIs and this has been unhelpful for their other more important roles of advice and consultation'. This makes no mention of inspection but it seems that: 'Other bodies took the line that the role of the inspectorate should be limited to advice and inspection' (p. 55).

Much the same might be said of the local inspectorate. But if to avoid undertaking significant administrative functions is one prerequisite for an effective inspectorate, equally important is the need to be at one and the same time the loyal servants of the national or local administration while retaining a more fundamental allegiance to the profession of education as a whole. This is no easy task and, for the most part, HMI has been much more successful in presenting this image of itself than has the local advisory service. Some have even gone so far as to see HMI as crucial defenders of education against the central government. Thus at the NAS/UWT conference of 1984, the conference was both warned that HMI might be asking 'unfair' questions and abusing their powers during school visits *and* that too much criticism should be avoided as such criticism might threaten the independence of HMI given that they were 'the most effective means we have for castigating the Treasury for failure to provide resources' (*TES* 4.5.84). In a sense Aitken puts the same kind of point even more tellingly and in doing so expresses a feeling which is probably widely shared amongst teachers: 'I don't agree by a long way with all the inspectorate says and does, but on the whole they are on our side, they are on the side of the children and the professionals' (Rogers 1983, p. 11). If local advisers are to be effective as inspectors they will have to earn the same respect.

Summary and conclusion

The importance of HMI and local advisory services as evaluators of systems, institutions and individuals within education is widely acknowledged, although much else about them is the subject of controversy. In an attempt to identify and clarify some of the issues involved, the model of relationships in evaluation outlined by Thomas in the last chapter has been used to analyse the role of HMI and the local advisory services. This model proved particularly useful in distinguishing three possible roles for the local adviser — consultancy, advice and inspection. 'Consultancy', a situation in which the adviser conducts evaluations for and at the request of teachers appears to raise few problems. The case of advice and inspection is rather more difficult. In one sense, as *Education* (1976) claims 'Whatever their title, these officers have both an advisory and an inspectoral function. It is difficult to advise without inspecting first, and there seems little point in inspecting unless it leads to advice for someone somewhere' (p. i). This may well be correct as far as it goes but it does matter what 'advice' means in this context and 'to' and 'for' whom it is offered. The role of the LEA adviser as an evaluator and an agent of change within educational institutions, while it may sometimes be viewed with scepticism, is rarely regarded with hostility. Recent attempts to push them into a more overtly inspectoral role has been viewed with growing suspicion within educational institutions. Why this should be so and how such suspicion might be diminished was the subject of much of the later sections of this part of the chapter. One solution might be to accept that the two roles are incompatible and to split them and have them performed by different groups of officials. While, as Winkley (1982) has demonstrated, some LEAs have done this, Kogan is surely right when he argues that such a solution is beyond the resources of most local authorities. Finally, it might be possible to demonstrate that the exercise of an inspectoral role does not necessarily arouse suspicion and hostility amongst those who are the subject of such evaluations in education. Thus it seems that HMI are both clearly recognised as 'inspectors' in Thomas's sense and yet retain the trust of most teachers. They retain this trust, it is suggested, mainly because they are not, normally, seen as exercising significant managerial functions and because they appear to exhibit a robust professional independence from the administration in what they do. Thus, during periods when they do seem to have exercised and/or served administrative purposes (such as during the period of 'payment by results' between 1868 and 1898, or in FHE today), HMI have generated the same kind of hostility as some advisory services pressed into inspection today have encountered. It is not that advice and inspection represent incompatible activities for the local adviser or for HMI but rather that to expect them to exercise simultaneously and effectively an advisory, an inspectoral and a managerial role is to expect too much.

Similar incompatible demands may be found in the role of senior managers as evaluators, considered in the next section.

DEPARTMENTAL REVIEW

Within a school or college superordinates have a right and an obligation to monitor and judge the performance of subordinates. It is a widespread activity, although it may often be done informally and somewhat unsystematically. The process of reviewing the performance of departments at Great Barr School, Birmingham, is interesting because it represents an attempt to make this process more formal and systematised and, in some respects, more open. It is also a well documented activity. One of the writers of this chapter reported upon it when he was the head of the school (Lambert 1980), one of the school's heads of department carried out an interview-based evaluative study as an MEd dissertation (Matthewman 1982 and 1984), and Open University teams have investigated the scheme in Clift et al (1982) and Clift (forthcoming). This amount of information on 'departmental review' allows a detailed analysis of the *conduct* of the evaluation relationship (Figure 15.2), once the relationship structure has been identified. As to the latter, evaluation of departments is clearly carried out by those based within the institution and located in a control relationship because, once agreed at a heads-of-department meeting, no single department could exempt itself from the scheme. *For whom* the evaluation was made, the critical issue for distinguishing 'internal assessment' from 'public audit', will be considered following the account of the main features of the scheme.

In writing of 'departmental review', Clift et al (1982, p. 11) suggest that it ' . . . must be seen in the context of the managerial orientation of the Headmaster and his espousal of the "objectives model" of curriculum planning and school management'. It must also be seen in the context of Lambert's view, developed during 15 years of headship by 1975, that a staff development policy was a pre-condition of introducing an evaluation process such as 'departmental review' (see also Lambert (1981) and Woods (1981)). It was in 1975 when the senior management team at the school concluded that, since systematic evaluation by HMI or LEA inspectors was so infrequent, some greater emphasis on internal evaluation by senior management was necessary. The idea of allowing individual teachers alone to do their own evaluation was rejected on the basis that, first, the criteria would not be adequate; second, if they did identify weaknesses they might not seek assistance and third, it was felt that teachers were not adequately trained for the task.

Initial proposals were put forward by the senior management team at heads-of-department meetings in the school year, 1975–76. Considerable discussion took place before agreement was reached and much of this fell into two broad areas, confidentiality and competence. Understandably, teachers were worried that the results of an 'inspection' might be passed to local inspectors or HMI and it was agreed, therefore, that the results of reviews would be confidential within the school. Anxieties about what would happen to the written reports from lesssons seen were met with the agreement that these would later be destroyed in the presence of the head of department. Many teachers also seemed worried about the competence of members of the management team when observing lessons in subjects in which they were not specialists. Agreement on this was reached by stressing that the review was not so much concerned with factual subject knowledge as with evaluating performance on criteria related to teaching and organisational skills, aspects which the senior management team felt themselves able to assess.

The process of review

The process of review falls into two principal phases, in the first of which all except one department were reviewed. The second phase was based on a revised plan agreed in 1980 and operative until 1983. This reviewed only one department, largely because during that time the school was short of one deputy for almost half the period. The principal stages are examined below.

Organisation of the department

In the first phase a series of interviews was held with the head of department by the deputy head in charge of the review to discuss the general organisation of the department, principally in terms of syllabus, records, assessments, marking policies, display work, examination results and staff development. This proved to be very time-consuming and in the second phase this was replaced by a detailed questionnaire which the head of department completed prior to discussions with the deputy head and also the director of studies. By shortening this stage time could be spent, before the review proper, 'getting the feel' of the department. This was a response to a request from the departments that time was needed for the reviewers to 'get under the skin' of each department to be reviewed.

The observation of lessons

In the first phase teachers were allowed to choose the lessons they wished to have observed but this led, perhaps not unnaturally, to an imbalance in classes observed. Consequently in the second phase it was agreed that, although staff would be informed in advance which lessons were to be observed, the choice would be that of the reviewing team. It has to be recognised that, to some extent, the presence of an observer was inhibiting. In particular, Clift (forthcoming) suggested that the presence of the head was particularly inhibiting and attempts were made to allow for this in the assessment of a lesson. The criteria for assessment were agreed beforehand and at its conclusion the reviewer discussed the lesson with the teacher. A written report on the lesson then went to the deputy head responsible for the review. All staff teaching the subject were seen, including members of the senior management team, and these reports then formed part of the draft report prepared for the senior management team.

Preparation of the report

From the discussions on departmental organisation and the lesson reports the deputy head then prepared a draft report for discussion at a special meeting of the senior management team. Following this meeting an agreed report was typed and sent to the head of department for his or her comments. Subsequently, discussions on the content of the report took place between the head of department and the responsible deputy head and, finally, between the head of department and the senior management team. This was especially important when there were explicit or implicit criticisms of departmental organisation and the performance of the head of department, because it was known how strongly the headmaster felt about the role of the head of department. Every effort was made not to be overtly critical of the head of department in the final report to the department. Some of the discussions with heads of department were amicable, others were not; critical reports predictably met with resistance. Amendments were certainly made when legitimate misapprehensions became apparent and additions made where previously undiscovered strengths were unearthed. The hope always was to produce an agreed report but the senior management team insisted on their right to produce a final judgement when agreement could not be reached.

Report to the department

The final report which went to the department was not a negotiable document and included recommendations for action by the department. Received at a specially convened departmental meeting, the reception of a report varied. Where it was a good report it often went through 'on the nod', but where critical it often faced opposition and a considerable degree of justification by the reviewing team was necessary.

Recommendations

Recommendations were set out at the end of the report and the department was expected to act on them. On at least one occasion this was not the perception of the head of department who, in the follow-up to the main inspection, queried the status of the recommendations. This was eventually formalised, making it clear that departments were required to act on the recommendations.

Follow-up

The follow-up investigation was a very time-consuming process and was not always as effective as the team would have liked, although it did have very positive results in some departments. Time was a problem throughout the period of the reviews, particularly as for one-third of the time under discussion the school was one deputy short of its complement, requiring the postponement of the review process until a new appointment was made.

Personal development interviews

These interviews were added in the second phase of the review process, partly as a result of comments made by staff. Each teacher in the departmental team was seen by the head and the deputy head responsible for staff development. The aim was to examine individual strengths and weaknesses, to suggest remedies for the former and explore how strengths might be developed to the advantage of the department and future career prospects of the individual. Only one departmental review was undertaken with this extra aspect and proved successful in relating individual needs to departmental needs.

Analysing relationships and structures

The opening paragraph of this section noted that only one doubt remained to be resolved in analysing the structure of the evaluation relationship, distinguishing whether it is an 'internal assessment' or a 'public audit'. The evaluated unit in this study is the department and the account given above indicates that from that level, 'departmental review' is a 'public audit'. The key factor indicating this conclusion is the status of the final report and the follow-up study. The evaluation was principally for the *senior management* who used it to decide the *policy* changes needed within the department, and then followed-up the recommendations in the report to ensure that action was taken. This still left it to the departments to *interpret* policy when deciding what action to take although, if satisfactory action was not taken, senior management reserved the right to intervene again. If the report had been principally intended for the *evaluated department*, one would have expected far more freedom on the part of the department to decide upon policy, and what action to take in the light of the evaluation report. This classification does not mean that the evaluated department might not benefit from the report, and many received support in terms of extra resources, job changes and job-enrichment programmes, as well as changes to the in-service programme to meet perceived problems.

The analysis of how the relationships were conducted is less straightforward. In an earlier account Lambert (1980, p. 211) recognised the nature of the problem of how the evaluation might be perceived. Describing departmental review as, ' . . . essentially "general inspections" of departments over a three or four week period by the senior staff', a central task would be to convince staff ' . . . that it was a positive constructive step and not a negative critical one'. Given that the structural location of the relationship is within the 'public audit' category, the notions of support and constructiveness might be generated through the conduct of the relationship, an analysis based upon Figure 15.2 which involves examining the negotiation of criteria and the openness of judgement. Identifying the conduct of the judgement made is the more straightforward of these two dimensions. It has already been noted above that the final judgement and report, made by the senior management team, was not negotiable. Since this places the conduct of the evaluation more towards the closed end of the 'judgement continuum' in Figure 15.2, it means that the category of conduct will be selected from either the consultative or inspectoral categories.

In selecting which of these latter two categories most appropriately identify conduct, the senior management team at Great Barr might claim that the criteria used had emerged over a long process of identifying and developing the role of the department within the school. Specifically, two papers had been presented at a meeting of heads of department early in 1974, the first concerned with categorising the responsibilities of heads of department into four functional areas, and the second an initial document on how the role of the head of department might be evaluated. This was followed by other documents refining and extending performance criteria for the role of heads of department and of work in departments. In 1975 a checklist for use in lesson observations was produced and widely distributed as part of the introduction of 'departmental review'. Since these formed the basis of the criteria for the evaluation, the senior management team might claim that the criteria were negotiated and that the 'consultative model' is the appropriate description of conduct. In relation to this, Matthewman (1982, pp. 64–65) notes that staff new to the school since 1974 may not have known of all these documents. Although he does not suggest that this ignorance is a defence, it does raise the issue of the nature of the discussion of criteria with at least some of the staff and suggests that the *perception* of some staff would locate conduct within the 'inspectoral model' of Figure 15.2. This perception of imposed criteria emerges again when we look at the checklists for lesson observation.

As one head of department commented to Matthewman (p. 64). ' "I wasn't aware of any criteria . . . There was nothing in print to which I could refer . . ." '. Even forgetfulness contributes to the perceptions individuals have of past events! And, of course, even with a widely distributed checklist for lesson observations, interpretation in use would still occur; as one of the senior management team commented to Matthewman (p. 65) on their use, ' ". . . we don't all agree on the order of priority".'[1]

What emerges from this account of how the criteria for the evaluation were fixed, is the importance of 'perceptions' in the conduct of relationships. What may *appear* to a head of department to be the imposition of criteria may *appear* to the head teacher only to be using previously adopted criteria which were negotiated at that time. Differing perceptions may arise from the position of an individual in an organisation, but they may also reflect different meanings attached to words. Consider the important word for this evaluation — 'supportive'.

At the end of the earlier paragraph on the structure of relationships within departmental review, reference was made to the availability of extra cash, or job and INSET changes to meet perceived problems. In one sense, this may be viewed as genuinely *supportive* of the work of the department and one head of department's view suggests a similar understanding of how the review was supportive, ' ". . . as it was explained . . . it was to have a supportive function . . . I can see that it could strengthen my hand vis-à-vis someone not pulling their weight" ' (Matthewman 1982, p. 35). This meaning of 'supportive' was not widely shared, as Matthewman (p. 110) summarises, 'The point has been made in various parts of the text that though the reviews were conceived to be supportive, they were not viewed as such by the majority of staff. They were viewed as being inspectoral' (p. 110). An awareness of that kind of anxiety contributed to introducing the 'personal development interviews' in the second phase of the review, an attempt at making the aspects of support more explicit.

In concluding this section, 'explicitness' provides an appropriate theme. 'Departmental review' makes formal and explicit much of the informal and unsystematic evaluations made by senior staff in schools, many of which will be based upon criteria which are implicit, and where the final judgement of the evaluator will not simply be 'closed', in the sense used in Figure 15.2, but where the evaluated will not necessarily be informed of the nature of the judgement. In addition, the senior staff engaged in 'departmental review' not only recognise their responsibility for the performance of the staff of their institution but also a readiness to act effectively in order to meet that responsibility. As argued at the end of Chapter 15 vigorous appraisal of institutions carried out by those within them may be a factor in improving the perceptions of a sceptical public about the quality of education in schools and colleges. This must be one reason why LEAs have sponsored the self-assessment schemes discussed in the next section.

LOCAL AUTHORITY SELF-ASSESSMENT SCHEMES

Self-assessment programmes with explicit structures have become more widespread. This has occurred as educational institutions recognise the need to be seen to be evaluating and as LEAs stimulate and encourage these trends, partly, to paraphrase Socket (1980, p. 10), to prove that something is being done to improve educational quality. Such programmes can be viewed as an attempt at reconciling the rights of non-teachers to information with the desire of teachers for professional autonomy where the origin of these documents is the LEA and, in relation to the issue of *who* are the evaluators, they would *seem* to be located on the external side of the internal/external parameter structuring evaluation relationships. However, these documents alone cannot tell us about the structures of relationships between the individuals and/or groups involved in evaluation. Despite their general description as self-evaluation schemes, analysis is needed to identify the structures which may actually arise and this can only be done by answering the questions: (a) are institutions able to reject the documents (autonomy or control?); (b) who does the evaluation; and (c) for whom is it done? This still leaves the further question of how the evaluations are conducted. Moreover, analysis is also needed even to clarify the use of the word 'self' in descriptions of the documents. These ambiguities are examined further below, using the analytical frameworks developed in Chapter 15 and in the context of the substantial documentary evidence, produced by G. Elliott et al (1981), of the trend towards the introduction of more formal self-assessment processes.

Out of 103 LEAs circulated in 1980, 69 were already ' . . . actively engaged in formulating self-evaluation schemes' (p. 6). By the end of that year 21 schemes had been published and these were examined in detail by Elliott and his collaborators. Eight of the 21 schemes contained no evidence to allow any conclusions about the nature of any links with external evaluation. Six schemes were linked to inspection by LEA staff. For example, the Dorset scheme was linked to ' . . . regular formal inspection of schools by local authority inspectors' (p. 11). Seven schemes indicated a range of informal links with LEA staff. The ILEA scheme, as an example, requests schools to discuss the outcomes of an evaluation with its inspectors in order to gain the benefit of an external viewpoint (p. 12).

The Dorset and ILEA documents are useful for examining how an appropriate analytical model helps in differentiating the relationships which can exist as between cases, all of which are known as 'self-evaluation schemes'. Thus, the link in Dorset with regular formal inspections would seem to make the document part of a larger 'inspection' relationship, where the work undertaken within the school using the document seems essentially to be a preparation for the later visit by the local inspectorate who, as argued in the earlier section on inspectors, undertake formal inspections principally for those external to the institution.

By comparison, the ILEA scheme seems more properly to fit the 'internal assessment' relationship. It is *expected* by the LEA that the evaluation will take place (control) and that it will be done by members of the institution. However, the results of the evaluation appear to be for the school's staffs' own use, and the role of the local inspector in discussing the *outcomes* of the evaluation seems only to add an extra viewpoint for the further illumination of the staff of the school.

The primary and secondary self-evaluation documents distributed in Solihull (Solihull 1979; 1980)[3] represent yet another structure of relationships, that of 'personal evaluation'. Although the documents are distributed by the LEA, the emphasis is upon institutional autonomy as to *whether* and *how* they are used; even the committees which prepared the documents were dominated by teachers. In this case, whether the document is used for an evaluation or not is for each school to decide (autonomy) and it would be done by the staff and for their own internal use. This example presents an opportunity for making a further point about autonomy and control which is related to the *level* at which the analytical model is applied. By this is meant that it is possible to analyse relationships treating an individual teacher as the evaluated unit, or a department and also an institution. Indeed, in the previous two sections of the chapter the institution and the department, respectively, have been treated as the evaluated unit. Given this, circumstances may arise where the *institution* is free to adopt or reject the use of an LEA evaluation document (as in Solihull) but, if it is adopted by the senior management of a school, they may *require* the staff to engage in the evaluation process. Thus, the school is in an autonomous relationship with the LEA over the use of the document, but teaching staff are in a control relationship with senior staff over its use.

It seems clear from this that even the meaning of the word 'self' in the title or preamble to the documents cannot be taken for granted. Its use might suggest that they focus upon evaluative activity by individual teachers, but such an assumption is rarely supported by an examination of published documents. Indeed, as Parkin (1984, p. 11) notes, 'The notion of self-evaluation is used rather ambiguously in that the "self" referred to varies from all individual teachers — as teachers or members of department — through to headteachers and finally the school as a unit'. As an example, the Surrey scheme is for the head and is ' . . . "a private document to assist your thinking" ' (G. Elliott 1981, p. 10). This focus upon the head is not uncommon 'because the head carries responsibility for running the school' (p. 17). Rightly, Elliott et al go on to comment about this focus on the head because of the head's responsibility, 'While this is not in question it opens up issues about styles of leadership' (p. 17). Despite these observations, they do go on to state that the 21 schemes ' . . . seem to be on the right lines emphasising teacher participation and curriculum improvement' (p. 19). They also note that the overall emphasis in all 21 documents is on partnership and ' . . . a consultative process which is open and collaborative' (p. 13). But such emphases must not be taken for granted as statements of practice, since our analysis of these LEA schemes suggests considerable diversity in the relationships between evaluators and evaluated.

Diversity might also be expected in the *conduct* of evaluation based upon LEA self-assessment schemes. The analysis of conduct is concerned with the setting of criteria and the openness of judgement, and the documents can themselves be influential in the first part of this process. Sixteen of the 21 schemes, including those of Solihull, listed objectives, many expressed as detailed statements or phrased as questions. This thoroughness has implications for the setting of criteria in at least two ways. Despite the emphasis in the documents that they should be adapted rather than adopted ' . . . it may be extremely difficult to adapt or modify schemes that are so thorough' (p. 15). In addition, checklists make value-laden assumptions about ' . . . the notions of the "good teacher" or "good head of department" ' (p. 24). Thus, even the dissemination of checklists can be viewed as an important stage in shaping the criteria to be used in an evaluation. How particular relationships which occur within these schemes are actually conducted can, finally, only be identified through empirical study.

What can be done here is to speculate on some of the alternative modes of conduct and also consider briefly the problems of perception. For example, consider the ILEA scheme which seems to be located within an 'internal assessment' relationship. Heads and senior colleagues in different schools may conduct their evaluations in quite diverse ways. Some may negotiate criteria with staff and share the process of judgement (the 'professional model of conduct'), while others may impose criteria and make their own closed judgement (the 'inspectoral mode of conduct'). But these initial examples only begin the process of unravelling the potential complexities of 'perceptions' in the actual and presented conduct of relationships, an issue explored to some extent in the earlier section of the chapter on 'departmental review'.

What is clear from this is that claims that schemes of self-evaluation sponsored by local authorities are consultative, collaborative and open should be treated with caution. There is considerable variation in practice, and it cannot necessarily be assumed that the existence of documents automatically guarantees that they are used in schools. Teachers who have strong misgivings in the matter may be able effectively to prevent their introduction. This is clearly a sensitive area in which issues cannot necessarily be resolved by purely rational means, as many heads of schools have discovered. In noting that appreciation is also necessary of the micro-politics of the evaluation relationships involving individuals and groups, we are in fact providing an anticipatory hint of the analytical framework offered by Slater in Chapter 19, which distinguishes between rational and political approaches to the management of change.

CONCLUSION

The previous chapter began by pointing to a paradox in relation to evaluation, in that the same phenomenon is apparently *both* well established and accepted *and* may yet be treated with hostility, scepticism and caution. The analysis which followed suggested that an explanation of this paradox is to be found in the different relationships of power and control which can exist between evaluators and evaluated. This chapter seeks to take that analysis a stage further by examining the question of 'whose interest' is served by the evaluation. In the case of the inspectorate, the analysis of this question of 'interest' suggests that 'advice' and even 'inspectoral' evaluations by inspectors may be far more acceptable to teachers where such inspectors are 'professionally' independent and are not obviously part of the system of administrative control. This is a conclusion which has interesting implications for evaluations carried out by the senior management within educational institutions in so far as their relationships with teachers in the school or the college bears a greater similarity to that of the local inspector than it does to HMI. The lesson to be learnt from the case of the inspectorate (national or local) is that if evaluations by senior management are to be viewed as supportive they must *manage* the relationship in a way which suggests that they, like HMI, preserve a degree of distance from and 'professional independence' of the LEA as employer. It is similarly helpful for school assessment schemes, even though the initial impetus may have come from the authority, to be seen to maintain a substantial element of discretion for the head and staff of the individual school. Even better when the perception corresponds with reality.

Finally, what relevance has all this to the management of change within educational institutions? Now while much of what is said in this and the previous chapter has focused more on the character of relationships and conducts in evaluation than upon the issue of what the purposes of evaluation might be, the implications for the management of change seem clear. In much of what is written and said elsewhere a simple dichotomy as to the possible purposes of evaluation is assumed, in which evaluation which is seen as externally orientated in the way discussed in these chapters is viewed as an instrument of control whereas evaluation which is seen as internally orientated is regarded as concerned with the management of change. Hence in the activities of 'inspectors' the distinction between the inspector as 'adviser' and the inspector as 'inspector' is considered to be crucial. Advisers, it is said, are thought to hold the interests of teachers as fellow professionals as fundamental in what they do and this, and their independence of those who employ teachers, makes it possible for them to act as welcome and effective agents of change. 'Inspectors', on the other hand, are often said to be 'agents of control', concerned essentially with monitoring levels and standards of performance for the employer, and, as such, to lack credibility with teachers when they attempt to present themselves as fellow professionals mutually engaged in the business of facilitating change within educational institutions. Now, while such a conception of the possible roles of the evaluator is deeply entrenched, there is some evidence that things may not be so simple and, certainly it does not fit with our analysis of evaluation. Thus, it does seem as if HMI, clearly 'inspectors' by our account, do in fact act as effective agents of change. How is this to be explained? In our analysis we have emphasised that how inspectors (and other 'externally' orientated evaluators) as evaluators relate to those whom they evaluate is crucially determined by the extent to which they manage to distance themselves from the employer. Where inspectors appears to exercise a significant degree of 'professional independence' it may well be possible for them to serve the needs of both those for whom they evaluate and those who are the subject of their evaluation. It is for this reason that 'inspectors', where they can avoid being seen as the creatures of administrators and politicians or, worse still, as administrators in their own right, can bridge the dichotomy and act both as agents of control and as change agents. Furthermore, what is true of 'inspectors' may well also be true of other 'external' evaluators (such as the senior staff engaged in departmental reviews or involved in local authority self-assessment schemes discussed earlier) whatever their status.

This is an area in which there is clearly considerable scope for further research and analysis. It would be helpful, for instance, to have an in-depth, systematic, contextualised, ethnographic study of both HMI and of an LEA advisory service, if such could be negotiated. That there are tensions between professional and systemic considerations in the practice of evaluation is indisputable. This is a characteristic, as other chapters in the present volume have amply shown, which evaluation has in common with other aspects of the management of educational systems and institutions. Their resolution is a continuing challenge.

NOTES

1. Her Majesty's Inspectorate is in fact separately organised for England, Scotland and Wales. Gatherer (1975) offers a useful comparison of the differences in approach and style between the Scottish and the English HMI and Rayner (1982) contains a chapter dealing specifically with the Welsh HMI.
2. Rayner (1982) observes that although in 1981 there were 1850 advisers in England (1982) (costing £45m a year) not all of them act as inspectors. Furthermore, the local advisers in Wales (139 costing £3m) "are not in general seen to have an inspectoral role" (p. 77).

3. Hywel Thomas has been engaged in two research projects in Solihull and some of the information used in this account is drawn from his discussions of the scheme with teachers and officers in the Authority.

REFERENCES

Auld, R. (1975) *William Tyndale Junior and Infant Schools Public Enquiry.* London: ILEA.

Bolam, R., Smith, G. and Canter, H. (1978) *Local Education Authority Advisers and the Mechanics of Innovation.* Windsor: NFER.

Clift, P. (unpublished) *Great Barr School. The Art Department: A Case Study of a Departmental Review.* Milton Keynes: The Open University Evaluation and Accountability Research Group.

Clift, P., Abel, B. and Simpson, G. (1982) 'Case Study 5: Great Barr School'. *Educational Studies: A Third Level Course, Curriculum Evaluation and Assessment in Educational Institutions E364.* Milton Keynes: Open University Press.

DES (1983a) *The Work of HM Inspectorate in England and Wales.* London: DES.

DES (1983b) *HM Inspectors Today: Standards in Education.* London: DES.

DES (1984) *Education Observed.* London: DES.

Edmonds, E. (1962) *The School Inspector.* London: Routledge and Kegan Paul.

Education Digest (1976) 'The Advisory Service'. *Education,* 20 February.

Elliott, G. et al (1981) *Self Evaluation and the Teacher: An Annotated Bibliography and Report on Current Practice, 1980, Part 2.* University of Hull/Schools Council.

Fiske, D. (1977) 'How advisers spend their time'. *Education,* 23 December.

Gatherer, W. (1975) 'Control and Guidance: The Role of the Inspector'. In Hughes, M. G. (ed.) *Administering Education: International Challenge.* London: Athlone.

House of Commons (1968) *Report from the Select Committee on Education and Science. Part 1: Her Majesty's Inspectorate.* London: HMSO.

House of Commons (1981) 'The Secondary School Curriculum and Examinations'. *Minutes of Evidence from the Education, Science and Arts Committee.* London: HMSO.

Kogan, M. (1971) *The Government of Education.* London: Macmillan.

Kogan, M. (1974) 'Advisers in Conflict'. *Times Educational Supplement,* 5 April.

Lambert, K. (1980) 'Evaluation at Great Barr School'. *Educational Administration,* 8(2).

Lambert, K. (1981) 'Staff Development: theory and practice'. *School Organisation,* 1(1).

Matthewman, M. (1982) 'Evaluation by Departmental Review'. Unpublished MEd dissertation, University of Birmingham.

Matthewman, M. F. G. (1984) 'The initial perceptions and reactions of staff on the announcement of a policy of institutional self-evaluation'. *Educational Management and Administration,* 12(3), 181–191.

Parkin, J. B. (1984) *School Self-Evaluation and the Management of Change.* Sheffield Papers in Education Management **37**: Sheffield City Polytechnic.

Rayner Report (1982) *Study of HM Inspectorate in England and Wales.* London: HMSO.

Rogers, R. (1983) 'HMI — whose servant?'. *Where,* **189**, June.

Salter, B. and Tapper, T. (1981) *Education, Politics and the State.* London: Grant McIntyre.

Sockett, H. (ed.) (1980) *Accountability in the English Education System.* Sevenoaks: Hodder and Stoughton.

Solihull (1979) *Evaluating the School: A Guide for Secondary Schools in the Metropolitan Borough of Solihull.* Solihull.

Solihull (1980) *Evaluating the Primary School: A Guide for Primary Schools in the Metropolitan Borough of Solihull.* Solihull.

Toogood, P. (1984) *The Head's Tale.* Shropshire: Dialogue Publications.

Weaver, T. (1979) 'DES: Central Control of Education'. *E222 The Control of Education in Britain.* Milton Keynes: Open University Press.

Winkley, D. (1982) 'LEA Inspectors and Advisers: a developmental analysis'. *Oxford Review of Education,* 8(2).

Wood, J. R. (1981) *Staff development in a large school.* Unpublished BPhil (Ed.) dissertation, University of Birmingham.

17

ACCOUNTABILITY VERSUS PARTICIPATION?

John Thorp

INTRODUCTION

Accountability and participation are among the most pressing problems today facing not only the education service but society as a whole. They are notions located within the concept of *democracy*. Democracy is a way of getting things done, a way of arriving at decisions, and by its very nature has 'accountability' built in — at least that is the theory. Representatives are elected to represent; to represent the people in governing and in so doing are held accountable to the people, even if only at election time. Government departments in turn engage specialised staff to carry out their work, to implement their policies and through their hierarchical organisation these are also held accountable. Critics, however, have identified distinctly undemocratic developments, such as in the case of the education service. For the critics the professionals engaged in education work have successfully insulated themselves from those bodies to which they ought to be accountable, either the people or their representatives, and have consequently failed to respond to those whose needs they are supposed to serve. And we should here be careful how we use the term 'participation'. Paradoxically, it seems that strong versions of 'professional participation' may deny the possibility of participation by the community, thus protecting professionals from accountability to the community.

In our contemporary pluralistic society then, notions of accountability and participation are themselves complex and confusing. Involved in their consideration are a number of basic issues like *power, ideology, values* and *responsibility*. Fundamentally problematic is the very nature of education in a plural society, its role as Silver (1980, p. 19) calls it, as a 'social instrument'. To this end education has a dual role — not only does it act as a distributor of life chances, it also functions as part of a cultural transmission of values. A focus on accountability and participation reveals the attempt to rescue

414

education from the undemocratic domination of professionals: in other words, the problem is one of control. As Silver (1980, p. 19) advises, we must 'constantly evaluate the motives of the makers and users of the instrument'.

Conventional usage of the terms in the literature of educational administration clearly reveals the differentiation made by Finn et al (1977, pp. 144–145) between ideologies *in* education of practising professionals and ideologies *about* education of various interest or power groups in society. It suggests that accountability has an external domain, involving the answerability of the school to the community, while participation has an internal domain, with professional involvement in decision-making. However, closer analysis suggests that this simple division is not so clear cut and that in fact there may be a considerable interpenetration of the concepts in practice. The notion of 'participation' itself demands very careful attention lest we confuse internal and external domains. It may refer to 'professional participation' within educational institutions or it may alternatively refer to 'community participation' and both have rather different consequences in their relationship to notions of 'accountability'. The climate in which discussion in these areas has developed should also be noted, spawning simultaneously as it has debate about the role of specialised 'professional' educational workers alongside notions of industrial democracy. Issues of 'control' in the workplace with its attendant discussion of 'power' and 'micro-politics' should not deflect us from a consideration of one other very important question, that of 'responsibility'. 'Responsibility' includes responsibility *for* something and responsibility *to* someone and it instructs us to consider the notion of consensus. As such then, it represents an opportunity to bridge that simple division noted above.

This chapter seeks to explore the notions of accountability and participation and particularly their inter-relationships. Analysis will be in three parts: first, notions of accountability as they relate to school and community relationships; second, notions of participation as they relate to the sharing of decision-making within schools among a wider body of professionals; and third, a section on accountability *versus* participation which examines the tensions involved in developing these notions in practice.

ACCOUNTABILITY, THE SCHOOL AND THE COMMUNITY

If, as we have suggested, 'accountability' is located within the wider concept of democracy, we must first examine how this is reflected in our system of education. We should inquire about the 'control' of one of our major publicly-funded social institutions, for if democracy is to work, and be seen to be working, then the people, the community, ought to have the chance to be involved in the control of its schools. In a general sense, schools ought to be responsive to the needs and wishes of the wider community, they should contribute to the common good of that society of which they are a part. And, in a more specific sense, school governing bodies might be seen as part of the wider structure of representative democracy, and it is they who should represent local community interest. Such a provision is embodied in the 1944 Education Act, which requires every maintained school to have a governing body, referred to either as 'governors' or 'managers'.

However, until well into the 1970s, the system of governing bodies did not, apparently, work very well. Baron and Howell (1974, p. 65) reporting their study of school governing bodies carried out in the late 1960s found that only 21 of the 78 county boroughs then in existence in England had separate governing bodies for each of their schools. A further 25 had governing bodies for small groups of schools, usually two or three, while 20 borough councils had a single governing body for all their schools. Such was the extent of a system of representative democracy.

But what of their responsibilities? According to Baron and Howell (1974, p. 40) the main functions ascribed to governors by the 1944 Act are:

> . . . finance, the appointment and dismissal of the head, assistant teachers and non-teaching staff, the general direction of the conduct and curriculum of the school, the care and use of school premises, school holidays, and the admission of pupils.

It would seem that their most significant responsibilities are those concerning the head teacher and the curriculum of the school, yet their potential for exercising this responsibility seems limited. During their study, these authors found that in most areas the governing bodies were involved in the appointment of head teachers, usually through involvement with interviews. It was found, however, that in most cases the governing body was not involved in drawing up short lists. It seemed a generally accepted principle (Baron and Howell 1974, p. 111) in the appointment of head teachers, 'that it is for professional administrators to ensure that proper weight is given to qualifications and experience'. This control of the shortlist can be seen as a significant factor in modifying and limiting the role of the governing body.

In the other significant, and perhaps the most contentious, area of governors' responsibility, that of the *curriculum*, Baron and Howell found a minimum of involvement by governing bodies. They noted the wording of the articles of government which establishes the responsibility of the head teacher for the 'internal organisation and discipline of the school' and pointed to 'the long standing tradition that the content of education should be left to the teachers, with the associated view that the head as a responsible professional should be left to get on with the job', as the reason why governing bodies did not take rather more seriously their role in 'the general direction of the conduct and curriculum of the school' (p. 125).

By the time the Taylor Committee had been appointed to inquire into the whole area of management and government in 1975, they were able to identify (DES 1977, pp. 8–9) 'very significant changes in the context and atmosphere of school government', its practice being 'modified by new forces which were only beginning to emerge during the 60s'. The 'forces' the Taylor Committee identified were those that came from the reorganisation of both local government and secondary education and from the growing demand for participation in educational decision-making from those both inside and outside the schools. 'Active public opinion concerning the schools', notes Taylor (DES 1977, p. 9) 'has become an element in the national and local political situation'. The context in which this change occurred clearly has some relevance to this discussion and the reader is referred back to the discussion in Chapter 4.

The Taylor Report recommended a considerable strengthening of the role of governors and it is useful to examine the extent to which strengthened bodies of accountability have actually altered the accountability of schools to the community. This is particularly relevant in view of the recently announced enhanced and more clearly defined functions of governing bodies, and a parallel proposed increase in parental representation (DES

1985), the latter falling short, however, of the parental majorities previously envisaged (DES 1984).

William Bacon's (1978) study of the Sheffield school-board system provides a suitable case for examination. Introduced into the city in 1970 it predates the kind of recommendations found in the Taylor Report and was a direct result of the local Labour Party's commitment to new forms of public involvement in the running of the schools. Each Sheffield school was given its own representative managing body, as Bacon (1978, p. 52) says 'so constituted that it would be flexible and sensitive to local needs and interests'. But it was how these new bodies actually worked and what kind of impact they had on the existing structures of power, that formed the basis of Bacon's study. His conclusions are particularly worthy of consideration.

Bacon found, not surprisingly he admits, that at first many head teachers were 'nervous' of the new Sheffield system. Many felt that their autonomy was threatened and their traditional leadership role undermined. Potentially of most concern was the now explicit requirement that the managers were 'through the agency of the head teacher to have general direction of the conduct and curriculum of the school'. Bacon (1978, p. 75) identifies the concern of heads that they might lose the opportunity to be powerful innovators as they would be circumscribed by conservative lay boards.

In practice it has not worked out like this, as Field notes in Chapter 12. In fact the reverse is true, with the head teacher's managerial role strengthened and the new school boards serving to insulate them from what Bacon calls (1978, p. 80) 'some of the worst tensions associated with their peculiarly isolated "man in the middle" position'. Bacon concluded that the school board reform did nothing to change existing power structures. Members of the governing bodies found themselves trapped in an unequal power relationship and dependent on the co-operation of the head teachers, who maintained their own control not only of the channels of communication but also the selection of information and choice of issues which would be discussed on their terms. Bacon was led to ask about the 'reality' of the democratic intent of the school board reforms and finds it chimerical. In its place he discovers a process he calls 'discrete manipulative co-option' (Bacon 1978, p. 198) which he says means,

> . . . that although a process of formal and elaborate consultation now takes place with all interested parties, teachers, parents, students, community groups, local political workers and so on, at the same time the differential knowledge of, or structural position occupied by certain key actors — the headteacher, the chairman, the officers of the local authority clerking the meeting — means that in the main the responsible officials of the organisation decide not only what issues are to be raised but also have a heavy influence upon the subsequent discussions and any final decision which is taken.

He refers to 'a new kind of people manipulating technology' (Bacon 1978, p. 193) which he suggests effectively achieves two objectives:

> Firstly, the appropriate deflection or diffusion of groups who may be critical of, or actively hostile to, the policies being pursued by the educational establishment. Secondly, the engineering of an effective level of client consent for and support of the local educational system.

He concludes (Bacon 1978, p. 201) that as a result of these 'co-optative techniques' and 'incorporative strategies', 'school boards are presently used as instruments of impression management and political obfuscation'.

If we are to understand by accountability the demands for change in schools which seem to emanate from an external source, and we note the seeming failure of existing structures of governance to make schools more accountable to the community, then we must examine further the source of this failure. We must consider this relationship of school and community in the context of changes in the process of decision-making *inside* schools, in particular the increased demand for professional participation.

PARTICIPATION AND SCHOOL DECISION-MAKING

Alongside the 'external' challenge to autonomy in education has been an 'internal' one, one which reflects the widespread growth in demands for greater democratisation of decision-making in many spheres of social life. While the external challenge may be seen as an attempt to redefine clear lines of responsibility or accountability, the internal one has seen rather the broadening-out of those lines with the development of notions of teacher participation in school decision-making.

Jennings provides us with a useful classification (1975, p. 73). He distinguishes between 'one-man rule', 'consultation', 'delegation' and 'participation'. The first of these would indicate a strong autocratic head who 'makes the decisions'. The teachers would operate within very strictly defined limits or 'zones' with little or no chance to 'participate' in decision-making at any level other than in their own classroom. With 'consultation', the 'zones' are perhaps blurred a little. The head may seek the opinions or recommendations of staff but having done so may just as easily ignore them. The possibility of teachers' views being considered is perhaps most likely in their own area of specialisation, particularly if it is not shared by the head. This would represent a form of participation very slightly broadening out from the level of 'the job' towards a 'team or department' level. In a more advanced form this might even lead to negotiation about a particular issue. A much more meaningful level of participation comes with 'delegation', when a head would empower a member of staff to act on his or her behalf. In these circumstances we can say that 'zones' of influence are tending to weaken, to overlap as the level of participation reaches the team/department stage and maybe even tends towards the level of the school. However, as with the previous two categories, in delegating the head still retains responsibility and in so doing may overrule decisions that are not his or hers at any time. Jennings reserves the term 'participation' for the conditions of joint decision-making when 'zones' become merged into one and decision-making becomes the responsibility of the whole school staff.

It is clear then that each of these forms of 'participation' has a different relationship to the location of power in the school and as such they are inextricably linked to the role or style of management of the head teacher. As Lortie (1967, p. 11) puts it, 'all teachers' authority is derivative, in official terms, from that invested legally in the head and the school managers'. Traditionally the head teacher in this country has enjoyed an inordinately powerful position and under those early autocratic or paternalistic heads 'participation' could only be said to exist at the most basic level noted above. However, as the educational enterprise has grown and developed, so too has the need for alternative styles of management for heads. In primary schools, developments like team-teaching and open-plan design have meant a move away from the traditional insulated classroom teacher role and a consequent need for more appropriate styles of management and leadership. In secondary schools, as Peters (1976, p. 2) suggests, 'it is no longer practicable for the head to exercise authority in a traditional way'.

The environment in which heads now have to operate has become so complex that, as Watts (1976, p. 127) suggests, 'Any head must delegate or disintegrate'. This creates the possibilities then for increased participation by staff, but the level to which this extends will be contingent on the way in which 'delegation' is managed. As Watts (1976, p.127) notes,

> ... delegation may be executed in such a way that no real authority, only workload, is passed out by the head. The crucial question is that of where the decisions are made and to whom decision-makers are accountable.

Opportunities do exist in the UK education system to view 'truly' participative decision-making even if they are few and far between. At Countesthorpe School, Watts describes the elements of such a participative organisation, of which he says, (Watts 1976, p. 131),

> The major policy decisions that have shaped the curriculum and discipline of the school have been made by the consensus of the staff. Increasingly students have contributed to this consensus and in some instances parents and governors have participated.

This 'consensus', he reports, is established in a general meeting open to all, the Moot, to which other decision-making groups are responsible. Moreover, '*any* individual may challenge their decisions through the Moot' (Watts 1976, p. 131). Watts accepted the headship at Countesthorpe because he says he 'found the policies and the means for determining them attractive' and furthermore he was 'prepared to answer for them externally while being accountable internally to the college'. In such a case Jennings (1975, p. 80) would question the possibility of accountability. He says,

> If the head no longer has the power to make the final decision he cannot be held responsible, i.e. he is not accountable to the LEA for such matters. Who then would be?

He presumes that the whole staff of the school may be held accountable and others like Dyer (1970, p. 442) see great merits in this view. However, Jennings (1975, p. 80) is led to suggest that 'it is not easy to see how such a body in practice could be held accountable effectively'.

Evidence from other sources even questions how much teachers want or are committed to share decision-making. The study by Belasco and Alutto (1972, p. 228) indicated the differences in attitudes of those teachers who participate in more decision-making than they want to, the 'decisionally saturated' and those who participate in less, 'the decisionally deprived'. This has obvious implications for systems of shared decision-making which must accommodate the different levels of participation needed by different teachers. It reinforces Hoyle's notions of extended and restricted professionality. A further study by Duke et al (1980, p. 93) concerned itself with what they called the 'costs of involvement' in shared decision-making. They found that most teachers felt 'less than anxious' to participate in school decision-making, deriving little satisfaction when they did. They suggest a reason (Duke et al 1980, p. 104),

> Since the teachers were less than enthusiastic about participation in shared decision-making even though they viewed the potential benefits of participation as high and the potential costs low, it is reasonable to conclude that they believed that the possibility of actually realising the potential benefits of participation was very low.

Does this then hint at another 'face' to participation?

At a time when a growing number of schools are being run on increasingly participative lines, it is pertinent to consider Noble and Pym's (1970) influential paper on 'collegial authority', which reflects on both the outcomes of participation in terms of account-ability, which troubled Jennings, and the relationships among the participants which concerned Duke et al. Noble and Pym (1970) considered the relationship of profession-alism and structures of authority. They noted, like Hughes (1978, p. 241) that professionalism does not easily 'fit' with bureaucratic control and they suggested that in an organisation where professionals dominate, then the Weberian concept of 'collegiality' might better describe the structure of authority. Although not in a school, their fieldwork in a similar public service organisation yields interesting observations about how professional autonomy and conflicting bureaucratic controls have been accommodated and leads us to consider the implications of participative management or collegial authority for the notion of 'accountability'. Their study revealed the extent of 'professional' control, of which they said that,

> . . . the claim inherent in professionalism to self-determination in the exercise of professional functions was extended beyond the areas of strictly professional competence into the sphere of general organisational planning. (Noble and Pym 1970, p. 433)

The form of organisation based on a committee structure of status equals ensuring professional consultation has, according to Noble and Pym, significant implications for the 'clients' of the organisation who, they suggest, are faced with what they describe as 'a receding locus of power'. This is a situation of which they say 'wherever and at whatever level one applies to the organisation, the 'real' decisions always seem to be taken somewhere else', a structure of decision-making described as 'an involuted hierarchy' (Noble and Pym 1970, p. 436). In the organisation considered, membership of a committee was an important source of power although, as Noble and Pym found, formal equality of status was by no means commensurate with equality of access to these committees. In other words, powerful figures within the organisation could preserve their positions of power within the structure of committees, as witnessed by the domination of these committees by a select few. Such forms of participatory decision-making may not alter *who* holds power but more importantly for the 'client', they do alter the degree to which they can be held accountable for the decisions they take.

Can we go further than this? Nias (1972, p. 175) distinguishes between what she calls 'genuine' and 'pseudo' participation. She says,

> When genuine participation takes place, power is shared. By contrast, pseudo participation implies interaction rather than equalisation of resources. Indeed, pseudo participation may even succeed in increasing the power of one party to the negotiation while preserving the illusion of exchange.

As Ramsay (1977, p. 496) indicates, the initiative for participation is usually a 'managerial' one, and so we are led to inquire again of the conclusion offered by Duke et al (1980, p. 104) that perhaps 'participation' is often 'pseudo participation'. But for what ends? Hughes (1978, p. 246) perhaps provides a clue. Having noted what he calls the professional's 'conditional organisational commitment', he considers 'staff participation in decision-making as a decisive factor in obtaining the co-operation of professional staff'. And so does Pratt, (1981, p. 76) who asks, Is 'participation' then granted as a concession by those with access to legitimated control strategies to those without such access'?

And why would such 'pseudo participation' persist? Noble and Pym (1970, p. 432) suggest that claims of 'professionalism' endow people not only with status inside the organisation in which they work but also with a social status outside it. At this level, all incumbents of roles within the organisation have an interest in maintaining the image of 'professionalism' inherent in a collegial authority structure. They extend this view (Noble and Pym 1970, p. 441) by pointing out that it is only through those participatory structures that the select few could maintain their domination. As they put it,

> . . . the powerful few could only act with authority while they maintained their equality of status. The structural resources from which their influence derived were the product of a committee structure made necessary by the equal claims to participation in decision-making of all the professional departmental managers.

The structures of participatory decision-making, then, may pose problems for the notion of accountability. As suggested by Jennings, it is very difficult to hold a collegial group responsible for their collective decision-making. What Noble and Pym showed is that what such collegial structures really achieve is the distancing or insulation of certain powerful individuals or groups inside the organisation from accountability to the community outside. In such manipulated structures 'participation' is in reality 'pseudo-participation' and becomes a 'strategy' for the 'engineering' of professional consent. But where does this leave 'accountability'?

ACCOUNTABILITY VERSUS PARTICIPATION

It was noted at the beginning of this chapter that the notions of participation and accountability in the literature seemed to reflect 'internal' and 'external' domains of educational administration. This section considers how discrete these domains may be and possible areas of interpenetration and tension.

A useful way of doing this is to look again at the 'zones' or 'spheres of influence' model (Lortie 1975; Hanson 1976) and consider their interaction. Drawing on the work of Lortie (1969; 1975), Hanson (1976, p. 28) suggests that at least two 'interacting spheres' can be distinguished in schools, with 'identifiable types of decision formally "zoned" (to use Lortie's term) to administrators and others informally zoned to teachers'. The teachers' 'zone' contains decisions affecting the instructional process inside the classroom. Hanson (1976, p. 28) noted that these administrative and professional zones he identified were characterised by 'identifiable constraints' which limited their decision-making autonomy, by 'decisional accommodation' which reduced conflict where decisions overlapped the spheres and by 'strategies' with which members could seek to influence the behaviour of members of the other sphere or to protect their own. This model, it was claimed, could perhaps better explain the management of an organisation staffed by professionals, as has been discussed in Chapter 10, in the way that it cuts across the idea of 'bureaucratic' organisation. It also reflects a kind of stability so that in a period of change or disruption those mechanisms of stability may well appear more visible.

The last decade, more or less, represents such a period of change: the climate has been one of questioning, criticism and reappraisal. The demands have been for the external accountability of schools, and one way to strengthen measures of accountability is to reinforce patterns of hierarchy. The whole period is characterised in this way by Salter and Tapper (1981, p. 219) who describe it in terms of 'the bureaucratisation of educational power', with which the central authority in education, the DES, intended to strengthen its capacity to initiate change. It had been heavily criticised in the mid-1970s in an OECD Report (1975) which urged greater rationality and there followed, as Salter and Tapper (1981, p. 223) have put it, 'a process of policy enclosure', with the result that,

> As policy-making was progressively internalised within the Department's 'rational' planning procedures, the LEA's and teachers' unions were increasingly made aware that they were subordinate, rather than equal partners.

The outcome of this process has led Pratt (1981, p. 73) to suggest that

> Today we need to understand the interactions between superordinates defending the interests of the providers of the education service and subordinates defending their opposing interests.

We may see therefore that the attempts at greater centralised control, or increased bureaucratisation provide a context of instability, uncertainty even, for the interaction of 'spheres of influence'. As we noted these are always subject to 'identifiable constraints' and these become more and more visible as attempts are made to reinforce or redraw them. Dale (1979, p. 104) characterises this as a change from what he calls 'licensed autonomy' to 'regulated autonomy' which has involved a 'shift along the continuum from the administration in the direction of government of education by DES' (Dale 1979, p. 109). How then could this be achieved? Elsewhere Dale (1981, p. 71) makes another useful distinction between procedures which contribute directly to the 'implementation' of the goals of the education system and those which indirectly 'facilitate' that implementation. As expectations of education change and goals are redefined, then the management of the education service has to adjust both facilities and implementive procedures. In other words, it must adopt 'strategies' to enlarge its sphere of influence, to penetrate the professional sphere. The first stage in making 'facilitating arrangements' is the 'organisation of policy-making' and we have noted the tendency towards greater centralisation. However, as Dale (1981, p. 71) notes, this must work, ' . . . in the context of arrangements orginally set up to facilitate quite different policies'. This inevitably leads to 'tensions' in moving forward from 'facilitation' to 'implementation' as the level of decision-making passes from one sphere to the other and 'strategies of defence' have to be overcome. Here lies the problem of legitimation.

One way to make increased demands for accountability 'legitimate' has been to make them appear the natural response to popular unease about education. The Great Debate has, according to Salter and Tapper (1981, p. 220), provided 'the appropriate ideological reinforcement', and what more appropriate tactic for increasing central power could there be than by seemingly strengthening *democratic* control. As Cockburn (1977) argued in her study of local government in Lambeth, the trend towards centralisation bypasses local representative democracy and therefore the use of participatory kinds of involvement can be seen as a front, a legitimation exercise. What it achieves is a kind of diversion of attention away from the real source of central authority decision-making. In accountability terms it appears that schools and teachers must face increasingly centralised prescriptions *about* education while having to manufacture their acceptability, or explain what happens *in* education to a wider community. Teachers then appear to stand at the interface of centralised/localised power relations, and what appear to be issues of management from one perspective can equally be seen as issues of control from another. In a more recent study of school governing bodies directed by Kogan (see Johnson 1983) the team found that one problem for many of them was the lack of any real role definition — certainly nothing so clearly stated as in Bacon's Sheffield. In these circumstances writes Johnson (1983, p. 119) 'the "woolly" definition of the governing body's role lends itself to manipulation by those interests that happen to be the most powerful — school or LEA, professional or political'. Moreover the team found that the lack of a clearly defined role or expectations resulted in a corresponding difficulty in relating to both the professionals in school and the local community, so much so that the team were led to consider (Johnson 1983, p. 131) 'that governing bodies do not represent a significant location for exchange between professional and lay interests . . . '. They go on to draw out some of the implications for 'accountability', suggesting that only when a governing body feels itself 'external' to the school, as opposed to an integral and therefore supportive part of it, can it then take on the accountability purpose.

In both of these studies of school governing bodies the proposition is considered that more effective accountability may be realised by means of increased democratic community participation in the governance and management of schools. Bacon's study revealed this claim to be unfounded, showing how the newly constituted school boards in Sheffield were manipulated to serve existing interests. Kogan's team suggests that participation by the community on governing bodies might in fact take them too 'close' to the schools, resulting in their 'incorporation' or 'integration' and thus denying them the distance for real accountability. In both cases the factor in common is the 'resources', or 'power' or 'strategies' which the institution of the school could muster to insulate itself from these outside pressures. In other words the setting-up of a system, the making of 'facilitative arrangements', was not enough and it failed to achieve an increased accountability by activity at the level of implementation.

What of these strategies then? Becker (1955, pp. 222–223) notes:

> Institutions try to become self-contained systems of power and protect themselves against interference from outside. Institutions are the means by which society delegates particular functions to specialised groups, always retaining the right to examine and pass judgement on that group's performance. Institutional functionaries feel that they understand the problems involved better than any layman and dislike any potential or actual interference, wanting to be left free to run things in their own way. Consequently, they erect defensive barriers designed to keep outsiders on the outside and prevent the surrounding society from directly affecting the institution's operation.

Hanson (1976, p. 37) elaborates this view, describing how teachers may defend the autonomy of their professional zone. Significantly though, he says, 'this type of power is one-sided in that it can be used only to block an attempt at outside intervention'. And he emphasises, 'it cannot be used by teachers to initiate change'. Woods (1983, p. 111) too reflects on the 'coping nature' of a particular action. Coping he says 'takes place at the intersection of biography and structure. It is where personal intention meets social constraint'. So 'strategies' in this sense are essentially tactics of internal *accommodation*, means by which 'spheres of influence' may be 'defended' or outside pressure 'coped' with. 'At the heart of coping', writes Woods (1983, p. 111) 'is the preservation of self'. Dale

(1981, p. 80) says that to understand the response of teachers to changing expectations it is essential to consider '. . . their effort to control as far as possible their work situation — to preserve convenient, acceptable and tested ways of doing things, even in the face of changing demands'.

An interesting possibility of doing this has presented itself in the recent developments of school self-evaluation schemes. The potential of these schemes as a means of increasing external control over schools is examined in Chapters 15 and 16. What is clear from that discussion is that the notion of 'strategy' enables us to examine the ways in which 'implementation' may be prevented, so that the penetration of the professional sphere may be resisted. Given that, as Elliott (1979, p. 6) suggests, 'Evaluation should be viewed as a participatory process rather than something that is done to teachers', facilitating measures of accountability for teachers which do not engage them in this participatory process seem doomed to fail at the level of implementation, and it is this level of implementation which is so crucial. As Becker (1955, p. 224) noted a long time ago,

> The results of the educator's effort to run his enterprise in his own way, with no interference from outside, is thus quite important for the kind of education the child receives . . .

a fact more recently emphasised by Welton (1980, pp. 26–27), who argues that accountability must deal with professional decision-making, 'professional judgements about their effect on the outcomes of learning situations'. For Hanson (1976, p. 33), this is the critical dimension since it is through the actions of teachers 'that the school succeeds or fails in its mission'.

It appears then that the reality of any kind of accountability depends on the level of professional participation within the institution. The greater the degree of professional participation the more problematic is the individual accountability of the head for the decisions of the institution, though the importance of the head's representative role is enhanced, as shown in Chapter 10. And, as the Noble and Pym study showed, at a high level of professional participation it may be possible for the professionals totally to insulate themselves from external responsibility in the short term, protecting their zone or sphere of influence to such an extent that real accountability becomes impossible. The example of school self-evaluation schemes also serves to show that while they may 'facilitate' measures of accountability, their implementation remains problematic. Clearly, the fundamental questions remain, who is answerable and how?

CONCLUSION

How do we breach this impasse? The conclusion to this chapter considers the notion of 'responsibility' and the possibilities it offers to clarify the complex inter-relationships of accountability and participation. Responsibility is particularly helpful in that it is a dual concept, involving as it does both responsibility *for* something and responsibility *to* someone. Being a teacher implies both.

Teachers feel primarily responsible to parents, to the community for the education of their children and they generally take this responsibility seriously. It is a 'responsibility' which is not only subject to vigorous evaluation by parents and the community, it is also for many teachers the primary source of their satisfaction and the basis of their self-image. For these teachers, responsibility is tied up in their relationships with children in the classroom. This is the teacher's 'zone' and the minutiae of what goes on there — can my children read, does Frank know his tables, has Jenny had any breakfast this morning — all transcend wider issues of prescription and expectation. In this instance responsibility is individualistic, particularistic and the basis of teachers' claim to autonomy.

Responsibility might also have a 'collective' dimension. As teachers develop an 'extended professionality' (Hoyle 1974) and increasingly participate in school decision-making, so responsibility becomes shared. In this way professional 'participation' refers to the *ways* in which the school gets its business done. It is at this level that we described an interaction of teaching and management zones or spheres of influence. Also at this level it is entirely appropriate that teachers are responsible — responsibility is owed to their clients and the community for the way in which they do the job. This is accountability *through* the participation of professionals.

However, the usual focus of accountability is not at this level. It is rather about what the education system is doing as a whole, what it is *producing* as the result of the massive investment it receives. In this way notions of accountability infer that teaching as a profession is responsible to society as a whole. Their responsibility is universalistic and hence they should be accountable. The turbulence of the last decade with its renegotiation of the teachers' professional mandate has seen the end of a period of sanctioning professional autonomy and a move to state heteronomy (Johnson 1977, p. 108). As such, accountability can be seen as an 'intervention' into the teacher–parent relationship. A strengthened central authority now issues guidelines on the curriculum and prescribes how schools should relate to parents (for example, Education Act 1980).

At this level the education system is deemed responsible for what 'society' wants and suggestions have been considered as to how to ensure its accountability, for example through strengthened governing bodies. However, such systems of 'representative democracy' might also be problematic. Representatives represent 'interests' or values and accountability in this sense must be considered a part of this. But where is the popular democratic debate about values? Where is the local or community dimension? Have we got a national level view of accountability for an education system which, given the manifestly differential local provision, is anything but a national system? This is accountability *against* participation by the 'community'.

But what then can teachers be responsible for? MacIntyre (1977, p. 3) provides a useful contribution. He distinguishes between *responsibility* and *intention*. For him, responsibility is something more than intention. In general, he says, 'acceptance of responsibility for something means that one can and will plan to meet given criteria', and also, importantly, that 'one is prepared to have one's performance evaluated in terms of those criteria'. It seems that those who talk about accountability in terms of some nationally imposed 'standards' do not fully appreciate its relationship to 'responsibility'. Teachers may have the intention to ensure a child's progress to a certain standard. They may even accept the responsibility for planning and providing the requisite experience for learning, although their planning will be contingent on the materials and resources available to them. But can they accept the responsibility for the standards attained by their children? MacIntyre thinks not. To hold the teacher responsible for 'standards' ignores the increasingly hostile environment in which they work — the lack of support they get from the community, the family, the media, the decreasing level of resourcing in schools. As Becher and Maclure

(1978, pp. 24–25) have put it:

> To be generally accountable for professional conduct in providing efficient instruction in socially approved subjects is one thing: to be held accountable for the success of particular policies adopted by cost-conscious managers is quite another.

Those who see accountability in terms of the sharpening of the managerial blade should recognise that it cuts both ways, which means that accountability in terms of 'standards' must also include accountability in terms of resources.

Teachers can and should be accountable for their own performance in school, and by participating in the decision-making in the school can be accountable to the school's clients for the total 'educational' experiences it provides. The reality of this accountability is, as we have shown, hard to achieve, but may be more readily facilitated as schools become increasingly 'open' — perhaps as 'community schools'. The more open to the community, the more the community participate in the educational business of the school, the sharper this accountability becomes (Thorp 1983).

Clearly though, high levels of professional participation must not be allowed to deny real participation by the community. Neither must demands for teacher accountability from a strengthened 'central' source deny the possibility of genuine popular debate about educational 'values'. As Elliott (1976, p. 193 and 199) concludes, at issue is educational justice:

> . . . people as members of the general public have the right to know if courses of action and policies result in the inequalities of liberty . . . similarly people have the right to know as members of the public if the pursuit of sectional interests infringes the principles of justice.

Accountability is a legitimate demand in democratic society and so is participation. If demands for accountability cut across real popular participation in the debate about values or if high level professional participation denies the possibility of accountability then a choice has to be made, because accountability *and* participation are not always legitimate demands.

REFERENCES

Bacon, W. (1978) *Public Accountability and the Schooling System*. London: Harper and Row.

Baron, G. and Howell, D. A. (1974) *The Government and Management of Schools*. London: Athlone.

Becher, T. and Maclure, S. (1978) *Accountability in Education*. Windsor: NFER.

Becker, H. S. (1955) 'Schools and systems of social status'. In Becker, H. S. (1970) *Sociological Work*. Aldine.

Belasco, J. A. and Alutto, J. A. (1972) 'Decisional participation and teacher satisfaction'. In Houghton, V., McHugh, R. and

Morgan, C. (ed.) (1975) *Management in Education*. London: Ward Lock.

Cockburn, C. (1977) *The Local State*. Pluto.

Dale, R. (1979) 'The politicalisation of school deviance: Reactions to William Tyndale'. In Barton, C. and Meighan, R. (ed.) (1979) *Schools, Pupils and Deviance*. Nafferton.

Dale, R. (1981) 'From expectations to outcomes in education systems'. *Interchange*, **12**(2–3).

DES (1977) *A New Partnership for our Schools — The Taylor Report*. London: HMSO.

DES (1984) *Parental Influence at School: a new framework for school government in England*

and Wales (Green Paper), Cmnd 9242. London: HMSO.

DES (1985) *Better Schools* (White Paper), Cmnd. 9469. London: HMSO.

Duke, D. L., Showers, B. K. and Imber, M. (1980) 'Teachers and shared decision making: the costs and benefits of involvement'. *Educational Administration Quarterly*, **16**(1) Winter.

Dyer, H. S. (1970) 'Towards objective criteria of professional accountability in the schools of New York City'. In Browder, L. H. (ed.) (1971) *Emerging Patterns of Administrative Accountability*. Berkeley, California: McCutchan.

Elliott, J. (1976) 'Democratic evaluation as social criticism: or putting the judgement back into evaluation'. In Norris, N. (ed.) (1976) *SAFARI 2 Theory in Practice*. CARE Occasional Publication No 4.

Elliott, J. (1979) 'Accountability, progressive education and school based evaluation'. *Education 3–13*, **7**.

Finn, D., Grant, N. and Johnson, R. (1977) 'Social democracy, education and the crisis'. *Working Papers No 10, On Ideology*. CCCS University of Birmingham: Hutchinson.

Hanson, M. (1976) 'Beyond the bureaucratic model: a study of power and autonomy in educational decision-making'. *Interchange*, **7**(2).

Hoyle, E. (1974) 'Professionality, professionalism and control'. In Houghton V. et al (ed.) (1975) *The Management of Organisations and Individuals*. London: Ward Lock.

Hughes, M. G. (1978) 'Reconciling professional and administrative concerns'. In Bush, T., Glatter, R., Goodey, J. and Riches, C. (ed.) (1980) *Approaches to School Management*. London: Harper and Row.

Jennings, A. (1975) 'The participation of the teaching staff in decision-making in schools'. In McHugh, R. (ed.) (1976) *A Case Study in Management*. Milton Keynes: Open University Press.

Johnson, D. (1983) *School Governing Bodies Project 1980— 1983: Final Report for the DES*. University of Brunel: Educational Studies Unit, Department of Government.

Johnson, T. (1977) 'The professions in the class structure'. In Scase, R. (ed.) (1977) *Industrial Society: Class, Cleavage and Control*. London: Allen and Unwin.

Lortie, D. (1967) 'Rational decision-making: is it possible today?'. In House, E. R. (ed.) (1973) *School evaluation: the politics and process*. Berkeley, California: McCutchan.

Lortie, D. (1969) 'The balance of control and autonomy in elementary school teaching'. In Etzioni, A. (ed.) (1969) *The Semi-Professions and their Organisation*. New York: Free Press.

Lortie, D. (1975) *Schoolteacher*. University of Chicago.

McIntyre, D. (1977) *What responsibilities should teachers accept*. University of Stirling, Occasional Papers No 1.

Nias, J. (1972) 'Pseudo-participation and the success of innovation in the introduction of the B.Ed.'. *Sociological Review*, **20**(2).

Noble, T. and Pym, B. (1970) 'Collegial authority and the receding locus of power'. *British Journal of Sociology*, **21**, December.

OECD (1975) *Educational development strategy in England and Wales*. London: HMSO.

Peters, R. S. (ed.) (1976) *The Role of the Head*. London: Routledge and Kegan Paul.

Pratt, S. (1981) 'Subordinates strategies of interaction in the management of schools'. *Educational Administration*, **9**(2).

Ramsay, H. (1977) 'Cycles of control'. *Sociology*, **11**(3) September.

Salter, B. and Tapper, T. (1981) *Education, politics and the State*. London: Grant McIntyre.

Silver, H. (1980) *Education and the social condition*. London: Routledge and Kegan Paul.

Thorp, J. (1983) *Coping with Community: A View of Management in a Community Primary School*. Unpublished MEd Dissertation, University of Birmingham.

Watts, J. (1976) 'Sharing it out: the role of the head in participatory government'. In Peters, R. S. (ed) (1976) *The Role of the Head*. London: Routledge and Kegan Paul.

Welton, J. (1980) 'Accountability in educational organisations'. *Educational Administration*, **9**(1 and 3).

Woods, P. (1983) 'Coping at school through humour'. *British Journal of Sociology of Education*, **4**(2).

18

SUSTAINING VIGOROUS EDUCATIONAL INSTITUTIONS IN A PERIOD OF RETRENCHMENT

Michael Matthewman

INTRODUCTION

For the two principal groups in the education service, the learners and their teachers, retrenchment is probably the critical problem of the decade. Retrenchment for learners, discussed more fully in Chapter 5, is related to the high levels of youth unemployment and means changing expectations regarding patterns of work and leisure with its consequential effect on their educational needs. Retrenchment for teachers, also discussed in Chapter 5, means adjusting to the effects of a service which is quite rapidly contracting in size following two decades of unparalleled growth. What are the implications of these twin pressures of retrenchment for the crucial task of sustaining vigorous educational institutions? Moreover, what exactly do we understand by the term 'a vigorous educational institution'? It is the purpose of this chapter to examine these problems, beginning with the next section which will attempt to describe the characteristics of a vigorous educational institution and which is followed by a section which distinguishes between the problems faced by different sectors of the education system. This leads on to an analysis of the difficulties of sustaining effective institutions and a typology of institutions which face different problems because of their particular circumstances. A penultimate section discusses selected institution-based strategies for sustaining institutional vigour. The chapter ends with a concluding discussion of the difficulties and opportunities faced by institutions in the 1980s.

VIGOROUS EDUCATIONAL INSTITUTIONS

Vigorous educational institutions can briefly be defined as those which are effective in meeting existing and changing client needs. Policy choices made by institutions and system managers, in relation to human resources (learners, teachers and ancillaries) and physical resources, must be subject to the acid test of their effect on pupils and students. The importance of sound policy choices places a high premium on the quality of an institution's processes of evaluation which, Hoyle (1980) argues, should focus on five specific areas of scrutiny:

(a) curriculum (balance, choice);
(b) organisation (grouping, pastoral structure);
(c) resources (buildings, equipment, staff numbers and range of competence, ancillary support);
(d) evaluation (proposed modes for internal evaluation);
(e) innovation (proposals, implementation and evaluation procedures, costs).

However, while these are all relevant, they do not comprise an exhaustive list. Other areas must also be scrutinised by an institution concerned to become or remain vigorous. These would include the liaison with the community (parents, industry and traders); professional support services (in-service training and specialist skill centres, advisers and HMI); outside agencies (social and welfare support services, courts); local institutions (feeder — primary, secondary, FE/HE); youth employment service (careers, training schemes).

Evaluation of the institution upon such a broad base would give an indication of its effectiveness over the whole range of its activities. An institution such as a primary or secondary school is very much a focal point for the community. Its vigour must therefore be assessed not only in terms of its academic effectiveness, but also in the manner in which it presents itself, and its student-clients, to the community.

It is of paramount importance that an institution is vigorous in attempting to meet existing perceived needs of the clients. It must also make assessments of how such needs will change in the future, and be sufficiently flexible in its organisation to accommodate such changes. From the above, it will be noted that client needs have to be divided into distinct groups; first the students, who are the current throughput of the system, and second, other users and providers of the system, parents, employers and the community.

Students need to benefit from a well-balanced or structured curriculum tailored to their individual ability and potential, taught by able and committed teachers within a well-regulated environment. The teachers should have at their disposal sufficient resources to discharge their responsibilities effectively. However, not only must the institution be seen to be effective in terms of the existing and changing intellectual and academic needs of its student clients, it must also be responsive to the changing environment or sub-system of which it is a part. It would, therefore, be inappropriate to establish one set of criteria by which to judge the relative vigour of all institutions, as each is striving to meet the needs of the community it serves. The problems to be managed in a relatively underprivileged inner-ring community place different constraints and responsibilities upon an institution to one which serves a more affluent commuter belt community.

The perceived needs of the students are often subject to the constraints placed upon the teaching institution by the requirements of examining boards, the professions and many other clients. These do not remain the same. For example, in addition to the traditional expectation that school leavers be numerate and literate, it is now expected that they have an understanding of aspects of information and computer technology. More difficult is the change in the labour market. Once, it was expected that students should proceed from school to further and higher education or to the work-place, but now young people must also be prepared for the possibility of unemployment and youth training schemes. The vigorous institution, therefore, is one which is sufficiently flexible to balance the perceived needs of all its clients by preparing its students to meet the multiplicity of changing demands which will be placed upon them as they enter the wider community.

SECTORAL DIFFERENCES IN THE PERIOD OF RETRENCHMENT

As indicated above, because institutions of similar types serve varying communities, each with differing specific needs, there can be no general criteria which can be developed to assess the relative vigour of all institutions. Moreover, even institutions serving one particular community can experience different challenges in meeting the needs of community so that, again, no general criteria can be developed to evaluate their relative success. Sectoral differences are particularly important in this respect.

Although primary enrolments have declined dramatically in recent years, the ACSET (1981) predictions indicate a rise in enrolments as from 1986. However, the decrease in the primary enrolments will continue to affect secondary enrolments until 1991 — the secondary population will begin to expand again in 1992. Therefore, while it is apparent that the previously declining primary rolls will continue to affect the secondary sector in the period 1986–1991, during this time there will be growth in the primary sector. Thus, there will be no uniformity in the manner in which retrenchment will affect institutions at either the primary or secondary levels. In the period 1986–1991 some 18 000 teachers are planned to be recruited for the primary sector, while approximately 42 000 fewer teachers will be required within the secondary sector by the end of the period. With regard to the tertiary sector, similar specific problems exist which are explained in part by demographic trends and in part by changing government policy, as is discussed more fully in Chapters 7 and 13.

Nevertheless, there are local policies and national trends which affect all institutions. The traditional academic sixth form is being replaced in many areas by open-access sixth forms or separate post-16 colleges. Lack of employment prospects for leavers, with the attendant shortage of apprenticeships, has resulted in a change of emphasis in the work of many colleges of further education. Many are now sustained in part by government-sponsored schemes for the young unemployed which are provided by the MSC and administered jointly with the LEA (see Chapter 7). In order to sustain their multiplicity of levels of work, and indeed to motivate staff, they have entered into more vigorous competition with the schools to attract more of the 16–19 age group to their institutions.

This fact of life is not necessarily helpful to those attempting to maintain and sustain the work of the 11–18 comprehensive. It is, however, in accordance with the philosophy expressed in the MacFarlane Report (DES 1981) that courses, whether of a general or vocational nature, do not belong to the domain of one sector or another. Thus, because young people seek to be amongst their peers, one of the likely consequences of the current retrenchment would appear to be an emphasis upon an institutional break between compulsory and post-compulsory education.

These distinctions between primary, 11–16 secondary and post-compulsory education illustrate that while there is contraction in one sector, there may well be growth in another. It also shows that changes in sectoral size can be encouraged by agencies other than the LEA, particularly the Manpower Services Commission. These sectoral differences have implications for teachers, who are likely to be encouraged by some LEAs to move from secondary to primary schools. Jackson (1983) also notes moves in the other direction in the case of a local reorganisation involving a change of primary transfer from age 12 to 11 in order to sustain secondary rolls and curriculum.

The desirability of such movement is, by implication, questioned by the DES (1983) proposal to introduce the practice of labelling the teaching qualification according to principal subject and age group. This suggests that teachers within each sector have specific skills and specialist subject knowledge which are not readily transferable. However, because retrenchment has a different significance and impact in the several sectors of education, it may be administratively expedient to move teachers between institutions to fulfil short-term staffing requirements. While to do so might make administrative sense for the decision-makers involved, in that teacher resources are deployed where most needed, it may not always be in the best interests of individual teachers or their clients.

These resource imperatives which shape the context within which institutions must work are one of the several issues considered in the next section, which examines the difficulties of sustaining vigorous institutions.

MEETING CLIENT NEEDS

The challenge of renewal

Since a vigorous institution is one which must be sufficiently flexible to meet pupil/student needs and to respond to the political and societal needs of the larger community, it must have a capacity to innovate. This creates an immediate problem because, as Taylor (1976) argues, it is the conventional wisdom that innovation and growth are inter-related, an argument which poses the question of whether or not there can be innovation without growth.

Responding to this problem of innovation without growth, Taylor suggests we reconsider the concept of growth. At the time of writing his paper, he argues, growth had become synonymous with its economic meaning of regular increments of additional resources, normally on a scale large enough to back projects of research and development, to recruit new staff, to establish new departments and provide buildings and equipment. He emphasises, ' . . . that we have come to associate innovation with increases in the size and scale of the educational operations'.

Therefore, with contraction — fewer numbers in many sectors and reduced financial budgets — the accepted concepts of 'growth' and 'innovation' must be re-examined, and a new understanding or appreciation of growth realised in which innovation may flourish. Taylor suggests that such a definition may be found not in the writing of economists, but rather in those of psychologists. It is in Rogers (1968) that such an approach to the perceived needs of the individual clients is found:

> . . . the goal of education must be to develop individuals who are open to change, who are flexible and adaptive . . . a climate conducive to personal growth . . . . Nearly all individuals have within themselves the capacity to move and grow in a socialised and self-fulfilling direction. . . .

Innovation must be viewed not only as a phenomenon supported by central funding for large-scale adoption, but rather as activities which can be internalised by particular or individual institutions. The need for innovation arises from several factors, including changes in the size and composition of groups or schools; changes in the types of societal skills and knowledge required by the community, and also those based upon responses to new techniques. Taylor also makes the point that while there has been — and still is — much secondary reorganisation, there has been little change in classroom technology or pedagogical technique; and despite all that is currently achieved through distance teaching (the use of audio-visual aids, etc.) most children are still taught by traditional methods.

He argues that there is no necessary or essential link between innovation (equated with improvement) and economic growth. He suggests that if growth, with its attendant concept of innovation, is equated with personal development and not solely economic factors, then there is considerable scope for the development of educational establishments as vigorous institutions. It is within such parameters that lies the challenge of renewal for institutions.

Taylor then presents a list of 11 specific ways by which we can stimulate or facilitate innovation within schools or colleges at a time when there is unlikely to be economic growth:

(a) redefine growth in psychological rather than economic terms;
(b) identify the good characteristics of one's own institution which might be transferable to another organisation;
(c) avoid committing resources on a permanent basis to activities or ventures which may have an uncertain future, and monitor or evaluate closely all those activities to which resources have been committed;
(d) ensure that staff development procedures incorporate a more open approach to promotion procedures, making provision for the development of 'intermediate statuses' for those whose professional development or promotion is effectively blocked; and also to allow provision for the early retirement of senior colleagues without loss of salary or status;
(e) maintain and enhance flexibility in the deployment of vacancies with the use of short-term contracts and secondments;
(f) endeavour to maintain maximum staff levels in the light of all known budgetary conditions to maintain staff morale;
(g) encourage staff to invest in their own education and to diversify their interest in order to minimise the effects of career frustration;
(h) generate effective administrative procedures and data-processing techniques to

maximise the useful deployment of all resources, particularly human, so that staff can concentrate upon the corporate educative task rather than the peripheral ones;

(i)   delegate responsibility for the utilisation of scarce resources to those most affected by their deployment;

(j)   maintain a balance, for the enhancement and continuity of staff morale, between security and reward for seniority and early and rapid promotion for the innovator;

(k)   devise means for the management of the inept and the appraisal of their performance vis à vis their accountability to the institution and its clients.

In short, the above indicates that Taylor believes that innovation can take place within an organisation, without any additional financial resources. However, it does mean that an institution requires both a comprehensive staff development policy and a strong administrative base. Many of the items identified also assume the existence of clear channels of communication for consultation and discussion, which are essential at all periods in the life of a vigorous institution, and are described later in the section on institution-based strategies.

This suggests that the challenges which face institutions at the present time are not essentially any different to those experienced in the past. They are concerned with managing the institution and ensuring its development together with its innovative role. The important difference lies in the absence of growth in resources to assist this activity. This calls upon the skills of managers or administrators to motivate staff to high levels of commitment towards the institution. However, such motivational skills will have greater or less success depending upon changes which are made at the system level to factors which will cause educational institutions particular difficulty. The following sub-section identifies some of the system-wide aspects of retrenchment which create problems.

Retrenchment as a systemic problem

Even if it is possible to contribute to the challenge of institutional renewal by redefining the concept of growth in a way which moves away from its resource meaning, this does not mean we can avoid consequences from the contraction brought about by falling rolls. At its crudest level, falling rolls appear to offer a logic for resource reductions: with fewer children in the classroom, the educational provision can be proportionately reduced (Stenning 1980). The attraction of this logic to decision-makers in central government is inevitably strong at a time of general economic difficulty and creates a poignant contrast to the eager anticipation with which the advent of falling rolls was once viewed. Wright (1980) noted that it was welcomed by many teachers as a time when the PTR could be improved and the quality of education improved, a view which itself appears to make a rather naive connection between levels of provision and standards of performance. However, even if the link between provision and quality must be treated cautiously, the importance of adequate provision for clients and teachers is widely recognised.

The problems encountered by clients and teachers are not dissimilar. Both require the provision of sufficient financial resources to maintain the operation of the plant and to supply the essential consumables for the learning activity — paper, textbooks, library books and other teaching materials. The lack of sufficient materials almost inevitably impairs the quality of the education provided. Learners require teachers most certainly; but they also need reassurance that continuity of education and teaching will be available. Anxieties are created in this respect by local authority rationalisation and re-organisation policies. They create an uncertainty which means it is not always possible to provide the client with such assurance. An institutional example of this is where a specialist subject teacher leaves an institution not to be replaced (Bailey 1982), because either the institution was operating at the maximum levels of the agreed pupil–teacher ratio or because valuable Burnham points have to be 'lost'. It can also be caused by LEA policies to redistribute special groups or by the operation of minimum group-size numbers which also have consequences for the size of other groups, thereby depriving clients of opportunities previously offered.

Uncertainty for learners is matched by the implications of falling rolls for teaching staff. As numbers within institutions fall, the spectre of redeployment or redundancy appears (Killick 1980). This, with the attendant lack of promotion prospects, has the effect of lowering morale.

The dearth of promotion opportunities is clearly demonstrated by Wright's (1980) analysis of the number of points available under the Burnham Unit Total System for allocation in the 20-year period culminating in 1992. Saran (1982) has suggested that this situation might be alleviated by the introduction of a professional salary scale for all experienced and competent teachers; second that there should be a salary scale offering higher rewards for those in managerial and administrative roles and, third, that salaries should be considered in relation to conditions of service. A contrasting view of the merits of these proposals for educational outcomes is taken by Hywel Thomas in Chapter 5.

One important similarity about the contexts of learners and teachers needs to be underlined because it illuminates the acute difficulties of educational institutions at the present time. The changing needs of learners require substantial change from educational institutions but at a time when the absence of promotion opportunities for teachers robs education managers of a traditional inducement for encouraging positive attempts to respond effectively to learner needs.

Much more could be written about these system-wide issues, but the focus of this chapter is on how institutions can respond to the problem using their own initiative. In so doing it is necessary to recognise that not all institutions face the same problems in the coming years. Accordingly, the next sub-section offers a typology in which institutions are classified in terms of their particular circumstances.

Retrenchment as an institutional problem

Written in the context of an analysis of falling rolls, Mercer's (1980) model of the five stages of organisational life is helpful in gaining an appreciation of retrenchment as an institutional problem. Each stage of the model presents its own management problems and appropriate management styles:

1. Managing the design and setting-up of an organisation.
2. Managing expansion.
3. Managing within a predictable organisational framework.
4. Managing cutback.
5. Managing a close-down. (Mercer p. 97)

Mercer makes the point that while the stages ' . . . can be considered sequential and often are so . . . in conditions of decline, retreat and turbulence they are likely to be confused, mixed up and unclear'. This confusion will certainly be the case for some educational institutions in the next few years. One example of this overlap has already affected the further education sector where the decline of courses for traditional apprenticeships has required the management of cutbacks within some college department while other departments experience rapid growth in the provision of MSC-sponsored courses. Moreover, like the development of the TVEI courses in schools, these MSC courses often require special organisational frameworks for their management.

Other institutions, depending upon the location of their catchment areas and local demographic trends, will be faced with the job of managing expansion, albeit within strict financial parameters. Different problems will arise where the management of merger will be the principal task, because this will lead towards either the closure of one or more schools and/or the amalgamation of the remnants, re-opening as a new institution. In such instances, while the opportunity to manage the establishment and design of an organisation within clearly defined parameters will be there, it will probably be particularly difficult to achieve because of the pre-histories of the several institutions. The examples mentioned here illustrate the range and complexity of the circumstances of particular institutions. However, this does not mean that no order can be identified from these cases and circumstances. In fact, it is suggested, that the typology given below offers a means of classifying educational institutions faced with retrenchment.

1. Institutions which are growing, either through the effects of local demographic trends or LEA organisational policy or combinations of both.
2. Institutions which will experience a reduction in size, either through the effects of local demographic trends or LEA organisational policy or combinations of both.
3. Institutions which remain constant.
4. Institutions which will face problems of the redistribution of client groups because of LEA policies: the loss or otherwise of sixth forms or special units; collapse of apprenticeships and growth of YTS.
5. Institutions which face the problems and prospects of re-organisation e.g. 11–18 school systems changing to 11–16 with 16+ colleges.
6. Institutions which face amalgamation.
7. Institutions which face closure.

It may be that within each type there are common problems and experiences and that managers of institutions, even from different sectors, may have something to learn from each other. In this respect the experiences of managers in and of primary schools may be of some value to colleagues in other sectors. It is also likely, given this range of institutional circumstance, that policies appropriate for one category of institution within the typology would be quite unsuitable for others. For example, if closure is a recognised and accepted fact and is also near at hand, an attempt to implement a major initiative on internal communication systems (see next section) would be inappropriate because of its orientation to the future needs of the institution. By contrast, work on a staff development scheme with a strong individual-needs perspective would be far more likely to benefit teacher morale and contribute to the effectiveness of the provision for the learners.

The typology presented here and its implications for management strategies shape the purpose and use of the next section in this chapter. In proposing and examining a range of institution-based strategies for sustaining vigour it is not suggested that they are appropriate for all institutions. They are suggested as a range of strategies from which institutional managers might select, given their needs and circumstances.

INSTITUTION-BASED STRATEGIES FOR SUSTAINING VIGOUR

Introduction

Attention has so far been given to some of the problems generic to retrenchment, and it has also been noted that vigorous institutions are those which maintain a flexible approach to the needs of the client and respond swiftly and sensitively to changing expectations. It is now appropriate to consider strategies which may be employed by which institutions can sustain this flexibility. The suggestions are not exhaustive and tend to apply particularly to the secondary sector.

Institutional-based self-innovated staff development policies

Taylor (1976) has expressed the view that there can be innovation without growth, although it was argued above that it requires the institution to have a comprehensive staff-development policy and a strong administrative base. It is also contended that staff development is equally important at all stages of organisational development, whether it be at a time of expansion or contraction, although in times of expansion staff-development programmes can flourish more easily, and are more obviously recognised as necessary to the development of the individual and to the development of the institution. However, at a time of cut-back, or for the management of institutions facing other retrenchment problems (see above section), staff-development programmes assume an *essential* role in the maintenance of organisational performance and morale. As Stenning (1980) notes, it appears logical to cut back financial expenditure and support at a time of falling rolls, yet it is necessary to train people to operate successfully under unusual conditions both at the managerial/administrative and classroom levels in a new situation.

Greenaway and Harding (1978) suggest that staff development may be said to have four aims, namely:

(a) to help staff perform as effectively as possible in their existing roles including support during probation;
(b) to provide opportunities for staff to prepare themselves for changing duties and responsibilities;
(c) to provide opportunities for members of staff to equip themselves for increased responsibility and career advancement;
(d) to enhance job satisfaction.

However, one obstacle to the implementation of the third aim of enabling staff to prepare for career advancement is the lack of promotion prospects for many teachers in the immediate future. Yet this does not detract from the view that institutions should develop such policies.

Writing in a somewhat different context, Spooner (1978) makes observations about the 'civilised management of professional staff', which add a further dimension to an appeciation of the aims of staff development. These are:

1. To involve in policy and decision-making those who have to carry out the policy and, as far as detail is concerned, giving scope for judgement to the person doing the job.
2. To treat staff as professional people relying fundamentally on their own standards, self-criticism and devotion to duty and refraining from nagging them about their peccadilloes.
3. To recognise that everyone has strengths and weaknesses and to discriminate sufficiently to exploit strengths and to avoid placing teachers in situations where their weaknesses are apparent to all.
4. To respect different views, diversity of approach and personal idiosyncrasy, recognising that these things add to the richness of living.
5. To create a relaxed atmosphere in which teachers willingly make voluntary contributions to school-life which are well above the call of duty.
6. To spend the maximum amount of time and energy on teaching and learning and to avoid in-fighting, intrigue, introspection and fruitless assessment.

It is argued, therefore, that staff-development policies must be initiated within an institution, even without LEA intervention, and that they would be an aid to the maintenance of staff morale and the work of the institution. A useful starting point could be an audit, an extension of Dennison's (1980) proposal, of teachers' second-subject specialisms. In most institutions this would reveal a wealth of untapped experience and talent which could be directed towards the goals of the institution. It would also mean that the consequence of redeployment for staff, as a result of strict curriculum-led staffing policies, would be less severe and result in a greater degree of security for the individual within the institution.

These second-subject skills could be developed afresh with the support of the heads of department in the appropriate subject who could devise in-service training courses for colleagues which would be open to colleagues from other departments. Such courses or seminars could draw upon the expertise of the departmental head and other members of the department. Their content would be such as to induct probationers and other teachers into the philosophy of the department; to consider matters pertaining to the most effective deployment resources within that subject; to share and update academic knowledge and matters pertaining to teaching methodology and skills (Bailey 1975). Other matters which could be discussed in such a forum might include, for example, grading and evaluation techniques and syllabus review processes. The desired outcome would be a greater understanding and appreciation of the academic discipline for all concerned, whether or not subject specialists, which could lead to either innovation within the department or inter-disciplinary co-operation.

Heads of department have the expertise and knowledge to devise and lead courses within their specialisms, as do those colleagues working within the administrative or management structure. Heads and deputies should be able to devise and lead courses which would give a greater appreciation and understanding of the work of the institution as a whole; the structure and philosophy of the pastoral care system; the philosophy of the school timetable and an appreciation of the significance of the detailed minutiae of its construction; the philosophy of the options system and other matters pertaining to curriculum design. The examination system of the school could also be the subject of scrutiny, with a consideration of the possible or probable impact the new national criteria for examining at $16 + /17 +$ will have on the institution and its curriculum. A wide range of services provided by other professionals which impinge upon the work of the institution can also be made the subject of in-service seminars: the role of the educational psychologist; the role of the HMI and the LEA inspectorate or advisory service; the role of the MSC in relation to TVEI and YTS provision (see Chapter 7), together with a consideration of the work of the feeder schools and other institutions to which pupils/students will proceed. The list of possible professional topics for a self-innovated staff-development programme of in-service training courses would appear to be endless, and could be staffed with the aid of visiting lecturers or speakers at no expense, or very little, to the institution.

While all of the above are relevant strategies to help staff perform more effectively and to prepare them for changing duties and career advancement (Greenaway and Harding 1978), they do not necessarily provide job satisfaction or enrichment. This is more likely to be achieved with Spooner's framework (1978) where staff are encouraged to act professionally, exploiting their strengths in the classroom situation for the benefit of their clients. However, teachers as well as heads of departments expect to have some element of control (Bailey 1973) over their immediate working situation and one way of developing this is through the practice of the rotation of jobs within a department, a scheme which can provide an element of job satisfaction and can also be viewed as a preparation for further promotion. For example, among the tasks which can be rotated within a department on an annual basis are requisitions, the allocation of resources, stock control, checking of exercise books, evaluation of examination results, assessment and grading techniques, preparation of internal examination papers and display work, etc. As tasks can be rotated within a department to ensure that individuals gain job satisfaction and increased professional experience, so also can the tasks which are performed by the senior management team, but perhaps on a bi- or tri-annual basis to preserve continuity of approach (Hodge and Martin 1984). Rotation of some of these senior management jobs might occur not only amongst the senior managers, but also provide an opportunity for a wider experience to be enjoyed by less senior members of staff. Thus, it is possible to note that, 'staff development implies the involvement of the whole staff in the operation and development of the school' (Bailey 1975).

Institutional-based research projects

It is to be expected that not all colleagues will welcome the type of in-service training or professional development outlined above. This may be for one or a combination of reasons. Some will be resistant because such activities normally take place after school hours and could intrude on commitment to lengthy part-time courses or other short courses; others may resist the contribution after school hours because of particular domestic arrangements, or simply lack of interest.

For those who see long courses as a staff-development opportunity, institutional-based research projects may be relevant. They could be encouraged to conduct research into aspects of the institution's organisation and management. Others might be encouraged to serve on locally organised subject-orientated curriculum development committees or examining board panels. The aim of such initiatives, using Hoyle's (1975) terms, is to encourage an extended-professional approach to their work, rather than that of the restricted professional.

Another idea comes from Stenhouse (1975) who observed that the future might hold a move toward 'institutionalised curriculum research and development'. An extension of this concept would be to see colleagues conducting within their own institutions both short and long-term research projects. Some of this research could perhaps be carried out under the supervision or auspices of departments of education in local institutions of higher education. Possible areas for research would include an examination of the decision-making processes within departments; an analysis of the decision-making processes by the senior management team with specific reference to some particular innovation or policy decision; an appraisal or analysis of the various student-assessment schemes employed within the institution; and evaluation of the effectiveness of the staff-development policy. Whatever the project, the research results should be published internally and so become the subject of scrutiny and debate. Indeed, they may influence future policy-making. In summary then, it is suggested that not only is there sufficient expertise within an institution to sustain a programme of self-innovated staff development, but there is also sufficient expertise to sustain a small research programme. The linkage of such research to long courses and to institutions of higher education brings benefits to the individual teacher who obtains a higher degree, facilitates dissemination of research findings and contributes to the development of the school or college on which the research was based.

A third strategy for development is based on the quality of evaluation processes.

Institutional-based self-evaluation schemes

Although Chapters 15 and 16 consider the concept and practice of evaluation, it is appropriate briefly to examine here the practice of institutional self-evaluation, as a further strategy for the maintenance of staff morale and the sustaining of vigour.

A large number of schemes for the evaluation of educational institutions are currently available. Chapters 15 and 16 consider the problems of taking these schemes at their face value, particularly as they relate to the relationships between evaluators and evaluated. In the classification which is developed in Chapter 15 (see Figure 15.1) the internal autonomy of teachers is maintained within processes of 'peer evaluation'. In writing about the internal evaluation of institutions, Stanton (1978) suggests what are effectively the prerequisites for Hywel Thomas's 'peer evaluation' relationships.

First, he notes that there must be full support for the procedures by members of staff; second, a climate in which it is accepted that evaluation is not concerned with awards or criticisms of individual professional competence, and third, an appreciation that such evaluation will not be used for the purposes of accountability. He also argues that such evaluation must take place within a climate of mutual trust between professionals.

However, if senior managers in schools become involved in this activity, it must become difficult for them not to act upon individual deficiencies which may be revealed in the course of the procedures. This can lead to the 'internal control' relationship discussed in

Chapters 15 and 16, reflecting a managerial ideology ' . . . where superordinates have a right and an obligation to monitor and judge subordinates' (p. 383). Whether evaluations within this relationship structure are viewed as threatening or supportive will partly depend upon how the relationship is conducted (see Figure 15.2) as illustrated by the case of Great Barr School examined in Chapter 16.

Should the supportive aspect not clearly be established some teachers will inevitably regard the procedures as being hostile. Nevertheless, the average conscientious teacher has little to fear from evaluation procedures of this type which seek to support and improve classroom performance for the benefit of both the teacher and the client. Indeed, Marland (1982) makes the case that teachers must get used to the idea of such evaluation when he writes, 'Teaching can be seen . . . as a professional lifetime devoted to reviewing, considering, discussing, and to some extent or other participating in decisions about the work of others as well as oneself'.

The whole purpose of the evaluative exercise is to provide feedback on every aspect of an institution's performance in order to ensure that strategies for improvement can be formulated and implemented. This concept of feedback raises the whole question of communication, which is considered in the following two sub-sections.

Staff communication and consultation systems

Writing about the management of contraction within an institution of higher education, Bone (1982) recalls the need for him to communicate all external policies affecting his college to the staff, in association with the professional bodies represented therein. Indeed, a committee was established whose members had considerable influence amongst their colleagues, and this brought all ' . . . to regard the problem of contraction as their problem, and not merely one which the management had to face'.

This is not the place to examine the concepts of participation or consultation as they relate to educational institutions (see Chapter 17), but rather to draw attention to the need for comprehensive communication policies. These can help to provide a sense of security for all within an institution, and are probably essential to the maintenance of high levels of morale. Sugarman (1975) notes: 'There is no aspect of the school whose functioning is not affected by the efficiency of communication, since this is a fundamental element in all social relationships'.

Hence, particularly at a time of retrenchment, there is a case for communicating, to all the teaching staff, information about any LEA policy which may affect an institution. The prudent head teacher will outline the implications of any such policy for the staff in detail, even if this is a task which has to be repeated at regular intervals.

It is the task of management within an institution to minimise the doubts and uncertainties which lie ahead. It is also the task of management outside the institution, the local education authorities, to make this possible by refraining from announcing in the media re-organisation schemes before informing the heads and staff of the affected institutions of their plans.

There are two basic modes for school or institutional communication. The first is a basic one-way, non-participatory system which can function through the use of a staff calendar. The second mode involves two-way communication with heads of department meetings, departmental meetings, house staff meetings, formal staff meetings and staff discussion-group meetings, all with formal minutes of which copies are sent to the head. The first mode of communication seeks to remind colleagues of their professional obligations and commitments. Halsall (1973) notes that the objective with respect to the large school is to ' . . . help everyone maintain contact with the school's life . . . in what would be an amorphous and anonymous institution'. One must, of course, add the comment: if they care to read! Failure to read or to observe instructions in any of the official documents must lead to a bureaucratic rebuke, because, as Watson (1978) notes: 'An individual teacher should be, and generally accepts that he is, accountable to his colleagues and the head for carrying out his duties responsibly and efficiently . . . '.

The second mode of communication is where the head and the management team pass agendas to colleagues to discuss at various levels of meeting, such as heads of departments, heads of houses and year tutors. These relate to matters of professional importance relevant to curriculum development, pastoral care and school organisation, and not least, at times of retrenchment, to matters of LEA policy regarding the future development of the institution. The two-way aspect of the process is evidenced by the fact that minutes are produced. For such meetings to be effective organs of communication, and indeed consultation, Jennings (1977) urges all relevant working or discussion papers be made available to the participants prior to the meeting to enable informed discussion to take place.

It is therefore contended that an institution with clear and precise channels of communication, which can be used effectively for consultation procedures, is one which has a strong administrative base. The next strategy develops the theme of communication in relation to parents and the wider community.

Community and parental communications

Where the existence of a school or institution is threatened by re-organisation policies, parental support for the institution is likely to increase. Parents have a right to be consulted about the future prospects for their children's continuing educational requirements. Parental support can be an added boost to the morale of both staff and student-clients. Izbicki (1983) notes that parental support can be used in a variety of ways in the primary classroom to support and sustain the work of professionals.

The school or college often forms a focal point for many activities within local communities, especially in rural areas, and hence its continued existence is the desire of a large proportion of the citizens. This is particularly so with respect to those who have had cause to benefit from their 'alma mater', as in the American experience quoted by Shattock (1979) where strong community support is forthcoming for the institution because of the costs involved in sending pupils to other schools. A similar phenomenon is alluded to by Briault and Smith (1980) in their analysis of falling rolls in secondary schools. They note the particular contradiction that parents, while being reluctant to send their children to a school under threat of closure or other pressures, generate a spirited defence of the institution.

Such parental support for an institution may be an indicator of the vigour and the quality of the esteem in which it is held by the community. This can pose a dilemma for the managers: it is obviously their task to sustain and manage the institution through all the periods of its life, yet they also remain the servants of the employing authority whose policies they must implement.

CONCLUSION

Emphasis has been placed in this chapter upon the need to maintain and sustain staff morale within institutions at a time of retrenchment. This is because the consequences of retrenchment will adversely affect teachers and the institutions they serve in two ways. First, teachers may experience feelings of personal alienation as they are confronted with anxiety over the continued security of their employment. As rationalisation and re-organisation procedures occur, fewer teachers within fewer institutions will be required. Those teachers who are retained, although protected against loss of salary, may face the prospect of loss of status in a closing or amalgamating institution. Some teachers in such circumstances may be invited or encouraged to accept early retirement, which may not always be welcomed. For those remaining in employment, the opportunities for professional advancement and career development will be significantly reduced. Second, all teachers will experience a lack of financial resources specifically available for classroom use, which will cause additional frustration as they become increasingly unable to provide appropriate teaching materials and aids to give their pupils/students a wide variety of stimulating learning experiences.

The problems experienced by institutions with regard to sustaining the morale and motivation of staff may be compounded by the difficulties of implementing LEA staffing policies. These may require that vacancies are advertised according to certain procedures which may mean that posts remain unfilled for longer periods than is usual or desirable (Bailey 1982). The situation is made worse by the fact that national recruitment policies have led to staff shortages in particular specialist areas.

On the other hand, this is a time when national developments present unique challenges to teachers and institutions. Amongst these are the moves towards providing rather specific guidance in relation to the school curriculum (DES 1985) and the implementation of a common system of examining at 16 + and of a new Certificate of Pre-Vocational Education (DES 1985), together with the MSC-sponsored changes discussed in Chapter 7. The list could be extended very easily. However, the principal challenge remains the pursuit of excellence, and the degree of success in achieving that objective may be measured by the extent to which pupils and students are attracted to an institution.

It is, therefore, appropriate to place emphasis upon the need to sustain morale and organisational hygiene in institutions to enable them to remain vigorous. It is argued, therefore, that a wide range of staff-development policies are needed which will engender high levels of staff morale, commitment to the goals and development of the institution. This can contribute to greater job satisfaction and high levels of professional development amongst teachers. It is a strategy which rests on the assumption: 'As is the teacher, so is the school' (USSR 1969).

REFERENCES

ACSET (1981) *The Future of the Teacher Training System: Initial Advice to the Secretaries of State*. ACSET 81/24, August. London: DES.

Bailey, P. (1973) 'The Functions of Heads of Departments in Comprehensive Schools'. *Journal of Educational Administration and History*, **5**(1) 53.

Bailey, P. (1975) 'Induction Year or Staff Development'. *Educational Administration*, **4**(1) 12.

Bailey, P. (1982) 'Falling Rolls in the Maintained Secondary Schools: Towards a Model for Management'. *Educational Management and Administration*, **10**(1) 25.

Bone, T. (1982) 'Problems of Institutional Management in a Period of Contraction'. In Gray, H. L. (ed.) *The Management of Educational Institutions*. Lewes: Falmer Press.

Briault, E. and Smith, F. (1980) *Falling Rolls in Secondary Schools*, I and II. Slough; NFER.

Dennison, W. F. (1980) 'The Education Audit as a Monitor of Institutional Effectiveness'. *Educational Administration*, **8**(2).

DES (1981) *Education for 16–19 Year Olds* (*The MacFarlane Report*). London: DES/CLEA.

DES (1983) *Teaching Quality*. Cmnd. 8836. London: HMSO.

DES (1985) *Better Schools* (White Paper), Cmnd. 9469. London: HMSO.

Greenaway, H. and Harding, A. E. (1978) 'The Growth of Policies for Staff Development'. *Research into Higher Education*, Monograph **34**, 13. University of Surrey.

Halsall, E. (1973) *The Comprehensive School: Guidelines for the Reorganisation of Secondary Education*. London: Pergamon Press.

Hodge, S. and Martin, J. (1984) 'The Implementation and Function of Job Rotation in a Secondary School'. *Educational Management and Administration*, **12**(3) 192–198.

Hoyle, E. (1975) 'Professionality, Professionalism and Control in Teaching'. In Houghton, V., McHugh, R. and Morgan, C. (ed.) (1975) *The Management of Organisations and Individuals*. London: The Open University with Ward Lock.

Hoyle, E. (1980) 'Evaluation of the Effectiveness of Educational Institutions'. *Educational Administration*, **8**(2).

Izbicki, J. (1983) 'Parents who run lessons overturn fears by teachers'. *The Daily Telegraph*, 18 April.

Jackson, M. (1983) 'Switch or risk sack, warning, to surplus primary staff'. *The Times Educational Supplement*, 1 July.

Jennings, A. (ed.) (1977) *Management and Headship in the Secondary School*. London: Ward Lock Educational.

Killick, J. (1980) 'Coping with Contraction: the management of teaching staff'. *Education 3–13*, **8**(2).

Marland, M. (1982) 'The Politics of Improvement in Schools'. *Educational Management and Administration*, **10**(2) 119.

Mercer, R. H. (1980) 'Declining Rolls: Some Management Issues in Secondary Schools'. *Educational Administration*, **8**(2) 97.

MSC (1981) *A New Training Initiative : A Programme for Action*. Cmnd. 8455. London: HMSO.

Rogers, C. (1968) 'A practical plan for educational revolution'. In Goulet, R. R. (ed.) *Educational Change: The Reality and the Promise*. New York: Citation Press.

Saran, R. (1982) *Reform of Teachers' Salary Structure*. University of Liverpool Occasional Papers.

Shattock, M. L. (1979) 'Retrenchment in U.S. Higher Education: Some Reflection on the Resilience of the U.S. and U.K. University Systems'. *Educational Policy Bulletin*, **7**(2).

Spooner, R. (1978) 'The Schools' Position in Relation to the "Great Debate" on Education'. In Lambert, K. (ed.) *The Education Service: In or Out of Local Government*. Proceedings of the Sixth Annual Conference of the British Educational Administration Society.

Stanton, M. (1978) 'School Evaluation: A Suggested Approach'. *Educational Administration*, **6**(2).

Stenhouse, L. (1975) *An Introduction to Curriculum Research and Development*. London: Heinemann.

Stenning, R. (1980) 'The Labour Relations

Implications of Contraction in the Schools Education Service'. *Educational Administration*, **8**(2).

Sugarman, B. (1975) 'The School as a Social System'. In Houghton, V. et al (ed.) (1975) *The Management of Organisations and Individuals*. London: The Open University with Ward Lock.

Taylor, W. (1976) 'Innovation Without Growth'. *Educational Administration*, **4**(2).

USSR (1969) *Report of the USSR*. Academy of Pedagogic Sciences.

Watson, K. (1978) 'Accountability in English Education'. *Educational Administration*, **6**(2) 15.

Wright, D. (1980) 'Management and Motivation in a Contracting Secondary School System'. *Educational Administration*, **8**(2).

19

THE MANAGEMENT OF CHANGE: THE THEORY AND THE PRACTICE

Derek Slater

INTRODUCTION: TWO APPROACHES TO THE MANAGEMENT OF CHANGE

There is considerable literature on the management of change. In this final chapter, an attempt will be made to survey some of the major studies as examples of different approaches to the subject. For heuristic purposes two main approaches will be identified, based on rational assumptions on the one hand, and political assumptions on the other.

Rational approaches may be regarded in the light of John Stuart Mill's definition: an end is selected with maximum care; science (or, in this case, social science) is used to determine the optimum way of achieving that end; and actions are then taken on that knowledge (see Nagel 1950, p. 66). Although such a 'hard' assumption of rationality is difficult to sustain in connection with the human sciences, nevertheless the notion of 'rational' in this connection implies that there are several components of the change process which are logically inter-related and are underpinned by certain premises from which they are derived (Walton 1976b, p. 95). Although the terminology varies in particular studies, these components in the change process are normally identified as a series of sequential stages: research, development, diffusion/dissemination, adoption and implementation. These components will be examined in the context of three different types of rational approach.

By contrast, political approaches assume the existence of alternative and possibly competing 'rationalities'. As Bachrach and Baratz (1970) p. 7 put it: 'Politics is that process whereby perspectives used, and solutions offered, are controlled by one frame of reference'. An attempt will be made to examine the issues of power and legitimation in the

445

context of competing interest groups, of which initiators and supporters of change are one political constituency.

Finally, some tentative interpretive conclusions will be drawn on the issue of order in relation to rational approaches, and the issue of control in relation to political approaches.

Although examples will be used from other countries, the majority of the studies surveyed relate to Britain; and the theory and practice of change derived from all studies will be applied to the British context, and in particular, to that of England and Wales. Moreover, although some studies have been derived from contexts other than education, they will be applied solely to the context of education in this chapter.

RATIONAL APPROACHES TO THE MANAGEMENT OF CHANGE

A framework for analysis

Many writers have attempted to construct theories on why and how change takes place at various macro and micro levels of government, from the national to the institutional. A number of both descriptive and prescriptive models have been constructed to explain the change process. In discussing these various models, I shall use a framework for analysis which assumes that there is evidence in different models of sets of related characteristics by which models may be grouped together in different categories which distinguish one approach from another.

This framework is based upon that first developed by Becher[1] (CERI 1973, especially pp. 9–10, and 23 et seq.) and further developed by Becher and Maclure (1978, especially pp. 64–80; 137–147). This framework posited three categories which reflected different approaches that different models and projects have taken: instrumental, interactive and individual. While originally formulated to explain change with specific reference to projects of curriculum development, these projects in their turn are illustrative, as Becher argued, of general models of change which may be fitted into each category.

From a purely empirical point of view, this framework is less than satisfactory: while some models fit neatly into each category, others demonstrate characteristics from each of the three categories (CERI 1973, p. 26). Nevertheless, conceptually it offers a useful starting point for the categorisation of the various models that have been developed to explain the process of change. None of the approaches is mutually exclusive, and it is arguable that each has evolved as a reaction to apparent defects in its predecessor (Becher and Maclure 1978, p. 65).

In its turn, this framework owes much to Havelock's (1971 a and b) work, which was the first major attempt to categorise and discuss models of educational innovations, and was based on a review of 4000 case studies.[2] Havelock suggested a classification based on three models as a descriptive analysis of what had hitherto taken place. Each of Havelock's models forms the basis of Becher's original categories, and will be used here, supplemented by other descriptive and prescriptive models which have the characteristics of each of the three categories.

Instrumental approaches

Instrumental approaches are characterised by technocratic assumptions (Becher and Maclure 1978 p. 68) and it is from these approaches that 'managerialism' — the notion that institutions can be changed from the outside — has grown (Stenhouse 1983, pp. 349–50).

The most common example of a model which claims to be descriptive of actual processes that have taken place was first developed systematically in the educational field by Brickell (1961 and 1968), and Guba and Clark (1976) and has been characterised by Havelock (1971a and b) as the Research, Development and Diffusion model (RD and D)[3].

The process of RD and D is a rational series of phases. Research communities produce new knowledge which a team then develops, as a project or series of projects, into a usable form of products and services, usually classroom materials and teacher handbooks. Trials are carried out in a number of areas (usually LEAs) and institutions (schools and colleges) to test the market and iron out any problems. The materials are then mass-produced as standard packages for general diffusion on the assumption that their self-evident merits will lead disinterested and passive practitioners (teachers) to adopt and implement them. Stenhouse (1975, p. 219) has argued that the first phase of curriculum innovation in Britain in the 1960s conformed to this model; and that the externally invented 'project' became part of the lexicon of education (Stenhouse 1983, p. 348).

The schematism[4] underlying this model is rooted in systems theory. Most commonly, the practitioners who were expected to embrace the projects were perceived as 'systems', referred to in the literature alternatively as the user, receiver, adopter, or client systems (Bolam 1974b, p. 40; 1975, p. 399). Moreover, this schematism is often portrayed in martial imagery (Becher and Maclure 1978, p. 110). An extreme example of this is quoted both by Becher and Maclure and Havelock (1971a) who cite Clark and Hopkins' (1966) prescription:

> Inform target systems; demonstrate solutions and programmes; train target system in use of solutions and programmes; service and nurture installed solution.

Those users who do not wish to embrace a particular change are characterised as 'resisters', and are compared unfavourably with those who do embrace the change, who are designated 'innovators' (Thomas 1975, pp. 47–48). Indeed, change is almost always described as 'innovation', which — as Dalin (1978, pp. 24–25) has pointed out — is defined in technical terms as 'better' than that which has gone before. Dalin's own definition of innovation is a case in point: he defines it as ' . . . a deliberate attempt to *improve practice* [my emphasis] in relation to certain desired objectives' (Dalin 1973, p. 36; 1978, p. 20).

Bolam (1975, p. 396) argues that the RD and D model is an example, following Chin and Benne (1974), of an empirical–rational strategy. This assumes that people are reasonable and will respond best to rational explanation and demonstration which shows that a particular situation or procedure makes sense under the circumstances, and is in any case in members' own interests. Typically, this has taken the form of meetings between project development teams and participating teachers to act as in-service training for the latter.

Certainly this assertion may be valid in pluralist societies such as the USA and the UK; but the model also has potential as, in Chin and Benne's (1974) typology, a power-coercive strategy[5]. As the nomenclature implies, a power-coercive strategy depends upon political, legal and economic power: compliance of those with less power is achieved by those with greater power by direction and manipulation. Dalin (1978, p. 72) expands House's (1974) argument that RD and D would only fully work in a situation where there is an 'integrated social system'; that is, according to Dalin,

> . . . where the incentive structures are compatible, where the structural relationships between R and D centres and schools are functional, where one can use power to force compliance and where diffusion patterns can be controlled.

Dalin further argues that this is not the case in the USA nor in other Western countries, and that even in more centralised countries like Sweden and the GDR there is still a long way to go before such an integrated social system is achieved.

However, in the cases of both the empirical–rational and power-coercive strategies, it is clear that an RD and D model is most appropriate at a macro-level of change, and is directionally a model of change from centre to periphery in Schon's (1971) typology, which is again a descriptive model. This model is based on three assumptions: that the innovation exists in all its essentials prior to its diffusion; diffusion is the movement of an innovation from a centre out to its users; and directed diffusion is a centrally-managed process of dissemination, training and the provision of resources and incentives (p. 81). He further argues that the effectiveness of the centre–periphery process depends, *inter alia*, on: the level of resources and energy at the centre; the number of points at the periphery; the length of the radii or spokes through which diffusion takes place; and the energy required to gain a new adoption.

Although instrumental approaches like this formed the basis of the curricular reform movement in both the USA and the UK in the 1960s, it is the diffusion part of the RD and D model which proved, in practice, its weakest link,[6] and led to a general disillusionment with the model as a whole.

As Becher and Maclure (1978, p. 70) note, the diffusion process

> . . . occurs almost as an afterthought; it is on the whole a peremptory affair, a matter of putting a few finishing touches to the overall design.

Goodlad (1976, p. 16) therefore casts doubt on whether the RD and D model, whatever its descriptive power as a model of change, is valid as a prescriptive model for change

> It is simply what the letters stand for: research, development, and diffusion, with what comes out to be diffused being more or less adrift, requiring some other force to pull it into close juxtaposition with persons who might have some use for it. A productive change strategy requires the inclusion of this latter element.

In assuming that the self-evident merits of a proposed change would ensure its spread, the notion of diffusion embraced a whole series of operations — such as adoption, implementation, institutionalisation, communication[7] — that were not fully worked out as active strategies. It is arguable that the diffusion phase is the most critical in societies where decision-making is dispersed, and casts doubt on the whole model as a heuristic device in this connection.

On the one hand, in practice, the history of many projects belied the empirical–rational assumptions of the model: Miles (1964), in an early analysis of the educational changes of the first part of the 1960s in the USA concluded that few educational innovations were installed on their merits. Political considerations were often equally, if not more, important[8] about which the RD and D model has little to say. Moreover, any empirical strategy does assume a consensus about values and goals that often does not exist in pluralist societies (Becher and Maclure 1978, p. 66; Dalin 1978, pp. 20 and 60–63). Again, many projects — as Stenhouse (1975, p. 219) points out — departed from the logic of the RD and D model — that it is the hypothesis and ideas behind the products, rather than the products themselves, which are being tested. Thus, frequently users equated the materials with the project, as happened with the Schools' Council Humanities Curriculum Project (School Council 1976, p. 14). Furthermore, the whole logic and language of the RD and D model precludes considerations of large-scale change other than its technical definition of innovation — for example, changes resulting from rising or falling school rolls on either curriculum or organisation of institutions; and it begs the question of how a change is to be judged an improvement.

On the other hand, dispersed decision-making functions weaken the potential for the use of the model as a power-coercive strategy: the bargaining powers of users at the periphery relative to the centre give the former greater freedom to reject or modify the centre's designs. In a number of projects of education innovation in the UK in the 1960s based on this model, teachers failed to act as predicted or desired by development teams, thus limiting or even negating the impact of the projects (see, for example, Becher and Maclure 1978, p. 68; Whitehead 1980, p. 51).

Moreover, dispersed decision-making often means that there is a marked lack of uniformity in the characteristics of users, making it difficult to transfer a change wholesale from one setting to another (House 1974, pp. 213–214); and this in turn gives users greater potential for what Schon (1971) has termed 'dynamic conservatism': a tendency to fight to remain the same.

In order to meet these objections other models in the same instrumental tradition have been formulated. Often these take the form of refinements or reformulations of the RD and D model, usually at the diffusion stage. This stage has been reformulated: from that of 'diffusion' to that of 'dissemination', to indicate the greater planning that this phase apparently needed. As Hoyle (1972a para. 2.16) writes:

> Whereas the term *diffusion* is neutral and simply connotes the spread of an innovation, *dissemination* is used . . . to connote a more deliberate pattern of diffusion. In this case, some agency takes specific steps to ensure that an innovation will reach the maximum number of people. [author's italics].

Other prescriptive models went further and added two more stages to the three existing ones. These new stages usually centred on the two concepts of 'adoption', i.e. the decision by the consumer to use an innovation and 'implementation' i.e. the realisation of the innovation in practice (Macdonald and Walker 1976, p. 28). Despite such modifications, by the mid-1970s there was general agreement among writers from various countries[9] that, whatever the descriptive merits of instrumental approaches as characterised by the RD and D model with its centre–periphery assumptions, they were — without serious qualifications — seriously deficient as prescriptive models because of their lack of success in achieving change at the user level.

Interactive approaches

Interactive approaches both extend and transform instrumental approaches, by concentrating on what has been perceived as the weakest point in the instrumental approaches — that of ensuring the spread of a change. While retaining many of the technocratic and managerial assumptions, and language, of instrumental approaches, these assumptions are modified and softened by other assumptions which may be termed 'ecological' (House 1974): that users belong to a network of social relationships, and that both informal personal contact and group-membership and reference-group identifications are important as indicators in influencing whether users embrace a change or not.

The most common example of a descriptive model incorporating this approach which is referred to in the literature is what Havelock (1971a and b) has termed the 'social interaction' model[10]. In this model, both research and development are assumed; as Becher and Maclure (1978, p. 70) note, dissemination is the central feature of the process — everything else is subordinated to it. As Morrish (1976) comments:

> In this . . . model the unit of analysis is the individual receiver, and the focus is on the receiver's perception of and response to knowledge emanating from the outside (p. 123).

Thus an innovation, usually already existing in a usable form, is brought to the attention of a potential user or receiver (a respected teacher, adviser or administrator in education). The reaction of the potential user in this awareness stage determines whether further stages take place. If such an awareness is followed by an expression of interest, the user will actively seek information, followed by a judgement or evaluation as to whether the innovation will fit present or anticipated circumstances. If it will, the user may well try out the innovation as a trial or pilot; and if successful, the innovation will be adopted, becoming increasingly internalised and routinised. Each member of the organisation or system will then proceed through the same stages (from awareness to adoption) as a result of contact with colleagues — hence the importance of personal contact and communication, through informal and formal networks, the latter of which would include, in the UK, in-service training courses at teachers' centres, or higher education institutions.

A number of commentators (e.g. Bolam 1974, p. 43; 1975, pp. 395–396; Hoyle 1975, pp. 332–333) have argued that a form of this interactive approach was, until the 1960s, probably the main way in which knowledge about educational changes spread, not only in the UK but in most countries with decentralised systems of decision-making as regards education. However, as Becher has pointed out (CERI 1973, p. 9; Hoyle 1975a, p. 333), it was not until the mid-1960s that the instrumental approach of the RD and D model, which had held sway in the early part of the 1960s, began to be supplemented by a more systematic and planned interactive approach along with the lines of the social-interaction model. Many of the later Schools' Council projects incorporated both instrumental and interactive approaches (see, for example, Jenkins 1974, p. 97; Whitehead 1980, pp. 8–12).

Although the schematism underlying interactive approaches retained much of the language, and many of the assumptions, of systems theory it is arguable that the schema is as much 'organic' (see below) as it is systematic; martial imagery is re placed by notions of growth. Thus, although interactive approaches in their most systematic form — as exemplified by the social-interaction model — may be categorised in Chin and Benne's (1974) typology as an empirical–rational strategy (Bolam 1975, p. 295), they do contain elements of another strategy which Chin and Benne (1974) typify as normative–re-educative. Such a strategy assumes that, if a change is to be effective, it has to be legitimised by invoking a whole range of social and cultural values, attitudes, relationships and skills, to ensure commitment on the part of initial users to adopt it. Rational argument is thus supplemented by affective appeals.

The social-interaction model assumes that the eventual implementer of change — the receiver or user of the innovation — still retains a relatively passive role whose needs are defined and determined exclusively by the 'sender', once the user has been committed to the change. However, other commentators on interactive approaches take a more organic view, claiming a much more active role for users to transform the change while using it, to suit the particular circumstances of their situation. In the words of a member of one such project (the Keele Integrated Studies Project) run along these lines, ' . . . the conditions of trial were open to negotiation and transaction' (Jenkins 1974, p. 71). House (1974), while locating his perspective within the social–interactive model, sees educational change as the result of factional groups competing for the control of resources, though he argues for 'ecological gentleness' to ensure a respect for the diversity which is the consequence of such processes.

In Schon's (1971) typology, such interactionist approaches exemplify either — in their more systematic form — a proliferation-of-centres model, or — in their more organic form — a shifting-centres model.

On the one hand, the proliferation-of-centres model still retains certain of the assumptions of the centre–periphery model:

> This system retains the basic centre–periphery structure but differentiates primary and secondary centres. Secondary centres engage in the diffusion of innovations; primary centres support and manage secondary centres . . . The limits to the reach and effectiveness of the new system depend now on the primary centre's ability to generate, support and manage the new centres. (Schon 1971, p. 85).

Each new secondary centre generates its own network of periphery and infrastructure. This model is particularly useful in explaining the intentions of the early Schools Council: in 1965, the latter sent a paper to teacher organisations, local authorities and universities proposing some 35 to 45 regional centres for curriculum development and in-service training, each of which would be linked to the Schools Council (Shipman 1974, p. 3). In the event, only one such area managed to get such a network actually operating (the North West Regional Curriculum Development Project).

On the other hand, more organic interactionist approaches have been closer to Schon's (1971) shifting-centres model. In this model, there is no clearly established centre; instead, centres appear, reach a peak and disappear to be replaced by new centres within short time periods. Nor is there a stable, centrally established message: the message is transformed as it evolves. Whitehead (1980, p. 8) has termed this a 'movement' model, and it is exemplified in the approach used by the Schools Council History, Geography and Social Science 8–13 Project[11].

All these interactive approaches emphasise the importance of the regional or local level rather than the central level; the importance of communication and negotiation in the interaction within the network; and the heterogenous nature of different sets of circumstances in terms of both time and space.

However, like the instrumental approaches which they succeed and arguably complement, interactionist approaches have been subject to serious criticisms.[12] Although such approaches do allow — more or less, depending on the model in question — for political factors in the form of negotiation and transaction in a way which more instrumental approaches do not, they still assume a certain consensus of view and values among practitioners regardless of time and place, if the 'network' of personal contacts is to work. The notion of 'communication' is seen as problematic only in so far as it is concerned with the efficiency and means of transmission of given 'facts', in the form of ideas or materials, which practitioners may then transform. Though political and value questions have a greater place in interactive than instrumental approaches, they are peripheral rather than central to them. Schon (1971) criticises the equation of 'diffusion' with 'communication' on just these lines: a change may well totally disrupt a 'technological–social system', leading to conflict, so that the diffusion process is less dissemination of information and more a sequence of related disruptions to complex systems. Certainly, such differences of interest and priorities between one project team and its potential clients were significant factors in preventing any progress towards the establishment of at least one regional centre for curriculum development as proposed by the Schools Council in 1965 (Shipman 1974, p. 4).

Even where thorough dissemination programmes had been carried out their effects have been debatable. Although there is ample evidence that particular projects, or material from particular projects, were being used in schools, their *systematic* impact was far more debatable, and disappointing from the point of view of the aims of project teams: at best, impact was uneven; at worst, negligible (see, for example, Nicodemus and Marshall 1975; Eggleston et al 1976; Elliott 1976; Simons and Humble 1978; Steadman et al 1978). Moreover, these surveys all contain common reasons for the failure of many schools to adopt projects: a lack of resources — in terms of time, finance, and support inside and outside the school — to commit themselves. In at least one project, this meant that, even in schools which adopted it, teachers' responses were ambiguous and confused — they simultaneously asked, on the one hand, for an instrumental approach with a clear blueprint and packaged materials, while on the other demanding a more interactionist approach to adjust materials and methods to their own classroom conditions (Shipman 1974, p. 89).

Moreover, like the instrumental approaches, interactive approaches failed to solve the problem of implementation — i.e. the internalisation and routinisation of changes after they had been initially adopted. There are numerous instances in the literature of the problem of lack of survival of projects when project teams have been withdrawn [13]. This therefore led to an increasing focus on implementation at an institutional level.

Individual approaches

Individual approaches focus on the contextual variables in the adoption and implementation of changes. A number of commentators have argued that the institution[14] is the essential unit of change (e.g. Becher and Maclure 1978, p. 169; Jenkins 1973, p. 85; Richardson 1973; Rudd 1973, p. 62; Dalin 1978, pp. 51, 97 and 103). By contrast, others have emphasised the place of the classroom[15] as the unit of change (e.g. Jackson 1968; Rudd 1973, p. 57; Reid 1975, p. 248; Galton et al 1980; Whitehead 1980, p. 26).

This has been accompanied by an awareness of the organisational complexity that is involved in an educational change at the institutional level. Hoyle (1975, p. 332)[16] summarises neatly:

> Curriculum innovation requires changes in the internal *organisation* [author's emphasis] of the school.

Change in the internal organisation of the school is a major innovation.

Other commentators have also stressed the importance of the organisational context of change[17].

The most common example of a model which describes and illustrates an individual approach is that referred to by Havelock (1971a and b) as a problem-solving model[18]. This model is based firmly on the assumption that change is but a part of a dynamic and continuous problem-solving activity which goes on at user level: the problems of the user are the starting place. The user or receiver perceives a need, which is then formulated as a problem and potential solutions diagnosed. This is then followed by a search and retrieval of ideas and information from the outside; but, in this case, the user remains fully in control. Outside help is non-directive, being rather on a consultancy basis, and the user makes full use of internal resources to adapt ideas and artefacts to fit the individual circumstances.

The underlying schematism of this model remains systematic: indeed, as Havelock (1971b, p. 86) points out, the 'user' may be of any size or complexity. Havelock (1971a and b) has suggested the notion of a 'linkage' model as a way of integrating the RD and D, social interaction and problem-solving models by emphasising linkage procedures between them. Conceptually, he tries to show how each model can overlie the other: for example, research and development teams interact in social networks, and are themselves problem-solving communities[19]. The picture thus offered is, in Bolam's words, a '. . . notion of a problem-solving macro-system containing fully defined and articulated micro-systems, each operating on a problem-solving basis [which] offers a helpful, if over-tidy and rational, theoretical basis . . . ' (Bolam 1974b, p. 38).

However, given the interest — noted earlier — in the institution as the essential unit of change, there has been an emphasis, using this model as a base, on its micro-level applications; in particular, the emergence of the concept of the 'problem-solving school'.

> In essence, the problem-solving school may be thought of as a self-monitoring, self-renewing system, which is, therefore, concerned with *all* [author's italics] aspects of a school's life, including the various curriculum development and innovation tasks (Bolam 1974b, p. 10).

Bolam (1974b, p. 43; 1975, p. 396) further claims that the 'problem-solving' model in this connection is both an empirical–rational and normative–re-educative strategy, in Chin and Benne's (1974) typology, consisting as it does, he argues, of three sub-models. The problem-solving user model, based on empirical–rational assumptions, describes a user who employs a cyclic problem-solving strategy. The task-consultant model, also based on empirical–rational assumptions, describes the role of an agency from without the institution, who helps it with a specific task. The process-consultant model, based this time on normative–re-educative assumptions, describes the role of an agency outside the institution which, in a non-directive way, attempts to help an institution develop its problem-solving procedures.

In this connection, there have been several attempts, as noted in the previous chapter, to suggest ways in which institutions as organisations can develop their problem-solving procedures. Collectively, these approaches have been termed organisation development (OD). One important example of an OD approach is that of Miles (1965; 1967; 1976)[20] and also Schmuck and Miles (1971). Miles's imagery is medical: he uses the concept of organisational health[21], and he posits ten dimensions[22] by which the health of an organisation can be measured. Failure to embrace change is therefore pathological: Hoyle

(1971, p. 69; 1975a, p. 336), for example, refers to the notion of 'tissue rejection' to describe the process whereby a change may be initially adopted but not implemented (i.e. institutionalised).

In certain respects, such individual approaches do take into consideration value and power questions, but as a technical exercise. In the form that Havelock propounds it, the problem-solving model, in common with similar instrumental and interaction approaches, does imply a consensus orientation, assuming as it does that individuals will ultimately adapt their values and behaviour to the needs of the institution. Dalin (1978, pp. 63–4) argues, however, that more recent attempts to build on a problem-solving model through organisational development do not necessarily seek to build a consensus, but, at a minimum, to clarify conflicts. Indeed, Miles (1967) has argued for instruments and methods for identifying areas of dissent about goals in institutions. Although Dalin (1978, p. 64) finds it hard to categorise such an approach as either a consensus or conflict orientation, it might be possible to term this orientation as 'dissensus': dissent, rather than conflict, is the characteristic of a 'healthy' organisation; conflict is indicative of a 'diseased' organisation.

As regards power questions, such approaches assume a power-equalisation concept as axiomatic — that is, that members of an organisation who must implement a change will oppose it less if they have been involved in formulating it (Gross et al 1971, p. 37). Morrish (1976, p. 129) notes that the notion of internal motivation is frequently used in the literature to legitimise participation — the active involvement of individuals who are affected by decisions, using group cohesiveness as a catalyst.

Like the preceding instrumental and interactive approaches, these individual approaches have been criticised. The individual approaches so far considered — again, like the instrumental and interactive approaches — take little account of an alternative schematism based on a phenomenological view of the world. As already made clear in this book, it is a matter of great debate as to whether systematic and phenomenological schemes offer competing or complementary views of the world[23]. The phenomenological perspective, unlike the systematic one, begins with the views and perceptions of an actor or group of actors who are the users. On the one hand, this schema would question the assumption that there is an objective view of rationality, in favour of what Hoyle (1982, p. 94) has termed 'alternative rationality'. This, in turn, calls into question any notion of an objective 'change' which is perceived in exactly the same way by all the actors in the decision-making process.

> Innovations do not exist in any unchanging, objective sense: they are constantly being defined, changed and redefined as a result of experience and the differing perceptions of the people who handle them (Bolam 1975, p. 397)[24].

Hence, whether a change is perceived as 'good' or 'bad' depends on the values and social formation of the individual. As Reid (1975, p. 249) points out, even syllabuses ' . . . are not unambiguous definitions of what has to be done: they are signals which set off a repertoire of acquired behaviours'.

In this connection, the clear presentation and transmission of the context of a proposed change may be a necessary condition of communication as a factor in the adoption and implementation of change; but it is not the sufficient condition which both the interactive and individual approaches, hitherto considered, assume. Macdonald and Walker (1976, p. 44) argue that ' . . . the innovator in education often solves his "communication problems" by altering the content rather than the form of his communication'.

On the one hand, Macdonald and Walker continue to argue plausibly that such an alteration of the content can contribute to successful implementation if the alteration gives a perception of reinforcing the values of those who are going to use it. However, this does presuppose that a consensus of shared values in an institution does exist: otherwise there is more likely to be a different effect. Hamilton (1975, p. 205) concludes, at the end of an empirical study, that this particular change under consideration was, in its implementation, ' . . . accompanied by a series of transformations which, ultimately, resulted in its serving ends directly opposed to those intended'. An alternative effect may be what has been termed the 'facade' phenomenon:

> the situation in which teachers, schools and inspectors present an image to each other and to outsiders which suggests that an innovation is working extremely successfully, whereas [outside] observers report differently (Bolam 1974b, p. 8)[25].

Bolam argues that such a facade phenomenon is the result of a lack of openness, which a problem-solving school could overcome, with the confidence openly to accept or reject a particular change on its merits.

However, this does assume some shared perception of the 'facts' of which the change consists, a perception which Bolam himself has elsewhere doubted. But more than this, it ignores the element of politics which a phenomenological schema acknowledges: actors — be they individual or groups — will adopt or employ defensive and aggressive strategies to operationalise changes in interest priorities to optimise overall survival satisfaction. The adoption, rejection or implementation of a perceived change may well be such a strategy, or part of such a strategy[26]. This may not only be true of a change that is internally generated in an institution, but also one that is externally generated: research communities, development teams and dissemination functionaries[27] are themselves actors in a political process.

Hence, reactions to change may be seen as both a political process, and the outcome of a political process.

POLITICAL APPROACHES TO THE MANAGEMENT OF CHANGE

A framework for analysis

Since the early 1970s, consideration has increasingly been paid in the literature to the recognition that the experience of political bargaining processes provide a major impulse for organisational change (Pratt 1982, p. 77).

Political approaches are based on a phenomenological schema, whereby initiators and supporters of change are seen as one or a number of individuals or groups, each with its own construction of reality and frame of reference. As Bailey (1982, p. 100) puts it 'One man's logic may be another man's confusion'.

As noted in Chapters 1 and 9, the operationalisation of these competing rationalities in an organisational context has been termed 'micropolitics'.[28]

> Micropolitics embraces those strategies by which individuals and groups in organisational contexts seek to use their resources of power and influence to further their interests . . . It is characterised more by coalition than by departments, by strategies rather than by enacted

rules, by influence rather than by power, and by knowledge rather than by status. (Hoyle 1982, p. 88)

Although, as yet, specific empirical studies of micropolitics within established theories of organisations are rare (Hoyle 1982, p. 96), there are a number of anthropological studies which, in the course of their exposition, do deal with micropolitical strategies (Reid 1975, p. 245; Bailey 1982, p. 99).

The notion of micropolitics raises two important issues. The first of these is power. Weber (1946, p. 80) argued:

> In general, we understand by 'power' the chance of a man or a number of men to realise their own will in a communal action even against the resistance of others.

In all organisations there are what will be termed, for convenience, superordinate and subordinate individuals and groups, whose power may be analysed in terms of its weight, domain and scope (Kaplan 1964). In educational institutions, superordinates (the head teacher or principal and the senior staff) have considerable control[29] over structure and discipline but less over what goes on in the classroom. Subordinates (teachers) have considerable control over what goes on in the classroom, but little over other institutional aspects.

The second issue is that of legitimation. Bailey (1982, p. 101) defines this as

> . . . . the way in which individuals are able to justify their actions as reasonable and normal and the way they persuade others that any power or influence being applied to them is authoritative.

He argues that the key as to whether actions are regarded as legitimate or not in any organisation is through an empirically-determined classification of 'proper' and 'improper' procedures. The continuum 'proper' – 'improper' may be seen as forming the basis of a useful typology. Certain actions in an organisation may be viewed as dubious but still within the bounds of the proper (and therefore the acceptable). Others may be perceived as totally improper, or worse: 'One must distinguish between the proper, the improper, the outrageous and the unthinkable' (Bailey 1982).

As regards educational institutions, Bailey gives three examples of what he terms logically distinct and competing 'systems of legitimation'[30]: the authority of management; the conventions of democracy; and the conventions of professionalism. These strategies are themselves neutral: in the context of the politics of change, they may be used by either supporters or opponents of change, as superordinates or subordinates, to legitimate their claims.

Taking these three examples as an ordering principle, it is now intended to examine each in further detail in the light of various studies in the literature about change.

The legitimation of change through the authority of management

The conventions of the authority of management stress that, while superiors should consult subordinates on issues, it is the superiors alone who are responsible for the rational direction of corporate action (Bailey 1982, p. 103). This legitimation strategy gives considerable power to the head teacher of a school or the principal of a college. This is particularly true in the UK: as Hoyle (1974, pp. 14–15) observed, authority is vested in the head by the articles of government, which usually provide the power to control the internal management, organisation and discipline of the school, together with the exercise of supervision over teaching and non-teaching staff. The same is usually true of principals of colleges. Furthermore, this authority is enforced by the head's hierarchical status, thus giving considerable power over school or college goals and administrative structure.

As an initiator or supporter of change — or as an opponent of change — this in turn gives the head considerable power. Dickinson (1975) in a case study of change in nine English schools argues that:

> The formal organisation that is found in schools means that nearly all curriculum change is channelled through the head teacher . . . The major re-inforcing impetus was that of the head teachers themselves (p. 173).

Other data support this conclusion. Galton (1983, p. 305) reports on the results of a survey of over 900 teachers, in which the latter were asked whether they would institute changes in the classroom without being assured of head teacher support. Almost 70 per cent said that they would not initiate such changes without first seeking and receiving the head's approval. Thus Galton concludes:

> An effective head teacher can transform a school with an average staff but it would seem doubtful whether even an enthusiastic staff can change a school without active leadership on the part of a head teacher (Galton 1983).

As was shown in Part 3 of the present volume, impetus for change may have to come from the head if a considerable number of teachers are conservative as regards change: many a change has foundered on the rocks of teacher reluctance (see, for example, Shipman 1971, pp. 13–14). But, *mutatis mutandis*, the impetus for change coming from teachers may well be quelled by a head legitimising his or her opposition by the authority of management.

Either way, if the head's authority is not used throughout the management structure to reinforce his or her views, he or she may become dangerously isolated from the staff (see, for example, Shipman 1971, p. 14; Dickinson 1975, p. 155). It is here that the head's considerable power of patronage can be used systematically to locate supporters into key positions of authority within the management structure (e.g. Dickinson 1975, pp. 159 and 160; Best et al 1983, p. 231). In this connection, Marland (1982, p. 122) criticising the lack of studies concerning the effects of the Burnham points system in schools[31], adds 'In fact, scale posts are a key part of the politics of improvement in schools.'

On the other hand, heads may well use coercion to remove those who are reluctant to support their plans, by shifting individuals to posts that are less important in terms of the changes they wish to support or oppose; or even sometimes by confrontation (Best et al 1983, p. 230). Thus this strategy of legitimation has considerable scope as a power-coercive strategy, whereby superordinate individuals (heads or principals) or groups (heads' or principals' allies in positions of authority) can legitimate their control over subordinate individuals or groups.

On the other hand, this strategy of legitimation can also be useful as a rational–empirical strategy: the prospect of economic and/or social reward (in terms of an up-grading of post or status) may well persuade individuals that it is in their best interest to support changes that a head and his or her allies wish to bring about.

The legitimation of change through the conventions of democracy

The conventions of democracy assert that individual members should debate issues openly and reasonably, revealing personal positions, interests and preferences and decide on corporate action by a majority vote (Bailey 1982, p. 103). This strategy can, in practice, give considerable influence to both superordinate individuals or groups (the head and allies) and to subordinate individuals or groups (teachers).

On the one hand, there is a growing expectation of participation in decision-making in education both inside and outside institutions of education[32]. However, paradoxically, this very change itself has certain negative implications for the impetus to other changes. As Parkes (1973) has pointed out, the forces involved in changing the form of government in education institutions have been political and social rather than primarily democratic; they have had more to do with pressures within a democratic society than with making institutional decision-making more efficient or effective. The benefit, he argues, has been in establishing stability rather than in promoting efficiency: the parliamentary model adopted has been concerned with setting up machinery (committees, working parties, etc.) by means of which conflict can be institutionalised and hopefully contained. Although he concedes that this may have brought about a greater commitment of staff to those policies which they have had a part in evolving, the cost has been in the speed of change: the demands of a fast-changing environment necessitate clear decisions free of the need for professional expertise to contribute to policy.

Although Parkes is referring specifically to the context of FE colleges, his arguments may equally well be applied to other educational institutions.

A further factor is that participation in decision-making may, on the whole, release forces in favour of conservation rather than change. Certainly, the evidence[33] from studies in participation in decision-making in general contexts does not suggest that the simple equation between participation in decision-making and propensity to change, that many proponents of power-equalisation have assumed, is valid (Bolam and Pratt 1976, para. 4.28).

In the specific context of education, therefore, the introduction of participatory structures in educational institutions which contain a majority of traditionally-minded staff will probably be to reduce the propensity to change. Indeed, Reid (1975, p. 249) suggests that, in general, teachers will tend to promote stability rather than challenge it because, lacking any generally accepted models, teachers will adjust to the value systems of the institutions they are in.

Moreover, as noted in Chapter 17, participatory structures in educational institutions may well enhance the monopoly of the professionals (teachers) and enable them to exclude even more effectively the views of other interested groups, such as parents and pupils (Bolam 1974b, p. 36; Bolam and Pratt 1976, para. 4.26). And even where participatory structures do encompass the views of others besides the professionals, the net bias may well be towards conservation rather than change[34].

A further point is that where participatory structures are introduced or established in educational institutions, they may well equally sustain the influence of superordinate individuals or groups as much as they enhance the influence of subordinate individuals or groups. If it is accepted that teachers are on the whole likely to conserve rather than change, then the implications for the impetus to change are considerable.

A number of studies have suggested that the participatory structures which are set up are, at best, structures of limited consultation or, at worst, forums for presentation of decisions already made. In Weston's (1980) study, meetings of heads of departments were used as a forum for the presentation of proposals already made by the head and his senior staff in an atmosphere which she terms 'deliberation under constraint'. In Bullock's (1980) study, this constraint was less marked, but still prominent: he quotes the head teacher as telling one convenor of a working party, 'I will say what will not happen, but you will say what will happen'. Best et al (1983, p. 249) conclude that the most successful head teacher in terms of negotiating change was the one who had ideals of democracy but who worked in undemocratic ways of manipulation and vetoing decisions in meetings which went against his philosophy (p. 232).

Even where there is a sophisticated committee system and an academic board — as in FE colleges — Noble and Pym's (1970) study has demonstrated how a democratic committee structure can produce a centralised oligarchy in what they term an 'involuted hierarchy'. Powerful 'vetting committees' emerged to act as gatekeepers in terms of what items went on to the political agenda. The oligarchy which controlled them was curiously meritocratic:

> Seniority and experience alone were insufficient. It was necessary that qualifications be allied with discretion, a tactfulness that in effect amounted to the capacity to preserve the opacity of the decision-making process. (p. 439).

It is in such an atmosphere of committee manipulation that micro-political techniques such as 'rigging' agendas, 'massaging' minutes, absorbing protest by co-optation etc. thrive (Hoyle 1975b, pp. 36–37; 1982, p. 90).

But they can only thrive if they are accepted by the majority of staff to be within the bounds of the conventions of democracy — that, though not totally 'proper' procedures, yet neither are they totally 'improper'. As Bailey (1982, p. 101) graphically puts it: •

> To nobble a committee member might be equated with driving at 35 mph in a built up area; to bribe or threaten him might be considered dangerous driving.

It is worth considering why the form of democracy rather than its substance may be a sufficient condition for legitimation. First, it may be argued that it may not even be a necessary condition. The evidence from a number of empirical studies certainly suggests that teachers' responses towards greater participation in decision-making is ambiguous, even contradictory. Belasco and Alutto (1972) found that, while some teachers felt themselves 'decisionally deprived', others felt 'decisionally saturated'. Bullock (1980) found that an attempt to involve teachers in decision-making in one school led to a 'marked division' in the staff: some criticised the head for abdicating his responsibilities when he should have been more authoritarian to create a stable atmosphere; while those taking part in the working parties criticised him for interfering too much. Again, Best et al (1983), studying change under three different head teachers in one school, found that the head teacher who was least successful in negotiating change was the one who attempted to introduce more democratic structures, only to be accused by many staff of lack of leadership and poverty of philosophy (p. 249).

Following from this, a second reason may be that the majority of staff collude in the exercise of power through participatory structures by superordinate individuals or groups. Bolam and Pratt (1976, p. 29), labelling this as 'power collusive' or 'power submissive', argue that many people assent to this because it 'frees' them from responsibility; to get involved in decision-making deflects energy from purposes more important to them. It may well be that many see their 'proper' domain as the classroom. This may involve a sort of suspension of disbelief; Bolam and Pratt (1976, p. 51 note 38), while acknowledging that some may regard this collusion or submission as improper, write:

> But there are others — we suspect it is the majority — who recognise the need for collusion in some of their own relationships in order to sustain a 'modus vivendi': to create the conditions under which a conditional system of belief can be frozen for long enough to get the action started.

More trenchantly, Best et al (1983, p. 249) conclude at the end of their study that it seems that teachers prefer a coherent philosophy and autocratic government behind a facade of democracy to democracy in practice:

> At the end of the day teachers prefer a strong leadership, and a resemblance of democracy, even when they know that the democracy is a sham.

It may thus be concluded that participation in decision-making by subordinates may not be a significant factor in the initiation and support of change; it is the 'top-down' initiation of change which is likely to be implemented in the institution as an organisation (Wheeler 1973, pp. 140–1; 1978, p. 5). But in order that this be so, superordinates may well have to offer the forms of participation to their subordinates rather than the actual practice of participation and to use micro-politics to maintain the distance between form and practice.

The legitimation of change through the conventions of professionalism

Legitimation through professionalism assumes that colleagues, regardless of their positions in the structure of authority, are all members of a fair-minded professional elite, and should discuss issues and seek a rational consensus for corporate action which does not impinge upon individual professional freedom of action[35] (Bailey 1982, p. 103). In so far as it stresses all staff as colleagues, and in its respect for the autonomy of the practitioner in the classroom, it is the most powerful strategy for subordinate individuals (teachers) or groups (of teachers) to influence, positively or negatively, the process of change.

Macdonald and Walker (1976, p. 50) argue that the mass of teachers are most likely to embrace a change if, among other things, it enhances a respect for their 'autonomy' with regard to classroom practice, and reinforces their professional identity. In this connection, Dalin (1978, pp. 28–29) argues that one of the reasons for the failure of early instrumental approaches was that curriculum development in the 1950s was taken over by university and research and development organisations which reduced the locally-controlled power of the teaching profession. On the other hand, Stenhouse (1980, p. 255) argues that few teachers have recognised the way in which the curriculum movement of the 1960s has once more placed power in the hands of the teacher through emphasising the importance of classroom practice (in the form of teacher and pupil materials) and putting a premium on the development of the teacher as professional: 'Curriculum development is about teacher self-development'.

Thus, by invoking a whole range of values, attitudes, skills and relationships implied by the notion of professionalism, this strategy has great potential as a normative–re-educative strategy, in positive and negative ways: Best et al (1983, pp. 229–230) note how one head was able to secure staff support and even convert opponents by an appeal to ideas which at that time had considerable professional currency (mixed ability teaching and integrated studies); while others remained unconvinced but felt constrained to accept them as it would be 'unprofessional to do otherwise'.

Nevertheless, the control that teachers have in the classroom means that their influence on the ultimate fate of a change is considerable. To enter a classroom to evaluate the effectiveness of any change is itself a political act which can be seen as improper: an affront to one of the tenets of professionalism — the autonomy of the practitioner. With its penetration into the classroom itself, this strategy of legitimation has in the end, perhaps, the highest currency of all.

RATIONAL AND POLITICAL APPROACHES TO THE MANAGEMENT OF CHANGE: SOME CONCLUSIONS

Rational approaches to the management of change: the issue of order

Although the different approaches that were identified have frequently been perceived by their advocates as alternative approaches, each critical of the others, I have also tried to show that it is possible to see these approaches as complementary, in the ways that are demonstrated in Figure 19.1.

As can be seen, the different approaches, which were, for convenience, labelled instrumental, interactive and individual, overlie specific stages in the process of change as conceived of as a rational activity: research, development, diffusion/dissemination, adoption, implementation. Each approach concentrates on different stages in the process.

Moreover, each approach and each stage can be located on the axis from central (macro) levels of government to institutional (micro) levels of government. As was argued

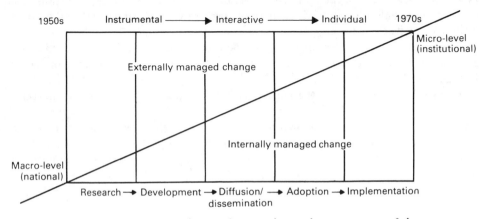

Figure 19.1 *A summary of rational approaches to the management of change.*

earlier, each was more appropriate to different levels. Instrumental approaches, concentrating as they have on research and development, have been more appropriate to central agencies (research communities and development teams). Interactive approaches, by contrast, in assuming that research and development had been carried out, and being concerned with the dissemination stage of the process, concentrated on building networks of institutions either at the regional (across LEAs) or local (within LEAs) level. Individual approaches, concentrating as they have on the contextual variables in the adoption and implementation of changes, have in their turn focused on institutions.

Furthermore, each approach and each stage can be seen as largely externally, or largely internally, managed. Instrumental and, to a lesser extent, interactive approaches, concentrating as they did on the different stages of research through to dissemination, assumed a managerial approach to change: institutions and individuals within them were assumed to be passive receivers, although some interactive approaches did assume a more active role for the receivers than others. Individual approaches, however, assume that however knowledge of the change is obtained, it is internally managed — either by the institution or indeed by the individual within the institution in his or her classroom.

Finally, to return from whence I began, each of these approaches may be seen sequentially: each is a development from, and transformation of, the one that preceded it in time; and indeed they may be located in historical time — instrumental approaches in the early 1960s giving way to interactive approaches in the late 1960s, while these in turn gave way to individual approaches in the 1970s.

Political approaches to the management of change: issues of control

It has been argued that political approaches to the management of change are based on a phenomenological schema. This assumes that there are a number of competing interest groups, or individuals, each with different constructions of reality. Initiators and supporters of change may be seen as one such interest group, as may opponents of change.

Political approaches raise issues both of power and of legitimation. Within organisations, there are superordinate and subordinate individuals or groups, either of which may be supporters or opponents of change, and each of which has different degrees of power, in terms of control and influence, over different aspects of the organisation. Each of these individuals or groups will furthermore use strategies to persuade the others of the legitimacy of its claims.

Three such strategies of legitimation, first identified by Bailey (1982), have been used as examples in order to demonstrate the operation of these strategies. These are summarised in Figure 19.2.

As regards legitimation by the conventions of the authority of management, this is largely the prerogative of superordinate groups or individuals, who, by virtue of their positions in the management structure, accrue to themselves certain ascribed powers. Here, control is firmly in the hands of superordinates; and this strategy enhances that control. By contrast, it is difficult for subordinates, unless they have certain authority roles, to use this strategy themselves, except, as has been demonstrated, in a paradoxical way: to accuse superordinates of abandoning the responsibility ascribed to them by their positions of authority.

The conventions of democracy, however, do offer scope for use by either super-

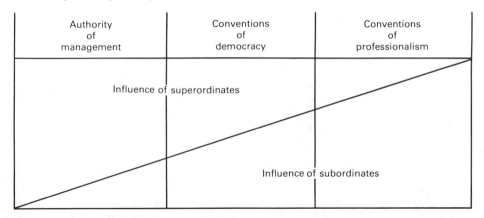

Figure 19.2 *A summary of political approaches to the management of change.*

ordinates or subordinates to legitimate support for, or opposition to, change. The evidence does suggest that, in practice, superordinates do subvert the conventions of democracy to retain their control by offering the form rather than the substance. But it does also appear that subordinates see this as within the bounds of the proper, preferring what is often a limited degree of influence rather than the control that is ideally implied in these conventions.

It is in the conventions of professionalism that subordinates have more power to promote or deny change in their control over the classroom, in so far as the conventions of professionalism offer a greater protection for subordinates than the conventions of democracy. In the final analysis, the classroom is the ultimate test of the success or failure of educational change; and the teacher the ultimate arbiter.

NOTES

1. Becher, T. (1972): *Three Styles of Curriculum Development* Unpublished paper for CERI, summarised in CERI (1973).
2. In his turn, Havelock (1971a) begins by acknowledging the work of Rogers (1962). See also Rogers and Shoemaker (1971).
3. For other summaries of this model, together with critical appraisals, see, for example, Becher and Maclure (1978) pp. 65–9 and 110; Dalin (1978) pp. 70–3; Goodlad (1976) p. 16; Havelock (1971a) pp. 10.41–10.42 and (1971b) p. 85; House (1974) pp. 213–4; Macdonald and Walker (1976) pp. 10 and 25–9; Morrish (1976) pp. 42–3, 109–10, and 119–23; Whitehead (1980) pp. 5–6.
4. I am here using concepts derived from structural anthropology. See Levi-Strauss (1981) especially p. 679.
5. c.f., however, Bolam (1975) p. 395 who argues that Havelock's work is not very relevant to understanding power-coercive strategies.
6. See also above, reference 3.
7. For example, Katz et al (1963) define the process of diffusion as '(1) acceptance, (2) over time, (3) of some specific item — idea or practice, (4) by individuals, groups or other adopting

units, linked by (5) specific channels of communication, (6) to a social structure, and (7) to a given system of values or culture'.

8. For example, the educational innovation movement of the early sixties in the U.S.A. was less the product of disinterested research and more that of the culmination of concern for trained manpower at a time of scientific and military competition with Russia, and triggered by the Russian launching of the first artificial satellite ('Sputnik') in 1957 ahead of the U.S.A. See CERI (1973) p. 9; Macdonald and Walker pp. 23 et seq.

9. See, for example, Bolam (1974b) p. 1, (1975) pp. 396 and 399; Macdonald and Walker (1976) p. 20; Munro (1977) p. 44; Thomas (1975) p. 54; Jenkins (1974) p. 118; Whitehead (1980) p. 6.

10. For other summaries of this model, together with critical appraisals, see, for example, Becher and Maclure (1978) pp. 69–74 and 110–111; Dalin (1978) pp. 69–70; Havelock (1971a) pp. 2.34–2.36, 6.33–6.34, 7.11–7.13, 10.12–10.14, and (1971b) pp. 85–6; House (1974) p. 6 passim; Macdonald and Walker (1976) pp. 9–10; Morrish (1976) pp. 43, 110–111, and 123–5; Whitehead (1980) p. 6.

11. Although Whitehead interprets this Project's dissemination strategy as an example of a proliferation of centres model, by his own description of the approach, it is clear that he is referring rather to the shifting centres model " . . . where dissemination has no clearly established centre, but a variety of foci which expand and contract. Such a project also has no stable, centrally established 'message' " (Whitehead 1980 p. 8).

12. See also above reference 10.

13. See, for example, Becher and Maclure (1978) p. 112; Bolam (1974a) p. 166; Gross et al (1971) p. 40; Hoyle (1969) p. 230; (1970) p. 2; (1971) p. 69; (1975a) p. 334; Macdonald and Walker (1976) p. 5; Shipman (1971) p. 15; Whitehead (1980) pp. 6, 11, 14 and 59.

14. The term 'school' is usually used in the literature, but the point equally applies to colleges also. See Tipton (1973), and Wheeler (1978).

15. The literature largely uses the word 'classroom', which may be taken as a generic term for any group learning situation.

16. Hoyle stresses this point about the importance of organisational implications at the institutional level in the management of change elsewhere: see Hoyle (1971) p. 72; (1972b) para. 3.3.

17. See, for example, Bolam (1975) p. 393; Gross et al (1971) pp. 139–42, 196 passim, and 214; Macdonald and Walker (1976) pp.7 and 45–6; Miles (1965, 1967); Reid (1975) p. 252; Shipman (1971) pp. 13–15; Thomas (1975) p. 59; Walton (1973) pp. 126–7 (1976) p. 25; Wheeler (1973) p. 138.

18. For other summaries of this model, together with critical appraisals, see for example, Becher and Maclure (1978) pp. 74–8; Dalin (1978) pp. 67–9; Havelock (1971a) pp. 2.40–2.41, 10.53–10.70, 11.12–11.15, and (1971b) pp. 86–8; Macdonald and Walker pp. 10–12; Morrish (1976) pp. 44–6, 111–112, and 125–9; Thomas (1975) pp. 49–50; Whitehead (1980) p. 6.

19. A number of commentators have attempted similar compromises. For example, Becher and Maclure (1978) p. 78, suggest a 'judicious amalgam' of all three models. On the other hand, Dalin (1978) pp. 100–9 suggests his own model which combines the three models, beginning with each individual school making out its own development programme, drawing on and contributing to a network of institutional relationships, with a degree of supporting policies and agencies in the macro-system.

20. For appraisals of this and other O.D. approaches, see, for example, Dalin (1978) pp. 67–9; Hoyle (1972b) paras 3.2–3.8; Newell (1973); Thomas (1975) pp. 61–4; Walton (1976b) pp. 23–4; Morrish (1976) pp. 104–8.

21. c.f. the geographical metaphors of Halpin's (1966) 'organisational climate'.

22. Miles' ten dimensions of organisation health are: goal focus; communication adequacy; optimal power equalisation; resource utilisation; cohesiveness; morale; innovativeness; autonomy; adaptation; problem-solving adequacy. There is however, a circularity about some of these dimensions; for example, it could be said that organisational health is itself a characteristic of problem-solving adequacy.

23. See also Chapter 9, and Burrell and Morgan (1979). In anthropological terms, each schema may be viewed as a myth, the product of different research and intellectual communities. Each community transforms (Levi-Strauss 1980 pp. 644–5 and 655) the myth of the other in order

to refute it. Both myths use the same phenomena; each is a transformation of the other.

24. Bolam takes as his assumption that the systematic and phenomenological perspectives are complementary (Bolam 1975 p. 393). He therefore tries to accommodate the different constructions of reality that actors will put on a particular change by defining an innovation as an 'open system' (ibid, p. 397). Elsewhere, however, he admits that this explanation is 'not entirely satisfactory' (Bolam and Pratt (1976) para. 2.13).

25. See also Bealing (1973); Goodlad et al (1970); Jenkins (1972) para 3.7, (1974) p. 100; Smith and Keith (1972).

26. House (1974) recognises the force of factional groups in the process of dissemination but he does not articulate any thoroughgoing political approach.

27. Such functionaries are often referred to, in approaches underpinned by systematic schema, as 'change agents': 'anyone outside the organisation who fosters innovation within it' (Hoyle 1972b p. 20). See also, for example, Bolam and Pratt (1974) para 3.16; Gross et al (1971) pp. 24 and 31–2; Hoyle (1971).

28. The conceptual difference between 'micro-' and macropolitics' is, in practice, hard to sustain. See Pratt (1982) p. 80.

29. Bolam and Pratt (1976) para 3.6 distinguish between control, whereby an individual or group determines the actions of others without the latter's consent; and influence, where the assent of others is essential in getting things done.

30. Although the term 'system' does suggest an internally consistent set of values and relationships, it is perhaps improper to use it in a phenomenological schema. The term 'strategy' will be used instead.

31. Although the system for generating and distributing posts is different in further education, there is a similar dearth of research studies of particular cases.

32. See above, Chapter 2.

33. For a summary of the relevant studies in this connection, see Bolam (1974b) pp. 32–7; and Bolam and Pratt (1976) paras. 4.8–4.12 and 4.24–4.27.

34. For an example of a case where teachers and parents together rejected a change by using participatory structures, see Whitehead (1980) p. 5.

35. This notion of professionalism subsumes the two aspects identified by Hoyle (1974) p. 14, who distinguishes between 'professionalism' as those strategies and rhetorics employed by members of an occupation in seeking to improve status, salary and conditions which enhances the eliteness of the professional; and 'professionality' as the knowledge, skills and procedures employed by teachers in the process of teaching, which justifies the autonomy of the practitioner. See also Hoyle (1975b).

REFERENCES

Bachrach, P. and Baratz, M. S. (1970) *Power and Politics: theory and practice*. London: Oxford University Press.

Bailey, T. (1982) 'The Question of Legitimisation: A Response to Eric Hoyle'. *Educational Management and Administration*, **10**(2) 99–105.

Bealing, D. (1973) 'Issues in classroom observational research'. *Research in Education*, **9**, 70–82.

Becher, T. and Maclure, S. (1978) *The Politics of Curriculum Change*. London: Hutchinson.

Belasco, J. A. and Alutto, J. A. (1972) 'Decisional Participation and Teacher Satisfaction'. *Educational Administration Quarterly*, **8**(1), Winter, 44–58.

Best, R., Ribbins, P., Jarvis, C. and Oddy, D. (1983) *Education and Care*. London: Heinemann.

Bolam, D. (1974a) 'The Experience of the project'. In Shipman, M. D. et al (1974) *Inside a Curriculum Project*, 136–68. London: Methuen.

Bolam, R. (1974b) *Teachers as Innovators*. Paper for the OECD. DAS/EID/74.53. Paris: OECD.

Bolam, R. (1975) 'The Management of

Educational Change: Towards a Conceptual Framework'. In Houghton, V. et al (ed.) *Management in Education: The Management of Organisations and Individuals*, 391–409. London: Ward Lock/Open University Press.

Bolam, R. and Pratt, S. (1976) 'The Management of Innovation in Schools'. *Units 4–5, Course E321: Management in Education*. Milton Keynes: Open University Press.

Brickell, H. M. (1961) *Organising New York State for Educational Change*. New York: Albany Press.

Brickell, H. M. (1968) 'Appraising the Effects of Innovation in Local Schools'. In Tyler, R. W. (ed.) *Educational Evaluation — New Roles, New Means*, 284–304. Chicago: University of Chicago Press.

Bullock, A. (1980) 'Teacher Participation in school decision making'. *Cambridge Journal of Education*, **10**(1), Lent Term, 21–8.

Burrell, G. and Morgan, G. (1979) *Sociological Paradigms and Organisational Analysis*. London: Heinemann.

(CERI) Centre for Educational Research and Innovation (1973) *Styles of Curriculum Development*. Paris: OECD.

Chin, R. and Benne, K. (1974) 'General strategies for effecting changes in human systems'. In Bennis, W., Benne, K. and Chin, R. *Planning of Change*. London: Holt, Rinehart and Winston.

Clark, D. L. and Hopkins, J. E. (1966) 'Roles for Research, Development and Diffusion'. CRP Project Memorandum 1.

Dalin, P. (1973) *Case Studies of Educational Innovation: Strategies for Innovation in Education*, **IV**. Paris: OECD.

Dalin, P. (1978) *Limits to Educational Change*. London: Macmillan/International Movement Towards Educational Change.

Dickinson, N. B. (1975) 'The Head Teacher as Innovator: a study of an English school district'. In Reid, W. A. and Walker, D. F. (ed.) *Case Studies in Curriculum Change: Great Britain and the United States*. London and Boston: Routledge and Kegan Paul.

Eggleston, J. F. et al (1976) *Processes and Products of Science Teaching*. Schools Council Research Studies. London: Macmillan.

Elliott, J. (1976) 'Preparing teachers for classroom accountability'. *Education for Teaching*, **100**, 49–71.

Galton, M. J. (1983) 'Classroom Research and the Teacher'. In Galton, M. J. and Moon, B. (ed.) *Changing Schools . . . Changing Curriculum*, 295–310. London: Harper and Row.

Galton, M. J. et al (1980) *Inside the Primary Classroom*. London: Routledge and Kegan Paul.

Goodlad, J. I. et al (1970) *Behind the Classroom Door*. Worthington, Ohio: Jones.

Goodlad, J. I. (1976) *The Dynamics of Educational Change. IDEA Reports on Schooling*. New York: McGraw-Hill.

Gross, N. et al (1971) *Implementing Organisational Innovations*. London and New York: Harper and Row.

Guba, E. G. and Clark, D. L. (1967) 'An Examination of Potential Change Roles in Education'. In National Education Association, *Rational Planning in Curriculum and Instruction*. Washington D.C.: NEA.

Halpin, A. W. (1966) *Theory and Research in Educational Administration*. London: Macmillan.

Hamilton, D. (1975) 'Handling Innovation in the Classroom: Two Scottish Examples'. In Reid, W. A. and Walker, D. F. (ed.) (1975) *Case Studies in Curriculum Change: Great Britain and the United States*, 179–207. London and Boston: Routledge and Kegan Paul.

Havelock, R. G. (1971a) *Planning for Innovation through the Dissemination and Utilisation of Knowledge*. Michigan: University of Michigan Centre for Research on Utilisation of Scientific Knowledge.

Havelock, R. G. (1971b) 'The Utilisation of Educational Research and Development'. *British Journal of Educational Technology*, **2**(2) May, 84–97.

House, E. (1974) *The Politics of Educational Innovation*. Berkeley, Ca: McCutchan.

Hoyle, E. (1969) 'How does the curriculum change?'. *Journal of Curriculum Studies*, **1**(3) 230–9.

Hoyle, E. (1970) 'Planned Organisational Change in education'. *Research in Education*, (3) May 1–22.

Hoyle, E. (1971) 'The role of the change agent in educational innovation'. In Walton, J. (ed.) *Curriculum Organisation and Design*, 68–75. London: Ward Lock.

Hoyle, E. (1972a) 'Facing the Difficulties'. *Unit 13, Course E283: The Curriculum —*

Context, Design and Development. Milton Keynes: Open University Press.

Hoyle, E. (1972b) 'Problems: A Theoretical Overview'. *Unit 17, Course E283: The Curriculum — Context, Design and Development*. Milton Keynes: Open University Press.

Hoyle, E. (1974) 'Professionality, professionalism and control in teaching'. *London Educational Review*, 3(2), Summer, 13–19.

Hoyle, E. (1975a) 'The Creativity of the School in Britain'. In Harris, A. et al (ed.) *Curriculum Innovation*, 329–46. London: Croom Helm/Open University Press.

Hoyle, E. (1975b) 'Leadership and Decision-Making in Education'. In Hughes, M. (ed.) *Administering Education: International Challenge*, 30–44. London: Athlone.

Hoyle, E. (1982) 'Micropolitics of educational organisations'. *Educational Management and Administration*, 10(2), June, 87–98.

Jackson, P. W. (1968) *Life in Classrooms*. New York: Holt, Rinehart and Winston.

Jenkins, D. R. (1972) 'Curriculum Development and Reference Group Theory: Notes Towards Understanding the Plight of the Curriculum Developer as Marginal Man'. In Bell, R. 'Perspectives on Innovation'. *Unit 14, Course E283: The Curriculum — Context, Design and Development*. Milton Keynes: Open University Press.

Jenkins, D. R. (1973) 'The Moving Plates of Curriculum Theory: A Speculator's Guide to Future Eruptions'. In Taylor, P. H. and Walton, J. (ed.) *The Curriculum: Research, Innovation and Change*, 81–7. London: Ward Lock.

Jenkins, D. R. (1974) 'Schools, teachers and curriculum change'. In Shipman, M. D. et al (1974) *Inside a Curriculum Project*, 94–120. London: Methuen.

Kaplan, A. (1964) 'Power in Perspective'. In Khan, R. L. and Boulding, E. (ed.) *Power and Conflict in Organisations*. London: Tavistock Publications.

Katz, E. et al (1963) 'Traditions of research on the diffusion of innovation'. *American Sociological Review*, 28(2).

Levi-Strauss, C. (1981) *The Naked Man: Introduction to a Science of Mythology*, 4. London: Cape; Paris: Librairie Plon.

MacDonald, B. and Walker, R. (1976) *Changing the Curriculum*. London: Open Books.

Marland, M. (1982) 'The Politics of

Improvement in Schools'. *Educational Management and Administration*, 10(2), June, 119–34.

Miles, M. B. (1964) 'Innovation in Education: Some Generalisations'. In Miles, M. B. (ed.) *Innovations in Education*, 631–62. Columbia, Ohio: Teachers' College Press.

Miles, M. B. (1965) 'Planned Change and Organisational Health: Figure and Grounds'. In Carlson, R. O. (ed.) *Change Processes in the Public Schools*, 11–34. Eugene, Oregon: University of Oregon Centre for the Advanced Study of Educational Administration.

Miles, M. B. (1967) 'Some Properties of Schools as Social Systems'. In Watson, G. (ed.) *Change in School Systems*. Washington D.C: National Training Laboratories, National Education Association.

Miles, M. B. (1976) 'Critique: Diffusing OD in Schools: The Prospects'. *Education and Urban Society*, 8(2), February.

Morrish, I. (1976) *Aspects of Educational Change*. London: Allen and Unwin.

Munro, R. G. (1977) *Innovation — Success or Failure?* London: Hodder and Stoughton.

Nagel, E. (1950) *John Stuart Mill's Philosophy of Scientific Method*. New York: Hafner.

Newell, T. (1973) 'Organisation Development in Schools'. *American Education*, 9.

Nicodemus, R. B. and Marshall, D. (1975) 'Familiarity of Headteachers with Twenty-five New Curriculum Projects'. *Educational Studies*, 1(3), 191–200.

Noble, T. and Pym, B. (1970) 'Collegial authority and the receding locus of power'. *British Journal of Sociology*, 21(4), 431–45.

Parkes, D. (1973) 'Circular 7/70 and the Government of Schools'. *Educational Administration Bulletin*, 1(2), 1–11.

Pratt, S. (1982) 'Editorial: Enter Micropolitics'. *Educational Management and Administration*, 10(2) 77–86.

Reid, W. A. (1975) 'The Changing Curriculum: Theory and Practice'. In Reid, W. A. and Walker, D. F. (ed.) (1975) *Case Studies in Curriculum Change: Great Britain and the United States*, 240–59. London and Boston: Routledge and Kegan Paul.

Richardson, E. (1973) *The Teacher, the School and the Task of Management*. London: Heinemann.

Rogers, E. M. (1962) *The Diffusion of Innovations*. New York: The Free Press.

Rogers, E. M. and Shoemaker, F. F. (1971)

Communication of Innovations: a Cross-Cultural Approach. New York: The Free Press; London: Macmillan.

Rudd, W. G. A. (1973) 'Teachers as Curriculum Developers: A Second-generation Viewpoint'. In Taylor, P. H. and Walton, J. (ed.) *The Curriculum: Research, Innovation and Change*, 52–67. London: Ward Lock.

Schmuck, R. A. and Miles, M. B. (ed.) (1971) *Organisation Development in Schools.* Palo Alto, Ca.: National Press.

Schon, D. A. (1971) *Beyond the Stable State.* London: Temple Smith.

Schools Council (1976) *Dissemination of Innovation: The Humanities Curriculum Project.* Working Paper 56. London: Evans/Methuen.

Shipman, M. D. (1971) 'Innovation in Schools'. In Walton, J. (ed.) (1971) *Curriculum Organisation and Design*, 11–16. London: Ward Lock.

Shipman, M. D. (1974) 'Problems in establishing an innovation'. In Shipman, M. D. et al (1974) *Inside a Curriculum Project*, 1–14. London: Methuen.

Simons, H. and Humble, S. (1978) *The Support from Council to Classroom: An Evaluation of the Diffusion of the Humanities Curriculum Project.* London: Macmillan.

Smith, L. and Keith, P. (1971) *Anatomy of Educational Innovation: An Organisational Analysis of an Elementary School.* London: Wiley.

Steadman, S. D. et al (1978) *First Interim Report to the Schools Council on the Inquiry into Impact and Take-up of Schools Council-funded activities.* London: Schools Council.

Stenhouse, L. (1975) *An Introduction to Curriculum Research and Development.* London: Heinemann.

Stenhouse, L. (1980) 'Reflections'. In Stenhouse, L. (ed.) *Curriculum Research and Development in Action.* London: Heinemann.

Stenhouse, L. (1983) 'The Legacy of the Curriculum Movement'. In Galton, M. J. and Moon, B. (ed.) *Changing Schools . . . Changing Curriculum*, 346–55. London: Harper and Row.

Thomas, A. R. (1975) 'Changing and Improving Educational Systems and Institutions'. In Hughes, M. (ed.) *Administering Education: International Challenge*, 45–70. London: Athlone.

Tipton, B. F. A. (1973) *Conflict and Change in a Technical College.* London: Hutchinson.

Walton, J. (1973) 'Some Restraints Affecting Curriculum Development'. In Taylor, P. H. and Walton, J. (ed.) *The Curriculum: Research, Innovation and Change*, 125–35. London: Ward Lock.

Walton, J. (1976a) 'Rational Curriculum Planning'. In Walton J. and Welton, J. M. (ed.) *Rational Curriculum Planning: Four Case Studies*, 5–27 London: Ward Lock.

Walton, J. (1976b) 'Curriculum development in practice — some observations'. In Walton, J. and Welton, J. M. (ed.) *Rational Curriculum Planning: Four Case Studies*, 95–124. London: Ward Lock.

Weber, M. (1946) *Essays in Sociology.* London: Oxford University Press.

Weston, P. (1980) *Negotiating the Curriculum.* Windsor: NFER.

Wheeler, G. E. (1973) 'Educational Need and Organisation'. In Taylor, P. H. and Walton, J. (ed.) *The Curriculum: Research, Innovation and Change*, 138–45. London: Ward Lock.

Wheeler, G. E. (1978) 'Management of Change'. *Coombe Lodge Working Paper 1312.* Bristol: F.E. Staff College.

Whitehead, D. J. (1980) *The Dissemination of Educational Innovation in Britain.* London: Hodder and Stoughton.

CONCLUSION
AND
INDEXES

CONCLUSION

Meredydd Hughes, Peter Ribbins and Hywel Thomas

In a field of study of such diversity and change as educational management, conclusions are likely to be as much about beginnings as endings. Our main aim in designing the book, as noted in the Introduction, was to demonstrate the value of analytical perspectives rooted in the social sciences as a means of understanding management structures and processes in education, and hence of assisting educational managers to cope with the diversity and change which exist in the educational system and its institutions. Diversity and change are equally evident, as was shown in Part 1, within the various disciplines of the social sciences which are of relevance to educational management. In a situation of such continuing flux and development in both practice and theory, it is thus prudent that our volume claims to be an introductory text rather than a definitive treatise.

Various perspectives and paradigms were presented in Chapter 1 (Hughes) and in Chapter 9 (Ribbins), the aim being to explain and clarify rather than to advocate or convert. This may not fully satisfy the firmly committed, whether their allegiance is to a systems viewpoint, to an action or interpretive paradigm, or to a radical change or conflict perspective, as the three were presented in Chapter 9. It seems to us that in facing new challenges, it is desirable that educational managers should be aware of the kind of issues which are likely to be highlighted through the adoption of a particular viewpoint, and equally important, the kind of issues which are likely to receive less emphasis. We have seen, for instance, that a consensual, functionalist approach may fail to take adequate account of power differentials and differences of perception within any given organisation, so that theory and practice become increasingly separated. On the other hand those whose emphasis is on conflicting social reality, subjectively constructed and interpreted, may underestimate the hidden strength of consensually accepted conventions, and the extent to which a rudimentary form of systems analysis is involved each time relationships are perceived and generalisations made, as the individual participant struggles to make sense of his or her organisational world. While no easy reconciliation can be expected between paradigms based on conflicting assumptions, the effort to appreciate the contribution to understanding which contrasting perspectives can provide brings an awareness of significant dimensions which might otherwise be missed.

Economics provides an example of a social science discipline, the potential contribution of which to management education has tended to be overlooked. It may be anticipated that in the current climate in the UK, as in other parts of the world, economics will be less on the sidelines than has hitherto been the case. Its perspectives on decisions in educational management, whether rooted in Human Capital theory or in the Screening hypothesis, or drawing on analyses of patterns and methods of finance, challenge much of contemporary practice. Moreover, as the analysis of an economic curriculum in Chapter 5 (Thomas) suggests, its insights can be supportive of those who emphasise a humanist tradition in educational provision, possibly an unexpected bonus for those who might be suspicious of an economic perspective.

In Chapter 1 (Hughes) the contribution of the micro-social sciences was briefly indicated, and on a number of occasions subsequently, particularly in Chapters 10 (Hughes) and 19 (Slater), the importance of political approaches to management and leadership was considered. In this regard it is well to remember that political activity may be entirely proper and even praiseworthy, and does not necessarily involve dubious intrigue or self-interested manipulation. Such activity does however raise important issues of power and legitimation, as Slater recognises in a passage which includes reference to Bailey's apposite observation on degrees of impropriety at the 1981 BEMAS Annual Conference (Bailey 1982). Subsequent discussion at the conference included several references to Machiavelli's *The Prince*, and there was an awareness that the ethical issues involved in politicising and in the use of power have been a perennial concern of artists and writers since classical times in ancient Greece.

Within the educational administration community in North America, there has been a similar appreciation for some time of the contribution which the arts and the humanities can make in the definition and the clarification of values:

> 'It is felt that classic and contemporary literature, philosophy, drama, music and art can be used effectively to portray crucial moral dilemmas and value conflicts, and that through examining these the prospective administrator will be in a better position to perform such essential functions as purpose definition, conflict resolution and cross-cultural communication.' (Farquhar 1978, p. 9).

A similar viewpoint has been expressed by Walker (1978, p. 96), who noted, however, that in practice, 'little attention is given in preparation programmes for school administrators to the question of values, while the literature in the field of philosophy and educational administration is miniscule'. The fact that, apart from Ohm and Monahan (1965) and Ostrander and Dethy (1968), hardly any substantial references could, at that time, readily have been cited tends to confirm Walker's observation.

Barrow (1976, p. 71) has suggested that philosophical competence, which includes 'the ability to recognise different kinds of questions for what they are and the ability to avoid conceptual muddle', is a quality much to be desired in heads of schools, while White (1984) has specifically called for sensitivity to what is morally permissible, as a necessary antidote to exclusive concern with what is managerially expedient. This is an area in which Hodgkinson (1978), as previously noted, has contributed significantly. Having defined values 'in a preliminary way as concepts of the desirable with motivating force' (p. 105), he concluded from a wide-ranging examination of the issues concerned that 'administrators need a technique for resolving value conflicts which is superior to the methods of avoidance, least resistance or lowest principle. To gain such a technique they must do some philosophy' (p. 146).

In chapters relevant to the unease noted above concerning the ethics of micropolitics, Hodgkinson's book also considered the potential contribution of administration to the insidious growth of moral pathologies (Chapter 9) and, alternatively, to shaping the development of the morally responsible organisation (Chapter 10). He suggested an administrative development programme, which would have at least four stages: to seek self knowledge of one's own values by private reflection; to review the meta and other values of the organisation; to analyse for conflict points the extension of the organisational interest into the social, national and cultural environment; and to seek to become as aware as possible of one's own self-interests. Such a programme, he concluded, might be expected to move administrators in the direction of Plato's philosopher kings.

In a recent study from a distinctly more radical position (which drew on Gramsci, Piaget and Freire), Codd (1984) followed Hodgkinson in seeing educational management as essentially philosophy in action. He distinguished three sources of ideas which shape and determine managerial practice: conceptual orientations derived from theory; 'the promptings of habit, convention, and intuition derived from personal experience and contained within the domain of commonsense' (p. 27); and 'a philosophical critique of practice in which deliberative action is derived from a combination of empirical and interpretive modes of inquiry that have been brought to bear upon both the public domain of extant theory and the private domain of commonsense' (p. 27). He argued strongly for the third of these alternatives.

There is still, of course, room for wide differences of view concerning the kind of philosophising that is appropriate, and some of the statements made by both Hodgkinson and Codd may well need to be questioned. We consider, however, that the general thesis— that the study and the practice of educational management has much to gain from philosophical analysis— has been convincingly propounded.

The particular practice with which we and our fellow authors have been specifically concerned has been the management of education in England and Wales, but it needs to be stressed that the ideas we have discussed have world-wide currency. It is of interest, for example, that of the specific references cited in the above discussion, three chanced to be from the U.K. (Bailey, Barrow, White), two were from the U.S. (Ohm and Monahan, Ostrander and Dethy), two were Canadian (Farquhar, Hodgkinson), and two were Australian (Walker, Codd). It may fairly be claimed that, within the international literature on educational management written in English, there is increasing recognition of the value of a multidisciplinary, analytical perspective which draws on varied intellectual traditions. With the encouragement of the Commonwealth Council of Educational Administration (CCEA) (of which incidentally Robin Farquhar and William Walker are respectively the current and former presidents) such multidisciplinary approaches are also currently being tried out and found relevant to the improvement of management practice in developing countries of the Commonwealth, as the continuing series of CCEA *Studies in Educational Administration* makes evident. Similar initiatives are being developed in Europe through the European Forum on Educational Administration (see, for instance, Association Francaise des Administrateurs de L'Education 1982) and through the Council of Europe (Hegarty 1983). UNESCO has also made substantial contributions through its Division of Educational Policy and Planning, its International Institute of Educational Planning and its International Bureau of Education (Haag 1982).

Given the wide range of disciplines in the social sciences and the humanities upon which students of educational management are now able to draw, together with the increasing richness of the relevant international literature which is available, it is encouraging to note that this is an area of study which in the UK, as in other parts of the world, is 'developing an identity and some coherence', a conclusion reached in the final report of a DES financial research project on professional development provision for senior staff in schools and colleges in England and Wales (Hughes, Carter and Fidler 1981, p. 214).

As the interlocking, changing pattern of the education service continues to evolve, its management development needs are increasingly being recognised. This is evident in relation to schools in DES Circulars 4/84 and 3/83 and in the creation of a National Development Centre at Bristol University, and in relation to further education in the strong recommendations of the ACSET (1984) education management working group. Meanwhile, at a conference aimed at university vice-chancellors and polytechnic directors as well as captains of industry, Mr. Richard Bird, a DES Deputy Under-Secretary, has made the interesting suggestion that 'it was the business of the Committee of Vice-Chancellors and Principals to encourage top administrators within the universities to go back to college' (*THES* 1984). The Jarratt Report (Jarratt 1985) has extended the proposal, recommending that deans and heads of department should receive management training. Given such unanimity of perceived need, there is clearly a special responsibility placed upon those involved in developing the study and teaching of educational management.

Our own response to this considerable challenge is a three-fold emphasis on the development of skills of description, analysis and explanation. It is these basic skills which are likely to assist students of educational management to develop a better understanding of their own complex organisations, and thereby to contribute to the effective achievement of educational objectives. The resulting approach is intended to encourage the asking and answering of those deceptively simple but fundamental questions of *what*, *how*, and *why*. We have seen that many conceptual frameworks are available for considering these questions, only some of which have been systematically applied to educational management in the UK. Such an array of alternative perspectives can threaten to overwhelm those new to the field, and we would suggest that tutors need to take this into account by cautiously recommending discrimination and selectivity and by correspondingly emphasising relevance and rigour in the application of particular conceptual frameworks.

Whatever the background and expertise of the practitioner group undertaking systematic study, a basic issue which has to be faced is the relationship of theory to practice. It will be remembered that at the end of Chapter 1 (Hughes) it was suggested that the unavoidable tension between them can be dynamic and creative, leading to deeper understanding and improved practice. A necessary corollary is that, for the theory-practice relationship to be effective, a continuing two-way process of action — learning is required, rather than a simple sequence of first learning the theory (which cannot be questioned) and then applying it (whatever the circumstances). One may thus warmly welcome the announced shift of emphasis of the National Development Centre from concentrated and highly structured management training to more comprehensive and experiential management development (NDC 1984). A more interactive mode avoids confrontation between inadequate prescriptive theory and 'narrow-minded, nose-to-the-grindstone parochialism and compartmentalisation, which can be rife and counter-productive unless active steps are taken to avoid it' (Everard 1984, p. 17).

It is of interest that though Everard's general viewpoint, which draws on his long experience of industrial management, is somewhat different from our own, his standpoint on the relationship of theory to practice is remarkably similar to that adopted in this book. On the basis of research undertaken for Shell, he picks out 'helicopter quality' as a major determinant of managerial success, the term being used to describe 'the statesmanlike attribute that enabled a manager easily to shift his position between the particular and the general and abstract, so that he could relate seemingly unrelated experiences in his day-to-day work and make a coherent pattern of them (seeing both the wood and the trees and how they relate)' (pp. 17–18).

Our own emphasis on alternative perspectives is again paralleled by Everard's advocacy of a multifaceted approach: 'Any situation that needs managing is many-sided, and while there will usually be a dominant framework of thought in which it is most appropriately and conveniently construed, the manager should always try to apply various templates to the situation in order to size it up fully' (pp. 7–8). The use of the term 'template' is particularly significant. According to the *Concise Oxford Dictionary* the first meaning of 'template' is "pattern . . . used as a guide in cutting or drilling . . .", which almost exactly duplicates, in an entirely different context, the original meaning of 'paradigm' as 'example, pattern, especially of inflexion of noun, verb, etc.', as noted in Chapter 1. It is through the informed attempts of practising managers (with such assistance and encouragement as are appropriate) to apply different templates or paradigms to situations of practice, that management can become more purposeful and more effective.

Templates have to be used with great care and accuracy, which again corresponds to our emphasis on rigorous analysis. Like Everard (1984, p. 18), who commends the aim of 'broadening mental horizons' in industrial management training 'especially in the middle to upper echelons', we have reservations concerning certain styles of prescriptive teaching. We are not convinced that prescriptive solutions to management problems of any complexity can be found which are universally applicable, and which do not need to take account of a whole range of contextual differences within educational systems and institutions. On the other hand, it will be noted that we ourselves are highly prescriptive in recommending an approach which encourages and prepares students to tackle and solve their own problems, rather than relying on pre-packaged general solutions of doubtful validity.

The viewpoint expressed can conveniently be summarised by noting what a student may learn from a book such as this, which claims to be more than a collection of loosely related readings. First, it is basic that the book offers adequate description, so that significant information may be acquired regarding important aspects of the educational system and institutions being examined. Second, it enables the reader to appreciate some of the different ways — Eastonian systems analysis, an economics perspective, loose coupling, or a social interactionist perspective, to name a few — in which situations can be structured and problems identified and considered. Third, it is hoped that readers will be encouraged to try out a perspective explained in one chapter in relation to situations and problems described in other chapters, and then in relation to *other* issues in the management of education of particular concern to themselves, which could not be included in a single volume because of limitations of space. The aim is therefore that the reader will come to consider, by the end of the co-operative exercise, not only that knowledge and understanding have been increased in specific areas, but that new competence has been gained, enabling him or her to tackle, more confidently and more creatively, new problems as they arise in personal experience, and to handle familiar situations undergoing significant change.

Long before the discovery of nuclear energy, Whitehead (1926) observed that 'nothing is more impressive than the fact that as mathematics withdrew increasingly into the upper regions of ever greater extremes of abstract thought, it returned back to earth with a corresponding growth of importance for the analysis of concrete fact'. Without claiming corresponding effects on such a dramatic scale, we would argue from our experience of jointly learning with our students, on the courses which gave rise to this book, that the rigorous development and critical application of theoretical perspectives can have the profoundly practical end-result of improving managerial competence. A substantial but flexible course is, of course, better placed to achieve significant improvement than any textbook, because of the opportunities provided for full discussion in seminar groups and individual tutorials, and the discipline involved in the requirement to produce written work (including projects or dissertations which can relate directly to the student's own area of managerial responsibility). To achieve long term improvement in the quality of educational management, we therefore attach great importance to the increased provision of opportunities for extended study, preferably on a full-time basis. In terms of promoting group learning, we regard it as a positive advantage for such courses to include students from different parts of the education service, and from both the UK and overseas.

Finally we would claim that the mixed authorship of this somewhat unusual volume itself provides cogent vindication of the approach adopted. Whether as practitioners or as university academics, we are all concerned with the use of explicitly theoretical perspectives to develop understanding of educational systems and institutions. We have sought to share our understanding and experience with others, in the belief that what we offer may provide a positive and promising approach to educational management. As the work progressed, we also came to appreciate that in the writing and the editing we were ourselves continuing to learn in a way which will, we hope, enhance our practice, for we are all, to a greater or lesser extent, educational managers.

REFERENCES

ACSET (1984) *Further Education Teachers Sub-Committee: Report of the Education Management Working Group.* London: DES.

Bailey, T. (1982) 'The question of legitimation: a response to Eric Hoyle'. *Educational Management and Administration,* **10**(2), 99–105.

Barrow, R. (1976) 'Competence and the head'. In Peters, R. S. (ed.) *The Role of the Head.* London: Routledge and Kegan Paul.

Codd, J. (1984) *Philosophy, Common Sense and Action in Educational Administration.* Victoria, Australia: Deakin University.

Commonwealth Council for Educational Administration, *Studies in Educational Administration* (continuing series). Armidale, NSW, Australia: University of New England.

DES (1983) *The In-Service Teacher Training Grants Scheme: Circular 3/83.* London: DES.

DES (1984) *The In-Service Teacher Training Grants Scheme: Circular 4/84.* London: DES.

European Forum on Educational Administration (1982) *Intervisitation Programme and Workshop in France, Grenoble 1982.* Paris: Association Français des Administrateurs de l'Education.

Everard, K. B. (1984) *Management in Comprehensive Schools — What can be Learned from Industry?* (2nd Ed.). York: Centre for the Study of Comprehensive Schools, University of York.

Farquhar, R. H. (1978) 'Recent developments in the professional preparation of principals'. *CCEA Studies in Educational Administration,* **11**, 1–18.

Haag, D. (1982) *The Right to Education: What Kind of Management.* Paris: UNESCO.

Hegarty, S. (ed.) (1983) *Training for Management in Schools.* Windsor, England: NFER-Nelson for the Council of Europe.

Hodgkinson, C. (1978) *Towards a Philosophy of Administration*. Oxford: Blackwell.

Hughes, M. G., Carter, J. and Fidler, B. (1981) *Professional Development Provision for Senior Staff in Schools and Colleges*. Birmingham: University of Birmingham Faculty of Education.

Jarratt, Sir A. (Chairman) (1985) *Report of the Steering Committee for Efficiency Studies in Universities*. London: Committee of Vice-Chancellors and Principals.

National Development Centre for School Management Training (1984) *NDC Newsletter No. 2*. Bristol: University of Bristol School of Education.

Ohm, R. E. and Monahan, W. G. (ed.) (1965) *Educational Administration — Philosophy in Action*. Norman, Oklahoma: University of Oklahoma.

Ostrander, R. H. and Dethy, R. C. (1968) *A Values Approach to Educational Administration*. New York: American Book Company.

Pratt, S. (ed.) (1982) 'The Micropolitics of Educational Improvement'. *Educational Management and Administration*, **10**(2).

Times Higher Education Supplement (1984) 'V.C.s should seek updating'. 14.12.84, p. 5.

Walker, W. G. (1978) 'Values, unorthodoxy and the "unscientific" in educational administration research'. *Educational Administration*, **6**(2) 94–106.

White, J. (1984) 'Managing heads'. In White, J. (ed.) *Education plc?*. Bedford Way Papers 20, London: University of London Institute of Education.

Whitehead, A. N. (1926) *Science and the Modern World*. London: Cambridge University Press.

NAME INDEX

Abell, P. 29
Abrahamson, M. 271, 282
Adair, J. 283
Adelman, C. 374, 375, 382, 390
Ahamad, B. 70, 79, 80
Ahier, J. 225
Albrow, M. 5
Allen, B. 309
Anderson, J. 8, 352
Andrews, J.H.M. 16
Anning, A. 294
Auld, R. 397

Bacharach, S.B. 28, 29
Bachrach, P. 445
Bacon, W. 319, 321, 387, 417, 423
Bailey, P. 357–8, 359, 361, 434, 437, 438, 442
Bailey, T. 28, 455, 456, 458, 459, 460, 462, 472
Baker, R.J.S. 5
Baldridge, J.V. 28, 29
Baldwin, R.W. 115
Ball, S. 248, 350
Balzac, H. de 5
Banks, M.H. 190
Banks, O. 16
Barber, B. 269, 270
Barnard, C.I. 7
Baron, G. 12, 17, 19–20, 60, 276–7, 308, 416
Barrow, R. 472
Barry, C.H. 314
Bassett, G.W. 9
Bassey, M. 366
Bates, A. 9, 308
Bates, R. 30, 227, 250, 253, 254
Batley, R. 164
Bauman, Z. 248
Baumgartel, H. 264

Bayliss, S. 59, 149
Bayne-Jardine, C. 351, 358
Becher, T. 8, 9, 56, 99, 100, 103, 104, 105, 107, 111, 114, 115, 118, 277, 425–6, 446, 447, 448, 449, 450, 452
Becker, H.S. 423, 424
Becker, S.W. 109
Bedeman, T. 190
Belasco, J.A. 9, 419, 459
Bell, L. 233, 352–3
Ben-David, J. 269–70
Benn, C. 152, 155, 314
Bennett, S.J. 308
Bennis, W.G. 267, 282
Benson, K. 225
Bernbaum, G. 9, 104, 308
Bernstein, B. 240, 349
Best, R. 225, 226–7, 231, 241, 243, 244, 245, 248, 344–8, 350, 355, 356–7, 358, 360, 361, 364, 365, 367, 457, 459, 461
Billingham, R. 334
Birchenough, M. 336
Birley, D. 167
Bittner, E. 30
Black, H. 377, 378
Blackburn, K. 257–8, 361
Blackstone, T. 193
Blau, P.M. 6, 273–4
Blaug, M. 26, 27, 79, 81, 144
Bloomer, K. 361–2
Blumer, H. 29
Boaden, N. 149
Bolam, R. 102, 398, 447, 450, 453, 454, 455, 458, 459–60
Bone, T. 283, 284, 285, 440
Bowden, K. 46, 47, 55, 58, 59, 60, 193
Bowles, S. 27, 251

Boyd-Barrett, O. 100, 101, 103, 104, 105, 107, 111, 113, 117, 118, 119, 120
Braybrooke, D. 25, 177, 189–92
Briault, E. 63, 128, 135, 138, 139, 441
Brickell, H.M. 447
Bridges, E. 31, 268
Bristow, A. 328
Brooksbank, K. 50, 52, 56, 102–3, 320
Brown, A.F. 265
Brown, R. 24, 150, 151, 160, 161, 170, 173, 333
Brown, R.J. 16
Browning, P. 59
Bruce, G. 114
Bullock, A. 459
Burgess, R. 248, 364, 365
Burghes, L. 183
Burnett, J. 228
Burnham, P.S. 264, 299, 355
Burns, T. 21, 32
Burrell, G. 7, 11, 22, 225, 226, 248
Burton, L. 243
Bush, T. 9, 172, 277, 297
Butler, R.A. 193
Buxton, R. 155

Callaghan, J. 99, 101, 105, 107
Callahan, R.E. 8
Campbell, R.F. 11, 13, 16, 268
Carlson, R.O. 14
Carter, C. 212
Cartwright, O. 263, 264
Cavanagh, D. 334–5
Charlton, D. 332–3
Chase, F.S. 9
Child, J. 29

Chin, R.   231, 447, 450, 453
Choppin, B.   136
Church, C.H.   383
Cicourel, A.V.   30, 248
Clark, D.L.   447
Clarke, M.   140
Clegg, S.   7, 22, 234, 240, 242, 246, 249
Clift, P.   404, 405
Coates, R.D.   58
Cockburn, C.   422
Cockcroft, W.   360, 361
Codd, J.   250, 253, 473
Cohen, L.   9, 308
Cohen, M.   22, 23, 25, 32, 351, 353
Cohen, S.   50
Coladarci, A.P.   11
Collins, R.   248, 249
Cooper, B.   350
Corbett, A.   180, 320
Corwin, R.   271, 272, 273, 282, 352
Cotterell, A.B.   181
Coulson, A.A.   293, 294, 299
Courtenay, G.   190
Cox, C.B.   106
Craig-Wilson, L.   303
Crispin, A.   69, 70, 72, 76, 77, 79
Croft, D.B.   14
Crowther, G.   178, 180, 182, 186, 187, 192
Cubberley, E.P.   8
Culbertson, J.   10, 12, 18, 227, 228, 253
Cullen, B.D.   140
Cumming, C.E.   135
Cunningham, L.L.   19
Cuthbert, R.   331
Cyert, R.M.   282, 284, 352

Daft, R.L.   109
Dale, R.   422, 423–4
Dalin, P.   447, 448, 449, 452, 454, 460
David, H.   360
David, M.E.   166, 167–8, 171
Davies, B.   233–4
Davies, J.H.   50
Davies, J.L.   281, 283
Davis, K.   241
Davis, M.J.   308
Dawe, A.   226
Dawes, L.   190
Dean, J.   136, 387
Deer, C.E.   16
Denison, E.F.   69
Dennison, W.F.   117, 319, 353, 437
Denzin, N.K.   30
Dewey, J.   10
Dickinson, N.B.   457

Doe, B.   159
Donaldson, L.   206, 209
Donnison, D.V.   165
Drake, K.   129, 133, 375
Drucker, P.F.   316
Duignan, P.   8
Duke, D.L.   419, 420
Dunham, J.   361
Dunleavy, P.J.   46, 52, 55, 57, 61, 62, 151
Dunsire   150, 151
Durkheim, E.   240
Dyer, H.S.   419

Easton, D.A.   24, 108, 161
Ebbutt, K.   333
Eckstein, H.   60, 171
Edmonds, E.   398
Eggleston, J.   104, 452
Eidell, T.L.   17
Elliott, G.   391, 409, 410
Elliott, J.   391, 424, 426, 452
Engel, G.V.   271
Eraut, M.   389
Erickson, D.A.   17, 18, 266
Erikson, K.   241
Esp, D.   322
Etzioni, A.   254, 267, 271, 282
Everard, K.B.   9, 263, 308, 474–5

Falk, G.   348
Farmer, C.   326, 329, 330
Farquhar, R.H.   17, 472, 473
Fayol, H.   4–5, 21, 31
Fearn, E.   165
Feigl, H.   11, 17
Feldman, S.   278
Fenwick, I.G.K.   152, 155, 158, 163
Fenwick, K.   158
Ferguson, C.   330–32
Fiedler, F.A.   267
Field, D.   151, 166, 169
Fielding, M.   9, 31
Fielding, R.   248, 249
Filley, A.C.   266
Finlayson, D.S.   16
Finn, D.   415
Fiske, D.   61, 137, 138, 298, 399
Fletcher, C.   226, 227
Ford, J.   257
Forrest, G.M.   115
Foster, W.   23
Fowler, G.   46, 50, 55, 62, 105, 134, 135, 138, 181, 183, 193, 200, 202, 205, 206, 208, 325, 326, 340

Gadamer, H.G.   30
Galton, M.J.   452, 457

Garfinkel, H.   30
Gatherer, W.A.   119
Geen, A.G.   165, 168
Gerstl, J.   285
Getzels, J.W.   11, 12, 13
Gibb, C.A.   263
Gibson, R.O.   18
Gintis, H.   27, 251
Giroux, H.   250, 253
Glassman, R.B.   107
Glastonbury, B.   271
Glatter, R.   xi, 20, 28, 52, 60, 62
Goffman, E.   245, 356
Goldberg, A.I.   273
Goldhammer, K.   32
Goode, W.J.   269
Goodlad, J.I.   448
Goodson, I.   348, 349, 350
Goodwin, F.J.   309
Gordon, A.   126, 130, 137, 138
Gordon, P.   109
Gorman, R.   248
Gouldner, A.   35, 229, 246, 272–3, 274
Graen, G.   268
Gray, H.L.   9, 308
Gray, J.   389
Green, A.   249, 251
Greenaway, H.   436, 438
Greenfield, T.B.   7, 13, 18, 232, 233, 239, 241, 242, 243, 244, 245, 256
Greenwood, R.   22, 23
Gregg, R.T.   11, 12
Gretton, J.   59
Griffith, J.A.G.   53
Griffiths, A.   55, 155
Griffiths, D.E.   9, 11, 14, 18, 19, 32, 223, 227, 241, 242, 248, 250
Grimes, A.J.   273
Gripps, G.   118
Gronn, P.   242, 244
Gross, N.   13, 355, 454
Guba, E.G.   12, 447
Gulick, L.   5, 31

Habermas, J.   30, 252–3
Hack, W.G.   19
Hage, J.   225
Hall, D.T.   271
Hall, J.   359, 361
Hall, R.H.   22, 267, 268, 270, 271–2, 274, 277
Halpin, A.W.   11, 14, 18, 32, 265, 266
Halsall, E.   441
Halsey, A.H.   92
Hamilton, D.   455
Hammersley, M.   28, 30, 243, 248

Handy, C.B.   9, 28, 236–8,
  263, 267, 280, 285, 315
Hanson, E.M.   283, 421, 423,
  424
Hanushek, E.A.   132
Hargreaves, D.   159, 233,
  248, 254, 354, 356, 364
Harlen, W.   375, 377–8, 386
Harman, G.   24
Harré, R.   30
Harries-Jenkins, G.   271
Harrison, R.   236
Hartley, O.A.   49, 51, 52
Harvery, J.   190
Haslegrave, H.L.   190, 192
Hatfield, D.   312
Havelock, R.G.   111, 446,
  447, 450, 453, 454
Hayes, A.E.   14
Heclo, H.   100, 150, 165
Hegarty, S.   322
Heidenheimer, H.   156
Heley, E.W.   181
Hemphill, J.K.   14, 263, 265,
  267, 300
Hencke, D.   70, 78, 79
Henniker-Heaton, C.   178,
  179–80
Hersey, P.   266
Heycock, C.   351
Hickox, M.   254
Hicks, J.   335, 336
Hill, D.M.   165, 166
Hills, J.   16, 17, 18, 20, 241,
  268
Hindness, B.   248
Hinings, C.R.   4, 22, 23
Hodge, S.   438
Hodgkinson, C.   xii, 8, 32,
  223, 231, 232, 257, 472–3
Holland, G.   184
Hollyhock, R.   339
Holt, J.   358
Holt, M.   8
Hopkins, A.   104, 106, 115,
  117
Hopkinson, D.   102
Horton, J.   226
Hough, J.R.   140
Houghton, Lord   85
House, E.   379, 449, 450, 451
House, R.J.   266
Howell, D.A.   xv, 24, 60,
  107, 151, 160, 161
Howson, J.   362
Hoy, W.K.   15, 263
Hoyle, E.   19, 20, 28, 224,
  227, 233, 267, 282, 322,
  358, 378, 380, 425, 429,
  439, 449, 450, 452, 453–4,
  456, 457, 459
Huberman, A.M.   61
Hughes, A.G.   9

Hughes, E.   269
Hughes, M.G.   8, 20, 276,
  278, 282, 292, 301, 308,
  316, 322, 420
Humphrey, C.   314, 315
Hunter, C.   298

Iannaconne, L.   32
Innes, J.T.   26
Izbicki, J.   441

Jackson, J.A.   269
Jackson, M.   183, 431
Jackson, P.W.   452
James, F.   181
James, P.H.   150, 156, 164,
  165, 167, 168, 169, 171,
  172
Jansson, D.S.   193
Jarratt, Sir A.   286, 474
Jauch, R.L.   273
Jencks, C.   105
Jenkins, D.R.   450, 451, 452
Jenkins, H.O.   8, 9
Jennings, A.   309, 418, 419,
  421, 441
Jennings, R.E.   165
John, D.   9, 281
Johnson, D.   423, 425
Johnson, N.   165
Johnson, T.J.   269, 275
Jones, G.W.   164, 165
Jones, P.   310
Jones, R.   8, 308
Jordan, B.   271
Joseph, Sir K.   101, 115, 149,
  158, 159, 214, 217
Judge, H.G.   308

Kaplan, A.   456
Katz, D.   265
Katz, R.   279, 312
Kay, B.   140
Keohane, K.   187, 190, 191
Killick, J.   434
King, G.   198, 203
King, R.   233, 234, 308, 328,
  352
Knight, B.A.A.   314
Knorr-Cetina, K.   30, 248
Kogan, D.   199
Kogan, M.   9, 46, 47, 55, 58,
  59, 60, 68, 100, 101, 104,
  107, 117, 152, 155–6, 165,
  169, 172, 180, 193, 199,
  200, 401, 402, 403
Kolakowski, L.   253
Koopman, G.R.   9
Kornhauser, W.   271

Lacey, C.   233, 248, 351, 364
Lambert, K.   285, 352, 361,

  362, 363, 404, 407
Lambright, W.H.   278
Landers, T.   9
Lane, T.J.   30, 253
Lang, P.   358
La Porte, T.A.   274
Larson, M.S.   270, 271
Lawrence, P.R.   21
Lawton, D.   99, 100, 101,
  103, 107, 110, 115
Layard, R.   198, 203
Leech, M.   328
Levin, P.H.   161
Levinson, D.J.   14
Levi-Strauss, C.   463
Lewin, K.   264, 301
Lewin, R.R.   165, 167
Lightfoot, M.   47
Lindblom, C.E.   25, 177,
  189–93
Lipham, J.M.   8, 268
Lippitt, R.   264
Litwak, E.   21
Lloyd, K.   298, 299
Locke, M.   208
Lodge, B.   367
Lodge, P.   193
Longman, B.   75
Lortie, D.   418, 421
Lucietto, L.L.   266
Luckman, T.   244
Lukes, J.R.   202, 207, 212
Lutz, F.W.   23
Lyons, G.   8, 308, 314

Macbeth, A.   119
McBride, P.   158
Macdonald, B.   449, 454–5,
  460
Macfarlane, N.   179, 181,
  182, 185, 187
McGregor, D.   265, 267
McGuiness, J.   364–5, 366
MacIntyre, D.   425
McMahon, A.   298, 318
McNay, J.   385
Maher, P.   364
Mangham, I.   29
Mann, J.   47, 52, 59, 79, 102,
  103
Mansell, J.   188, 190, 191
Manzer, R.A.   43, 57, 58, 63
March, J.G.   22, 23, 24, 25,
  32, 107, 109
Marland, M.   311, 343, 346,
  357, 360, 361, 363, 364,
  440, 457
Marsland, E.   219
Martin, W.J.   8
Masterman, M.   10, 257
Matterson, A.   199
Matthewman, M.   404, 407–8
Mayo, E.   6

Mercer, R.H.   434–5
Merton, R.K.   6, 17, 273
Meyer, J.W.   22, 108
Miles, M.B.   448, 453, 454
Millerson, G.   269
Milroy, P.   55, 62
Milstein, M.M.   284
Mintzberg, H.   8
Miskel, C.G.   15, 263
Mitchell, P.   309
Moody, G.C.   276, 277
Moore, W.   241, 276, 282
Morgan, C.   xvi, 279–80, 293,
   309, 312, 313, 318, 353,
   354–5
Morris, Lord   284, 285, 286
Morrish, I.   450, 454
Moser, R.F.   264
Mosher, F.C.   284
Mouzelis, N.   257
Musgrove, F.   8, 308, 312,
   322, 348, 352

Nagel, E.   445
Nash, R.   254
Neuse, S.M.   271
Neve, B.   166
Newell, C.A.   9, 263, 295
Nias, J.   9, 295, 301, 322, 420
Nicodemus, R.B.   452
Nisbet, J.   388, 390
Noble, T.   271, 334, 420, 421,
   424, 459
Norwood, C.   277
Nuttall, D.L.   115

Ogilvie, D.   359, 363
Ohm, R.E.   472
Oleson, V.   270
Organ, D.W.   274
Ostrander, R.H.   284, 472
Ouston, J.   280, 308
Oxtoby, R.   337–8

Packwood, T.   308, 351
Padgett, J.F.   23
Paisey, A.   9
Parkes, D.   329, 340, 458
Parkin, J.B.   410
Parkinson, M.   156, 165, 168
Parlett, M.   387
Parnes, H.S.   80
Parsons, T.   234, 235, 236,
   240
Passmore, B.   158, 159, 340
Pateman, T.   378
Pattison, M.   46, 49, 50, 57–8,
   62, 149, 150, 151, 152,
   155, 156, 157, 159, 163
Pedley, R.   115
Peeke, G.   354
Pelz, D.C.   268
Perrow, C.   7, 223–4, 249

Peston, M.   26, 392
Peters, R.S.   419
Peters, T.J.   29, 237
Pettigrew, A.M.   165
Pfeffer, J.   28, 29
Piele, P.K.   17
Pile, W.   53, 62, 68, 79, 101,
   117
Prandy, K.   270
Pratley, B.   330
Pratt, J.   201, 203, 205, 206,
   207
Pratt, S.   28, 420, 422, 455
Price, C.   59
Pritchett, G.R.   59
Pugh, D.S.   4, 22

Rabb, C.D.   119
Raison, T.   52, 53, 55, 180
Raleigh, M.   360
Ramsay, H.   420
Ransom, S.   22, 23
Reddin, W.J.   266
Regan, D.   53, 160
Reid, W.A.   452, 454, 456,
   458
Reissman, L.   272, 273
Revell, J.   102–3
Rhodes, R.A.W.   165
Ribbins, P.M.   150, 151, 166,
   173, 243, 245, 358
Richardson, E.   308, 343,
   350, 364, 452
Richardson, J.J.   193
Richmond, A.   335–6
Robinson, E.E.   202, 207
Roethlisberger, F.G.   6
Rogers, C.   432
Rogers, R.   399, 400–1, 402
Ross, J.M.   107, 115
Rotondi, T.   271
Rudd, W.G.A.   452
Rutter, M.   136, 316, 385

Sallis, J.   60, 102
Salter, B.   59, 202, 211–19,
   401, 422
Saran, R.   55, 59, 90, 152,
   154, 165, 167, 169, 434
Schein, E.   354
Schmuck, R.   281, 453
Schon, D.A.   111, 448, 449,
   451, 452
Schultz, T.W.   26
Schutz, A.   244, 248
Schwab, J.J.   17
Scott, P.   200, 202, 203, 204,
   205, 206, 207–8, 209, 210,
   216
Scott, W.R.   271, 272, 273–4
Scribbins, K.   57
Self, P.   164
Shackle, G.L.S.   375

Sharma, C.L.   9
Sharp, R.   249, 251
Shattock, M.L.   441
Shipman, M.   234, 236, 238,
   240, 251, 252, 284, 379,
   451, 452, 457
Siddle, J.   343, 344, 359, 360,
   361, 364
Silver, H.   414, 415
Silver, P.   278
Silverman, D.   6, 7, 241–2,
   243, 246–7, 256, 354
Simkins, T.   128, 135, 138
Simon, H.A.   11–12, 24, 25
Simon, J.   118
Simons, H.   452
Skilbeck, M.   116
Sloman, P.   52, 53
Smith, G.   173
Smith, R.   138
Snyder, R.C.   20
Socket, H.   379, 408
Sorenson, J.E.   271
Spooner, R.   437, 438
Stagles, R.   183
Stake, R.E.   388, 389, 390
Stanton, M.   439
Start, K.B.   117
Steadman, S.D.   452
Stenhouse, L.   439, 447, 449,
   460
Stenning, R.   317, 433, 436
Stevens, A.   183
Stoddart, J.   335
Stogdill, R.M.   263, 264
Straughan, R.   377
Sugarman, B.   233, 440
Susman, G.   227
Szreter, R.   277

Taylor, F.W.   4, 7, 8, 31
Taylor, T.   60
Taylor, W.   284, 308, 431,
   432–3, 436
Thomas, A.R.   8, 447
Thomas, H.   144, 314, 315,
   361
Thomas, N.   296
Thomas, W.J.   31
Thomason, G.   9, 231, 277,
   308
Thompson, N.   326
Thornton, R.   273
Thorp, J.   426
Tipton, B.   58, 248, 253, 254,
   332–3
Tomlinson, J.   297
Toogood, P.   400
Trethowan, D.   9, 308
Trow, M.   13
Tuma, N.B.   274, 275
Turner, C.   23, 338, 351, 352
Turner, G.   233, 249

Turner, L.T. 31
Turner, R. 354, 356

Urwick, L.F. 5

Vaizey, J.E. 25
Van den Berghe, V. 242
Vaughan, M. 181
Venables, E. 328
Vickers, Sir G. xvi, 24

Waddell, J. 186, 190
Walker, W.G. 472, 473
Waller, W. 252
Walsh, K. 134, 137, 139
Walton, J. 445
Warwick, D. 9
Waters, D. 299, 303
Watkins, P. 250, 252–3
Watson, K. 441
Watson, L. 316, 341, 351
Watts, A.G. 188
Watts, J. 282, 317, 419
Waven, H. 327
Weaver, T. 53, 54, 401

Webb, C. 337, 338
Webb, P.C. 8
Weber, M. 5–6, 8, 21, 32,
    242, 243, 245, 257, 456
Weeks, J.C.S. 316, 321
Weick, K. 22, 23, 99, 107,
    108–9, 111, 112, 117, 119,
    120
Weindling, R. 322
Welton, J. 424
Wenger, M.G. 285
West, J. 111
Weston, P. 459
Westwood, L. 351
Whitaker, P. 292, 293
White, J. 9, 349, 472
White, R.K. 264
Whitehead, A.N. 32, 475
Whitehead, D.J. 449, 450,
    451, 452
Whitty, G. 248, 249
Wilby, P. 158, 159
Williams, G. 26, 27, 28
Williams, S. 47, 115, 157,
    181, 213

Williets, D. 338–9
Willis, P. 233, 241, 251, 252
Willis, Q. 8
Willower, D.J. 8, 17, 18, 23,
    241, 242
Wilson, D.J. 118
Winkley, D. 398, 399, 403
Wirt, F. 270, 275, 285
Wolcott, H.F. 17, 284
Wood, J.R. 404
Woodhall, M. 26, 79, 80
Woodland, D. 355
Woods, P. 241, 243, 248,
    249, 423
Wright, D. 433, 434

Yauch, W.A. 9
Young, M. 349
Yukl, G. 266, 300

Zabalza, A. 81, 82, 83, 85,
    88, 90, 91, 92, 94
Zaleznik, A. 28

SUBJECT INDEX

Accountability 414–26
  and participation 283, 421–6
  in primary schools 297
  in secondary schools 320–1
Action theories 243–9
Administrators, professionals as 276–85
Ancillary staff 134
Assessment of Performance Unit (APU) 389

Bureaucracy 5–6, 8–9, 22, 32, 273–4, 351–2

Catholic Church, influence of 170
Central government
  and the education sub-government 45, 46–56,
    62
  and educational policy-making 150–9
Change
  in higher education 213–15
  management of 445–63
  political approaches to 455–61, 462–3
  rational approaches to 446–55, 461–2
Chief Education Officers (CEOs) 162, 164–6
Classical management theory 4–5, 31
Clerical staff 134
Communication 316–17, 440–2
Comprehensive secondary
  reorganisation 148–74, 229–31
Conflict
  in schools 238–40, 251–2
  theories 249–54
Consensus theories 231–42
Contingency model 21–2
Critical theory 30, 227, 253
Crowther Report 178, 182, 186–7, 190
Culture in schools 236–8
Curriculum
  changes in 309–10
  and class size 139–40
  content and control 99–121, 128–9, 140–4
  in primary schools 296
  in secondary schools 348–51
  for sixteen to nineteens 185–9

Departmental reviews 403–8
Departments, heads of see Heads of
  departments
Deputy head teachers 299
DES (Department of Education and Science)
  and curriculum control 99, 101–2, 105–7,
    110–14, 117–18
  and the education sub-government 43–56, 60,
    62–3
Disjointed incrementalism 25, 189–93

Economics of education 25–8
  and changing enrolment 125–45
  and teacher supply 79–95
Education sub-government 43–65
  and sixteen to nineteens 182–5
Enrolment, changes in
  economics of 125–45
Equipment, expenditure on 135–6, 314–15
Ethnomethodology 30, 255, 282
Ethogenics 30
Evaluation
  definition of 374–6
  perspectives on 373–92
  practice of 394–412
  structural relationships in 380–6, 395
  techniques of 388–91
Examination systems 114–16, 119–20, 186–7,
    438
  and evaluation 389

Further education (FE)
  management and leadership in 325–41
  see also Higher education policies

Garbage can model
  organisational structure 23, 29, 353
Getzels–Guba model 12–13, 264
Goal attainment 234–5
Governors, role of 59–60, 320–21, 333
  and accountability 415–17, 423
Grammar schools, numbers of 148–9

Head teachers
  authority of 456–7
  dual model 278–80, 286
  and governing bodies 417
  in primary schools 291–306
  in secondary schools 230–1, 308–22
  style of management 418–19
Heads of departments (HODs)
  in comprehensive schools 351, 357–64
  in FE colleges 333, 337–8
  and review processes 404–8
Hermeneutics 30, 227–8
Higher education policies 198–220
HMI (Her Majesty's Inspectorate)
  and curriculum control 102, 105–6, 113, 115
  evaluation by 385, 390, 396–403, 412
Human capital theory 26, 81–3, 471
Human relations theories 6–7, 9, 31, 282
Human resources development (HRD) 284

Ideal type, concept of 257
Incrementalism 25, 192–3
Inspection 390, 395, 396–403; *see also* HMI

Latency 235
Leadership
  action-centred 283–4, 306
  behaviour 265–6
  in further education 325–41
  personality traits 263–4, 276–7
  in primary schools 291–306
  in professionally staffed organisations 262–86
  roles in educational institutions 275–85
  in secondary schools
    head teachers 230–1, 308–22
    middle managers 343–67
  situational approaches to 266–8
  styles 264–5, 294–5, 299–306
LEAs (local education authorities)
  and curriculum control 102–3, 110
  and the education sub-government 43, 45, 46,
    48–57, 60–3
  self-assessment schemes 408–11
  see also Local authority policy-making
Local advisory services 396–9, 403
Local authority policy-making
  comprehensive secondary reorganisation
    148–75
Loose coupling 22–3, 107–19, 120–1, 268, 475

Management
  cycle of 281
  in further education 325–41
  in primary schools 291–306
  in secondary schools 309–21
  theories of 3–33
Management training
  in FE 338–40, 474
  lessons from industry 7–9, 474–5
  National Development Centre (NDC) 322,
    474
Manpower planning 79–84
Marxist theories 250–1, 254, 255

Micropolitics 28–9, 33, 224, 262, 455–6, 472
Micro-social sciences 28–30, 33, 249, 472
Middle managers
  in secondary schools 343–67
Ministry of Education *see* DES
MSC (Manpower Services Commission)
  and the education sub-government 48, 51,
    58–9, 63
  and further education 328–9, 335
  and sixteen to nineteens 182–5, 188, 190, 191,
    192
  TVEI 140–1, 143, 185, 188, 329
  YOP 112, 184–5, 329
  YTS 185, 188, 190, 191, 329

National local government system 45, 57–62, 151
New Movement theory 9–10, 11–19, 31, 32

Organisation development (OD) 284
Organisational climate studies 15–16
Organisational structure 19–24
  comprehensive schools 344–53
  FE colleges 330–32
Organisations
  leadership in 262–86
  theory of 223–57
Organised anarchy 23, 32, 353

Paradigm, concept of 10–11, 257
  template as synonym 475
Parents 168–9, 171, 321, 441–2
Participation
  and accountability 283, 421–6
  in decision-making 418–21, 458–60
  in primary schools 295, 297–8, 304
  in secondary schools 316–17
Pastoral care 310–11, 344–8, 357–9
Plowden Report 91, 117
Policy-making
  comprehensive secondary
    reorganisation 148–74
  higher education 198–220
  models 24–5
  sixteen to nineteens 177–95
Political systems
  and policy-making 160–71
Polytechnic directors 277, 281
Polytechnics 199, 202–3, 204, 207–9
Polyversities 216
Primary schools
  leadership in 291–306
Principals
  FE colleges 277, 333, 334, 335–7, 456–7
Professionalism
  and organisational management 269–75
  and participatory decision-making 420–21,
    460–1, 463
Pupil–teacher ratio (PTR) 69, 75, 80, 83–4, 85,
  138, 139–40
Pupils
  age structure 136–7
  falling rolls 430, 433
  numbers of 72–4, 126–9

relationships with teachers 318–19
Rayner Report 396–7, 398, 399–400, 402
Research, Development and Diffusion model
    (RD and D) 447–9
Retrenchment, problems of 428–42
Robbins Report 198, 200, 205, 214, 215, 218
Role structure 235–6, 353
Role studies 13–14
Role theory 14, 235, 353–7

Schools
    buildings 134–5, 315
    closures 128, 135
    equipment 135–6
    organisation structure 224–5, 229–31, 233–56
    size 137–9
Scientific management 4, 7–8
Scotland
    curricular policy-making 118–19
    higher education 216
Screening hypothesis 27–8, 471
Secondary schools
    comprehensive reorganisation 148–74,
        229–31
    head teachers 230–1, 308–22
    middle managers 343–67
Self-assessment schemes 390–1, 408–11, 439–40
Sixteen to nineteen policies 177–95;
    see also Higher education policies
Sixth forms 136, 177–8, 180, 182, 186
Social-interaction model 450–1
Social theory
    and organisation structure 225–8
Socialisation in schools 236, 240
Staff development policies 436–8
Structural functionalism 18, 226, 231–42, 263,
    471
Structural relativism 21–2, 32
Sub-government *see* Education
    sub-government
Subject departments
    comprehensive schools 348–51
Symbolic interactionism 29, 226, 282, 356
Systems theory 17, 18, 231–42, 255

Task achievement 281–2
Teachers
    and accountability 424–6
    characteristics of 130–4, 141–3
    and comprehensive secondary reorganisation
        167–8, 171
    and curriculum 103–4
    and evaluation 377–8, 380–1, 392, 439–40
    in further education 330
    numbers of 75–6, 129–30
    organisations 58, 60, 103, 317
    pay and conditions 57, 81–3, 85, 88–94, 133–4,
        145, 330, 434
    in primary schools 297–99
    qualifications 133
    regional distribution of 94–5
    role in decision-making 418–21, 424–5
    in secondary schools 312–14, 317–18
    staff development policies 436–8
    subject shortage areas 70–1, 89–91, 133–4,
        142–3
    supply of 68–96
    training 69–70, 77, 78, 87, 141
    see also Head teachers
Tertiary colleges 181–2
TVEI (Technical and Vocational Initiative)
    140–1, 143, 185, 188, 329

United States 8, 9–10, 11–12
Universities 200, 203, 204, 205, 206
University vice-chancellors 276–7, 281, 283, 474

Vocational courses
    in higher education 205–6

Wales
    constitutional position 63

YOP (Youth Opportunities Programme) 112,
    184–5, 329
YTS (Youth Training Scheme) 185, 188, 190,
    191, 329